AQA A-level

Sociology 2

David Bown
Laura Pountney
Tomislav Marić
Natalie Meadows

Approval message from AQA

This textbook has been approved by AQA for use with our qualification. This means that we have checked that it broadly covers the specification and we are satisfied with the overall quality. Full details of our approval process can be found on our website.

We approve textbooks because we know how important it is for teachers and students to have the right resources to support their teaching and learning. However, the publisher is ultimately responsible for the editorial control and quality of this book.

Please note that when teaching the *AQA A-level Sociology* course, you must refer to AQA's specification as your definitive source of information. While this book has been written to match the specification, it cannot provide complete coverage of every aspect of the course.

A wide range of other useful resources can be found on the relevant subject pages of our website: www.aqa.org.uk.

DYNAMIC LEARNING

HODDER EDUCATION
AN HACHETTE UK COMPANY

Dedication

David: to Mary

Laura: with love to my parents, Tom, Flick, Emma and last but definitely not least, little Bela.

Tomislav: to Skyler

Natalie: to Grandad – I hope this fuels your love of sociology.

The Publishers would like to thank the following for permission to reproduce copyright material.

Photo credits p.1 © Tyler Olson/Fotolia, **p.2** © Jim West/Alamy Stock Photo; **p.8** © VALERY HACHE/AFP/Getty Images; **p.38** © Ingram Publishing/Alamy Stock Photo; **p.44** © LevT/Fotolia; **p.45** © REX; **p.49** © Marmaduke St. John/Alamy Stock Photo; **p.50** tl © Brian Jackson/Fotolia, bl © Janine Wiedel Photolibrary/Alamy Stock Photo, r © PYMCA/Alamy Stock Photo; **p.52** © rh2010/Fotolia; **p.53** t © Monkey Business/Fotolia, c © ablestock.com via Thinkstock/Getty Images, b © SyB/Fotolia; **p.70** © Andrey Popov/Fotolia; **p.72** © Sipa Press/REX; **p.73** © REX; **p.76** l © contrastwerkstatt – Fotolia; r © Show-Shot-Foto – Fotolia; **p.77** © Marmaduke St. John/Alamy Stock Photo; **p.80** © racorn - 123RF; p.98 l © blas – Fotolia; tr © Roger Bamber/Alamy Stock Photo; br © Damian Dovarganes/AP/Press Association Images; **p.101** © Britpix/Alamy Stock Photo; **p.114** © Dimitri Otis/Getty Images; **p.115** © Imagestate Media (John Foxx) /Clouds, skies & aerial views BS24; **p.119** © Steven Hunt/Getty Images; **p.122** © Clichesdumonde – Fotolia; **p.125** © nmann77 – Fotolia; **p.127** © Michael Debets/Alamy Stock Photo; **p.128** © Boaz Rottem/Alamy Stock Photo; **p.131** © DYLAN MARTINEZ/Reuters/; **p.137** t © MASSIMO SESTINI/REX; b © Everett Collection/REX; **p.139** tl © fabiomax – Fotolia; tr © Paul Mounce/Corbis; bl © Richard Ellis/Alamy Stock Photo; br © Christopher J. Morris/Corbis; **p.140** l © Ullsteinbild/Topfoto; r © Topfoto/ImageWorks; **p.143** © gudrin – Fotolia; **p.144** © Frances Roberts/Alamy Stock Photo; **p.145** tl © epa european pressphoto agency b.v./Alamy Stock Photo; bl © RosaIreneBetancourt 7/Alamy Stock Photo; r © INTERFOTO/Alamy Stock Photo; **p.148** © Agencja Fotograficzna Caro/Alamy Stock Photo; **p.150** © Dan Yeger/Alamy Stock Photo; **p.161** © Jeffrey Blackler/Alamy Stock Photo; **p.162** © The Kendal Project; **p.168** © AP Photo/Sunday Alamba; **p.170** © jdavenport85 – Fotolia; **p.174** © John Warburton-Lee Photography/Alamy Stock Photo; **p.175** © KaYann – Fotolia; **p.176** © jdavenport85 – Fotolia; **p.179** © Laboko - iStock via Thinkstock/Getty Images; **p.180** © WorldFoto/Alamy Stock Photo; **p.189** © Sipa Press/REX; **p.190** © Gianni Muratore/Alamy Stock Photo; **p.201** © graja – Fotolia; **p.204** © PIUS UTOMI EKPEI/AFP/Getty Images; **p.206** © André Quillien/Alamy Stock Photo; **p.210** © ZUMA/REX; **p.217** © Jenny Matthews/Alamy Stock Photo; **p.221** © APAImages/REX; **p.229** © FAYEZ NURELDINE/AFP/Getty Images; **p.230** © Cylonphoto/Fotolia; **p.233** © dbimages/Alamy Stock Photo; **p.238** © Jack Picone/Alamy Stock Photo; **p.239** © Reuters; **p.242** © Paul Grover/REX; **p.244** © KPA/Zuma/REX; **p.256** © Terry Harris/Alamy Stock Photo; **p.260** © Gabriel Olsen/Getty Images; **p.277** tl © ddp USA/REX; tm © Matt Baron/BEI/REX; tr © Jim Zuckerman/Alamy Stock Photo; b © ablestock.com via Thinkstock/Getty Images; **p.292** © Africa Studio – Fotolia; **p.293** © REX; **p.295** t © Company Pictures via Ronald Grant Archive; b © REX; **p.298** © LEON NEAL/AFP/Getty Images; **p.299** © Imagestate Media (John Foxx)/Male Topmodels SS96; **p.302** l © Ray Tang/REX; r © REX; **p.304** © AF archive/Alamy Stock Photo; **p.308** © DHSB Psychology; **p.310** © rrruss – Fotolia; **p.311** © Random House; **p.319** © Sophie Bassouls/Sygma/Corbis; **p.320** © Heidi Safia Mirza; **p.327** t © Alan Crowhurst/Getty Images; b © RTimages – Fotolia; **p.328** t © Brad Pict – Fotolia; b © Xavier MARCHANT – Fotolia; **p.347** © Dave Higgens/PA Archive/PA Images; **p.348** © Beth Moseley Photography and #ToyLikeMe; **p.350** © c.HBO/Everett/REX; **p.354** © ITV/REX; **p.355** © Alexander Raths – Fotolia; **p.361** © Jimmy Sime/Getty Images; **p.366** © PA Photos/Topfoto; **p.381** tl © Picture-Factory – Fotolia; tr © Allan Danahar - Digital Vision via Thinkstock/Getty Images; bl © MaxRiesgo - iStock via Thinkstock/Getty Images; br © Matt Cardy/Getty Images; **p.383** © goodluz – Fotolia; **p.385** © Chris Lofty – Fotolia; **p.393** © shazman – Fotolia.

Every effort has been made to trace all copyright holders, but if any have been inadvertently overlooked, the Publishers will be pleased to make the necessary arrangements at the first opportunity.

Although every effort has been made to ensure that website addresses are correct at time of going to press, Hodder Education cannot be held responsible for the content of any website mentioned in this book. It is sometimes possible to find a relocated web page by typing in the address of the home page for a website in the URL window of your browser.

Hachette UK's policy is to use papers that are natural, renewable and recyclable products and made from wood grown in sustainable forests. The logging and manufacturing processes are expected to conform to the environmental regulations of the country of origin.

Orders: please contact Bookpoint Ltd, 130 Milton Park, Abingdon, Oxon OX14 4SE. Telephone: +44 (0)1235 827720. Fax: +44 (0)1235 400454. Email education@bookpoint.co.uk Lines are open from 9 a.m. to 5 p.m., Monday to Saturday, with a 24-hour message answering service. You can also order through our website: http://www.hoddereducation.co.uk

ISBN: 9781471839429

© David Bown, Laura Pountney, Tomislav Marić, Natalie Meadows, 2016

First published in 2016 by

Hodder Education,

An Hachette UK Company

Carmelite House

50 Victoria Embankment

London EC4Y 0DZ

www.hoddereducation.co.uk

Impression number   10 9 8 7 6 5 4 3 2 1

Year   2019 2018 2017 2016

All rights reserved. Apart from any use permitted under UK copyright law, no part of this publication may be reproduced or transmitted in any form or by any means, electronic or mechanical, including photocopying and recording, or held within any information storage and retrieval system, without permission in writing from the publisher or under licence from the Copyright Licensing Agency Limited. Further details of such licences (for reprographic reproduction) may be obtained from the Copyright Licensing Agency Limited, Saffron House, 6–10 Kirby Street, London EC1N 8TS.

Cover photo © simon2579/iStockphoto

Illustrations by Integra Software Services

Typeset in 10.5/12.5pt ITC Berkeley Oldstyle Std Book by Integra Software Services Pvt. Ltd., Pondicherry, India

Printed in Italy

A catalogue record for this title is available from the British Library.

Contents

Introduction	v
1. Theory	**1**
Different types of data	2
Consensus, conflict, structural and social action theories	8
How do the concepts of modernity and postmodernity relate to sociological theory?	21
To what extent is sociology scientific, objective and value-free?	25
The relationship between theory and methods	31
Debates about subjectivity, objectivity and value freedom	37
2. Crime and deviance	**49**
Crime and deviance, social order and social control	50
The social distribution of crime and deviance	70
Globalisation and crime in contemporary society	84
Crime control, surveillance, prevention and punishment	97
3. Beliefs in society	**114**
Ideology, science and religion	115
Religion as social change or conservative force	131
Religious organisations	139
Social groups and religious beliefs and practices	149
Religion in the modern world	158
4. Global development	**170**
Development, underdevelopment and global inequality	171
Globalisation and its influence on relationships between different societies	189
The role of different organisations in strategies for development	201
Development in relation to aid and trade, industrialisation, urbanisation, the environment, and war and conflict	216
Employment, education, health, demographic change and gender as aspects of development	238

5. The media — 256

- The new media — 257
- The relationship between ownership and control of the media — 268
- The media, globalisation and culture — 277
- What makes the news? — 281
- Media representations of social groups — 292
- The effects of the media on audiences — 303

6. Stratification and differentiation — 310

- Theories of stratification and differentiation — 311
- How do different factors impact life chances? — 326
- Definitions and measurements — 349
- Structural changes — 366
- Patterns of social mobility — 381

7. Tackling the A-level exam — 393

- Overview of the A-level — 393
- The skills you will be expected to demonstrate — 394
- The types of questions you will be expected to answer — 397
- How the A-level is different to AS (including how to tackle longer questions) — 401
- Tackling A-level Paper 1 — 404
- Tackling A-level Paper 2 — 416
- Tackling A-level Paper 3 — 420

Key terms — 430

References — 437

Index — 447

Introduction

This book has been written specifically to cover the new AQA specification introduced for first teaching in September 2015. The writers are all experienced authors, teachers and subject specialists who provide comprehensive and up-to-date information that is both accessible and informative.

As a textbook it has been written to build student understanding through a concept-driven approach to the AQA AS and A-level specifications. Each chapter is self-contained, providing the content to generate knowledge and skills required. It has been carefully written to develop student skills to enable them to evaluate theories and research, as well as build up their knowledge to master sociological topics.

The content of this book covers all topics in the new specification. Each chapter has a range of features designed to give students the confidence that the content of their course is covered in a clear and accessible way as well as supporting them in their studies.

Summary of the specification and its coverage in *AQA Sociology for A-level* books 1 and 2

Content	Covered in
AS compulsory content	
3.1.1 Education	AQA Sociology for A-level 1
3.1.2 Methods in Context	
3.2.1 Research Methods	
AS optional – one of these topics must be studied:	
3.2.2.1 Culture and Identity	AQA Sociology for A-level 1
3.2.2.2 Families and Households	
3.2.2.3 Health	
3.2.2.4 Work, Poverty and Welfare	

A-level compulsory content	
4.1 Education with Theory and Methods 4.1.1 Education 4.1.2 Methods in Context 4.1.3 Theory and Methods	All covered in AQA Sociology for A-level 1 *except* Theory, which is covered in AQA Sociology for A-level 2
4.3 Crime and Deviance with Theory and Methods 4.3.1 Crime and Deviance 4.3.2 Theory and Methods	All covered in AQA Sociology for A-level 2 *except* Methods, which is covered in AQA Sociology for A-level 1
A-level optional – one topic from each set of options must be studied:	
Option 1 4.2.1 Culture and Identity 4.2.2 Families and Households 4.2.3 Health 4.2.4 Work, Poverty and Welfare	AQA Sociology for A-level 1
Option 2 4.2.5 Beliefs in Society 4.2.6 Global Development 4.2.7 The Media 4.2.8 Stratification and Differentiation	AQA Sociology for A-level 2

This title (Book 2) covers the second year of A-level, including all the options. This book includes a full Theory chapter, which expands on the introduction to theory section in Book 1, both of which will help you to understand all the different sociological concepts.

The book has been meticulously designed to strengthen learning through each stage of the course with plenty of practice and extension exercises. As an innovative textbook it offers the following qualities:

The AQA specification
Each chapter begins with a table illustrating how the content reflects the AQA specification. Every topic in the AS/Year 1 A-level AQA specification has a full chapter in this book. The content of every chapter has been carefully chosen in conjunction with the AQA specification to develop knowledge and understanding of key sociological concepts in a contemporary context.

GETTING YOU STARTED
Each chapter begins with an opening activity involving text or images with questions designed to develop sociological skills with practical activities. A combination of open and closed questions is used to stimulate thinking about key ideas appropriate to the chapter. The questions may be completed individually or used to stimulate discussion and group work.

Key terms

Key terms are written in bold type and defined in a simple way in the glossary towards the end of the book. The terms are mainly sociological but also cover important terms from other disciplines that are relevant but may need explaining.

IN THE NEWS

This section includes articles adapted from contemporary newspapers, websites and journals; it is used to discuss topic events that you may have seen in the news. It is designed to demonstrate the application of sociological ideas to the applied social world around us.

STUDY TIP

These are designed to give pointers towards improving students' knowledge of sociology and skills development. They offer careful and balanced advice on concepts, ideas and theories to consider in ways that will add depth and quality to students' work.

CONTEMPORARY APPLICATION

This section offers a contemporary example of how each section within a chapter can be applied to the social world we live in. The content is designed to provoke thought and possibly offer examples and evidence that can supplement students' written work.

RESEARCH IN FOCUS

These extracts offer an insight into interesting and relevant contemporary research. The questions that follow them are designed to provoke understanding of the findings as well as consideration of methodological approaches and issues.

Check your understanding

This end of chapter section offers a set of questions designed to test knowledge and understanding of the chapter's content.

Practice questions

These are designed to offer study practice. A range of questions are asked along with the provision of items as appropriate.

Introduction

Theory

Understanding the specification

AQA Specification	How the specification is covered in this chapter
The distinction between primary and secondary data, and between quantitative and qualitative data	**Section 1: What are the quantitative and qualitative methods of research?** What are the distinctions between primary and secondary data? What are quantitative and qualitative methods of research?
Consensus, conflict, structural and social action theories	**Section 2: What are consensus and conflict theories?** What are consensus and conflict theories? What are social action theories?
The concepts of modernity and postmodernity in relation to sociological theory	**Section 3: How do the concepts of modernity and post-modernity relate to sociological theory?** How do the concepts of modernity and postmodernity relate to sociological theory?
The nature of science and the extent to which sociology can be regarded as scientific	**Section 4: To what extent can sociology be regarded as scientific, objective and value-free?** To what extent can sociology be regarded as a science?
The relationship between theory and methods	**Section 5: What is the relationship between theory and sociological methods?** What is the relationship between positivism, interpretivism and sociological methods? What theoretical considerations influence research?
Debates about subjectivity, objectivity and value freedom The relationship between sociology and social policy	**Section 6: Debates about subjectivity, objectivity and value freedom** To what extent is sociology value-free? What is the relationship between sociology and social policy?

Section 1: The distinction between primary and secondary data, and between quantitative and qualitative data

This section will explore:
- What are the distinctions between primary and secondary data?
- What are quantitative and qualitative methods of research?

GETTING YOU STARTED
What makes good research?

What makes good sociological research was covered in Book 1 (pages 7–8). It defined good research as capturing or measuring what was set out to be examined in the first place. The following guidelines are not from a sociological source but a publication from London Borough of Richmond Upon Thames Council.

Figure 1.1 Collecting data in the field

However, the principles outlined as guidance to its Local Government Officers are as relevant as if it had been written by the British Sociological Association for sociologists. It highlights factors that are common to all good pieces of research, irrespective of the fact that each piece of research is different:

- There is a clear statement of research aims, which defines the research question.
- There is an information sheet for participants, which sets out clearly what the research is about, what it will involve and consent is obtained in writing on a consent form prior to research beginning.
- The methodology is appropriate to the research question. So, if the research is into people's perceptions, a more qualitative, unstructured interview may be appropriate. If the research aims to identify the scale of a problem or need, a more quantitative, randomised, statistical sample survey may be more appropriate. Good research can often use a combination of methodologies, which complement one another.
- The research should be carried out in an unbiased fashion. As far as possible the researcher should not influence the results of the research in any way.
- From the beginning, the research should have appropriate and sufficient resources in terms of people, time, transport, money etc. allocated to it.
- All research should be ethical and not harmful in any way to the participants.

Adapted from White (2006).

Questions

1. Why are research aims important in any piece of research?
2. In what situations might it not be appropriate for sociological researchers to give out an information sheet for participants and to get their informed consent?
3. Why is it that good research often uses a combination of methodologies?
4. Why is it important for the researcher to ensure they have appropriate and sufficient resources?

1.1 What are the distinctions between primary and secondary data?

When studying the distinction between primary and secondary data, you should have an awareness of the difference between these two types of data.

Theoretical perspectives will inform each sociologists' choice of data source based on their skills, and factors like practical and ethical considerations. Those adopting a realist approach (see page 33) will seek, as a matter of good practice, both quantitative and qualitative data, which may require them to use both primary and secondary sources.

Primary data

Primary data is collected first-hand by the researcher and is unique. It is collected by the researcher personally, or using a team, through methods such as those described in Section 2. For the researcher, the advantage of collecting primary data is that:

- they have control over how the data is collected;
- they can adjust their research strategy and research questions to obtain data specific to aims of their research or hypothesis; and,
- it is up-to-date data that does not currently exist within the public domain.

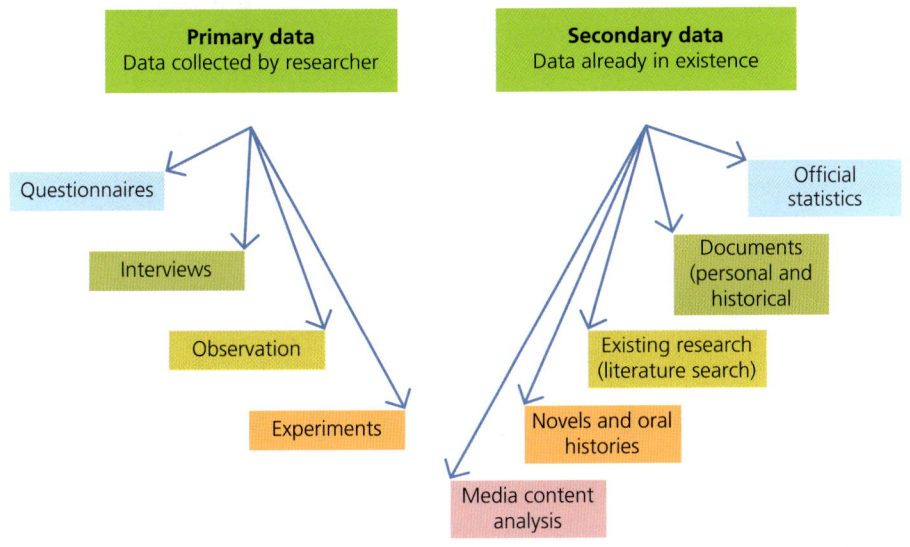

Figure 1.2 Primary versus secondary data

Secondary data

Secondary data is data that has been collected by someone else that is used by a sociologist to ask new questions or to pool with other research. Secondary data can include:

- literature searches of existing academic published research
- historical and personal documents
- official statistics
- journals and academic papers
- novels

- oral histories
- media content analysis of newspaper and magazine articles
- transcripts of audio/video recordings.

One of the key problems in using secondary data is that sociologists have no control over the research procedures used to collect it. Researchers need to be alert to the fact that secondary data is highly variable in terms of its quality. If a researcher is confident that the data has been produced by a dependable source, it can offer significant benefits saving both time and money. There is little point in replicating data that already exists, unless to check the reliability of the data. Secondary data needs to be used carefully, but can be a useful component in the researcher's strategy. **Meta-studies** will rely heavily on published secondary material on a given subject.

When sociologists use any secondary sources they must be aware that the motive behind its construction may reflect bias. Documents may well reflect a desired viewpoint or official statistics may have been constructed to reflect government policies more favourably.

Oral history

Oral history occurs when the researcher spends a significant amount of time with participants listening to the stories they tell about their life. It is a collaborative process of narrative building rather than an in-depth interview. Getting people to reflect on their life experiences is becoming more popular in certain areas of sociological research. Such individuals are seen as an important asset with important stories to tell about the social world while they are still living. By empowering subjects to see their experiences as important, interviews can yield rich qualitative data, high in validity.

Some feel that there is a danger of people exaggerating, selectively remembering or possibly putting a subjective slant on their recollections. Any of these factors would serve to undermine the validity of the data and render it biased. Equally, if individuals give a slightly different version of the past each time they are interviewed, the data becomes low in terms of reliability. An example of using oral histories is Rachel Slater's (2000) study of how four black South African women experienced urbanisation under apartheid.

Media content analysis

The mass media offers a colossal amount of potential data. This data can be either quantitative or qualitative. Through adopting a systematic content analysis it is possible to produce high-quality and **objective** data by analysing media content.

It is important to remember that media content is often biased, especially media that is allowed to openly support political parties. The Marxist Glasgow Media Group (GMG) (see page 285) adopted highly sophisticated techniques to ensure that their analysis was scientific and objective. Not all researchers are this thorough in their analysis with the risk that a researcher's analysis ends up being little more than a subjective (personally biased) interpretation of the content.

Novels

Novels must be used with extreme care in sociological research. The usefulness and validity of novels will depend on the integrity and authenticity of the research the author has undertaken. Sometimes sociologists will use respected novels in order to verify information obtained from more traditional sources. A feminist might use the representation of gender in novels to offer an insight into gender relations and how these might be influenced by age, social class, ethnicity and location.

CONTEMPORARY APPLICATION

It is worth noting how both academics and the public are benefiting from the growing accessibility of secondary sources as more become available as they are published, particularly on the internet. In addition, the government is frequently subject to mandatory publication of information following Freedom of Information requests.

STUDY TIP

When discussing secondary methods and data, be sure to include official statistics and documents, discussed in Section 2, as well as novels, oral histories and media content analysis discussed in this section.

RESEARCH IN FOCUS

Using secondary data in the form of archival sources

Knight *et al.* (2015) collected secondary data in order to study everyday food and families in periods of low income and poverty. The method they used was to analyse narrative archival sources. They studied the content of three diaries written for the Mass Observation Archive in the 1950s. By examining the everyday food practices expressed in these diaries, they were able to gain an understanding of how people ate in times of austerity.

The researchers were aware of the implications of using secondary data – in this case from narrative archives. For example, they talk of the challenges presented because of the 'muted, moral and mundane' aspects of food practices: surrounded as they are by the personal and private as well as the social and public. Also, perceptions of what constitutes 'the everyday' vary. However, the researchers state that the data allowed them to gain an understanding of habitual food practices and describe how this was achieved.

They found that that presentation of the diary material varied considerably. Typed entries were mostly still legible, but in some hand-written ones the ink had faded or the writing was difficult to read. The narratives also varied in terms of style, and depth and breadth of content.

The researchers took an epistemological standpoint that emphasised the importance of context in their analysis. They aimed to contextualise the diary entries in a number of ways. They included statements from other accounts of the period as well as photographs and other Mass Observation data from the time. However, they observe that they could never fully understand or make sense of the data, as post-war circumstances were very different to those of 21st century Britain.

Adapted from Knight, Brannen and O'Connell (2015)

Questions

1. Briefly outline some of the problems the researchers found in using secondary data.
2. What benefits did they find they gained from using secondary data?
3. Using the item and your wider sociological knowledge, what general problems can be associated with using diaries as a source of data?
4. What problem is highlighted in the last sentence of the item with regard to using historical documents generally?

1.2 What are quantitative and qualitative methods of research?

When thinking about quantitative or qualitative methods, you should have an awareness of each of these approaches, the research methods that are associated with them and how they are associated with the respective approaches of positivism and interpretivism.

The quantitative approach

When sociologists accumulate data for their research they can collect either quantitative data or qualitative data (or both). Quantitative data refers to data that is essentially factual and generally takes a numerical form. It is the type of data that is traditionally associated with positivist sociologists.

Most sociologists in the nineteenth century adopted the positivist position. Positivists believe that people's behaviour is shaped by factors that are directly observable, so they undertake a scientific method of collecting 'social facts'. As a consequence, quantitative data is often numerical in nature expressed in the form of statistics. Because it is easier to replicate quantitative research the data is said to be higher in reliability.

Some research methods are more appropriate than others for collecting quantitative data. The most common research method is using a social survey, based on a closed question questionnaire or structured interview. When sociologists collect their own data this is known as primary data. However, they can also simply use data that has already been collected by someone else. This is known as secondary data and is comprised of findings from existing research and official statistics. Often secondary data will come in the form of quantitative data, such as official crime statistics, marriage rates, or the percentage of pupils who attain 5 A*–C GCSEs. The quantitative approach is favoured by researchers who are studying trends or statistical truths.

The qualitative approach

In contrast to quantitative data which is usually numerical, qualitative data is made up of words. Those who gather and use qualitative data are known collectively as interpretivist sociologists, adopting an approach modelled on social action theory, originally devised by Max Weber. Researchers can interpret the motives and meanings behind people's experiences by exploring their behaviour and feelings.

The most common research methods used to collect qualitative data include unstructured interviews and participant observation. Whereas collecting quantitative data involves the objective accumulation of factual and measurable data, qualitative data is subjective; essentially it is data about how people feel. Qualitative data consequently tends to be viewed as richer in detail than data obtained by quantitative means. Because it gets to the heart of the matter, qualitative data is generally considered higher in validity.

It is important to recognise that while quantitative data is associated particularly with a positivistic approach, all sociologists will inevitably collect some numerical data in the course of their research.

KEY SOCIOLOGIST

Emile Durkheim (1897) sought to collect quantitative data through a positivist approach in his study of suicide. It was a ground breaking analysis of statistical data from which Durkheim concluded that social factors rather than individual personalities caused suicide. Later, interpretivists argued Durkheim's positivistic approach overlooked the meanings that lay behind not just suicidal behaviour but also how statistics were interpreted by people like coroners.

STUDY TIP

As you study this topic, make a note of examples of methodological pluralism as you come across them. Being able to cite them will strengthen your work.

RESEARCH IN FOCUS

Imitating Casanova

Schuurmans and Monaghan (2015) undertook a qualitative investigation into what they refer to as the 'seduction community' (SC). This comprised young heterosexual men who shared a forum and embodied the Casanova-myth by operating as pick-up artists. The qualitative data was derived from life history interviews of a sample of 29 males undertaken during fieldwork in California in 2009 and 2013. Such men, it is claimed, act as an ideal type as judged by other young men. They are deemed to represent adventurous urban male heterosexuality pursuing a fantastic vision of an enviable sex life – an image, the researchers point out, interestingly promoted by the commercialised dating industry.

Most interviewees were recruited via snowball sampling. The interviews conducted in 2009 were fully transcribed and those from 2013 were part-transcribed, with the material analysed using an inductive approach. It became apparent early in the research that these SCs had a pyramid organisational structure: a large body of novices at the bottom, a smaller amount of medium-term members (1–3 years) and a few long-term members (over 3 years). This latter group mainly consisted of pick-up coaches and the forum moderators.

The findings were that while the SC promoted the view that men should become skilled at picking up beautiful women, the reality was that as part of a longer-term quest for emotional intimacy, many decided to abandon their 'playboy lifestyle' in favour of heterosexuality with a special, deserving and attractive partner.

Adapted from Schuurmans and Monaghan (2015)

Questions

1. What is a snowball sample?
2. What issues are associated with transcribing recorded interviews?
3. In what ways will qualitative data offer advantages in this research, compared to the collection of quantitative data?
4. What is meant by the term 'reliable'?

Check your understanding

1. What is primary data?
2. What is secondary data?
3. Make a list of as many sources of secondary data as you can think of.
4. What is meant by the term organic analogy?
5. What is quantitative data?
6. What methods would typically be used to collect quantitative data?
7. What is qualitative data?
8. What methods would typically be used to collect qualitative data?
9. What is a positivist approach?
10. What is an interpretivist approach?

Practice questions

1. Outline and explain two advantages of using official statistics in sociological research. [10 marks]

Read Item A on page 8 and answer the question that follows.

Item A

Qualitative data tends to be made up of words, from which researchers can extract meanings, especially to explain the actions of actors. While all researchers can collect qualitative data, it is generally associated with non-positivistic sociologists.

Applying material from Item A and your knowledge of research methods, evaluate the strengths and limitations of adopting a qualitative approach to studying aspects of society. [20 marks]

Section 2: Consensus, conflict, structural and social action theories

This section will explore the following debates:
- What are consensus and conflict theories?
- What are social action theories?

GETTING YOU STARTED
Defining 'pimp'

Figure 1.3 The pimp's role in prostitution often flies under the radar

Holly Davis (2013) felt that while the topic of prostitution received a lot of coverage, the focus tended to be on the sex workers rather than the pimps. She argues that the word pimp is used in an ambiguous manner, making it difficult to make consistent and clear comparisons within the growing body of literature on prostitution. She states it is important to **operationalise** the term pimp and offers a more robust definition drawing from history, cultural context, mainstream usage, academic applications and feedback from pimps themselves. Her new definition of pimp is: 'an individual who financially profits from, and manages the activities and income of, one or more individuals involved in prostitution'.

While prostitution is perennial, pimps are exceptionally under-studied, not least because of the inaccessibility of the population. As a consequence research into this group has been restricted, resulting in very limited, both historical and current.

Adapted from Davis (2013)

Questions

1. Why is it important to generally have clear-cut and shared definitions of terms?
2. Davis calls pimps 'inaccessible'. What typical problems are researchers faced with when their subject matter is elusive and operate in the underground?
3. Using the item and your broader sociological knowledge discuss some of the dangers associated with researching sex work.

2.1 What are consensus and conflict theories?

Remember that functionalism and the New Right are examples of consensus theories and theories like Marxism, neo-Marxism and feminism are examples of the conflict theories.

Structural consensus theory

'Consensus' means a shared view or agreement between people. Consensus theories argue that society works effectively – consequently it benefits both the individual and society. The main source of consensus is the socialisation process whereby norms, values and appropriate behaviour are taught and learnt. This is a lifelong process but occurs particularly in the early years of childhood. Without some form of consensus human society would not be possible. The key consensus theory in sociology is functionalism (originally called 'structural functionalism'). Functionalism is a structural theory as well as being a macro-theory, concerned with understanding human behaviour through the way in which society operates as a whole.

What is the functionalist perspective?

This theory is centred on how the component parts that make up society operate in a way that is both functional to its members and the maintenance of society as a whole. The origins of functionalism go back to influential thinkers of the nineteenth century, including Herbert Spencer (1820–1903) and Emile Durkheim (1858–1917).

Spencer, heavily influenced by Charles Darwin, emphasised the evolutionary development of society and its component parts. Through his '**organic analogy**' Spencer compared society to the human body. Just as an organism is made up of organs that are interrelated and interdependent, then so is society made up of social institutions (such as family, education, work) that are interrelated and interdependent.

Durkheim, a contemporary of Spencer, developed a key understanding of the role that consensus values played in reinforcing social order and stability in society. Emile Durkheim is often viewed as the key influence on the development of functionalism. Functionalists share many of Durkheim's ideas such as **value consensus**; the role core values play on sustaining consensus. Durkheim emphasised the importance of a socially integrated society, held together by the **collective conscience** of the people. Durkheim stated that, 'the individual is the point of arrival, not departure' which implies that individuals have little control over their own lives let alone the ability to change society. Durkheim also used the organic analogy of comparing society to a body (see page 10).

Such ideas were to prove highly influential to a group of sociologists in the mid twentieth century in the USA who developed 'structural functionalism'. As a theory, it is heavily influenced by Durkheim's consensus view of society. As a theory it also reflects Spencer's ideas though its focus on integration derived from inter-relationships between institutions and their members.

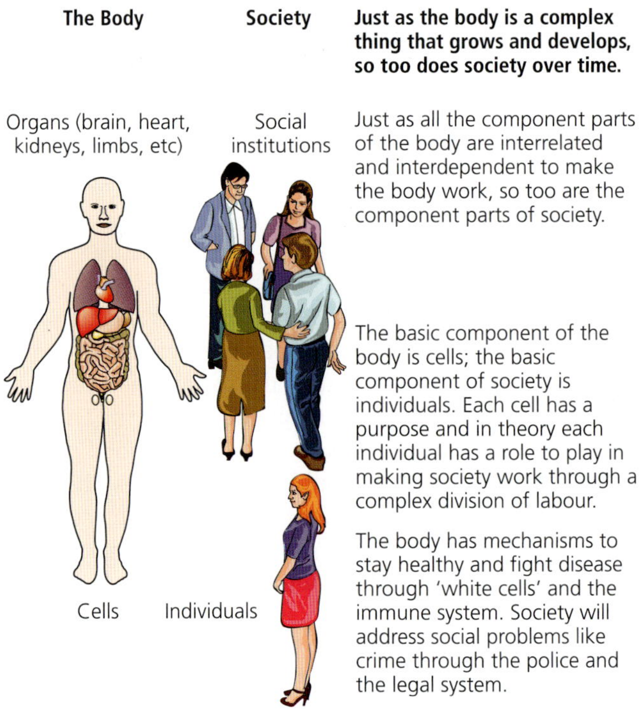

| The Body | Society | Just as the body is a complex thing that grows and develops, so too does society over time. |

Organs (brain, heart, kidneys, limbs, etc) — Social institutions

Just as all the component parts of the body are interrelated and interdependent to make the body work, so too are the component parts of society.

The basic component of the body is cells; the basic component of society is individuals. Each cell has a purpose and in theory each individual has a role to play in making society work through a complex division of labour.

The body has mechanisms to stay healthy and fight disease through 'white cells' and the immune system. Society will address social problems like crime through the police and the legal system.

Cells — Individuals

Figure 1.4 The organic analogy

The person most credited with the development of structural functionalism is Talcott Parsons (1902–1979). He supported Durkheim's emphasis on the role of core values in reinforcing social order and stability in society. In addition, Parsons also saw the agencies of socialisation as the key promoter of these core values. Parsons' biggest contribution to understanding society is probably his social systems theory, which embraces both structure and functioning. Parsons viewed society as a system made up of four sub-systems (economic, political, kinship and cultural) each specifically there to meet essential human needs. These needs are referred to by Parsons as imperatives or prerequisites. Society is in social equilibrium when these needs are met and a balance exists within the system and its sub-systems.

He developed key concepts, such as '**collective conscience**' to describe the moral values that were core to any society, serving to bind people together. Within this structural consensus theory the importance of unity and social order is seen to come from the sharing of **core values** held throughout society. Such core values serve to integrate society together, for example by establishing and reinforcing cultural rules and a moral code. The primary and secondary socialising agencies (**social institutions** like the family, education, religion, mass media, etc.) each help to promote conformity. They do this through reinforcing the core values of society (such as respecting authority, hard work and achievement, valuing the family). Failure to conform is addressed by these agencies through sanctions of disapproval or punishment.

Within the system of society, Parsons argued there were four sub-systems: economic, political, kinship and cultural. Each of these sub-systems functions to meet essential human needs. So important are they that Parsons refers to them as imperatives or prerequisites of society. For society to be healthy and survive, it has to deal with four problems: adaptation, goal attainment, integration and latency (also called pattern maintenance).

Functionalism dominated sociology until the 1960s, when it became increasingly challenged by Marxist and interactionist thinking. Its critics argue that it is a naïve and overly optimistic theory; choosing to over-emphasise consensus while ignoring the widespread conflict that exists in society. As a theory it also struggles to adequately explain social change.

Criticism of functionalism

Functionalism rapidly lost support following its decline in the 1960s. Critics argue that functionalism declined because it failed to account for the growing diversity and conflict in society. The New Right perspective, although rooted in political neo-liberal ideology, shares many ideas with functionalism. Specific criticism of functionalism includes:

- There is simply too much emphasis on consensus and not enough recognition of the degree of conflict that exists in society between social classes, ethnic groups and men and women.
- The organic analogy, which effectively reifies society (turns it into a living organism), serves to ignore the divisive nature of the class system and the unequal distribution of power.
- Unlike Marx's historical materialism which portrays the development of human society in stages, functionalism fails to see society as an historical system, shaped by the conflicting interests of its participants.

What is New Right theory?

Although New Right theory is, strictly speaking, a political ideology centred on neo-liberal principles, its contribution to the sociological debate simply cannot be ignored. Its neo-liberal support for free-market capitalism offers a polar opposite to the anti-capitalist Marxist perspective. Although it is criticised for being ideologically blinkered, it is by no means the only sociological perspective to be accused of this.

The New Right perspective adopted many, but not all, of the ideas of functionalism. The decline of functionalism's influence after the 1960s created a vacuum of right-wing political ideas in sociology. In the 1980s writers like Friedrich Hayek (1944) became influential, particularly with the Thatcher government in the UK and the Reagan administration in the USA. The political influence of right-wing neo-liberal politics spread globally and the New Right quickly established a presence in sociology.

New Right thinking has always been something of a controversial perspective. For example, it has received negative criticism for adopting a rather dogmatic approach to things like lone-parent families, the underclass and homosexuality. Nonetheless, its ideas penetrated, and challenged, many of the prevailing ideas of sociology in relation to Year 1 topics: the family, education and poverty, work and wealth. In Year 2 topics it plays a significant role in crime and deviance, and global development.

The New Right has influenced social policy in contemporary governments globally. For instance, it has almost become a received wisdom of consensus opinion that it is no longer possible, or even desirable, to go back to the social democratic welfare state of post-war Britain. This era of cradle-to-grave government intervention and support is sometimes described as 'the golden age of the welfare state'. It went hand in hand with Keynesian demand management economic policy. This was implemented by post-war governments in the 1950s and 1960s and is credited with securing full employment for over 20 years. Any shortfall in consumer spending was compensated for by an increase in government spending. Keynesian economics became discredited because of rising inflation in the 1970s. Prime Minister Thatcher, by embracing New Right ideas in the 1980s, set a theme of British politics that argued that the free market, rather than government, was the most efficient allocator of resources.

> **KEY SOCIOLOGIST**
> **Friedrich von Hayek** (1899–1992) grew up in early twentieth-century Austria. He was shocked by the totalitarianism of the communist Soviet Union and the fascist regime of the Nazi government in Germany. His book *The Road to Serfdom* (1944) was a response to the growth of economic planning in the wartime economies of countries like Great Britain. Hayek fiercely supported the free market in allocating resources, claiming that state planning was inevitably 'coercive'. He argued that strong states damaged society, by restricting personal freedoms.

After just under 20 years of Thatcherism, Tony Blair effectively carried on the same theme. Although officially he advocated a 'third way', midway between neo-liberalist economic efficiency and social democratic compassion, his social and economic policies were fundamentally those of the New Right. For example, as a long-term supporter of blaming crime on structural causes ('tough on crime, tough on the causes of crime'), once Prime Minister he quickly converted to the familiar New Right concern with the 'problem family' as the main cause of crime. Government policies advocated New Right solutions of zero tolerance policing and more prisons. Wider social policy scapegoated lone mothers, teenage pregnancy, dysfunctional families, the work-shy and the substance abuser. Blair's 'solution' to crime was welfare to work policies and cutting benefits.

The Thatcher legacy of cutting back the state and welfare and embracing neo-liberal socio-economic policies became ever more obvious in the coalition government (2010–2015) and apparently remains so in the 2015–2020 Conservative government.

As a sociological perspective, New Right thinking has been largely isolated and commands limited support other than from its few enthusiastic advocates. Politically, however, New Right thinking has been massively influential in shaping government policies globally since the 1980s. Such influence means that it would be naïve and simplistic for sociologists to simply dismiss it.

Criticisms of the New Right
- Many of their ideas are seen as simplistic and short-sighted, ignoring the complexities of modern society and reinforcing stereotypes that lack evidence.
- For example, Charles Murray's views on lone mothers and the underclass have been denounced by Alan Walker (1990) as reliant on little more than 'innuendos, assertions and anecdotes' rather than firm evidence.
- Others challenge the naïve assumptions of the New Right that we have equality of opportunity and live in a **meritocracy**.

Structural conflict theory
An alternative view to consensus theory is conflict theory. Note this is also normally a structural theory so has the same macro-theory characteristics of making sense of human behaviour through trying to understand how society works. As the name implies, its starting criticism of consensus theory is that it ignores the considerable amount of conflict that exists in society. Conflict theory sees society as being comprised of different groups who each possess unequal amounts of power. This power imbalance applies to any inequality in society such as gender, ethnicity and particularly social class. Society, they argue, is characterised by inequality because of the domination of disadvantaged groups by more advantaged ones. The key structural conflict theory in sociology is Marxism, derived from the work and ideas of Karl Marx (1818–1883).

What is the Marxist perspective?
Like functionalism, Marxism is a response to modernism. Karl Marx was able to observe, first-hand, the new industrial society of capitalism. Like functionalism, this theory is structuralist in that it places a lot of emphasis on the structures that make up society. The two theories have also been described as macro-theories, as they are top-down theories that explain the operation of society as a system. Politically, functionalism and Marxism are poles apart, and in contrast to the consensus basis of functionalism, Marxism is based on a conflict analysis of society, especially that centred on class conflict. Marxism is preoccupied with the economic system of capitalism.

Marx also viewed society as a system, but in his case an economic system he called **capitalism**. Capitalism is made of two classes, the **bourgeoisie** (who own the wealth; expressed as the **means of production**) and the **proletariat** (who do all the work and therefore generate all the wealth). Crucially, Marx argued, the interests of these two classes will never coincide; therefore conflict is endemic within capitalism. But as with the gender inequality that was accepted until feminism raised women's consciousness, society gives the impression of a social class consensus, with most of the proletariat accepting and even supporting the blatant inequalities that exist in society.

Despite the fact that society is fundamentally divided and unfair, with life chances very much shaped by the income and wealth of your parents, most people openly support society as it is. Consider how there is little support for any radical political party in elections, and how the major parties, who secure the bulk of the votes, offer 'more of the same' with minor adjustments. To explain people's '**false consciousness**' (of their true exploited position), Marx recognised that social institutions such as the family, religion and the media act as **diversionary institutions**. Marx's famous phrase 'religion ... is the opiate of the people' implies that religion has functioned primarily to befuddle people to accept their lot in life in return for the promise of a better afterlife. Workers are too busy becoming slaves to paying the bills and putting food on the family table to bother about their true class position. The media offers escapism, such as the consolation that our lives haven't got half the problems of the characters in *EastEnders*, or by generating unsatisfied wants by advertising the next 'must have' product. Either way, the fact that the very privileged are born to rule and provided with institutions to facilitate this, such as an exclusive private school system, goes largely unnoticed.

Marx used the phrase '**bourgeois ideology**' to reflect the fact that dominant ideas in society reflect the interests of the dominant class. An ideology is simply a set of ideas used to shape people's attitudes and behaviour and inevitably reflecting the interests of dominant groups. Marx used the analogy of the **camera obscura** to show that ideology is a set of ideas capable of making circumstances 'appear upside down' and 'inverting' our perception of reality. The workers end up supporting capitalism, the very economic system (or '**infrastructure**') that exploits them and fills them with a sense of **alienation**. Ideology that pervades the '**superstructure**' therefore alters and distorts the individual's perception of the outer world – their objective social reality.

Ideas are shaped by the economic system

Cultural, political and ideological ideas	Superstructure **(ideas and beliefs)**
Social classes (social relations of production) Economy	Infrastructure **(invisible economic system)**

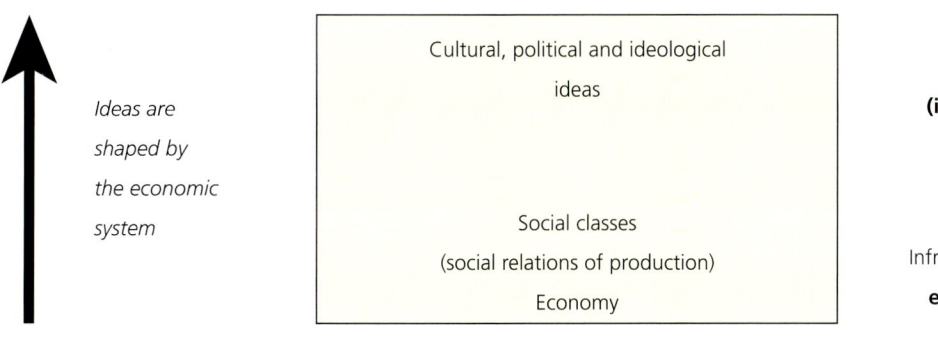

Figure 1.5 Infrastructure versus substructure

Marxism is much better equipped than functionalism to deal with and explain social change, as this is a cornerstone to Marx's theory. Through his theory of historical materialism, Marx portrayed capitalism as merely a stage or 'epoch' in the history of human development. The end of history, he argues, will be a truly equal communist society. The driver of social change, Marx argued, is class conflict. He shows that all societies are class societies with a dominant and a subordinate class. The interests of these two classes can never coincide, and ultimately the subordinate class will seize power and overthrow the dominant class. Under capitalism, the dominant class is the 'bourgeoisie' and the subordinate class the 'proletariat'. However, Marx showed that the subordinate class can be duped and fooled into supporting the society that actually exploits it. He referred to this process as 'false consciousness'.

Marx was clearly aware of how **ideologies** can distort reality and prevent workers seeing their true class position – exploited, alienated beings. Institutions like the media, religion, education and the family all divert people's attention away from revolutionary thought.

Neo-Marxism

Neo-Marxists took Marx's ideas and interpreted them in light of the changes they saw between the world in which Marx made his observations and the world they saw around them. They also can offer some criticisms of traditional Marxist analysis, particularly its economic **determinism**. Three broad neo-Marxist traditions evolved in the twentieth century; each is discussed below.

Gramsci's concept of hegemony

Antonio Gramsci (1971) argued that ideology was just as important as economic class structure in maintaining the ruling class's political dominance. This was Gramsci's concept of **hegemony** – that dominant groups exercise control over minority groups through ideas. Hegemony is a subtle form of control: winning people's support for capitalism avoids the need for coercion by agents of control such as the police, courts and prisons. Hegemony is therefore achieved through the legitimation of power within popular culture. Social institutions, such as the media, education and religion, are used to justify, explain and win support for the system that is actually exploiting the working class. Gramsci's work, because it distances itself from the class structure and is embedded within people's ideas, is sometime called 'humanist neo-Marxism'.

Althusser's ideological state apparatus

Louis Althusser's (2005) description of the role of ideology is similar to Gramsci's, but Althusser places greater importance on the structures that support and transmit such ideologies – ideological state apparatuses. These apparatuses are the major social institutions that make up society such as the family, education, religion, media and even things like health organisations like the NHS. Althusser argues that such institutions legitimise inequalities by subconsciously introducing a particular set of ideas (see Book 1, Education page 52 and Health page 225). The ruling class maintains its power by having these apparatuses socialise the norms and values that preserve the *status quo*.

Should these everyday apparatuses prove inadequate in fulfilling this ideological role then the state will draw upon its repressive state agencies – the coercive power of the riot police and, if policing proves inadequate, the armed forces. Because of its emphasis on the ideological role of social institutions, Althusser's work is sometimes called 'structuralist neo-Marxism'.

The Frankfurt School

The third important neo-Marxist influence has been the Frankfurt School who are credited with the development of **conflict theory**. The School established itself in the USA in the 1930s after fleeing Nazi persecution. Critical theory attempts to explain the perpetual power of the ruling class as stemming from subtle ideologies of consumerism and individualism which promote false consciousness. One of the best applications of the School's work has been to the mass media (see Book 1, page 119, and the Media chapter page 256). An important idea is that of culture industry whereby all forms of culture get reduced to mass culture; manufactured and superficial, devoid of artistic merit but produced to entertain and keep the proletariat under control. More widely, critical theory has been credited with encouraging a questioning of everything. Such has been the influence of the Frankfurt School over the post-war decades that the author Michael Walsh (2015) claims they are responsible for being a leading influence in the social justice movement and even the drive for political correctness.

Criticisms of Marxism

- Critics argue that Marxism over-stresses conflict and underestimates the extent of consensus in society.
- As a theory it is criticised for being over-negative and crudely deterministic in that all social problems are inevitably blamed on the capitalist system.
- Critics argue that people (not the economic system) make their own history and, for that reason, the assumed future of communism cannot be predicted.
- Functionalists argue that Marxism places too much emphasis on conflict at the expense of recognising the fair amount of consensus in society.
- Feminists argue that the focus solely on class ignores gender relations.
- The proletariat show no appetite for a revolution, although Marxists explain this away through false consciousness.

	Structural Consensus Theory Functionalism	**Structural Conflict Theory Marxism**
Links to 'founder'	Emile Durkheim	Karl Marx
Similarities	Macro-theory: society is structural (bigger than the individual) and seen as a social system made of component social institutions.	Macro-theory: society is structural (bigger than the individual) based on the economic system of capitalism.
Analogy	Organic analogy of comparing society to a body with organs (social institutions) made up of cells (people).	Building analogy of economic foundation of the infrastructure that supports the superstructure of social institutions, culture and ideas.
Role of socialisation	Importance of socialisation to instil consensus of shared core values.	Importance of socialisation for the imposition of bourgeois ideology to instil false consciousness.
Social change	Change is slow and evolutionary because consensus means everyone works together to maintain equilibrium.	Society moves through stages or 'epochs'. Change derives from conflict because the interests of the subordinate class never coincide with those of the dominant class.
Fairness	Society is fair, with meritocratic principles that reward the talented and hard-working.	Society is fundamentally unfair with the class system serving to reproduce inequalities in society.
Inequality	Seen as a good thing encouraging ambition and hard work.	Seen as a bad thing reflecting unequal chances and oppression.
Summary	Helps us understand how society is integrated to function as a whole.	Helps us understand how society reflects the interests of one class and the degree of inequality and exploitation that exists in society.

Table 1.1

KEY SOCIOLOGIST

Jürgen Habermas (1929–) is a neo-Marxist who revitalised the Frankfurt School into its second generation. He adopts an optimistic appraisal by predicting that capitalism will undergo a series of crises. In particular, he predicts a legitimation crisis whereby, unable to finance welfare spending, states embark upon a laissez-faire (free-market) approach. This, he predicts, will only serve to disillusion the people not only with politicians and political parties (who increasingly offer the electorate similar policies) but with the capitalist system itself. He therefore promotes an optimistic view of the development of an increasingly class-conscious working class.

STUDY TIP

Both consensus theory and conflict theory have strengths and weaknesses. While students often favour one theory over another, it is important to retain balance to be able to write critically about each. This is especially so when they are being applied to specific sociological perspectives such as functionalism, Marxism and feminism.

CONTEMPORARY APPLICATION

Parsons' idea of society as a 'system' made up of component parts is a useful idea to this debate. Think of a car engine as basically comprised of pistons, spark plugs and a fuel pump. Each of these component parts does nothing on its own, but when combined together they operate as a system and make the engine work. Society is also like a system, made up of component parts (such as family, education, the state) and together they make society work. However, if one component fails then this stops society operating efficiently.

Feminism as a conflict theory

Conflict theory's central focus is on the conflict they see as inherent in society. Yet this conflict of interest is not always recognised or resented, even by the disadvantaged in society. The reasons for this, conflict theorists argue, is that socialisation operates as a means of sustaining and justifying the inequalities that exist in society. Thus, feminists argue, women put up with oppression from **patriarchy** in the past because from childhood they had been socialised into accepting the subordination of women as somehow natural and normal. Men, girls learnt, were the logical and appropriate choice to be head of households, breadwinners while women stayed at home, paid more in the workplace, occupiers of all the senior religious positions and dominators of politics and public life. It was not until feminism raised women's consciousness about the fundamental unfairness of the way society has been gendered in the interests of men, that women began to sit up and question the assumed consensus and 'normality' of male domination.

What is the feminist perspective?

Feminism developed as a specific theoretical perspective within sociology because its supporters claimed that especially before the 1960s the subject often rendered women invisible by ignoring them and their experiences. Feminists argued that even if women were considered, sociology frequently marginalised the importance of women's roles. Feminists argue that this was largely as a result of the systematic biases and inadequacies of what they refer to as '**malestream**' theories. A feminist theory was necessary as a check to such male domination as illustrated across the chapters in both this volume and Book 1 (see page 318).

Feminism also offers an alternative view and constructs reality by drawing on women's own interpretations of their own experiences and interests. Feminist theory can be complex. It is a structural theory in the sense that it is centred on how patriarchy shapes the experiences of women (and men) across society. However, it is also interpretive since it seeks to make sense of women's experiences by portraying the meanings of being a woman in patriarchal society. The evolution of feminism is often described in terms of 'waves':

- **First wave feminism**: associated with the campaign for votes before and after the First World War.
- **Second wave feminism**: associated with the women's liberation movement of 1960s and 1970s.
- **Third wave feminism**: associated with postmodernist ideas of individualism and differentiation (see Table 5.2 in Book 1, page 179). Women were recognised as having a variety of experiences and outcomes associated with income, wealth, ethnicity, age, locality and belief systems (see Religion chapter, page 129).
- Fourth wave feminism: activist campaigning to build a strong, popular reactive movement particularly by embracing online technology (see Media chapter, page 256).

As a perspective it is divided into different types of feminisms, reflecting disagreement on the nature, causes and solutions to patriarchy.

Liberal feminism

This type of feminism views gender inequality as stemming primarily from the ignorance of men that derives primarily from the strength of socialisation and 'sex-role conditioning'. The solution to gender inequality is simply the education and reform of men, although they recognise this sometimes needs the 'stick' of anti-discrimination legislation. This is therefore the least radical of all the feminisms and is often criticised by other feminists for glossing over the true oppression and exploitation which women experience. Other feminists also claim that men are not simply ignorant, but have a vested interest in maintaining the patriarchal ways of living and thinking that empower them. Liberal feminism is usefully applied to social policy and education in Book 1 (page 80).

Marxist-feminism

As their name implies these are feminists who adopt the Marxist view that the economic dependence women have on men has been created by capitalism. This serves two functions: firstly, to provide cheap female workers who can be exploited even more than men, and secondly to ensure that household chores are done cheaply. When women did enter the workforce; they traditionally worked in low-paid, low-status, mainly part-time jobs (although this can now be viewed as somewhat simplistic and changing). Marxist-feminists argue that the solution to women's oppression is the abolition of capitalism. This would eradicate the double oppression of patriarchy in the home and economic exploitation in the workplace. The Marxist-feminist perspective is usefully applied in the Global Development chapter in the context of 'exploitation thesis' (see pages 241 and 253) which emphasises how the global spread of capitalism involves the systematic exploitation of women.

Radical feminism

This is the most extreme form of feminism. Radical feminists focus their attention on the power relations between men and women, which is referred to as 'sexual politics'. They argue that all women are oppressed by men, in particular within the home, and need to break this imbalance of power through a collective identification of their interests through a sense of 'sisterhood'. Radical feminists see gender as a shared class identity. They argue that women share the same sex-class position because they are controlled and sometimes abused by the violence of men. Women's liberation can only be achieved by actively challenging and eradicating the prevailing systems of patriarchy. An interesting and extreme expression of radical feminism is that of separatism which argues that women can only be free when men are isolated entirely from their lives.

Black feminism

Black feminism derived because black women felt white feminists failed to recognise some women were oppressed not only by feminism but by racism as well. Black feminists criticised the ethnocentricity of most feminism, which was blinkered and focused on just white women's experiences. Therefore, in order to eliminate women's subordination, the system of racism must be challenged, alongside patriarchy and capitalism. Black feminism plays an important role in differentiating different women's experiences of family life. Recognising that racism can be a frequent experience for women from Black and Minority Ethnic Groups (BMEs) they are more positive about the institution of the family, seeing it as a potential haven for its members in a racist world.

Postmodernist feminists

The claim of some that we now live in a postmodern society has led to two polar strands in feminism. Some people, called post-feminists, argue that the shift towards an increasingly gender-equal society has made feminism no longer relevant. The battle has largely been won! Clearly the bulk of feminists would challenge this assertion.

The other strand of postmodernist feminism embraces the essential argument of postmodernism that we are now living in an increasingly fragmented and pluralistic society centred on individuality and multiple identities. While they recognise that gender is clearly a very important determinant of life chances, the experiences of individual women differ. Factors like social class, age, ethnicity, physical appearance and even locality all shape and individualise women's experiences. Clearly some women are more oppressed by men than others, so a more individualistic approach is necessary, rather than a one size fits all approach. An example of postmodernist feminism being applied to a social context is the discussion and comparison of difference feminism's contribution to our understanding of the family (see Book 1, page 179). Both Linda Nicholson and Cheshire Calhoun are described as difference feminists. Difference feminism recognises that women's experiences of family life varies depending on their type of household. They are critical of feminist perspectives that overlook this simple point.

Criticisms of feminism

- The strength of feminism is that it redresses the way in which women have been systematically ignored from malestream sociology. As a perspective it focuses on the issues and meanings of being female, and the oppression of women (possibly as a sex-class) by patriarchal forces.
- It is ethnocentric, largely ignoring black women. It ignores the fact that for black women racial oppression may be of equal or greater significance.
- It is orientated to Western society and largely ignores Third World women.
- It ignores the positive way in which many women view the family and relationships with women.

> **STUDY TIP**
>
> In elaborating the differences between consensus and conflict theory, focus on consensus theory's defence of the status quo and the positive aspects of society. Conflict theory, in contrast, is much more focused on the negative aspects and the ever-changing nature of society.

2.2 What are social action theories?

The origins of action theory lie with Max Weber (1864–1920). It is very different to the structural/macro approaches of functionalism and Marxism. Instead, action theory focuses on the micro-level of social life – the way in which individuals interact with one another. Society is seen to be the end-product of all this, whereas to a structural theorist society is seen as the starting point. So instead of seeing a system into which individuals are born and are socialised into the prevailing norms and values, action theory argues that only by looking at how individual humans are able to interact can we come to understand how social order is created. So just like any sociological theory, the purpose of action theory is to explain human behaviour, but it avoids making assumptions of the determinism of the constraining social structure. Instead it examines the personal meanings that lie behind actions and recognises the importance and influence of other individuals in shaping behaviour. Action theory argues that the nature of society lies not in the fact that it is a system but the extraordinary ability of humans to work out what is going on around them. From this they can then choose to act in a particular way, in the light of this interpretation. Hence action theory is also called interpretive theory.

Since people's actions stem from their conscious engagement in what are perceived to be meaningful encounters, the result is social order (the shared imagination in people's minds of a society that seems to work). But this order is not derived from the imposition of cultural rules, as consensus theorists see it. Nor is it the result of the constraints of a world where advantages are unequally distributed as the conflict theorists see it. Instead, society is the result of interactions, carried out by actors interpreting and giving meaning to the social settings they find themselves in, and choosing courses of action accordingly. Action theory has been most closely developed into the sociological perspective of interactionism.

What is the interactionist perspective?

Interactionism, also called symbolic interactionism, derives particularly from Max Weber's action theory. It was developed by sociologists at the University of Chicago, in particular Herbert Blumer and George Herbert Mead in the mid twentieth century. As a perspective it is fundamentally different to both functionalism and Marxism. It rejects any attempt to make sense of society as a system, choosing instead as its starting point to try and understand the meanings behind individual actions. As a consequence it is described as micro-sociology because its starting point is how individuals make sense of the world, not how society works. It has three key characteristics:

- It focuses on the interaction between the individuals (who it calls actors) and the world (effectively the actors' 'stage' on which they perform a variety of roles).
- It is interested in the actions of individuals (such as why people choose to behave the way they do as '**voluntaristic**' behaviour), rather than the structures in which they operate (such as family obligations, compulsory education, speed cameras, etc.).
- It stresses the importance of an actor's ability to interpret the social world, arguing there is no objective reality, instead the world is real inside the head of each individual.

Much of interactionism centres on the concept of self, which is at the very hub of this perspective. As individuals we are very conscious of the people around us and how they think about us and our behaviour. As such, the self can be interpreted in three ways:

- how we imagine we appear to others
- how we imagine their judgement of that appearance; and
- our response to those perceived judgements, such as pride, anger or humiliation.

Erving Goffman (1959) developed the idea of the self. He recognised the discrepancy between our 'all-too-human selves and our socialised selves'. The tension is between what people expect us to do, and what we spontaneously want to do.

The concept of power relations and labelling theory were introduced by Howard Becker (1963). He noted how powerful groups can impose labels on the less powerful. Such labels often stick and can become self-fulfilling, so a teacher may negatively label a student as 'stupid' or 'troublesome' which can become a shared meaning and even internalised by the student who may feel an obligation to live up to the label.

To interactionists, there is no such thing as objective reality. Reality is what is inside people's heads – individual's interpretations of the world. This is an idea that would be adopted subsequently by postmodernists. Both functionalists and Marxists criticise interactionism for neglecting social structures which they argue impact directly on people's lives and shape life chances and opportunities. Marxists argue that the structure of social class is particularly important, whether or not actors are consciously aware of it.

	Positivist/structural approach		**Interpretive/social action approach**
Sociology perspective	functionalism, New Right	Marxism, neo-Marxism, feminism*	interactionism, labelling theory, feminism*, phenomenology
Emphasis on	consensus	conflict	meanings and motives
Views on behaviour	determinism – behaviour is determined by structures that surround individuals		voluntarism (agency behaviour) – behaviour reflects free will and derives from within the individual
Characteristics	scientific, value-free, objective, quantitative data, high in reliability		non-scientific, value-laden, subjective, qualitative data, high in validity
Giddens' contribution (see page 362)	structuration theory (structure + agency)		

* Feminism can be viewed as both structural (focusing on the structure of patriarchy) and interpretive (focusing on the meanings of gender oppression)

Table 1.2 Comparison between structural and action theories

Check your understanding

1. What is meant by the term organic analogy?
2. What did Durkheim mean by the collective conscience?
3. What ideology underpins New Right theory?
4. What do Marxists mean by diversionary institutions?
5. What point is being made with Marx's analogy of the camera obscura?
6. What do the terms infrastructure and superstructure mean?
7. What did Gramsci mean by hegemony?
8. Why is feminism seen as both a structuralist and an interpretivist theory?
9. Which sociologist developed social action theory?
10. What do the terms macro-sociology and micro-sociology mean?

Practice questions

1. Outline and explain two advantages of using personal documents in sociological research. [10 marks]

Read Item A below and answer the question that follows.

Item A

Feminists have contributed a lot to broadening the knowledge base and using knowledge to change society. Because feminism is a radical and different perspective it effectively 'deconstructs' existing knowledge that is 'malestream'.

Applying material from Item A and your knowledge of research methods, evaluate the strengths and limitations of adopting a feminist approach to studying aspects of society. [20 marks]

Section 3: How do the concepts of modernity and postmodernity relate to sociological theory?

This section will explore the following debate:

- How do the concepts of modernity and postmodernity relate to sociological theory?

GETTING YOU STARTED
What is meant by modernity?

The modern period is generally agreed to have developed following the Enlightenment in the eighteenth century. This was a fertile academic and intellectual movement of rational and scientific thinking. It challenged the religious ideas that had prevailed for centuries replacing faith with reason. At the same time, the modern world was being shaped by three other significant forces. The Industrial Revolution had begun in Britain transforming rural agricultural societies to urban industrial ones. Modernity described the development of early capitalism with an industrial proletariat or waged labour replacing the rural peasants or serfs.

Politically, modernity also saw the creation of many nation states. Within Europe countries like Germany and Italy evolved from component principalities into nations; and new states were created in Africa, Asia and the Americas in the race to colonise the world.

The third key area which modernism is associated with is culture. Modernity challenged traditional culture, often shaped by legend, superstition and stories, replacing it with a rationality centred on scientific and technical knowledge.

Sociology itself can be viewed as a legacy of the Enlightenment and a product of modernity. This is reflected in the ideas of positivism together with the grand theories developed by Marx, Durkheim and Weber. Anthony Giddens (1987) saw the development of modernity, and its new intellectual expression through these three 'founders' of sociology as serving to challenge the very essence of knowledge and what it was for. Sociology in this period of modernity had a belief in progress and embraced science both as a characteristic of modern thinking, but also as a means to bring about reform and, in the case of Marx, the goal of revolution. Sociological theory was portrayed as the means to understand society in order to improve human lives through the pursuit of progress.

Adapted from 'Introduction to Social Theory' (unpublished: Itchen College)

Questions
1. Briefly explain the Enlightenment.
2. Identify and explain the three significant forces that helped shape the modern period.
3. In what ways can sociology itself be viewed as a product of modernity?

3.1 What is modernity?

To understand modernity or postmodernity, you need to understand the characteristics of each in order to make comparisons and contrasts.

Postmodernity literally means 'after modernity'. This implies it was preceded by a period of modernity and before that there was a period we can call pre-modernity. In sociology modernity reflects the era of industrialisation.

It is also associated with positivism, and the '**grand theories**' developed by classical sociologists like Karl Marx and Emile Durkheim. Indeed sociology itself can be viewed as a product of modernity. Modernity is often discussed in relation to three key areas: economics, politics and culture. Economically, modernity is associated with industrialisation and early capitalism. This came about from market trading, both within countries and globally as **colonialism** and the slave trade developed. Politically, modernity is associated globally with the development of the nation state and internally with the centralised bureaucratic nation state and class-based political party systems. Culturally, modernity is associated with traditions and the accumulation of rational, scientific and technical knowledge. It is therefore no surprise that sociology itself was a product of modernity. The 'founders' of sociology (Durkheim, Marx and Weber) all shared a common intellectual interest in making sense of human behaviour in this period of industrialisation.

Some sociologists, like Anthony Giddens, prefer to use the term '**high modernity**' to postmodernity in order to stress the continuities with modernity. The implication is that we are in a mature stage of modernity, rather than a distinctly new type of society after modernity. Marxists argue that however society implies it has changed superficially, it is fundamentally the same old economic system of capitalism that underpins it.

3.2 What is postmodernist theory?

As noted above, the period of modernity is associated with industrialisation. Since society today is very different to that of the Industrial Revolution, some argue that we are now living in a postmodern society. It is worthwhile stating here that not everyone supports this view. Marxists, for example, argue that society is fundamentally the same capitalist system, with the same economic relations of class exploitation. Sometimes those who believe we are still in the modern period use the term 'late modern' to concede some social and cultural differences to the nineteenth century.

Supporters of postmodernism argue that society is fundamentally different now from what it was during the era of industrialisation. They argue it is now characterised by its preoccupation with consumerism, shopping and style, which is fundamentally different to the old society centred on production and work. Postmodernists argue that society has become considerably fragmented and individualistic – there is so much diversity, allowing people to make personal choices in almost every field of life. Like interactionism, postmodernism does not recognise objective reality. Reality is what is inside people's heads. Since there are multiple versions of reality, postmodernism rejects the very idea of 'grand theories' like the ones discussed above, although it is ironically a theory (of sorts) itself.

At the same time people are increasingly using their choices to construct their identity. Under modernity identity was linked to production: typically the job you did and consequently the social class you belonged to. In postmodernity identity is linked to consumption with surface images and style becoming important defining features. So identity is about wearing labelled clothes which now conveniently have the labels outside so everyone can see them, the brand of car you drive, the neighbourhood you live in, the media you consume, the stylish shopping malls, clubs, pubs and eating places you frequent, even down to the 'trophy wife'. Icons and signs are therefore increasingly consumed for their appearance rather than for their utility.

Many therefore see postmodernity as a superficial society with little depth as style takes precedence over substance. For example, Jean Baudrillard (1985) sees the proliferation of signs and symbols as so extensive that reality becomes confused with fiction. The images are everything, the reality nothing: a condition Baudrillard terms 'simulacrum'. His ultimate vision of the future is one of a society that has 'imploded' and become like a black hole with humans trapped in a type of powerless uniformity, not liberated as other postmodernists believe by diversity and choice.

Globalisation has resulted in global brands and icons that are recognised across the world, with people choosing as if from a 'global cafeteria' (Bruce, 1999). Global brands like McDonald's and Coca-Cola are available in all parts of the globe. In the developing world they are consumed almost in terms of sharing the 'American Dream', that is, their consumption conveys a symbolic message that the individual is emulating people in the Western world and is on a journey that implies one day they will have all the materialist trappings of Western society. The media is increasingly global and offers now hundreds of channels of choice. Technologies like the internet, email and Skype all serve to shrink the world in terms of communication into what Marshall McLuhan (1962) imaginatively described over 50 years ago as a 'global village'. Globalisation is also credited with political change such as encouraging the downfall of the Soviet Union and communism in Eastern Europe. Some see it as undermining nationalism as a source of identity, but at a local level nationalism may be strengthening, such as the independence movement in Scotland. Globalisation has also spread knowledge and ideas. Postmodernity challenges the grand theories of modernity (including sociological theory), arguing that there is no such thing as objective truth. Instead the only truth is the pluralistic character of knowledge. Truth is relative; reality is what is real to individuals.

It is important to recognise that many academics do not recognise postmodernity as a distinct and new era that has replaced the period of modernity. Instead they see society as possibly different, but essentially a continuation of modernity, perhaps in a mature or twilight stage. Marxists are particularly critical of postmodernity being a new era.

Pre-modernity	Pre-literate, tribal societies where myths, legends, superstition and tradition formed the basis of social life. There was little conception of social change. Pre-modern society ended with the decline of medieval society in Europe and the development of Enlightenment in the eighteenth century.
Modernity	Characterised by the industrialisation and urbanisation associated with the huge shift of population to the cities in the nineteenth century. The evolution of the nation state and a centralised and increasingly bureaucratic government state engaged with the welfare of the population. In contrast to the superstition and traditions of pre-modern society modernity is characterised by the rational and scientific thinking that came in with the Enlightenment. Modernity is shaped by science and reason. Sociology is a product of modernity with its grand theories ('big stories' or metanarratives) derived from the production of objective knowledge of scientific status, value-freedom and positivism. Identities are based on social class and work, a person's place in the production system. Politics centred on social class divisions.
Postmodernity High/Late modernity*	Society has become a post-industrial society increasingly shaped by service industries, consumerism and globalisation. Advances in technology and communications have increased geographical mobility and resulted in a media-saturated society. Postmodernity rejects the very idea of 'grand theories', since it does not believe there is objective truth, but rather multiple versions of reality: relativism. Identities based on consumption: a person's spending and lifestyle choices. Politics become more issue-based: environmentalism, animal rights and individual concerns over gender, sexuality, ethnicity, age.

Table 1.3 Stages of modernity

STUDY TIP

You should be able to look at postmodernity critically. Many sociologists argue that postmodernists overstate the degree of change that has occurred in society. So while most ordinary people appear to accept the postmodernist mantra that 'class is dead', sociological research shows it is still a real and valid concept impacting on life chances. Consumption may be a more important driver of identity, but consumption still depends on income.

KEY SOCIOLOGIST

Jean-Francois Lyotard (1984) coined one of the classic definitions of postmodernism: 'incredulity toward metanarratives'. By this he means that no one believes the narratives that technology can solve all our problems. He describes the postmodern era as having two characteristics: Firstly, the search for truth is abandoned as knowledge fragments. No longer is there one great truth (religion, communism, nationalism, etc.) that unites and justifies all knowledge. Secondly, statements are judged not by whether they are true, but whether they are useful.

CONTEMPORARY APPLICATION

There is no doubt that society has changed quite radically in the past 50 years or so. The workplace has seen a decline in manufacturing and heavy industry to be replaced by the service sector jobs of a post-industrial society. Identity has shifted from being production-based to consumption-based. Culture has become diverse and fragmented as people pick and mix components from around the world. People increasingly engage in 'identity-work' as they invest time and effort into constructing their persona through grooming and styling themselves through consumption and leisure activities. However, whether this amounts to a new type of society is debatable.

RESEARCH IN FOCUS

New ways of studying the family

Castrén and Ketokivi (2015) adopted a new approach to studying family relationships. They argue that on the one hand the family is viewed as a subset of any personal relationships. At the same time, they argue, the family has a special dynamic of its own that requires a 'language of family'. Their research proposed a qualitative approach of using both interviews as well as an understanding of how significant webs of relationships both constrained and enabled people.

They argue that combining these two aspects highlights the complex family dynamics and lived ambivalences between personal affinities and relational expectations. Their research examined significant life events, including marriage and biographical disruptions, such as bereavement, divorce and illness. They describe their methodology as relational: bringing together the personal and the more structural aspects of family dynamics.

By drawing on Norbert Elias's notion of figuration their research combines insider and outsider perspectives. Through the use of interviews they gained qualitative data in relation to the "I" perspective' as well as using questionnaires and circles maps to build up knowledge of the structural webs of relationships that exist within all families.

Adapted from Castrén and Ketokivi (2015)

Questions

1. What does a relational methodology mean with regard to this research?
2. How did Elias's notion of figuration influence the methods used?
3. Using the item and your broader sociological knowledge, discuss some of the problems researchers have in studying family life.

Check your understanding

1. What kind of society was pre-modern?
2. How did the Enlightenment influence the development of sociology?
3. In what ways can sociology be viewed as a product of modernity?
4. What three key areas is modernity associated with?
5. Why do some sociologists prefer terms like 'late modernity' or 'high modernity' to postmodernity?
6. Why is postmodernism associated with consumerism and consumer society?
7. Why does postmodernism reject the idea of grand theory?
8. What is the Marxist response to the idea of a postmodern society?
9. What does Lyotard mean by metanarrative?
10. Identify three characteristics of postmodern society.

Practice questions

1. Outline and explain two advantages of using a multiple methodological approach in sociological research. [10 marks]

Read Item A below and answer the question that follows.

Item A

Because change is ongoing, it is not clear what the future aims, objectives, content, pedagogy, evaluation and direction of the school curriculum will be in the future. One of the educational challenges according to postmodernists is to design a curriculum that both accommodates and stretches, a curriculum that has the essential tension between disequilibrium and equilibrium.

Applying material from Item A and your knowledge of research methods, evaluate the strengths and limitations of bringing in a postmodernist analysis to society. [20 marks]

Section 4: To what extent can sociology be regarded as scientific, objective and value-free?

This section will explore the following debate:
- To what extent can sociology be regarded as a science?

GETTING YOU STARTED

Modernity and the evolution of sociology as a science

The so-called founders of sociology (Comte, Durkheim, Marx and Weber) lived during the period of modernity when reason and rational thinking was replacing faith in explaining the world. Sociology itself can be viewed as a product of modernity and it is no surprise that these founders each took a great interest in science. For example, Auguste Comte (1798–1857) argued that a science of society was possible and advocated that sociology should adopt the methods of the natural sciences (positivism). Emile Durkheim (1858–1917) was heavily influenced by the earlier work of Comte. Durkheim advocated **empiricism** which involved seeking observable evidence. He famously employed a comparative historical method to study the phenomena of suicide. He undertook a systematic comparison of suicide both between societies and social groups within societies. Durkheim was seeking to find observable **correlations** so that he might establish **causal explanations**. He argued that social phenomena could be studied scientifically and that '**social facts**' could be established and measured the same way as physical things. Following his research, he concluded that evidence showed that the personal act of suicide is affected by 'external' social conditions. By embracing the positivistic approach, Durkheim attempted to objectively show the causal relationship between the degree of integration in society and the suicide rate.

Karl Marx (1818–1883) shared this positivist view, believing that by adopting a scientific approach to his work, he could demonstrate the reasons for change and achieve political progress. However, his work differs from Durkheim's in a fundamental way. Marx was no empiricist; he spent his life studying the invisible economic forces of capitalism that are not directly observable and only understood at the level of theory. However, like Durkheim, he too used historical comparisons as major sources of evidence. In order to develop his theory of how society evolved in a series of stages or 'epochs' (historical materialism), he embarked on a systematic comparison of historical evidence. Like Durkheim's, Marx's methodical approach could be described as scientific.

Max Weber (1864–1920) also used historical comparisons, such as his study of world religions. However, he fundamentally opposed the positivistic approach of Durkheim and Marx. As a modernist he believed sociology could come up with scientific findings that could be used for humanity's benefit; but not by copying the methods of the natural sciences. Weber's science was instead interested in revealing the role of social action. For Weber, science was about the interpretation of the real world by using *verstehen* (putting oneself in the place of the subject matter). Unlike positivists, Weber saw objective accounts of the world as essentially based on subjective (ideal-type) interpretations of reality. The ideal-type was developed in conjunction with Weber's belief in the possibility of 'value-free' sociology. The ideal-type allows for a value-free sociology because it can be used as a methodological tool to analyse society. It highlights what to look for by focusing on what is relevant, or a key feature of society, its institutions or its processes.

Questions

1. Why is the period of modernity associated with scientific advancement?
2. What does the word empiricism mean?
3. What were Durkheim's findings from his study of suicide?
4. How was Marx's approach different to Durkheim's?
5. Why did Weber reject the scientific approach of positivism?

4.1 To what extent can sociology be regarded as a science?

Make sure you understand clearly the arguments for and against sociology as a science. Positivism versus interpretivism will form the basis of your thinking, along with the view of the natural sciences not being very scientific anyway, despite their claim to be.

In attempting to answer this question it is important to establish what the methodology of the natural sciences is and whether the subject matter of sociology lends itself to a scientific approach to study. The word science is derived from the Latin *scire*, which means 'to know'. Scientific knowledge is claimed to be objective because it is derived from a methodology centred on the collection of facts. The debate that forms the title above has tended to focus on firstly whether sociology can be a science, followed by the supplementary question whether it *should* try to copy the natural sciences. Section 3 showed that the period of modernity was concerned with the development of scientific and rational thought and how sociology itself became a product of modernity. This was because most of the early classical sociologists supported the scientific approach of positivism *per se*, while others saw identification of sociology with science as important in establishing it as a new subject with credibility.

Positivism developed as an approach that highlighted the similarities between both the natural and social world and how these respective areas could be studied scientifically. Commonly shared words like 'facts', '**correlations**', '**causal relationships**' and 'laws' were stressed. In addition, just as natural phenomena are the product of laws of nature, so people's ideas and actions were seen to be caused by the external social forces which make up social structures. The social philosopher Karl Popper (1959) advocates for all social research the **deductive approach** whereby support for hypotheses is strengthened by constantly trying to disprove or falsify them. Popper believed that sociology could be viewed as a science provided it subjected itself to continual testing or **falsification**. Sociology, he argued, can proceed just like a natural science, by using the **hypothetico-deductive method**:

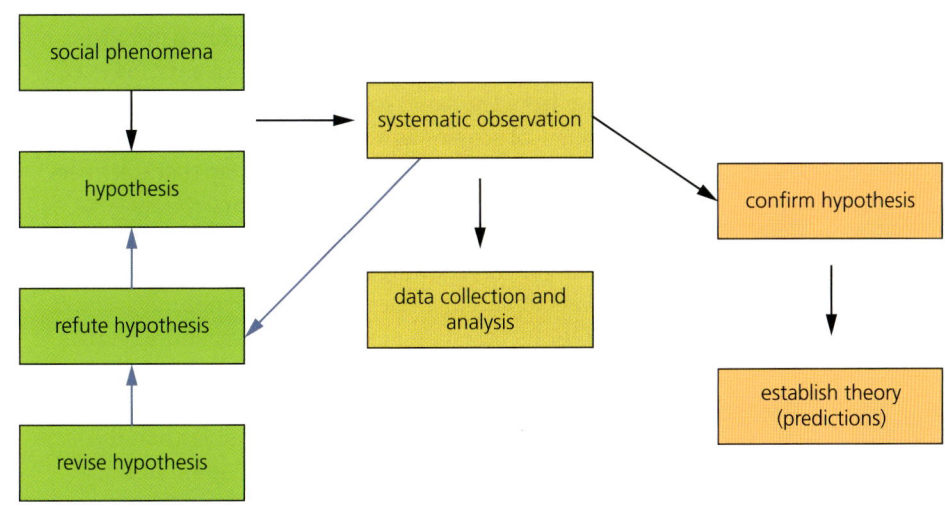

Figure 1.6 The hypothetico-deductive method

The essence of the hypothetico-deductive method is that hypotheses can be tested against empirical evidence (data collected) in order to make predictions based on theories. However, interpretivist sociologists argue that such an approach is inappropriate because it is fundamentally flawed. Their argument is that sociology should abandon any attempt to be scientific because firstly humans have consciousness, and secondly human behaviour is not determined by observable structural forces. The nature of sociology's subject matter is nothing like that of a natural scientist. Instead, they argue, it is the product of how people interpret the world around them. Consequently, sociologists should use methods like Weber's *verstehen* to understand these interpretations. Their argument is that good sociologists are able to understand their subjects' actions by operating in an empathetic manner towards them, understanding the structural circumstances that the people they are studying find themselves in, and taking account of their subjects' goals.

In response to this criticism, positivists refute the idea that just because humans have consciousness adopting a scientific approach to their research is invalid. They argue that while it is true that sociology's subject does have consciousness, people do not behave randomly. Rather they behave in a predictable patterned way that is capable of scientific study. While interpretivists talk about individuals having 'free will' and a voluntarism to act how they wish, the reality is that they do not; generally behaving in a predictable and conformist manner. The fact that this predictability of behaviour is quite marked implies there must be underlying causes (in the form of structures) to this patterning. This too is capable of being studied, they argue, in a scientific way by studying the social world at the level of structures (the family, education, religion, work, etc.). However, as Section 1 demonstrated realists argue that the causes of behaviour are not always directly observable. Therefore the task of science is not necessarily to take social structures at face value, but understand their underlying and hidden characteristics. To achieve this, an interpretive approach may become necessary to understand people's behaviour.

The fact that sociology is divided into theoretical perspectives is also used by its critics to argue that it is not worthy of scientific status. The argument is simple. If an objective truth could be found about human behaviour then all sociologists would share this worldview. The fact that there is a fundamental division within structuralist theory (consensus and conflict) and then between structuralists and action theorists undermines, they argue, the credibility of sociology. However, natural scientists do not all sing from the same song book either! They too have competing 'world views'. The view of science as a united body of knowledge was challenged by Thomas Kuhn (1962). He argues persuasively that scientists belong to distinct scientific communities and often let their conceptions and assumptions about the world blind them to contradictions that appear in their investigations. Over time revolutions in thinking occur and a new **paradigm** becomes dominant, until it too is replaced. Understanding the natural sciences also involves making interpretations based on personal choices, and scientists make judgements at all stages of their research. Driven by the profit motive of capitalism generally, and specifically the chemical and arms industries, it is difficult to see natural scientists as either objective or neutral. Rather, the way in which 'big science' works renders it open to the accusation that it too accumulates 'knowledge' in a selective and partisan way.

The postmodernist position from the above is that if science is not scientific, then what claim can sociology make to be a science? Postmodernists claim that all positions, including the natural sciences, are ideological in the sense that they merely offer a story (in competition with other stories). No form of knowledge is inherently scientific without facts to back it up. Karl Popper, with his theory of falsification, makes the useful point that the best anyone can claim about knowledge is that it is not false. Very rarely, even in science, can something be shown to be true. So in the absence of hard facts, most science faces questions about its own scientific credentials. The history of science is littered with naïve and premature predictions, the concealment of 'inconvenient' statistics, and downright cheating. Postmodernists defend their position by pointing to the refutation that comes from within science itself about its limitations. The scientific community is highly divided and, as Kuhn pointed out, a paradigm prevails until it is shot down by a new paradigm. However, this postmodernist relativist assumption that all knowledge is ideological becomes problematic, since it implies that all knowledge is equal.

Empiricism is an important concept relevant to this debate. Empiricism is the view that scientific knowledge derives from evidence. Such evidence in the natural sciences derives especially from experiments, but in sociology empirical evidence can come from the field, such as through the collection of measurable and testable data. All hypotheses and theories must be tested against collected evidence. Hence, for sociology to be considered a science, it must be considered to be methodologically empirical in nature.

	Positivism	Interpretivism	Postmodernism
Is sociology a science?	Yes	No	No
Justification	Sociology adopts methods of natural sciences to collect facts and develop theories and eventually laws.	Sociology's subject matter is fundamentally different to the natural sciences. People have consciousness.	Sociological theories are no more than metanarratives: simply 'big stories'.
Response	Even if people do have consciousness, they still largely behave in predictable ways, shaped by structures which can be studied.	Only a non-scientific antipositivist approach of *verstehen* can lead to a sound understanding of human behaviour.	No form of knowledge is inherently scientific: not even science is, so what hope is there for sociology?

Table 1.4 Is sociology a science?

It is worth bearing in mind that whatever methodology is adopted, including 'scientific' approaches, it will have an ideological dimension in the sense that it will be chosen on the basis of the type of knowledge it is able to produce. Therefore no methodology is completely objective.

KEY SOCIOLOGIST

Andrew Tudor (2008) has an important contribution to this debate. His influential book *Beyond Empiricism*, originally published in 1982, argues the case that sociology should be allowed back into the scientific fold. One of Tudor's arguments is how philosophers of science have recently broken with the empiricism that was once so fundamental to their discipline. At a time when alternative methods pervade the world of science, Tudor argues that these developments are significant for sociologists and advocates a new approach paying detailed attention to questions about the nature of theory, explanation and demonstration.

STUDY TIP
When considering whether or not sociology is a science, challenge the simplistic assumption of positivist versus interpretivist positions and recognise approaches like that of realism which embraces elements of each approach in order to get closer to the truth.

CONTEMPORARY APPLICATION
Textbooks in the past tended to emphasise the polarised and oppositional position of positivism versus antipositivism in the field of methodology. In contemporary sociology, realism has made an important contribution to the debate recognising that while structures do exist independently of us, they often have hidden mechanisms, not directly observable. However, like interpretivists, realism sees reality as whatever experiences an individual has and therefore sees as real in their head. Things individuals believe to be real become constructed as their reality.

RESEARCH IN FOCUS

Feminist analysis of science

Some types of feminism are equivocal about science and technology, both because of their different positions in relation to gender roles, and the interaction between gender and other forms of control. Some feminists have criticised the science establishment for either exploiting women or failing to meet their needs. In particular they raise concerns about medical science for its tendency to perpetuate social defined roles of women as the natural carers and mothers, yet to restrict or negatively influence the means of carrying out these roles (for example, natural childbirth, IVF debates.). Science is seen to support patriarchal control. It is also considered that women are entitled to the solutions that science offers to fundamental issues (for example, contraception and abortion).

It clear is that many feminists believe that science has something to offer women - however, as science is largely in hands of men, it could be inherently controlling for women. The issue is how (and if) this oppressive element to science could be eliminated, with the aim of making science more conducive to women's lifestyle choices.

Adapted from Bloor (2000)

Questions
1. Why have some feminists been highly critical of science and technology?
2. Why do some feminists believe science is 'inherently controlling'?
3. How could the oppressive element of science be removed?
4. Why do you think so few scientists are female, both in school and the workplace?

Check your understanding

1. What is positivism?
2. What subject area did Durkheim study in a scientific way?
3. Why did Weber argue a scientific approach was inappropriate for sociology?
4. What is a correlation?
5. What is a causal relationship?
6. What is meant by the deductive approach?
7. Why did Popper advocate falsification?
8. What is the hypothetico-deductive approach to research?
9. What point does Kuhn make about the development of knowledge?
10. How would postmodernists respond to the idea of sociology being a science?

Practice questions

1. Outline and explain two advantages of using a quantitative approach in sociological research. [10 marks]

Read Item A below and answer the question that follows.

Item A

Auguste Comte founded the doctrine of 'positivism' in his Course in Positive Philosophy (1830) in which he argued that scientific knowledge should replace religious and metaphysical (theoretical) thinking. He argued that sociology should adopt the same positivist approach that had enabled natural scientists to establish laws of nature.

Applying material from Item A and your knowledge of research methods, evaluate the strengths and limitations of adopting a positivist approach to studying social phenomena. [20 marks]

Section 5: The relationship between theory and methods

This section will explore:
- What is the relationship between theory and sociological methods?
- What theoretical considerations influence research?

GETTING YOU STARTED

Theory and research

The close connection between theory and research lies with each of their functions. It is often said that the basic impetus for research is the search for theory since theory development relies on research. The corollary of this is that research simultaneously relies on theory.

Hegel's concept of the dialectic can be useful in understanding the relationship between theory and method. Hegel talked about the dialectic as the beneficial outcome of new knowledge that derives from polarised and conflicting ideas (thesis versus antithesis). Such new knowledge is valued because it takes our understanding of the social world forward.

Theory therefore determines what data is to be collected and the nature of the research. In order for theories to be developed it is necessary to gather evidence data. The purpose of research can therefore be summarised as either to generate a theory or to test one. Research can test theories and take our knowledge and understanding further since findings can sometimes provide challenges to accepted theories. When the purpose of research is theory generation then the researcher's focus will often be influenced by a selective interpretation of things to look for.

Adapted from Fawcett and Downs (1986)

Questions

1. From the extract and your own knowledge briefly outline the function of theory.
2. According to the article what are the two functions of research?
3. Does the article imply research can take place without reference to theory? Explain your answer.
4. What are the implications of the last sentence in terms of bias and lack of objectivity?

5.1 What is the relationship between theory and sociological methods?

When considering the relationship between positivism, interpretivism and sociological methods, you will need an awareness of each of these two approaches but equally how sociologists typically embrace them both in contemporary research. Because these theoretical approaches to research were covered in some detail in Book 1 (pages 12–14 and also on pages 42–3) they receive a relatively brief coverage here. Refer back to Book 1 for more on the positivist–interpretivist debate.

Positivism

Most of the early sociologists in the nineteenth century felt that to achieve the two key conditions of research, rigour in its execution and based on **empirical** evidence, then it had to adopt the methods of the natural sciences. This scientific approach, which had been advocated by Auguste Comte (1798–1857) somewhat earlier, was known as **positivism**. It argued that only by adopting a rigorous methodological approach based on the scientific principles of collecting objective evidence in the form of facts could sociology stand up to academic scrutiny. Such research was based on evidence, subject to verification (it could be tested) and was considered truly objective. The approach and results were believed to be genuinely value-free and like scientific research could be cross-referenced, that is, checked against existing research findings. Positivism researches society by focusing on the **macro level**; it does this by observing how the social structures of society influence and shape the behaviour of individuals.

Interpretivism

However, this approach was challenged by Max Weber (1864–1920) who made the simple, but obvious, point that sociology's subject matter was not the same as that of the natural sciences. Unlike crystals, cells or earthquakes, human beings have consciousness and are normally aware when they are being studied. Therefore they tend to stop behaving naturally, simply because they know they are being researched. To truly understand human behaviour, Weber advocated a totally new approach. He said we should try to understand ('*verstehen*') human behaviour by putting ourselves in the shoes of those we are studying and focusing on interpreting the meanings behind people's actions. Weber's 'action theory' therefore focuses on the **micro-level** of social life – the way in which individuals interact with one another. Behaviour is seen as **agency** driven, being shaped by personal choice and hence **voluntaristic**, as opposed to constrained by structures. However, this approach still stresses the importance of adopting a rigorous and systematic approach, stressing that making sense of human behaviour derives from a careful interpretation of it – hence this alternative approach is known as **interpretivism**.

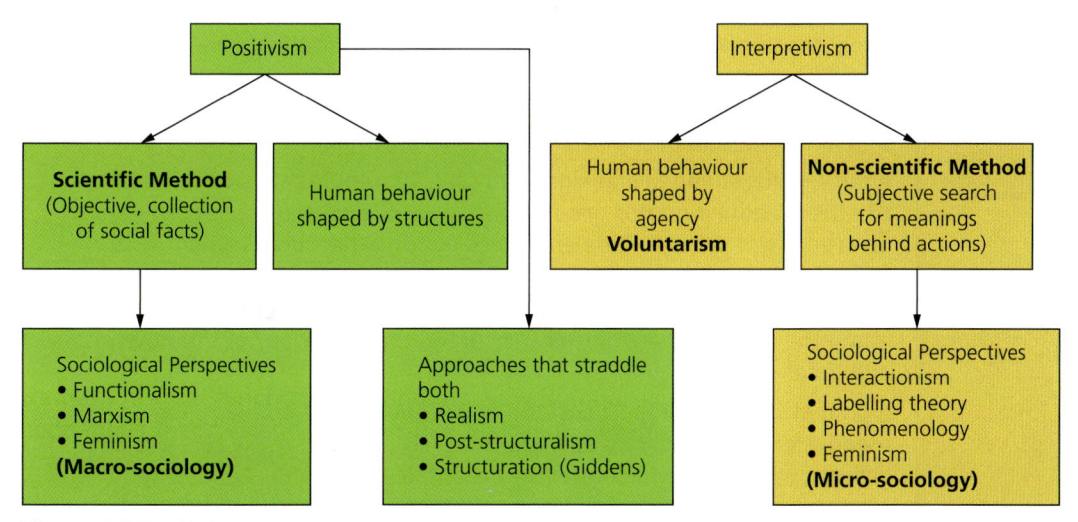

```
                    Positivism                              Interpretivism
                   /         \                             /              \
     Scientific Method    Human behaviour        Human behaviour    Non-scientific Method
  (Objective, collection  shaped by structures   shaped by          (Subjective search
    of social facts)                             agency              for meanings
                                                 Voluntarism         behind actions)

  Sociological Perspectives   Approaches that straddle   Sociological Perspectives
  • Functionalism             both                       • Interactionism
  • Marxism                   • Realism                  • Labelling theory
  • Feminism                  • Post-structuralism       • Phenomenology
  (Macro-sociology)           • Structuration (Giddens)  • Feminism
                                                         (Micro-sociology)
```

Figure 1.7 Positivism versus interpretivism

Realism

As noted in Section 1 (see pages 6–7) sociological researchers rarely fall neatly into the positivist or interpretivist approaches. The reality is that when undertaking research sociologists use a combination of the two approaches. The approach of realism recognises both strengths and weaknesses within each of positivism and interpretivism and seeks to use their respective strong points. The analogy of an onion is sometimes used to illustrate the strengths of a realist approach. Positivist approach is centred on the observation of structures. If this approach was applied to an onion, it would conclude that onions are dry and papery. Realists believe that a structured reality exists but, unlike positivists, disagree that this reality is necessarily observable directly. Sometimes you have to probe beneath the surface, and if applied to onions would reveal their moist texture and the ring structure. Realists also identify with the interpretivist view that people are conscious beings. They are aware of their position in the world and consequently behave in a meaningful and voluntaristic way. By doing this they help create the social world and its structures.

KEY SOCIOLOGIST

Michel Foucault is associated with post-structuralism which argues that to get to the truth researchers need to go beneath the surface of society. The post-structuralist criticism of the structure/agency polarisation is that all perspectives actually include both. They conclude that the sensible conclusion to draw from the structure versus agency debate is that the agency/structure distinction does not so much present a problem to be solved but rather is a way of describing reality.

STUDY TIP

Knowing and understanding the table above will help ensure that you have a joined-up understanding of the different approaches to sociological research.

Questions

1. Why was consent for students' involvement sought from the deputy head teacher and parents?
2. What is a pilot study?
3. What benefits were gained in this research from using pilot studies?
4. Why is this research a good example of a realist approach to undertaking research?

Application to contemporary society

It would probably be fair to say in the twenty-first century that sociology has risen above the stale and polarised debate of positivism versus interpretivism. Today most sociological research involves elements of both approaches. This is known as a realist approach and involves collecting quantitative and qualitative data, discussed on the next page.

RESEARCH IN FOCUS

Tackling underage drinking

Locke and Jones undertook research in order to evaluate an innovative local authority project in Eastleigh, Hampshire, intended to reduce underage drinking. The project had been running for over two years aimed at diverting young people (8–14 years) from drinking. It sought to do this by educating children early about the effects of their longer-term drinking habits by providing health advice and raising awareness of the effects of alcohol.

Their research method involved distributing a questionnaire to local Year 8 students. This particular year group was sampled as they had already been involved in the local project while at primary school. Consent was obtained from parents and teachers.

A survey questionnaire designed to take 10 minutes was completed by 67 students during tutor group time. Students were asked about their awareness of the activities of the project and their involvement with it. Questionnaires were also completed by 39 parents of children who were taking part in the survey. They answered questions on their views about the project and whether it affected the behaviour of their own and other children.

A pilot study resulted in revisions to the surveys. In addition, the feedback from the pilot was used to develop ideas for the three focus groups, which were facilitated by project leaders who represented the various agencies involved with the project.

Quantitative data was generated from the completed questionnaires and analysed. Qualitative data was obtained from open questions on the survey and from the focus groups.

Adapted from Locke and Jones (2012)

5.2 What theoretical considerations influence research?

Sociological theories are either structural or social action and this can shape research techniques, choice of research area and interpretation of results.

While researchers should strive to be objective and neutral in their research, inevitably their prejudices and values may shape what they research, their approach to the research, their method choice and finally the interpretation of their findings. For example, Marxists and feminists have an open political agenda: they would both like to change society and make it more equal, with regard to class and gender inequalities respectively. Functionalists, however, will use evidence selectively in order to reinforce their consensus view that a common set of values exists in society. It is therefore important to remember that behind a lot of sociological research lies an agenda with an interest in being supported.

Structural approaches

Structural theorists explain the order and predictability of social life by seeing human behaviour as learned behaviour shaped by external forces. They are sometimes referred to as macro-theories which adopt a top-down approach because of their large-scale vision of seeing society-wide structures or institutions as the starting point for explaining human behaviour. Examples of such structures would be family, education, religion, work and the state. Examples of macro, structural, top-down sociological perspectives would be functionalism/New Right, Marxism/neo-Marxism and some aspects of feminism. The favoured methodological approach of structural theorists is quantitative methods aimed at generating facts and statistics. There is an overlap between structuralist approach and positivism.

Social action theory approaches

The alternative to the macro, structuralist approach are theories based on the social action approach, originally conceived by Max Weber. Action theory sees society not as the starting point, but as the outcome of individuals engaging in an infinite number of meaningful encounters. It is precisely because these encounters are meaningful to the people concerned that they create social order with the semblance of an apparently stable society. These theories argue that society is generated by the sum of social actions, in which people actively interpret and give meaning to social encounters.

Because of the focus on the individual (rather than society) as the starting point from which to make sense of human behaviour, social action theories are sometimes described as micro-theories generating a bottom-up, small-scale view. Action theory argues that making sense of society starts with the extraordinary ability of people to interpret what is going on around them. They then embrace agency in order to make choices and act in a particular way, in the light of this interpretation. Examples of micro, agency-based, bottom-up sociological perspectives are interactionism, postmodernism, and some elements of feminism. The favoured methodological approach of action theorists is qualitative methods aimed at generating an understanding of meaning behind behaviour. Action theory is therefore closely associated with the interpretivist approach or phenomenology.

KEY SOCIOLOGIST

Phil Hadfield (2006) applied a Marxist analysis to the 'nocturnal economy' of pubs and clubs. Hadfield sought evidence to support his view that capitalist enterprises, in following their natural profit-making goal, may end up creating an environment in which certain types of crime flourish. Hadfield demonstrated the irresponsibility of the drinks industry which ignored the repercussions of their profit-driven behaviour.

CONTEMPORARY APPLICATION

It is rare in contemporary research for researchers to be constrained into either a purely positivistic or interpretivist approach. Significant amounts of research involve a triangulation or realist approach, collecting quantitative and qualitative data.

STUDY TIP

Make sure you are clear on the basic arguments outlined here: Demonstrating a good understanding of the relationship between theoretical approaches and methodological approaches will add depth and content to any writing on this topic.

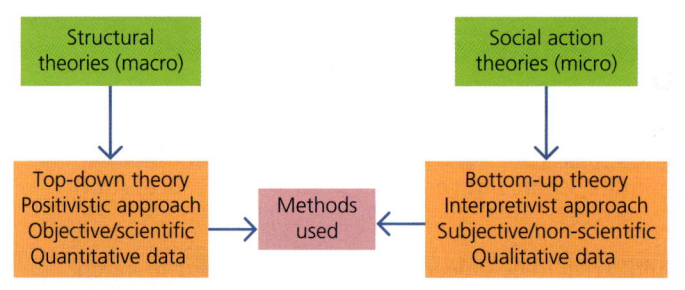

Figure 1.8 Structural theories versus social action theories

RESEARCH IN FOCUS

Using the Millennium Cohort Study

Researchers, from the University of London's Institute of Education have found that parents' social class has a greater impact on how well their children perform at school than 'good parenting' techniques such as reading bedtime stories. In a study of 11,000 7-year-old children, drawn from the Millennium Cohort Study, they found that those with parents in professional and managerial jobs were at least eight months ahead of pupils from the most socially disadvantaged homes, where parents were often unemployed.

The team from the Institute of Education took advantage of the Millennium Cohort Study (MCS) to provide an opportunity to answer major questions about the social class prospects of children born in 2000–01. The MSC's sample was selected from all births in a random sample of electoral divisions, disproportionately stratified to ensure suitably comprehensive representation across the UK, including areas of deprivation. In contrast to the preceding studies (in 1946, 1958 and 1970) the MCS sample design took in a whole year's births, and covered the whole of the United Kingdom.

There have, so far, been four surveys (also known as 'sweeps' or 'waves'): at age 9 months and at 3, 5 and 7 years. At each sweep interviews were carried out with both resident parents, collecting a wide range of socio-economic and health data. The three most recent sweeps included evaluation of the child's cognitive development.

Alice Sullivan, the main author of the study, said the research showed that while parenting is important, a policy focus on parenting alone is insufficient to tackle the impacts of social inequalities on child development.

Adapted from Sullivan, Ketende and Joshi (2013)

Questions

1. What was the size of the sample used?
2. Why was the sample 'disproportionately stratified'?
3. How does the sample design of the MCS differ from previous cohort studies?

Check your understanding

1. What does empirical mean?
2. What do sociologists mean by structures?
3. What do sociologists mean by the term agency?
4. What did Weber mean by *verstehen*?
5. What is meant by post-structuralism?
6. What is meant by a top-down approach?
7. What is meant by a bottom-up approach?
8. What is the realist approach?
9. What did Giddens mean by structuration theory?
10. How would postmodernists respond to the idea of sociology being a science?

Practice questions

1. Outline and explain two advantages of using a realist approach in sociological research. [10 marks]

Read Item A below and answer the question that follows.

Item A

Triangulation refers to the methodological approach of using more than one method. Even Howard Becker, who was a prominent interpretive sociologist, supplemented his observational study of doctors in *The Boys in White* (1963) with an appendix of statistics to give it 'scientific weight'

Applying material from Item A and your knowledge of research methods, evaluate the strengths and limitations of adopting a triangulation approach to studying social phenomena. [20 marks]

Section 6: Debates about subjectivity, objectivity and value freedom

This section will explore:

- To what extent is sociology value-free?
- What is the relationship between sociology and social policy?

GETTING YOU STARTED
Value freedom in sociology

Is it possible for sociologists to be completely objective, that is, not allowing their opinions and feelings to influence their work? A key question for sociologists like Marxists and feminists is should they be concerned with changing the social world? If so, this inevitably entails making value judgements. Firstly, because these conflict sociologists see the world as unequal, they conclude that the social world needs changing in order to bring about class and gender equality. Secondly, by implying how it can be changed for the better, this is an inevitable reflection of their core values. An alternative view is that the role of sociology should not try to change society but merely attempt to make sense of it.

However, here again there is a difference of opinion. Some sociologists, reflecting the positivist position, argue that it is their duty to be as objective as possible. Their argument is that sociology should be like natural science, where the scientific researchers are not influenced by their values (in theory at least). However, to be truly objective is harder in sociology because it is about people. An alternative view is that of the interpretive position which argues that sociologists should accept that they are bound to be influenced by their values. Consequently they should be open about these, leaving the reader to judge how far their work has been influenced by their values.

Adapted from Blundell and Griffiths (2003)

Questions

1. Explain why some sociological perspectives would argue that values should be celebrated and fully incorporated into sociology.
2. How is the subject matter and approach of the natural sciences different to that of sociology?
3. Evaluate the implication behind the claim that every sociological researcher has been socialised into believing a certain viewpoint.
4. Is it possible for qualitative research to be value-free?

6.1 To what extent is sociology value-free?

When discussing the value freedom of sociology you could explore the positivist versus interpretive debates about how they respectively feel values can be excluded from research. (You could also include the postmodernist critique of this since they argue that everything is ideological and that some sociologists have a political agenda therefore are happy to express their values.)

Figure 1.9 Women today have more opportunities to pursue careers and independent travel

In addressing the question whether sociology can be value-free, the previous debate about whether sociology is a science inevitably overlaps. The question actually promotes two supplementary questions: is a value-free sociology firstly *possible* and secondly is it a *desirable*? After all, many sociologists, such as feminists, Marxists and interactionists are openly value-laden in their analysis of both their findings and the desired outcome of their research. In addressing the first question, about the practicalities of a value-free sociology, we have to consider differing theoretical perspectives and their position as to whether it is actually possible to produce objective knowledge about the social world. With the second question, the first one gets thrown on its head. Here we are looking at how and why value-freedom is discarded in the name of progress of respective goals: gender equality, class equality or the plight of the underdog.

Is value-free sociology possible?

Postmodernists would argue that no value-free sociology is possible since all theoretical positions, including the natural sciences, are ideological. The portrayal of knowledge, they claim, is little else than story-telling. Adopting the principle of relativism, no one story is necessarily better than another. It follows then that the very essence of value freedom is not whether the sociologist has values, since all human beings are influenced by values of some sort. Therefore the real question with regard to value freedom is whether or not the sociologist can suppress their personal values and whether they *want* to?

Adopting an objective approach to research was envisaged by the positivist approach of Auguste Comte and Emile Durkheim. By modelling themselves on the methods of natural science, they embarked on what they claimed to be an empiricist and objective (and hence value-free) approach to the study of society. They argued, however, the purpose of studying society scientifically was to change it for the better. This was not a matter of personal judgement, but to find the true principles for a good, ordered and integrated society. They believed that once the laws of society had been discovered then this would show the way to the natural and correct state of social integration and social order. This was not imposing the sociologist's values, but using science for the establishment of a better society. To achieve this Comte referred to sociology as the 'Queen of the sciences' with sociologists as the 'priests' of a golden age of proven truth!

The objective principles of positivism were actively embraced in the twentieth century by the structural consensus theory of functionalism. It advocated methodological objectivity (objectivism) which argued that to understand how society worked it was only necessary to study its social structures. However, the counter view of methodological subjectivity (subjectivism), shared by interpretivists, fundamentally criticises the idea that only 'social structures' should be studied. The interpretivist view maintains that human behaviour can only be understood through understanding the motivations and meanings that lie behind individual's actions.

These American functionalists actively distanced themselves from suggesting any reforms of society; it was not the role of sociology to prescribe how society ought to be. Instead they threw themselves into the process of collecting facts. For them, only the collection of facts through the adoption of a scientific positivistic approach could be truly objective and establish the truth about society. Adopting a scientific approach meant sociology must be neutral, not take sides and produce value-neutral knowledge. So in contrast to the classical positivists of the nineteenth century, who saw themselves as the architects of the perfect society, twentieth-century positivists saw themselves as mere information gatherers. However, they were misguided to equate their objective approach with value freedom, since all sociologists are influenced by values of some sort. Secondly, to view sociology merely as 'information gathering' has been described as naïve and even immoral.

The reality of sociology in twentieth-century USA was that 'value-free' sociologists were increasingly used by government and big business to promote highly value-laden causes. For example, the US army employed sociologists in Project Camelot (1964). Sociologists were located in Latin American countries in order to reveal the origins of social instability. The USA had a vested political and economic interest in stability in Latin America and stated it had a 'responsibility to assist friendly governments in dealing with active insurgency problems'. Another example of value-laden scientific research was that involving the eugenics movement in the 1920s and 1930s. Eugenics influenced the United States immigration policy and served to justify the institutionalised racism that prevailed, especially in the southern US states. Sociologists were also used by big business in ways that promoted profits. For example, the US Ford Corporation employed sociologists to investigate and reduce industrial disputes. The criticism of this kind of research is that it is not value-free. Sociologists, who saw themselves simply as 'information gatherers', were actually employed to undertake research that reflected the values of their employer.

Conflict sociologists like C. Wright Mills (1956) and Alvin Gouldner (1962) attacked this 'positivistic' information gathering for what it was. Mills, for example, argued that it was impossible for sociologists to avoid values and implying them in their work. According to Gouldner these 'amoral positivists' were engaging in cynical self-improvement: attempting to address their degraded status and acquire professional and academic credibility. The establishment ceased to see sociologists as a threat and began using them for their own purposes. Gouldner points out that by refraining from criticising the agenda and the tasks they were set, the sociologists became morally complicit. By insisting on value freedom they were declaring a clear message 'we will not rock the boat' or 'bite the hand that feeds us'. Either way this is a very value-laden approach.

Is value-free sociology desirable?

Following Gouldner's lead, much of sociology in the 1960s and 1970s rejected the inherent conservatism of positivism/functionalism. Instead it argued for a more radical and committed approach to social life. This has taken one of two forms. Firstly, inspired by the work of Max Weber and his social action theory, interpretive sociology argued that truth could only be gained by adopting subjective research methods to understand meanings. Weber agreed with the principle that no values can be regarded as ultimately correct, but felt the sociological researcher should still be a responsible citizen. The investigator could be value-free in the choice of topic or the application of knowledge, just so long as neutral testing procedures are used. Ethical and political responsibility cannot be shirked. Weber believed that it was possible for sociologists to be personally objective in their research and that knowledge could therefore be cleansed of values. However, critics argue that the problem with this approach is that it runs the risk of being subjective and prone to the personal biases of the researcher. In addition, the choice of subject matter and the use of knowledge are both areas where values must unavoidably be involved.

One response by interactionists to this criticism was to openly declare their values. For example, Howard Becker advocated a 'compassionate sociology' that took the side of the underdog. He argued, firstly, that we can only know about social behaviour by seeing reality from the point of view of the actor. Secondly, that the most disadvantaged in society are only ordinary people subject to the impact of unfavourable circumstances. Becker argued that since the world is generally seen from the powerful (overdog's) point of view, it is the obligation of sociologists to balance things up by taking the underdog's point of view. However, some Marxist sociologists have become contemptuous of what they consider the rather romantic and sentimental approach of the interactionists. For example, Gouldner has attacked Becker for taking too 'safe' an attack on the inequalities of power: [Becker] looked at people 'on their backs' (the underdog) rather than those 'fighting back' (the radical).

	Positivism	**Interpretivism**	**Postmodernism**
Can sociology be value-free?	Yes, by adopting the methods of the natural sciences (positivism)	Yes, by carefully interpreting the meanings behind people's actions (*verstehen*)	Never, because all theories are ideological

Table 1.5 Different views on value-free sociology

Marxist conflict sociology advocates a self-conscious politically radical approach. Generally, conflict sociologists argue that sociologists should be true to their own values, by seeing the world as wrongly unequal. Values must therefore be followed through and the wrongs of capitalism identified and righted. Although the French sociologist Louis Althusser (2005) saw sociology as a science, he saw its role as to explicitly expose the ways in which the ruling capitalist class dominate and control society. He therefore saw the role of sociology as promoting class consciousness and exposing the truth about the inequalities and unfairness of capitalism.

The origins of feminist theory in sociology lie in the fact that until the 1960s gender issues and inequalities were rarely discussed within the discipline. Along with the Women's Liberation Movement, academic feminist writing developed to become an indispensable part of critical sociology. Section 1 pointed out that feminism is both structural and interpretive. Like the Marxist perspective it is political – its goal is to change society for the better – and like interpretive sociology it is compassionate, focusing on the 'underdog' position of women. Thus, feminist sociology is openly value-laden. In addition, feminists see knowledge as power, and actively promote a feminist perspective to challenge 'malestream' knowledge that abounds in all academic and popular areas. Feminists clearly make no apology for their overt values, arguing they are necessary in the furtherance of the emancipation of women.

The New Right perspective may also be viewed as value-laden in its overt support for neo-liberal principles in favour of the free market and its opposition to all forms of government intervention, including the welfare state.

Funding is a concept that is relevant to this debate about value freedom. We saw in Section 4 how access to funding can influence the choice of topic a sociologist researches. Those funding research usually have a pre-conceived idea of the findings they expect. This can therefore influence how the sociologist interprets the data and the selection of what findings to include in the report. The values of the researcher clearly become compromised if this happens.

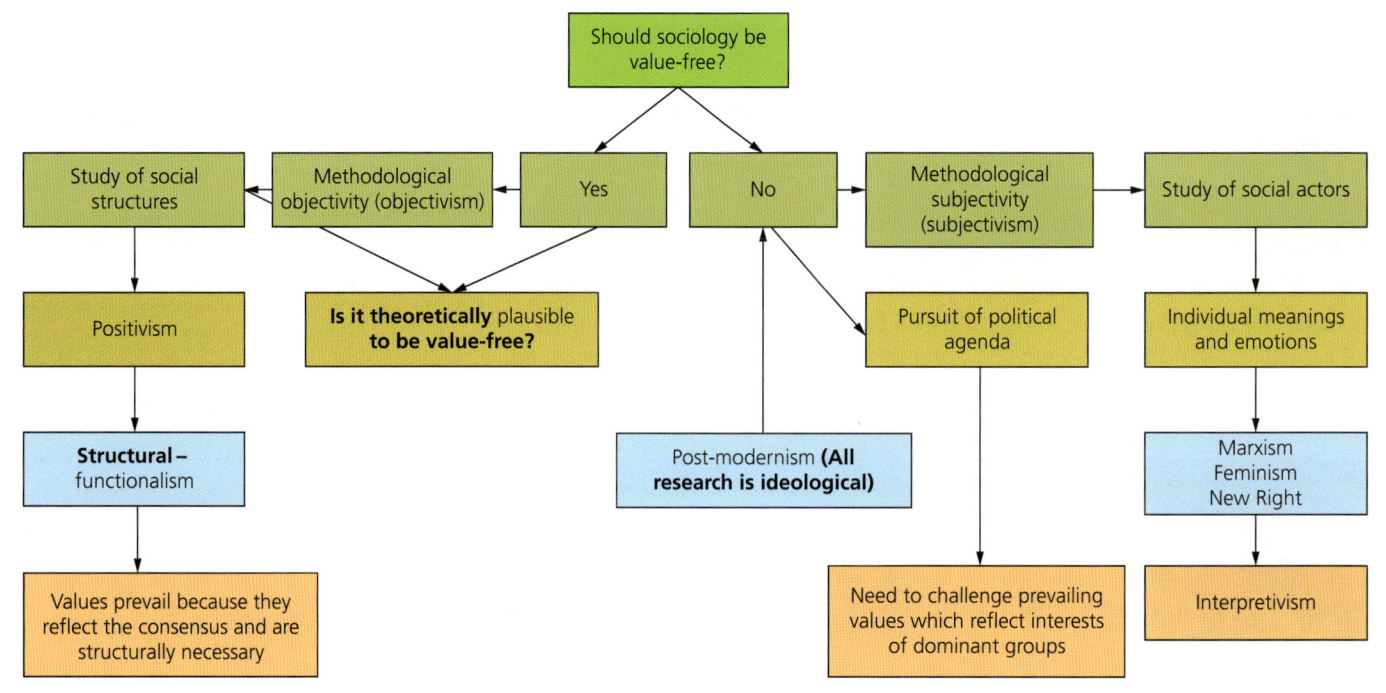

Figure 1.10 Objectivity of research

Evaluation

It is worth remembering that a significant amount of sociological research results in criticism about the quality of its validity, reliability and representativeness. Therefore, this has implications for the extent to which it is purely objective and value-free. It is easier for the natural scientist to practise methodological objectivity because their subject matter does not have consciousness.

KEY SOCIOLOGIST

The classical early sociologist **Auguste Comte** has an important contribution to make to this debate. Comte set himself the task of establishing sociology as a 'positive science of society' and argued that by adopting a positivist approach society could be studied in a value-free way in order to reveal the laws of social life. He predicted that with this accumulation of objective knowledge that sociologists would come to understand and control human behaviour, eradicate social problems, and produce a society that would benefit all.

CONTEMPORARY APPLICATION

Sociologists know they will not obtain government funding for certain sensitive areas of research, including researching poverty, inequalities in income and wealth, and inequalities in life chances associated with social class. By not providing funding for the research of these areas governments are effectively banning the study of areas it finds politically embarrassing. Government funding of research is clearly value-laden as they will only fund research that has a potentially positive outcome.

Different perspectives

Postmodernism makes an important contribution to this debate. Postmodernists argue that all sociology is value-laden since knowledge is culturally constructed. Postmodernists argue that all sociological positions are value-laden because they are little more than ideological story-telling. However, as Jürgen Habermas notes, the postmodernist position lacks any claim to validity since by refuting all sociological theories as 'metanarratives' they end up creating a metanarrative of their own!

> **STUDY TIP**
>
> It is important to have a good knowledge and understanding of both sides of this debate. Figure 1.10 shows methodological objectivity is normally associated with structuralist perspectives, whereas methodological subjectivity is normally associated with interpretivist perspectives.

RESEARCH IN FOCUS

Improving pupil attainment through parental involvement

Research by the Joseph Rowntree Foundation (JRF) has found that there was a reasonable case to be made for parental (family) involvement in their children's education having 'a causal influence on children's school readiness and subsequent attainment' (Carter-Wall and Whitfield, 2012: p.5), compared with all the other interventions it reviewed.

This research points to four areas of parental involvement which have had success: improving at-home parenting, involving parents in school, engaging parents in their children's learning and in their own learning, and aligning school–home expectations.

The research identifies the key features of successful interventions in these areas, but could not isolate which of these, singly or in combination, actually led to improved educational outcomes for young people. However, the researchers suggest the greatest improvements appear to be gained from providing parents with better information and access to appropriate support and advice. They conclude that simply raising parents' aspirations for their children are unlikely to result in real advances, whereas those which 'enable and encourage parents actively to engage with their child's learning and the education system more generally' are usually successful (Carter-Wall and Whitfield, 2012: p.6).

The researchers acknowledge that robust evidence for the impact of extra-curricular activities and mentoring on students' achievements is lacking, but suggest that these kinds of intervention offer great potential.

For example, the JRF research gave examples of practices that resulted in successful mentoring of young people. There is some evidence that mentoring results in improved achievement, although how or why the improvement occurred was not made clear in the evaluations.

The JRF studies propose that if AAB-type strategies (those that focus on the aspirations, attitudes and behaviours of disadvantaged children and their families) are to be cost-effective, then carefully designed and rigorously evaluated funding should be concentrated on parental involvement, extra-curricular provision and mentoring. They do not rule out other creative approaches, but argue that such interventions should have a strong evidence base, with in-built robust evaluations of student achievement and that they should be trialled at a small-scale level before it is decided to apply them on a larger scale.

Adapted from Egan (2013)

Questions

1. What intervention was found to be unsuccessful if implemented?
2. In what ways could parents be encouraged to actively engage with their child's learning and the education system more generally?
3. What were the findings about mentoring?
4. What concerns does the JRF raise about future research and interventions?

6.2 What is the relationship between sociology and social policy?

Social policy has a complex relationship with sociological research.

Figure 1.11 Palace of Westminster

Social policy refers to the activities and legislative outcomes of central and local government and their agencies. They generally have some bearing on human welfare. The relationship between sociology and social policy is a complex one. Ken Roberts (2012) talks of a golden age in the 1940s and 1950s when sociologists actively supported reforms of the newly established welfare state. At the time, he claims sociology had the ear of governments and could recommend policy changes on the basis of the extensive research it was undertaking to measure the ways and extent people's lives were being improved. Therefore sociology can claim some credit for raising awareness about social problems and instigating a social policy response from the government. For example, some feminists claim that raising awareness about gender inequality led to the Equal Pay Act (1970) and the Sex Discrimination Act (1975). Cynics might respond that these two important acts of legislation came in because they attracted a lot of votes from women.

Therefore, others see social policy influenced primarily by other factors such as ideology, self-interest and electoral popularity (policies that are vote-winning). Social policy can be influenced by sociological research, but only when it suits and benefits central or local government. For example, the political preoccupation with winning elections results in the dismissal of any sociological findings that are not vote winners. In addition, there has been a lot written recently about the influence of **lobbyists**. Government policy is increasingly shaped these days by powerful and well-funded interest and pressure groups, rather than sociologists. Therefore it is big business and rich individuals who shape social policy, rather than humble academic sociologists.

In addition to the issue of to what extent sociology *does* influence social policy, there is another debate about what the relationship between social policy and sociology *should* be. On the one hand, the broadly consensus theorists argue that sociology should underpin social policy and contribute to the reform of society. In other words sociologists should work with government and its agencies to make society better. However, critical sociologists are critical of the relationship between sociology and social policy and argue that the role of sociology should be to bring about radical change rather than piecemeal reforms. Finally, some argue that since sociology is an academic subject, its relationship to social policy should be independent. The value of sociology lies with its specific use-value to the discipline itself. For example, postmodernists argue that sociology has no contribution to make to social policy. This is because, they argue, its function is simply to make sense of individual lives. They reject the usefulness of sociological knowledge, especially in the form of metanarratives, since they challenge any modernist idea that knowledge can be used to make society better. This is because they do not recognise the concept of an orderly society in the first place; one that is capable of being studied and reformed by the scientific rational method.

Consensus theorists attempt to explain the basis of sociology's relationship to social policy in terms of how knowledge reflects and shapes the consensus, shared values and a reformist response from the authorities. The social theorist Anthony Giddens argues that one of the key roles of sociology is to inform policy makers and assess the results of policy in order to promote an understanding of society. Giddens himself is credited as being influential in policymaking. His work on the 'third way' was very influential and shaped many of the policies of Tony Blair's New Labour government.

Figure 1.12 Anthony Giddens

Sometimes pioneering sociology highlights issues previously hidden or ignored and demands a response. So it is suggested that the work of Peter Townsend (1966) on poverty was responsible for social policies like the minimum wage and family and working tax credits. Townsend claimed to have 'rediscovered' poverty in a Britain which had assumed poverty had largely been abolished. He redefined poverty as 'relative' when 'resources are so seriously below those commanded by the average individual or family' rather than the old-fashioned view of lacking basic necessities. It is claimed by his supporters that Townsend's 'relative poverty' raised the profile of the poor, resulting in a social policy response. However, governments have never taken poverty seriously – partly because the poor have a notoriously low turn-out at elections. Instead, it is a problem they like to sweep under the carpet and pretend is not significant, or victim-blame by putting the responsibility for poverty onto the poor themselves (such as being lazy, feckless, work-shy and welfare dependent). If Townsend was responsible for the minimum wage and tax credits, these were introduced in 1999 and 2003 respectively, at least 33 years after his research! In addition, following pressure from employers the minimum wage has always been set at too low a level to help eradicate low-wage poverty. Pressure to cut welfare, and to make firms rather than the government subsidise low wages, led to plans to cut working family tax credits with the National Living Wage by 2020.

Sociologists have a long list of social policy reforms they claim sociology has been at least partly responsible for bringing in. For example, it is said that sociological research into attainment *levels* resulted in the introduction of the comprehensive school system. However, the evidence suggests that it was pressure from middle-class parents that was the key driver of this reform. Because there were so few grammar school places available, the middle class fought for the better of two evils. Sending their children to a comprehensive school was infinitely better than the secondary modern schools. Thus, ex-grammar school champion of the middle classes, Conservative Secretary of State for Education Margaret Thatcher (who had no truck with sociologists, whom she despised), was responsible for establishing the majority of comprehensive schools in the 1970s. Another example of a government choosing to ignore clear-cut evidence was the dismissal of the 'Black Report' (1980) into inequalities in health. Despite Sir Douglas Black making 37 far-reaching policy recommendations the government partly implemented just two and again resorted to victim-blaming for their explanation of health inequalities. Despite clear-cut evidence to the contrary, people were accused of bringing about their own poor health through unhealthy behaviour and lifestyle choices.

Nonetheless sociologists argue that research can still contribute to effective social policies. Sociologists have always championed marginalised and stigmatised groups. Consequently sociologists may take some credit for the Equality Act (2010), designed to criminalise discrimination and harassment related to certain personal characteristics such as gender, race, age and disability. A logical outcome of the spirit of the Equality Act is the right for same-sex couples to get married which became effective in 2014. Sociologists can also take some credit for highlighting the extent and impact of domestic violence, resulting in the Home Office instructing the police to treat domestic violence as seriously as any other form of violence.

Marxists are fundamentally opposed to all forms of social policy on the grounds that they are an ineffective and inefficient response to the injustices of capitalism. They also serve to muddy the waters; by appearing to be benevolent they serve to promote a sense of false consciousness. So despite some social policies reflecting substantial expenditure, they are criticised by Marxists because people lose sight of the fact that the problems social policy seeks to remedy are actually caused by the economic system of capitalism that underpins them. In treating the symptoms with social policy, the state promotes false consciousness and deflects any radical thinking or action to transform society.

Marxists are therefore very critical of the idea that sociology should help governments to address social problems, arguing it is not sociology's role to engage in reforming society. For example the criminology theory of Left realism, developed by Jock Young and John Lea, sought to provide a theory of crime that would provide credible and relevant solutions for the government to limit the harm crime was doing to lives of particularly the poorer members of society. However, traditional Marxist sociologists responded that Lea and Young had 'sold out' implying they had accepted the role of sociology was to help formulate social policy. It should not be the role of sociologists to help governments, Marxists argued, especially when crime exists because of the unfairness and inequalities of the capitalist system. Unless capitalism is abolished, crime will always be present as an issue anyway, so any reforms are just scratching the surface of the problem. In addition, by focusing on working-class offenders Left realism diverts attention from the greatest rule breakers in society: white-collar criminals and the corporate crime of big business.

The concept of social quality is important to this debate. It was devised by Alan Walker and is designed to provide an independent rationale for social policy in Europe. The concept comprises social inclusion/exclusion, social cohesion/anomie, socio-economic security/insecurity, and social empowerment/subordination.

> **KEY SOCIOLOGIST**
>
> **C. Wright Mills** (1956) has an important contribution to make towards this debate. He argued that sociology should be more than the accumulation of facts. Instead it is the duty of sociology to not only explain social problems but also to offer policy solutions.

CONTEMPORARY APPLICATION

John Williams (2013) argues that a lot of contemporary social policy and new legislation is shaped by sociology. He cites the examples of public inquiries into the racism and the murder of Stephen Lawrence, the policing of the Hillsborough football stadium disaster, and the Leveson inquiry into media regulation as all influenced by materials and evidence provided by sociologists.

STUDY TIP

Remember the postmodernist idea that it is impossible for sociology to contribute to social policy. Because they reject the modernist position that knowledge can be used to make society better, the only contribution of sociology is therefore to make sense of individual lives.

Different perspectives

Marxists argue that social policies provide ideological legitimisation for capitalism. Social policies, like welfare provision, give capitalism a 'human face' and promote false consciousness by implying that the government actually cares about the people. What people forget is that all welfare is funded out of taxation, so they are financing it themselves.

RESEARCH IN FOCUS

Closing the attainment gap in education

An example of sociological research driving social policy is that of Sosu and Ellis (2014). In their research they outlined what teachers, schools, local and national government and other education providers can do to close the education attainment gap associated with poverty in Scotland. They also looked at attempts that have been made to tackle the issue and considered the evidence for which ones have proved successful. The research makes recommendations for educators and policy makers about what is likely to work. In terms of methodology, the research took place in three main phases: initial trawl, screening and selection and analysis and synthesis.

Initial trawl: involved a systematic search of existing databases using pre-specified search terms such as 'poverty and educational attainment'. A snowballing strategy that involved following up interesting references cited in articles retrieved was also adopted. Electronic searches were complemented by email and telephone enquiries with key stakeholders, ensuring comprehensive coverage of existing evidence.

Screening and selection: pre-specified inclusion and exclusion criteria were used to determine which materials were selected for inclusion in the final report. The criteria were guided by the terms of reference of the project and judgements about the quality/strength of the evidence to support claims made.

Analysis and synthesis: This third stage involved identifying and summarising key elements/findings from each review. It also addressed gaps in existing evidence. It entailed bringing together the key issues addressed in order to construct a viewpoint. The focus was on specific recommendations for actions to become social policy in order to reduce the attainment gap between children from the poorest and richest backgrounds.

Adapted from Sosu and Ellis (2014)

Questions

1. What were the three stages of the research?
2. In the 'initial trawl' what was meant by the 'snowballing strategy'?
3. In the second stage what criteria guided the selection process of materials?
4. What became the focus of the third stage?

Check your understanding

1. The word science is derived from the Latin *scire*, what does this word mean?
2. Explain how sociology itself became a product of modernity.
3. What did Karl Popper mean when he advocated the deductive approach?
4. What did Thomas Kuhn mean by paradigms of knowledge?
5. Name three sociological perspectives that can be value-laden in their approach to research.
6. What was the approach adopted by classical sociologists like Comte and Durkheim?
7. Why did Gouldner refer to the twentieth-century sociologists as 'amoral positivists'?
8. What is meant by the term social policy?
9. What type of sociologist argues sociological research should underpin social policy and contribute to the reform of society?
10. Why are Marxists fundamentally opposed to reformist social policies?

Practice questions

Read Item A below and answer the questions that follow.

Item A

Any study of education cannot be purely scientific since all researchers will bring pre-conceived ideas to their work. It is not possible for any researcher to completely divorce themselves from attitudes and values derived from their own schooling experience, their attitudes about education as parents (if they have children) and their personal values about the government's education policies.

Applying material from Item A and your knowledge of research methods, evaluate two reasons why sociological research cannot be value-free. [20 marks]

To what extent can sociology claim to be a science? [10 marks]

Crime and deviance

2

Understanding the specification	
AQA Specification	**How the specification is covered in this chapter**
Crime, deviance, social order and social control	**Section 1: Crime, deviance, social order and social control**
	What are the definitions of crime, deviance, social order and social control?
	How do functionalists, the New Right and Marxist sociologists explain crime and deviance?
	How do labelling theorists explain crime?
	How do left and right realists explain crime?
	What is the postmodernist perspective of crime?
The social distribution of crime and deviance by ethnicity, gender and social class, including recent patterns and trends in crime	**Section 2: The social distribution of crime and deviance**
	What are the different rates of crime among different social groups, and how have these trends changed over time?
	What is white-collar crime and corporate crime?
Globalisation and crime in contemporary society; the media and crime; green crime; human rights and state crimes	**Section 3: Globalisation and crime in contemporary society**
	How has globalisation affected crime in contemporary society?
	What is the relationship between the media and crime?
	What is green crime?
	What are human rights and state crimes?
Crime control, surveillance, prevention and punishment, victims, and the role of the criminal justice system and other agencies	**Section 4: Crime control, surveillance, prevention and punishment**
	How is crime controlled? What are the possible responses to crime and how might it be prevented?
	How is crime measured?
	Who is more or less likely to be a victim and why?
	What is the role of the criminal justice system and the agencies that work alongside it?

Section 1: Crime, deviance, social order and social control

This section will explore the following debates:

- What are the definitions of crime, deviance, social order and social control?
- How do functionalists, the New Right and Marxist sociologists explain crime and deviance?
- How do labelling theorists explain crime?
- How do right and left realists explain crime?
- What is the postmodernist perspective of crime?

GETTING YOU STARTED

Figure 2.1 Are these examples of crime and deviance?

Questions

1. Which of the images on the right shows someone breaking a law?
2. Which of the images are not breaking a law, and how are these behaviours treated?
3. Which of the behaviours shown are seen as wrong?
4. How have attitudes towards crime changed over time?

1.1 What are the definitions of crime, deviance, social order and social control?

Make sure you understand how these definitions, and the positions of their critics, may have changed over time.

Crime, deviance and social control

A **crime** is any form of action which results in breaking a written, formal rule in society – for example, a bank robbery, or burglary. Crimes are socially constructed, which means that they are defined within a specific cultural time and place. Definitions of crime change over time and from place to place.

Deviance is behaviour which, at a specific time and in a specific place, is seen as wrong. A deviant act may or may not be a crime – it deviates from what is socially acceptable, but may not be against the law. A good example of deviance is young children swearing – it is not illegal but it is usually considered wrong, or 'deviant'.

Social control can be either formal or informal. Formal social controls include laws; informal social controls might be anything from residents' groups pressuring people to maintain their gardens, or asking people breastfeeding to leave cafes.

The nature of social control is changing. Whereas people used to be controlled through physical punishment, today punishment for criminal or deviant actions has become more psychological. For example, people's behaviour is now regulated through surveillance such as CCTV.

Feminists regard social control as a mechanism of patriarchal ideology – men reminding women of their subordinate position through responses to crime and deviance. For instance, when women stray from expected 'female' nurturing and caring behaviour, they are regarded as doubly deviant, and are often given a more harsh punishment.

Sociologists agree that crime is culturally constructed: crimes reflect a particular set of values in a specific place at a specific time. For example, smoking in a car with children present was not seen as deviant until relatively recently and has now become criminalised. This reflects the socially constructed nature of crime.

> **STUDY TIP**
> Make sure that you can define these key concepts clearly and carefully, and recognise that crime and deviance are different and socially constructed. This is particularly relevant when considering change and, for example, newly emerging forms of crime such as green crimes.

IN THE NEWS

The Home Secretary announces a new form of crime

A new domestic abuse offence of 'coercive and controlling behaviour' is to be introduced carrying a penalty of up to five years in prison, the home secretary has announced. While the government's definition of domestic violence recognises the impact of coercive control and threatening behaviour, this has not previously been reflected in law.

The decision to make this behaviour a crime follows a long fought campaign by organisations who argue that domestic violence is not simply physical. However Refuge, one of the largest national domestic violence charities, said that coercive and controlling behaviour would be extremely difficult to prove, and police were not implementing properly the existing laws against serious physical violence.

Adapted from Evans (2014)

Questions

1. How does this article show that crime is socially constructed?
2. Why might controlling and coercive behaviour be difficult to prove?
3. Can you think of any other deviant behaviour that might become a crime in the future?

1.2 How do functionalists, the New Right and Marxist sociologists explain crime and deviance?

In considering how a particular group of sociologists explain crime, make sure that you evaluate their views using other theoretical perspectives. In particular it is important for you to understand when the theory emerged and the social context in which it was created. It is important as well to assess the extent to which a particular theory may or may not be useful in the context of contemporary society.

Structural consensus theories

Consensus structural explanations of crime and deviance formed some of the earliest theories of crime. These theories were chiefly developed by functionalists who claim that crime, in small amounts, is necessary for society to function.

They argue that boundaries, based on **value consensus**, are necessary for society to maintain social order.

Durkheim (1947) was an early functionalist who believed that, to a certain extent, crime is inevitable: he claimed that it was inevitable that not everyone can be fully integrated into the norms and values of society. These individuals can remind others of the importance of **social solidarity**, where people have a sense of the importance of the social group they find themselves in. For example, when someone commits a crime, and is punished, it serves as a reminder for others of the boundaries of society. In fact Durkheim argues that without this form of boundary maintenance, crime rates might increase, leading to anomie or normlessness.

Later, the structuralist functionalist Merton (1968) developed the earlier ideas of Durkheim, arguing that crime occurs as a result of the tension or strain arising from people trying but failing to attain the goals society has set for them. He acknowledges that these goals are stratified, depending on a person's starting point, and that there are socially acceptable ways of achieving these goals. When people are unable to achieve their goals by these socially accepted means, they may look for other routes – some of which will be criminal. For example: many people share the goal of financial success and if this is not possible by the socially accepted means of work, they may turn to crime to achieve it. Merton calls these responses to strain 'modes of adaption'.

There are problems with Merton's approach: he assumes that people's motivations for crime are individual and ignores the fact that crime often occurs in groups. Further, Merton's approach does not explain why some individuals are more likely to commit crime than others. Merton's ideas also do not explain why some people who have achieved the goals of society still go on to commit crimes.

Durkheim and Merton's ideas may not apply to the contemporary UK: there have been many significant changes to UK society since these ideas were developed. Take, for example, the idea that people within contemporary society share similar views on what is considered right and wrong: this view has been seriously challenged in recent years for example, through different attitudes towards crime that now co-exist. Similarly, new forms of crime have emerged since Durkheim and Merton were writing. Despite the fact that society has become far more diverse, for example through increased rates of migration, functionalist ideas still offer an interesting explanation for crime that may still be useful to some extent.

A summary of Merton's responses to strain

Type of adaptation to strain	Do these individuals accept the conventionally accepted ways of achieving success?	Do these individuals accept the goals of society?	Example
Conformity	Yes	Yes	Someone who abides by the rules and works to achieve the goals of society in the conventional way.

Type of adaptation to strain	Do these individuals accept the conventionally accepted ways of achieving success?	Do these individuals accept the goals of society?	Example
Innovation	No	Yes	People without the means for success, for example, the poorly educated, find alternative ways of achieving success, through crime.
Ritualism	Yes	No	People who accept that they will not achieve the goals of society but go through the motions of work, for example people just working for the sake of it, not trying to get promotion or people who do not care about their work.
Retreatism	No	No	People who give up on achieving the goals and simply drop out of society all together.
Rebellion	Yes and No	No	People who refuse to accept the goals of society and seek radically different alternatives.

Table 2.1 Merton's responses to strain

Functionalist subcultural theories

Partly in response to the criticisms of Durkheim and Merton's ideas, newer forms of functionalist theory emerged in the 1970s. These were functionalist subcultural theories. These theories reflected the social changes of the time, with the emergence of youth subcultures and more liberal attitudes and behaviours, such as promiscuity, along with less pressure on people to conform to traditional social structures. Cohen, writing in 1971, argued that the young working class felt a sense of frustration because they lacked the job opportunities to enable them to achieve society's goals. Cohen calls this '**status frustration**'. Cohen argued that status frustration led to the development of an alternative set of values, a 'delinquent subculture', which ran counter to the values of the rest of society. The idea of status frustration may still be relevant to today's society where young people lacking employment and status may commit crimes. Since Cohen wrote, this frustration may even be greater. Contemporary society has become more materialistic and many young people may feel pressured to buy expensive items such as trainers and designer clothes. For example, the riots in London in 2012 might have been a good example of status frustration.

> **IN THE NEWS**
>
> ### London Riots One Year On
>
> In this article, Jones explores the aftermath of the riots a year on. Owen claims that rather than improving things, the riots have actually been followed by even greater social problems. He claims that increasingly high levels of unemployment led to the riots due to the high levels of frustration particularly among young people. Owen argues that it is lower-class men and some ethnic minority groups who feel as if they are treated as if they are different and therefore cannot 'get on' in life. Owen describes how this leads to such young men joining gangs and lacking ambition in the conventional sense. Instead they seek status in other ways, namely through crime.
>
> Adapted from Jones (2015)

Questions

1. How does this example support the idea that status frustration leads to crime?
2. How useful are functionalist subcultural theories in explaining crime?

Cohen suggests that within this delinquent subculture, deviant behaviour allowed the working class to experience an alternative form of status and respect from their peers. For example, risk-taking behaviour such as stealing cars, vandalism and **antisocial behaviour** don't help achieve social goals but can help achieve status within the peer group. Cohen's study (1955) overcame the criticism against functionalists that they overlooked crime that takes place more socially, in groups (see page 79).

Cloward and Ohlin (1961) offer an alternative view, claiming that there are a number of responses to the strain of status frustration. They argue that there is a range of **criminal subcultures**, such as conflict subcultures (where it is common to find violence) and retreatist subcultures. These subcultures might be applied to today's society; for example, conflict subcultures might involve a violent gang, restreatist subcultures might be groups of young people spending time together but not interacting with other groups, such as those sharing a particular interest in a type of music. Cloward and Ohlin's explanation is very useful as it highlights the complexity of working-class subcultures and acknowledges that crime has a social aspect.

Both Cohen and Cloward and Ohlin tend to ignore that people are not necessarily permanently within these subcultures, rather they move in and out of them.

Matza (1964) criticises other functionalist subcultural theories for suggesting that a delinquent is somehow different to other people. Matza argues that people belonging to such subcultures use '**techniques of neutralisation**', justifying their behaviour by removing themselves from taking any responsibility for the act. For example, someone suggesting that they committed an act of violence because they were provoked or felt that they had no choice. Matza also argues that there is a process of '**delinquency and drift**' whereby individuals are not in a permanent state of delinquency, rather that they drift in and out of being a delinquent, before they are settled and established as adults in mainstream society. Matza suggests that the lack of commitment that young people have makes it possible for them to feel that they can take greater risks. Matza refers to this set of values, based on deviant behaviour, as 'subterranean values' and says they are particularly attractive to certain members of the working class. This idea might still be considered relevant to today's society, despite Matza's ideas being developed over 50 years ago.

An interesting contrast to these theories can be found in the work of Lyng (1990) who suggests that young people commit crimes in order to take risks and experience excitement. Lyng calls this kind of crime '**edgework**'. The idea of 'edgework' challenges the notion that there is some form of structural cause of crime among young people. Contemporary examples of this might include 'urban explorers' (see In the News, below). Rather, he suggests that crime might simply be committed for the thrill and risk, and the criminal may or may not be experiencing frustration, marginalisation or social exclusion.

> **IN THE NEWS**
>
> ### 'Urban explorer' scales London's 1,000ft Shard
>
> Bradley Garrett, 31, is an urban explorer. Urban explorers sneak into London landmarks at night – skyscrapers or disused Tube tunnels, for instance – despite the threats to their safety, and the threat of arrest.
>
> Tonight, Garrett, who has written a PhD thesis on what he calls 'place-hacking', is found clinging tightly to a crane 1,000ft up, perched at the top of London's Shard.
>
> Garrett said his group, the London Consolidation Crew, had climbed up the Shard a number of times over the past 12 months. The stunt will dismay the security operation that surrounds the huge construction project amid claims just one guard was on duty each night. Garrett said his group had first scaled the building to watch New Year's Eve fireworks over London in December 2010.
>
> 'We don't break in – we sneak in,' he said. 'We never cause criminal damage and we leave everything exactly how we find it. We're doing it because we love the building. Ninety per cent of the time no one even knows we have been in and out of the place.'
>
> Adapted from Andrews (2012)

Questions

1. What is place hacking?
2. How is place hacking a good example of edgework?

Cloward and Ohlin's three types of delinquent subculture

Type of subculture	Explanation	Example
Criminal	Crimes which result in something being gained for the person carrying out the crime (utilitarian crime).	Burglary, or theft, which provides the perpetrator with an alternative career and network.
Conflict	Where there is instability and a high rate of movement of people in and out of the area, a lack of shared norms and values, leading to little social cohesion. In this context young people seek an alternative status through violent crime, to gain respect from their peers.	Gang culture, gang related crime.
Retreatist	For those who have had no success in either conventional mainstream culture and criminal subcultures, these individuals retreat from society, often turning to drugs and alcohol.	Drug-related petty crime, such as theft, shoplifting, burglary.

Table 2.2 Types of delinquent subculture

The New Right

New Right thinkers, emerging around the late 1980s picked up and developed some of the ideas of functionalist thinkers. They argued that there are a group of people who do not work and whose values run counter to the rest of society – the underclass. Key New Right thinker Murray (1989) argues that this underclass is responsible for a large proportion of crime that is committed in society. Murray argues that an overly generous state has led to people becoming reliant on welfare benefits, which in turn encourage people to turn to crime rather than go to work and earn money. New Right views are heavily criticised, for example by left realists for failing to see that some people experience structural inequalities from which they cannot escape, and for example, individuals who cannot overcome their poverty through education as they were unable to go to good schools and raise their social position.

Echoes of the New Right ideology are still found very much in evidence in contemporary society: many of the ideas of the New Righthave been picked up again by the current Conservative government and right-wing media who claim that an overgenerous welfare state and the breakdown of traditional attitudes has led to 'broken Britain', including rioting and other crimes.

Marxist theories

Classical early Marxists also argue that crime is a product of structural forces: Crime reflects inequalities that exist within capitalist society – the types of crime that exist are inevitable, only to be resolved with the overthrow of capitalist society. Capitalism, they argue, breeds the values of greed and competition which lead to the need for consumer goods and products, which leads people to commit crimes.

Marxists argue that the problem lies in the fact that because the ruling class create the law, these laws protect their interests. More recently the classical Marxist Snider (1993) argues that laws still do not curb the interests of big business. This means that either legislation is not written to stop massive amounts of profit being made by the wealthy or that laws are written in such a way as to allow the rich avoid them, for example, they avoid paying taxes. Snider argues that big businesses are important and necessary within capitalist society and therefore they are given certain concessions which benefit them. Banks, for example, controversially, pay their senior staff huge bonuses, despite some being part-owned by the state, for example the recent case of The Royal Bank of Scotland which was controversially given government-based financial assistance. There are many other examples of conscious decisions to avoid creating laws and regulations for the wealthy; Chambliss (1973) calls this 'non-decision making'. Although these arguments were developed some time ago, it is clear that their relevance today remains clear.

Marxists argue that crime occurs at all levels of society, for example, white-collar crime which is crime carried out by the ruling class, such as embezzlement of money, money laundering, or corporate crime. Snider argues that these types of crime actually cost society far more than the crimes carried out by the poor such as burglary.

There are problems with the traditional Marxist view of crime and deviance; for example, not all crime is utilitarian, meaning that not all crimes are committed for personal gain or material wealth. Examples of non-utilitarian crimes are hate crimes and crimes of passion. Furthermore, Marxists do not explain why crime exists in non-capitalist societies. Nor do Marxists account for the fact that crime rates vary within and between capitalist societies. Feminists argue that Marxists ignore the different patterns of crime between men and women and the importance of patriarchal ideology in influencing the legal system. Finally, it could be argued that class is no longer such a relevant factor in deciding who commits crime, and perhaps other factors are more relevant to a person's identity such as ethnicity.

Neo-Marxist views on crime and deviance

More recently, neo-Marxists have attempted to develop Marxist theories of crime to go beyond the traditional view that it is the structure of capitalist society that is the main cause of crime. Instead, neo-Marxists argue that the individual has a degree of choice or agency in their decision to commit a crime. Taylor, Walton and Young (1973) were influenced by both Marxist and interpretivist theories of crime and argue that there are several factors involved with understanding crime, including:

The New Criminology (Taylor, Walton and Young 1973)

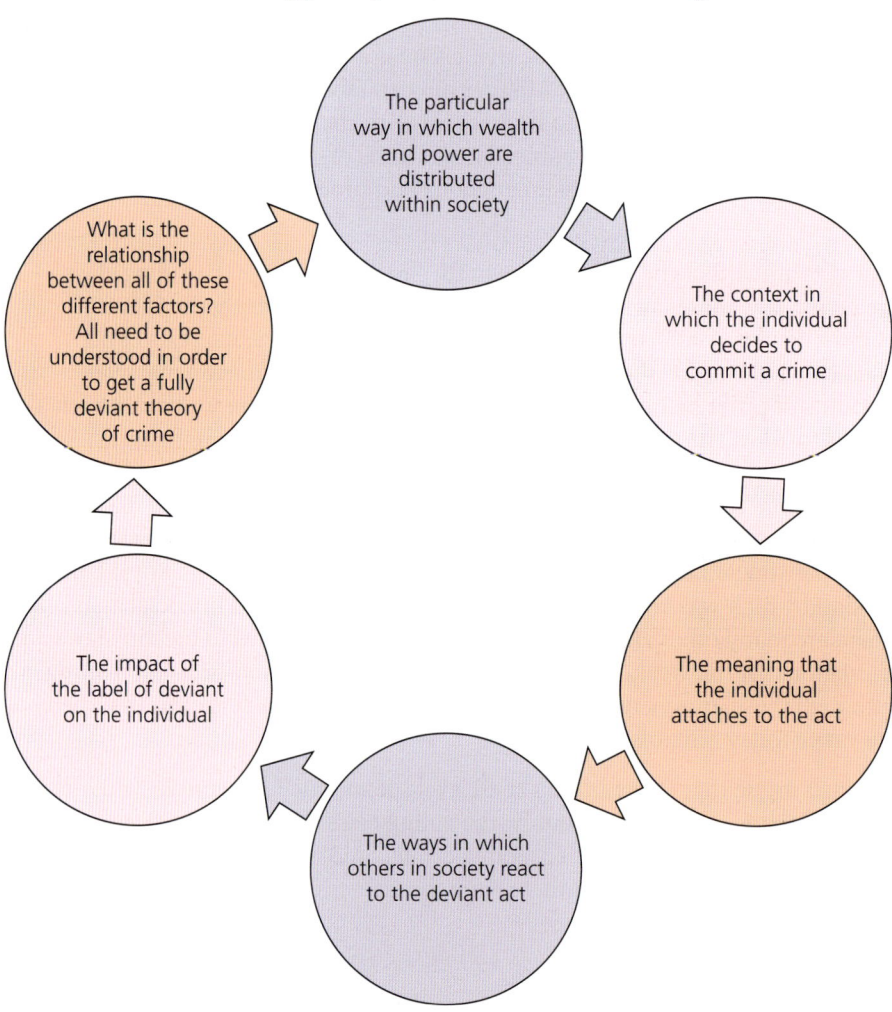

- The particular way in which wealth and power are distributed within society
- The context in which the individual decides to commit a crime
- The meaning that the individual attaches to the act
- The ways in which others in society react to the deviant act
- The impact of the label of deviant on the individual
- What is the relationship between all of these different factors? All need to be understood in order to get a fully deviant theory of crime

Figure 2.2 Theory of crime

This theory of crime has been criticised for failing to examine the impact of gender and ethnicity. In fact, more recently Young and Walton acknowledge that this is a problem with their earlier ideas.

Stuart Hall (1978) attempted to address some of these issues through his 'fully social theory of deviance' which attempts to explore how crimes are blown up to distract people from economic problems caused by capitalism and turn attention away from structural causes of inequality. Hall's study, *Policing the Crisis* (1978), focused on a moral panic surrounding mugging in Britain in the 1970s.

The concept of 'mugging' was imported from the USA and referred to being robbed in the street by black men. During the 1970s, several British newspapers repeatedly reported incidents of mugging. This led to a wave of concern about an issue which threatens society, known as a **moral panic**. In this case, the moral panic was built on the idea of a collective fear of an 'enemy within', namely young black men.

Hall's study explored the idea of the black mugger as a scapegoat for other social ills of the period. Between 1945 and the late 1960s, Britain had prospered with full employment and improved living standards. However, the 1970s brought about an economic decline. This led to a series of strike actions which resulted in civil unrest and, according to Hall, a challenge to social order and the power of the capitalist state.

Hall's ideas are more comprehensive than simply blaming capitalism as they show how economic conditions with labelling, societal reaction, moral panics and deviancy amplification combine into a complete 'social theory' of deviance. Hall shows the **social processes** involved in 'becoming criminal' or 'victim'.

The wider origins of the deviant act	The 1970s was a period of considerable social crisis in Britain, the result of an international downturn in capitalist economies.
The immediate origins of the deviant act	This turmoil was shown in a number of inner-city riots, as well as conflict in Northern Ireland and dissatisfaction generally expressed through strikes. The government was searching for a group that could be scapegoated, to draw attention to them and away from the looming economic crisis.
The actual act	Mugging, which according to the police, was more likely to be carried out by those from African Caribbean backgrounds.
The immediate origins of social reaction	Media outrage at the extent of muggings, linked to racism among the Metropolitan Police (and wider racism in society, e.g. growth of the National Front).
The wider origins of social reaction	The need to find scapegoats and the ease with which young men from African Caribbean backgrounds could be blamed.
The outcome of social reaction on the deviants' further action	A sense of injustice among ethnic minorities and a loss of confidence by ethnic minority communities in the **criminal justice system**.
The nature of the deviant process as a whole	The real causes of crime were not addressed and were effectively hidden by the criminal justice system.
CCCS	Birmingham Centre for Contemporary Cultural Studies which carried out research into subcultures forming much of the research discussed in this section.

Table 2.3 Hall's 'fully social theory' of crime: Mugging

Traditional Marxists criticise Hall's study and argue that the new criminology is too removed from the Marxist tradition. Feminist criminologists argue that the new criminology has merely continued the omission of women from criminological discussion, ignoring the power of **patriarchy** in the analysis. Left realists (including Young!) argue that the new criminology tends to 'romanticise' the view of criminals, seeing them all as fighting against the system. There is, as with traditional Marxism, little discussion of the victims of street crimes such as mugging, most of whom are themselves working class. It is also problematic that many new forms of crime have emerged which do not occur at street level, such

CONTEMPORARY APPLICATION

New Right ideas are very visible through the ideas of David Cameron, leader of the Conservative Party and UK Prime Minister since 2010. He argues that workless families contribute to what he calls 'Broken Britain' where 'troubled families are much more likely to raise children who turn to crime'. Cameron draws a strong link between workless families, delinquency and crime.

STUDY TIP

Make sure that you can draw out the different interpretations of each theoretical perspective. For example, that functionalist subcultural theorists build on Durkheim's ideas. It is a good idea to criticise each set of ideas.

Questions

1. How is crime marketed to young people, according to Hayward?
2. What is 'brandalism'?
3. Why are consumer products important to young people today?

as cybercrime (see page 86). Hall's study after all relates to the 1970s economic crises which is in some ways similar and in other ways different to the kinds of economic problems found today.

New criminology played an important role in challenging traditional Marxist views and in part led to the development of left realism, which may be considered to be more relevant to contemporary society.

KEY SOCIOLOGIST

Miller (1961) argues that a unique, predominantly male working-class subculture characterised by 'focal concerns' has long existed. These relate to behaviour which is seen as particularly important within these subcultures – 'toughness' and masculinity, hostility towards authority, risk-taking behaviour and rule-breaking. Miller suggests there is a continual drive to be the dominant figure within the subculture by showing the strongest focal concerns.

Edwin H. Sutherland (1960) supported the idea that crime is a product of social interactions, claiming that differential association leads to criminal behaviour. In other words, people who associate with other criminals throughout their early life will begin to learn how to commit crimes and see a criminal lifestyle as normal and acceptable.

One of the largest high street banks, HSBC, was recently exposed for encouraging some of its wealthiest customers to avoid paying taxes by 'playing the system'. This has caused huge controversy as many argue that those earning much less are forced to pay tax on all their earnings and are therefore at an even greater disadvantage, widening the gap between the rich and the poor. This leads to the wider question of why the wealthy and rich are 'above the law' while the poor are heavily regulated and policed.

RESEARCH IN FOCUS

Youth crime and consumer culture

Hayward (2006) argues that there is now a strong relationship between consumer culture and youth crime. In fact, he proposes that crime is 'marketed' through branded goods, especially to young people whose identity in society is linked to the possession of particular products. While various representations of criminality and the pursuit of stylised excitement have always held a certain draw, Hayward argues that designer goods, such as particular items of clothes and jewellery, have become synonymous with risk-taking behaviour and a deviant lifestyle. Hayward further contends that the stakes have risen: while in the past some celebrity rappers sang about branded trainers, today they rap about luxury cars.

Major companies design marketing campaigns that seem to promote resistance to established culture (for example the graffiti-style placing of logos). Hayward suggests that this practice of 'brandalism' contributes to social control of young people, offering a discussion of crime that is concerned with 'status frustration'.

Hayward (2006)

1.3 How do labelling theorists explain crime?

Both functionalist and Marxist theories of crime point to structural causes. Interactionist theories of crime, which were developed around the 1960s, are different as they suggest that it is more important to explore how people come to be considered deviant, and the effect of being labelled deviant on a person's future behaviour. Thus this theory is commonly known as labelling theory. Most labelling theorists argue that everyone acts in ways which are deviant. Therefore the point of interest is why some acts become determined as deviant while others do not. All crimes are clearly socially constructed: official statistics on crime simply tell sociologists about the stereotypes that the police hold (which are interesting and revealing). There are different parts to this approach, exploring what kinds of interactions occur between deviant people, what defines a person as deviant and the process through which someone becomes defined as deviant.

Becker (1963) is a key figure in labelling theory. He suggests that an act only becomes deviant when others perceive and define it as such and whether or not the deviant label is applied depends on societal reaction. Becker calls groups such as the mass media and the police, who have the power and resources to create or enforce rules and impose their definitions of deviance, **moral entrepreneurs**. Agencies of **social control** use considerable discretion and selective judgement in deciding whether or how to deal with illegal or deviant behaviour, leading to selective law enforcement. Becker suggests that the police operate with pre-existing conceptions and stereotypical categories of what constitutes 'trouble', criminal types, criminal areas, and so on, and these factors influence their response to behaviour that they come across. Any action they then take reflects the stereotypes they hold, rather than reality. Lemert (1972) distinguishes between **primary deviance** and **secondary deviance**. Primary deviance is defined as deviance that has not been publicly labelled as a crime. For example, people might break traffic laws, or use illegal drugs which may have few consequences for the person as long as no one knows about it. Secondary deviance occurs once an offender is discovered and publicly exposed and the label of 'deviance' is attached.

The ideas of Becker and Lemert have considerable relevance to contemporary society, for example, the recent negative labelling of some asylum seekers and refugees as 'immigrants' and vulnerable people said to be 'scrounging' on state benefits. The media has an important role to play in labelling crime and deviance in a way which can increase the actual occurrence of the crime in official statistics, a process known as deviancy amplification (see the work of Cohen on page 90).

Labelling theorists explore and develop the idea that police officers' decisions to arrest are influenced by their stereotypes about offenders. For example, in the classical study by Cicourel (1968) it was found that officers' assumptions led them to concentrate on certain 'types' of people, namely the working class. This resulted in law enforcement showing a class bias. In turn, this leads police to patrol working-class areas more intensively, resulting in more arrests and confirming their stereotypes. This theory has considerable use not just for exploring police labelling of groups in contemporary society, for example some ethnic minority groups.

Cicourel also found that other agents of social control within the criminal justice system reinforced this bias. For example, probation officers held the common sense theory that juvenile delinquency was caused by broken homes, poverty and lax parenting. Therefore they tended to see youths from such backgrounds as likely to offend in the future and were less likely to support alternative punishments to prison sentences for them. In Cicourel's view, justice is not fixed but negotiable. For example, when a middle-class youth was arrested, he was less likely to be charged. This was partly because his background did not fit the idea of the police's 'typical delinquent', and partly because his parents were more likely to negotiate successfully on his behalf, convincing the control agencies that he was sorry, that they would monitor him and make sure he would stay out of trouble in future etc. As a result, typically he was 'counselled, warned and released' rather than prosecuted.

Cicourel's study has serious implications for how we interpret police statistics – he argues that they are not valid. Instead, Cicourel argues that we should investigate the processes that create the police statistics. Despite this study being written in the 1960s it still has much relevance today. It remains the case that working-class people, and people from ethnic minorities, are over represented in crime statistics. Further, cases of police bias have been exposed in far more recent times, for example the Stephen Lawrence case. However, some sociologists argue that social class is less relevant as a marker of identity than other variables today such as gender, ethnicity and age for example.

STUDY TIP

Make sure that you draw out the differences between each interpretivists view of crime and deviance. Avoid the tendency to write about them as similar. Make sure you explain the fact that labelling theory is still very much applicable to society today, giving examples.

RESEARCH IN FOCUS

In his research Cicourel used participant and non-participant observation in more than four years study of juvenile justice. He went on patrol with the police as an observer and sat in the courtroom during proceedings. As a participant he took on the role of an unpaid probation officer. He argued that his first-hand experience enabled him to uncover the often unconscious assumptions of control agents in a way that methods such as interviewing would not have revealed.

Cicourel (1976)

Questions

1. What were the strengths of Cicourel's research methods?
2. How is Cicourel's study relevant to contemporary society?

CONTEMPORARY APPLICATION

Braithwaite and Drahos (2000) argue that labelling theory need not just be applied to people but also more broadly to the environment. For example, they argue that crimes against the environment ought to be re-identified as 'harm', to ensure that any legally acceptable form of behaviour which is damaging to the environment is punished. Braithwaite and Drahos argue that this is much more of an effective way of understanding crime than through laws alone.

1.4 How do left and right realists explain crime?

Make sure that you explain how realism is different and similar to other social theories of crime. Realism is a relatively new theoretical perspective, emerging around the 1980s.

Until relatively recently sociological theories of crime generally (apart from labelling theory) sought to explain the reasons for crime at a structural level without considering practical strategies for reducing crime. Realists, however, are different:

- they acknowledge that crime exists and usually affects the poor
- they focus not just on understanding the causes of crime, but offering solutions and responses to crime.

Realist views have had considerable influence on present and past policies and strategies to reduce and respond to crime. There are two main branches of realism which are known as left and right realism. These largely reflect the political views of left and right-wing political parties although they sometimes overlap.

Left realism

Left realism is a more contemporary response to traditional Marxist and neo-Marxist explanations. They agree that structural inequality in society is largely to blame for the crime that occurs, and they argue that for crime to be reduced there needs to be greater social equality and a stronger sense of community. But left realists considered Marxist and neo-Marxist views too focused on romanticising the working class and failing to take account of the effects of crime on victims.

Lea and Young (1984) suggest that there are three causes of crime:

1. **Relative deprivation** refers to how people regard their position in relation to others that causes crime, not deprivation per se.
2. **Subcultures** of various types form among the working class who may begin to see offending behaviour as normal.
3. **Marginalisation** is the process through which some people find themselves on the edges of society and unable to access rights and services available. This in turn leads to crime becoming seen as more acceptable.

Left realists claim that the following strategies should be used to reduce and prevent crime rates:

- Increase trust between the public and the police. Left realists feel that communities are important for taking some responsibility in policing the streets and they would encourage the public to get involved with policing local communities, for example neighbourhood watch. This in turn, they argue, would reduce any unrealistic fear of crime.
- Develop a greater understanding of the role of victims. They argue that understanding the reasons why some people become victims offers insight into reducing crime.
- Develop greater understanding by the police and other agencies of the meaning given to the crime by the offender.

In essence, to truly understand crime, Lea and Young argue that it is important to understand the causes of social inequalities in society. Similar to right realists, left realists acknowledge that most victims of crime are poor or working class.

There are limitations of left realist approaches to crime – they fail to recognise or explain that not all working-class or marginalised groups respond to their situation by committing crime. Furthermore, this theory fails to acknowledge the existence of crimes committed by the powerful and wealthy.

Left realists also tend to focus too heavily on victims' evidence: victim surveys can lack validity, as people can tend to present their experiences in a biased way, consciously or subconsciously omitting certain facts.

Right realism

There is a strong link between right realism and New Right ideology. For example, both believe that individuals should take responsibility for themselves. Right realists argue that social order is crucial in society and that value consensus regarding what is considered right and wrong is essential. They also feel that the state plays a strong role in maintaining social order, through laws and policies. Right realists argue that crime will always exist but, unlike left realists, right realists feel that there is little point in looking for structural causes – that energy should be put into prevention and reduction of crimes.

These ideas link closely with the views of Murray (1984), a key New Right thinker, who claimed that the breakdown of other institutions in society, such as the family, along with an over generous welfare state, leads to children being inadequately socialised. The lack of strong male role models, for example, Murray claims, leads young children to be more likely to commit crimes. Murray's ideas subsequently influenced welfare reforms in the USA in the mid 1990s and to some extent, the UK.

The basic starting point of right realism is the belief that people are naturally selfish and will commit crime for their own personal gain if they feel that they can get away with it. Right realists argue that people commit crime based on a rational choice, where an individual assesses the risk of getting caught: if the risk of getting caught is low they will then commit the crime. Their ideas are very influential; several governments in many parts of the world have adopted their ideas. They generally argue that the best solution to crime is to punish people harshly to reduce the likelihood of people being tempted to commit crime and act as a deterrent.

Some specific examples of their suggested strategies to reduce crime include:

- stricter, military-style control of the socialisation of young people
- target hardening (zero tolerance to small-scale crimes)
- situational crime prevention, where strategies are introduced to deter people such as CCTV and harsher punishments for crimes.

They also suggest that the local community should be involved in policing local people. These ideas resonate within Conservative government policies. For example, the Prime Minister David Cameron describes Britain as 'broken' and clearly draws links between the breakdown in traditional values and crimes, for example, the London riots in 2011 as well as 'troubled families' (see In The News, pages 54 and 65).

There are strengths of right realist views; they offer a strong set of clear solutions for reducing the opportunity for crimes to occur. Similarly to left realism, this approach acknowledges the importance of community control in policing and reducing crime. It also recognises that small-scale crimes may lead to larger-scale worse crimes.

However, there have been many criticisms of this approach. For example, it assumes that people are inherently selfish which may not always be the case.

It also ignores the role of structural inequalities in creating the context for crime. Furthermore, like Left Realism, this approach ignores the crimes of the powerful. New Right thinkers also argue that crime tends to be rational, premeditated and therefore ignore crimes which are not based on rational thought processes such as crimes committed in anger or crimes of passion or crimes that have no monetary reward. Many argue that right realist strategies do not help marginalised groups improve their situation in a positive way, rather they simply demonise the poor and vulnerable who see themselves as having to commit crime as they have few opportunities to legitimate means of success.

IN THE NEWS

David Cameron vows to mend 'broken Britain'

Referring to a spate of gang killings, David Cameron spoke of the need to address 'anarchy in the UK'.

Mr Cameron argues that Britain is a 'broken society' as a result of a breakdown in traditional family values. His analysis of 'Broken Britain' has been criticised by some as excessive. However, there is much support for his core political message about the need for increased social responsibility.

Mr Cameron's sees the solution as the strengthening of families and communities. He wants family life to be encouraged through the tax system, and for communities to be supported by allowing police and head teachers to do their jobs without interference from government.

Helm (2007)

Questions

1. What does Cameron mean by the term 'Broken Britain'
2. What is Cameron's solution to the problems he describes?

KEY SOCIOLOGISTS

The key left realist thinkers are **Lea and Young** (1984) who argue that crime is a product of structural inequalities as well as the way people perceive these inequalities. They draw attention to the fact that it is the working class who are most likely to be the victims of crime.

KEY SOCIOLOGIST

Wilson (1985, 1975) argued that, to reduce the effects of crime on people's lives, solutions to crime need to be clearly defined and acted on. Wilson suggested the best way to deter people from committing crimes was increasing the perception of the risk of getting caught for a crime, both before and after the event.

KEY SOCIOLOGISTS

Right realists **Wilson and Kelling** (1982) argue for a tough stance with small offences – a 'zero tolerance' approach to crime. They claim that multiple small scale crimes lead to a growing sense of a breakdown in social order which contributes to a sense of social disorder where crime is possible. This set of ideas has become known as the 'broken windows thesis' whereby the small visible signs of crime need swift and harsh punitive action.

> **STUDY TIP**
> Make sure that you know the strengths and weaknesses of realist approaches. Also make sure that you acknowledge the influence of Marxist ideas for left realists and the New Right ideas for right realists. Learn some contemporary examples of left and right realist strategies.

> **STUDY TIP**
> There are certain views that realists share – for example, the view that community policing is important and that strategies need to be developed to prevent and deter further crime. Both approaches ignore the crimes of the powerful and wealthy. Make sure that you can draw out similarities as well as differences between the two approaches.

> **KEY SOCIOLOGIST**
> The right realist **Felson** (1998) posits that three things must occur: a motivated offender, a suitable target and an absence of the police or an authority figure. Interestingly Felson believes that members of the public work far better at preventing crime than the police, as they may have a greater understanding of the criminal's background. Felson argues that to reduce crime these three things must be tackled.

Social policy

The coalition government have introduced policies which ensure that the police publish crime statistics locally so that the public can see how much crime is occurring in their area. They claim this leads to the police being more directly accountable to the public which reflects their right realist approach to crime prevention.

> **Questions**
> 1. Identify three strategies above which reflect right realist views on crime
> 2. How might local businesses help prevent crime?
> 3. Name one criticism with the strategies mentioned above.

1.5 What is the postmodernist perspective of crime?

When thinking about 'contemporary society' it is helpful to be able to understand postmodern approaches to crime. This might include theoretical ideas as well as suggestions for reducing and preventing crime. It is worth exploring how postmodern theories of crime go beyond other theories of crime.

Postmodernists argue that traditional theories and explanations, sometimes known as metanarratives, are no longer able to explain or understand the society that we live in today, as they offer singular often structural explanations. Postmodernists argue that in contemporary society, there is no single explanation of crime. Thus new ways of understanding crime are necessary. These ideas are therefore particularly useful for understanding contemporary forms of crime.

Explaining crime

Postmodernists do not seek structural explanations of crime; rather, they seek to explore ways in which postmodern society has led to the emergence of certain new forms of crime and new responses to crime. Postmodernists argue that society today is fragmented, characterised by increasing individualism, **diversity**, fluidity and in some respects, chaos and that this is useful in thinking about the reasons why people commit crime.

Postmodernists are not generally interested in any patterns of crime, nor are they interested in looking for one structural cause of crime. They argue that crimes reflect highly individual experiences and choices, which cannot be generalised or explained through one explanation alone. In this respect, crime is seen to be the product of the individual who has free will to decide whether to commit a crime or not.

Postmodernists argue that 'crime' in fact is no longer a useful concept. It simply reflects socially constructed ideas about certain behaviours that fall into a legally defined narrow category. They argue that many laws are out of date and no longer applicable to many of the forms of deviant behaviour that exist today. This is because community ties and social norms are weaker today: people no longer have such a strong sense of social cohesion and are likely to place their own individual needs and wishes above those of others. For example, consider applying the concept of 'crime' to religious extremism, which is complex, controversial and some might suggest, problematic. Postmodernists would argue that for many types of behaviour, conventional forms of punishment such as incarceration are simply no longer appropriate or effective.

To add to this, society is increasingly diverse – there is a whole range of social norms co-existing. Postmodernists argue that laws are narrow also in the sense that those who create them do so from one particular cultural and social perspective. Therefore there is difficulty in applying them to many crimes that actually occur.

Rethinking crime prevention and punishment

Postmodernists' solution for this is to create a broader concept of crime which includes any form of social wrong, or harm, which makes it easier to apply to a diverse and complex contemporary society.

The postmodernists Henry and Milovanovic (1996) suggest that the concept of crime should be replaced with the concept of '**social harm**'. They claim that crime reflects a narrow range of legally defined behaviours and that this cannot deal with the vast array of deviant behaviours causing social harm within a culturally diverse and fast-changing world. These forms of harm fall into two main categories:

- Harms of reduction – where someone uses their power in a way which results in an immediate loss of a possession or causes some form of harm to the person. This would include conventional current forms of criminal offence such as burglary, murder, or theft.
- Harms of repression – where people's future growth and development are threatened. This includes the kinds of behaviour which are harder to police and prevent within the current legal system such as actively disrespecting people of a particular culture, treating groups and individuals with less dignity, hate crimes and sexual harassment.

Approaches to reducing crimes and social harm

Postmodernists suggest that the way to reduce crime or social harm in society today is to have a number of strategies in place which may be both small and large-scale, publicly and privately funded; for example, private security firms using CCTV cameras. The post-structuralist Foucault argues that surveillance is likely to become an effective means of regulating behaviour and reducing crime in contemporary society. People who know that they are being watched are less likely to commit a crime as their chances of being caught are that much greater. Foucault was correct in his prediction: the UK has become the country with the most CCTV cameras in Europe. However, this has not resulted in crime disappearing altogether.

Postmodernists also point to the way in which crime prevention has become much more localised with some areas having high rates of particular crimes. For example, in areas where there are high numbers of some ethnic groups, there might be higher or lower rates of certain crimes. Therefore crime strategies can no longer be generalised.

Bauman and Lyon (2013) present the concept of liquid surveillance and argue that it can help to understand how people interact with various forms of surveillance. Bauman and Lyon argue that there are many forms of surveillance, including mobile phones or passports or identity chips for example, which people willingly buy and use, which enable them to be watched by the state and other organisations. They suggest that this makes our lives increasingly transparent, to the point that surveillance becomes invisible to us: we are not conscious of being under surveillance. This erodes our sense of civil liberties (including our right to privacy). Postmodernists suggest that surveillance is changing the dominant belief from one of a right to privacy into the idea that nobody should have anything to hide, therefore nothing to fear. This suggests how powerful and pervasive surveillance is as a mechanism of social control.

An evaluation of postmodern views of crime

Postmodern views provide an explanation of crime which shows how definitions of legally defined crime are narrow. Postmodernists are correct in pointing out that legal definitions of crime fail to take into account the multiple new forms of deviant behaviour that occur today. Postmodernists also take into account the changing social context of UK society, including the complex sets of social norms and values that co-exist.

However, postmodern theories of crime do not address the major cause of a lot of crimes which lie in structural inequalities. They also fail to explain why many people do not commit crime. Nor do postmodern theories of crime offer any suggestion about how social harm might be operationalised. Further, postmodern explanations ignore the issue of selective law enforcement. Finally, if crime prevention strategies are linked to understanding consumer behaviour for example, then people who choose not to participate as fully in certain forms of consumerism may not be detected nor observed. In fact some people might argue that surveillance is a violation of individual privacy in itself.

> **KEY SOCIOLOGIST**
>
> **Henry and Milovanovic** (1996) argue that the concept of crime should be replaced with social harm. They claim that crime simply reflects a narrow range of legally defined behaviours that is no longer useful for dealing with the vast array of deviant behaviours that exist within a culturally diverse and fast changing social world.

> **IN THE NEWS**
>
> ### Social media mass surveillance is permitted by law, says top UK official
>
> The government have recently revealed that there is extensive surveillance of individuals through their use of Google, Facebook and Twitter, including private messages between people. The government have confirmed that they can check people's social media accounts without a warrant.
>
> However, some civil rights groups have challenged this form of surveillance arguing that it damages privacy rights. Some groups argue that these new forms of surveillance do not have the consent of those being watched and that the new rules allowing surveillance are there to benefit the government only.
>
> Adapted from Bowcott and Ball (2014)

Questions

1. Explain how the surveillance of individual social media accounts reflects postmodern ideas about crime and deviance
2. How might this form of surveillance prevent criminal acts?
3. Do you think this is an effective way of preventing crime?

Different perspectives

Functionalists and Marxists would argue that there remains a strong sense of value consensus in society; people on the whole continue to share beliefs about what is right and wrong. Also, individuals continue to be shaped by structural factors. Functionalists would argue that a certain amount of crime is both necessary and useful, while Marxists would claim that crime is a product of capitalism.

CONTEMPORARY APPLICATION

In 2000, the Regulation of Investigatory Powers Act (RIPA) came into force to regulate, among other things, covert surveillance. Together with associated secondary legislation and codes of practice, it provides a framework designed to ensure that public authorities comply with the European Convention on Human Rights.

STUDY TIP

Postmodern theories assert that crimes are changing due to the increasing information sharing, and the social and geographic mobility. Crimes in postmodern society are sometimes the product of an increase in conflict between different sets of ideas and values, such as Islamophobic hate crimes.

Check your understanding

1. What is the difference between consensus and conflict theories of crime?
2. How are right and left realist approaches different and how are they similar?
3. What are subcultural theories?
4. Identify and briefly explain two criticisms of Marxist theories of crime.
5. Why might the concept of social harm be more useful than crime as a way of understanding deviant behaviour?
6. What is status frustration?

Practice questions

1. Outline two ways in which the crime is socially constructed. [4 marks]
2. Outline three ways in which Marxists argue that crime is a product of capitalism. [6 marks]
3. Outline two problems with labelling theories of crime. [4 marks]
4. Outline two ways in which postmodernists explain crime. [4 marks]

Section 2: The social distribution of crime and deviance

This section will explore the following debates:

- What are the different rates of crime among different social groups, and how have these trends changed over time?
- What is white-collar crime and corporate crime?

GETTING YOU STARTED

Figure 2.3 Who do you think is most likely to commit a crime?

Questions

1. Who do you think is most likely to commit a crime and why?
2. Think about who is least likely to commit a crime.
3. Have these patterns changed over time, if so how?

2.1 What are the different rates of crime among different social groups, and how have these trends changed over time?

When writing about crime rates among different groups, make sure that you consider a range of different social groups, as well as considering the intersections between these groups; that is, how a combination of various variables leads a person to be more or less likely to be a perpetrator or victim of crime. It is also important to describe variables as dynamic and not fixed; patterns change over time.

Although official crime statistics vary, there are some patterns which appear to be consistent; some groups appear to be overrepresented in prisons for example, while others appear to be more likely to be the perpetrators or victims of crimes. This section explores the variables of ethnicity, gender and social class.

Ethnicity and crime

Data	Type of ethnicity (1)	Time period (2)	White	Black	Asian	Mixed	Chinese or Other	Unknown	Total
Population aged 10 or over	Self-identified	2011	87.1 %	3.1 %	6.4 %	1.7 %	1.7 %	-	49,443,451
Stop and Searches (s1)(3)	Self-identified	2011/12	67.1 %	14.2 %	10.3 %	2.9 %	1.3 %	4.2 %	1,120,084
Arrests	Self-identified	2011/12	79.5 %	8.3 %	5.9 %	3.0 %	1.4 %	1.8 %	1,235,028
Penalty Notice for Disorder	Self-identified	2012	68.8 %	2.1 %	5.5 %	0.6 %	3.8 %	19.3 %	106,205
Cautions	Officer-identified	2012	83.9 %	7.0 %	5.2 %	-	1.4 %	2.6 %	188,610
Court Proceedings (indictable)	Self-identified	2012	71.4 %	7.8 %	4.7 %	1.9 %	1.1 %	13.1 %	375,874
Convictions (indictable)	Self-identified	2012	73.2 %	7.5 %	4.5 %	1.8 %	1.1 %	11.9 %	308,124
Sentenced to immediate custody (indictable)	Self-identified	2012	70.6 %	8.9 %	5.5 %	1.9 %	1.7 %	11.4 %	81,082

Table 2.4 Overview of race and the criminal justice system: proportion of individuals in the criminal justice system by ethnic group compared to general population, England and Wales. Adapted from Table A in Ministry of Justice (2013)

Questions

1. Describe the differences in crime rates among different ethnic groups.
2. How might these differences be explained?

There are two key issues relating to the patterns of crime in terms of ethnicity: the way that different ethnic groups engage with the criminal justice system as perpetrators or victims, and the behaviour of different ethnic groups. This section also explores the extent to which the police hold racist views of particular groups in society which results in differential treatment and policing styles. The 2012/13 Crime Survey for England and Wales shows that adults from Mixed, Black and Asian ethnic groups were more at risk of being a victim of personal crime than adults from the White ethnic group.

Victimisation
- According to the BCS 6 per cent of white adults report having been the victim of crime, whereas 8 per cent of ethnic minorities report having been a victim
- The highest proportion of victimisation was reported by the mixed ethnic group at 11 per cent
- A higher proportion of children from ethnic minority groups stated that they avoided travelling on buses as they were worried about their personal safety, compared with white groups

Criminalisation
- According to the BCS the average prison sentence length in 2010 was the highest among the black population, 20.8 months, followed by Asian people at 19.9 months, while the average among the white population was 14.9 months
- In 2010, the total prison population was 85,002, of which 25 per cent were ethnic minorities. In the general population ethnic minorities account for 11.3 per cent of the population

Ethnicity and Crime

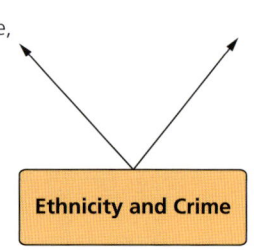

Figure 2.4 Ethnicity and crime

Many sociologists argue that it is likely to be a combination of ethnicity and class-based inequalities combined with racist policing which result in the overrepresentation of some ethnic minorities in crime statistics.

Bowling and Phillips (2002) acknowledge racial discrimination occurs throughout the criminal justice system and that it is cumulative. Some ethnic minorities experience both greater victimisation and criminalisation and this reflects in their overrepresentation in crime statistics. They argue that this is a result of wider inequalities in society. Higher levels of robberies carried out by black people, for example, reflects their lower economic position and marginalisation and offers them a powerful sense of identity. Bowling and Phillips use these statistics to argue that the use of the powers against black people reveals discrimination and they argue that if these cannot be regulated to be used more fairly, then they should be seriously questioned.

Sociology, ethnicity and crime

Until the 1980s ethnicity was generally overlooked in terms of crime; however, from the mid 1970s onwards there was a breakdown in relations between ethnic minority communities and the police and growing tension in communities between some ethnic groups. In 1981 the Scarman Report into the Brixton riots highlighted the role of resentment felt by the African Caribbean community against the police whom they felt they were being harassed by. Furthermore, the Home Office in the same year revealed that South Asian people were fifty times more likely to be the victims of racially motivated crime than the white population.

Figure 2.5 A riot in the 1980s

More recently, the Macpherson Report (1999) on the police investigation of the murder of the teenager Stephen Lawrence found that **institutional racism** in the police force was widespread. Macpherson argues that it may not simply be outright discrimination but rather the collective failure of the police and criminal justice system in a subconscious way. Macpherson therefore argues that the culture of the police, who are mainly white, tend to label particular groups and take some ethnic minority groups less seriously. This has led to some ethnic minorities being more likely to become victims of crime and also more likely to become criminalised.

Explaining patterns in ethnicity and crime

There have been many explanations put forward for the overrepresentation of some ethnic groups in crime statistics. **Cultural derivation theorists**, for example, argue that one reason may be inadequate socialisation of some ethnic minority groups.

However Paul Gilroy (1983), a neo-Marxist, presents a strong argument against the view that black criminals are inadequately socialised, leading to them becoming criminals. Rather, he claims that ethnic minorities become criminal as a result of needing to defend themselves against a society that discriminates against them. Both British Asians and African Caribbeans originate from former colonies of Britain and carry the weight of historical violence in other parts of the world, for example, through slavery. Gilroy argues that once they arrive in Britain, some ethnic minorities use similar techniques to resist exploitation, for example, marches, demonstrations and riots.

The Marxist Reiner (1993) argues that a combination of discrimination and victimisation leads to the overrepresentation of ethnic minorities in crime statistics. This idea is supported by the left realists Lea and Young (1982) who claim that both crime and victimisation rates are higher for some for ethnic groups than others because they are likely to be marginalised, and that this marginalisation is made worse by discrimination. Some ethnic minorities feel a sense of relative deprivation and a strong sense of being unable to access conventional routes to gaining material success due to discrimination. These factors conspire to create subcultures, particularly among young black males who may be tempted to turn to street crime as a result of status frustration.

Labelling theory can also be applied to patterns of ethnicity and crime. Certain ethnic groups become labelled as deviant or criminal and thus the police become more suspicious and these groups are likely to be stopped and searched, for example. These ideas are very much supported by the statistics on crime.

Social policy

In 1999 there was a drive to increase the number of police officers recruited from ethnic minorities. This followed the racist murder of a black London teenager, Stephen Lawrence, in April 1993 and the subsequent Macpherson inquiry into his death. The Macpherson Report published in February 1999 concluded that the police handling of the murder investigation had been marred by institutional racism and called, among other things, for targets to be set to increase the recruitment and retention of ethnic minority officers.

A decade later numbers had increased with minority ethnic officers accounting for around 4.4 per cent of the total police force. However, this was still far short of the 7 per cent target figure set by the Home Office to reflect the proportion of ethnic minorities in the population as a whole. In February 2009 it was felt that the 7 per cent target was not realistic and it was replaced with individual targets for each police force to reflect the ethnic make-up of their local communities.

Figure 2.6 Stephen Lawrence

Different perspectives

In his classical work 'Policing the Crisis' based on the work of various contributors, the Marxist Hall (1979) explores how supposedly deviant groups, in this case young black males, are periodically singled out and placed at the centre of a series of moral panics which allow the state to demonstrate that it has the people's consent to maintain the status quo through an increasing reliance on an authoritarian state model of society. Hall argues that the black British represent some of the most exploited proletariat. In this case, the UK was experiencing an economic crisis and unemployment levels were high, as well as there being a high level of social and political unrest. Hall argues that to avoid any threat to the dominant ruling-class ideology, a moral panic about 'black muggers' who became a folk devil, a scapegoat for societies' problems, which helped to justify more aggressive forms of policing in city centres.

CONTEMPORARY APPLICATION

In 2009/10, according to the British Crime Survey, per 1,000 of the population, black people were stopped and searched seven times more than white people compared to six times more in 2006/07. This suggests that despite the Macpherson report in 1999, the practice continues to reflect discrimination by the police.

IN THE NEWS

Metropolitan police still institutionally racist, say black and Asian officers

In a striking statement on the eve of the 20th anniversary of murdered teenager Stephen Lawrence's death, Scotland Yard's black and Asian police officers have declared that the Met is still institutionally racist.

The Metropolitan Black Police Association (BPA), the biggest group representing minority officers in the force, says Scotland Yard has failed to tackle the institutional racism in the criminal justice system, despite the training and community initiatives put in place over the last two decades.

BPA chair Bevan Powell said: 'Institutional racism is not about labelling individuals racists but rather police practice and procedures that bring about disproportionate outcomes for black and minority ethnic communities and police personnel.'

The disproportionate incidence of 'stop and search' carried out in black and minority ethnic communities continues to be an issue.

In comparison to their white colleagues, minority ethnic officers remain longer in the lower ranks and are subject to more disciplinary actions.

The BPA stated that the current position was unsustainable and that it: ' ... severely impacts on police legitimacy and more importantly erodes trust and confidence in ethnic minority communities.'

Adapted from Muir (2003)

Questions

1. What do the BPA say about the police following the twentieth anniversary of the death of Stephen Lawrence?
2. Give reasons why the police have had little success in meeting their targets to recruit police from ethnic minorities.
3. Why do you think that ethnic minorities disproportionately occupy lower positions in the police?

Explaining patterns in crime and gender

Gender remains significant in terms of rates of both criminal behaviour and victimisation. The statistics reveal complex patterns of female offending as until fairly recently women committed very few crimes, so there has been a small but not insignificant increase in the number of all crimes committed by women.

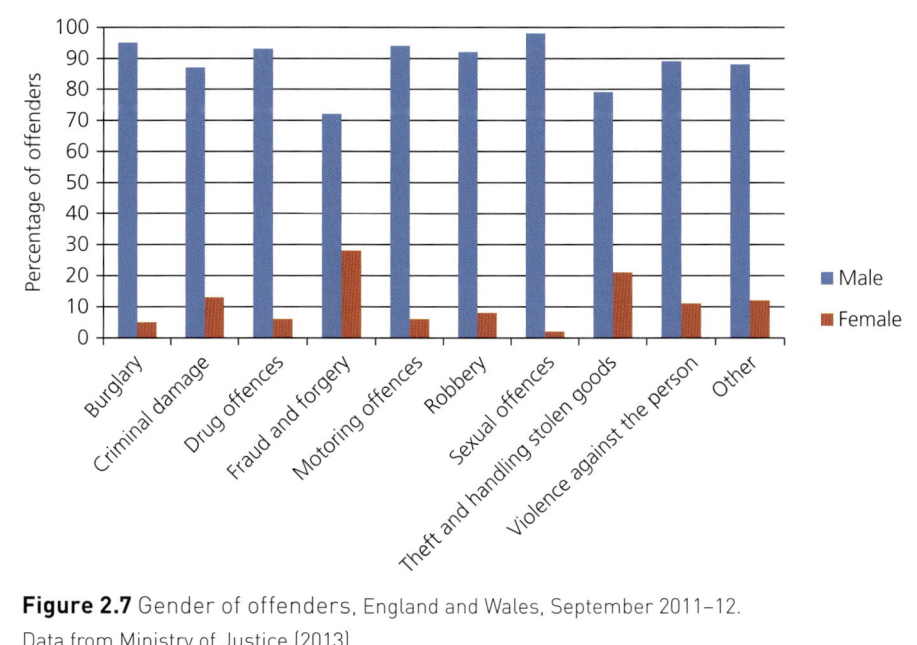

Figure 2.7 Gender of offenders, England and Wales, September 2011–12.
Data from Ministry of Justice (2013)

- Official arrest data for 2012–13 show that of all arrests, 85 per cent were men and 15 per cent were women.
- However, a higher proportion of men reported being a victim of violence than women.
- Men are more likely to be a victim of violence by an acquaintance or stranger and women more likely to be a victim of domestic violence.
- Interestingly, the male prison population has increased over the last ten years, while the female prison population has decreased, with females making up just under 1 in 20 prisoners in 2014 (Ministry of Justice 2014).
- The relationship between victims and perpetrators also differs by gender. For example, homicides against men were most likely to be committed by a friend or acquaintance (39 per cent), while homicides against women were most likely to be committed by a partner or ex-partner, (51 per cent) (Official National Statistics 2013).

Victimisation
- Women are most commonly the victim of crimes by someone they know, unlike men
- By self-report, a greater proportion of women were victims of violence (7 per cent) than men (5 per cent). This is mirrored in girls (11 per cent) and boys (5 per cent)

- Women are underrepresented in the criminal justice system: they make up 27 per cent of police, 23 per cent of the judiciary, 15 per cent of senior police. This represents a small increase

Criminalisation
- Shoplifting is the most common offence for women
- Drunk and disorderly behaviour is the most common offence for men
- Ten per cent of men were sentenced to immediate custody in 2011, compared with 3 per cent of women
- The average length of prison sentence is 17.7 months for men and 11.6 months for women

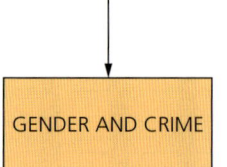

GENDER AND CRIME

Figure 2.8 Gender of offenders spider diagram

National Office for Statistics (2011)

Sex-role theory and socialisation

Figure 2.9 What does this image say about sex roles at an early age?

Sex-role theorists, such as Parsons (1995), tend to be functionalists. They argue that boys tend to be socialised to be physical, competitive, aggressive, macho and risk-taking, while girls tend to be socialised into being compliant, conformist and reserved.

Feminists such as Carlen (1988) and Heidensohn (1996) argue that the patterns in relation to crime and gender can be understood by looking at the opportunity to commit crime. Women have fewer opportunities to commit crime, as they are often caring for children or husbands, which explains their lower crime rates.

Men, on the other hand, have greater opportunities to commit crime. Heidensohn argues that this is because of gendered patterns of social control, formal and informal, which reinforce the control that men have over women. For example, women are not expected to go out alone at night, whereas this is seen as more acceptable for men.

Pollak explores women's involvement in violent and property crime, noting that violent crime rates continue to show large differences in the rates of participation between men and women, while property crime rates are becoming increasingly similar between men and women. Pollak suggests that, placed in similar social settings, men are more likely than women to develop criminal behaviours. Pollak explains female crime and the gender gap through a mix of biological, psychological and sociological factors.

Pollak argues that men and women actually commit a similar number of crimes. However, he argues that the types of crimes women commit such as shoplifting are underrepresented in crime statistics, for a range of reasons. For example, women commit crimes that are easily concealed and under-reported, or unlikely to be reported as they might cause embarrassment for the male victims.

Feminist perspectives

Feminists argue that patriarchal ideology encourages men to dominate women. Therefore it is no surprise that women are much more likely to be the victims of crime. Pat Carlen (1988) argues that women's crimes reflect their powerlessness – they lack the opportunity to change their repressed position. Carlen argues that women are likely to experience abuse at the hands of men in their families and beyond, who use violence to assert their control over women. Since women are also powerless in their jobs, there is little legitimate opportunity to improve their situation. Therefore, women commit crimes in a rational way, to overcome their position.

The liberation thesis

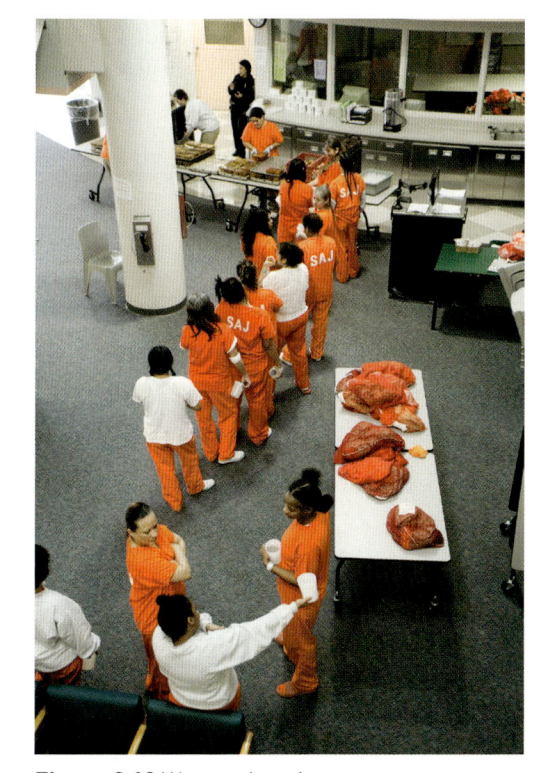

Figure 2.10 Women in prison

Women in the criminal justice system

There are very few women that work within the criminal justice system; for example, women only made up 25 per cent of all judges in 2014, which is actually a significant increase on previous years, but a long way from equal. Smart (2002) argues that in rape trials male judges judge men and women very differently, seeing men's need for sex as acceptable and women's behaviour as capricious, calculated. Feminists argue that women who are the victims of sexual violence often end up feeling as if they are going on trial themselves. In situations where it is unclear if a woman wanted to have sex or not, it is often suggested that a woman was somehow 'asking for sex'.

Where women deviate from their expected gender roles they are often considered to be doubly deviant and punished much more harshly. They are punished for deviating from being a female and for committing a crime.

Feminists such as Smart argue that women are treated in a paternalistic way by the police and the courts which may result in them being treated more leniently (known as the **chivalry thesis**, see page 112). This has found to be the case with motoring offences, for example.

> ### Questions
> 1. Why might working-class women feel more powerless than working-class men?
> 2. What are the reasons for working-class women committing crime according to Carlen?
> 3. What does it mean when Carlen says crime becomes a 'rational choice'?

> ### RESEARCH IN FOCUS
> Carlen (1985) carried out research using unstructured interviews with 39 female, working-class convicted offenders aged 15–49. Carlen found that her respondents had committed crimes as a response to feeling frustrated and powerless. Carlen argues that women are encouraged to be conformist and controlled by men, for which they receive two rewards: the class deal, whereby they receive material rewards, a reasonable standard of living and some leisure time; and the gender deal which means women receive emotional rewards from their role in the family as the primary caregiver. Women who do not feel the class or gender deal has been met and who have little reward in their lives and very limited opportunity to improve their situation in a legitimate way end up committing crimes. Therefore Carlen argues that crimes were committed as a rational choice.
>
> Adapted from Carlen (1988)

Social class and crime

Victimisation
The poor are much more likely to be the victim of crime than other more affluent groups

For example, the unemployed are more than twice as likely to be burgled than employed people

Middle class, more affluent people are more likely to be victims of plastic card fraud

SOCIAL CLASS AND CRIME

Criminalisation
There has been a significant increase in middle-class crime, including fraud and embezzlement

The socially deprived are much more likely to commit crimes such as antisocial behaviour

One in two people on Jobseeker's Allowance have a criminal record

Offenders leaving prison spend significant periods of time out of work

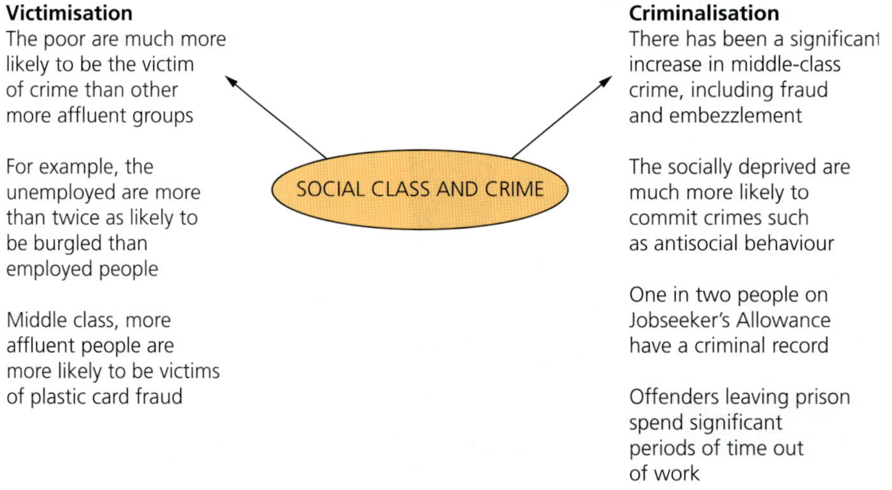

Figure 2.11 Social class and crime

Official statistics show that there is a strong relationship between social class and crime. The poor and the working class are overrepresented in the roles of both victims and perpetrators. This is not to suggest that the wealthy do not commit crimes – they certainly do and sociologists are interested in exploring the reasons why affluent people commit crimes and why they are underrepresented in official statistics.

There are some interesting facts about social class and crime, uncovered by the British Crime Survey (2014). For example, households headed by someone who was unemployed were over twice as likely to be victims of domestic burglary compared with those households headed by an employed person. Alternatively, respondents in higher-income households were more likely to be victims of plastic card fraud. For example, 7.1 per cent of respondents in households with a total income of £50,000 or more were victims of plastic card fraud compared with 3.5 per cent in households with a total income of less than £10,000.

Functionalist and functionalist subcultural theories

There are a number of explanations for these patterns. Functionalist and functionalist subcultural theorists argue that the working class or the poor have weak ties with society. They suggest that because poor groups are marginalised and experience social deprivation, they face **social exclusion** and poor life chances.

Subcultural theorists such as Merton (see pages 52–3) and Cohen (see page 90) argue that working-class men in particular feel a sense of status frustration. Cohen says that young men seek out others who share this frustration to engage in criminal behaviour with. Cloward and Ohlin (1960, see page 55) argue that when the young working class are unable to achieve the goals of society, in areas where there are high levels of social deprivation, it is likely that members of this group will turn to crime. Miller identifies some working-class subcultures as having 'focal concerns' which are shared values such as excitement and toughness that lead to crime (see page 60).

New Right explanations

As we saw earlier in the chapter, the New Right thinker Charles Murray (1989) argues that the group of people who do not work and share similar values, known as the underclass of society, are likely to turn to crime (see page 64). For Murray and other New Right thinkers, there is a very strong relationship between crime and socio-economic position.

Marxist explanations

Marxist explanations of the relationship between social class and crime are linked to capitalist society. According to the Marxist Pearce (1976) laws are created by the ruling class to protect their private property. Marxists argue that crime occurs among all social classes but that corporate crimes committed by the middle class are largely ignored, even though they claim that they cause most damage to society (Snider 1993). For example, Snider points out that corporate crime costs more than street crime. Gordon (1976) argues that the police practise selective law enforcement in the USA leading to the attention being turned from the ruling class to the working class. This prevents the system being challenged for being unfair and ensures that the status quo is maintained.

Left realist explanations

Lea and Young (1984) claim that the relative deprivation experienced by the poor or marginalised results in them being much more likely to commit crime. This means that poorer groups in society feel that they have less than other groups in society and, lacking any legitimate means to gain status or wealth, they commit crime. Lea and Young add that as living standards increase and the media reinforce relative deprivation, crime too increases, although they argue that relative deprivation can be experienced by anyone, not just the poor. Lea and Young also argue that poorer groups form their own subcultures as a group solution to their frustration.

Labelling theory explanations

Labelling theory also goes some way in explaining the link between social class and crime. Because poorer groups are more likely to be the victims and the perpetrators of crime, it is likely that the police label those at the bottom of the social class scale more readily. This is likely to extend to the rest of the criminal justice system who are predominantly middle class too. The poor are more likely to commit the kinds of crimes which tend to be more visible such as antisocial behaviour, vandalism and theft, while the middle class are more likely to commit crimes such as fraud and embezzlement which are very much hidden from the public.

These explanations, however, do not reveal why many poor people do not commit crimes, and why some are more likely to than others. There is also the combined impact of ethnicity, gender and class which can lead to higher or lower levels of crime, and these must be taken into account together.

There are many strengths of Marxist explanations of the overrepresentation of the working class in crime statistics, however Marxists do not explain why some working-class people do commit crimes while others do not.

The sociological study of the ruling-class crimes is discussed below, in the section on white-collar and corporate crime.

Questions

1. How does this article challenge traditional views of patterns of crime?
2. Give two reasons for these recent patterns in crime.

IN THE NEWS

Meet criminals who cost UK £14bn: the middle class

Figure 2.12 Middle-class criminals now cost the UK £14 billion a year (posed by model)

Statistics suggest that middle-class crime is costing Britain up to £14 billion a year – almost five times that of burglary – in undetected forgery and fraud.

In a crime survey, well over half of people in England and Wales admitted that they had padded their insurance claim, paid to avoid taxation or not spoken up when handed too much change.

Furthermore, scientists from the University of Keele told the British Association science festival at Salford that 70 per cent of Britons questioned said they felt they had been ripped off or duped by businesses, banks and tradesmen.

These 'crimes' were carried out at the kitchen table and home computer, from offices and call centres and in supermarkets and restaurants.

Adapted from Radford (2003)

RESEARCH IN FOCUS

Per-Olof H Wikström (2012) of Cambridge University carried out a study of teenagers and the community in Peterborough over ten years. He shows that most adolescent crime is the result of a lack of morality which he regards as having a strong link to social deprivation. The research involved an in-depth longitudinal study of the lives and habits of 700 young people, along with a survey of over 6,000 local residents and large amounts of cross-referenced census data. Wikström concluded that a lack of clear morals is more often found in backgrounds where people are from a lower social class.

Wikström *et al.* (2012)

Questions

1. What is meant by social deprivation?
2. What sort of preventative measures might be put into place to reduce adolescent crime, based on the findings of this study?

STUDY TIP

There is an intersection between class, gender and ethnicity; it is impossible to untangle ethnicity from class and gender for example, so remember that all three variables need to be explored together as well as separately.

2.2 What is white-collar crime and corporate crime?

Link your discussion of corporate crime to social class and Marxist theory as corporate crime relates to crimes of the powerful. This area is difficult for sociologists to research as it focuses on elite groups that can be hard to gain access to.

Much sociological theory and research focuses on crimes committed by the working class. This section explores crimes which are carried out by the powerful. It can be difficult for sociologists to find out about these types of criminal activities as these individuals and groups can use their power to hide their illegal activities. Sutherland (1960) was among the first sociologists to identify that crime occurred among those with power, status and wealth. He calls this kind of crime **white-collar crime**. Examples of white-collar crime include money laundering, embezzlement, claiming expenses in a dishonest way.

Corporate crimes are carried out at an organisational level, using the business as a front for criminal behaviour. It can be difficult to identify which individuals should take responsibility for a corporate crime. Both white-collar crime and corporate crime often involve huge amounts of money and wealth and yet they are often under-reported and unpunished.

Marxists argue that capitalism leads to white-collar crime and corporate crime by creating a drive for profit meaning that some companies commit crimes out of desperation to make big profits. Functionalist subcultural theorists would argue that strain theory operates at all levels, so that even among the more affluent in society, people may feel a sense of status frustration, or relative deprivation, which may drive them to innovate and commit crimes to achieve their goals. Control theorists might suggest that as people become more and more wealthy they begin to feel they can act 'above the law'. Individuals may forget or overlook the fact that there are victims of their crimes. There is a fine line between acceptable competitive behaviour in business and illegal acts. For others there might be a sense of risk-taking or 'edgework' as Lyng (1990) suggests which exists not just among working-class men but also more affluent men who might, for example, take risks on the stock markets for pleasure. Another reason for the prevalence of white-collar and corporate crime is that they are often undetected. There are several types of crimes committed by companies including:

- Tax evasion and concealing profits or losses

HSBC bank recently got into trouble for encouraging its customers to avoid paying taxes through certain loopholes in the law, for example. The US company Enron hid its losses and ended up collapsing causing great losses for its customers and stakeholders.

- Breaking employment laws

For example allowing workers to work in poor or dangerous conditions. Once again, it is very difficult for workers to complain as they are often poor and need the work and unlikely to be able to successfully challenge the company.

- Ignoring or avoiding policies and regulations

For example not gaining permission or permits, refusing to follow health and safety regulations. This is a problem because the only people who are likely to know that this is happening are the workers who are in a less powerful position and are unlikely to be able to challenge senior business people.

- Misinformation and dangerous goods and services

Companies may lie about their products, label them incorrectly or produce goods that are dangerous or fake. For example, drugs companies lied about test results on a drug called thalidomide, which was then given to pregnant women for nausea resulting in birth defects in the 1970s.

- Breaking trade agreements and unfair trade practices

For example, price fixing. Major supermarkets have had to pay large fines for 'rigging' prices meaning that customers have to pay more than they should for good because the supermarkets all agree to keep certain products at a fixed price.

Why are white-collar and corporate crimes difficult to police?

They are difficult to detect	Large companies are often private and it can be hard for investigators to gain access to information. Where access is gained, people are likely to be able to cover their tracks to ensure that no one finds out about the crime.
They are hard to punish	Large companies are often very wealthy and can afford expensive lawyers and law suits so that they stand a very good chance of defending themselves. Also, individuals working at this level are likely to be perceived as hard-working and middle class, meaning they may be let off more leniently.
Once punished, individuals often escape punishment	There is a range of different ways of punishing companies that include fines or enforcement notices. This often means that individuals who were responsible for making decisions or acting against the law go unpunished. Wealthy companies can absorb the costs of fines.
These crimes often involve wealthy individuals or groups	These individuals or groups are powerful and have networks of support, who may use their power to persuade law keepers to punish them more leniently or not at all.
These crimes may not have a victim	For example, where two powerful groups are benefiting each other through money laundering there is no immediate victim which makes it difficult to detect the crime.

Table 2.5 The difficulties of policing white-collar and corporate crimes

CONTEMPORARY APPLICATION

With headquarters in Zurich, Switzerland, FIFA (the world governing body for international soccer) claims that it is a non-profit organisation and as a result does not have to pay taxes. However in 2012 the company reported $89 million in net profit and $1.378 billion in financial reserves. FIFA is guilty of a number of violations of **human rights** of its low-skilled labourers including their right to adequate housing, right to free movement, right to work, and right to protest.

Additionally, FIFA is guilty of profiting from forced evictions and exploitation of the people living in the area where the football matches were played. The Brazilian government spent $14 billion of taxpayers' money on the 2014 World Cup in the face of poverty and inequality while FIFA took home $4 billion in untaxed revenue. Because FIFA does not have to pay taxes, Brazil lost out on tax money totalling $400 million from the 2014 World Cup.

STUDY TIP

In writing about corporate crime, make links to Marxism and also other emerging types of crime, such as global crimes. Many major companies today are multinational and therefore different rules and laws are applied in different parts of the world. This topic can also draw links with globalisation.

Social policy

Companies are preparing for tougher punishments if they break the law. Under new rules that came into force in October 2014, UK companies can be fined as much as 400 per cent of any profits accrued from bribery, making the UK's fining regime one of the toughest in the world.

Check your understanding

1. Give three reasons why women appear to commit less crime than men.
2. Why do you think that men are more likely to be the victims of crime?
3. What is institutional racism?
4. Why is the Stephen Lawrence case so significant?
5. Name one problem with cultural deprivation theories for explaining crime rates among different ethnic groups.
6. Why does white-collar crime often go undetected?
7. Suggest some reasons why women only make up 25 per cent of all judges.

Practice questions

1. Outline two reasons why some ethnic minorities are overrepresented in official crime statistics. [4 marks]
2. Outline three reasons why working-class people may be less likely than middle-class people to commit crimes. [6 marks]

Section 3: Globalisation and crime in contemporary society

This section will explore the following debates:

- How has globalisation affected crime in contemporary society?
- What is the relationship between the media and crime?
- What is green crime?
- What are human rights and state crimes?

Questions

1. Why do you think that hoodies are being banned?
2. Do you think it is true that socialising with others after they have been convicted leads to further crime? Why?
3. Do you think that the measures suggested will reduce crime? Why?

GETTING YOU STARTED
'Gang members banned from wearing hoodies'

Adapted from De Graaf (2013)

In measures to curtail their activities, gang members are to be banned from wearing hoodies, riding push-bikes and having pay-as-you-go phones in their possession. They will also be banned from the postcode area in which their gang operates.

This new set of court orders was announced today by the head of the Crown Prosecution Service. The idea is that preventing people from socialising after they have been convicted is an important way of preventing further crimes. However, community leaders argue that many of the methods set out are likely to make matters more difficult.

3.1 How has globalisation affected crime in contemporary society?

Consider the impact of the process of globalisation not just in terms of new forms of crime emerging but also in terms of new forms of policing and punishment. There are many connections between globalisation and postmodernism.

Globalisation has had an interesting effect on crime and deviance. Two notable effects of globalisation have been:

- greater geographic mobility leading to greater cultural diversity
- the twofold effect of Western ideas spreading and engulfing other forms of local culture, while simultaneously allowing local ideas, customs and practices to be protected, shared and reaffirmed.

Globalisation has given rise to new forms of crime and a range of sociological explanations for them.

Financial global crimes

Globalisation and the growth of transnational companies working across legal jurisdictions (see page 189) have led to greater opportunities for corporate crime, including money laundering, tax avoidance, illegal waste disposal and illegal employment practices.

Like companies, criminal networks have formed or have extended as a result of globalisation. For example, international credit card fraud networks extend all over the world.

Taylor (1997) explored new ways in which the deregulation of financial markets led to the creation of new opportunities for new forms of crime to emerge, such as the collapse of Barings Bank in 1996 after a key trader took huge risks and lost £860 million. Taylor points out how globalisation has allowed the wealthy to use different parts of the world with different tax rules to avoid paying taxes and to hide money and wealth. Taylor also point out how much changing practices in work, due to globalisation, have led to more and more tasks being carried out by technology, leading to higher unemployment rates and subsequently higher levels of crime as well as illegal immigrants working for less than the minimum wage.

Human trafficking

The buying and selling of people for exploitation is prolific. People are smuggled illegally from one part of the world to another. The people trafficked are used for slavery, prostitution and sexual exploitation, forced labour and sometimes even for organs.

Illegal drugs trading

The trade of illegal drugs is increasingly globalised as drug smugglers operate across national boundaries. According to data from the United Nations Office on Drugs and Crime (2013) and European crime-fighting agency Europol, the annual global drugs trade is worth around $435 billion a year. This represents nearly 1 per cent of total global trade. Countries such as Colombia have struggled to stop powerful drug cartels from producing and supplying drugs: their wealth and influence are considerable.

Crimes connected to the new technology – cybercrime

Cybercrime refers to crimes related to the internet and computers which have become possible over the past few decades. Since the internet is comparatively new and widespread it has been very difficult for lawkeeping agencies to police and regulate. This includes crimes such as identity theft, computer theft, fraud and phishing as well as abuse against people such as children through exploitation. Although strategies are now in place to deal with many of these crimes, many continue to go undetected. There have been notable examples of high-level corruption such as the misuse of computer software by security agencies who have gained access to people's private internet accounts without their consent. Therefore cybercrime still has a long way to go to be fully understood.

Global crime control

There have been attempts to address the recent surge in international crimes, such as the development of the international Interpol and Europol. These are crime agencies which involve 190 countries working together within the existing legal framework of each country to try to catch criminals on the run and co-operate in major cross country investigations. They also collect statistics and examine patterns of crime to suggest global strategies for member countries. This is very much a response to the recent years of global crime.

> **KEY SOCIOLOGIST**
>
> **Castells** (1997) argues that the power of the nation state is fading, being undermined by the globalisation of core economic activities, the media, technological communication and crime. Crime, Castells argues, is like a shadow economy whose main market is illegal drugs. In countries which are emerging into the newly forming Western economies (such as Russia) criminal networks are becoming integrated within the capitalist networks.

KEY SOCIOLOGIST

Held (1999) says globalisation has changed the scope and content of international law. Twentieth-century forms of international law – those governing war, crimes against humanity, environmental and human rights – have created the a newly emerging 'cosmopolitan law'. This law defines and limits the political power of individual states. In principle, states are no longer able to treat their citizens as they think fit. Although, in practice, many states still ignore these internationally agreed standards.

RESEARCH IN FOCUS

Hobbs and Dunningham (1998) carried out an ethnographic study of organised crime in the UK in the 1990s and found that crime is changing in some ways in response to globalisation. For example, criminals can now extend their networks and illegal activities across national boundaries. However, they argue that crime continues to focus primarily on local issues, with only some criminal activities becoming linked to global activities. They found that criminals tend to be entrepreneurial, mixing criminal and legal projects simultaneously. Thus they argue that organised crime in the UK is glocal.

Questions

1. Give some examples of how crime might be changing as a result of globalisation.
2. What is meant by glocal crime?

STUDY TIP

Remember that globalisation has a complex effect on crime; acknowledge that globalisation both reduces certain forms of crime as well as leading to new forms of crime emerging. Globalisation also involves the spread of Western ideas and capitalism and the crimes that go with it, which can be interpreted from a Marxist perspective.

CONTEMPORARY APPLICATION

Glenny (2009) argues that over the last 20 years organised crime has reflected changes in society and also experienced the effects of globalisation and development. Glenny describes the social structure of the global criminal underworld, which he calls 'McMafia'. Glenny compares the food company McDonald's, which has come to represent the essence of a globalised brand, with the criminal world. He estimates that the crime economy is worth around 20 per cent of world economic output. Those benefitting from this include those who run the global criminal network. Those losing out include those who are exploited, such as the trafficked women of Moldova or Britain's cockle pickers, who pay with the loss of their basic human rights, sometimes even their lives.

Glenny explains that the changes in the ex-Soviet zone demonstrated how the collapse of countries during the transition to capitalism created a vacuum that was rapidly filled by organised crime. The Balkans (the former Yugoslavia) saw the rise in the skills of criminal networks that were transporting illicit goods and people. Glenny points out that all too often these global criminal networks are one step ahead of governments and the police.

IN THE NEWS

Organised crime worth £560bn

Organised international crime is worth up to $870bn (£560bn) a year, the United Nations has estimated. The criminal networks are estimated to be worth more than six times the global aid budget, or around 7 per cent of the world's legal exports, the UN Office on Drugs and Crime (UNODC) said. There is also a high cost in human lives and economic stability with crime groups bringing 'increasing domestic corruption, extortion, racketeering and violence'.

'Criminal groups traffic women for sexual exploitation and children for purposes of forced begging, burglary and pickpocketing. Fake medicines and food products enter the legal market and not only defraud the public but can put their lives and health at risk,' the UN claim. By far the most profitable trade, worth over a third of the total, is in narcotics, which has an annual value the UN estimates at $320bn. Second is the trade in counterfeit goods, which generates around $250bn. Human trafficking generates $32bn a year, with an estimated 2.4 million victims affected at any one time.

Police and other security officials needed more sophisticated tools to fight criminal networks that were taking full advantage of technological improvements, the UN said.

Adapted from Harrison (2012)

Questions

1. According to this article, what are the top forms of global crime?
2. How might sociologists explain the emergence of these recently emerging forms of global crime?

3.2 What is the relationship between the media and crime?

Be aware that there is a complex and fluid relationship between crime and the media. The media can inform people about crimes, it can distort or wilfully misrepresent crime and this affects the perception that people have of crime and even the way that people behave as a result.

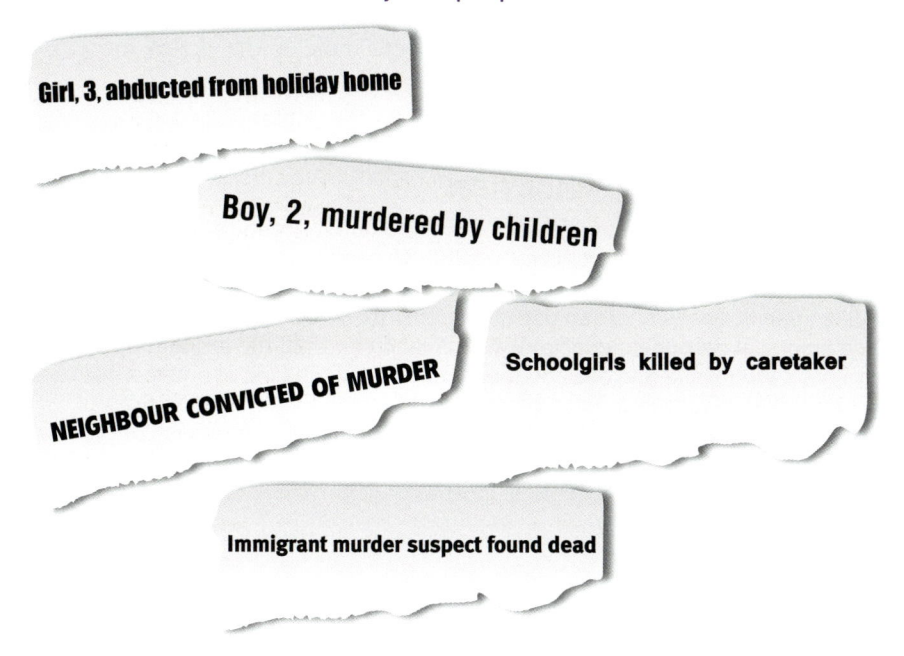

Girl, 3, abducted from holiday home

Boy, 2, murdered by children

NEIGHBOUR CONVICTED OF MURDER

Schoolgirls killed by caretaker

Immigrant murder suspect found dead

Figure 2.13 Some media representations of crime

Crime occupies a considerable proportion of the news; this section explores the extent to which crime covered reflects the kinds of crimes that actually occur and why. The media are powerful: they decide about what does and does not get reported; the media set the agenda in terms of what is considered to be important.

There are two types of crime coverage in the media: fictional and non-fictional. The process of choosing how crime is represented results in shaping ideas that people have about crime and deviance. Sociologists explore what the media consider to be newsworthy and what does not get reported and consider the reasons behind these decisions. Because it is not possible for all crimes to be reported, the view that people have of crime can be distorted or they can perceive there to be more or less crime than there actually is.

What is reported in the news – news values

Reiner (2007) claims that journalists reporting crime have the role of creatively interpreting real life events almost as if they were writing a play or a drama. The process of deciding what does and what does not get considered to be worth reporting is known as **news values**. News values are what journalists consider to be valuable and important enough to select to report in the news. There are a number of reasons why something might be considered to be suitable for reporting, but generally these things are what are felt will appeal to the readers or viewers, and will therefore increase or maintain the readership or viewing numbers.

Katz (1990) discusses the limitless appetite for crime news that the public apparently have. He argues that crime news is characterised by a collective, ritualistic aspect which elicits a strong emotional response which he claims is why crime is newsworthy. Katz argues that the crime is not really the issue – it is more the moral dilemmas created by crime through which people like to think about their own morals and lives.

Katz argues that the media focuses much more on criminals, rather than the victims of crime or the police. Katz claims that the public are encouraged to see risk-taking behaviour as attractive and exciting. The media also encourages viewers to imagine how they might feel in the same situation that the criminal finds themselves. However, the work of Katz has been criticised for failing to relate to the media today which does tend to focus more on the victim, for example, exploring the effects of the crime in people's lives.

CONTEMPORARY APPLICATION

The United Nations Convention against Transnational Organized Crime, adopted by in 2000, came into force in 2003. This is the main international instrument in the fight against transnational organised crime. The Convention targets specific areas of organised crime: the prevention and punishment of trafficking in persons, especially women and children; the smuggling of migrants by land, sea and air; and the illegal manufacturing of and trafficking in firearms. The Convention represents a major step forward in the fight against transnational organised crime and signifies the seriousness of the problems posed by it, as well as the need to encourage close international co-operation in order to tackle these problems.

How does the media distort crime?

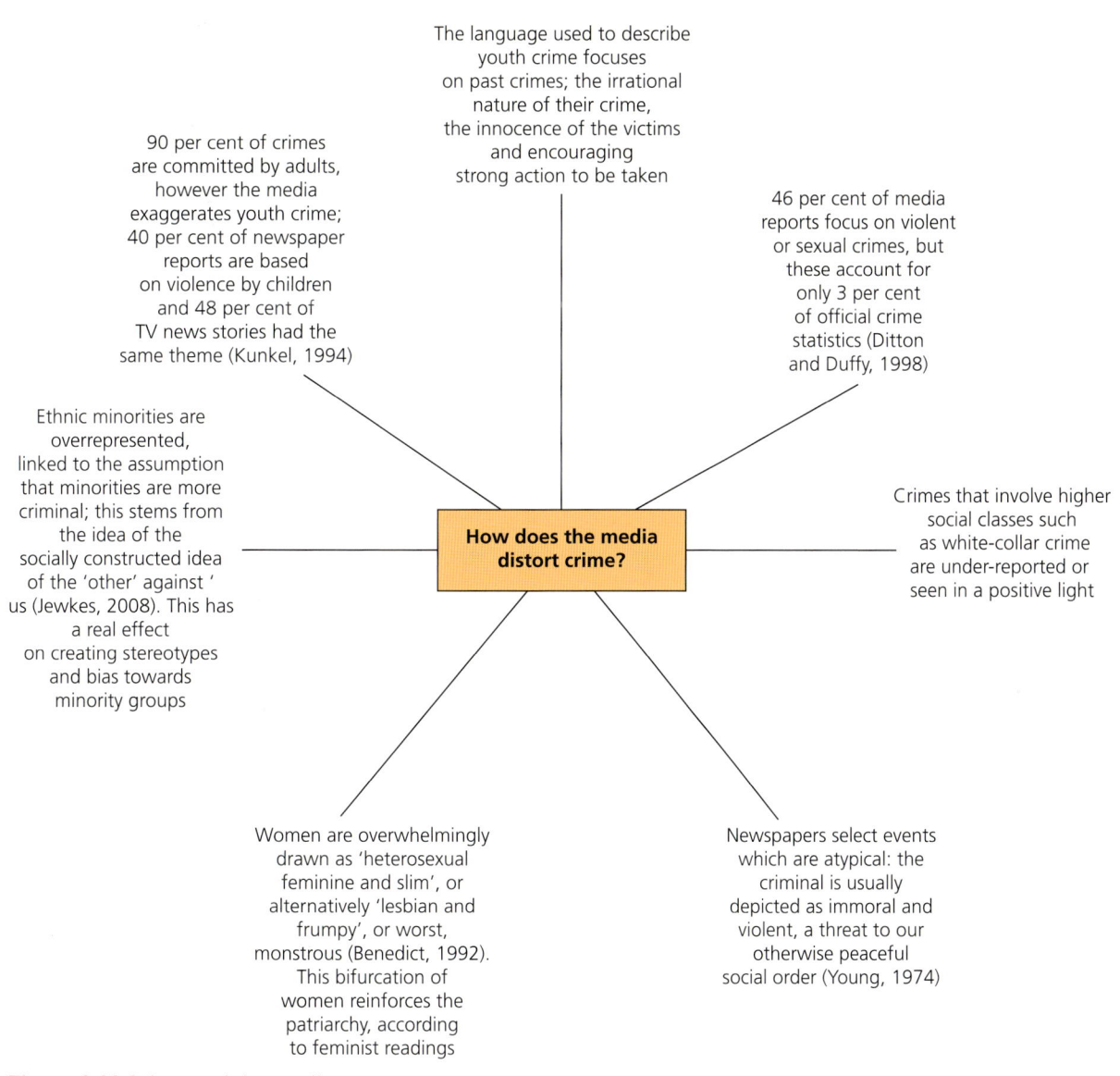

- 90 per cent of crimes are committed by adults, however the media exaggerates youth crime; 40 per cent of newspaper reports are based on violence by children and 48 per cent of TV news stories had the same theme (Kunkel, 1994)

- The language used to describe youth crime focuses on past crimes; the irrational nature of their crime, the innocence of the victims and encouraging strong action to be taken

- 46 per cent of media reports focus on violent or sexual crimes, but these account for only 3 per cent of official crime statistics (Ditton and Duffy, 1998)

- Ethnic minorities are overrepresented, linked to the assumption that minorities are more criminal; this stems from the idea of the socially constructed idea of the 'other' against ' us (Jewkes, 2008). This has a real effect on creating stereotypes and bias towards minority groups

- Crimes that involve higher social classes such as white-collar crime are under-reported or seen in a positive light

- Women are overwhelmingly drawn as 'heterosexual feminine and slim', or alternatively 'lesbian and frumpy', or worst, monstrous (Benedict, 1992). This bifurcation of women reinforces the patriarchy, according to feminist readings

- Newspapers select events which are atypical: the criminal is usually depicted as immoral and violent, a threat to our otherwise peaceful social order (Young, 1974)

Figure 2.14 Crime and the media

How does media coverage affect the actual crime rate?

According to Jewkes (2013), one of the most enduring questions among academics and the wider public is the extent to which television programmes, films, DVDs, websites and computer games can be said to cause antisocial, deviant or criminal behaviour. In some academic circles, and certainly in popular discourse, it is believed by many that media images are responsible for eroding moral standards, subverting consensual codes of behaviour and corrupting young minds. The relationship between media and audiences is sometimes referred to as the 'hypodermic syringe' model because it is seen as a mechanistic and simple process, by which the media 'inject' values, ideas and information directly into the passive receiver, producing direct and 'effects' which, in turn, have a negative influence on thoughts and actions.

RESEARCH IN FOCUS

Cohen's well-known study, *Folk Devils and Moral Panics* (1972) refers to the way that the public and politicians react to minority or marginalised groups, led by the media, a process he calls deviancy amplification. This study can be located within labelling theories which focus on the process by which an act becomes assigned as deviant, then criminal, thus reinforcing the idea that crime is socially constructed. Cohen comments that the issues given attention in the media usually concern young people, who appear to be some kind of threat to societal values and interests. This study, although carried out some time ago, has resonance with contemporary society, for example with concerns over youth crimes such as antisocial behaviour or drug taking.

The subjects of Cohen's analysis are mods and rockers: two rival youth groups who emerged in England in the 1960s and whose different styles of dress, taste in music, and preferred modes of transport (scooters and motor bikes respectively) marked their sense of subcultural identity and negativity towards each other. The result was that in 1964, in Clacton, there was damage to beach huts and some objects thrown leading to minor injuries.

Cohen reflects on why the media reacted so strongly to a relatively minor level of disorder between the mods and the rockers. Cohen argued that the media exaggerated and distorted events to raise levels of fear about young people.

This led to the amplification of the deviance as young people responded by reinforcing their ideas about youth subcultures and acting them out more strongly, leading to a moral panic in the public. The media then used this to create the idea of young people as folk devils, a shared target for public concern. According to Cohen, such moral panics and folk devils created by the media are a way society coping with concerns about broader social changes. For example, the rise of youth subculture presented a real challenge to society at a time when traditional ways of life were changing and transforming. This could equally be applied to today's society where significant social changes such as economic downturn and migration could be seen to be contributing to media concerns over young people which may be disproportionate to the actual crimes occurring. Also, with the rise of different forms of news platforms and the rise of social media, ideas about crime are communicated to an ever wider audience instantaneously.

Questions

1. What is a folk devil?
2. Can you think of any other folk devils in today's society?
3. What is the amplification of deviance?

KEY SOCIOLOGIST

Young (1971) argues that news is not discovered, but created or manufactured. Factors influencing the likelihood of an event becoming news are: violence; status of those involved in the event; immediacy – how recent the crime was, drama and intimacy – how closely the victim knew the criminal. Similarly, if the event is simple, or has a high degree of risk, it is more likely to be covered.

McRobbie and Thornton (1995) challenge Cohen's ideas about moral panics. McRobbie and Thornton's work takes a more contemporary perspective, written at a time when the UK media had expanded and a whole range of magazine titles and broadcast channels became available, but before internet news services and social networking sites took off and the social world became multi-media. McRobbie and Thornton argue that moral panics are no longer rare events but continuous features of the mass media coverage of crime, reflected by 24/7 news. McRobbie and Thornton argue that moral panics have become subtle and complex and need to be understood in terms of the reasons people might have for marginalising certain groups.

Marxists and neo-Marxists, such as Hall (1979), argue that the media is used as a way to exaggerate crimes to distract people from the problems with capitalism. By blaming the working class, the real cause of problems in society, created by the ruling class, capitalism continues unchallenged. Hall argues that the moral panic surrounding mugging in the 1970s distracted the public from the economic crisis that was occurring. Contemporary examples would include teenage binge drinking, knife crime or antisocial young people.

Social policy

In June 2014 the government's most senior security official, Charles Farr, announced that searches on Google, Facebook, Twitter and YouTube, as well as emails to or from non-British citizens, could be monitored by security services. That is, the UK government admitted that communications in and out of the UK, sent via 'private' channels on social media, can be intercepted without a warrant. This important decision reflects the way in which new forms of social media are being used by both the public and security services in detecting and creating crimes.

3.3 What is green crime?

Until recently damaging the environment was not considered a crime. Even now, many forms of harm to the environment continue. This reflects the culturally constructed nature of crime.

In recent years, sociologists have become increasingly interested in a deviant behaviour which has in part become a criminal act – the direct or indirect damage to the environment. Laws are now in place to cover some forms of green crime, but not all and not everywhere. This is a very good example of a new form of the socially constructed nature of crime. Like other forms of crime, there is not necessarily any consistency in laws across different countries.

There is much debate about what constitutes a green crime, since the environment can be defined in a number of different ways. Green crimes can also be very difficult to detect and police, and deciding who is responsible can also be a hard as there may not be a direct link to the person or people responsible.

In the past, traditional sociologists, such as Marxists, have argued that damage to the environment simply reflects another way in which the powerful exploit for their own profit to serve their own interests. Marxists would argue that the fact that laws were not made until recently to protect the environment reflects the dominant class whose selective law enforcement favours them.

More recently, sociologists such as White (2007) have attempted to understand and explain green crime in the context of broader changes in society. White suggests that green crime should be defined as any action that harms the physical environment and any animals (including humans) within it, regardless of whether there is a law in place for that particular issue or not. This would include taking a more global perspective of crime, since green crimes are often committed in a particular place yet their effects are often felt much further away. For example, atmospheric pollution from industry from one country turns into acid rain which can fall in another country and poison its watercourses and destroy forests.

Therefore this topic cannot be fully understood without considering the process of globalisation. As companies and countries have increasingly worked together in business and governance, there have been more and more examples of green crimes being linked to different parts of the world.

One example of the global nature of green crimes is an accident in the nuclear industry, the Chernobyl disaster of 1986, in the Ukraine which led to the spread of toxic radioactive materials over a geographic area of thousands of miles, having multiple effects on the soil and people's health. The damage affected not just the Ukraine but also Russia and Belarus, which have had to

> **STUDY TIP**
> Make sure that you understand the ways that both victims and offenders are portrayed by the media. Consider the ways that new forms of social media are used to reinforce or challenge stereotypical ideas about particular individuals or groups.

deal with the continuing and substantial decontamination and health care costs of the Chernobyl accident. The effects included a battle to contain the nuclear contamination to avoid a greater catastrophe which involved over 500,000 workers and cost an estimated 18 billion roubles. During the accident itself, 31 people died and long-term effects such as cancers are still being investigated, as well as contaminated soil.

South (South and Beirne, 2004) states that there are two forms of green crime. **Primary green crime** involves actions that are not (yet) illegal under international law, but are considered as environmental issues. Despite not being criminal these actions cause direct harm to the environment. Deforestation is a good example of this. One-fifth of the world's tropical rainforest was destroyed between 1960 and 1990. Much of this destruction was legal, with governments selling the land to companies for development.

Another example of damage to the environment which is considered to be legal currently is air pollution. The burning of fossil fuels, for example, adds billions of tons of carbon dioxide to the atmosphere every year, contributing to global warming. Currently it is estimated that air pollution contributes to around 25,000 deaths a year globally.

Further examples of primary green crime include water pollution and species decline. Water pollution accounts for the deaths of approximately 40 per cent of all deaths per year, while South notes that 50 species are lost a day. There are further threats to species which are becoming endangered such as fish stocks that are at risk due to overfishing.

Secondary green crime includes actions that are considered to be illegal under national or international law, which may or may not be enforced. In fact, these actions often openly occur and go unpunished. An example of this might be animal poaching and trafficking, which goes on often without being policed despite being illegal. Dumping toxic waste to save the cost of disposing of the waste responsibly is illegal yet happens regularly all over the world. Secondary green crime also includes opposition to groups who are committed to saving the environment.

Different perspectives

Marxists point out that Marx himself saw humans as connected with their physical environment and claimed that part of avoiding the feeling of alienation involves developing a connection with the natural environment. Marxists argue that capitalism works against this process and actually removes the individual from their environment and exploits the natural environment in the pursuit of profit.

The post modernist Beck (1992) argues that contemporary society is characterised by risk and competition for scarce resources. Beck claims that at no other point in history has there been such risk for humans posed by humans themselves. He cites the reason as being the result of mass production of goods and services which has led to environmental damage. However, he argues that people do not necessarily understand the threat to the environment posed by companies for example.

CONTEMPORARY APPLICATION

At around midnight on 2 December 1984, an accident at a Union Carbide pesticide plant in Bhopal, India, resulted in 45 tons of poisonous methyl isocyanate escaping from the facility. Thousands of people died within hours. More followed over subsequent months, about 15,000 in all. In total, about half a million people were affected in some way. Many of those who survived suffered blindness, organ failure and other serious bodily malfunctions. A very high number of children in the area have been born with a range of extensive birth defects. In 1989, Union Carbide paid out about half a billion dollars to victims, an amount the afflicted say is not nearly enough to deal with the decades-long consequences. Bhopal remains the worst industrial disaster in history.

Social policy

There is increasing pressure for the United Nations to accept 'ecocide' as a fifth 'crime against peace', which could be tried at the International Criminal Court. This idea comes from the British lawyer-turned-campaigner Polly Higgins. This would have a profound effect on industries blamed for widespread damage to the environment like fossil fuels, mining, agriculture, chemicals and forestry. After a successful launch at the UN in 2008, the idea has been adopted by the Bolivian government, and there is growing pressure on other countries to adopt it as well.

IN THE NEWS

World's top firms cause $2.2tn of environmental damage, report estimates

A major unpublished study for the United Nations has found that most of the cost of pollution and other damage to the natural environment caused by the world's largest companies is not paid for by those responsible. Concerns are increasing that damage to the environment is reaching crisis proportions in the form of pollution and the rapid loss of freshwater, fisheries and fertile soils.

Estimated at over $2tn dollars, the amount would reduce company profits by more than a third. Emissions of greenhouse gases blamed for climate change account for more than half of the total amount. Other major issues were local air pollution such as particulates, and the damage caused by the over-use and pollution of freshwater.

Adapted from Jowit (2010)

KEY SOCIOLOGIST

Potter (2010) explores Ulrich Beck's (1986) position that social problems were previously divided along class, ethnicity and gender lines, whereas today's problems, such as green crime, affect everyone indiscriminately. Potter argues that social inequalities are reinforced by environmental issues and green crimes because the green crimes are mainly committed by the rich and powerful. Potter also suggests that women and the poor also suffer disproportionately as a result of green crimes.

STUDY TIP

Be aware that green crime may affect the poor more than the wealthy, and that people in developing countries may be (but not always) more likely to experience the effects of green crime due to their reliance on fossil fuels for their industrialising economies. These ideas link to corporate crime as well as globalisation.

Questions

1. Why are companies currently not held accountable for green crimes according to sociologists?
2. Why is it seen as difficult to introduce laws that regulate and punish green crimes?

3.4 What are human rights and state crimes?

Remember that the UK is influenced by other governing bodies that cross national boundaries such as the European Union and the United Nations. Until recently human rights did not exist and the state could commit crimes on its own people or other countries often without detection or punishment.

Despite setting the agenda for law keeping, governments also at times commit illegal acts – these are state crimes. These may be war crimes – such as genocide, murder, enslavement or false imprisonment, property theft, torture of citizens, terrorism, or other human rights crimes. State crimes can also include failing to take action to prevent harm to its citizens or citizens from other places.

Following Sutherland's claim that crime occurs in all levels of society (see page 81), including among the powerful, critical sociologists have been exploring the crimes which occur among the powerful and the wealthy. The difficulty in studying state crimes is of course that the state decides what is to be considered a crime and what is not. Therefore there is a great danger that state crimes go undetected and unpunished.

State crimes have only recently been prosecuted through human rights and war crimes courts. It requires significant effort and evidence to prove that a state is accountable for a criminal activity and therefore state crimes are significant and interesting to sociologists. Until fairly recently these crimes have been overlooked by sociologists but recently they have become more central. One reason for this is that the common characteristic of many conflicts in the past century has been ethnicity; either the suppression of ethnic minorities or the threat of terrorism as a result of ethnic conflict. For example, the rise of Islamic fundamentalism has presented a new form of ethnic conflict that has challenged the West both in terms of human rights and in terms of the role of the state.

Different perspectives

The Marxist Chambliss (1989) argues that sociologists should be critical of the role of the state in terms of its potential to commit crimes and for these crimes to go undetected. Through an exploration of crimes such as piracy and smuggling, Chambliss reveals how the state can play an important role in organising and supporting activities which break their own state laws and international laws, with the objective of meeting their own financial aims. Marxists point out that governments are able to remain secretive about much of their deviant behaviour, ensuring that where possible it is not defined as criminal behaviour.

Social policy

In 1998, the Rome Statute of the International Criminal Court (ICC) established the first permanent international criminal court. The Rome drafting process and the ICC's ongoing case against the president of Sudan have added further points to ensure the efficiency of the international law of genocide. In 2007, the International Court of Justice (ICJ), which hears cases between states, issued a landmark decision addressing state responsibility to prevent and punish genocide in the case of Bosnia and Herzegovina vs. Serbia and Montenegro.

KEY SOCIOLOGIST

McLaughlin (2001) argues that Weber's ideas are useful; Weber himself argued that the state claims a 'monopoly of the legitimate use of physical force within a given territory'. In other words, within a democracy, the government can use the argument that it is the public who wish to use force in their interests.

KEY SOCIOLOGIST

H & J Schwendinger (1973) argue that the state should not impose social control in any form without the careful scrutiny of sociologists and other agencies. Schwendinger and Schwendinger suggest that the definition of crime ought to be broadened to include all human rights violations or harm and argue that if sociologists simply explore legally defined crimes alone then their understanding of deviance is limited and partial.

STUDY TIP

Avoid being too descriptive of human rights and examples of state crimes. Make sure that you understand the sociological explanations of these.

CONTEMPORARY APPLICATION

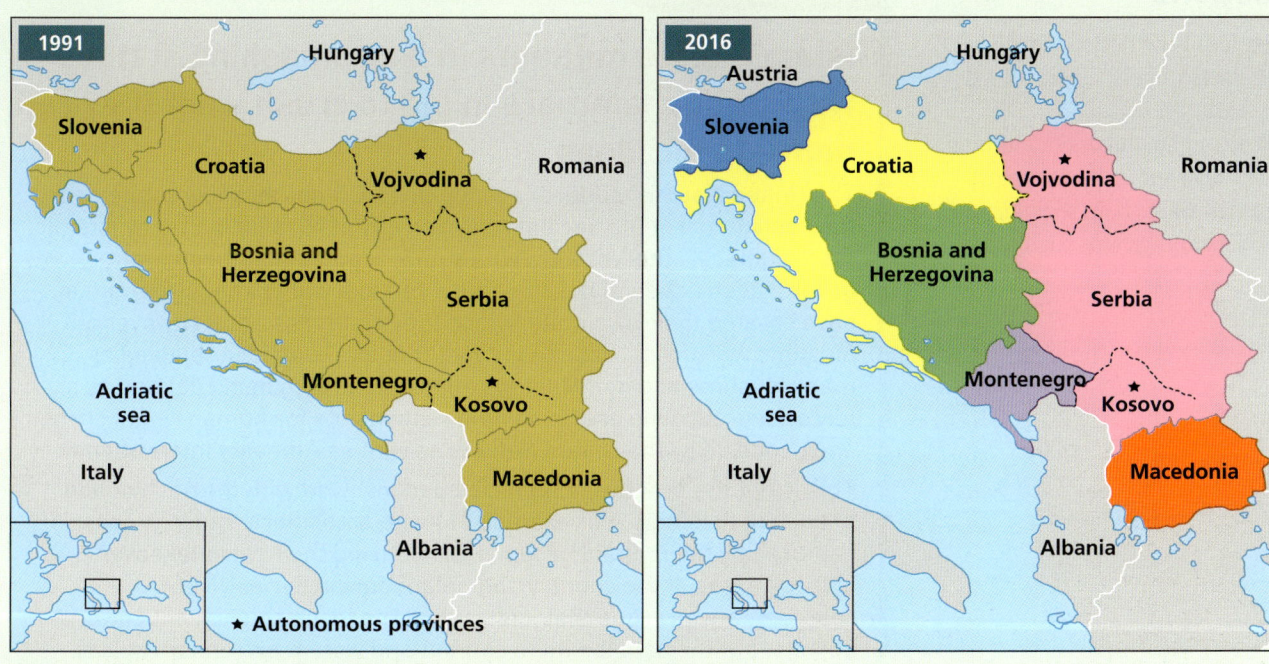

Figure 2.15 The former Yugoslav Federation and the region today

Between 1991 and 1995, a bitter and bloody war raged in Bosnia and Herzegovina, part of the former country of Yugoslavia. The conflict was based on religious and cultural differences between various ethnic groups, which had largely been suppressed until the collapse of communism. The United Nations tried to settle the conflict, with very limited success.

Often described as Europe's deadliest conflict since the Second World War, this ethnic conflict has become infamous for the state crimes and war crimes it involved, including mass ethnic cleansing. These acts were the first since 1945 to be formally judged genocidal in character. Many key state figures were subsequently charged with war crimes, including for the first time, the former president of Yugoslavia, Slobodan Milosevic. Milosevic was sent to The Hague for trial on charges of crimes against humanity and war crimes. Milosevic, a Serb nationalist leader, was indicted by the tribunal in May 1999 on allegations of murder and ethnic cleansing of ethnic Albanian civilians in Kosovo as well as several other powerful figures. He died in prison in 2006 while on trial. Many others committing war crimes, however, remain unpunished.

RESEARCH IN FOCUS

There have been a number of attempts to link the media to antisocial or criminal behaviour with controversial results. While it has been difficult to link specific media to actual crimes, sociologists have highlighted the ways that the media contributes to a desensitisation (in other words to make crime seem normal) of violence and crime that can potentially make it seem more acceptable or even exciting and glamorous to commit crime.

Questions

1. Explain how destroying ancient artefacts might be considered as a war crime.
2. How might a broader definition of state crime as harm against human rights help sociologists understand groups such as ISIS?

IN THE NEWS

Islamic State militants in Iraq smashing statues with sledgehammers in bid to crush what they call non-Islamic ideas

The United Nations' cultural agency UNESCO has strongly condemned the destruction of the ancient Assyrian city of Nimrud in Iraq by Islamic State fighters, otherwise known as ISIS, arguing that the militant group's destruction of the site amounted to a war crime. ISIS claim to have created their own state, which they claim has authority over all Muslims worldwide, despite the fact that this is an idea rejected by many Muslims and non Muslims alike. ISIS is also being defined as a terrorist group who are being held responsible for human rights crimes and genocide by the United Nations as well as Amnesty International.

This is not the first time ISIS have been involved with the destruction of ancient artefacts. For example, Mosul, a northern Iraqi city, was captured by the militant group in 2014 during their rapid takeover of large areas of the country and neighbouring Syria. UNESCO representatives argue that it is not just the loss of significant cultural objects, but the act also fuels conflict and violent extremism in Iraq.

Adapted from Shaheen (2015)

Questions

1. Explain why the following crimes have received a lot of media coverage using Jewkes' criteria:
   a) the disappearance of Madeleine McCann
   b) the plane crash/suicide in the Alps, which killed the 150 people on board
   c) the trial of Oscar Pistorius
   d) the trial of Amanda Knox, who was accused of murdering Meredith Kercher.

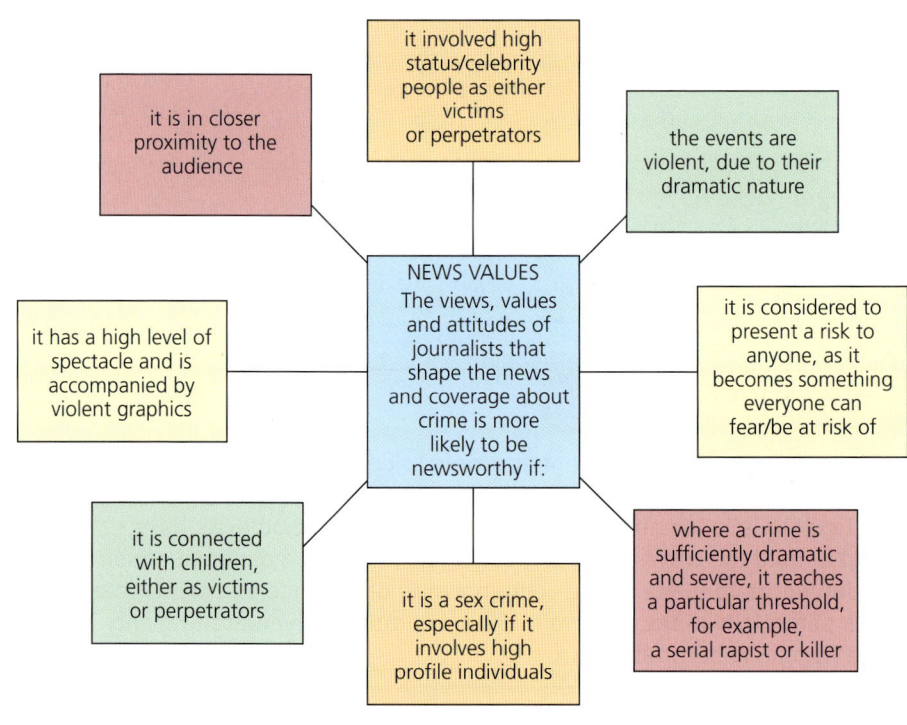

NEWS VALUES
The views, values and attitudes of journalists that shape the news and coverage about crime is more likely to be newsworthy if:

- it is in closer proximity to the audience
- it involved high status/celebrity people as either victims or perpetrators
- the events are violent, due to their dramatic nature
- it has a high level of spectacle and is accompanied by violent graphics
- it is considered to present a risk to anyone, as it becomes something everyone can fear/be at risk of
- it is connected with children, either as victims or perpetrators
- it is a sex crime, especially if it involves high profile individuals
- where a crime is sufficiently dramatic and severe, it reaches a particular threshold, for example, a serial rapist or killer

Figure 2.16 Jewkes' criteria for newsworthiness

Check your understanding

1. Green crimes are often more likely to occur in developing countries rather than wealthy countries. Why do you think this is?
2. What are the problems with trying to define and police green crime?
3. What is the difference between primary and secondary green crimes?
4. What are state crimes?
5. Why are state crimes so difficult to punish?
6. What is Interpol and what does it do?

Practice questions

1. Outline two ways in which the state can commit crimes. [4 marks]
2. Outline two reasons why a crime may be considered newsworthy in the media. [4 marks]

Read Item A below and answer the question that follows.

Item A

Globalisation has affected many areas of life including crime and deviance. The effects are complex, in some cases leading to new forms of crime to emerge. One reason for this is the declining importance of national boundaries so that there is greater communication possible between different criminal networks.

On the other hand, globalisation has led to greater co-operation and collaboration between different law enforcers in different parts of the world, the International Criminal Police Organisation, known as Interpol, for example.

Applying material from Item A, analyse two ways in which globalisation has led to the emergence of new forms of crime. [10 marks]

Section 4: Crime control, surveillance, prevention and punishment

This section will explore the following debates:

- How is crime controlled? What are the possible responses to crime and how might it be prevented?
- How is crime measured?
- Who is more or less likely to be a victim and why?
- What is the role of the criminal justice system and the agencies that work alongside it?

GETTING YOU STARTED

Figure 2.17 Crime prevention and punishment

Questions

1. What are the forms of punishment and prevention taking place in each image above?
2. Which of these methods of punishment and prevention are most effective and why?

4.1 How is crime controlled? What are the possible responses to crime and how might it be prevented?

Remember that there are both theoretical and practical approaches to crime prevention and punishment.

This section explores the different ways to prevent crime and how to respond to crime once it has been committed. Crime control is a form of formal social control and as such it plays an important role in reflecting norms and values, which may change over time. Responses to crime inevitably reflect the ideology of the particular government who are in power at the time, which are also informed by academic research and ideas. For example, some laws reflect left and right realism.

Realist crime prevention strategies

Situational crime prevention

Section 2 looked at left and right realist approaches to crime prevention (see page 79).

Situational crime prevention is an extension of the right realist approach to crime. Right realists assume that everyone is potentially likely to commit crime, especially when the potential crime is part of someone's everyday routine. They argue that crimes are based on a rational choice – a person decides if the risk is worth taking then they will commit the crime (see page 64). Therefore situational crime prevention works to reduce the opportunity for crimes to be committed and for the risk of being caught to increase.

There are problems with the right realist approach to the prevention of crime: they do not focus on the social causes of crime, for example, social inequalities. Their approach also cannot account for the selective policing which occurs in certain groups (some ethnic minorities for example). Situational crime prevention has been criticised for simply resulting in crime moving to other places that are not under surveillance, for example. This is known as displacement.

Left realist crime prevention strategies	Right realist crime prevention strategies
Building positive, trusting relationships between the police and the public, e.g. more public involvement in choosing senior police personnel, public meetings to discuss issues. Making the police more accountable and transparent in their actions. These ideas can be seen within recent governments, with the development of police commissioners who are publicly accountable positions.	Greater police presence and especially making sure that the police are perceived to be effective and tough on crime, e.g. statistics available about the efficiency of the police.
Policies to reduce cultural and material deprivation, such as Sure Start, to encourage better parenting, to reduce social exclusion and to increase social mobility. In both the coalition government and the Conservative government Sure Start has been all but abandoned.	Policies to encourage parents to be stricter with their children. For example, controversially giving fines to parents who allow their children to truant from school.
Community building, working together with the police with schemes such as Safer Neighbourhoods which encourage individuals to pre-empt crimes, for example through securing their homes more effectively.	Encouraging schemes that encourage local communities to watch and report each other, such as Neighbourhood Watch.
Police to liaise with other agencies such as social workers, schools and doctors to create a multi-agency approach to understand better the social issues facing criminals and victims, to support and encourage the vulnerable to report crime for example.	Strategies which aim to make crime harder, for example, introducing CCTV and anticlimb paint.

Table 2.6 Left and right views on crime prevention strategies

Environmental crime prevention

This approach argues that it is possible to prevent crime through making crime less acceptable or normal in the environment. This is based on the argument that a tough stance on crime deters others from believing that they can commit crime. Right realists Wilson and Kelling (1982) put forward their **'broken windows' theory**. Their argument is that obvious signs of decay in an area left unrepaired suggest that there is little social control and that criminal or deviant behaviour is acceptable.

Wilson and Kelling argue that this can lead to the police feeling less able to tackle smaller scale issues, and communities feeling fearful and unable to do anything to improve the situation. Wilson and Kelling suggest a **zero tolerance** style of policing where visible signs of crime are resolved immediately and at the same time police tackle any form of criminal behaviour. This approach has been proved to have had success in some cases, such as antisocial behaviour orders in the UK; however, it is difficult to know if it was the zero tolerance approach or other factors (such as a greater presence of police on the street) which in fact led to the reduction in crime.

Punishment

Similarly to crime prevention, there are different views on what form punishment should take. According to The Prison Reform Trust (2014), on 23 May 2014, the prison population in England and Wales was 84,305. Between June 1993 and June 2012 the prison population in England and Wales increased by 41,800 prisoners to over 86,000. The prison system as a whole has been overcrowded in every year since 1994. At the end of March 2014, 77 of the 119 prisons in England

> **KEY SOCIOLOGISTS**
>
> The Marxists **Rusche and Kirchheimer** (1939) argue that comparatively, each particular society has a punishment system based on the way that the economy is organised. They argue that in capitalist society, punishment is carried out through incarceration, or imprisonment. The working class sell their wage labour and imprisoning the working class is an appropriate punishment as it means that they can no longer sell their wage labour.

> **KEY SOCIOLOGIST**
>
> **Felson** (1998) explores the strengths of situational crime prevention and argues that reshaping the physical environment to 'design out' crime can be proven to reduce crime rates. Felson cites the example of New York City where a major bus station was redesigned in such a way that all areas were visible and clean. In doing this, Felson argues that the crime rate dropped significantly.

> **KEY SOCIOLOGISTS**
>
> **Chaiken et al.** (1974) challenge the effectiveness of situational crime prevention and argue that rather than reducing crime through changing the physical environment, crime simply becomes displaced. So for example where an area is improved and CCTV is put into place, crime simply moves to another area where it is less visible and noticeable

Questions

1. What evidence is there that prisons are in crises?
2. How is Gove proposing to change prisons?

and Wales were overcrowded. This suggests that either there are a growing number of crimes or that prison simply does not work in acting as a deterrent.

Durkheim, the functionalist, argued that punishment is a very important part of maintaining boundaries in society. Therefore punishment should be visible, to remind members of society what happens if those boundaries are crossed. This also increases social solidarity and gives people an opportunity, when a crime occurs, to express their views on the crime and share these, thus reinforcing social solidarity. Durkheim thought that a little crime in society therefore played a positive role in reinforcing social solidarity and maintaining value consensus.

Marxists argue that punishment is a way to maintain capitalist society. By punishing those who seek to challenge the system, which is so exploitative and negative towards the working class, the ruling class can exert their formal social control. According to Marxists it is the ruling class who create laws, and this avoids them being policed and caught for their own crimes. The Marxist Althusser regards prisons as part of the Repressive State Apparatus, which coupled with Ideological State Apparatus (shaping people's minds to accept capitalist ideology) makes sure that capitalism continues unchallenged.

Right realists agree with functionalist views on the importance of the law as a mechanism of social control. They argue that where social control is weak, crime occurs. They argue that prison is effective and that the threat of prison is a deterrent to would-be criminals. Right realists pursue a policy of zero tolerance. Right realist approaches have also included less expensive alternatives to prison such as curfews and the use of electronic tagging devices. This is because prisoner numbers have grown, costing the state a huge amount of money, and making cheaper, alternative punishments attractive. Right realists do not necessarily see swollen prison numbers as a sign that prison does not work, however. The ideas are reflected in recent Conservative government reform which seeks to encourage people to take greater responsibility for their own behaviour or else face punishment.

Left realists, however, differ and argue that punishment is also connected with rehabilitation and reducing the risk of the person reoffending through tackling the causes for them offending in the first place, usually material and cultural deprivation. This means for example, re-educating offenders, working with them to ensure that they find a place within the community once they have come out of prison to avoid them ending up reoffending, reducing their sense of marginalisation and social exclusion. Left realist approaches to punishment include alternatives to incarceration such as community service orders.

> **IN THE NEWS**
>
> ### A vision for reforming prisons – and justice
>
> Michael Gove, the new Justice Secretary and Lord Chancellor, argues that prison should be a place of reform, where education and rehabilitation should be the goal.
>
> One of the proposals to address the crisis in prisons was to use proceeds from selling inner-city prisons to improve education and insisting that the system can take no more cuts. 'In any single week, there are four or five deaths, 300 assaults and 70 assaults on prison officers, of which nine are serious,' he said.
>
> Hutton (2015)

Retributive justice is the idea that someone who omits an offence actually tries to make up for the crime that they committed. This form of 'paying back' might include apologising to the victim or the victim's family and is a way of ensuring that the criminal is seen to be apologising for their decision and changing their views. This approach is sometimes supported by right realists and is highly controversial.

Different perspectives

The post-structuralist Foucault argued that punishment has changed over time. Hundreds of years ago, punishment used to be focused on the torture or murder of the body, providing a visible demonstration which acted as a deterrent for others. Foucault argued that punishment has become increasingly focused on the mind, focusing on surveillance as a mechanism of social control. The panopticon is a good example: in the late eighteenth century, Bentham, a prison reformer, designed a prison in which there are no doors, just the knowledge that as a prisoner you are being watched all the time. This more sophisticated approach to punishment, according to Foucault, is far more effective and allows the state much more control over the individual.

> **STUDY TIP**
> Make sure you can highlight the different theoretical responses to crime prevention and punishment and draw out contemporary examples which reflect these different approaches.

> **CONTEMPORARY APPLICATION**
> The Crime and Courts Act 2013 allows courts to defer at pre-sentence stage in order for the victim and offender to be offered restorative justice at the earliest opportunity. Eighty-five per cent of victims surveyed as part of a government funded £7 million seven-year research programme were either 'very' or 'quite' satisfied with their restorative conference. Eighty per cent of offenders were 'very' or 'quite' satisfied. Twenty-seven per cent fewer crimes were committed by offenders who had experienced restorative justice, compared with those offenders who did not. Restorative justice approaches are also considered to be cost effective. As a result of reductions in the frequency of offending Restorative Justice Council projects saved nine times what they cost to deliver (The Prison Reform Trust 2014).

> **Questions**
> 1. Suggest two reasons why prison may not be an effective form of punishment.
> 2. What alternatives to prison might reduce reoffending rates and why might this be?
> 3. How would a left realist respond to this article?

IN THE NEWS

Prison doesn't work

Figure 2.18 Is prison an effective form of punishment?

Government figures show that half of criminals commit another crime within a year of being discharged. The figures for young offenders are even worse: 70 per cent of under-18s who are given a prison sentence reoffend within 12 months.

If a major purpose of prison is to stop people committing more crimes, clearly it is not succeeding.

Community-based sentences give slightly better results: they have been found to reduce reoffending by 6 per cent. Similarly, people who are handed a suspended sentence are 9 per cent less likely to reoffend than someone who committed a similar crime but was sent to prison.

Restorative justice programmes have a better record in terms of reducing reoffending. Government research estimates the reduction at 14 per cent, but campaigners for the programmes place the improvement much higher, at 27 per cent. In restorative justice, perpetrators consider the impact of their crimes and in some cases meet the victims in a controlled environment to see the effect of their crime, helping them to take responsibility and work towards making amends.

Adapted from Leach (2014)

4.2 How is crime measured?

If sociologists are to explain patterns of crime it is important that they are aware of the amount of crimes that are occurring as well as identifying the types of crime. Sociologists are interested in both the number of crimes recorded by the police and also the crimes and deviant acts that are not recorded by the police. This offers interesting information not just about crime but also about policing practices. We have already seen that the way that people perceive crime does not always match patterns of crime created through police recorded official crime statistics.

To gain a detailed view of the crime that occurs in society therefore several methods are used in order for sociologists to build up an accurate picture of crime:

- police recorded statistics
- victim surveys
- self-report studies.

Police recorded statistics (official crime statistics)

Official crime statistics are drawn from the records that are kept by the police and other official agencies. These records are published every six months by the Home Office. Official statistics are useful for revealing long-term patterns in crime as they have been collected since 1857.

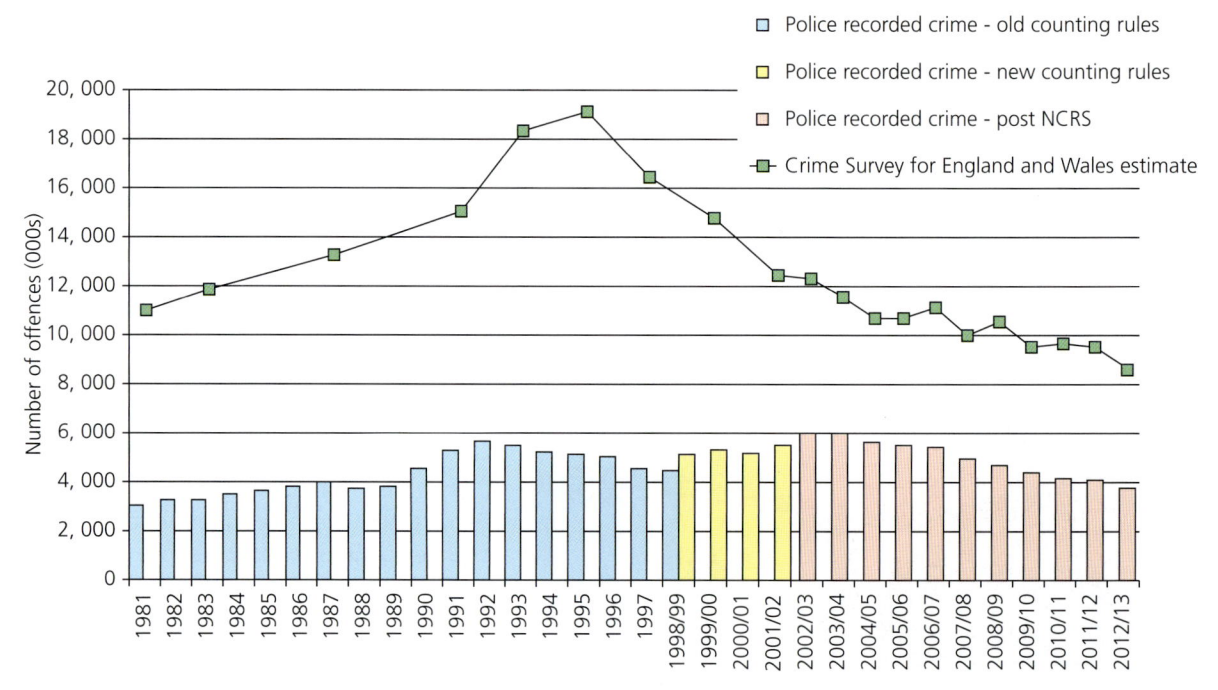

Figure 2.19 Trends in crime, 1981 to year ending June 2013. Adapted from *Crime in England and Wales, Year Ending June 2013*, Office for National Statistics (2013).

Strengths of official crime statistics

Positivists argue that official crime statistics are useful for understanding large-scale macro crime patterns. This includes the fact that the statistics can be used to understand trends over time. Official crime statistics also allow sociologists and the public to explore the police clear-up rate to measure police efficiency. The statistics also reveal where the police might need to concentrate their resources to reduce crime. The official crime statistics provide the public (often via the media) with information on crime patterns, which may warn them or educate them about their own behaviour; for example, being more vigilant about certain forms of crime. Official crime statistics also provide a basis for sociologists to explain crime including what is and what is not shown in the statistics. Furthermore, official crime statistics reveal police assumptions and stereotyping, as the statistics are in part generated by the activities of the police themselves and the offenders they choose to pursue and the offences they choose to record.

Criticisms of official police statistics

Police-recorded statistics are based on information that the criminal justice agencies collect. However, crimes cannot be recorded if they are not reported in the first place and, in reality, a high proportion of crimes are not reported to the police. For example, people may not trust the police or feel that the crime will be taken seriously. Some people may assume the crime is not important enough to be reported or they may feel embarrassed to come forward. Also as discussed earlier in the chapter, statistics may reflect the attitudes of the police; for example, consider the overrepresentation of particular ethnic minority groups in crime statistics (see page 72 on crime and ethnicity), pointing to some cases of racism among the police.

Furthermore, not all crime is recorded even when it is taken to the police. When people actively report an offence to the police, we would assume that these actually make it into the official police statistics. However, in any one year it is estimated that only 57 per cent of all the crimes reported to the police make it into the official statistics.

There is also the issue of police interpretation of a crime. Clearly the police play an important role in filtering the information supplied to them by the public, according to what they see as important. There are many factors which may affect their decision to record the crime including: how serious the crime is, how the crime is categorised, police discretion (their own view on the importance of the crime), the social position of the person reporting the crime and if the police feel that they might benefit their own career by following up the crime.

The courts also play an important role in determining the official crime statistics. The processes that occur in court are also inevitably socially constructed, the result of numerous social processes. British courts work on the assumption that many people will plead guilty. In fact only 75 per cent of the people going through court, on average, do plead guilty. Therefore it is down to the judges and the jury to decide if a person is guilty or not. This can be based on or influenced by personal appearance, judgements based on a person's gender, ethnicity or social class, for example.

The government influences definitions of crime and subsequently the way that they are recorded. What is considered to be a crime changes over time also in response to cultural changes and the influence of powerful groups such as the media. So comparing crime rates over time can be difficult because definitions of crimes change. For example, the use of cannabis; as its use is more widespread, the numbers of offences for possessing it have dropped. The police statistics make it look as if cannabis use is dropping when in fact the opposite is happening.

Victim surveys

A victim survey is a sample of the population, either locally or nationally, who are asked about which offences have been committed against them over a period of time.

There are many strengths of victim surveys. For example, this approach overcomes the fact that a significant proportion of offences are never recorded by the police. It also gives an excellent picture of the extent and patterns of victimisation, something that is less clear within official accounts. Since 1982 the British Crime Survey has been collecting information about the victims of crime every year. The sample is large with almost 40,000 people being interviewed annually. Supporters of the survey believe it is more 'valid' than the police statistics.

The British Crime Survey is a good example of a general victim study; it is useful but not focused on providing detailed information about particular places. This led to a number of detailed studies of crime, focusing on particular areas. These studies provide specific information about local problems. The most well known of these were the Islington Crime Surveys (1995 and 1996). These showed, among other things, that the British Crime Survey under-reported the higher levels of victimisation of minority ethnic groups and domestic violence.

Strengths of victim surveys

Victim surveys reveal the kinds of crime which people think are not worth reporting to the police. Due to the anonymous nature of victim surveys people may be more comfortable to reveal more personal embarrassing crimes. They allow the victim to define the crime in their own terms and therefore there is no imposition of police bias in the reporting or classification of the crime.

This method also provides greater understanding of the perspective of the victim. Garland (2001) suggests that in the past, most people believed that the government had crime control in hand. However, Garland suggests that in late modernity, there is a much greater sense of uncertainty and risk, and governments are no longer believed to catch and punish all criminals.

Criticisms of victim surveys

One problem of victim surveys is that they rely on victims' memories and recollections which may be faulty or biased. The categorisation of the crimes that has been committed against them is left to the person filling in the questionnaire and this can lead to considerable inaccuracy in categories. Furthermore, victim surveys overlook a range of crimes, such as fraud and corporate crime, and any crime where the victim is unaware of or unable to report a crime. In addition, even though victim surveys are anonymous, people still appear to under-report sexual offences.

Victim surveys are dependent on people being aware that they are victims. The media play a key role in this as they provide illustrations of 'crimes' and generally heighten sensitivity towards certain forms of behaviour. This is known as sensitising the public towards (certain types of) activity that can be seen as a crime worth reporting.

Victim surveys may not include a wide range of the population. The British Crime Survey has the problem of not collecting information from those under the age of 16. However, this is now partly overcome by the British Youth Lifestyles Survey (2000) which was carried out specifically to obtain detailed information on crimes against younger people.

Self-report studies

A self-report study is where a sample of the population are selected and, usually using questionnaires and interviews, asked what, if any, offences they have committed. Self-report studies are a useful way of gaining access to information about crimes such as antisocial behaviour, and often hidden crimes such as domestic violence or white-collar crime. These self-report studies have had many aims other than to study criminal careers and the causes of offending. In particular, they have been used to evaluate the effectiveness of prevention and intervention programmes, for example Painter and Farrington (2001).

Steven Box (1981) carried out a review of the results of 40 self-report studies of delinquency and found that on the basis of these findings, antisocial behaviour is not only a working-class phenomenon, but that middle-class youths also commit antisocial behaviour as well. The results can be used to compare with official crime statistics and reveal interesting patterns about actual crime and police bias and interpretation.

Criticisms of self-report studies

People may not tell the truth about the crimes they have committed. They may cover up crimes for fear of being punished for them. They may also forget and misinterpret their own behaviour for various reasons. For example they play up or play down a crime. The respondents may not understand what is and what is not classed as a crime and therefore the results may be inaccurate.

Official crime statistics are drawn from the records that are kept by the police and other official agencies which are regularly published for the public to read.

Victim survey is research carried out into specific or general areas about the kinds of crimes people have been a victim of.

Self-report study is research carried out, usually in the form of an interview or questionnaire that asks people about the crimes which they have committed.

Different perspectives

Positivists would favour the use of official crime statistics to understand crime, while interpretivists would see these as invalid and socially constructed rather than being a valid picture of crime rates. Interpretivists are more likely to favour self-report studies and victim surveys as they potentially involve less bias.

> **CONTEMPORARY APPLICATION**
> The government are now acknowledging that official crime statistics may not provide a valid picture of crime and are now looking to use victim surveys as a way of understanding crime rates.

IN THE NEWS

The government acknowledges that statistics are not the only measurement of crime

Published crime statistics have often been viewed with scepticism. Now the UK Statistics Authority has announced that it has formally dropped police recorded crime figures as the only standard measurement, suggesting that at times the published figures were manipulated.

According to many, this change is long overdue. Published figures are almost meaningless, as they do not show the true extent of crime. Many crimes of all kinds go unreported, and police figures are kept artificially low by presenting them in ways that reflect well on the management of crime levels.

Many argue that the Crime Survey for England and Wales gives a more accurate measure of crime trends. The CSEW is a public survey and looks at about 50,000 households per year. It asks people whether they have experienced various types of behaviour in the past year, including violent assault, theft, burglary and other crimes. Crucially, and in contrast to other estimates, the CSEW includes offences that victims did not report for whatever reason, and incidents of crime where victims did not perceive them as offences.

The CSEW shows that many forms of crime have declined significantly since the mid 1990s, in particular violent crime, which it estimates as being at early-1980s levels.

Adapted from Fogg (2014)

Questions

1. What are the problems with official crime statistics according to this article?
2. Identify two strengths of the Crime Survey of England and Wales.

4.3 Who is more or less likely to be a victim and why?

Consider both positivist and critical perspectives in victimology, the study of victims as well as considering the fact that crimes have changed over time. For example, there have been many new forms of crime emerging over the past 30 years, which have meant the concept of 'victim' has also changed.

Sociologists can learn a lot about crime and deviance from the victims of crime. This section explores who is likely to be a victim of crime and why, as well as exploring the dominant sociological explanations for these patterns.

Christie (1986) argues that 'victim' is a socially constructed concept and so what it means to be a victim varies from time to time and place to place. Sometimes it is very clear when a person is a victim, such as through murder or robbery, whereas at other times people may not even have been aware that they were the victims of a crime at the time it occurs, such as through identity theft. Christie reminds us that attitudes towards victims and how they should be dealt with are likely to be shaped by the assumptions we make about them, which may not always be based on factual evidence.

In the past, the victim of crime has often been invisible or of little interest. However, since victims have become more visible in public discourse and through the media, there have been greater efforts made to understand the experiences and nature of the victim. The study of the victim is known as victimology and there are two major schools of thought, positivist victimology and critical victimology.

Positivist victimology

Positivists believe that social problems and issues are discoverable and to some degree can be improved through the use of scientific methods. Positivist victimology is based on an exploration of the victim as somehow different to other people in their general make-up, putting them at greater risk than others. Miers (1989) claims that in identifying people who have characteristics which predispose them to becoming victims, patterns can be established. Miers argues that this is possible particularly in crimes which involve a level of violence between individuals, and claims that the individual themselves are partly responsible in becoming a victim.

In what are now considered controversial studies, Von Hentig (1941, 1948) and Mendelsohn (1956, 1974), suggested that certain people could be identified as being more likely to be the victim of a crime. They were interested in observing and identifying particular types of victim who could then be categorised within various typologies. According to this approach, the victim could be seen as potentially partly guilty themselves for allowing or encouraging others to make them a victim of a crime.

A major weakness with positivist victimology, however, is that it assumes that the identity of the victim is known, and that there is a law in place to prevent that particular form of harm, which is not always the case. Thus, there is a tendency to concentrate almost exclusively on victims of conventional interpersonal crimes, particularly those involving violence and predatory attitudes towards the property of others.

Critical victimology

As the name suggests, critical theorists seek to challenge the existing social order and wish to see changes in society to make it more fair and just. Critical victimologists include Marxists and feminists, who argue that victims are constructed in such a way that reinforces and justifies structural inequalities. Critical victimologists argue that the state looks after its own interests and uses its power to apply the label of victim in a way which deflects the real inequalities in society. Mawby and Walklate (1994) are feminists who claim that women are often denied the possibility of becoming victims as crimes against them such as domestic violence are often unrecognised. When cases of domestic violence go to court, they are often unsuccessful therefore reinforcing patriarchy and undermining women's ability to challenge the structural inequalities that they face.

The critical victimologists Tombs and Whyte (2003) go further and argue that sometimes the victim in the existing legal framework almost becomes to blame for the crime that is committed against them. For example in rape cases, it is the (usually female) victim of the rape whose sexual behaviour comes under scrutiny, not the perpetrator. This puts other victims off from coming forward and reporting similar crimes. Tombs and White argue that this type of process plays an ideological function and sends a clear message to victims, who are often already marginalised and powerless, that they are unable to seek or gain justice for the crimes that have been committed against them.

However, critical victimology has been criticised for ignoring the fact that not all crimes are committed by the powerless, and at times the powerless do seek and get legal redress. It also ignores the fact that at times, people do behave in a less responsible way which means they are partially responsible for being a victim. However, critical victimology is useful in highlighting the way in which victim status is applied by the powerful to reinforce structural inequalities.

Patterns of victimisation: who are the victims of crime?

Official statistics and other forms of research into crime reveal that certain social groups are much more likely to be the victims of crimes than others. There are primary victims to whom the crime is directed and secondary victimisation, which refers to the negative experiences which people have when going through the process of reporting the crime. For example in rape cases, the victims (usually female) may be made to feel as if they were partly to blame for the rape and also feel violated by having their sexual behaviour scrutinised in a public way.

People close to the victim may also be affected by the crime, and these are known as 'indirect victims', for example, where someone is murdered and the family subsequently has no breadwinner. Children and adults may also be disturbed and distressed by witnessing a crime, which can leave long-term psychological effects.

Another factor to consider is the effect that the victims of crime have on people who are not victims. The wide coverage of crime and victims in the media has led to increased fear of becoming a victim, often significantly disproportionate to the actual risk of becoming a victim. The proportion of adults who are very worried about being the victim of crime is much lower than a decade ago: for burglary, 10 per cent compared with 19 per cent a decade ago; for violent crime, 13 per cent compared with 24 per cent a decade ago (The Poverty Site 2014).

For example, young women may be afraid to go out alone at night whereas it is young men who are at a significantly higher risk of becoming the victims of violent crime. Equally, the fear surrounding strangers is disproportionate to many violent crimes, which are often committed by someone known to the victim.

The table below summarises the major patterns in relation to victimisation among different social groups. Interestingly, there are other social groups who experience very high levels of victimisation and these include children in care and people with mental health problems which until recently has not been fully recognised.

Variable	Evidence	Explanation
Class	Lone parents and the unemployed are more than twice as likely to be burgled as the average household. In 2004, 67 per cent of the homeless population suffered a theft, compared to 1.4 per cent of all adults in England and Wales	Mack and Lansley (1985) argue that poor people suffer disproportionately from victimisation, as well as from the effects of victimisation. There is a known link between inequalities increasing in income and an increase in crime. Marxists would argue that the working class are the victims of crime as part of their exploited powerless position within capitalist society. It is the ruling class who have the power to decide what constitutes a victim and to apply the label of victim.
Ethnicity	People of mixed ethnic origin were also at higher risk of becoming a victim (11 per cent) of a personal crime than people from Asian (6 per cent) and White (6 per cent) ethnic groups. More than half of people from Bangladeshi and Pakistani ethnic backgrounds still live in low-income households, making them more prone to being victims.	Some ethnic groups are more likely to be the victims of crimes and this is often linked to the cultural and material deprivation that they are more likely to experience. Hate crimes and racially motivated crimes are further reinforced by police behaviour and public stereotypes. However, some ethnic minorities are less likely to report crimes, as they do not trust the police who they may see as being institutionally racist.
Gender	In 2011/12, as in previous years, more than two-thirds of homicide victims (68 per cent) were male. In contrast, women were more likely to be a victim of domestic abuse.	Women are much more likely to be the victims of domestic violence, men are much more likely to be the victim of a violent crime by a stranger.
Age	Households headed by young people are more than twice as likely to be burgled as the average household. 8 per cent of children aged 10 to 15 have experienced violent crimes in the last year; 5 per cent have experienced violence with injury.	Contrary to some views held by the media, young people are much more likely to be the victims of crime than middle-aged people. The elderly are more likely to be the victims of crimes; this may be because the elderly are less likely to be able to report crimes against them such as abuse in care homes due to their age and status.

Table 2.7 Victims of crime

It is important to note that the patterns above are based only on the crimes that are reported; according to the Office for National Statistics (2012) 44 per cent of people not reporting a violent crime did not report it because the incident was trivial or they thought that the police would not or could not do anything. Some 35 per cent of non-reported crimes were not reported because they were felt to be private or to be dealt with by the victims themselves.

KEY SOCIOLOGIST

Miers (1989) is a symbolic interactionist who explores victimology from a critical perspective, asking who has the power to apply the label of victim? Miers is interested in looking at the range of factors which influence the decision to apply the label of victim at any given time. Miers emphasises the socially constructed nature of the status of 'victim'.

STUDY TIP

Make sure that you acknowledge that victimology ignores many of the victims of crime who either choose not to report a crime or those who do not realise that they are, in fact, a victim of the crime.

Different perspectives

Postmodernists argue that the law is narrow and does not reflect all forms of deviant behaviour. Therefore social harm is seen as a better concept through which to understand victimisation.

> **CONTEMPORARY APPLICATION**
>
> There is a Code of Practice for the Victims of Crime which was written by the Ministry of Justice (2013) which sets out the rights of the victim, taking them through what they can expect to happen at all stages. This includes both adults and children and aims to make sure that everyone gets treated fairly and equally. This includes information on how to make a complaint and also how to get in touch with victim support groups.

> **IN THE NEWS**
>
> **Change is long overdue for sex abuse victims**
>
> Concern that the court process can be traumatic for accusers in sex abuse cases is increasing, following a case in which a woman fell to her death when she stepped off the roof of a shopping centre, three days after the alleged attacker was acquitted of rape.
>
> A close friend said the woman had appeared desperate when she heard the news, and that she had found her court experiences highly traumatic. The woman had complained that she found police support inadequate, from when she reported the incident through to when the first trial collapsed and a retrial was ordered. A police spokesman said that following the verdict the woman had been 'angry and upset'. Officers tried to talk her down from the shopping centre roof, but were unsuccessful.
>
> The tragedy came as work began on how to improve the experience of the criminal justice system. The death has represented for many, including former director of public prosecutions, Keir Starmer, an added conviction that the criminal justice system offers a poor service to those who go through it as apparent victims.
>
> Adapted from Gentleman (2014)

Questions

1. What does this article reveal about the problems that victims of sex abuse may face?
2. How might a positivist criminologist explain this case? How might this be different from a critical criminologist's explanation?

4.4 What is the role of the criminal justice system and the agencies that work alongside it?

Consider the differences between the intended role and the actual role of the criminal justice system. Think about the social characteristics of the people who run the criminal justice system and whose interests they might seek to protect.

According to the *Barrister Magazine* (2008), the role of the criminal justice system is to deliver justice for all, by convicting and punishing the guilty and helping them to stop offending, while protecting the innocent. The criminal justice system works in partnership with the police, courts, the Home Office, the Ministry of Justice and other agencies throughout the criminal justice system. The criminal justice system is made up of a number of composite parts, which are highlighted in Figure 2.26. There are different views on the role of the criminal justice system.

THE POLICE
There are 43 police forces across England and Wales responsible for the investigation of crime, collection of evidence and the arrest and detention of suspected offenders

THE LAW OFFICES
Crown Prosecution Service
Serious Fraud Office
Attorney General, legal advisor to the government and overseas, the prosecution authorities

THE HOME OFFICE
Has responsibility for immigration, passports, drug policy, crime, counter terrorism and police

THE SERIOUS FRAUD OFFICE
Prosecutes serious or complex fraud and corruption

CRIMINAL JUSTICE SYSTEM

THE NATIONAL OFFENDER MANAGEMENT SERVICE
Provides administration of correctional services in England and Wales through prisons and the probation service

THE COURTS
Most cases are heard within the Magistrates' Courts and the Crown Courts. Magistrates' Courts deal with less serious criminal offences. Youth Courts deal with youth crimes, with defendants aged between 10 and 18 years old. Crown Courts deal with the most serious offences which are triable by judge and jury

THE MINISTRY OF JUSTICE
Has responsibility for courts, prisons, probation services and attendance services, including criminal and family justice as well as democracy, rights and the Constitution

HER MAJESTY'S CROWN PROSECUTION SERVICES INSPECTORATE
An independent organisation that inspects and reports on the Crown Prosecution Service

Figure 2.20 The criminal justice system

Functionalists believe the criminal justice system reflects the value consensus within society, the dominant ideas about what is considered to be right and wrong. They argue that ideas about crime change over time and as such the criminal justice system reflects these socially constructed ideas about what is considered illegal and deviant at any given point. This optimistic perspective is challenged by many who regard the criminal justice system as reflecting the views and interests of particular dominant groups in society.

Marxists argue that the criminal justice system reflects the values and aspirations of the ruling class who dominate the criminal justice system. Marxists point out that the majority of crimes are committed by the working class, while ruling-class crimes go undetected and unpoliced. The Marxist Chambliss (1989) explains that the police are more likely to judge a working-class person as a criminal than a middle-class person and that middle-class people are much more likely to be let off for minor crimes.

Foucault, the post-structuralist, argues that the state controls the individual and has the power to define who becomes a criminal and who does not. The criminal justice system, according to Foucault, has expanded throughout the development of modernity and has become a way of the state controlling individuals and regulating their behaviour. Foucault argues that rather than punishing the body, as was common in the Middle Ages, punishment now focuses on the mind. This involves the surveillance of the individual through the state and private control systems. Foucault argues that the knowledge that a person is being watched acts as a powerful deterrent to committing crime.

Racism within the criminal justice system

Phillips and Bowling (2002) argue that the criminal justice system reflects racist views that are deeply embedded in the practices of its various branches. For example, they point out that discrimination against particular ethnic groups begins with policing priorities and practices. Phillips and Bowling argue that since the 1970s the police have targeted African and African Caribbean populations taking an inappropriately heavy-handed approach, sometimes using excessive force. Following the murder of Stephen Lawrence, despite serious complaints and concerns being raised about the institutionally racist practices of the police, black minority groups are still seven times more likely to be stopped and searched than their white counterparts. Similarly, black men in particular are more likely to be given prison sentences and for longer periods of time. Phillips and Bowling argue that although it is difficult to know how much the overrepresentation of ethnic groups is linked to racism, it is clear that institutional racism does play a significant role in the criminal justice system.

Women in the criminal justice system

According to the **chivalry thesis**, women get treated leniently by the criminal justice system and there is some evidence to support this view with women often being less likely to receive prison sentences for manslaughter than men for example, as well as being much less likely to be stopped and searched. However, there is also evidence that women are treated more harshly by the criminal justice system when they are accused of committing more serious crimes. The feminist Walklate (1998) argues that rape trials, for example, put female victims themselves on trial by judging them for any behaviour which strays from being conformist and virtuous while men's sexual exploits are typically celebrated and seen as acceptable.

Heidensohn (1985) agrees and argues that double standards exist within the criminal justice system with any girl or woman who deviates from societal norms of female sexuality being punished more harshly. At the same time courts are less likely to put mothers with children into prison than fathers. Therefore the criminal justice system can be seen to be operating on a highly gendered set of assumptions.

Different perspectives

New Right thinkers such as Charles Murray (1984) believe that the state should play a key role in social control by reforming welfare benefits which encourage individuals to take more responsibility for their own welfare. Therefore social control is likely to take place not just through the criminal justice system but as Garland points out through the welfare system, where social control is economic and ideological.

> **KEY SOCIOLOGIST**
>
> **Garland** (2002) explores the role of welfare policies in social control. Garland argues that although there have been many changes in laws in late modern society, the most significant shift has been in the attitudes that people have towards control. Garland argues that social control has changed from being limited to traditional penal sentencing to regulating people through welfare reform.

> **KEY SOCIOLOGIST**
>
> **S. Cohen** (1972) examines the way public and private social control mechanisms are merging, alongside traditional forms of punishment for crime. Cohen argues that this is due in part to the emerging forms of criminal behaviour. Therefore, Cohen says, there needs to be a range of ways of punishing crime, which are growing more complex and sophisticated.

> **STUDY TIP**
>
> Consider the way in which the criminal justice system supports or does not support the interests of particular social groups. Apply these ideas to different theoretical groups.

> **KEY SOCIOLOGISTS**
>
> **Wilson and Kelling** (1982) are right realists who claim that community-based programmes reduce crime. These include long-term strategies such as strengthening social control through more disciplinarian parenting and increasing employment levels to provide strong working role models for children as important long-term ways of reacting to crime.

> **CONTEMPORARY APPLICATION**
>
> The Anti-social Behaviour, Crime and Policing Act 2014 intended to introduce simpler, more effective powers to tackle antisocial behaviour that provide better protection for victims and communities. Within the Act there is greater emphasis on giving control to local communities on the basis that it will empower them, giving them a greater say in how agencies respond to complaints of antisocial behaviour and in out-of-court sanctions for offenders.
>
> The Act will also tackle irresponsible dog ownership and the use of illegal firearms by gangs and organised criminal groups and strengthen the protection afforded to the victims of forced marriage and those at risk of sexual harm.

IN THE NEWS

Prison overcrowding blamed on 'getting tough on crime' policies

A senior figure in the prison system has claimed that increasing competition between political parties to show they are tough on crime is holding back progress in improving jail conditions in England and Wales. Many politicians believe that there are votes in being toughest on crime.

The prison population has risen from 45,000 in the mid 1990s to a record 85,000 in England and Wales. As a result, in many prisons, nearly half of the prisoners are still 'doubled up' with two men being held in cells designed for only one inmate.

The Woolf report, which was published in February 1991, made more than 200 proposals for reform including the introduction of telephones on landings so inmates could keep in closer touch with their families. However, many point out that these reforms have not occurred and that prisons are overcrowded and unsafe.

Adapted from Travis (2015)

Questions

1. What kinds of solutions would left realists suggest to resolve growing numbers of prisoners?
2. What kinds of challenges might the criminal justice system face in the future?

Check your understanding

1. What are the different forms of punishment?
2. Give two examples of behaviours which have recently changed from being seen as deviant to becoming criminalised.
3. Explain the difference between positivist and critical victimology.
4. What happens to the crime rate when there are new counting rules introduced, and why?
5. Why do some people claim that prison is not an effective form of punishment?
6. Who is more likely to be a victim of crime, and why?

Practice questions

1. Outline two problems with prisons. [4 marks]
2. Outline three different views on the role of the criminal justice system. [6 marks]

3 Beliefs in society

Understanding the specification	
AQA Specification	**How the specification is covered in this chapter**
The ideology, science and religion, including both Christian and non-Christian religious traditions.	**Section 1: Ideology, science and religion, including both Christian and non-Christian religious traditions** What is religion? Issues with defining religion. How is science a social construct? Are religion and science belief systems and ideological influences? What are the different theoretical views on the role and function of religion?
The relationship between social change and social stability, and religious beliefs, practices and organisations.	**Section 2: The relationship between social change and social stability, and religious beliefs, practices and organisations.** Religion as a conservative force Religion as a force for social change
Religious organisations, including cults, sects, denominations, churches and New Age movements, and their relationship to religious and spiritual belief and practice.	**Section 3: Religious organisations** What are the types of religious organisations? What are new religious movements and new age movements?
The relationship between different social groups and religious/spiritual organisations and movements, beliefs and practices.	**Section 4: The relationship between different social groups and religious organisations, beliefs and practices** How do age, gender, ethnicity and class affect religious beliefs and practices?
The significance of religion and religiosity in the contemporary world, including the nature and extent of secularisation in a global context, and globalisations and the spread of religions.	**Section 5: Religion in the modern world** Are we still religious? What impact has globalisation had on beliefs?

Section 1: Ideology, science and religion, including both Christian and non-Christian religious traditions

This section will explore the following debates:

- What is religion? Issues with defining religion.
- How do sociologists explain religion and its social functions? Different theoretical views on the role and function of religion.
- How is science a social construct?
- Are religion and science belief systems and ideological influences?

GETTING YOU STARTED

Figure 3.1 What happens after death?

Questions

1. What existed before the universe?
2. Where do we come from?
3. Who am I (essentially)?
4. What is my true nature/essence?
5. What is my true identity?
6. What is the meaning of life?
7. What is my greater purpose?
8. How should I live my life?
9. What is death?
10. What happens after death?
11. Is there a god, and, if so, what is his/her nature?

Think about where you got the answers to the questions above.

Think of the ways in which an individual's life can be shaped by their religious beliefs in the following ways:

- family life
- education
- politics
- culture.

1.1 What is religion? Issues with defining religion

Consider how different sociologists have defined particular concepts of religion, and how sociological definitions might differ from the everyday meaning assigned to them.

Religion is something that is hard to define precisely. Exactly what constitutes a religion is contested and depends mainly on the criteria used to define it. Because the boundaries of where religions begin and end can be so blurred it makes defining it extremely difficult. Using too narrow a definition, such as belief in God or performing certain rituals, can exclude recognised religions, while too broad a definition can result in certain non-religious belief systems becoming included.

Sociologists are not concerned with whether religious beliefs are true or false, but with how religions are organised, whether religious beliefs constitute sources of social solidarity or conflict, and what social forces are at work which keep religions alive or lead to their decline.

Most sociologists agree that anything resembling the phenomenon we call religion is comprised of three main characteristics:

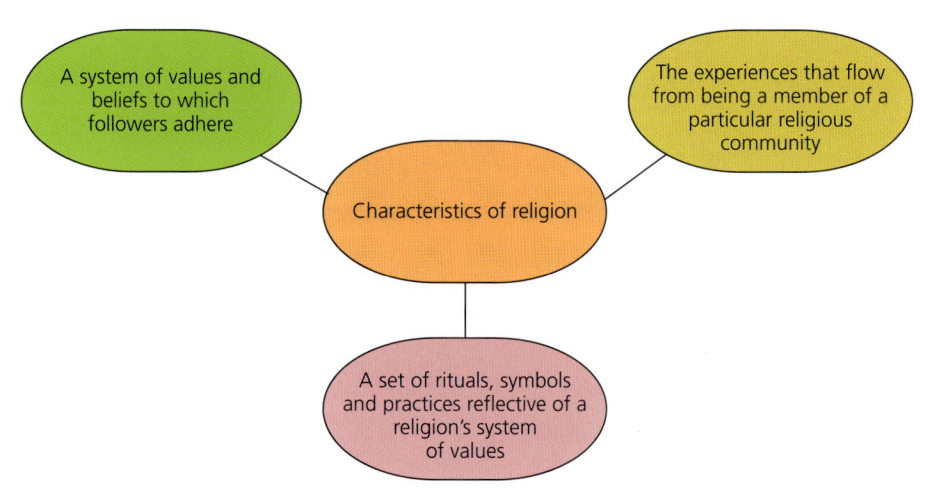

- A system of values and beliefs to which followers adhere
- The experiences that flow from being a member of a particular religious community
- A set of rituals, symbols and practices reflective of a religion's system of values

Figure 3.2 The main characteristics of religion

Sociologists define religion in three main ways: substantive, functional and social constructionist.

	Definition	Evaluation
Substantive	This definition emphasises what religions are about and places a significant emphasis on the existence of **supernatural forces**. Substantive definitions are exclusive – they draw a clear line between religious and non-religious beliefs. Bruce (2002) offers an exclusive definition of religion in his work *God is Dead*: 'beliefs, actions and institutions that assume the existence of supernatural entities with powers of action, or impersonal powers or processes possessed of moral purpose.'	The substantive definition is too exclusive and has Western bias, for example it excludes religions such as Buddhism, which do not have the Western idea of a god. Defining religion in this way leaves no room for beliefs and practices that perform similar functions to religion but do not involve belief in God, such activities as devotion to football team, idolising celebrity, having political commitment, or seeking meaning through consumerism and other secular activities.
Functional	This definition focuses on what the religion does for people (its functions). The functional definition was developed initially within the work of Durkheim who saw religion as providing a basis for community. According to Durkheim the key function of religion is to strengthen social solidarity and integration (see page 123). Functional definitions stress how religions contribute to societies in terms of social and psychological function. John Milton Yinger argues that religion performs functions for individuals such as answering questions about the meaning of life and what happens when we die.	Defining religion in this way allows us to include a wide range of beliefs and practices that perform functions such as integration. By not specifying belief in God there is no bias against non-Western religions such as Buddhism. However, just helping to integrate individuals into groups does not make an institution a religion. This definition is too broad and too inclusive encompassing all sorts of phenomena – from football fandom to nationalism – that can not be seen as religion.
Social constructionist	This definition focuses on what religion means to each individual person (a micro approach). Social constructionists are interested in how definitions are constructed, challenged and fought over. Adopting an interactionist stance, Berger and Luckmann (1966) argue defining religion should be centred on how people make sense of the world around them. It is not possible to produce a definition of religion that applies to all situations, as the term 'religion' means very different things to groups and to individual people. Also, debate concerning religion is affected by those in a position to influence it. For example, Aldridge (2007) shows that to its followers, Scientology is a religion. However, it is not recognised as such by several governments, which have also tried to ban it.	This definition does not assume that religion always involves a belief in a god or the supernatural, or that it performs similar functions for everyone in all societies. However, this approach allows us to get close to the meanings people themselves give to religion. However, this makes it impossible to generalise about the nature of religion, since people may have widely differing views about what counts as a religion.

Table 3.1 Sociologists and religion

Sociologists face a major challenge when they try to make sense of the role that religion plays in modern societies. Religion is identified with experiences indicating that there are dimensions of human life and the natural world which are deeper or more significant than everyday reality. The extensive diversity of religious ideas and distinction between the official and unofficial forms of religion means there is no easy answer to the question about the role of religion in any society today. Here we explore different theoretical perspectives on the role and function of religion.

Ideology and religion

Religion, like ideology, also offers a vision of and a means of understanding, interpreting and explaining the world. However, unlike ideology, religious beliefs are not necessarily tied to the interests of a particular social group, and as Antony Giddens (2006) put it, religion involves 'shared beliefs and rituals that provide a sense of ultimate meaning and purpose by creating an idea of reality that is sacred, all-encompassing and supernatural.' There are three main aspects to religion:

- belief in the spiritual and supernatural – a person, entity or other extra-worldly spiritual force or being of some kind, which ultimately provides a sense of meaning and a means of interpreting and explaining the world
- faith on the part of believers – a strong sense of trust and conviction in a person or entity that is not based on observable, testable or falsifiable evidence
- a body of unchanging truth – religion usually contains certain fundamental and unchangeable beliefs, like Christ being the son of God, or Mohammed being Allah's Prophet, and new discoveries are fitted into these existing frameworks.

Religion differs from ideology in that ideologies are not necessarily based on faith in supernatural beliefs, but on the interests of social groups. However, religion may become part of an ideology, as a social group may seek to use religion for its own ends, such as promoting and protecting its own interests. Marx, for example, regarded religion as part of the ideology of the dominant class in society (what he called dominant ideology), forming part of the worldview and helping to justify the interests of that class, and acting like the drug opium to dull the senses and pain of those that it exploited (see Marx theory of religion, page 125).

More recently, fundamentalist Christians in the United States, and increasingly in Europe, have transformed some religious beliefs into a campaigning ideology called intelligent design (sometimes also called creative design). Intelligent design is a religious belief that the universe and living things, including the human race, are not products of the scientifically accepted process of natural evolution, but are, rather, created by an intelligent force (God). This religiously based ideology is aligned to conservative American politicians and seeks to remove the teaching of the scientific theory of evolution in schools.

It is unclear that religion has been displaced by science in contemporary society. This is due to the problematic nature of measuring religious influence, despite the growing influence of science and rational thinking. Science and religion can be viewed as competing ideologies in society. While ideas of secularisation support the growth of influence of science, the debates surrounding globalisation, beliefs in postmodern society and fundamentalism all support the continued influence of religion.

IN THE NEWS

Evolutionism versus intelligent design

Figure 3.3 What are the origins of life?

In the USA, a fierce battle was being waged over what children in state schools should be taught about the origins of life. In December 2004, The American Civil Liberties Union of Pennsylvania, on behalf of 11 parents, filed a federal lawsuit, arguing that the way science is being taught in state schools violates their religious liberty; the trial started in September 2005. The trial arose out of a decision by a local school board in Dover, Pennsylvania, which required biology teachers to present 'intelligent design' to their students as an alternative to the scientific theory of evolution. Intelligent design is a set of beliefs based on idea that life on earth is so complex that it can not be explained by the theory of evolution, and therefore must have been designed by intelligent, supernatural entity. Proponents of intelligent design argue that they do not wish to prevent the theory of evolution being taught, but that students should be presented with alternative theories and allowed to make up their own minds.

In the Dover area schools must present intelligent design as a bona fide scientific theory competing with the scientific theory of evolution in order to develop a balanced science curriculum. Many scientists and civil rights liberties lawyers attacked the decision to treat intelligent design as a scientific theory on the same level as evolution. They point out that the idea of intelligent design is fundamentally untestable and unprovable, because it relies on inserting a supernatural force – God, or an intelligent designer – into a scientific theory. They say that intelligent design has no explanatory or predictive power; it simply says that some things seem to have happened through natural causes, so must have been created by supernatural entity. This, say scientists, is dogma, not science.

The 11 parents involved in the Pennsylvania lawsuit say that presenting intelligent design in state schools science classes violates their religious liberty by promoting particular religious beliefs to their children under the guise of science education. They claim that making teaching of such views in state schools compulsory entangles government with religion which violates the US constitutional separation of church and state.

Adapted from Garrod (2006)

Questions

1. What is intelligent design?
2. Why are parents in Pennsylvania unhappy about science being taught in their school?
3. Is intelligent design a scientific theory?

1.2 How is science a social construct?

For a long time, science was confused with religious beliefs, superstition and magic. Even now science and religion are seen as having competing ways of explaining the world. It is, however, generally accepted that science aspires to objectivity and value freedom, and is based on impartial research methods, producing explanations that are based on empirical evidence.

Characteristics of science

The first characteristic of science is its **objectivity**. This is derived from the fact that scientific research should be free from any bias and through the control of all variables. The goal of all science is cause and effect relationships, rather than mere correlations.

The second characteristic of science is that it is logical and rational. Scientific knowledge is rooted in the rationalist approach that such knowledge must be based on reason. However, this approach, in itself, does not guarantee scientific knowledge is correct or of good quality.

The third characteristic of science is that it is based on evidence derived from rigorous research methodology, notably that experiments should be repeatable under similar circumstances. The significance of this is that it renders knowledge verifiable (testable).

The social, political and economic context of science

Science developed in eighteenth century Europe during a period known as the Enlightenment. The two key principles behind the Enlightenment were:

- that human reason and rational thinking replaced faith in explaining the unknown and providing an understanding of the world, and
- human beings can use this understanding to improve the world to make it a better place to live in.

These principles formed the guidelines for the scientific method – the procedure for 'doing science'. These views were considered radically different at the time, especially in parts of Europe where the Catholic Church was powerful. According to Catholics and Christians the world was created by God and could not be explained by reason.

Social construction of knowledge

How do we know that scientific theories provide accurate explanations? According to Karl Popper theories can be tested through observation and experiment. In this respect, they are superior to everyday knowledge and beliefs. Any theory that can be falsified (proven wrong) is a scientific theory. Science is defined not by the discovery of the final truth but by the elimination of untruths. So Popper argues that researchers should aim, not to prove their hypotheses true, but to falsify them, or prove them wrong. Popper's argument that all hypotheses should be subject to falsification implies that religious argument will increasingly be displaced by scientific argument since religious ideas cannot be proven, being reliant solely on faith. As a contemporary supporter of the secularisation thesis, Bruce argues that scientific explanations are replacing superstitious ideas. However, supporters of religion argue that religious and scientific ideas need to be viewed as competing ideologies.

Popper suggests that science involves the **hypothetico-deductive method**. This involves testing a **hypothesis** (a testable statement). There are five stages to the scientific method, shown in Figure 3.4.

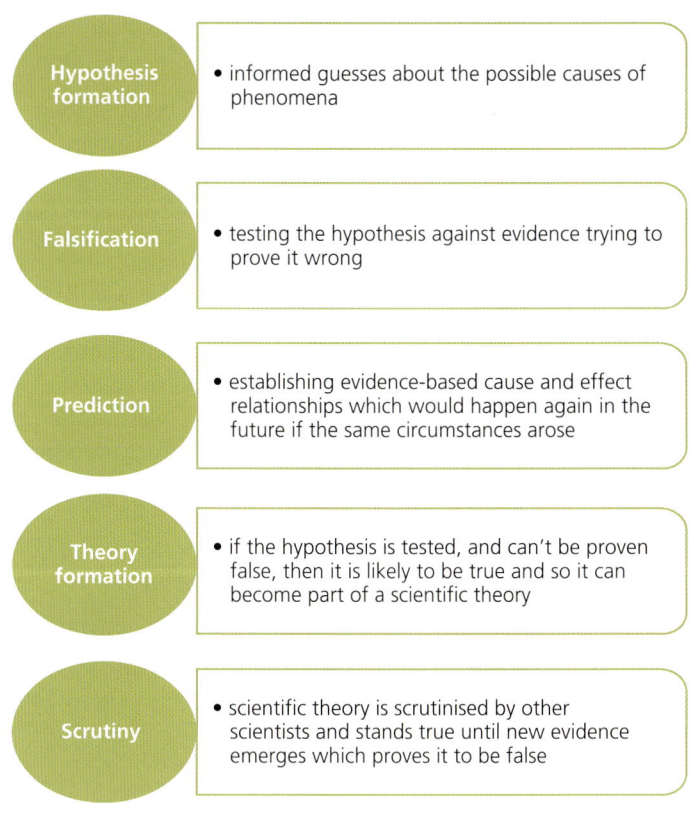

Hypothesis formation
- informed guesses about the possible causes of phenomena

Falsification
- testing the hypothesis against evidence trying to prove it wrong

Prediction
- establishing evidence-based cause and effect relationships which would happen again in the future if the same circumstances arose

Theory formation
- if the hypothesis is tested, and can't be proven false, then it is likely to be true and so it can become part of a scientific theory

Scrutiny
- scientific theory is scrutinised by other scientists and stands true until new evidence emerges which proves it to be false

Figure 3.4 The scientific method

Thomas Kuhn (1962) challenges the traditional view of science. He saw science as socially constructed within scientific communities. This rejects the view that science is based solely on rationality and objectivity. According to Kuhn, scientists work in communities centred on particular branches of science and particular research projects. Kuhn argues that scientists work within a **paradigm** – a set of values, ideas, beliefs and assumptions about what they are investigating which is not questioned until the evidence against it is overwhelming. Kuhn argues that most scientists in their experimental work try to fit observations into the paradigm rather than actually attempting to falsify their hypotheses, as Popper suggests. The power of the paradigm means that scientists focus on what they are looking for and therefore might overlook evidence which doesn't fit into the existing paradigm. So, what might be seen as a scientific 'truth' might simply be an act of faith in scientific values of scientific rigour. Only when there are a number of anomalies or things that can't be explained does the paradigm break down, to be replaced by a new one until it is challenged.

Following the period of the Enlightenment, some commentators predicted that religion would one day be displaced by science. However, in the twenty-first century, while science has gained in influence and knowledge, it would be wrong to say that religion has been displaced, as it still plays an important role. Therefore the debate surrounding religion and science is one of competing and fluctuating ideologies and beliefs.

1.3 Are religion and science belief systems and ideological influences?

Develop your awareness of how both religion and science are ideologies as well as similarities and differences between two.

Sociologists argue that science can be interpreted as a form of belief because there are so few scientific 'laws' and 'facts'. There are still very few irrefutable laws in science, such as Newton's law of gravity. Most scientific theory has not been proven yet and therefore requires the scientists' 'faith' that their findings are correct.

Religion as a belief system

Peter Berger suggests that religion has lost its role as providing a 'sacred canopy' sheltering and protecting us against events in life that we cannot understand. In a media-saturated postmodern society, with increasingly fragmented ideas and beliefs, religion has lost its role of providing theodicy to supply answers to the big questions in life. According to Berger, religion helps us to construct our own personal universe of meaning. He believes that religion makes life meaningful through providing us with predictable rules and guidelines, for example, religious symbols, rituals and identities.

Berger suggests that there is no longer a single truth about religion or a way of living your life. As such society has become confusing; an individual's world has become more fragmented. Many people no longer use religion to provide their universe of meaning as the rise of reason, science and logic gives individuals a different way to understand their social world.

Max Weber stated that religions will always have a hold over the population as long as the 'big questions' need to be answered. What is the meaning of life? What existed before the universe? What happens after death? However, scientists argue that science has steadily replaced – often correcting – previous religious explanations. An example of this would be Darwin's theory of evolution that has replaced the religious account of creation. Nonetheless, creationism is still taught in several states of the USA and many faith schools across the world.

Figure 3.5 Durkheim claimed that totems symbolise both god and society at the same time

1.4 What are the different theoretical views on the role and function of religion?

Functionalist theory of religion

Functionalist theory assumes that society is primarily harmonious and that social order is maintained through a consensus or widespread agreement between people on important goals, norms and values of society. It is a consensus theory.

Functionalists are interested in how religion meets society's **functional requirements** for certain levels of value consensus, social solidarity and integration. According to this theory, religion contributes to all these functional prerequisites: religion provides shared values and beliefs, gives meaning to life, helps individuals to cope with stress, promotes social solidarity, helps the continued existence of society and is a conservative force.

Durkheim argued that religion was a social construction. According to Durkheim people divide their world into things that are profane (things that are 'ordinary' and non-sacred) and sacred (things or people that evoke strong emotions of awe and respect). They represent the collective consciousness. Durkheim focused on the symbols or totems that most religions use, for example, statues, carvings. He claimed that totems symbolise both god and society at the same time. Religion demonstrates the moral superiority of society over the individual, where individuals accept the importance of society and their dependence on it.

Durkheim based his work on studies of the religion of one tribe of Australian Aborigines, which he called totemism. Each clan had a totem – a symbol, usually either a plant or an animal – and this distinguished the clan from the others and was sacred. The totem is the 'outward and visible form of god'. Therefore, Durkheim argues that when members worship the god (totem), which represents their clan/society, they are worshipping society. Durkheim believes that society cannot survive without **collective conscience** and religion reinforces it. Because the shared values and beliefs are sacred they are powerful. He claimed that religion was important in forming a value consensus or collective consciousness by providing regular opportunities to establish and reinforce social values and integrate people into society, that is, religious ceremonies surrounding birth, marriages, death, etc.

Talcott Parsons shared the view that religion reinforces consensus values, even for those who were not particularly religious, but who share the prevailing norms and values of society that are often rooted in religious traditions. He claimed that religion provides and legitimises core values that enhance social solidarity (for example, the ten commandments). Religion is the primary source of meaning for individuals: it provides meanings to 'eternal' questions about humanity and life. The function of religion is to act as a 'mechanism of adjustment' (it provides meaning and answers in difficult times), for example, when individuals are 'hit' by events they cannot foresee, or when individuals are faced with uncertainty for example, weather, war. These events defy our sense of justice and make life appear meaningless. This may undermine our commitment to society's values.

According to Parsons religion offers answers to these:

- suffering tests a person's faith and can make them stronger
- those who do not follow norms and values will get their punishment in the afterlife.

So this helps people make sense of the 'meaningless' and promotes social stability. Religion also provides core values and norms – both of which are made sacred. Religion can help people to adjust to situations and strengthens solidarity.

Evaluation of functionalist theories of religion

- Functionalist theory of religion gives a clear explanation of the relationship of the individual to the society, via the secondary socialisation obtained from religion.
- There is evidence that in times of stress/crisis people turn to religion for comfort, for example during the 9/11 event in USA.
- In contemporary society there are many competing religions. It is therefore difficult to see how diverse religions unite society.
- With evidence of secularisation there is a case that religion is no longer a social glue.

Other sociologists have challenged the assumptions of functionalism (and to a lesser extent Marxism) that religion promotes social integration, pointing out that it often lies at the heart of conflict. For example, Northern Ireland is a very religious place, but divided by two communities doggedly intolerant and distrustful of the other. Far from integrating the people of Northern Ireland, religion serves to promote conflict, intolerance and violence between the communities. This is repeated in examples across the globe and over time.

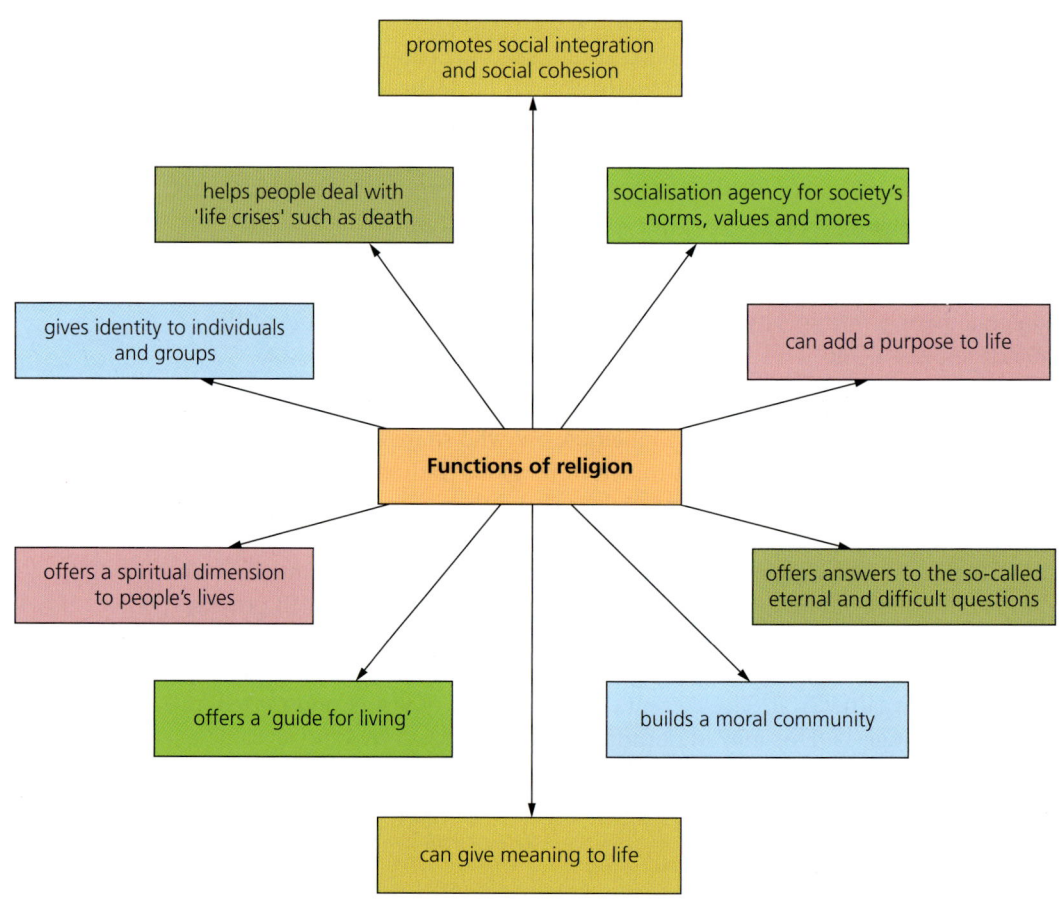

Functions of religion:
- promotes social integration and social cohesion
- helps people deal with 'life crises' such as death
- socialisation agency for society's norms, values and mores
- gives identity to individuals and groups
- can add a purpose to life
- offers a spiritual dimension to people's lives
- offers answers to the so-called eternal and difficult questions
- offers a 'guide for living'
- builds a moral community
- can give meaning to life

Figure 3.6 Functionalist theory functions of religion

Marxist theory of religion

Figure 3.7 Karl Marx

Rather than functioning to benefit society and the individual, Marxists see religion as preventing individuals from having a true understanding of themselves and their situation. Rather than working to benefit society as a whole by providing social solidarity and acting as 'social glue', Marxists see religion working to maintain class divisions and the power of the ruling class.

Marx identified two key functions of religion:

- It is used by the ruling class as an instrument of oppression.
- It is used by the working class to cushion the effects of oppression.

While Marxists agree that religion can act as an important agency of socialisation and can be seen to help bind society together through the promotion of false consciousness, they disagree with the premise of functionalism that this is both good and desirable. Describing religion as the '**opium of the people**', Karl Marx saw it as a dangerous set of beliefs that distorted reality by persuading people to tolerate life now in return for rewards in the afterlife. This type of theory takes the opposite view to that of functionalism; rather than seeing society as based on harmony, it sees society as primarily conflict-ridden and unstable, emphasising social inequality between groups. It is concerned with issues such as power and the inequality and control of dominant groups or classes. It is an example of a conflict theory.

How does religion legitimise the power of the ruling class?

According to Marx religion helps to reproduce, maintain and justify class inequalities. It fulfils an ideological role; for example, it provides a set of ideas, beliefs and values which benefit the ruling class. It acts as a means of social control. Religion legitimates and justifies inequalities by suggesting that the existing social order (with its inequality and class divisions) is 'God given' (God created the world and placed people in their positions within it). If the world is given by God it is impossible (and sinful) to try and alter it.

The Hindu caste system can be seen as religion justifying and legitimating inequality. In the Hindu caste system if you are in a low caste this may be a consequence of an impure former life. For Marxists religion is an instrument of oppression because it blinds people from their true position – it produces **false class consciousness**. Rather than seeing themselves as having the power to change the world, the working class are persuaded to accept their place in society.

How is religion the opium of the people?

Religion acts to cushion the effects of oppression. It achieves this in a number of ways. It promises an afterlife which is much better. For Christians this is heaven and for Muslims paradise. Suffering is seen as virtuous and will be rewarded. While the rich may enjoy life on Earth, at the 'day of judgement' the poor will have their reward. As the Bible teaches: 'It is easier for a camel to pass through the eye of a needle than for a rich man to enter the kingdom of heaven'. Religion offers the possibility of supernatural intervention. Hence through prayer deprivation and hardships may be eased.

Evaluation of Marxist theories of religion

- Marx predicted that with communism religion would disappear because people would no longer suffer false class consciousness and there would be no need for it – as there would be no ruling class there would be no oppression and religion would not be needed either as an instrument of oppression or to cushion the effects of oppression. However, despite attempts by the former Soviet Union to restrict religious activity (by closure of churches and the banning of religious teaching), religion continued to flourish.
- It is difficult to see religion as a major tool of ruling-class power if relatively few people regularly attend church.
- There are plenty of examples of religion not supporting or legitimating the ruling class, but of religion being used to overthrow them – Catholicism in Latin America and Islam in the revolution in Iran – see your later notes on Neo-Marxism and **liberation theology**.
- Traditional Marxism fails to address the secularisation issue or explain why so few working-class people are seriously religious in the first place.
- If religion is such a strong ideological apparatus, why do less than 10 per cent of the population attend church on a Sunday?

Neo-Marxist theory of religion

Antonio Gramsci

Gramsci argues that beliefs are no less real or important than economic forces. Gramsci argues that for a revolution to occur, the working class must shape its ideas to explain working-class experience and so help shape working-class consciousness (the Roman Catholic Church has done this in certain parts of the world; see Section 2 Examples of liberation theology). This control over the consciousness he called **hegemony**.

Louis Althusser

Althusser argues that religion is an ideological state apparatus: it spreads the dominant ideology and creates hegemony (acceptance and dominance of bourgeois ideas – the working clless believe social class hierarchy is inevitable and unchangeable). Althusser describes any institution as an ideological state apparatus (ISA) when it serves to reinforce ruling-class ideas while at the same time preventing the proletariat from recognising their true class position as exploited and oppressed. Religion as an ISA therefore serves to reinforce false consciousness and the status quo.

> **KEY SOCIOLOGIST**
>
> **Lenin** (1870–1924) agreed with Marx. He used the term 'spiritual gin' to describe the ways in which religion is seen as a form of escapism which numbs and blinds people's awareness to the reality around them.

Feminist theory of religion

Figure 3.8 Pat Storey became the UK and Ireland's first female bishop when she was consecrated at a ceremony in Dublin in November 2013

Feminists tend to be critical of religion as patriarchal in terms of its ideological messages as well as its roles and structures. For example, Browne refers to the women's barriers to promotion within religions, especially to the top clerical roles, as the 'stained-glass ceiling'. While some religions are more liberal than others in terms of gender attitudes and expectations, they are collectively seen as helping to maintain male domination over women.

Discussion of gender and women in religion was largely ignored until the feminist Simone de Beauvoir began discussing the significance of religious ideology in the 1950s. She argued that religion served to reinforce and justify the traditional roles within the family, particularly that of women as wives and mothers. Given the imbalance of domestic work and how many women felt unfulfilled and trapped in the home, these clearly benefited men at the expense of women.

Although many denominations and some sects have had female clergy for some time, it is only recently that the Church of England has allowed women to become initially curates and then vicars. However, the Roman Catholic Church refuses to accept women as priests. In non-Christian religions the picture of exclusion or **marginalisation** is a familiar one. By excluding women these religions undermine the position of women by reinforcing their status as inferior and second best.

Feminists accuse religions of being patriarchal by the way in which they tend to provide divine justification for the oppression of women. An illustration of how religion undermines women can be seen in the attitude of many religions to menstruation and childbirth. Jean Holm argues that both are regarded across a wide range of religions as 'polluting'. For example, Muslim women cannot touch the Koran, enter a mosque or even pray while they are menstruating. Such misguided ideas, in a rational scientific modern age, have to be interpreted as religion being used to control women.

Many feminists adopt a view of religion parallel to the Marxist concept of false consciousness. They see it as encouraging women to be passive and tolerant of their inferior position in return for rewards in the afterlife. The Egyptian feminist

Nawal El Saadawi describes how religious justification of female circumcision blatantly serves the interests of men, enhancing their enjoyment of sexual intercourse while limiting women's sexual pleasure, although she blames a misinterpretation of the Koran for this practice rather than Islam itself.

Figure 3.9 Is the veiling of women a religious instruction or a form of liberation?

The veiling of women is often interpreted as a religious instruction, enforced by men and a means of controlling women by husbands. Sociologist Alan Aldridge sees women as trapped and locked within the burka. Aldridge argues that veiling associated with Islam is a powerful symbol of **patriarchy** and oppression since it denies females the opportunity to express themselves in an individualistic way and is a form of control by their husbands. However, many feminists, such as Helen Watson, see the burka as liberating since women are no longer judged by their appearance, hair or make-up. It is also a way of avoiding the oppression of the male gaze and male sexual harassment.

It seems that women are more spiritual and participate more in religious activities than men. The evidence seems to suggest that religion can be viewed as serving men at the expense of women. If religion itself is not patriarchal it still serves to reinforce patriarchy in other aspects of life such as the family and public life.

There are different types of feminists and each one explains religion as different forms of oppression of women.

Liberal feminists are the most optimistic feminists who see education and occasionally legislation as necessary to move society towards greater equality. They would look at changes within the Church of England and many denominations that have female clergy. There are now female bishops in the Anglican Church in the USA, UK and many denominations. However, within some religions, such as Roman Catholicism, there has been no gender progress.

Radical feminists see all religions as patriarchal, serving to oppress women in a way that benefits men. They see the family as the key source of oppression of women and radical feminists like Sylvia Walby note how religions embrace an ideology that justifies and legitimises the traditional roles within the family. Within the organisation of religions, women encounter the 'stained-glass ceiling' (Browne, 2009) by being prevented from rising up the hierarchy and gaining roles in the priesthood, as bishops and above. In many religions, women's bodies are portrayed as 'polluting' in the sense that they menstruate and promote promiscuity.

Marxist feminists share the Marxist view that religion is a significant force, inhibiting social change and acting as a diversionary institution promoting false consciousness. Marxist feminists point out that women are more likely to be marginalised and experience poverty than men. They therefore recognise how religion can be seen to act as a compensator to women's oppression, offering solace and redemption for being a person, and particularly a domestic servant to their husbands on Earth. Religion acts as a compensator for their exploitation as both workers and women, but Marxist feminists argue that this is merely at the level of false consciousness.

Some feminists argue that religion can have positive functions because not all women accept that religion is oppressive, for example in some religions like in ancient Greece, in Hinduism and in Modern New Age religions, (for example, the pagan witchcraft-based Wicca), there are female goddesses. However, these goddesses have mainly been replaced by monotheistic (single god) religions such as Judaism, Christianity and Islam. For example, Badawi argues that some aspects of Islam are positive, for example, women keep their own name, and so their own identity, when they get married.

> **KEY SOCIOLOGIST**
> **Mary Daly** (1928–2010) suggests that Christianity is an ideological force that spreads a 'patriarchal myth'. Daly argues that the Church is a powerful and ideological force which perpetuates the view of women being passive and obedient.

Evaluation of feminist theories of religion

Woodhead (2002) is critical of those feminists who equate religion with patriarchy and the oppression of women. While she accepts that some traditional religions are patriarchal, she also believes that there are 'religious forms of feminism' (ways in which women use religion to gain greater freedom and respect).

Women also use religion to gain status and respect for their roles within the home and the family, for example evangelicals believe that men should respect women. In addition women use church-based activities such as Bible study groups to share their experiences and to find support.

Postmodernist theory of religion

Postmodernists think that the classical perspectives and their views on religion are out of date. Many were from a long time ago; for example, Marxism in the 1800s and society has changed a great deal since then. Postmodernists such as Lyotard say that religion is becoming very personal to the individual due to all the complexities in our society. We cannot generalise it as one thing as there are too many explanations for it. Postmodernists generally agree that society is changing and with it religion. Our beliefs are not spiritual and mystical anymore so we need to adapt to this. The postmodernists also think that religion is becoming increasingly influenced by science. This is what has led to the development of new religious movements and new age movements (see later in this chapter). This increase in science is also affecting individuals because they must ensure that they can balance both their view of religion and their view of science to fit in with their understanding of society.

Foucault, another postmodernist, argued that religion is one of the metanarratives that are breaking down, leading to the destruction of what sociologists Durkheim, Marx and Firestone see as society. The postmodernists also say that as our society is so diverse religion cannot be a conservative force or a force for social change. We need to accept that there are many religions from which people pick and choose what they want in order to create their identities.

Evaluation of Postmodernist theory

Postmodernism is a sceptical explanation, it discriminates all the other theories and while saying we don't need a theory it is itself seeming to become one. Postmodernists do not recognise ideas such as the functions religion gives us, how it is ideological and how it uses different institutions to hold control over us. Therefore postmodernism doesn't see religion's role as very important – we can use it as part of our identity if we want to, but it is not necessary.

Interpretivist theories of religion

For interpretivists, belief systems help us as individuals to make sense of the things we experience in our daily lives (see pages 125–30 for more on interpretivists' theory of religion and page 134 for more on the Weberian view).

Check your understanding

1. Why is it difficult to define religion?
2. What are the main characteristics of science?
3. Explain how science is ideology.
4. What is difference between religion and science?
5. How does religion legitimise the power of the ruling class?
6. List all of the criticisms of functionalists' theory of religion.
7. How does religion encourage women to be passive and tolerant of their inferior position according to feminist theory?

Practice question

Read Item A below and answer the question that follows.

Item A

Both science and religion are belief systems that involve sets of knowledge-claims: that is, statements that claim to offer explanations of why things are as they are. For example, science uses concepts such as germs to explain why people fall ill from infectious diseases, while some religions use ideas such as the will of God to explain human illness and suffering.

Assess the view that science has replaced religion as the main ideological influence in society today. [20 marks]

Read Item B below and answer the question that follows.

Item B

Sociologists disagree about the role of religion in society. Functionalists, for example, see religion mainly as a positive force. However, Marxists see religion as a tool of capitalism. They argue that it acts to justify inequality, helping to keep the poor satisfied by giving them hope of better times to come and preventing social unrest and revolution.

Assess the contribution of Marxist theories to our understanding of the role and functions of religion in the world today. [20 marks]

Section 2: The relationship between social change and social stability, and religious beliefs, practices and organisations

This section will explore the following debates:
- What is the relationship between social change and social stability, and religious beliefs, practices and organisations?
- Does religion cause stability or conflict?
- What are sociological views on religion as a conservative force and, as a force for social change, for stability or conflict?

GETTING YOU STARTED

Figure 3.10 The 7/7 London bombings

Christian Dominionism is a contemporary theocratic ideology, primarily in the USA, that is based on a fundamentalist view of Christianity. The ideology is totalitarian in that it seeks to have every aspect of human life (government, education, culture and relationships) subject to conservative biblical principles.

Though the prevailing religion in the USA is Christianity, fundamentalists represent a relatively small proportion of the American public. However, proponents of the ideology are organised and focused. The Republican party is largely composed of supporters, making Christian conservatives highly influential in the political arena.

Adapted from Monnier (2010)

Questions
1. What is totalitarian ideology?
2. Why are they called fundamentalist Christians?
3. How do Christian Dominionists want to change US society?

Religion and conflict

Sociologists face a major challenge when they try to make sense of the role that religion plays in modern societies. The risk of serious conflict is higher in parts of the world where deep religious divisions coincide with strong political and social divisions. In many cases the social basis for the divisions is ethnicity, tribalism or 'race'. For example, outright warfare has occurred between Muslims in the north of Sudan and Christians in the south. Nigeria has also suffered a split between the Muslim north and the Christian south. The tensions between the Orthodox Christians of Serbia and religious minorities contributed to the collapse of the former Yugoslavian state. The virtual war between the state of Israel and the Palestinians owes much, but not everything, to conflicts between Jews and Muslims. Meanwhile, the hostility that has been simmering between Hindus and Muslims since 1974 has erupted into violent conflict in recent years. Finally, the long history of conflict between Protestants and Catholics in Northern Ireland has its roots in ethnic and political divisions as well as in religious differences (McGuire 2002).

Some aspects of all these conflicts confirm the ideas about the capacity of religion to legitimate and to challenge political, social and economic power structures. Religion is no longer at the root of the most serious conflicts in advanced industrial societies but can still generate tension and divisions. However, it would be wrong to conclude that religion is invariably associated with conflict. There is ample evidence of successful attempts to promote inter-faith dialogue and multi-faith activities in the public realm. Religious differences recede into the background on occasions of public grief.

Diversity of religions, indifference to religion, and individualised forms of religious belief and practice are characteristic of many societies today. As a result, religion is a rarely a source of complete consensus or outright conflict. It remains central to the collective identity of some communities; and it still has the capacity to provoke conflict and to attract hostility on occasion.

Religion and conflict in the UK

1. Values arising from religious sources are among factors motivating the activists in a range of moral protests against abortion, nuclear arms, threats to rural life and so on. Some religious organisations help to mobilise the protests and to co-ordinate campaigns.
2. Religion itself is at the centre of the conflicts that have been raging for decades over controversial religious movements such as Scientology. Relatives and friends of people who joined Scientology make allegations about 'brainwashing', financial deception and break-up of the families. Anticult groups try to keep stories about cult controversies in the mass media and on the political agenda.
3. The potential for conflict is ever present when religious and ethnic minorities assert the right and the necessity to do things that break the law or offend against majority public opinion. This happens when minorities argue that their religious obligations require them, for example, to slaughter animals in particular ways, to impose strict discipline on young people, to wear certain clothing or hairstyles, to smoke marijuana or to avoid the use of computers. These conflicts can become especially intense in public institutions such as schools, prisons and military establishments, where the regulations require uniformity of conduct.

Whether religion reacts to or creates social change is a big debate in the sociology of religion. Contemporary research acknowledges that religion can be both change-promoting and change-inhibiting. The focus of research now is exploring the conditions in which religion promotes and/or inhibits change. (See also the discussion of cultural defence on page 164.)

2.1 Religion as a conservative force

Explore the extent to which religion acts as a source of conflict or consensus in society and you have to provide several useful empirical examples of each argument.

Sociologists disagree about the relationship between religion and social change. For instance, some Marxists, feminists and functionalists argue, in different ways, that religion acts as a force to prevent change, while Max Weber put forward the view that under certain circumstances religion could actively lead to change in society.

Marxist and functionalist theories entirely reject the fact that religion can bring about change in society.

The Marxist view

Traditionally, Marxists see religion as a diversionary institution that promotes false consciousness. Marx saw religion as maintaining the status quo in the interests of the ruling class rather than of society as a whole. According to Marx religious ideas mirrored the deceptiveness of capitalism and, consequently, prevented the working classes from seeing that their problems would be solved only when alienation and exploitation were abolished. The abolition of religion was a necessary precondition for the success of social and political revolution.

Religion gave the impression that the privileges of dominant classes were divinely ordained, that is God's will. The oppressed accepted this philosophically as they believed there was nothing that they could do about it. Marx acknowledged that religion offered consolation and hope to the oppressed, emphasising the existence of an afterlife of eternal bliss – giving the oppressed something to look forward to. But he denied that it could ever lead to real emancipation. Religion made the present more bearable as it gave hope of supernatural intervention in the future when the problems on Earth would be sorted out by God. Religion encourages the oppressed to wait for this deliverance in death instead of rebelling and overturning the system in the present.

Religion sometimes offers hope of supernatural intervention to solve problems on Earth. For example, the Jehovah's Witnesses believe that survivors of the battle of Armageddon between God and Satan will form a new paradise on Earth where they will live forever ruled by a heavenly government. This promise for the future, found in many of the world's religions, can encourage people to accept their position and not act to change society.

The growth of fundamentalism challenges the Marxist position. Fundamentalism is about traditions and keeping constant values, but implementing fundamentalist views can cause radical change, for instance, implementing a fundamental return to the traditional values of holy texts. For example, Islamic fundamentalists challenge Western values and seek to reverse changes that have happened in Islamic states. Sometimes fundamentalists are prepared to engage in extreme action, such as global terrorism, to cause or further such a return to traditional values.

The functionalist view

Functionalists believe that religion is a conservative force, acting to bring society closer together through social integration of norms and values (see page 123). Functionalists see religion as a conservative force, helping individuals to realise the 'collective conscience' and a 'we're all in this together' mentality. Functionalists argue that this way of thinking deters people from going against the norm – a conservative force.

Malinowski argues that religion supports society through times of life crisis: religion supports, comforts and helps people cope during times of crisis or change, such as death or puberty, by associating rituals with these events. These rituals provide a framework for behaviour at these times, which helps people cope, and, in turn, helps prevent radical change. A modern example of this would be the 7/7 terrorist attack in London.

Despite being constitutionally outlawed in the 1950s, the caste system in India remains one of the best examples of religion as a conservative force. The caste system is fully supported by the Hindu religion. Another very obvious example is the medieval European monarchs. Their right to rule was said to be their divine right. Their right to be the rulers was believed by the people of those times to be God-given. They had all the power and there was no one who could challenge them or any decision made by them.

Different perspectives

A number of feminists have seen religion as a conservative force. Where Marxists have seen religion as maintaining the power of the ruling class, feminists have seen it as maintaining patriarchy – the domination of women by men. For example, many religions don't allow female religious leaders and the many religions endorse the idea that women should marry and be solely caregivers; this shows a prevailing conservatism, which wishes that the role of women should be subservient. Also religious laws and customs may give women fewer rights than men, for example in access to divorce, how many spouses they may marry, decision-making, dress codes etc.

Religious influences on cultural norms may also lead to unequal treatment, such as genital mutilation or punishments for sexual transgressions. Many religions legitimate and regulate women's traditional domestic and reproductive role. For example, the Catholic Church takes a dim view of abortion and artificial contraception. Woodhead (2002) argues that the exclusion of women from the Catholic priesthood is evidence of the Church's deep unease about the emancipation of women generally. (See more on gender and religiosity on page 152.)

2.2 Religion as a force for social change

The Weberian view

Max Weber (1864–1920) argues that religion can shape economic systems. Weber's view was that religion can act as a powerful force for change and revolution, especially when associated with a charismatic leader and ethical prophecy. In his work on Calvinism he argues that Protestant ethics revolutionised economic activity from the seventeenth century onwards. Weber's insights into the potential of religious beliefs and organisations to drive social change as well as to approve existing inequalities of wealth, power and status are still applicable to many aspects of religion today.

> **STUDY TIP**
> When constructing arguments for or against religion as a conservative force include arguments from the relationship between different social groups and religious organisations, beliefs and practices from pages 150–157.

Weber argued that the Protestant branch of Calvinism encouraged the development of capitalism through their belief in **predestination** and the **Protestant work ethic**. The uncertainty of predestination led people to look for signs of elevation such as wealth – encouraging the poor to work harder and the rich to constantly reinvest their profits. The Protestant work ethic encouraged a hard-working and God-fearing character creating a docile proletariat.

According to Weber, Calvinists were faced with a dilemma – were they one of God's chosen, 'the elect'? Were they going to heaven or hell? They could never know, but they believed that living an exemplary life in their calling, working hard, being successful and making money, was a sign that they were one of the chosen. The same self-discipline which drove Calvinists to work hard also required them to live very simply, abstaining from life's 'pleasures'. Rather than spending it, profit is reinvested to make more profit. A single-minded emphasis on being successful combined with living frugally was a religious duty. Calvinists' lives were given meaning through the pursuit of entry into heaven which they sought through work and the continued attainment of profit. According to Weber, this single-mindedness is at the heart of capitalism – the search for profit and forever renewed profit. The combination of Calvinism's doctrine of predestination and the spiritualism of work were the perfect complement to capitalism and consequently encouraged its rapid expansion.

Weber's key ideas:

- Religion provides meaning to help people make sense of the world.
- Religion can lead to social change if there are the right beliefs and the right economic circumstances.
- Rationalisation: Religion as a belief system would be replaced by science which results in a disenchantment of the world.

Weber was interested in the origins of capitalism and wanted to know why the economic system of capitalism had developed in Western Europe but not elsewhere. He carried out a detailed, comparative study of major religious belief systems including Confucianism in China, Hinduism in India and Calvinism in Europe.

For Weber, capitalism required both the right economic conditions and the right values. It needed natural resources, a money economy, a legal system, relevant technology and so on, but above all a set of values which emphasised the pursuit of profit for its own sake. While China and India may have had the right economic conditions for capitalism, they did not have the necessary values. For Weber these values were to be found in Western Europe and especially among Calvinists.

Roland Robertson challenges Weber's work, arguing that many of the beliefs that Weber attributed to Calvinists were shared by other religions, including even Roman Catholics. In the eighteenth and early nineteenth centuries British evangelicals were responsible for a vast amount of social reforms. They ended child labour in factories and mines, stopped young boys being chimneysweepers, restricted the length of the working day, ended slavery and founded schools and public libraries.

The Marxist Karl Kautsky (1982) also mounted a converse argument – that capitalism pre-dates Calvinism and even encouraged its growth in order to justify and legitimatise the exploitation of the proletariat by the capitalist class.

> **KEY SOCIOLOGIST**
>
> **Antonio Gramsci** (1970) argued that religion can empowerment the proletariat. For example, the Roman Catholic Church supported Polish trade unions against the Soviet Union-backed communist government in the 1980s (see page 137). This challenges the traditional Marxist view that religions inevitably support the dominant groups in society. Although the economic liberation of Poland from state-controlled communism would therefore mean that the Catholic Church would become free too.

The neo-Marxist view

Several neo-Marxists distance themselves from the traditional Marxist view (see page 125). Rather than seeing religion as opium for the masses, they argue that religion can act to support and reflect the interests of the marginalised and deprived. Neo-Marxists use the concept of relative autonomy to refer to the apparent independence of the ruling class from cultural institutions like the media and religion. They argue that this enables religion, under certain circumstances, to promote social change. Neo-Marxists also use the idea of relative autonomy to explain why some religious groups seem to be more engaged in the promotion of change than others.

According to the neo-Marxist Otto Maduro, religion can be a force for change – it can undermine stability and challenge power. It can be a revolutionary force, used to support the proletariat to challenge the ruling class. Maduro developed the concept of **liberation theology** to describe the mixture of Marxist ideology and Christianity that occurred in many Latin American countries in the 1950s and 1960s. This view proposes that the poor take control of their situation and accept responsibility for the end of their poverty. Local Roman Catholic priests condemned the poverty and inequality that characterised so many countries and advocated peasant uprisings to eradicate this impoverishment.

In this sense, liberation theology adopts an essentially Marxist approach, but differs by being a belief system that promotes rather than inhibits change. Liberation theology, by trying to empower peasants to transform their circumstances, illustrates the potential for religious institutions' ideas to raise consciousness. It also shows that religion can take the side of the marginalised and the oppressed rather than reflect **ruling-class ideology**.

Despite local encouragement from priests, the Roman Catholic Church officially opposed liberation theology. The actions of the Church in this instance reinforce the traditional Marxist position.

> **KEY SOCIOLOGIST**
>
> **Meredith McGuire** (2008) identifies that where religious beliefs are central to the culture of society, they can be used to justify or legitimate demands for either stability or change. She also says that if religious institutions are closely integrated with other parts of the social structure – for example, the political and economic systems – they have greater power to produce stability or change.

IN THE NEWS

Irish vote yes to gay marriages

Ireland has voted by an overwhelming majority to legalise same-sex marriage, becoming the first country in the world to approve gay marriage by popular vote. Official figures show that over 1.2 million people backed an amendment to the constitution - some 62 per cent of the Republic's electorate. The vote represented the highest turn-out at a referendum vote in Ireland in over 20 years.

The Yes vote is a strong indicator of movement towards a more liberal and secular society. While the UK made gay sex legal in 1967, homosexuality was not decriminalised in predominantly Catholic Ireland until 1993.

Adapted from Gillman and Mullin (2015)

Sociologists identified many instances in history when social change and even revolution have been directed by religious beliefs. According to Nelson (1986) in certain times or places religion can either be a conservative force or revolutionary force. Here are three examples which demonstrate when religion has promoted change, or undermined a society's stability. These examples show how authority was undermined and a change was brought in:

- opposition to communism by the Catholic Church in Poland
- Churches played an important role in the civil rights movement in America in the 1960s, for example, Reverend Martin Luther King
- Taliban and Afghanistan.

Examples of religion supporting and creating social change

Catholic Church and communism

The state-communist country of Poland in the 1980s was particularly undermined by the support the Catholic Church gave to the trade union Solidarity, which was organising protests and strikes in order to oppose the communist government. It has been suggested that the degree of support offered by the Catholic Church stemmed from its oppression under the communist regime: the economic liberation of Poland from state-controlled communism would also free the Catholic Church from state controls.

Figure 3.11 Pope John Paul II

Reverend Martin Luther King and civil rights

In the black civil rights movement in the USA in the 1950s and 1960s, clergy and the churches provided an organisational focus. In particular, the Reverend Martin Luther King became a charismatic leader. His 'I have a dream' speech was to be a great motivator to ordinary people, as was his assassination. Protests led by the Reverend Martin Luther King influenced the government to pass civil rights laws which banned segregation on the basis of skin colour. Geoffrey Nelson (1986) argues that an example such as this indicates how religion can 'spearhead resistance and revolution'.

Afghanistan and Taliban

Religion can act as a form of resistance to the powerful, and as an agent of social change, and not simply as a conservative force. Islam, particularly Islamic fundamentalism, is often a vehicle for resisting the global influence of Western cultural imperialism, fighting the Americanisation of the world's culture, and resisting the dominance of Western corporations in the world economy.

Not all social change is necessarily progressive. The Taliban regime in Afghanistan during the 1990s set up possibly the most extreme form of religious regime ever witnessed, based on an extremely harsh interpretation of the Koran. Women were forced to dress themselves head to foot in traditional dress to hide their identity, men were forced to grow beards, children were forbidden to fly kites, all music was banned, and people were forbidden to own any pictorial representation of any living being. Harsh punishments such as amputation for theft, beatings for not wearing traditional dress, and executions for adultery were common. Girls were forbidden from receiving any education after the age of eight, and all women were excluded from employment, even widows.

Figure 3.12 Martin Luther King

Only Afghanistan, under the control of the Taliban, has come close to becoming another Islamic theocracy. A more common pattern, repeated in other predominantly Muslim countries such as Egypt, Pakistan, Bangladesh and Indonesia, is for some political parties and movements to identify themselves closely with Islamic values and policies. This creates only partial consensus, however, because other political parties resist the growth of so-called Muslim fundamentalism.

Examples of religion causing conflict and instability might include:

- **Conflicts within the same religion.** For example, Northern Ireland is a very religious place, but divided by two communities (Protestant and Catholic Christians) stubbornly intolerant and distrustful of the other. Far from integrating the people of Northern Ireland, religion serves to promote conflict, intolerance and violence between the communities. This is repeated in examples across the globe and over time such as disputes in the Anglican Church over homosexuality, and between Sunni and Shia Muslims in Iraq.
- **Conflicts between religions.** In the Indian subcontinent, warfare between Muslims and Hindus was in part responsible for the division of a once united India into two separate countries, India and Pakistan. In the 1980s and 1990s, these divisions were added to by conflicts between Hindus and Sikhs. In the 1990s, the former Yugoslavia disintegrated into warring factions of Serbs, Croats and Bosnians, often aligned on religious grounds. In contemporary Britain, there are tensions within the Muslim community, and internationally there are links between terrorism in the predominantly Christian West and Islamic fundamentalism.

Check your understanding

1. In what way is religion a conservative force according to Marxists?
2. Is religion change-inhibiting or change-promoting?
3. Does religion act as a conservative force or a force for social change?
4. How did Protestant ethics caused capitalism according to Weber?
5. In what way and under what conditions does religion promote rather than inhibit change?
6. What is liberation theology?
7. Give three examples of religion as a force of change.

Practice questions

1. Outline and explain two criticisms of the view that religion always acts as conservative force. [10 marks]
2. Assess the view that the main function of religious belief is to promote social stability. [20 marks]

Item A

While both functionalism and traditional Marxism see religion as functioning to inhibit social change, functionalists are essentially positive about this role of religion whereas with traditional Marxists the emphasis is on the negative aspects of religion. Although functionalists view religion as essentially conservative, this is justified as it promotes social integration and cohesion. In contrast, traditional Marxists see religion inhibiting change as a means of social control for the exploiters, serving to delude the exploited through the socialisation of false consciousness.

Using material from Item A and elsewhere, assess the view that religion is a force for social change. [10 marks]

Item B

Many sociologists argue that religious beliefs and organisations act as conservative forces and barriers to social change. For example, religious doctrines such as the Hindu belief in reincarnation or Christian teachings on the family have given religious justification to existing social structures. Similarly, it is argued that religious organisations such as churches are often extremely wealthy and closely linked to elite groups and power structures.

Applying material from Item B and your knowledge, evaluate the view that religious beliefs and organisations are barriers to social change. [20 marks]

Section 3: Religious organisations

This section will explore the following debates:
- What are religious organisations, including cults, sects, denominations, churches and new age movements.
- What are religious organisations?
- What are new religious movements and new age movements?
- What is their relationship to religious and spiritual belief and practice?

GETTING YOU STARTED

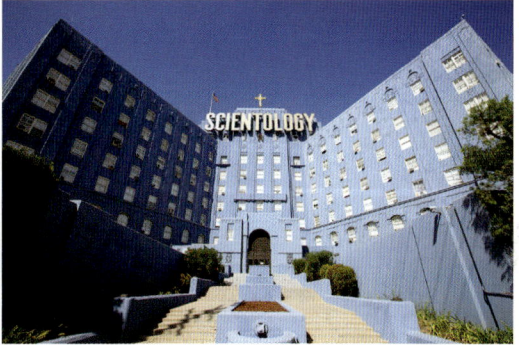

Figure 3.13 Clockwise from top left: A church (St Peter's Cathedral, Vatican City), a sect (Scientology), a cult (UFOland) and a denomination (Baptist Christianity)

3.1 What are the different types of religious organisations?

Know the differences between different types of organisations, why different religious organisations appeal to different social groups, how influential different organisations are, and the changing shape and development of new types of religious movements.

There have been a number of attempts to categorise the different types of religious organisations, but no system fits perfectly the enormous variety of organisations that have existed throughout the world. Nevertheless, it is possible broadly to distinguish some main types of religious organisations. Traditional religious organisations have faced many challenges over the past 30 years.

Questions

1. What are similarities and differences between the different religious organisations above?
2. What are religious organisations? List as many as you can.
3. How do people practise their religion?

In the past, their influence in society was considerable and they were seen as the mainstream spiritual movements. These organisations also had substantial political power and influence. However, changes in society over the past few decades have presented considerable challenges to the traditional roles and status of these organisations. Similarly, some sociologists argue that many people have reassessed their personal commitment to traditional religious organisations. As a result, such organisations have lost both support and membership.

Sociologists are interested in the different types of religious organisation – especially how they develop and who joins them. Sociologists have distinguished four religious organisations: **churches**, **sects**, **denominations** and **cults**.

Religious organisations differ in many ways, such as:

- organisational structure
- relationship to wider society
- size of membership
- the commitment required of their members
- the social class of their members
- attitude to other beliefs/religions.

Sociologists have used these differences to help them define the characteristics of religious organisations – using the concept of ideal type. These are 'pure types' – they may not actually exist in an ideal form, but they allow sociologists to categorise and compare religious organisations.

What is a cult?

Figure 3.14a The cult of Mary?

Figure 3.14b Scientology is not a mainstream religion but is it a cult?

A cult is a highly individualistic, loose-knit and usually small grouping around some shared theme and interest. Cults are usually led by practitioners or therapists who claim special knowledge. Cults do not demand strong commitment from their followers, who are often more like customers. There is some disagreement among sociologists on how to classify a cult, but most agree that it is a less coherent religious organisation which focuses on individual experience, bringing like-minded individuals together. Cults also have flexible membership.

The word cult usually includes the idea of devotion to someone or something. Most of the time, tabloid newspapers portray cults as evil organisations that destroys people's lives – 'sex cults' or 'suicide cults'. They represent them as dangerous, depraved organisations that have problems with sexual abuse, financial corruption or violence, and then list all the negative factors about them. Once it has been suggested that a non-mainstream religious movement is a cult, it becomes stigmatised as deviant and dangerous.

These characteristics, stereotypically attributed to cults, have been observed from time to time in mainstream religious organisations. For example, cases of financial exploitation, manipulation by unscrupulous clergy, sexual abuse, racism and cruelty towards children have been documented in some of the world's largest Christian denominations.

Examples of cults are Raelians, Company of Avalon, New Age ideas and movements (N.B. differentiating between cults and sects can sometimes be difficult. For example, some would classify Scientology as a cult rather than a sect).

What is a sect?

According to Anthony Giddens (2006) sects are often comparatively smaller, less well-organised groups of very committed believers. They usually aim at discovering and following 'the true way', and some withdraw from the surrounding society into communities of their own. Members of sects often regard the established churches as corrupt. They are usually set up in protest at what a church has become. Most sects have few or no officials, and all members are regarded as equal participants.

Cults resemble sects, but differ in some ways. They are the most loosely knit of religious organisations and are often short-lived. They are composed of individuals who reject what they see as the values of the outside world, and their focus is on individual spiritual experience. Like sects, cults often form around a charismatic leader. Usually sects would have no more than a few hundred members. Unlike churches, sects are hostile to wider society and they expect a high level of commitment. Their members are likely to be the poor and oppressed. Sects have one characteristic in common with churches – sects also believe they have a monopoly of the truth.

Many sects form around the inspirational leadership of an individual who has presence and a strong personality and can attract people to the movement. Young people are attracted to sects because the organisations are often new and different from the old, established religious movements and suit a modern lifestyle. Many join sects because they are looking for something, but leave the movement when they do not find what they were after.

Is a sect short-lived?

While churches tended to remain fundamentally unchanged for generations, sects tended to be short-lived. Niebuhr argued that sects would either evolve into a denomination or they would die out because members of sects tend to come from the margins of society, and on joining the sect, they usually lead frugal and ascetic (strict, self-denying) lives. As a result, their social status is likely to rise and their wealth increase. Their new situation no longer fits with their rejection of the wider society – and it brings greater public acceptance. As their contact with mainstream society grows, they modify their more unconventional beliefs. This process is accelerated by the next generation. They were not converted into the sect, they were merely born into it. As a result, they are unlikely to show the same enthusiasm and commitment as their parents. They are more likely to make compromises with, and be less critical of, the wider society.

The very success of a sect can lead to its downfall: the more its membership grows, the greater the need for full-time officials to manage the organisation. This, coupled with the toning down of its more 'extreme' views and the rise in its members' status, leads the sect down the road to a denomination, sitting comfortably within mainstream society. There is evidence that some sects follow the route outlined by Neibuhr. For example, the Quakers began as a sect in the seventeenth century. Within a few generations they had moderated their beliefs and entered mainstream society, so much so, that several Quaker families played a major part in the development of the British banking system – Barclays Bank, for example. Similarly, the Methodists began as a sect, moderated their strict beliefs and their criticisms of the wider society, and developed into a denomination. The early Methodism was viewed suspiciously and began as a small sect of the Church of England. Eventually it evolved from a sect into a denomination – partly a matter of size, but also one of social acceptance.

Death or denominations are not the only alternative outcomes for sects. Some survive as sects – they become 'established sects'. J. Milton Yinger (1946) says they often do so by isolating themselves from the outside world – for example, the Amish in Pennsylvania isolate themselves from the rest of American society. And the leaders of the sect keep outside influences at bay by banning their members from watching television and using computers.

Wilson argued that the crucial factor which determines whether a sect develops into a denomination or remains a sect is the way it answers the question, 'What shall we do to be saved?' The answer from some sects is to convert as many people as possible. These conversionist sects are likely to develop into denominations. They are typically found in the USA where they use large-scale revivalist meetings to generate conversions. They can become a denomination without compromising their primary aim – they can still save souls.

Other types of sect cannot maintain their basic position in a denominational form. The primary aim of adventist sects, such as Jehovah's Witnesses, is to prepare themselves for the Day of Judgement. To do this, they must separate themselves from today's sinful and corrupt society and await the second coming of Christ. Only membership of the sect will guarantee them a place in the new world order. Becoming a denomination would compromise their position – they need to be separate from society, not integrated with it.

> **KEY SOCIOLOGIST**
>
> **Bryan Wilson** explains the growth of sects as a response to social change: sects are a reaction to the uncertainties that derive when rapid social change challenges prevailing norms and values. It is suggested that the rapid growth of Methodism (originally a sect) in the nineteenth century can be explained as a response to the breakdown of the traditional ways of life when challenged by industrialisation.

In the twenty-first century people are only experimenting with their spirituality. Some sociologists argue that people today shop around and experiment with various religious and spiritual movements without ever committing themselves to long-term membership. Many people join sects to help them cope with personal crises in their lives – when the crisis is over they have no further need for the religious sect. Many sects impose strict discipline and rules on their members. Some find such rules hard to cope with and eventually leave the sect.

What is a church?

The term 'church' has a distinctly Christian connotation, and does not include the other great faiths such as Islam, Buddhism or Hinduism. In the USA the term 'church' generally refers to religious organisations we could call denominations in the UK. All churches claim a monopoly on the truth. Examples of churches include the Church of England, the Roman Catholic Church, and the Greek Orthodox Church.

The first person to identify the key features of a church and a sect was Ernst Troeltsch (1931). According to Troeltsch, churches are:

- large organisations, often with millions of members
- run by a hierarchy of professional priests
- well-established religious bodies
- mainstream organisations that represent the major world religions
- inclusive – they aim to include the whole of society
- often linked to the state.

Figure 3.15 St Mark's Church, Zagreb

Troeltsch characterised churches as possessing a formal hierarchical structure with a professional clergy. Churches tend to have a close relationship with social elites, although they claim to reflect consensus norms and values and are welcoming to society generally with few restrictions on membership. However, their worship tends to be restrained and makes much use of ritual, especially in what is termed 'high church', which adheres to orthodox traditions and values of the religion. These churches often have a limited appeal to the masses and are made up of the middle class and above.

Churches tend to have a clear relationship with the state and are characterised by their bureaucratic organisation. They also tend to have a close relationship with politics. For example, the 26 Church of England bishops sit in the House of Lords and consequently have an influence on legislation and the political process. In addition, the Archbishop of Canterbury periodically makes pronouncements on political, social and cultural issues as well as officiating at state occasions like royal weddings, state funerals, Remembrance Day and other ceremonial events. The Queen is Head of State as well as Supreme Governor of the Church of England.

England	Scotland	Wales
Church of England, (Anglican) Roman Catholic, Protestant (Methodist, Pentecostal, Baptist, etc), non Christian (Muslim, Hindu, Sikh, Jewish, Buddhist)	Church of Scotland (Presbyterian), Roman Catholic, Free Presbyterian, Anglican	Calvinist, Methodist, Anglican

Figure 3.16 Main religious groups in Great Britain

What is a denomination?

Figure 3.17 Pentecostalists praying in church

According to Becker (1950), a denomination is a sect that has cooled down to become an institutionalised body rather than a protest group. Sects become denominations due to the necessity of a bureaucratic, non-hierarchical structure once the charismatic leader dies. They no longer claim a monopoly of truth. Denominations are tolerant of wider society and require a low level of commitment. In a study of religion in the USA, H.R. Niebuhr (1929) was the first sociologist to differentiate clearly between denominations and churches. Denominations lie midway between churches and sects (an example is the Methodist church).

Denominations broadly accept society's values, but are not linked to the state. They may impose minor restrictions on members, such as forbidding alcohol, but they are not as demanding as sects. Unlike both church and sect, they are tolerant of other religious organisations and do not claim a monopoly of the truth. Denominations cover a wide range of organisations, from Jehovah's Witnesses to Methodists, from Pentecostalists to Baptists. Some of these organisations are classified as sects by some sociologists, but as denominations by others. Steve Bruce sees the lack of a claim to a monopoly on religious truth as the defining feature of denominations. However, the blurring of boundaries between religious organisations as they change has made the concept of the denomination no less problematic than that of the church.

3.2 What are new religious movements and new age movements?

While attendance at established churches has, on the whole, declined, new religious movements (NRMs) have experienced a growth in recent years particularly in Western societies. The growth of sects, cults and other movements has presented challenges to the traditional teachings and organisation of the established churches.

New religious movements (NRMs)

NRMs are mainly sects and cults; they have little in common with churches and denominations. Some do, however, draw on traditional religions like Christianity, Buddhism, Islam or Hinduism. The number of new religions and organisations has increased significantly after the 1960s. This led to new attempts to classify them. Many of them did not fit into the traditional church-denomination-sect-cult typography. Bruce Wallis categorises these new religious movements (NRMs) into three groups based on their relation to the outside world. Wallis describes three broad categories of NRMs – world-rejecting, world-accommodating and world-affirming.

Figures 3.18 (Anti-clockwise from top left) Moonies, Hare Krishnas and transcendental meditation

World-rejecting NRMs

World-rejecting NRMs are similar to sects and include examples such as the Moonies, the Children of God and the People's Temple. World-rejecting NRMs are, by definition, isolationist and highly critical of the increasingly secular nature of society. Their members live apart from society, often in tight-knit communities whose leaders exercise a lot of control over their members such as imposing a dress code and giving them new names. Conversion to such groups is often sudden, involving a complete break with previous lives and families. In the past, world-rejecting groups have been accused of abducting people against their will and engaging in 'brainwashing'. However, Eileen Barker found no evidence of this in her extensive study of the Moonies (1984). Occasionally such groups are associated with violence, such as the attack on innocent civilians on the Tokyo underground in 1995, or mass suicides, such as the Waco siege.

World-accommodating NRMs

World-accommodating NRMs are often breakaways from existing mainstream churches or denominations – an example being Neo-Pentecostalism which split from Catholicism. Such NRMs focus on restoring the spiritual purity of religion.

World-accommodating NRMs tend to be more conventional, with stronger links with mainstream religions. These groups are often characterised as 'charismatic' (meaning members have a 'sense of grace', rather than a charismatic leader) because the focus is on the personal religious experience of members. Their acts of worship tend to be enthusiastic and vital, offering a spiritual element, which many members believe is absent in traditional religious organisations. Members strive to cultivate a sense of inner divinity to compensate for and protect them from an increasingly secular world.

World-affirming NRMs

World-affirming NRMs often lack the conventional features of religion, such as collective worship. They claim to offer special knowledge or techniques that enable followers to unlock their own spiritual powers and achieve success or overcome problems. Examples include Scientology and Transcendental Meditation (TM). World-affirming NRMs tend to be the most respectable groups, sharing a positive view of society. They tend to be characterised by offering individuals ways to self-improvement, as well as unlocking hidden powers. They often appeal to people from the professions and management who see such groups as offering a means to relate to the world more effectively. The Church of Scientology, for example, includes many celebrities such as Tom Cruise.

What is the appeal of NRMs?

Sociologists say the appeal of NRMs lies in their offering – a means to self improvement, and a response to **relative deprivation**, rapid social change and the associated collapse of social norms. Joining a sect might help people cope by providing strict guidelines to live by. Many individuals seem to be attracted particularly to the world-affirming NRMs, which often claim to provide an individualised route to self-fulfilment, happiness and even monetary success. This is in marked contrast to traditional religions, which are often accused of suppressing individualism and current self-fulfilment by promising rewards in the afterlife rather than the present.

Heelas *et al.* found that most traditional religions were contracting in terms of size and membership, whereas many NRMs, which emphasise individualism, were prospering. Some sociologists see the continued attraction of NRMs as stemming from a search for meaning in an increasingly shallow, complex postmodern world. Traditional religious organisations are seen as too conservative or old-fashioned; they seem slow to change and adopt ideas that fit society today and are thus felt to be too conservative. In society today postmodernists might argue that people have faster, more fragmented lifestyles in which traditional church activities and belief no longer fit. Some sociologists, such as the postmodernist John Drane, see the spread of secularisation in contemporary society as a reflection of a spiritual void which mainstream churches and denominations seem either unwilling or unable to challenge.

People seeking answers to the problems of contemporary society may turn against both scientific and traditional religious organisations. Within postmodernism there is a distrust of experts and some individuals find the grand **metanarratives** from both science and established religion an inadequate response. Therefore, for many people, joining an NRM is a logical response.

The new age religion

According to Steve Bruce (1996) the new age spiritualities have emerged as consequences of the changing nature of contemporary Western societies, particularly the cultural changes that have allowed people the freedom to adopt lifestyles of their own choice. The term new age covers a range of beliefs and

> **KEY SOCIOLOGIST**
> **Colin Campbell** (1999) coined the term 'Easternisation' – the increasing impact of Eastern mysticism, principally from Hinduism and Buddhism, which includes belief in unity of humankind and nature. Holistic views of mind, body and the spirit stress the limits of science and rationality and challenge some of the core values of Western society, as in the Hare Krishna and Bhagwan Rajneesh movement.

> **KEY SOCIOLOGIST**
> **Wallis** has suggested that NRMs can offer young people status, particularly if they feel they are in a situation of '**status frustration**' with regard to their position within school or family. However, he conceded that the appeal of NRMs can be quite transitory and wears off as young people move into adulthood and status frustration disappears.

> **KEY SOCIOLOGIST**
> **Weber** suggested that the appeal of sects lay in their connection to marginalised or deprived groups in society. He argued that underprivileged people often develop a '**theodicy of disprivilege**', whereby religious beliefs and values are developed to justify their socio-economic status. Churches are rarely inclined to do this, instead ignoring the plight of the poor and remaining unattractive to the marginalised in society.

activities that have been widespread since the 1980s. New age movements (NAMs) appeal to the individualism valued in modern society, and they include belief in tarot, crystals, various forms of alternative medicine, meditation and magic. NAMs tend to be unstructured, and often exist independently of any organisation. Instead they tend to be centred more on sets of beliefs or activities associated with a range of lifestyle activities or therapies associated with the mind or body. These can often contain a spiritual element, but others may have nothing to do with a supernatural dimension.

NAMs are inclusive in that they stress unity within diversity. These movements have a strong sense of individualism and reject the model of all-embracing communities, both of which are essential features of life in the postmodern world. Unlike followers of traditional religions, in which worship is seen as part of one's obligation, the new agers are consumers, who are exercising their right to buy their own religiosity. The **religious pluralism** enables new age movements to bypass Christianity, Islam and Judaism, which have for centuries revered a single all-powerful God. A huge number of new spiritual beliefs and practices now exist alongside theologies that many currently regard as restricting and old-fashioned.

How do NAMs fit in the wider society?

New age spirituality became popular because, in some ways, it is very well suited to our circumstances.

- NAMs accommodate cultural diversity.

In our modern, diverse cultural landscape, to continue to insist that only one religion is right and the rest are all wrong generates endless arguments and conflict. The solution is to become relativist: if it works for you then it is your truth. There is no need to argue or fight. In that sense relativism gives us an effective solution to the problem of diversity. Individuals now 'shop' in a global cultural marketplace for competing means of salvation.

- NAM mirrors the modern stress on the right individual to choose.

We claim the right to decide what we believe. It is worth noting that the same individualism appears in the mainstream Christian churches: there is no longer the old belief that the priest or the minister knows the best.

- The new age empowers the consumer to pick and choose as they like from a **holistic milieu**.

In contrast to traditional religious participation, engagement with the broader holistic milieu is growing, appealing particularly to women and the professional middle class. The holistic milieu can be understood in terms of a postmodern society, the notion of a **spiritual shopper** and the **global cafeteria**. It is part of a spiritual revolution where people are not only seeking spirituality in areas other than traditional religion but are doing so in search of truths being interpreted as increasingly individualistic and personal rather than objective.

Most new agers don't become followers or members of anything. Some join mutual interest groups but many express interests by buying ideas and therapies. They pay for a residential week at the Findhorn Foundation (a spiritual community, learning centre and eco-village) in Scotland, for example. They learn meditation by attending few classes and buying a few books. Buying and selling spirituality does not offend new agers – they like it because it establishes who is in charge. The buyer decides what revelations to follow and what therapies to practise: we decide what ritual to practise and what belief to commit to in the same way we decide where to go on holiday, what appliance to buy for the house.

> **KEY SOCIOLOGIST**
>
> **Stark and Bainbridge** (1985) distinguish between sects and cults in different way. They regard both of them as being deviant in the view of society. However, in their definition, sects are breakaway groups from established religious movements, with radically new ideas – not schism from previous mainstream organisations.

- The new age interest in personal therapy perfectly mirrors the modern obsession with self-improvement and pampering.

The modern world obliges us to improve ourselves. If you are fat, you diet and exercise. If you can afford it, you can pay for liposuction and plastic surgery. If you don't like your personality, change it. You can get counselling, psychotherapy, join a self-help group, and take assertiveness training. Demands of the postmodern world are such that people tend to pick and mix and choose what is the most convenient to their lifestyles.

IN THE NEWS

Lessons in meditation?

Figure 3.19 Children meditating

Children in the UK could soon be trained in meditation techniques at school to help them cope with the pressures of life and improve their ability to learn.

Education Ministers are considering introducing lessons in supporting 'mindfulness' – a calm, accepting mental state achieved by focusing the mind on the present moment. Mindfulness techniques were developed by US doctors in the 1970s to reduce the effects of stress and are based on ancient traditions of Buddhist meditation.

Evidence suggests that mindfulness sessions help reduce stress, which in turn encourages positive attitudes and motivation. Thousands of mindfulness sessions are prescribed to NHS patients every year to help treat anxiety and depression.

Adapted from Clarke and Chorley (2014)

Different perspectives

A key feature of the postmodern world is that there is a loss of faith in 'metanarratives' such as science and traditional religions. These metanarratives have brought about war, genocide, environmental damage and global warming. This has disillusioned people and as such they turn towards NAMs for answers and a as a source of identity.

Sects and cults are both individualistic organisations and tend to be relatively small compared with churches and denominations. Postmodernists, like Jean Lyotard, challenge the existence and validity of metanarratives which churches and to some extent denominations traditionally peddled. So they are not necessarily surprised that they are in decline at a time when people can shop around for the individualism that sects and cults appear to offer. Postmodernists would see sects and cults as reflecting an increased choice and diversity for individuals as 'spiritual shoppers', increasingly disillusioned with mainstream churches and denominations. Postmodernists would see religions as increasingly competing against each other in a form of 'spiritual supermarket'.

> **STUDY TIP**
> Take note of how different sociologists have defined particular concepts.

Check your understanding

1. Using the following characteristics compare similarities and differences between sect, cult, church and denomination:
   a) Organisational structure
   b) Relationship to wider society
   c) Size of membership
   d) The commitment required of their members
   e) The social class of their members
   f) Attitude to other beliefs/religions.
2. What are three different NRMs?
3. Why do people join NRMs?
4. What is the difference between NRM and NAM?
5. Conduct research and explain the main practices of the following NAMs:
   a) astrology, belief in aliens, crop circles, Green Party, ley lines, magic, near-death experiences, organic foods, paganism, spirit guides, tai chi, witchcraft, yoga, aromatherapy, colour therapy, herbalism, hypnosis, Indian head massage, massage, Reiki, or palmistry, clairvoyance, Feng Shui.

Practice questions

1. Outline and explain two reasons why membership of sects may be short-lived. [10 marks]
2. Outline and explain two differences between church and cult. [10 marks]

Section 4: The relationship between different social groups and religious organisations, beliefs and practices

> **This section will explore the following debates:**
> - What is the relationship between different social groups and religious/spiritual organisations and movements, beliefs and practices?
> - What are patterns of religiosity among different social groups, such as social class, ethnicity, gender and age?
> - What are the reasons for these changes?

GETTING YOU STARTED

Jewish Hasidic sect in Stamford Hill 'bans' women from driving

Figure 3.20 Hasidic Jews are the strictest sect of their religion

The leaders of an Orthodox Jewish sect in north London have reportedly declared that women should not be allowed to drive in a letter sent out to the community. In a letter sent to parents, Belz rabbis said that having female drivers goes against 'the traditional rules of modesty in our camp' and against the norms of Chasidic institutions. The letter, which was signed by Belz educational leaders and endorsed by rabbis, also said children could be barred from their schools if their mothers drove them from August onwards.

According to the letter – which was signed by leaders from Belz educational institutions and endorsed by the group's rabbis – the leaders believe that driving a vehicle is a high pressured activity where their values may be compromised by exposure to selfishness, road-rage, bad language and other inappropriate behaviour.

They said that the Belzer Rebbe in Israel, Rabbi Yissachar Dov Rokeach, has advised them to introduce a policy of not allowing pupils to come to their schools if their mothers drive.

Dina Brawer, UK Ambassador of the Jewish Orthodox Feminist Alliance, said that the instinct behind such a harsh ban is one of power and control, of men over women. In this sense it is no different from the driving ban on women in Saudi Arabia.

Adapted from Saul (2015)

Questions

1. Why would women driving to school offend some Jewish groups?
2. What is the purpose to this driving ban?

4.1 How do age, gender, ethnicity and class affect religious beliefs and practices?

Be aware of the different social groups such as age, ethnicity, gender and class and how they relate to religious observance. You have to be aware that religious participation varies across the spectrum of ethnic groups and that with each group it may also vary according to social locations such as age, gender and social class.

Different social groups have different social and spiritual needs and use religion and religious organisations in very different ways. For some people religion is an important part of their lives. It can provide contact with others as well as participation in the local community. This section explores the relationship between different social groups and religious/spiritual organisations and movements, beliefs and practices.

Age and religiosity

Church attendance has been in rapid decline in recent decades, with young people less and less likely to be regular churchgoers. More generally young people in the UK tend not to hold traditional religious beliefs, and in studies such as the annual British Attitude Survey, more than half of them say that they regard themselves as not being religious. In general, people seem to develop a greater attachment to religion as they grow older. Belief in God is lowest among those under 34, and highest among those over age 55. Young people are not only less likely to participate in mainstream religious activity than older people; more than half of them say they don't regard themselves as religious at all. Under 15s have high participation rates as they are made to attend by parents, while over

65s are more likely to be sick/disabled and so unable to attend. Bruce argues that the age gap between churchgoers and non-churchgoers has widened in all Christian denominations with 30 per cent of churchgoers now over the age of 65.

The attachment of older people to religion is often explained by three main factors: disengagement, religious socialisation and ill health and death.

Disengagement	Religious socialisation	Ill health and death
Disengagement means that as people get older they become detached from the integrating mechanisms of society, such as participation in workplaces through paid employment. Older people may face a growing privatisation of their lives, with increasing social isolation as partners and friends die. Participation in religious organisations provides a form of social support in this situation, and a network of people to relate to.	Older people are more likely to have had greater emphasis placed on religion through the education system and socialisation in the family when they were younger. This may have laid foundations that thrive, as they grow older, as they rediscover a religiosity they may previously have ignored.	Older people tend to be faced with declining health, and they are more close to death. These are the very things that religion concerns itself with. The ageing process may therefore generate an engagement with religion for comfort, coping, meaning and support.

Table 3.2 Older people and religion

Young people and religiosity

Young people are undoubtedly less religious in terms of their expressed religious belief in surveys and their participation in the mainstream Christian religions. The explanations suggested below for the apparent lower religiosity and religious practice of young people may be because these are simply being expressed in new, private ways which are difficult to record in statistical surveys.

The mainstream religious organisations are very unattractive to most young people. In many cases, they find services to be boring, repetitive and old-fashioned, full of old people, and out of touch with the styles and attitudes of younger people. Controversial issues such as abortion, contraception, the ordination of women priests and bishops, gay rights, sex before marriage and so on seem bizarre to many young people, and alien to the values they hold.

Sociologists have identified some of the reasons why young people are less religious: secular spirituality, declining religious education and pragmatic reasons.

Secular spirituality	Declining religious education	Pragmatic reasons
Lynch suggests that, although young people may be diverted from religion as normally conceived, they may be finding religious feelings inspired in them by aspects of what is generally regarded as non-religious or secular life. Lynch suggests, then, that young people may not have lost all religiosity, but that it is simply finding new forms, many of which are associated more with the secular and non-religious world than with religion as it is presently understood by most people.	Church is increasingly unable to recruit young people by socialising them into religious thinking through such things as church Sunday schools or religious education. Sunday schools are in a state of decline. Christian Research says that a century ago over half of all children attended a Sunday school, but by 2000 this had reduced to just 1 in 25 children.	There are range of practical or pragmatic explanations for the decline of religious belief and commitment among the young. Leisure has become a much bigger part of life, and shops, clubs and pubs all open for very long hours, including Sundays. Young people have more demands on their time, and they may simply have more interesting and enjoyable things to do. It is also seen as not popular to be religious in many young peer groups, which exerts peer pressure not to be religious.

Table 3.3 Younger people and religion

KEY SOCIOLOGIST

Lynch (2008) suggests that young people may be turning away from conventional ideas of religion as there is now what Roof (2001) called an 'expanded spiritual marketplace'. This involves growing exposure and accessibility to a wide diversity of religious and spiritual ideas. These have opened up new avenues for exploring religion and spirituality.

RESEARCH IN FOCUS

Children's perspectives on believing and belonging

In July 2005 the National Children's Bureau published a report for the Joseph Rowntree Foundation, which detailed research on children's perspectives of 'believing without belonging'. The study was carried out by Greg Smith and a team from the University of East London, examined the views of more than 100 children aged between 9 and 11 years. The research into children's beliefs and practices took place in two schools in a city in the north of England and one school in an east London borough. The schools in the north were church primary schools serving multi-ethnic, multi-faith neighbourhoods, and the east London school was a local primary school in a culturally diverse part of the borough. Qualitative methods were used, including interviewing, classroom discussions and worksheet exercises; questionnaires and school-based ethnographic observation over an 18-month period.

The researchers found that school is often one of the few places where children from different religious and ethnic backgrounds meet on a regular basis. In school, friendships developed across and between religious and ethnic groups, whereas friendships outside school were more likely to be shaped by family circumstances and religious affiliation.

The children described their beliefs in terms of both social practice and teachings and morality and ethics. Researchers developed threefold typology to organise children's accounts of their experiences (religious identity, social practice and belief and spirituality). The children were identified as belonging to one of the five following groups: highly observant, observant, occasionally participating, implicit individual faith and not religious.

The researchers found that the amount of time spent on religion by the more devout and observant children affected their out of school relationships; they had less social interaction with children outside their particular religion than did less devout children.

Adapted from Smith (2005)

Questions

1. What are the main findings of the research?
2. How reliable are qualitative data in this research?
3. Are the schools in this research representative of the all young people in the UK?

Gender and religiosity

Statistical evidence shows that women tend to be more religious than men across most cultures globally. Social Trends (2008) showed 13 per cent of men and 15 per cent of women attended religious meetings or services once a week or more. It is suggested that women have greater interest in religion and they are more committed to participate because they have a stronger faith and a greater belief in life after death. Men tend to hide their emotions more and adopt a more rational, sceptical and questioning worldview, whereas religion requires faith. Finally, being religious is not particularly macho. Congregations across the UK tend to be made up of two-thirds women and one-third men. This is common across cultures, but the gap seems even wider in cultures where traditional values, such as with regard to abortion, cohabitation and working women have weakened.

Women are the biggest consumers of religion and they are more likely to have religious beliefs and practise their religion. This is true across all faiths and religious organisations including NRMs and NAMs. The exception is Islam where men show greater commitment and involvement.

There are many reasons why women appear to be more religious than men. It would seem that these are connected to their role, life expectancy and attitudes.

Longevity/life expectancy	Traditional roles	Nurturing role	Status frustration
Women live longer than men, and this means they are more likely to be widowed and living on their own as they grow older. Many women may turn to religion as an element of insurance for the afterlife, as well as seeing religious communities as a source of company and comfort.	Women tend to have a traditional role of carer or part-time worker, which gives them more time and opportunity for religious-related activities. Again this could be criticised as out of date, with more women becoming full-time workers or with Sunday retailing being introduced so that many women now work on Sundays.	Women's greater religiosity can be linked to their closer association with birth and death. Giving birth and dealing with the sick, disabled and dying within families make women more spiritual as they are more conscious of the vulnerability of human life.	Women are more likely than men to face social deprivation and marginality, and may experience more disillusionment and alienation from wider society. Status frustration may be experienced by some women, who lack personal fulfilment or status as a result of being confined to the home by the constraints of housework and childcare, or are in unsatisfying lower middle-class jobs, which are mainly done by women.

Table 3.4 Women and religion

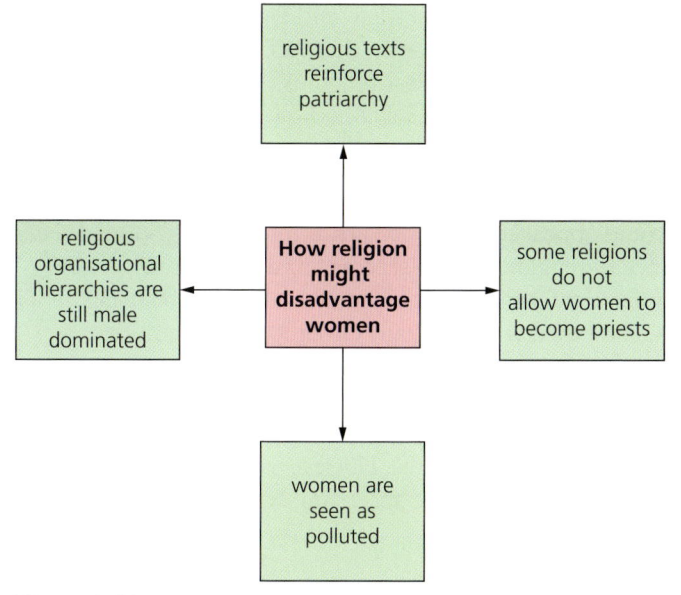

Figure 3.21 Reasons why women may be disadvantaged by religion today

Centre: How religion might disadvantage women
- religious texts reinforce patriarchy
- religious organisational hierarchies are still male dominated
- some religions do not allow women to become priests
- women are seen as polluted

Young people today may regard their religion, faith and beliefs as a private matter. They may not consider themselves to belong to a particular religion, or to possess any particular religious beliefs, even if they have some faith or spiritual principles. They may choose not to make public displays of their beliefs, to belong to religious organisations, or to admit to being a member of a religion in surveys. Grace Davie (1994) referred to this as 'believing without belonging'.

> **KEY SOCIOLOGIST**
>
> **Paul Heelas** found women were more attracted to NAMs and alternative spirituality. Women are more likely to engage with NAMs as they tend to believe more in some form of spirituality and engage far more with the 'holistic milieu' of activities associated with mind, body, spirit and healing such as alternative therapies.

> **KEY SOCIOLOGIST**
>
> **Grace Davie** (1994) claims that not only do more women than men attend Christian services but that women and men view God differently. Whereas men view their God in terms of power and control women view God in terms of love, comfort and forgiveness.

Different perspectives

Many feminists argue that religion can be seen as a mechanism of social control (see more page 127). Feminists view religions as patriarchal because in their hierarchy, clergy and ideology, officials tend to be male and religious organisations are male-dominated. The patriarchal structure in most religions (male mullahs, bishops, priests and rabbis) enforces the notion that women should remain in the home and not concentrate on professional careers in religion. Feminists argue that religious institutions and beliefs help to legitimise gender inequality.

> **KEY SOCIOLOGISTS**
>
> **Miller and Hoffman** (1995) suggest that men are less religious than women because they have a greater taste for risk — in this case the risk that they might not go to heaven. If women are more risk-averse than men, they are more likely to be religious as a safeguard against the possibility of eternal punishment.

Ethnicity and religiosity

An important element of the identity of minority ethnic groups in the UK is their religious faith. Following immigration from a variety of countries – mainly Pakistan, India, Bangladesh and the Caribbean in the 1950s and 1960s – Britain has become a pluralistic society, with a diversity of religious faiths and practices. Research has consistently shown that the minority ethnic groups in Britan – specifically African Caribbean, Bangladeshi, Indian and Pakistani – are more religious that the white ethnic majority. However, there are similarities between all groups in that younger people tend to be less religious than older people and, except in Muslim communities, women usually show more commitment to religion than men do.

One reason for greater levels of participation by ethnic minority groups could be socialisation. This would appear to be particularly strong among South Asian families, whose adherence to religion is often seen as an issue of family honour. Family structures are much tighter-knit in Asian communities, with strong extended families. This, combined with generally closer-knit communities, may result in pressure to conform to religious values and behaviour. There are therefore strong pressures from parents to be religious and to ensure that their children are seen as being religious. However, not all ethnic groups embrace religion and participate in it to the same degree. However, religious participation within ethnic groups may vary across the age spectrum, with youth participating less than their elders.

Why might religion be more important to ethnic minorities?

Many explanations focus on the idea that religion may perform different functions for different groups:

Cultural defence	Cultural transition	Social deprivation and marginality	Social and cultural identity
Religion may offer a source of support and provide a sense of identity in an uncertain or hostile world. It may provide a means of maintaining traditions and developing social solidarity and group cohesion.	Religion can ease the transition into a new culture. Religious organisations can help others to settle by providing very practical support. For many Muslim, Sikh and Hindu migrants religious organisations become a basis of support – religion was socially functional, it aided adjustment to a new society. Mosques, temples and churches became community centres when people moved into new areas.	Members of ethnic minorities are disproportionately among the poor and disadvantaged. Religion may provide an explanation for this but also provide a sense of hope and belonging which can restore pride. Black Muslims may provide an example as may Rastafarians with their belief that they are the lost tribe of Israel and are 'special'.	Religion in minority ethnic groups can provide individuals with many markers of identity, such as their customs, dress and food, and also rituals and festivals, such as Diwali (Hindus and Sikhs) or Ramadan and Al-Hijrah (the Muslim new year). By asserting an identity drawn from religious elements of their cultures, members can resist the denial of status and the devaluing of their own culture by racism.

Table 3.5 Religion and ethnic minorities

KEY SOCIOLOGIST
Modood et al. (1994) found that religion was important in the lives of minority ethnic communities as a source of socialisation, and as a means of maintaining traditional morality, such as conceptions of mutual responsibility, trust, and right and wrong. It also helped to cope with the worries and pressures in life, perhaps arising from the hostility and discrimination arising from racism in the wider society which many from minority ethnic groups encounter.

KEY SOCIOLOGIST
Butler (1995) conducted interviews with 18–30-year-old Muslim women in Bradford and Coventry and found out that young women had attachment to the religious values of their culture, and saw religion as important in shaping their identities but they also challenged some of the restrictions that traditional Asian Muslim culture imposed on them and wanted more choice and independence in their lives.

A growth of Islamic identity among the young may be seen as a response to Islamophobia. However, it should be noted that the religious values of young Muslims may also be a **hybrid** – while they may wear the veil and attend the mosque, they reject arranged marriages and other customs.

Different perspectives

Many sociologists have used a Weberian approach to explain how migrant interest in religion is connected to their marginalised position in society. In addition, from a Weberian point of view, Pentecostalism could be viewed as reinforcing the values of individualism, hard work, prudent saving and sexual morality, all of which contribute to the success of capitalism.

KEY SOCIOLOGIST
Ken Pryce (1979), in his classic study of the St Paul's area of Bristol, found that Pentecostal religion acted as a compensator for the poverty and oppression experienced by African Caribbeans. From a Marxist point of view, Pentecostalism could be interpreted as a diversionary institution – promoting false consciousness while giving purpose and meaning to the hardship and racism that minority ethnic groups experience under capitalist society.

> **RESEARCH IN FOCUS**
>
> ### What does the Census tell us about religion by ethnicity in 2011?
>
> - In 2011, England and Wales became more ethnically diverse with more people identifying with minority ethnic groups. Despite the White ethnic group decreasing in size, it was still the majority ethnic group that people identified with (86 per cent).
> - In 2011, over nine out of ten Christians in England and Wales were White (93 per cent) accounting for 30.8 million people. Within this group White British was the largest group (28.7 million people, 86 per cent). Over 1.6 million people (5 per cent) identified with Other White.
> - Muslims were more ethnically diverse. Two-thirds of Muslims (68 per cent) were from an Asian background, including Pakistani (38 per cent) and Bangladeshi (15 per cent). The proportion of Muslims reporting as Black/African/Caribbean/Black British (10 per cent) was similar to those reporting as Other ethnic group (11 per cent).
> - 93 per cent of people (13.1 million) with no religion were from a white background.
> - The majority of Hindus and Sikhs were from an Asian ethnic background (96 per cent and 87 per cent respectively). As with Muslims, Buddhists were also ethnically diverse.
> - In England and Wales, over nine in ten Christians (93 per cent) were White and nine in ten (89 per cent) were born in the UK, though the numbers have fallen since 2001.
> - Nearly four in ten Muslims (38 per cent) reported their ethnicity as Pakistani, a 371,000 increase (from 658,000 to over a million) since 2001. Nearly half of all Muslims were born in the UK.
> - The majority of people with no religion were White (93 per cent) and born in the UK (93 per cent) and these groups have increased since 2001.
>
> Adapted from data from the Office for National Statistics, licensed under the Open Government Licence v3.0

Questions

1. What are the most religious ethnic groups?
2. Which groups are the most ethnically diverse?
3. Which group forms are the majority of Christians?
4. Which majority groups are the least religious?

Social class and religiosity

The majority of the upper and middle classes show the most commitment to churches. This continues the long historical trend: in Victorian times the least religious social group in terms of religious practice was the urban working class. In contemporary times the situation is complex with some churches and denominations attracting more middle classes, others more working class. The Church of England, for example, attracts more middle classes, while Catholicism attracts more working class. While Methodism attracts more working class, Quakers attract more middle classes. More middle classes attend established religious institutions because, in the main, they tend to support and be integrated with wider society.

New age movements are overwhelmingly middle class. Steve Bruce argues that 'spiritual growth appeals mainly to those whose more pressing material needs have been satisfied. Unmarried mothers raising children on benefits tend to be too concerned with finding food, heat, etc. to be troubled by finding their inner lights and when they do look for release from their troubles they usually prefer the brighter outer lights of bars and nightclubs'. Bruce argues also that NAMs appeal specifically to 'university educated middle classes working in the "expressive professions": social workers, counsellors, actors, writers, artists, and others whose education/work cause them to have an articulate interest in human potential.'

Different perspectives

Marxists suggest that the ruling-class ideas and interests are reflected in religion. The working class are subdued into a state of false consciousness by making the true extent of their exploitation by the ruling class invisible. Religion is a form of social control keeping the rich rich and the poor poor. (See page 125.)

> **KEY SOCIOLOGIST**
>
> **Halevy** argued that the Methodist religion was pivotal in preventing working-class revolution in nineteenth-century Britain. He argued that working-class dissatisfaction with the establishment was instead expressed by deserting the Church of England which was seen as the party of the landed classes. Methodism attracted significant numbers of the working-class worshippers and Halevy claims that Methodism distracted them from their class grievances by encouraging them to see enlightenment in spirituality rather than revolution.

> **STUDY TIP**
>
> When writing about social groups and religiosity explore the range of issues relating to different social groups and religious belief and practice. Do not focus predominantly on one group. Make sure you use mainly empirical material.

Check your understanding

1. Why are young people less religious than older people?
2. Why are old people disengaged with society?
3. What are the main reasons that make ethnic minorities more religious?
4. What are the main findings of the 2011 Census in relation to ethnicity and religion?
5. What are the main criticisms of religion from the Marxist perspective?
6. What is cultural transition?

Practice questions

1. Outline and explain two reasons why older people seem to have a higher participation rate in religion than other social groups. [10 marks]
2. Outline and explain two reasons why women seem to have a higher participation rate in religion than men. [10 marks]
3. Assess the view that, for minority ethnic groups, the practice of religion and membership of religious groups is mainly a form of cultural defence. [20 marks]

Section 5: Religion in the modern world

> **This section will explore the following debates:**
> - Secularisation debate – are we still religious?
> - What impact has globalisation had on secularisation?

GETTING YOU STARTED

The 31st annual British Social Attitudes Survey (BSA) was conducted in 2013 and asked 'Which religion or denomination do you consider yourself as belonging to?'

The survey was published on the same day as David Cameron reiterated his claim that Britain is 'a Christian country'. The British Humanist Association (BHA) has pointed to the survey as showing this is not the case.

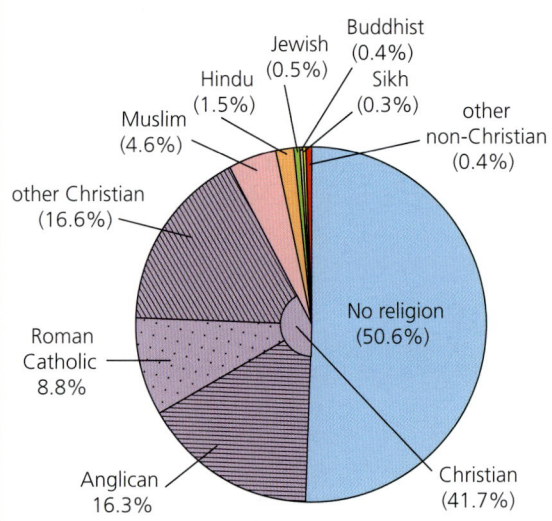

Figure 3.22 The results of the British Social Attitudes Survey (BSA) 2013

Adapted from British Humanist Association (2014)

Pie chart values: No religion (50.6%); Christian (41.7%) – Anglican 16.3%, Roman Catholic 8.8%, other Christian (16.6%); Muslim (4.6%); Hindu (1.5%); Jewish (0.5%); Buddhist (0.4%); Sikh (0.3%); other non-Christian (0.4%).

Questions

1. Is Britain still a Christian country?
2. Why does David Cameron claim that Britain is a Christian country?
3. How can we measure religiosity?
4. Why did 50 per cent of people declare that they are not religious?
5. Do we need religion?

5.1 Are we still religious?

When discussing secularisation you should be able to identify the key measures of secularisation using relevant concepts and evidence. Be aware that the secularisation debate depends on the definition of religion used (functional or substantive).

Assessing religiosity is difficult: the occasional head counts of worshippers can be misleading and surveys on belief lack validity meaning statistics are unreliable. And secularisation is one of the most complex of all sociological concepts. According to Bryan Wilson, secularisation is a 'process by which religious institutions, actions and consciousness lose their social significance'.

The secularisation thesis

Secularisation is an extremely contested concept. The secularisation thesis is supported by three factors:

- the decline in religious practice, specifically church attendance
- the institutional dominance of secular authorities over religious bodies
- the privatisation of religion – it is no longer part of the public sphere.

The evidence of decline in church attendance is not straightforward. If we look at religion more broadly and include Islam and Pentecostalism then there is evidence of growth in attendance globally. Even taking traditional European religions of Protestantism and Catholicism there is evidence of healthy church attendance in inner city areas in Britain. This is in part due to migrants from Poland and other Eastern European countries bringing vitality to declining UK congregations.

Some sociologists, such as Davie, have argued that church attendance is an unreliable guide to religious faith. She says the nature of religious membership and practice has changed and that belief has become a more private affair, in line with other aspects of society which have become more individualised and privatised. However, just because people choose not to engage in collective worship, it does not mean that they are not religious: they might worship their god at home.

In order to operationalise the concept of secularisation, sociologists of religion have looked at three significant areas.

Religious practice	Religious institutions	Individuation and belief
Refers to things people do to carry out their religious commitment, such as the extent to which they actively participate in religious worship, e.g. attending a mosque.	Refers to the extent to which religious institutions have maintained their social influence in wider society, and how far they are involved in the day-to-day running of society.	Refers to the influence of religion on people's beliefs and values, such as the importance of religion on their lives, whether they see themselves as a religious person, whether they believe in things like God, spirits, etc.

Table 3.6 Significant areas to consider in relation to secularisation

The evidene of secularisation mainly refers to Christian faith, but Britain is a **multi-faith society** where the minority population have increased their religious participation. As Britain's population has become more ethnically and culturally diverse the idea of established church has become outdated. To assume increasing secularisation is to dismiss the importance of other major faiths. In this way cultural and religious pluralism clouds debate about religious decline.

Steve Bruce (2001) argues that before very long, Christianity in Britain will decline past the point of no return, and that many denominations will become extinct by 2030. He suggests that Christianity has been in a state of decline for at least the last 150 years and definitely over the course of the last century. During the twentieth century, church attendance dropped from almost 30 per cent of the population to 10 per cent. In the same time the number of children attending Sunday schools fell from 55 per cent of the population to 4 per cent. Not only are those who attend religious services predominantly in older age groups but also there is little statistical evidence for any significant religiosity among the young who could one day replace them. According to Bruce, in the Middle Ages the Church was the dominant social institution in Europe. Bruce argues the decline of Christianity in the modern world is not a result of people becoming more rational and less superstitious. In today's society religion no longer provides education, welfare and social control. Nowadays the specialised agencies provide these services. Also modern societies based on nation state make local communities, in which religion once acted as social glue, disappear. The third factor is increasing rationalisation through science. The growing prestige of science undermines the status of religious explanations of life, the universe and everything.

Charles Glock and Rodney Stark (1999) argue opposite to Bruce by suggesting that religion is not in decline quite simply because it was never that popular anyway. Stark claims that in fact we are more religious than ever before. He strongly disagrees with Bruce that the Middle Ages was an age of faith in which religion was dominant and everyone believed in God and went to church. He suggests that the historical record shows widespread indifference to religion among the general population. Stark also criticises Bruce in claiming that religion is in decline in the modern world because it is, in fact, not only persisting but flourishing. In the USA, he states, church membership has not declined but trebled.

Grace Davie (1994) developed the thesis 'Believing without belonging' and argues that many of us may not belong to a religion but may still cling to religious beliefs. According to Davie the fact that religious participation and the power of religious institutions are in decline does not mean that personal religiosity is in decline also. She believes that great numbers of individuals are believers without necessarily being belongers. This means people may have given up on religious institutions but they have not abandoned religious belief completely.

Davie argued that limited pluralism was the best way to describe the religious life of Britain. This resulted from the multi-faith nature of British society and increasing number of Eastern Europeans settling in the UK who are committed Catholics, for example young Polish migrants.

The 'disenchantment of the world'

Weber (1905) called the process of secularisation the 'disenchantment of the world'. More recently, Bruce (2002) argued that the decline of religious influence could be linked to the growth of technology. Not all sociologists agree with these views. For example, Norris and Inglehart (2004) link religiosity to survival and to the need for a feeling of security. Other sociologists argue that religion is not declining but changing. For example, some postmodernists hold the view that people no longer need to belong to or have a lifelong commitment to a religious organisation. Instead, they pick and mix, or adapt various aspects of different religions to suit their own personal lifestyles.

Weber, Durkheim and Marx argue that decline in religion was an inevitable part of the process of modernisation. They saw the raise of rationality, scientific theories and technology as the necessary challenge to religious beliefs. However, in many societies in the world today, religious institutions are still extremely powerful and have a considerable number of followers.

KEY SOCIOLOGIST

Casanova (1994) has challenged the notion of disengagement. He maintains that religion still plays an important political role especially in such conflicts as those between Protestants and Catholics in Northern Ireland, and Sunni and Shi'ite Muslims in Iraq and Syria. He argues that rather than religion withdrawing into the private realm, in some countries it is becoming the more public and political.

Figure 3.23 A 2011 Census billboard on religious beliefs

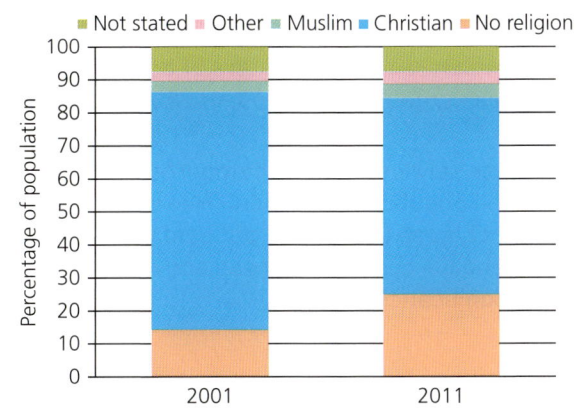

Figure 3.24 Changing picture of religious affiliation over the last decade in England and Wales

Different perspectives

Postmodernism does not claim that religion is good or bad but simply seeks to explore some of the characteristics of society today, and hence, religion. In today's postmodern world people 'pick and mix' their religion making hybrids, thus there are many different forms and no 'metanarrative'. According to Jean-Francois Lyotard (1984) in the postmodern society there is a loss of faith in the big stories or grand explanations provided by science, religion and politics. Their authority and certainty have been undermined; their claim to the truth has been questioned.

> **KEY SOCIOLOGIST**
>
> **Lyon** (2000) claims that we have become spiritual shoppers as religion has relocated to the sphere of consumption. Lyon uses the example of a Christian rally held at Disneyland in California to show how there has been a blurring of boundaries between different aspects of social life. Popular culture has merged with religion, maybe giving people a less traditional, more familiar environment in which to explore religion.

> **CONTEMPORARY APPLICATION**
>
> **New atheism** is a new cultural movement associated with Richard Dawkins, Sam Harris, Daniel Dennett and Christopher Hitchens. New atheists make substantial use of the natural sciences in both their criticisms of theistic belief and in their proposed explanations of its origin and evolution. They believe empirical science is the only basis for genuine knowledge of the world, and they insist that a belief can be justified only if it is based on adequate evidence.

> **STUDY TIP**
>
> Start with a specific definition of religion. An inclusivist interpretation is unlikely to find secularisation is occurring. An exclusivist definition works from a Eurocentric, mainly Christian focused position of modernity.

RESEARCH IN FOCUS

The Kendal Project – Testing the Spiritual Revolution Thesis

the Kendal project

Figure 3.25 The company logo

The Kendal Project 2003, led by Paul Heelas, set out to test the 'Spiritual Revolution Thesis' which claims that there is a 'spiritual revolution' occurring, resulting in significant growth in new age spirituality.

The researchers identified two possible trends:
- Secularisation theorists argue that there is a decline in traditional Christianity, with a god who tells people how to live their lives.
- Sacralisation theorists argue that there is a growth in new age practices such as yoga and tai chi.

Gathering data – methodology

Kendal is a regional centre of approximately 28,000 people south east of the Lake District in northwest England. It was small enough to be able to investigate thoroughly but large enough to have a range of traditional religions and new age spiritualities.

The research compared the congregational domain (where people come together in designated places of worship to engage with religious traditions) and the holistic milieu (where people come together in groups or one to one encounters to explore interconnected body – mind – spirituality). The number of people in congregations of Kendal on a particular Sunday was compared with the number of those participating in the holistic milieu during an average week.

Adapted from Heelas and Woodhead (2003)

The study took a headcount of those who attended the 25 Christian churches and chapels in Kendal on Sunday 26 November 2000 (there were no temples or mosques).

The study used a questionnaire to count those involved with new age spiritualities, the holistic milieu – activities which they see as involving the mind, body and spirit. The inclusion of 'spirit' is critical: if an activity such as yoga or tai chi is not seen as spiritual, then that person is not included.

The findings

Church attendance: 7.9 per cent of the population of Kendal – exactly the same as the percentage for Britain as a whole. Attendance for Kendal from the 1950s onwards showed a significant decline. The holistic domain, however, shows strong growth. In the 1970s there were three providers of holistic spiritual services in the Yellow Pages. In 2000, there were 95.

Those using these services in 2000 numbered 600 – 1.6 per cent of the population of Kendal. However, only 55 per cent of those users – 0.9 per cent of the population of Kendal – considered these activities to be of spiritual significance.

Conclusion

Heelas and Woodhead found that 'the spiritual revolution clearly has not taken place in Kendal'. If present trends continue, however, the revolution will take place in 20 or 30 years, when numbers involved with the holistic milieu will overtake those in the congregational domain.

Questions

1. Explain what is meant by the term 'Spiritual revolution thesis'.
2. Explain the difference between 'secularisation theorist' and 'sacralisation theorist' approaches.
3. What research method have sociologists used in the Kendal project?
4. What did the researchers mean by the terms 'congregational domain' and 'holistic milieu'?
5. Summarise the findings of the research.
6. What is the conclusion of the study?
7. What are the criticisms of the Kendal Project?

> **Questions**
> 1. Investigate further the Kendal Project at www.kendalproject.org.uk and consider how they might try to improve the study. You could also check out the research opportunities for A-level students as part of this website.
> 2. Conduct an interview with a member of the older generation. Have they noticed a decline in religiosity since they were children? How has the role of Christianity in society changed since they were young?

5.2 What impact has globalisation had on beliefs?

When considering the impact of globalisation on beliefs, explain the relationship between secularisation, postmodernism and fundamentalism and how secularisation might be an ethnocentric if not a Christocentric view.

Secularisation is taking place at different rates in different parts of the world and the range of religious expressions is growing and changing fast. Over the past 100 years, many societies have become more complex and differentiated. Religious diversity has increased, even in countries in the Middle East, Europe and Asia where the dominance of one religion is still protected by the state. The acceleration of international and global trade, travel and communication means that diverse religions and religious communities co-exist in varying degrees of harmony and tension.

Religion has been described as the original globaliser: for centuries the major religions have spread across the world, through conquest, colonisation and migration. As societies and religions come into closer contact with one another, there is the potential for religious conflict and for religious diversity and change. When one society or state dominates another, people may use religion to explain and resist this domination. Religious ideas lead some people to act in new ways that encourage economic development in less technologically developed societies.

More recently sociologists have examined what role religion may play in development in today's globalising world. Until recently many sociologists believed that religion was in decline in the West. Postmodern sociologists, however, believe that some forms of religion are enjoying a measure of growth (see page 149). While Christianity may still be the designated mainstream religion in the Western world, it is more and more difficult to argue that it has a monopoly of religious life.

Religion as defensive reaction to globalisation

Modernisation and globalisation have led to mass migration and rapid social change, resulting in social disruption, disorientation and threats to identity for many migrants. The certainties of their old way of life are replaced by the uncertainties of their new environment. They are increasingly part of a global economy which shapes their lives, but over which they have little or no control (Davie 2007). Religious resurgence, especially within the developing world, has been seen as a response to modernisation and globalisation.

Conservative religious movements can be a retreat into a religious haven, providing certainty in an uncertain world by selectively retrieving traditional religious truths. Globalisation undermines people's traditional sense of self, religion helps to build 'resistance identities', based in part on traditional doctrines (Castells, 1996). Globalisation often involves Westernisation – the spread of Western norms and values. Conservative religions can provide 'cultural defence' for local societies. This can be seen in Iran since the 1979 revolution when the religious leaders saw a return to traditional Islam as a cure for the 'disease' of 'Westoxification'. What's more, globally, there are forces that make religion important and actually reverse the process of secularisation. For example, the rise of Islam since the reinstatement of Ayatollah Khomeini in Iran in 1979, and the rise of more conservative or even orthodox religious observances by Bosnian Muslims following the ethnic cleansing of Muslims by Bosnian Serbs in the former Yugoslavia since 1992.

The rapid growth of Pentecostalism in Central and South America illustrates how conservative religion can be seen as a practical response to the problems resulting from modernisation and globalisation. Pentecostal churches impose a strict regime and morality. There is an emphasis on self-improvement – the churches offer business classes and teach congregations how to save. People are encouraged to better themselves, start their own businesses and pull themselves out of poverty. For example, machismo is widespread in Central and South America, particularly in the poorer, urban areas. The strict morality of Pentecostalism works against this: the roles of husband and father become central, money spent on wine, women and song increasingly goes into the family, resulting in a better diet and education for the children (Brusco, 1995).

Developing societies are often former colonies. For many, neither colonial rule nor independence has encouraged a positive national identity. Attempts at modernisation has been based on Western models and globalisation have been largely directed by Western corporations. Religion offers an alternative, helping to build a secure, positive identity. For example, the resurgence of Islam can provide a positive, non-Western identity which draws on traditional culture. It can create an Islamic identity which crosses national boundaries and can mobilise Muslims to take political action in a global context (An-Na'im, 1999).

Different perspectives

Postmodernists view religion as an indicator of social change. They argue that change in religion reflects the shift from modernity to postmodernity. For Lyotard (1984) post-industrial society and postmodern culture are essentially associated with a number of important technological, scientific and economic changes. However, he suggests that the most significant transformations are related to the undermining 'metanarratives' especially those which stress authority, certainty and the conviction that this is possible to identify absolute truths in the world.

Client cults

A key feature of postmodern society is consumerism. In Western countries there has been a shift from economic production to consumption of goods and services. It is frequently argued that the resurgence of religion in postmodernity may result from the fresh emphasis on culture and its dominant consumer ethics (Lyons 1996). Consumerism, with its concern with taste and choice, means that religion is a matter of personal preferences and a product to be packaged for the **spiritual marketplace** of competing religions. Postmodernists see a link between spirituality and sides of the self and body, all of which are related to choice of lifestyle and construction of self-identity. This is evident in a preoccupation in new forms of religion with self-improvement, healing and therapeutic techniques. In this regard there seems to be a growth of what Stark and Bainbridge (1978) call **client cults** which offer services to their followers that involve personal adjustments, such as holistic therapy, healing and techniques to fulfil human potential.

'Self-religions'

Paul Heelas (1996) argues that disintegration of certainties of the past has left a situation in which postmodern religion – particularly new age spirituality and what he terms 'self-religions' – emerges to fill the spiritual vacuum and satisfy the need for meaning. The emphasis on self in this context is particularly significant. Postmodernity brings a desire to create self-identity with an emphasis on experience and an on/off-the-shelf image. It establishes the freedom for individuals to create and sustain the self-image of their choice. Related to the growth of consumer culture is the tendency of religion in the postmodern age to be expressed in terms of individualistic religious experience. Such an emphasis of experience might be at the expense of beliefs and practices that informed traditional religion.

Quasi-religions

Quasi-religions appear to be part of the postmodern scene. There are various beliefs and practices which can be put under the broad or substantive definition of religion. They are ways of social life that have at least some qualities in common, although not always obviously, with more traditional forms of religion – the numerous cults of film, rock music television personalities, UFO cults, sports fans, human potential movements and even shopping. These examples would seem to take definitions of religion to extraordinary lengths; however, those cults have the same functions as religion, since they may be central to people's lives and provide greater meaning and significance – as more traditional forms of religion have done.

Quasi-religions include search for meaning and identity in the world which finds them increasingly difficult to provide them. The search originates in the individual's life experience or expresses itself in a form of retreat from an alienating society. For example if football is central to a person's life it might be said to be his/her religion.

Postmodernity challenges many of the constricting traditional sociological theories and categories. In short, forms of religion anchored in supernatural views of the world have declined and have been replaced by those which are more focused upon this world. From this point of view quasi-religions appear to be some of the most interesting and controversial expressions of religious life.

Fundamentalism

The concept of fundamentalism is properly applied to any religious group that has as one of its aims a desire or commitment to go back to what are regarded as the original and true beliefs and practices. These beliefs and practices are usually found in a sacred text. Fundamentalist groups often arise in times of rapid social change, when some members claim that following of the original beliefs and practices of the group has been corrupted or compromised in some way.

The emergence of fundamentalist groups and their commitment to their beliefs is often used as evidence against the process of secularisation. Similarly a discussion of fundamentalism is also relevant to the debate regarding whether religion is a source of social stability or social change. Many people associate fundamentalism with violence, and religious and political extremism. However, while fundamentalists may have views that differ greatly from the mainstream, this does not automatically make them violent or antisociety. Fundamentalists

> **KEY SOCIOLOGIST**
> According to **Zygmunt Bauman (1991)**, the crisis of postmodernity is critically related to the self and identity. New expression of religiosity can restore the concept of self and identity by linking them to a moral and cosmic framework.

usually seek a return to what they would see as the 'true path'. They reject modern interpretations of faith as having lost their way because teachings have been watered down over the decades. Fundamentalists seek a return to a literal interpretation of their holy book and strict obedience to religious teachings.

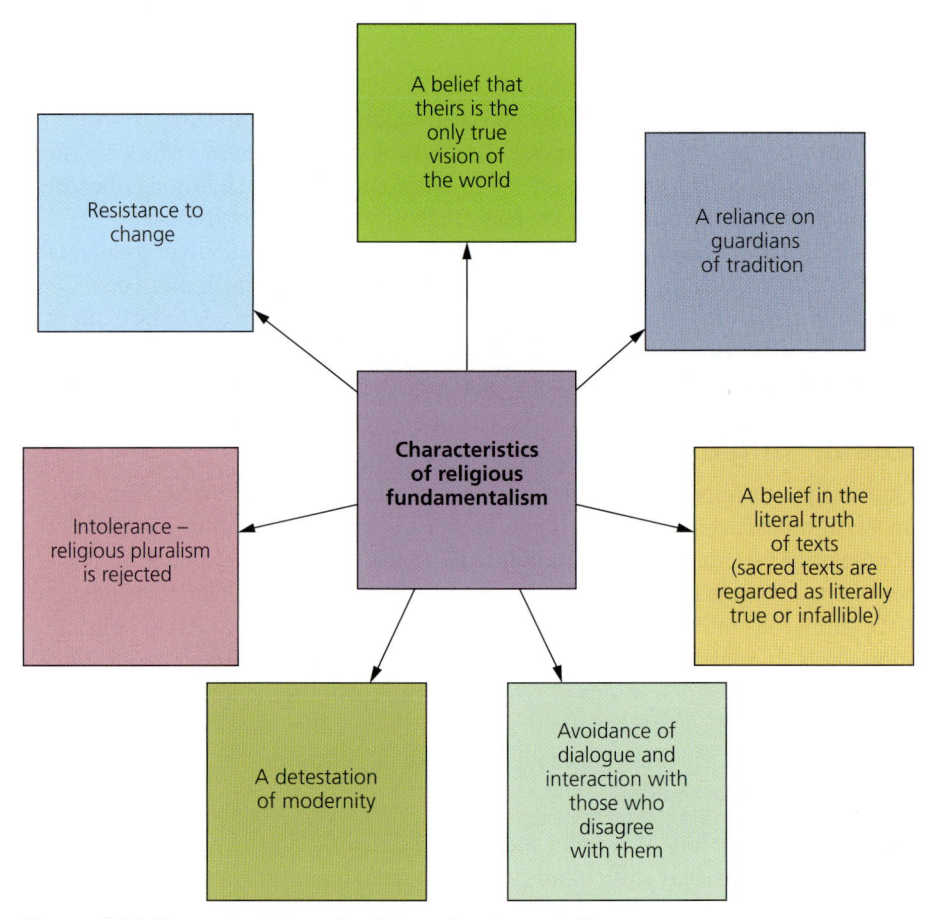

Characteristics of religious fundamentalism:
- A belief that theirs is the only true vision of the world
- A reliance on guardians of tradition
- A belief in the literal truth of texts (sacred texts are regarded as literally true or infallible)
- Avoidance of dialogue and interaction with those who disagree with them
- A detestation of modernity
- Intolerance – religious pluralism is rejected
- Resistance to change

Figure 3.26 Characteristics of religious fundamentalism

Christian fundamentalism

In the USA, modern Christian fundamentalism emerged at the end of the nineteenth and beginning of the twentieth century. Emphasis was placed on the literal truth of the Bible, in particular the creation story, and challenges to the teachings of Darwinist evolution theory continue to occur even today. Christian fundamentalism came back into prominence in the USA in 1970s, and since then fundamentalist sects have played an increasing role in American society, particularly in the political sphere. Fundamentalists have been instrumental in challenging liberal reforms in areas such as divorce legislation, abortion, gay rights and civil liberties, especially for blacks. The political conservatism of such groups has led to their being labelled the New Christian Right.

During the 2012 USA presidential election run-up, candidate Mitt Romney's campaign for the presidency was one long exercise in giving dangerous, harmful, extreme policies a place right at the top of the presidential ticket. Whether the topic is economics, women's health, LGBT equality, religious liberty, the role of government, or the future of the Courts, Romney sided with the far right. Romney pledged his loyalty to religious right leaders' agenda and echoed their concerns about secular government.

Bauman (1990) argues that the Western societies' Christian fundamentalism may fulfil a spiritual desire for some people. The forces of postmodernism erode certainty and taken for granted views of the world, but fundamentalism provides a clear set of beliefs and practices and strict moral conduct. As a mainstream Christianity declines, some people may choose a lifestyle in which religion has greater significance for them.

Reactionary Islamic fundamentalism

Islamic fundamentalism is a political, religious-ideological movement and trend, with different branches, variations, and organisational expressions that is spreading across North Africa, the Middle East, and Central Asia in particular, but also globally. The most prominent reactionary Islamic fundamentalist group is ISIS. The Sunni extremist group the Islamic State in Iraq and Syria (ISIS) has waged a violent campaign in recent months, capturing large areas of territory in both countries. In June 2014, the group declared itself a new Islamist caliphate, or formal Islamic state, and proclaimed leader Abu Bakr al-Baghdadi as the caliph.

ISIS is a jihadist group, committed to holy or religious war across national boundaries. Recruiting fighters from around the world, its programme is not forming a Sunni-dominated state in Iraq, but an Islamic caliphate first encompassing the entire area from Iraq, across Syria and Lebanon to the Mediterranean, and then expanding to other countries having a predominantly Muslim population.

They forcibly impose religion, in particular a fundamentalist or absolutist, literalist interpretation of the Koran and Sharia law (the body of religious rulings made by Islamic clerics) on society as its governing law and ideology – in short by creating a theocracy and obliterating any separation of religion and state. This means imposing and violently enforcing patriarchal, separate and unequal laws for women, including forced veiling, forced control by male family members, and denial of equal legal rights. It includes society-wide indoctrination in religious obscurantism and discrimination and often attacks other religions or non-believers. The group adopted a very fundamentalist and exclusionary interpretation of Islam, saw itself as the only 'victorious sect' in Islam, and considered Shias (Shiites, who constitute 55–60 per cent of Iraqis) deviants and legitimate targets of its attacks.

Not only are there threats to those who do not follow the group, they also have created videos, statements, and have killed a lot of people in many villages and towns across Iraq and Syria. The group continues to spread and the violence continues to worsen – in November 2015 the group carried out a series of terror attacks in Paris, targeting a concert hall, a stadium, restaurants and bars. People are increasingly fearful of what ISIS is capable of.

None of this is to say – or imply – that all Muslims or everyone living in the Middle East or Central Asia is an Islamic fundamentalist, or that Islamic fundamentalism is part of the 'identity' of the peoples in these regions. Nor does it mean that Islam is 'inherently violent', or any more reactionary than literal or absolutist interpretations of Christianity or Judaism.

IN THE NEWS

Teenage girls abducted in raid on Nigerian secondary school

Figure 3.27 Protests about the 2014 kidnapping of the Nigerian schoolgirls were widespread

On 14 April 2014, the Islamic extremist group Boko Haram abducted 276 girls from a boarding school in Chibok, a town in northern Nigeria. The heavily armed militants – witnesses estimate about 200 of them – arrived at night in vehicles, kidnapped the girls and stole supplies. Over 50 of the girls later escaped.

Boko Haram, which means 'Western education is forbidden' in the Hausa language, promotes the view that women should not be educated. The school was hosting final year exams and has Christian and Muslim students. In a video released in May 2015, girls are shown wearing Islamic dress and reciting verses from the Koran and the Boko Haram spokesman says that some of the Christian students have converted to Islam. Boko Haram has killed thousands of people in its campaign for an Islamic state since it was founded in 2002.

Adapted from Chothia (2014)

RESEARCH IN FOCUS

The rise of Pentecostalism in Brazil

In terms of numbers, Pentecostalism is the fastest growing Christian religion. For example, in Rio de Janeiro in Brazil between 1990 and 1992 a new Pentecostal church was registered every single weekday. Within the churches the Pentecostals are told that they can escape poverty with the help of God and by their own efforts, their mission: 'Our greatest dream is that they all become entrepreneurs.'

Berger argues that Pentecostalism in Latin America acts as a 'functional equivalent' to Weber's Protestant ethic; it encourages the development of capitalism today as Calvinism did in the sixteenth century. Latin American Pentecostalists embrace a work ethic and lifestyle similar to that of the Calvinists. It encourages it members to prosper and become upwardly mobile, thus Pentecostalism has a strong link with modern capitalism. As a result in Chile and southern Brazil there is now a growing and prosperous Pentecostalist middle class leading capitalist development.

Lehmann attributes the success of Pentecostalism as a global religion in part to its ability to 'plug into' and incorporate local beliefs. Although it preaches a similar message worldwide, it uses imagery and symbolism drawn from local cultures and existing religious beliefs. Pentecostalism has also been successful in developing countries because it is able to appeal in particular to the poor who make up the vast majority of the population, and because it uses global communications media to spread its message, along with 'road shows' and world tours by 'celebrity' preachers.

Adapted from David Kristoffer and Lannemyr Andersen (2012) 'From Victim to Victor' The Rise of Pentecostalism in Brazil – An empirical study of reason for growth

Questions

1. Why is Pentecostalism the fastest growing religion?
2. How is Pentecostalism equivalent to Weber's ideas of Protestant ethics?
3. Is Pentecostalism a global religion? Explain your answer.

Millenarianism

According to Holden (2002), Millenarian movements have developed within most of the major world religions. Such movements promise a future paradise for people who are suffering social injustice. In Christianity, the basis of these movements comes from the Book of Revelation, which prophesies that there will be major change in society after Christ's second coming, when he will reign for 1,000 years on Earth before the Day of Judgement.

Jehovah's Witnesses, The Mormons (the Church of Jesus Christ of Latter Day Saints) and the Seventh Day Adventists all have similar beliefs about millenarianism and consider it to be their mission to promote evangelical messages about the end of time. These communities can provide hope, encouragement, focus and, ultimately, increased self-confidence to people who feel let down by the modern world.

The Jehovah's Witnesses' core belief is that the Bible is interpreted literally as the word of God and can therefore be used to justify disasters such as famine, war and genocide on the grounds that they have been prophesised in the Bible. Biblical prophesies about the end of the world support their beliefs about the positive transformation of society that they believe is coming in the near future.

Check your understanding

1. Identify and explain two problems associated with the use of statistics to examine the decline of religious belief in Britain today.
2. Explain in your own words what is meant by 'belief without belonging'.
3. Do you think we live in a secular society? Explain your answer.
4. How can we measure religiosity?
5. What is quasi-religion?

Practice questions

1. Outline and explain two arguments against the view that secularisation has occurred worldwide over the past 30 years. [10 marks]
2. Outline and explain two reasons that support the claim that society is becoming increasingly secular. [10 marks]
3. Outline and explain two ways in which postmodern views of religion have undermined the secularisation thesis. [10 marks]
4. Assess the view that the growth of religious fundamentalism is a reaction to globalisation. [20 marks]

4 Global development

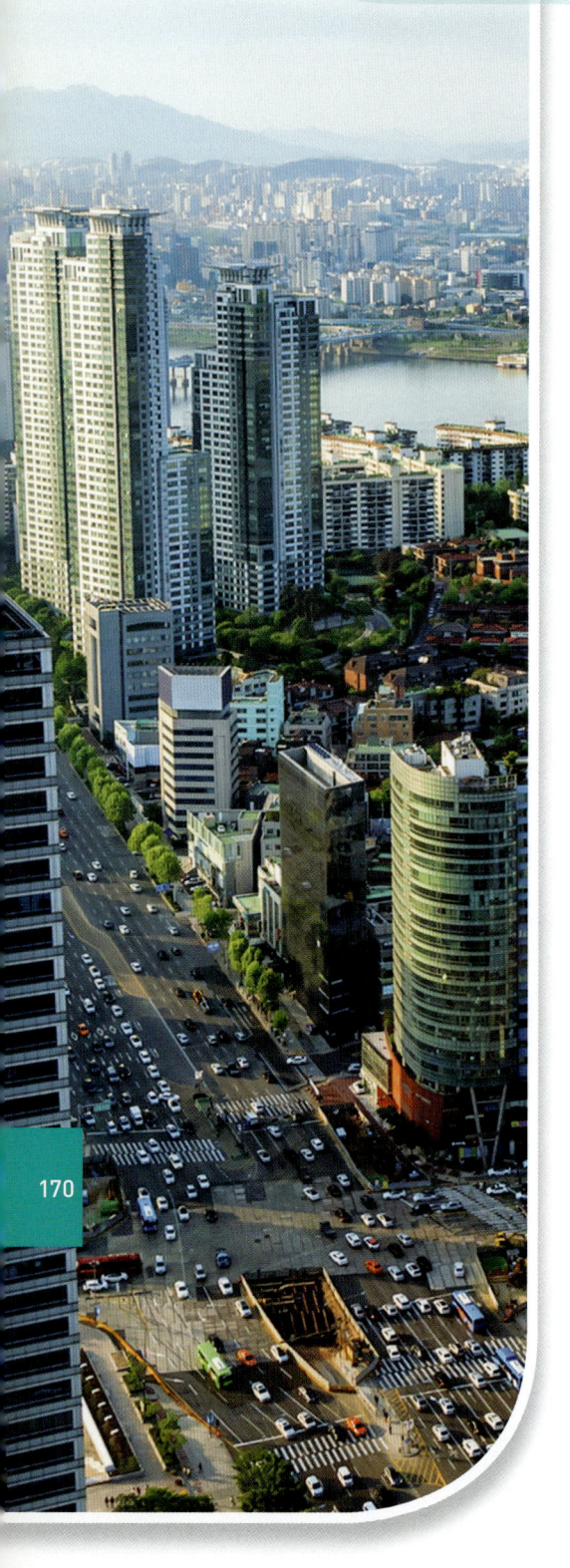

Understanding the specification	
AQA Specification	**How the specification is covered in this chapter**
Development, underdevelopment and global inequality	**Section 1: Development, underdevelopment and global inequality** What is development? How does modernisation theory explain development? How does dependency theory explain development? Are there contemporary alternative theories of development? Competing definitions and measurements of development, underdevelopment and global inequality.
Globalisation and its influence on the cultural, political and economic relationships between societies	**Section 2: Globalisation and its influence on the cultural, political and economic relationships between societies** What is globalisation? How is globalisation expressed? How unequal is global society?
The role of transnational corporations, non-governmental organisations and international agencies in local and global strategies for development	**Section 3: The role of transnational corporations, non-governmental organisations and international agencies in local and global strategies for development** The role and effectiveness of these organisations What power do TNCs exert? What is the role of non-government organisations (NGOs)? What is the role of international governmental organisations (IGOs)
Development in relation to aid and trade, industrialisation, urbanisation, the environment, and war and conflict	**Section 4: Development in relation to aid and trade, industrialisation, urbanisation, the environment, and war and conflict** What is aid? What are the arguments in favour of aid? What are the arguments against aid? Industrialisation and development Urbanisation and development The environment and development How do war and conflict impact upon the developing world?
Employment, education, health, demographic change and gender as aspects of development	**Section 5: Employment, education, health, demographic change and gender as aspects of development** Employment in the developing world, The role of education in development Health care systems and the nature of health and illness in developing countries The significance of demographic change The significance of gender in relation to development

Section 1: Development, underdevelopment and global inequality

This section will explore the following debates:

- What is development?
- How does modernisation theory explain development?
- How does dependency theory explain development?
- Are there contemporary alternative theories of development?

GETTING YOU STARTED

What is development?

When the largest gathering of world leaders in history met at the Millennium Summit in 2000 they adopted the UN Millennium Declaration. This committed their nations to a new global partnership to reduce extreme poverty and set out a series of time-bound targets. These targets have become known as the Millennium Development Goals (MDGs). The deadline for their achievement was 2015.

The MDGs are many dimensional aimed at addressing key global inequalities in poverty, hunger, disease, lack of adequate shelter, and exclusion – while promoting gender equality, education, and environmental sustainability. They also offer basic human rights to each person on the planet with regard to health, education, shelter and security.

The world has made significant progress in achieving many of the goals. For example, MDG1 the number of people living in extreme poverty and hunger was halved by 2010. However, progress for all the goals has been far from uniform across the world. There are huge disparities across and within countries. Within countries, poverty is greatest for rural areas, though urban poverty is also extensive, growing, and under-reported by traditional indicators.

Sub-Saharan Africa is the epicentre of crisis with the widest shortfall for most of the MDGS, with continuing food insecurity, a rise of extreme poverty, high child and maternal mortality, and large numbers living in slums. Other regions have mixed records, notably Latin America, Asia and the Middle East.

Adapted from United Nations Millennium Project (2006)

Questions

1. What was the original timescale for the MDGs?
2. Outline the intentions of the MDGs.
3. What progress has been made in achieving the goals?
4. Where is there most concern about lack of achievement of MDGs?
5. What does the very existence of MDGs imply about the nature of the world?

1.1 What is development?

To understand the meaning of development you should aim to demonstrate a critical awareness of the different ways, outlined below, of measuring it.

Defining 'development' is far from straightforward. It is measured primarily in terms of the size and growth of a country's economy, but also culturally and politically. Different countries are clearly at different stages of development and within each developing country there can be an enormous gulf in income and wealth. For example, India has the most millionaires of any country in the world, yet significant numbers of people living in **absolute poverty** defined by the United Nations (UN) as people living on less than $1.25 USD a day. Benjamin Selwyn (2014) makes the point that the discrepancy between the dynamism of global capitalism and the existence of global poverty demands a rethinking and questioning of what is actually meant by development.

Measuring development – economically

The most straightforward way to define development is to say that it reflects **economic growth** whereby the size of a country's economy (its **Gross National Product** – GNP) gets bigger. This measure assumes that growth in GNP will positively impact on the country's residents, but this is not necessarily the case. For example, what if economic growth leads to:

- a polarised society with the gap between rich and poor widening
- environmental destruction
- displacement of indigenous people from their ancestral lands
- replacing subsistence food production with cash crops for export
- rising living standards but a reduction in the quality of life.

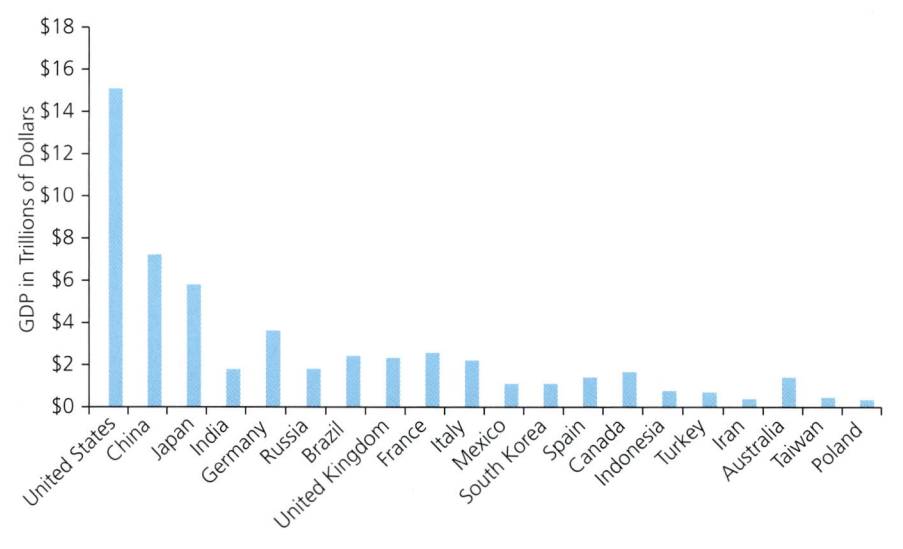

Figure 4.1 Ranking of countries in terms of GDP (note how China is second, reflecting the phenomenal growth of its economy). For this topic GDP and GNP can be interchanged

Data from International Monetary Fund (2012)

Problems with comparing GNP

While all of these examples might contribute to economic growth and possibly prosperity, they also cause problems, often for the poorest and most vulnerable people in society. For example, feminists are critical because GNP does not value the unpaid (and hence invisible) work undertaken in the home mainly by women, such as baking bread, rearing chickens, keeping a pig for consumption, etc. Another problem with measuring growth in GNP is that two countries might have the same GNP, but if one has twice as many people, they have less to spend per person. An alternative and slightly more informative measure is therefore GNP per capita (Gross National Product per head). This allows for differences in the sizes of populations between countries. The GNP per capita figures below for the ten richest and ten poorest countries highlight the huge gulf between the developed and developing world.

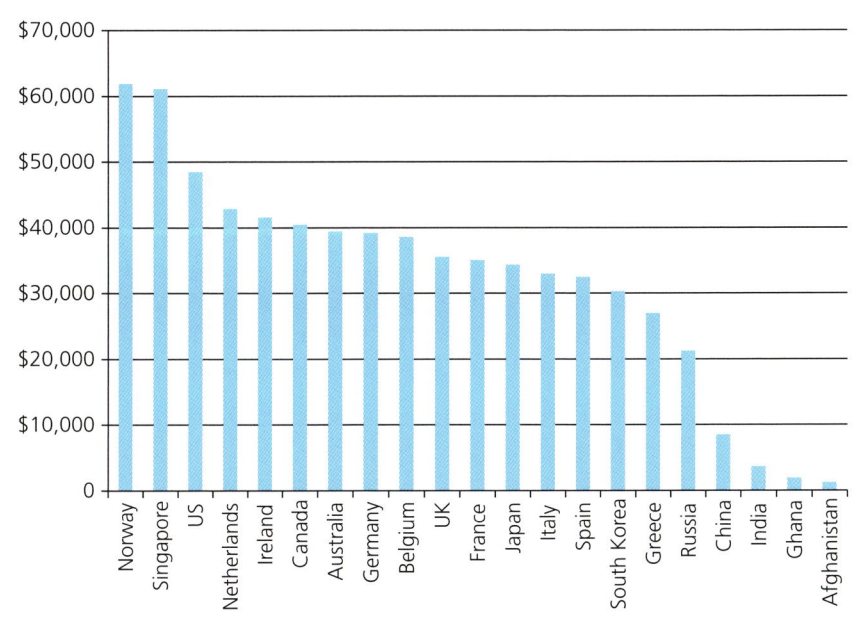

Figure 4.2 GDP per capita of countries by ranking, 2011. Note how India and China are near the bottom because of the size of their populations.

Data from economicshelp.org (2012)

Problems with comparing GNP per capita

The above graph shows income per capita, but such measurements only give an indication of the average income available per person. It does not show the degree of equity with how that income is distributed or to what extent that income is spent on public services, such as free health and education. Therefore it is important when comparing countries of similar GNP per capita incomes to recognise that their people's quality of life can vary considerably. Sociologists consequently use GNP and GNP per capita figures with caution.

Further problems with economic measurements

Besides the factors above, there are a number of other reasons for exercising care with such economic data.

> **KEY SOCIOLOGISTS**
>
> **Kingsbury et al.** (2004) offer an important contribution to this debate. They argue that development as a process has been promoted by the West for purely selfish economic reasons. As poor countries develop, their increased purchasing power generates more international trade and opens up new markets for Western manufactured goods. Kingsbury et al. also note that countries like the USA have made a connection between poverty and global terrorism.

> **CONTEMPORARY APPLICATION**
>
> Countries like the Himalayan kingdom of Bhutan and the South Pacific island nation of Vanuatu, have received quite a bit of attention recently because they both score highly as happy places to live. They top the Happy Planet Index because their people are satisfied with their lot, live long and healthy lives and do little damage to the planet. Using only economic measurements of development ignores these factors. Unfortunately Vanuatu experienced widespread damage in 2015 when Severe Tropical Cyclone Pam hit with gusts of up to 320 kilometres (200 miles) an hour.

> **STUDY TIP**
>
> You should aim to understand the limitations of comparing GNP alone. Comparing GNP per capita takes into account population size but does not indicate how equitably the GNP is distributed. The Human Development Index covers a much broader range of factors associated with the quality of life. The Happy Planet Index goes further including factors like human well-being and happiness.

- Firstly, environmentalists argue that GNP should take account of the using up of non-renewable resources and the creation of social costs such as pollution and rubbish.
- Secondly, GNP does not include what Maggie Black (2002) refers to as 'invisible economies' whereby people generate valuable goods and services but these are not recorded in official figures, thus making countries seem poorer than they actually are. Examples would include the value of people growing their own vegetables and keeping livestock for personal consumption. These activities are commercialised in developed countries and therefore are included in GNP statistics, whereas in developing countries this is frequently not quantified.
- Thirdly, GNP figures do not take account of typical working hours or working conditions like 'sweatshops'; how long people have to work on average to produce the economic output that makes up this national income.
- Finally, comparing production between developed and developing countries is difficult. In very poor countries production is often about essentials and subsistence whereas in richer countries production is geared to indulgent consumption.

Non-economic measurement of development

One of the most vocal opponents to measuring development solely in economic terms is Amartya Sen (1999). He feels development should be measured in terms of the 'removal of various types of unfreedoms' which leave individuals with little choice or opportunity to exercise agency. Sen became one of the key figures responsible for the **Human Development Index** (HDI). This was developed within the United Nations precisely to take into consideration factors like the provision of education, health care, life expectancy and childhood mortality.

Although it uses GNP as one-third of its index, it covers broader factors that shape people's quality of life such as measuring poverty, health chances (measured by infant mortality and life expectancy), numbers who have access to basic services such as clean water and sanitation, access to technology (such as phone ownership, access to internet, etc.), male/female equality in terms of outcomes (school attendance, qualifications, jobs, and so on) and what the government spending priorities are.

Although the HDI index offers many advantages in comparing the quality of life of people, some have gone much further and suggested that far more comprehensive 'green accounts' of economies are needed. An innovative global measure of progress, the **Happy Planet Index**, has been constructed by the New Economics Foundation (NEF) and Friends of the Earth. They argue that we need a different way to measure human well-being and happiness in order to recognise environmental concerns.

Figure 4.3 Bhutan currently tops the Happiness Index

IN THE NEWS

Why Asia is probably poorer than we think

Figure 4.4 The reality of Asian poverty

Global organisations are currently defining absolute poverty as living on less than the equivalent of $1.25 a day. However, a report from the Asian Development Bank (2014) suggests that this measurement is inadequate to capture the true meaning of the nature of poverty across Asia. It argues that three additional things need to be taken into consideration: the higher costs of consumption for poor people; food price inflation (the price of food is rising much faster than general prices), and the particular vulnerability of the poor to natural disasters and economic crises. Finally, the $1.25 poverty line falls below most Asian developing counties' national poverty lines.

Adapted from Ghosh (2014)

Because the poor tend to spend a higher proportion of their meagre incomes on food than wealthier people, the rate of food price inflation is a far more accurate measure than a general consumer price index. This is because the latter does not capture the full impact on the poor when rising food prices go up faster than other prices. Using this index it is estimated that the number of extremely poor people in Asia rose by 140 million in 2010.

People living in poverty are particularly vulnerable to economic shocks and climate change, moving them from poverty to extreme poverty. The Asian Development Bank estimates that an additional 418 million people (12 per cent of Asians) became poor in 2010 following the global banking crisis of 2007/8. Therefore when the United Nations claims that the number of people living in absolute poverty has fallen globally, in Asia it may well have increased. For example, in China following the banking crash the number of people living in poverty increased from 16 per cent at the $1.25 benchmark to 29 per cent in 2010. India has a poverty rate of 40 per cent, while Bangladesh and Nepal are even higher with 50 per cent in absolute poverty. It is estimated that if the rate of $1.25 was revised to a more realistic $1.51 a day, then the number of very poor people in Asia would be 1.75 billion (2010); not the 733 million reported.

Questions

1. What is the current global measurement of absolute poverty?
2. According to the Asian Development Bank what three additional things need to be taken into consideration to gain a true picture of the plight of the poor?
3. Why is a food price index more relevant to measuring poverty than a general price index?
4. How many people are living in absolute poverty in India and Bangladesh?
5. How does the article's estimate of the number living in absolute poverty in Asia differ to the official view of the United Nations?

How does modernisation theory explain development?

When studying modernisation theory, you need to understand its origins within functionalism and how it was used to promote capitalist ideology during the Cold War. It is important to show how internal factors, especially traditional values, explain why some countries have developed less than others.

Figure 4.5 Skyscrapers in Seoul

Modernisation theory was the first and one of the most important theories of development. It evolved out of the functionalist perspective around the 1960s. Modernisation theory's pro-capitalist basis became its selling point for the USA during the Cold War. By committing to free-market capitalism and a desire to modernise, promoted by the USA, countries were promised what Samuel Huntington (1993) describes as 'an evolutionary process'. By adopting Western cultural values and social institutions, developing countries would go through several stages to finally bring about a modern society of mass consumption: the American dream. The USSR, in contrast, offered help in developing infrastructure, agriculture and industry rather than the promotion of mass consumption.

Traditional society holds back development

Modernisation theory explains why some countries appear to have developed quicker and further than others on internal factors, particularly traditional values. The classical work of both Emile Durkheim and his concept of 'mechanical solidarity' (discussed in Book 1 page 318) and Ferdinand Tönnies' concept of 'gemeinschaft' have been used within modernisation theory to highlight the importance of traditional values. When traditional values are very strong they act as a brake to development.

Recognising this, Talcott Parsons stressed the necessity for developing countries to embrace cultural change if development was to happen. He used the concept of 'shifting equilibrium' to describe how societies evolve and change. For example, while traditional values serve traditional societies, they hinder development by restricting both geographic and social mobility, which Parsons saw as essential features of a developing society. Parsons saw development reflecting a shift in what he called pattern A variables to pattern B variables:

Pattern A variables	Pattern B variables
1. **Affectivity** (i.e. direct gratification)	1. **Affective neutrality** (i.e. indirect gratification)
2. **Particularism** (i.e. favouring family and friends)	2. **Universalism** (i.e. judging people according to the same standards)
3. **Ascription** (i.e. being given a role or status)	3. **Achievement** (i.e. position/role through merit)
4. **Diffuse roles** (many roles in society)	4. **Specific roles** (e.g. division of labour)
5. **Collectivism** (putting the group first)	5. **Individualism** (putting yourself before the group)

Table 4.1 Parsons' pattern variables

When countries shed traditional values and embraced the desire to modernise, Walt Rostow (1960), saw their development as an evolutionary process in which countries progressed up a development ladder of five stages of varying length, as shown in Figure 4.6.

traditional society
- With aid and direct investment, countries shed their old traditional values and ways to enter stage 2, pre-conditions for take-off.

pre-conditions for take-off
- Traditional values become less important, infrastructure of roads, railways, electricity, etc. expanding, development of education and health care systems.

take-off
- The crucial stage, according to Rostow is 'take-off'. Using the analogy of a plane, this is where the country has so much development momentum that it leaves the ground.

drive to maturity
- Economic growth and investment tends to be high in new technology and the infrastructure.
- There is export of manufactured goods to the West.

society of high mass consumption
- In this final stage, life expectancy and living standards are high for the vast majority of people. Most enjoy welfare provision in the form of education and health care. Such is the extent of living standards that people practise conspicuous consumption.

Figure 4.6 Stages of development

Evolution into neo-liberalism

Like functionalism, modernisation theory has lost influence and popularity over time. However, the pro-capitalist ideology that underpins modernisation theory has resulted in it being replaced by neo-liberal theory. Neo-liberalism retains some of modernisation theory's key ideas. For example, Rostow's idea of stages or steps was subsequently adopted by neo-liberalists with the global market often portrayed as a ladder of opportunity. Once they begin moving up the bottom rungs of this ladder, this opens up the possibility of climbing further and thereby achieving development. However, there are also some differences. Whereas modernisation theory blamed lack of development on internal factors, especially traditional values, neo-liberals explain lack of development more by an exclusion from the capitalist world system. As such they advocate ideas like liberalisation of trade and the deregulation of financial, labour and commodity markets in order for developing countries to harness the dynamism of global capitalism. Nevertheless, some writers like Anthony Giddens (2000) still blame countries themselves for slow or lack of development. He particularly identified 'authoritarian government, corruption, conflict, over-regulation and the low level of emancipation of women' as key factors.

Criticisms of modernisation theory

The biggest criticism is that it is **ethnocentric**, assuming that everyone aspires to the 'American Dream'. Secondly, there is evidence from Japan and the '**Asian Tiger economies**' that the traditional values in the form of non-Christian religious beliefs and the extended family can exist successfully alongside the modern. Modernisation theory conveniently ignores what is known as the '**crisis of modernism**', the social and economic problems that are common in mass consumption societies such as mental illness and suicide, high divorce rates, crime, drug abuse, poverty and homelessness. Modernisation is often associated with **polarisation** whereby the gap between rich and poor widens. The creation of rich elites is frequently linked to **kleptocracy** (corruption) where political leaders defraud their own people by pocketing and taking bribes as well as overseeing **human rights** abuses. Through its emphasis on internal obstacles, modernisation theory underestimates the external obstacles to development. For example, ecological limits – there are simply not enough resources on the planet for every country to become a society of mass consumption. In addition, modernising development can encourage **false needs**; activities such as cigarette and alcohol consumption that are actually harmful. Finally, **postmodernists** challenge the idea that you can make generalisations about the developing world. They argue development can only be understood in relation to historical conditions and the individual characteristics of any one developing country.

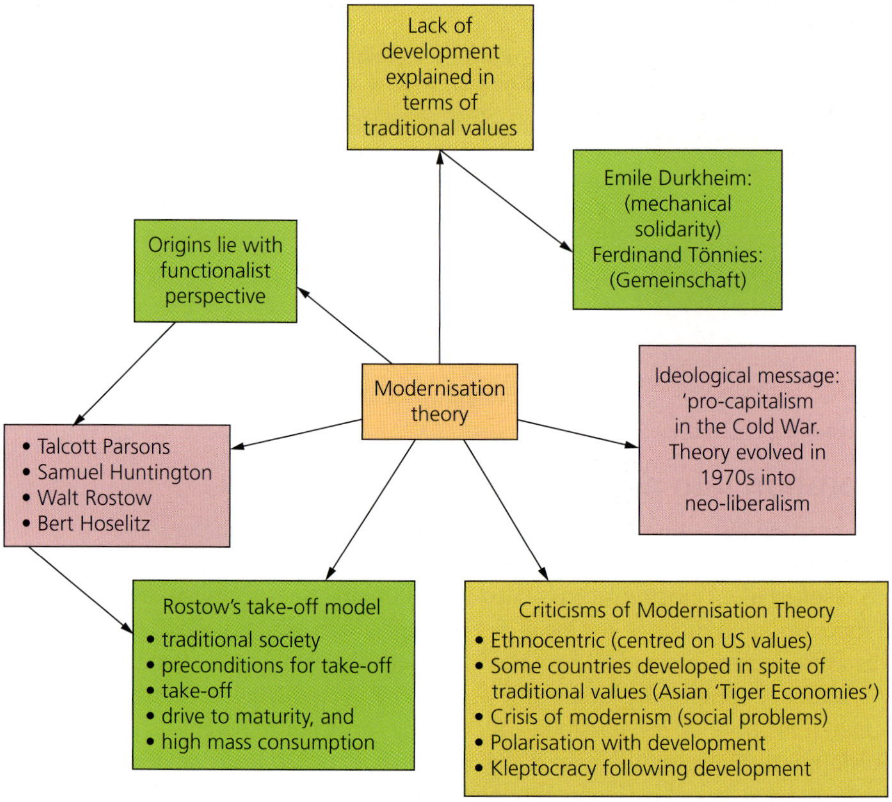

> **KEY SOCIOLOGIST**
>
> **Samuel Huntington** (1993) is an influential neo-modernisation theorist. He saw modernisation as an evolutionary process. He affirms the importance of culture as the primary variable for both development and the conflict generated by that development. He argues that developing countries resent the economic success of the West and the West's attempt to impose its version of modernity upon them through institutions like the United Nations and the World Bank. He notes that resistance to Western forms of modernisation are likely to provoke a return to fundamentalism and the sponsorship of international terrorism (such as '9/11' and organisations like the Islamic State).

Figure 4.7 Making sense of modernisation theory

We have seen that modernisation theory tends to be dismissed as no longer relevant. However, despite its criticisms it laid foundations that proved durable and are now expressed through neo-liberal theory. In this way, modernisation theory exerts a considerable influence today on organisations like the United Nations, World Bank and International Monetary Fund (IMF).

CONTEMPORARY APPLICATION

The 'people first' policies of global charities or non-governmental organisations (NGOs) are based on the modernisation principle of 'intervention'. These NGOs act as external agents, often seeing themselves as the necessary catalyst needed to stimulate change in attitudes and hence encouraging development. However, critics of NGOs argue this approach is paternalistic and patronising, with an attitude of 'knowing what is best for people'.

STUDY TIP

Remember that modernisation theory blames lack of development on internal factors, particularly adherence to traditional values. Make sure you have a good idea of the nature of these traditional values which could include: **patriarchy**, religious ideas (especially **fundamentalism**) and support for the extended family.

IN THE NEWS

The World Bank calls for a new focus in global development

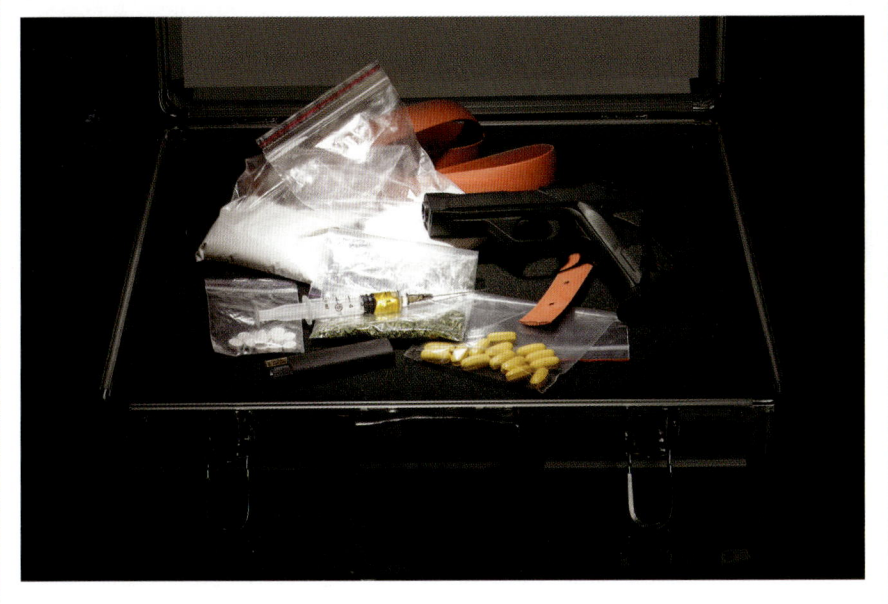

Figure 4.8 Drug trafficking and violence often go hand in hand

The World Bank reported in its *World Development Report 2011* that, since the end of the Cold War, there has been a growth in violence, often driven by cross-border crime, such as drug trafficking. For example, more people are dying in Guatemala from criminal violence and drug trafficking than previously when it was engulfed in a civil war. In such circumstances, conventional development spending, as advocated by modernisation theory, may do little or nothing to improve the situation for ordinary people.

The report notes that unless there is a basic functioning justice system then more sophisticated plans to improve education or health systems or infrastructure tend not to work, because they get undermined by turbulence and instability. However, it takes time to escape from cycles of violence where they occur. The report cites Ethiopia, Mozambique and Rwanda as countries that have successfully emerged from violent conflict and are making rapid progress towards reducing poverty.

The report advocates people-centred development alongside traditional humanitarian and development aid workers. The international community has a role in trying to cushion affected societies from the external stress of conflicts on its borders or drug trafficking.

Adapted from Borger (2011)

Questions

1. According to the World Bank what key problem has developed since the Cold War?
2. What tends to be the consequence of violence according to the report?
3. What policy initiatives does the World Bank offer to help redress these problems?

1.2 How does dependency theory explain development?

To explain dependency theory you should aim to understand how, in contrast to modernisation theory, it explains lack of development in terms of external factors; most notably the combined forces of neo-colonialism.

Figure 4.9 Woman working in a garment factory

Dependency theory is a neo-Marxist theory that was developed particularly by Andre Gunder Frank (1969) as an alternative to modernisation theory. The theory examines how the forces of global capitalist society operate against and oppress the poorer countries that have yet to develop. Compared to modernisation theory, dependency theory sees the key obstacles to development as imposed from outside rather than 'internal factors'. Developing countries lack development, not through any internal shortcomings, but because they have been forced into a position of dependency on the developed world.

Dependency theory rejects the evolutionary view of development supported by modernisation theory. Instead, dependency theory argues that the cause of the low levels of development in developing countries is their reliance (dependence) on more economically developed countries. The argument is that developing countries remain underdeveloped because it is not in the interest of the developed countries to let them develop. By keeping such countries underdeveloped, developed countries consequently benefit from their cheap land, labour and resources.

The slave trade and colonialism

Frank argues the origins of this oppression stem from mercantile capitalism and the **slave trade**. He notes that this early trade took place among countries often as economically and socially advanced as their European trading partners. However, the Europeans had greater military power and could dictate unequal terms. Many European countries went further and used their military power to command direct control and turn these lands into **colonies**. This political control facilitated further their exploitation for cheap cash crops, minerals and labour. In addition, colonies provided new markets for the manufacturing industries of the colonial power. By the 1970s most colonies had acquired independence from their colonial powers. However, the trading links between colonial powers and their ex-colonies often remained strong and still not necessarily equal.

Neo-colonialism

Frank makes the important point that ending colonialism did not end exploitation. Instead, developing countries became subject to a new form of economic exploitation, which he called **neo-colonialism**. This embraces three forms of oppression: world trade, transnational corporations (TNCs) and aid. Frank separated the world into the exploitative '**core**' and the exploited '**periphery**'. In contrast to modernisation theory, the powerful developed countries now become the problem rather than the solution to development. The rich countries, it is argued, have a vested interest in keeping the developing countries dependent and poor, making it easier to exploit them.

Two solutions to dependency have been suggested:

- Isolation – which suggests that the only way to escape from a position of exploitation and underdevelopment is by escaping the capitalist system altogether. However, examples which include China in the past or North Korea in the present, suggest that this approach is not particularly successful. In contrast, modernisation theorists would see China's subsequent embracement of global capitalism as the key to its recent success.
- 'Dependent development' – which advocates a shift towards import substitution industrialisation (ISI) whereby local industries produce goods that would normally be imported from the developed world. Duncan Green (1995) has documented how ISI advanced Latin America's economic development in the past. For example, in the 1960s domestic production provided 95 per cent of Mexico's and 98 per cent of Brazil's consumer goods.

Criticisms of dependency theory

- The very meaning of 'dependency' has been questioned. Frank never clearly defined the term or showed how it could be quantified.
- It plays down the role of internal factors in holding back development. These would include both the kleptocracy of elites and cultural factors.
- It cannot explain the rapid development of countries like the Asian 'tiger economies' or emerging economies such as Mexico, Brazil and Argentina. Why were these countries not kept 'dependent' and underdeveloped?
- Modernisation theory would argue that aid and inward investment by **Transnational Corporations** (TNCs) do bring some benefit to developing countries often taking them to 'take-off' and turning them into emerging economies.
- Some, like John Goldthorpe, have defended colonialism arguing that it frequently provided developing countries with a basic infrastructure in terms of transport and communications.
- It implies all developing countries are homogeneous, sharing the same experiences and predicament. Clearly this is simplistic and naïve. A country's experiences and development will depend upon factors like politics, elite priorities, resources and culture and values.
- Finally, postmodernists challenge the idea of any grand theory and argue the only way to understand a specific country's development (or underdevelopment) is to examine its own individual characteristics.

Traditional Marxist criticism

Despite their relationship, there is a fundamental difference between how neo-Marxist dependency theory and traditional Marxists view the impact of global capitalism. Ironically a fundamental criticism of neo-Marxist dependency theory comes from traditional Marxism.

In his writing, Karl Marx clearly viewed capitalism as a dynamic and progressive force constantly looking for new markets to saturate in the pursuit of profits. Therefore, in contrast to dependency theory's view that countries are kept underdeveloped, Marxists would argue that the capitalist class have a vested interest in encouraging global development, since this creates new markets for suppliers. The Marxist Bill Warren (1980) noted that in several developing countries an indigenous capitalist class is developing causing them to 'emerge' with rapid economic growth. The seeds of this development were often sown in the eras of colonialism and neo-colonialism. Failure to develop this is largely due to internal factors such as kleptocracy or poor governmental policies. Supporting this, Graham Hancock notes that a great deal of the aid that remains within developing countries ends up in the bank accounts of their elites.

Dependency theory

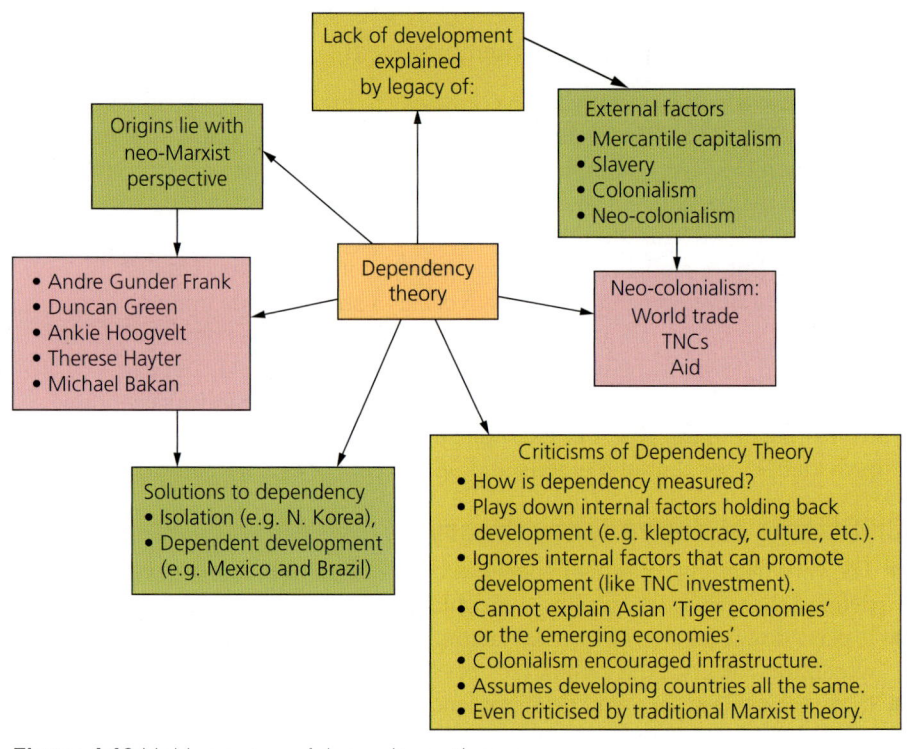

- Lack of development explained by legacy of:
- External factors
  - Mercantile capitalism
  - Slavery
  - Colonialism
  - Neo-colonialism
- Neo-colonialism:
  - World trade
  - TNCs
  - Aid
- Origins lie with neo-Marxist perspective
  - Andre Gunder Frank
  - Duncan Green
  - Ankie Hoogvelt
  - Therese Hayter
  - Michael Bakan
- Solutions to dependency
  - Isolation (e.g. N. Korea),
  - Dependent development (e.g. Mexico and Brazil)
- Criticisms of Dependency Theory
  - How is dependency measured?
  - Plays down internal factors holding back development (e.g. kleptocracy, culture, etc.).
  - Ignores internal factors that can promote development (like TNC investment).
  - Cannot explain Asian 'Tiger economies' or the 'emerging economies'.
  - Colonialism encouraged infrastructure.
  - Assumes developing countries all the same.
  - Even criticised by traditional Marxist theory.

Figure 4.10 Making sense of dependency theory

STUDY TIP
Don't focus too much on the dualism between dependency theory and modernisation theory since some criticise both. Postmodernists argue that both modernisation and dependency theory ignore the unique characteristics and individual features of each country, making generalisations difficult.

KEY SOCIOLOGIST
Ankie Hoogvelt (2001) notes how the interests of elites in the developing world often become 'intertwined' with both TNCs and the interests of developed countries. She also discusses the ways in which international 'management of instability' emerges as contemporary forms of imperialist globalism. However, she notes how there is a growing 'mosquito cloud' of local resistance movements challenging aspects of this neo-colonialism.

CONTEMPORARY APPLICATION
The Fairtrade movement and the availability of fair trade goods has grown in recent decades. The very term 'Fairtrade' is loaded and implies normal trade is not 'fair'. When developing countries frequently rely entirely upon one or two cash crops it is important that their farmers receive a sufficient price for their goods. The Fairtrade movement argues it is necessary because, too often, world trade is balanced in favour of the developed countries.

> **IN THE NEWS**
>
> ### The only new jobs are service ones like flipping burgers
>
> Mainstream news media implies the US economy is slowly improving. However, this message is highly questionable: many companies are going into liquidation, being forced to sell up or scrabbling around for investment. Most new jobs are low-paid service jobs such as those in catering – great for teenagers wanting spending money, or for pensioners looking to top up their income – but nowhere near what is required to fund a family's needs. And what about graduates? Most jobs being created do not allow new workers to pay living expenses and at the same time repay their student loans.
>
> The reality is that far from getting better, the situation is becoming much worse. US government debt has risen to an unprecedented high of $17tn. The trade deficit has resulted in huge foreign debt, a drastically reduced manufacturing industry, unemployment, and wages that don't keep track of inflation so mean less is real terms. The Economic Policy Institute estimates that for every 1bn dollars in trade deficit, 9,000 jobs are lost in the USA, with the result that consumer spending is further reduced. Failed trade policies with China alone are estimated to have cost the US 2.7mn jobs. Because goods can be manufactured more cheaply in other parts of the world where workers are paid a fraction of US wages, transnational businesses are faced with the difficult choice between outsourcing labour to countries with a lower wage rate, or greatly increasing their risk of going out of business.
>
> The so-called 'free trade' agreements such as the North Atlantic Free Trade Agreement (NAFTA) and the United States-Korea Free Trade Agreement (KORUS) as well as the USA's membership of the World Trade Organization (WTO), demonstrates that the USA has all but relinquished its economic supremacy to the rest of the world.
>
> It is time for us to urge the government to tackle the implications of all of this on our businesses, jobs, and trade deficits. If we don't, the US economy will continue on its downward journey.
>
> Adapted from Elkis (2014)

Questions

1. What evidence is there to question that developed economies like the USA are recovering?
2. According to the article, what kind of jobs are being created in developed countries like the USA?
3. What arguments does the article make to explain this impact on developed economies like the USA?
4. How does this article contradict dependency theory?

1.3 Are there contemporary alternative theories of development?

When discussing alternative and contemporary theories of development you should demonstrate knowledge and understanding of neo-liberal theory, world systems theory and postmodernist theory.

Neo-liberalism

As noted on previous pages, many of the ideas of modernisation theory became rejuvenated in contemporary neo-liberal theory. This ideological view became prominent from the mid 1970s, with the ideas of economist Friedrich Hayek (1949) proving particularly influential. Neo-liberals present capitalism as both dynamic and benign, offering prosperity and reward to those who demonstrate initiative and hard work. The neo-liberal response to issues like the inequalities and cyclical booms and slumps that inevitably spring from free global capitalism is to resort to Hayekian arguments that capitalist outcomes are still better than any other system.

Neo-liberal ideas currently command the support of most governments, transnational corporations and leading international organisations such as the IMF and World Bank. It therefore exerts a lot of influence in the contemporary world. Such is this influence that it is referred to as the 'Washington Consensus' because its ideology dominates the worldview of US-based IMF and World Bank. Like modernisation theory it believes that internal factors still serve as the key obstacle to development. However, as Anthony Giddens (2000) notes, the focus has shifted from culture and traditional values to economic policies and institutions. Neo-liberals argue the route to development is simply the embracement of free trade within global capitalism alongside cutting taxes, dismantling welfare services and the privatisation of government-owned assets.

Criticisms of neo-liberalism

Critics point out that neo-liberalist policies tend to polarise societies, generating both wealth and poverty at the same time. Consequently, the economic success in the form of GNP growth and TNC profits has to be weighed up against the costs of economic deprivation, exploitative low wages, long working hours and often limited health and safety legislation. Sometimes capital is attracted to countries with poor human rights records, where trade unions are banned and militia exist to break up any industrial disputes or worker demonstrations. When these human costs are factored in, they argue, the neo-liberal argument becomes less positive. A common outcome of neo-liberalism is the widening of the gap between the rich and the poor, not just globally but within developing countries as well.

In addition, neo-liberalism underpins IMF/World Bank structural adjustment programmes that deliver loans in return for cuts in state spending, replacement of crops for domestic consumption with cash crops for export, and the privatisation of key industries. Any cuts to welfare provision invariably hit the most vulnerable and poorest people in society hardest. Developing countries point out both an irony and contradiction of neo-liberalism: while the Washington consensus is obsessed with cutting government spending of developing countries, countries in the developed world are either unable or unwilling to address their own fiscal responsibility and have huge budget deficits. For example, for the fiscal Year 2015 the federal budget deficit for the USA is $564 billion.

Another contraction of neo-liberal development models is the way the European Union and USA protect their agriculture and industries with tariffs and trade barriers, but do not allow developing nations to do so.

World systems theory

Over time dependency theory came under increasing criticism for its focus upon nations rather than wider global capitalism. To address this, world systems theory was developed by Immanuel Wallerstein (1979) who argued that individual countries exist within a broad political, economic and legal framework he calls the 'modern world system' (MWS). Wallerstein uses the ideas of the core and the periphery, but goes much further than Frank by adding a semi-periphery and claiming that the modern world system transcends national boundaries. The powerful core states exploit the semi-periphery and the periphery by introducing trade barriers and quotas, exploiting cheap labour and resources and dumping unsafe goods. The semi-periphery likewise exploits the periphery. The economic, political and military power of the core facilitates the accumulation of capital in the hands of the few.

Wallerstein recognised how TNCs, in the interest of maximising profits, embrace what Folker Froebel (1980) termed a **new International division of labour** (NIDL) – they shift manufacturing to the developing world and take advantage of cheap labour and lax health and safety legislation. Production often occurs in purpose-built **export-processing zones** (EPZs) which are specifically built to facilitate TNC production to be exported back to the developed world where the consumer markets are strongest (see page 224).

Criticisms of world systems theory

Critics of Wallerstein's work argue that, like most Marxist analysis, it is economically deterministic and ignores the influence of political and cultural factors. Secondly, he has been criticised for ignoring the active agencies which feature in the 'new international division of labour', such as trade unions and workers' organisations in the developing countries.

Postmodernism

Postmodernists criticise both modernisation and dependency theory for treating developing countries as homogeneous. Instead, postmodernists emphasise each country's individualism and unique characteristics. They reject any theory that attempted to apply a 'one size fits all' approach as a **metanarrative**. In fact postmodernists are critical of the very notion of development itself; since this implies evolution and progress. Any attempt to assume change as evolutionary and progressive is a flawed idea since there is no such thing as truth and knowledge, only what has been socially constructed. The nature and extent of development appears to be dependent upon the specific characteristics of a country's space, time and power relations that exist within it. So the postmodernist approach explains development on an individualistic basis. In addition, it is particularly useful, with its emphasis on discourse and power, for understanding the conflicts that can hinder development, especially where there is a diversity of ethnic identities.

Criticisms of postmodernism

The strength of postmodernism is its focus on culture, discourses, values and identities. However, critics argue that since it requires tools from other disciplines, not least recognition of the role structures, it cannot be applied as a single tool for the analysis of development. There simply are general factors that play a role in shaping development. From these general theories can be constructed. Such factors include debt, TNCs, kleptocracy, the IMF and World Bank's Structural Adjustment Programmes, and trade restrictions like import tariffs and quotas.

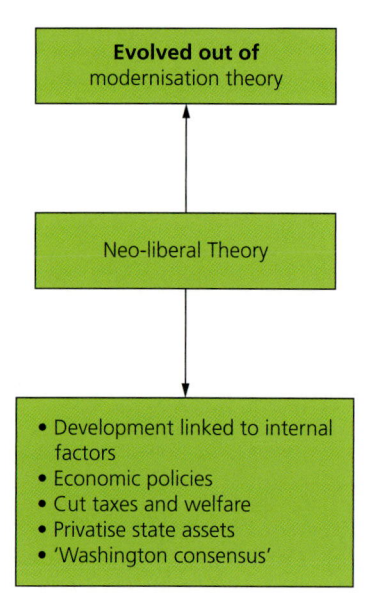

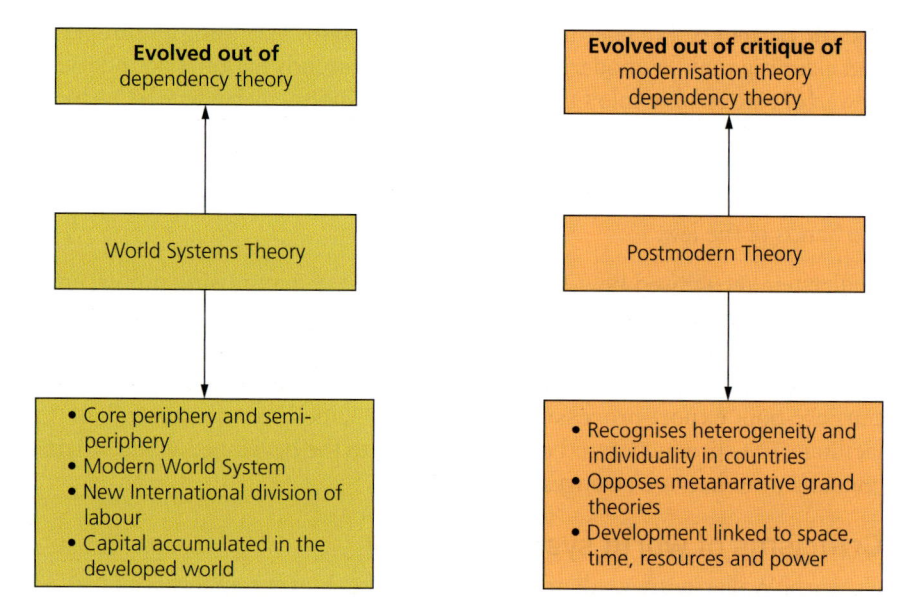

Evolved out of modernisation theory	Evolved out of dependency theory	Evolved out of critique of modernisation theory dependency theory
↑	↑	↑
Neo-liberal Theory	World Systems Theory	Postmodern Theory
↑	↑	↑
• Development linked to internal factors • Economic policies • Cut taxes and welfare • Privatise state assets • 'Washington consensus'	• Core periphery and semi-periphery • Modern World System • New International division of labour • Capital accumulated in the developed world	• Recognises heterogeneity and individuality in countries • Opposes metanarrative grand theories • Development linked to space, time, resources and power

Figure 4.11 Alternative and contemporary theories of development

It is important to recognise that these alternative theories emerged as a result of the 'theory impasse' whereby modernisation and dependency theories were seen as outdated and no longer capable of explaining forces like globalisation and a post-Cold War global world.

Post-development

Influenced by the pioneering work of Ivan Illich and his criticism of colonialism and post-colonialism, sociologists like Arturo Escobar (1995) developed post-development theory as a critique of the **ethnocentric** way development has taken place. For example, he asks how did the industrialised nations of the Northern Hemisphere, especially the USA, come to be seen as the appropriate model for development. His answer is that development policies were just as pervasive and effective as the practice and ideology of colonialism. The drive for development was, he argues, little more than a mechanism to control the developing world since, at the same time, poverty and hunger became widespread. Consequently while modernisation theory fought it out with dependency theory, no one dared to question whether development was even desirable, let alone achievable.

It was not until the 1980s that anyone even dared to deconstruct just exactly what 'development' was, when the social reality of what was happening to the poorer countries was becoming apparent. Escobar stresses the role played by economists in development discourse. In rejecting the Western model of development towards the American dream and mass consumerism, he advocates a more individualistic approach of 'pluriversal studies', which he illustrates with examples from recent Latin American movements. For example, in Colombia he demonstrates how attempts by experts to make food production more economic resulted in more hunger. Peasants, women and nature, he argues, become objects of knowledge and targets of power under the 'gaze of experts'.

Environmentalism

The economic advance of development, both globally and with regard to individual countries, inevitably gives rise to the question of sustainability. Despite advances in food technology, the number of hungry people is at a record level and rising. There are also environmental trends that pose a threat to the planet and therefore the fauna and flora on it, including humans. In Latin America the term '**extractivism**' is used to describe a reliance on the use of natural resources (such as timber and minerals) to promote export-based economies in that continent. Such ideas can challenge the myth of infinite growth, and lead to a growth in the **divestment** in unethical companies such as those involved in logging or the extraction of fossil fuels. For example, globally 11 million hectares of forests are destroyed yearly, while desertification eats up 6 million hectares of productive dryland each year. If these trends continue over the next 30 years then the world will deforest an area the size of India and deserts will expand to cover an area roughly as large as Saudi Arabia. Much of deforested land is converted to low-grade farmland unable to support the farmers who settle it. In Europe, acid rain kills forests, lakes and may have irreparably damaged vast amounts of soil. Global warming continues from the burning of fossil fuels as a result of the greenhouse effect. If the polar caps melt at their current rate then sea levels will rise, flooding coastal cities and disrupting national economies. Further depletion of the ozone layer may cause a sharp rise in cancers. Finally, industry and agriculture put toxic substances into the human food chain and into underground water tables.

KEY SOCIOLOGIST

Paul Collier (2000) coined the term 'bottom billion' to describe the poorest one billion people trapped in 50 societies, many in sub-Saharan Africa, that are stagnating, failing and in decline. He is firmly opposed to aid, arguing that the inability of aid to eradicate poverty stems from the four traps of conflict, natural resource, landlock and bad governance. However, he does concede that aid has helped the 'bottom billion', adding one percentage point to annual GNP growth figure.

CONTEMPORARY APPLICATION

Divestment is the opposite of an investment. It involves organisations removing stocks, bonds and investment funds that are increasingly viewed as unethical or morally ambiguous from their investment portfolios. For example, the Church of England announced in 2015 that it would sell its holdings of £12m in thermal coal and tar sands whose extraction in Canada has caused huge environmental damage. Divestment supporters hope to drive fossil fuel companies out of business to be replaced by sustainable alternatives, helping to save the planet.

STUDY TIP

Remember that sociological analysis has proceeded beyond the modernisation versus dependency theory debate. Neo-liberalism, world system theory and postmodernism theories, as well as post-development and environmentalism, can all be used to evaluate modernisation and dependency theory.

Check your understanding

1. Define development in its most conventional meaning.
2. What is Gross National Product?
3. Why is the measure GNP per capita a better way of comparing countries?
4. What is the Human Development Index?
5. How does modernisation theory explain lack of development due to internal factors?
6. In what ways has modernisation theory evolved into neo-liberalism?
7. What did Frank mean by 'neo-colonialism'?
8. How would a traditional Marxist view challenge the assumptions of neo-Marxist dependency theory?
9. What is meant by the terms North and South?
10. Which organisation developed the Millennium Development Goals?

Practice questions

1. Outline and explain **two** ways in which development can be measured between countries. [10 marks]

Read Item A below and answer the question that follows.

Item A

The Human Development Index (HDI) was developed in order to provide a better comparison between countries that looked at factors that reflected quality of life, rather than just economic measurements.

Applying material from Item A, analyse two reasons why using the HDI results in a more accurate picture of a country's state of development. [10 marks]

Read Item B below and answer the question that follows.

Item B

Measurements of global inequality show not only that a significant gap exists between the developed and developing countries but that there is a huge income gap within most developing countries. Not only does inequality inhibit economic growth, but it can generate many social and political problems as well.

Applying material from Item B and your knowledge, evaluate the view that inequality is holding back development in the **majority world**. [20 marks]

Section 2: Globalisation and its influence on the cultural, political and economic relationships between societies

This section will explore the following debates:
- What is globalisation?
- How is globalisation expressed?
- How unequal is global society?

GETTING YOU STARTED
The 'Battery' Textile Workers

Figure 4.12 Textile workers

Recently two shoppers came back from shopping in Swansea, South Wales and noticed unconventional labels stitched into their dresses. One said 'Degrading sweatshop conditions' and the other: 'Forced to work exhausting hours'. These labels were assumed to be 'cries for help' by workers in the garment industry in Dhaka, Bangladesh. But to do so would risk detection from pin-sharp inspectors and the immediate sack. It is now thought that they are the work of an activist, holed up in a South Wales fitting room, hastily darning her protests.

Whoever is responsible, it triggered days of media and social network discussion about the costs of cheap fashion. The shops in the malls prefer us to wander the aisles with our eyes wide open and our minds shut tight. The whole point of shopping is seduction, not dwelling on inconvenient headlines, such as 1,134 dead and another 2,500 injured textile workers in Rana Plaza when their factory collapsed in 2013.

There are thousands of workers in the garment industry who work in similarly precarious and punishing conditions, making the clothes we wear. Outsourcing and globalisation may have brought down the price of our shopping, but it has also enabled retailers to engage in the blame-game. For example, when the high suicide rate was revealed at a factory which made iPhones in China, Apple quickly passed the buck to the outsourced firm Foxconn who employed them. By law you are entitled to more information about the production of your eggs than the label sewn into your underwear. Forcing businesses to admit exactly the wages paid to production line workers and how much tax they pay would be a good start. Otherwise, we're entirely dependent on activists in fitting rooms.

Adapted from Chakrabortty (2014)

Questions
1. Outline the nature of working conditions associated with 'sweatshops'.
2. What benefits to Western consumers are implied in the article from globalisation?
3. What ways can transnational corporations avoid responsibility for working conditions in the developing world?
4. What are Chakrabortty's suggestions about how the situation could improve?

2.1 What is globalisation?

You should aim to understand how globalisation manifests itself economically, culturally and politically.

Figure 4.13 A real-life example of global 'culture'

Introduction

Globalisation is a widely used term used to describe the flows and interconnections that are pulling the global world together in terms of time and space. Held and McGrew (1999) describe the way that economic, cultural and political processes now extend to the 'four corners' of the world as '**stretched social relations**'. Through technology and communication, they argue that the world is metaphorically shrinking as distance is no longer the barrier it was to trade, travel or tourism. In addition, there have been '**intensification of flows**' around the world – of goods, services, money, people as well as negatives like crime (such as drugs, money laundering and the trafficking of people) and environmental damage (such as global warming).

Held and McGrew argue that the growing volume, intensity and velocity of global interactions can be associated with their deepening impact. Because of globalisation, distant global events can and do have an impact locally. Globalisation has been made possible by the spread of free-market capitalism. It is economically tied in with the global dispersion and growth of TNCs and Folker Froebel's (1980) concept of the new international division of labour, whereby manufacturing is increasingly outsourced to the developing world. This not only necessitates huge ships transporting goods back to the developed world, but has also contributed to the development of consumerism and a market for goods in the emerging economies of the developing world as incomes rise with economic growth.

Cultural, political and economic

It is important to see globalisation as cultural and political, as well as economic (see page 193). In terms of the cultural flows, to many, globalisation can look like Westernisation or, particularly, Americanisation. This is because most of the iconic global brands derive from the USA, such as Coca-Cola, McDonalds, Microsoft, Apple and Disney. In addition, cinemas around the world are showing Hollywood films which traditionally convey the values of the 'American dream'. Marxists are very critical of this dissemination of Western or American culture, seeing it as firstly destroying local cultures and secondly by creating '**false needs**'. This occurs when impoverished people in the developing world are duped into buying expensive Western goods, simply because of their iconic value. A further irony is that such goods are often harmful; such as junk food burgers, high-sugar soda drinks or American brand cigarettes. However, countering the destruction of local culture argument, globalisation has been known to rejuvenate identification with local areas and goods in something of a backlash. It can also cause a hybridisation of global with local cultures or goods, resulting in what Roland Robertson (1992) calls 'glocalisation'.

Theoretical perspectives on globalisation

Although the evidence for globalisation is strong and all around, it may be surprising to learn that some academics are still sceptical or unconvinced that it is a real phenomenon. The main theories, advocating and challenging globalisation, are discussed below.

Neo-liberal perspective ('positive' or 'optimist' globalists')

As key supporters of free-market economics and global capitalism, neo-liberals see globalisation as a key driver in expanding world trade and the economic growth of individual countries. They further argue that countries actively embracing the global free market are the ones developing most quickly and furthest. Nigel Harris (1987) saw the emergence of a 'global manufacturing system' as levelling inequalities in the world. Countries in the previous agricultural periphery were experiencing rapid industrialisation, which to Harris is analogous to development. Industrialisation offered hope to previously poor countries, paving the way for a more equal world system. Neo-liberalists see capitalism as both benign and dynamic, offering a potential source of real human development by encouraging entrepreneurialism.

Neo-liberals argue that globalisation:

- encourages the eradication of poverty as wealth is assumed to 'trickle down' and eventually benefit the whole global population
- encourages the spread of Western values, including the political system of democracy, around the world.

Neo-liberals are called 'positive globalists': they paint an optimistic picture of everyone benefiting and no one losing out in the globalisation process.

Marxists ('pessimist globalists' or 'radicals')

Marxists see the present global capitalism as an inevitable development of the mercantile capitalism that began centuries ago. Sometimes referred to as 'pessimist globalists' Marxists see globalisation as real, tangible and inevitable; promoting polarisation whereby rich countries get richer relative to poor countries. Even if some emerging economies seem to benefit, the world trade element of globalisation inevitably benefits the developed world and their TNCs at the expense of the oppression, exploitation and impoverishment of the developing world. Marxists view the cultural element of globalisation as cultural imperialism, meaning that a homogenised culture reflecting Western and particularly American culture and interests is being imposed across the world at the expense of local cultures. In terms of global politics, Marxists see the neo-liberal 'Washington consensus' as particularly strong, shaping not only economic policy but a New Right political agenda of privatisation and the cutting back of state services.

The work and ideas of the Marxist Wallerstein are introduced on page 184. Wallerstein described the global system as being in a state of constant evolution in a search for profits, leading Frobel to describe the NIDL seen most clearly in

EPZs. Other effects of the MWS are commodification, whereby a price is attached to everything. An interesting observation of Wallerstein is that development can be two-way: for example, a core country like Britain could one day decline to become a semi-periphery country, just as a periphery country can quickly develop and become semi-periphery like the Asian Tiger economies have.

Marxist Joseph Schumpeter (1951) explains that this global MWS will result in the **polarisation** of countries whereby the rich West gets richer, while poor countries become relatively poorer. He used the term '**creative destruction**', by which he meant the inherently unstable nature of capitalism, to argue how any entrepreneurial innovation and technological development in the developing world is inevitably short-lived as TNCs eliminate or absorb new rivals. As predominantly Western companies, TNCs are thus able to maintain and extend their dominant self-interested and monopoly positions. Subsequently Marxists, drawing on World Systems Theory, use creative destruction to explain how developing countries have converged in terms of industrialisation, but not in terms of income. This is because the profits gained from manufacturing in the developing world return to the developed world, boosting their economies.

Transformationalists

Transformationalists believe that the case for globalisation has been exaggerated. For example, they emphasise how individual nation states remain politically, economically and militarily autonomous. They concede that global forces are at play: it would be naïve to simply dismiss globalisation or to underestimate its economic, cultural and political impact.

Transformationalists argue that individual nations and people may react differently to aspects of globalisation, reflecting the extent to which autonomy and sovereignty matter. In response to the Marxist criticism that globalisation is causing a bland Americanised homogeneous culture, transformationalists point to the often innovative and exciting hybrid cultures that evolve from cultures mixing. They also reject the simplistic Marxist idea of polarisation. They see that the global world is unequal but not necessarily in terms of its old cleavages: as countries develop and emerge they gain power and countries like the UK who used to dominate the world stage may see their influence decline.

Internationalists

Internationalists are sceptical about globalisation and challenge the idea that there has been a shift in social relations that has brought in a new global phenomenon. They cannot deny that global flows of goods, money and people have increased; however, they argue that these changes are not substantially different to what occurred in the past.

Internationalists see an imbalance in global power relations, with the powerful states acting solely in their interests, as they have always done. Internationalists, rather than talking about globalisation, say that most economic and social activity is still essentially regional: trade within the European Union or American Free Trade Association (AFTA) should be seen as reflecting the increased importance of regionalisation rather than economic globalisation.

It is important to grasp the key processes by which globalisation is witnessed, as well as an awareness of the different theoretical perspectives towards this phenomena.

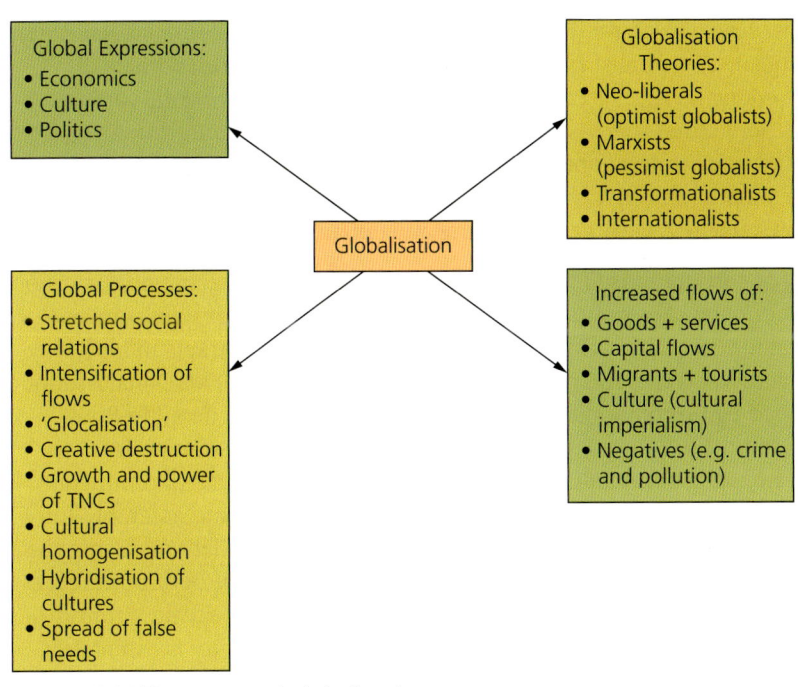

Figure 4.14 The nature of globalisation

> **CONTEMPORARY APPLICATION**
>
> The Transatlantic Trade and Investment Partnership (TTIP) is a proposed free-trade agreement between the European Union (EU) and the USA subject to a degree of public opposition in 2015. They are concerned about increased TNC power – who will be allowed to run public services like the NHS. In addition, the provision of an 'investor-state dispute settlement' will allow TNCs to sue a future government if it decides to return such services to the public sector. However, both the EU and the USA claim it will lead to economic benefits on both sides of the Atlantic. For example, the British government claims TTIP could add £10bn to the UK economy, £80bn to the USA and £100bn to the EU every year.

> **KEY SOCIOLOGIST**
>
> **Anthony Giddens** (1999) summed up his feelings about globalisation in the title of his book: *Runaway World: How Globalization is Reshaping Our Lives*. He shared the view that the most visible expressions of globalisation were American since most TNCs are located in the USA. He also coined the term 'global pillage' (a take on Marshall McLuhan's (1962) more romantic term 'global village') to describe the growth of poverty and debt in the developing world as global inequalities widen.

> **STUDY TIP**
>
> When evaluating the role of TNCs it is important to be aware of both sides of the argument. Modernisation theory's view is that TNC's inward investment in developing countries promotes growth and moves them towards 'take off'. Dependency theory, in contrast, argues the motive is one of neo-colonialism; primarily profit maximisation from cheap labour, tax breaks and lax health and safety controls.

2.2 How is globalisation expressed?

When studying how globalisation is expressed, you can look at it in terms of the three areas of economics, culture and politics. You could then explore the extent to which these aspects of globalisation have taken place.

Cohen and Kennedy (2013) argue that all the dimensions of globalisation – economic, technological, political, social and cultural – appear to be coming together at the same time, each reinforcing and magnifying the impact of the others. In addition, they argue that globalisation is best thought of as a multidimensional set of social processes that resists being confined to any single thematic framework.

Economic globalisation

Evidence of economic globalisation comes from the following factors:

- world trade
- transnational corporations and the World Trade Organisation (WTO)
- new international division of labour (Folker Froebel, 1980)
- global financial markets
- role of speculation in global markets
- McDonaldisation.

It is difficult, given the above list, to challenge the idea that economic globalisation is not significant. A capitalist free market exists around the world, with ex-communist countries like Vietnam and China now actively embracing capitalist enterprises. Sometimes there is pressure from the World Bank and IMF for pro-capitalist enterprise to be adopted. They will loan money but only if neo-liberal policies are adopted through 'structural adjustment programmes' that advocate privatisation, cuts in government spending and expansion of the free market.

Transnational corporations (TNCs) have embraced the new international division of labour and increasingly outsource the manufacture of their products to developing countries. Goods are then shipped to the major markets in both the developed world and the 'emerging' economies. The concept of McDonaldisation was developed by George Ritzer (1970) and discussed in more detail in Book 1 (pages 171 and 324). Ritzer uses the McDonald's company as the perfect example of how global capitalist firms have transformed patterns of production, distribution and consumption. He discusses how technology and assembly-line production techniques remove control from the worker while dehumanising the work process. As a result of global trade it could be argued that both production and consumption have been globalised. However, it is worth bearing in mind the internationalist's point that most economic and social activity is essentially regional rather than global (see page 192).

Finally speculators are a phenomenon of economic globalisation. They are accused of influencing the price of currencies, money markets, raw materials and traded commodities. Historically, the price of commodities (say wool, for example) reflected the cost of domestic production, but now the price of commodities like it are increasingly shaped by the global market including the input of speculators who buy and sell according to which way they think market prices will go. This speculation, however, just makes the changes in global prices even greater.

Cultural globalisation

Cultural globalisation overlaps with economic globalisation in that it can refer to the spread of global goods and services. For example, trends in taste, such as for American brand fast food, are linked to economic globalisation and living standards. This is wonderfully illustrated by Pakko and Pollard (2003) with their concept of '**Burgernomics**' whereby they calculate how long workers have to work in order to purchase a McDonald's Big Mac. Since such food is still expensive in the developing world, regular access to American brand fast food can only be achieved through rising wages. Examples of cultural globalisation include:

- global products and consequent patterns of consumerism
- cosmopolitan lifestyles
- global religions such as Islam, Christianity, Hinduism
- the existence of global technology and communication systems
- world sport
- world tourism.

Pessimist globalists (see page 191) emphasise how **global culture** takes the form of cultural imperialism – they see globalised culture dominated by a bland, homogenised, Westernised culture heavily centred on American values, products and icons. While the omnipresence of Coca-Cola, McDonald's, Western TV programmes and Hollywood films supports this, it is also important to recognise an element of '**interpenetration**' – cultural flow is two-way. For example, the success of 'Bollywood' films or restaurants and fast food outlets on global high streets from cultures within the developing world. Supporters of modernisation theory would argue that given the pursuit of the American dream being fairly widespread, support for American culture is welcome and its presence evidence of development. However, many actively resist it, especially in countries where religious fundamentalism is strong and Western cultural values rejected. Transformationalists would argue that the meeting of cultures often results in new hybrid cultures, rather than necessarily one culture dominating. In other examples, traditions may be sustained, or resurrected for tourists.

Political globalisation

Advocates of neo-liberal political ideologies feel that political globalisation and the spread of democracy will naturally expand as capitalism dominates the global economy. Further evidence of the spread of political globalisation is reflected in the following list:

- supra-national political entities such as the European Union and United Nations
- global financial institutions like the IMF and World Bank (with their neo-liberal agenda)
- growth of democracies with 'free and fair' elections and decline of dictatorships
- growth of problems too great for nation states to handle (for example, refugees, terrorism, global warming, AIDS)
- increasing number of global summits: such as G8, G20, NATO
- the growth of global new social movements such as 38 Degrees or change.org.

While this political globalisation has a momentum, it is ironic that the opposite is occurring with some aspects of politics moving towards a local rather than a global base. For example, many nation states are conceding some power to smaller and localised political structures. For example, the passing of power to the Scottish Parliament, the Welsh Assembly and the Northern Ireland Assembly through devolution are good examples of this process.

Globally, not all political systems and elections are free and fair, with the opposition allowed to organise freely. However, where elections take place they are almost always now observed by international monitors and there are procedures to try to reduce bribery, vote rigging and so on. To promote liberal democracies, free and fair elections is now often a condition of receiving structural adjustment programmes or aid. Consequently, the number of dictators and totalitarian states has declined with many countries wanting to be seen to embrace democracy to meet these criteria. However, critics argue that often such elections are little more than token gestures and do not bring tangible benefits to voters.

Irrespective of structural adjustment and aid conditions, the West continues to support many non-democratic countries if they have desirable assets or can offer strategic facilities for NATO forces. For example, many Arab countries around the Gulf are not democracies but are openly accepted as they are generally pro-West and, cynics might add, have lots of oil.

Held and McGrew (2007) raise important questions about political globalisation. For example, they ask whether the trend towards globalisation is being eclipsed by resurgence in geopolitics. They question whether the post 9/11 'war on terror' denotes the end of globalisation, or, alternatively beckons a new era of 'militarised globalisation'. However, they discount such ideas as premature, arguing that globalisation is protected by the primary structures of world order. Globalisation, they argue, should still be taken seriously as both a description and explanation of our current global condition.

> **Questions**
>
> 1. According to the article what two important ideologies, once strongly advocated by the USA, are in retreat?
> 2. What have been recent political and economic trends according to the article?
> 3. What examples are given to highlight how globalisation has changed?
> 4. This editorial clearly laments the decline of US influence. Do you share this view? Explain why.

In contrast, both transformationalists and internationalists question the extent to which political globalisation exists, arguing that national governments still exercise significant sovereignty and have autonomy over their own affairs. Yet generally speaking participation in national elections is declining in developed countries. In the 2015 General Election the turn-out was just 66.1 per cent, although slightly higher than 2010 when it was 65.1 per cent. At the same time, there has been an expansion of global interest and pressure groups. Clearly supporters of neo-liberal ideology would claim that it is influencing all aspects of globalisation. The economic spread of free-market capitalism is also shaping cultural and political globalisation. However, it is worth remembering the transformationalist and especially internationalist argument that the case of globalisation is overstated.

IN THE NEWS

America in retreat

Recent events make it clear that we have entered a post-American age. Liberalism and democracy are both in retreat, the two biggest ideas the USA stands for. Around the world, liberalism and democracy (two key US tenets) are under threat, and globalisation – the means of promoting such principles – has slowed. In the years following the Second World War up until recently, advances towards democracy were achieved through the driving force of social movements in countries such as Greece, Spain, Argentina, Brazil, Russia and South Africa. However, the gains achieved towards democracy, such as those by the civil uprisings of the 'Arab Spring', are now reversed, with a harsh backlash across the region, including a catastrophic civil war in Syria. Countries with authoritarian governments such as Russia and China are on the rise.

The global financial crash has undermined economic confidence and the worldwide recovery is mostly slow with an emerging pattern of stagnant wages and rising prices. Workers across the world see the rich getting richer while their share of wealth is falling everywhere. Voices in favour of protectionism are increasingly voiced over the free-trade argument.

Globalisation, which promised so much in the 1990s, is rolling back too. The global capital flows are less than half what they were before the 2007–8 financial crisis. The internet, which promised McLuhan's 'global village' by bringing the world together, is being censored in Burma, Cuba, Saudi Arabia, Turkey, Iran, China, Russia, Vietnam and Tunisia. Even once mighty transnational organisations, from NATO to the EU, have an air of desperation about them. With new crises emerging across the world, we would be unwise to depend on the USA for mediation and protection.

Adapted from Rajan (2014)

KEY SOCIOLOGIST

Ankie Hoogvelt (2005) describes a three-tier social structure arising from globalisation: the rich and affluent elites at the top (the 'bankable'), the 'insecure' in the middle and the 'excluded' at the bottom, but says these operate across countries, rather than within them. Globally, the rich and the poor live adjacent to each other in large cities.

STUDY TIP

Looking at economic, cultural and political globalisation, their nature and extent is strengthened when your approach includes theoretical analysis. Be aware of how neo-liberalist thought underpins all three of these expressions of globalisation, but equally subject this ideology and its open support for global capitalism to critical evaluation.

CONTEMPORARY APPLICATION

The flow of illegal immigrants across the Mediterranean into Europe is an example of globalisation. They comprise refugees from Syria, Egypt and the many war-torn countries of Africa. They are aware of better living standards and welfare provision in the developed world and consequently are prepared to pay money to people smugglers and risk their lives to reach Europe. Many see countries like Germany and the UK as particularly attractive hence the 'jungle' camp in Calais and the mass attempt to get to Germany in the autumn of 2015.

2.3 How unequal is global society?

To understand how global inequality is measured it is important to recognise inequalities exist between the developed and developing world as well as within each country.

Neo-liberal 'residualist discourse'

Global inequality refers to the extent to which income and wealth is distributed in an uneven manner among the world's population. In the past 40 years or so the ideology of neo-liberalism has become influential, defending global capitalism and its expression through the free global market. According to neo-liberalists, the poverty associated with the bulk of the developing world stems not so much from the nature of capitalism, but rather from their effective exclusion from it. Poor countries, they argue, can achieve prosperity providing they embrace the spirit of capitalism and harness the dynamism of the global market. This idea of poor countries being left behind has become known as the 'residualist discourse' whereby capitalism is portrayed as providing the solution to poverty. Therefore the problem of development is not the capitalist system itself but exclusion from it. (For a detailed summary of neo-liberal ideas see page 184.)

Marxism and the role of capitalism

Marxists reject both this benign view of capitalism and the idea that development policy is engaged in by enlightened and well-meaning players. There is no doubt that capitalism is capable of delivering economic growth, innovations in technology and wealth – the developed world, Asian 'tiger economies' and the emerging markets are testament to this – but this benefits a minority, not the majority of the world's population.

Mahatma Gandhi once described poverty as 'the worst form of violence' and it is the nature of capitalism to generate both great wealth and poverty. This is evidenced by the financial crisis of 2007/8 which, according to the World Bank (2009), resulted in an extra 90 million people becoming 'extremely poor'. This contrasts with the world's richest 100 individuals whose wealth grew by $241 billion in 2012 (Miller and Newcombe, 2013). Oxfam estimates that just $214 billion would remove everyone from extreme poverty (living on $1.25 a day) four times over. Therefore Marxists argue that development is founded upon the systematic exploitation and repression of the developing world's labour force by the states and capitalist classes of the developed world.

The global income gap

The gap between rich and poor nations is widening, not shrinking, and given present trends and institutional arrangements, there is little prospect that this trend will be reversed. Tracking the extent and nature of this divide between the developed and developing world poses a variety of statistical challenges. This is because of inequalities not only between the developing world and the developed world, but within them too (see Ankie Hoogvelt (2005), page 196).

Developing countries are often highly polarised societies with very rich people alongside the very poor. For example, Indonesia has one of the largest and fastest-growing economies in South East Asia yet half the population live on less than two dollars a day. Alongside shanty towns there are expensive shopping malls, luxury cars with blacked out windows and lots of new high rise buildings. The extent of the gap between the rich and poor is illustrated by the estimate that the combined wealth of Indonesia's 40 richest people is equivalent to that of about 60 million of its poorest citizens.

Looking at Indonesia's GNP (or even its GNP per head) as a measure of its development can give a very misleading picture of the real life experiences of significant numbers of its citizens. As noted on previous pages (see pages 173–5), measuring the true picture within countries is challenging: different nations tally income and wealth in different ways and some nations barely tally reliable statistics at all. Fortunately, there are an increasing number of good sources of summary data on global inequality such as the United Nations, the World Health Organisation and even the World Bank.

The Millennium Development Goals (MDGs)

As their name implies, these goals were agreed at the turn of the last century, when world leaders at the United Nations agreed on eight Millennium Development Goals (MDGs). The MDGs were intended to bring together the three policy initiatives of economic development, social well-being and sustainable development. In addition, they were a pledge to uphold the principles of human dignity, equality and free the world from extreme poverty. By setting these MDGs the United Nations made a commitment to significantly reduce global inequality by halving the proportion of people living on less than $1.25 USD a day.

> **STUDY TIP**
> You should aim to be aware of the ideological arguments surrounding this inequality, supported by some up-to-date statistics to illustrate its nature and extent.

> **KEY SOCIOLOGIST**
> **Joe Remenyi** (2004) argues that since the 1980s, Western governments have cut back on aid. At the same time, organisations like the World Bank have focused on making sure countries repay their loans to commercial banks. The International Monetary Fund (IMF) has increasingly lent money only if countries agree to cut back on their welfare policies through **structural adjustment programmes**. He argues such cuts in welfare spending will only add to, rather than remove, a country's problems.

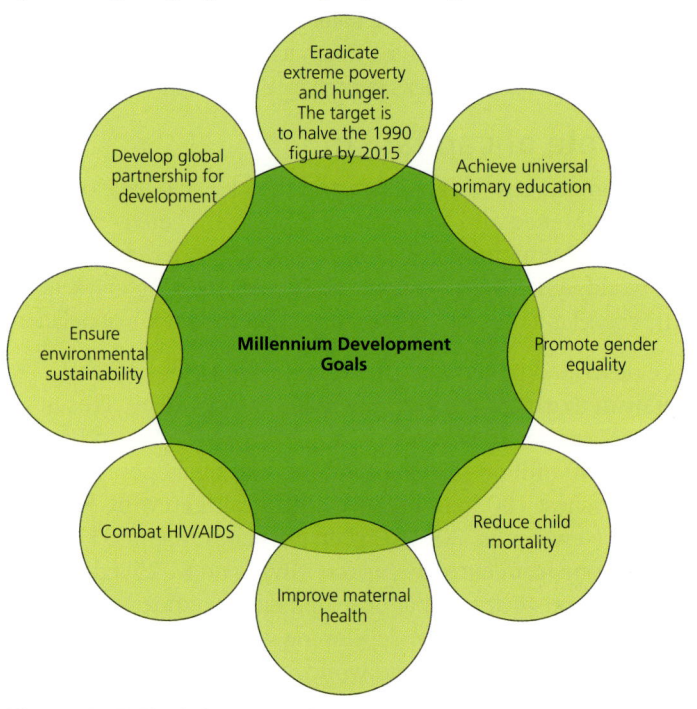

Figure 4.15 The Millennium Development Goals

Whether or not these goals will be achieved is difficult to say: much of the information available is projections and estimates, rather than actual data. The United Nations claims credit for achieving MDG1 five years ahead of the target year of 2015. In 2010 the number living on the global absolute poverty rate of $1.25 a day fell by 700 million to less than half the 1990 rate. However, at the global level 1.2 billion people, what Paul Collier (2008) refers to as the 'bottom billion,' are still currently living in extreme poverty. There has also been good progress in getting all children into school and drastically reducing child mortality.

Sociologists have expressed a concern that the Millennium Development Goals simply reflect a desire to impose Western values and institutions upon developing countries. Marxists would argue that the goals could be seen to be rooted in neo-liberal free-market ideology, designed to persuade countries to adopt the industrial-capitalist development pathway. They argue that the real rationale behind the goals is to ensure that the capitalist system continues to be dominated by the developed countries. In addition, less developed countries continue to be the source of cheap raw materials and labour markets as well as potential new consumer markets for Western goods.

CONTEMPORARY APPLICATION

At the Rio +20 conference (2012) the world discussed a new set of targets: 'Sustainable Development Goals' (SDG) to be monitored up to 2030. It was decided to establish an 'inclusive and transparent intergovernmental process open to all stakeholders, with a view to developing global sustainable development goals to be agreed by the General Assembly of the United Nations. While these goals are made with the best of intentions, some see them as an example of cultural imperialism as the developed world helps shape the developing world in its image.

STUDY TIP

When writing about global inequality use supporting evidence whenever you can: including examples, statistics and theory all adds depth to writing.

IN THE NEWS

Research that led to the Gini coefficient

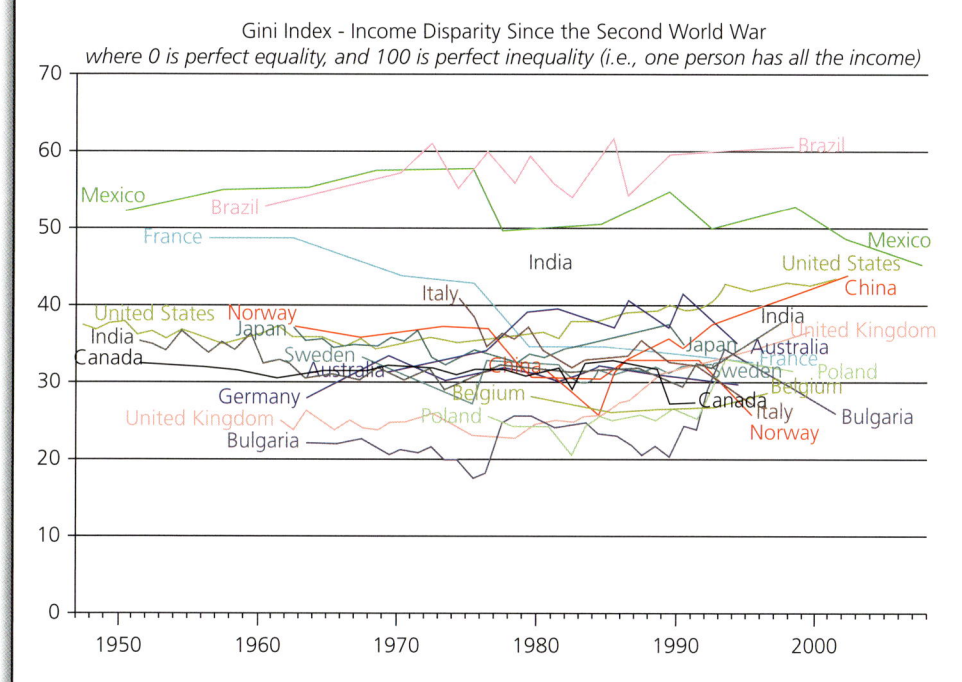

Figure 4.16 Different Gini values of countries (1950–2010)

The Gini coefficient is a measurement of how equally income is distributed within a country. If the Gini coefficient is 0, meaning a country's income is distributed totally equally, this could be plotted on a graph as a 45 degree line. The extent of inequality in wealth or income is calculated and drawn as a 'Lorenz Curve'. The space between the curve and the 45 degree line represents the Gini coefficient: the closer the curve to the diagonal line the closer the Gini coefficient will be to zero (perfect equality). A completely unequal society would have a Gini coefficient of one.

In terms of the contemporary global situation, middle-income countries appear the most unequal. Latin America remains the region with the highest level of income inequality, although there has been a significant improvement since 2000. Going in the opposite direction and showing a trend towards increased inequality are the Eastern European countries and Russia (formerly the Soviet Union). Many countries in Asia have experienced large increases in inequality between 1990 and 2008. Low-income countries show mixed results; Sub-Saharan Africa is highly unequal but appears to have reduced its Gini index by almost five points, on average, since 1990.

Such is the extreme inequality in the distribution of the world's income that it is raising questions about the current development model. When development leads to the polarisation of society into rich and poor – are we developing a country or just the privileged rich elite? If development seems to be benefiting the wealthiest billion, then what hope is there for the bottom billion?

IN THE NEWS

Critics argue everyone loses in the face of inequality: Not only does inequality slow economic growth, but it generates health and social problems and can easily lead to political instability. Inequality is potentially dysfunctional, according to reformists, who argue that a deliberate policy of redistribution should be at the centre of the development agenda. The United Nations development agenda aims to strike a balance between growth and equitable development.

Adapted from Ortiz and Cummins (2011)

Questions

1. What does the Gini coefficient measure?
2. Which region has the highest level of income inequality?
3. Which countries have experienced the greatest shift towards inequality since 1990?
4. Why do critics argue that everyone is a loser from inequality?
5. How might a neo-liberalist respond to this article?

Check your understanding

1. Outline and explain the differences between the two types of globalists.
2. What did Robertson mean by the term 'glocalisation'?
3. Explain the difference between a transformationalist and an internationalist.
4. Summarise some key characteristics of economic globalisation.
5. Summarise some key characteristics of cultural globalisation.
6. Summarise some key characteristics of political globalisation.
7. What is meant by the neo-liberal 'residualist discourse'?
8. What is a shanty town?
9. What are the Millennium Development Goals?
10. What is meant by the term the 'Washington consensus'?

Practice questions

1. Explain what Marshall McLuhan meant by the term 'global village'. [3 marks]

Read Item A below and answer the question that follows.

Item A

Globalisation has been described as the process of international integration. It reflects an intensification of flows of products and people as well as ideas and other aspects of culture. Notions of a shrinking world are associated with advances in transportation and telecommunications.

Applying material from Item A, analyse two ways in which globalisation may be expressed. [10 marks]

Read Item B below and answer the question that follows.

Item B

Modernisation theory focuses upon development as a process. It attempts to locate the cultural and economic factors that are holding countries back from development.

Applying material from Item B and your knowledge, evaluate the view that modernisation theory cannot adequately explain why some countries have not developed. [20 marks]

Section 3: The role of transnational corporations, non-governmental organisations and international agencies in local and global strategies for development

This section will explore the following debates:
- The role and effectiveness of these organisations
- What power do transnational corporations (TNCs) exert?
- What is the role of non-government organisations (NGOs)?
- What is the role of international governmental organisations (IGOs)?

GETTING YOU STARTED
How TNCs frequently ride roughshod over countries

Figure 4.17 Cigarettes

The US tobacco giant Philip Morris International has a geographically diverse portfolio that enables it to exploit the growing cigarette sales opportunities in the emerging markets. The company is bringing a lawsuit against Uruguay for $25 million. It is angry about the government's introduction of legislation requiring an increase in the size of the graphic health hazard warnings on the company's cigarette packets.

Over recent years there has been a rapid expansion of warnings on Uruguayan cigarette packets. The requirement is now to cover 80% of the area of both faces of the packet with graphic warnings, plus all of one side panel with text warnings. Philip Morris is basing its lawsuit on the contravention of a 1991 investment treaty between Uruguay and Switzerland. Although its headquarters are in the USA, the company has an operations centre in Switzerland.

TNCs like Philip Morris increasingly outsource production to the developing world through the new international division of labour. TNCs are a major factor of economic globalisation, since they create the material base for the international economy. A TNC has the following characteristic features. Firstly, they are active participants in developing countries through the new international division of labour. Secondly, they are relatively independent of the capital flows and other processes within nation states. Thirdly, they play a significant role in influencing the world economy by operating in many countries.

Adapted from Trefis Team (2014)

Questions

1. Why are tobacco companies like Philip Morris so interested in emerging markets?
2. What are the three 'characteristic features' of TNCs outlined in the article?
3. What is meant by the new international division of labour?
4. In what ways would modernisation theorists view TNCs positively?
5. Why is dependency theory so critical of TNCs?

3.1 The role and effectiveness of these organisations

Be aware of the role of organisations like transnational corporations, non-governmental organisations and international agencies in the development process then you need to unpack the differing and contrasting views sociologists have on their relative merits.

The impact of neo-liberalism

Wayne Ellwood (2001) offers a strong critique of the neo-liberal valorisation of a free-market model of globalisation. He associates the rise of neo-liberalism in the 1980s with the pro-free-market Thatcher government in Britain and the Reagan government in the USA. Under this new pro-capitalist ideology TNCs began to flourish under a philosophy that argued companies must be free to move their operations anywhere in the world in order to minimise costs and maximise returns to investors. A new six-step plan to national prosperity was proposed that advocated: free trade, unfettered investment, deregulation, balanced budgets, low inflation and privatisation of publicly owned enterprises. This new philosophy encouraged the spread of globalisation whereby every aspect of life was increasingly affected by this new global structure of communication and economy.

Ellwood goes on to argue that the spread of free trade in goods and services encouraged the deregulation of world financial markets. This led to the unleashing of financial institutions like the banks, insurance companies and investment dealers. Prior to this they had been confined within national borders but now had access to global markets. The big financial corporations from Europe, Japan and North America expanded into each other's markets as well as quickly dominating the fragile financial markets in the developing world. Ellwood argues that finance capital became a profoundly destabilising influence on the global economy. It also coincided with the growing influence of supra-national regulatory bodies (such as IMF, **GATT**, World Bank) and the transformations of trade and debt through the traumas of structural adjustment programmes (SAPs). Ellwood is critical of these bodies for their high-handed approach and their imposition of neo-liberalist policies. Neo-liberalism is explained in detail on page 184.

TNCs and horizontal and vertical flexibility

Ankie Hoogvelt (2001) argues that transnational corporations (TNCs) seek to make alliances with local landed elites. In doing so, they lower resistance to the exploitative nature of their production processes. In addition, they gain access to facilities like purpose-built EPZs (see page 224). Hoogvelt talks about the benefits to TNCs of **horizontal flexibility**. This refers to the increasing global interconnectedness of TNCs with other local firms. To quickly establish production TNCs can discreetly outsource fabrication activities to local firms for short-term services such as finishing products. This can also mask sweatshop working conditions, even though they are directly associated with the TNCs. Over time, horizontal flexibility may result in take-overs and mergers across borders. When mergers involve TNCs taking over companies from the developing world, they can be aggravated by tensions between organisational cultures.

Hoogvelt also recognises the impact of **vertical flexibility** which refers to changes within global firms, especially with regard to the treatment of workers. She describes how TNCs particularly employ semi-skilled labour, decreasing their security and rewards. Through the international division of labour, TNCs increasingly employ workforces from developing countries in a variety of tenuous capacities. For example, workers have limited employment rights, insecurity of employment and frequently endure the uncertainties of self-employment and piecemeal work. At the same time, the high status and remunerated positions, such as marketing experts, IT consultants, legal affairs specialists, financial accountants and top managers are typically supplied from the developed world.

Moyo and African Development

Dambisa Moyo (2009) has criticised the government aid programme that amounts to $1 trillion over the last four decades. She argues that it has singularly failed to develop Africa. She is sometimes mistakenly accused of criticising NGO aid, but is actually a supporter of humanitarian and charity aid.

She has little time for celebrity-led aid, arguing that it perpetuates a negative view of Africa. By focusing very much on the negative, they reinforce images of Africa as a place of conflict, disease, corruption and poverty. Moyo rhetorically asks, 'where is the voice of African governments?' But she responds that they cannot be bothered to say anything, since they are sitting on an endless supply of governmental aid and World Bank loans. Another problem for Moyo is debt relief. She questions giving debt relief if it just gets replaced by new aid and debt simply reinforcing rather than breaking the aid cycle. Across the African continent, most countries have at least 70 per cent dependency on aid.

Moyo advocates for countries to build up their own government bond rating in order to finance their own development. But she argues, 'why go to the trouble of getting a bond rating when I can just go to the World Bank? Or go to the G20? Or actually, have Bono go to the G20 and ask for you'. She also promotes the role of microfinance – lending to small local initiatives to help them progress in business or farming. She is also a big supporter of the Chinese presence in Africa, pointing out how they have transformed the infrastructure in many African countries, something the West has shown no interest in doing since its colonies gained independence.

Moyo disagrees that democracy is a prerequisite for economic growth, citing countries like China and Singapore. She supports the view of Przeworski *et al.* (2001) who argue that long-term stable democracy is not possible unless the population earn at least $6,000 a year. It is therefore a false hope even trying to establish democracy in countries where poverty is widespread.

> **KEY SOCIOLOGIST**
>
> **Naomi Klein** (2000) is a Canadian journalist who made an important sociological contribution with her antiglobalisation book *No Logo* (2000). Since then she has argued that the globalised free-market economy has become a doomsday machine, pumping out ever increasing quantities of carbon and setting our civilisation up for a head-on collision with environmental disaster (*This Changes Everything*, 2014).

> **CONTEMPORARY APPLICATION**
>
> Since the collapse of the Soviet Union, Cuba struggled to cope with the isolation imposed by US sanctions. Despite this it developed organic agriculture, established an excellent education system and a world-class health care system. Despite struggling to find trading partners and its population enduring poverty, it acted as a model that defied most, if not all, conventional ideas around development and how it is possible to avoid the neo-liberal intervention of the World Bank and IMF. On 14 August 2015 the USA reopened its embassy in the capital Havana. Renewed US diplomatic relations with Cuba means its economic and political days of trade embargoes and isolation are effectively a thing of the past.

> **STUDY TIP**
>
> The three authors discussed above (Ellwood, Moyo and Hoogvelt) are all critical to different degrees of the supra-national bodies like international NGOs, TNCs, World Bank and IMF. Their criticisms allow you to evaluate the activities of these global bodies.

3.2 What power do TNCs exert?

You need to differentiate TNCs from national and multinational companies, as well as demonstrating an awareness of their power and domination of world trade. Bringing in applied examples as well as concepts like 'creative destruction' will add depth to your answer.

Figure 4.18 An oil and gas terminal in Nigeria

TNCs and politics

While TNCs are primarily involved in economic activities (which this section reflects) Leslie Sklair (2007) makes the important point that it is impossible to ignore their engagement in political activities of various types. He highlights the complex and varied engagement TNCs have at all levels of the political sphere, from community and urban, through national to global politics. TNCs can be involved with many different political groups including governments, political parties and what he calls the 'service industries' of politics (such as interest groups).

The economist Joseph Schumpeter (1943) used the concept of '**creative destruction**' to describe how industrial innovations serve to continually reshape capitalism. An obvious example of this is the decline of heavy industry and manufacturing in the West which has been replaced with service and high-tech jobs. As a visionary of global processes, he predicted both monopolisation as well as the growing size of firms. Therefore, even after many decades, his work can explain the nature of TNC penetration into developing countries. Globally the world is dominated by a minority of powerful companies in positions of economic and political power.

The increasing influence of TNCs

Froebel *et al.* (1980) describe how the new international division of labour led to a substantial movement of industrial capital from the industrialised world to the developing world. The NIDL developed in the 1970s when rising labour costs together with high levels of industrial conflict in the Western industrial societies was reducing the profitability of TNCS. At the same time developing countries were beginning to set up Export-Processing Zones (EPZs) or **free-trade zones** (FTZs) where TNCs were offered many incentives to locate their factories in order to produce goods for export back to the West.

From a modernisation/neo-liberal perspective, TNCs provided inward investment, jobs and by implication economic growth to the developing world. However, Linda Weiss (2005) notes how TNCs effectively operate in a way that denies developing countries the 'right' to develop their own infant industries. In addition, TNCs are content to exploit the cheap labour; tax breaks for relocation, lax health and safety rules and the fact that trade unions were often banned. At the same time, they often paid little, if any, taxes to developing countries on their earnings and profits, which invariably flowed back to the developed world.

Environmental influence

Naomi Klein (2014) condemns TNCs for their reckless destruction of the environment and the world's ecosystem and avoiding their **corporate responsibility**, paying only lip service to such responsibilities. She describes their rhetoric about fair trading, sustainability and indigenous people as '**green wash**'. Corporate decision-makers rarely consider the financial, social and environmental impact upon local communities of their actions, seeking only to maximise their profits.

She argues that if we really valued all lives equally across the world then TNCs and governments would transform how they respond to the climate crisis. She points to the hypocrisy of green and charitable organisations that profess great concern about climate change but actually invest in fossil-fuel-producing TNCs. For example, the (Bill) Gates Foundation has at least $1.2bn invested in oil giants BP and ExxonMobil (as of December 2013) among a vast portfolio of fossil fuel holdings.

> **KEY SOCIOLOGISTS**
>
> **Ivan Illich** (1987) argues that TNCs create '**false needs**' in the way they market products that are either harmful (cigarettes) or have minimal nutritional value (carbonated drinks and junk food). Baby milk formula is a classic example, since breast milk is by far the better option for new born babies. **Susan George** (1976) exposed the scandal of how new mothers were manipulated into using formula in the developing world in the 1970s – it still seems to be an issue in the twenty-first century.

> **CONTEMPORARY APPLICATION**
>
> Such is the power of TNCs that some are even allowed to create their own enclaves within the developing countries. In such enclaves the country's national laws become secondary to the rules and regulations of the TNC. Because TNCs are often bigger than nation states, they exercise considerable muscle power and can play one developing country off against another in order to secure the most cost-effective location for their production.

> **STUDY TIP**
>
> Application of TNCs is elevated when they are discussed through applied examples and in the context of theory. The obvious debate is between the neo-liberal (positive) position and the Marxist (pessimist) position. But consider also how transformationalists and inter-nationalists would view TNCs.

RESEARCH IN FOCUS

Infidel brands: Alternative meanings to global brands

Elif Izberk-Bilgin undertook research in Turkey to examine how Western global brands like Nestlé, McDonald's, and Coca-Cola were received. Such brands are firstly associated with powerful nation states, coupled with their immense financial resources and cultural influence. He argues that such global brands became tangled in a complex web of socio-political dynamics, subjecting these brands to religiously charged interpretations and frequently labelled as 'infidels'. He also found that religious ideology impacted upon consumer behaviour. Religion and ideology intertwined in complex way, often informing consumer identity and attitudes toward brands.

Izberk-Bilgin found that in less industrialised countries, a lack of access to resources and power, coupled with eroding faith in modern institutions, left some consumers seeking meaning in religious ideology to cope with growing resentment of daily socio-economic problems. He found the articulation of Islamic teaching found a particularly fertile ground as a soothing rhetoric to locals' discontent with the International Monetary Fund's and World Bank's neo-liberal interference through their strategic adjustment plans.

He suggests that the Marxist undertones of Islamism have been fostering resentment to the ideals of 'market society' and which often culminates in antagonistic attitudes to global brands. For example, branches of McDonald's, Kentucky Fried Chicken and HSBC in Turkey, Egypt, Pakistan, and Palestine have been vandalised. In all of these areas Islamism has been on the rise. The explanation is that the poor are the most adversely affected by globalisation and the most likely to be susceptible to religious rhetoric. Popular Islamic beliefs praise the moral superiority of avoiding material ostentation which is believed to contaminate the soul. Many thus actively seek to minimise their participation in consumer culture and to particularly see these iconic Western brands of global capitalism as 'infidels'.

Adapted from Izberk-Bilgin (2014)

> **Questions**
> 1. Why do you think Western brands are viewed as 'infidels' by some in Islamic countries?
> 2. Why do you think Islamism is more influential in less industrialised countries?
> 3. In what ways might Islamism have 'Marxist undertones'?

3.3 What is the role of non-government organisations (NGOs)?

It is important to recognise the aspirations of NGOs, the different forms they take and the important success they can achieve at local level. The proliferation of NGOs means they exert an important contribution to global politics. Inevitably they offer, at best, only a small improvement into the global situation.

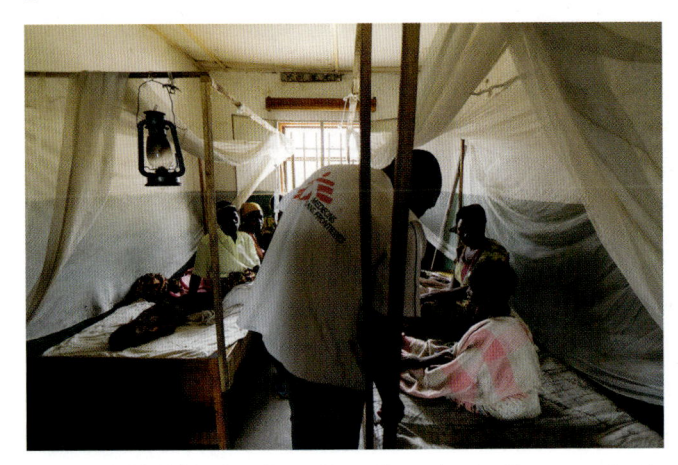

Figure 4.19 Médecins Sans Frontières in the Democratic Republic of Congo

Introduction

The term non-governmental organisation (NGO) refers to any non-profit citizens group which is organised to provide humanitarian help. They are better known simply as 'charities'. The activities of NGOs vary widely. They can exist on a local, national or international level. We focus here on the latter – international non-government organisations (INGOs). INGOs are independent of government or business, but often work closely with either to deliver humanitarian help to people in need.

NGOs vary tremendously in size. There are small specialist NGOs, sometimes operating in just one country, as well as the large organisations like Oxfam, Save the Children and Médecins Sans Frontières (MSF). Whatever their nature, NGOs must reconcile the fact that despite their lofty goals and aspirations, they will never have sufficient resources to transform the lives of all individuals and communities in the developing world. This, however, is not to deny the significant impact their work frequently achieves at a local level. Often overlooked are the unintended consequences of their work. For example, NGO aid can stimulate new streams of income, indirectly create employment, and can unintentionally stimulate more cosmopolitan and tolerant societies.

What do NGOs do?

Some NGOs are focused on achieving change person by person, often through micro-projects. Robert Chambers (1993) is a strong advocate of what he terms '**participatory rural appraisal (PRA)**' whereby he argues NGOs have significant advantages over government agencies in developing new methods to analyse what people need. NGOs, he argues, are:

- good at working with people in what he terms 'the process mode'
- able to start small projects and grow, adapt and improve them gradually
- successful in developing organisations that can serve local communities and their people.

Such organisations can then take the work forward and act as village development catalysts. Bebbington *et al.* (2008) share this view arguing that the major strength of NGOs is the grassroots linkages that NGOs can offer. This enables them to design services and programmes using innovative and experimental approaches centred on community participation.

Other NGOs focus on educating, campaigning and lobbying politicians and governments. While global inequality means that this activity is inevitably focused on the developing world, some NGOs (like the Red Cross) can help the vulnerable and those in need in the UK also.

The public image of NGOs is often of their work providing disaster relief in emergencies around the world. They are particularly visible in crises that can follow earthquakes, tsunamis, droughts and the build-up of refugees from conflict zones. Fundraising for such disaster relief is often co-ordinated with the Disasters Emergency Committee (DEC). Over the years, aid from governments and **intergovernmental organisations** (IGOs) has often been siphoned off by politicians and elites through kleptocracy. A response to this has been for NGOs to be increasingly used for the distribution of Official Development Assistance from governments and IGOs. Besides diminishing the potential for corruption, governments can send a signal to sceptical donors that their money is being used by responsible organisations to directly benefit ordinary people rather than swelling the elite's Swiss bank accounts.

Criticisms of NGOs

Some of the biggest NGOs have been criticised for becoming detached from their founding principles and operating more like businesses than charities. For example, Graham Hancock (1989) describes their highly paid executives as 'lords of poverty'. CEOs of NGOs typically get paid six-figure salaries, while their workers frequently receive low wages or are volunteers. In 2013 Britain's 30 executives working in the 14 leading foreign aid NGOs were each paid more than £100,000. In response to public condemnation, some like MSF operate a pay policy whereby the highest employee never earns more than three times the lowest-paid employee. The global food charity Mary's Meals pays its CEO the organisation's average salary of around £32,000 (2014). It argues that it is difficult to justify a 'genuine partnership' with people living and working in impoverished conditions if its own workers are highly paid. In addition, money donated by the public often goes to pay for smart NGO headquarters (frequently in central London), administration costs and attendance for their workers to be delegates at expensive international conferences. The charity watchdog website 'aliveandgiving.com' claims that some NGOs can have a charitable spend of as little as 71 per cent of their revenue (August, 2015).

NGOs have come in for close scrutiny from Edwards and Hulme (1992) who concluded that: 'it is none too soon for NGOs to put their house in order'. They argue that NGOs' ability to attract support, and consequently act legitimately in the field of development, rests fundamentally on their ability to demonstrate effective performance and accountability: the chain of operations and funding can be quite extensive. The process often starts with INGOs who will then contract one or several medium-sized NGOs to undertake beneficial work on their behalf. These NGOs may then make contact with national NGOs in the capitals of the developing countries involved. The actual delivery may then be undertaken by small local NGOs using low or unpaid volunteers and local people. Clearly, the longer the chain between the INGO and the ultimate beneficiary villages, the greater the chance of money being used for bureaucratic procedures. In addition, the more organisations money passes through the greater the risk that some will be siphoned off by corrupt officials.

Therefore NGOs are increasingly under the spotlight in terms of the impact their money has in transforming people's lives on the ground. In addition, they are increasingly judged on their contribution to sustainability. Therefore, besides addressing issues from agriculture and food security to the crises of malnutrition and absolute poverty, they have to demonstrate innovation with regard to ecology and the environment.

The United Nations (2012) recognises that poverty reduction is far more successful when it is accomplished through a holistic, sustainable approach. Some NGOs are involved in small-scale lending through initiatives like microcredit and microfinance. Despite some excellent projects, the work of NGOs serves only to scratch the surface: global inequalities and the need for assistance and help remain huge demands upon those relatively better off in both the developed and developing world.

It is important to remember that NGOs are all different, each with its own agenda, principles and altruistic goals. They face uncertainties associated with the cultural, political and ecological environment in which they operate. The success of their activities will depend upon factors like:

- their internal efficiencies
- how realistic their goals are and
- the social and material technologies being employed.

As Watkins et al. (2012) note: 'they are shaped as much by how they are imagined as by what they actually do. These organisations confront a profound contradiction between the global visions of transformation that animate them and the complex, obdurate material and social realities they encounter on the ground'.

Global civil society

Bebbington et al. (2008) have drawn attention to the accountability of NGOs through the concept of **global civil society**. The term refers to the vast assemblage of groups operating globally, frequently beyond the reach of governments. Global civil society includes INGOs, NGOs, global social movements, tourists, academics, artists, cultural performers and ethnic and linguistic groups. Some see global civil society as an autonomous coherent group with potential power to change and exert influence. Others see it as little more than a reflection and representation of Western liberal society. Those with a particular focus of concern, such as women's issues, possibly have a greater chance of bringing change. Because of the heterogeneity of the groups who

> **KEY SOCIOLOGISTS**
> **Swidler and Watkins** (2009) have made an important contribution to this debate through highlighting how the ideal of sustainability has become dogma in many aid programmes. Sustainability aims to avoid recipients becoming dependent, but instead self-reliant. It also goes down well with donors. By announcing from the outset that programmes are of limited duration and must be sustainable, donors feel they are avoiding a long-term commitment.

comprise the global civil society they have been described as everything and nothing. What is true is that the global civil society is an evolving entity.

It is important to recognise that while these organisations are driven by altruism and a desire to make the world a better place, in evaluating their success it is important to note that they are often just one of many factors at work in an area where the change has occurred. Equally, in other areas where similar programmes were in operation, no change may be recorded.

> **STUDY TIP**
> While NGOs are viewed very positively by the population at large, it is important to be able to evaluate them critically. Take the opportunity to research examples of NGOs.

> **CONTEMPORARY APPLICATION**
> NGOs are something of a contradiction. They have to reconcile grand goals, modest techniques and frequently difficult environments. While each NGO has specific goals and objectives, their collective agenda seems to be representing the needs and aspirations of the global citizenry. Because NGOs do not operate in a social, political and economic vacuum, there is inevitably going to be some form of agenda behind their activities.

> **RESEARCH IN FOCUS**
>
> ### The impact of tourism on the developing world
>
> Saarinen and Lenao (2014) undertook research into the impact of tourism on poverty in the developing world. They wanted to investigate evidence for the claimed link between tourism and poverty alleviation. This correlation is summed up in the term 'pro-poor tourism' (PPT). The aim of PPT is to create net benefits for the poor in developing countries.
>
> The extent of these benefits is predominantly economic but can also benefit poor people in terms of social, environmental and cultural issues. However, the PPT model has received harsh criticism from those who question to what extent the benefits of tourism extend beyond the private tourist businesses.
>
> Saarinen and Lenao found that tourism development often caused conflicts and issues of inclusion and exclusion in rural areas and poor communities.
>
> They concluded that tourism can represent a viable tool for rural development but, as noted also by the World Bank, tourism 'comes with its own set of risks and challenges'. Thus, their research argues that governmental or other similar structures should provide support for the communities to control and benefit from tourism activities. In this way tourism can be viewed as a tool in which Integrated Rural Tourism (IRT) could provide a useful framework for implementing the elements like sustainability. The IRT framework, by emphasising the core elements of networking, sustainability and empowerment, could aid in the understanding of the different dimensions and contexts tourist development can take in the developing world. However, so far the IRT framework has been developed and mainly utilised in the European context.
>
> Adapted from Saarinen and Lenao (2014)

Questions

1. Suggest ways in which tourism could benefit the poor in developing countries.
2. Why has pro-poor tourism come in for criticism?
3. What were the conclusions of Saarinen and Lenao?

3.4 What is the role of international governmental organisations?

Highlight the growing importance of IGOs in shaping global affairs since the Second World War. They need to be differentiated from NGOs and particularly with organisations like the IMF, World Bank and WTO, how they openly promote a neo-liberal agenda, with all its consequences.

Introduction

The role of the international governmental organisations (IGOs) has developed significantly since the end of the Second World War. The most significant IGO is the United Nations (UN) which was created in 1947. IGOs are also known as supra-state organisations, since they exist outside nation states and represent global rather than partisan state interests. Critics argue they tend to reflect, if not US interests, certainly the pursuit of a pro-capitalist agenda. This is particularly the case with the IMF, World Bank and World Trade Organisation (WTO) whose appetite for neo-liberalist economics and politics has labelled them the 'Washington consensus' (see page 184). As an ex-employee of the organisations, Ariel Buira (2003) is very critical of the World Bank, the IMF and the WTO arguing that they have grossly overstepped their mandate by imposing political and economic directions that violate the sovereign will of states. A common thread that runs through the writings of Buira is his concern for the lack of 'ownership' developing countries have with regard to the imposition of policies by the World Bank and IMF.

Figure 4.20 The World Bank in Washington DC

The United Nations (UN)

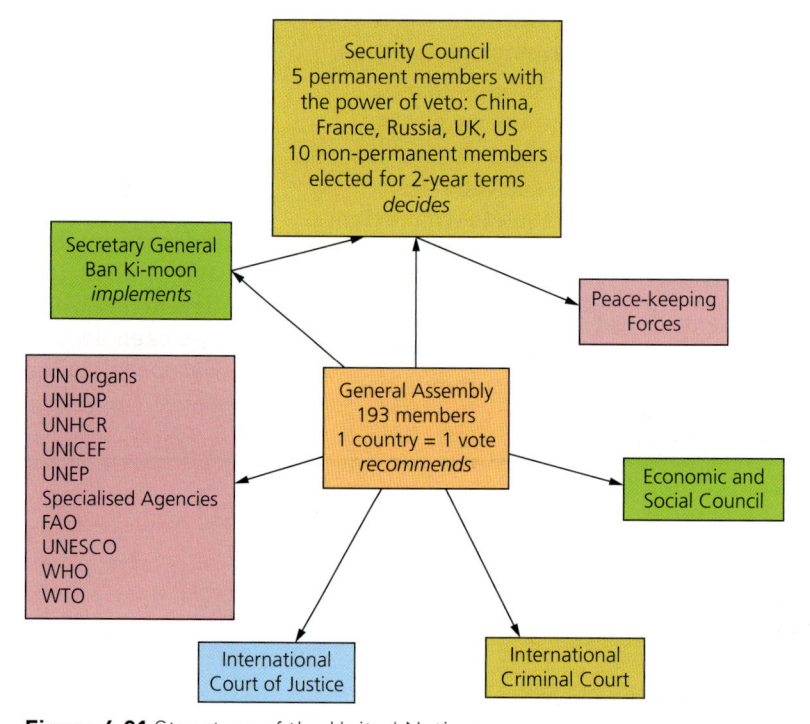

Figure 4.21 Structure of the United Nations

The United Nations (UN) was founded in 1945 and created in 1947 after the Second World War by 51 countries. It made an early commitment to maintain international peace and security. It also sought to develop friendly relations among nations along with the promotion of social progress, economic development and human rights. Today the UN has five areas of responsibility: fostering peace and security, promoting development, guarding human rights, monitoring humanitarian affairs and the upholding of international law. It works on these through its 15 agencies such as UNICEF (United Nations Children's Fund). The UN Secretary General is an influential global figure and often will take a prominent personal stand in order to help resolve global conflicts, address humanitarian issues and highlight environmental disasters.

Over time the influence and voice of developing countries has become louder and more influential within the UN as they gained independence from colonial rule and represented themselves at the General Assembly of the UN in their own right.

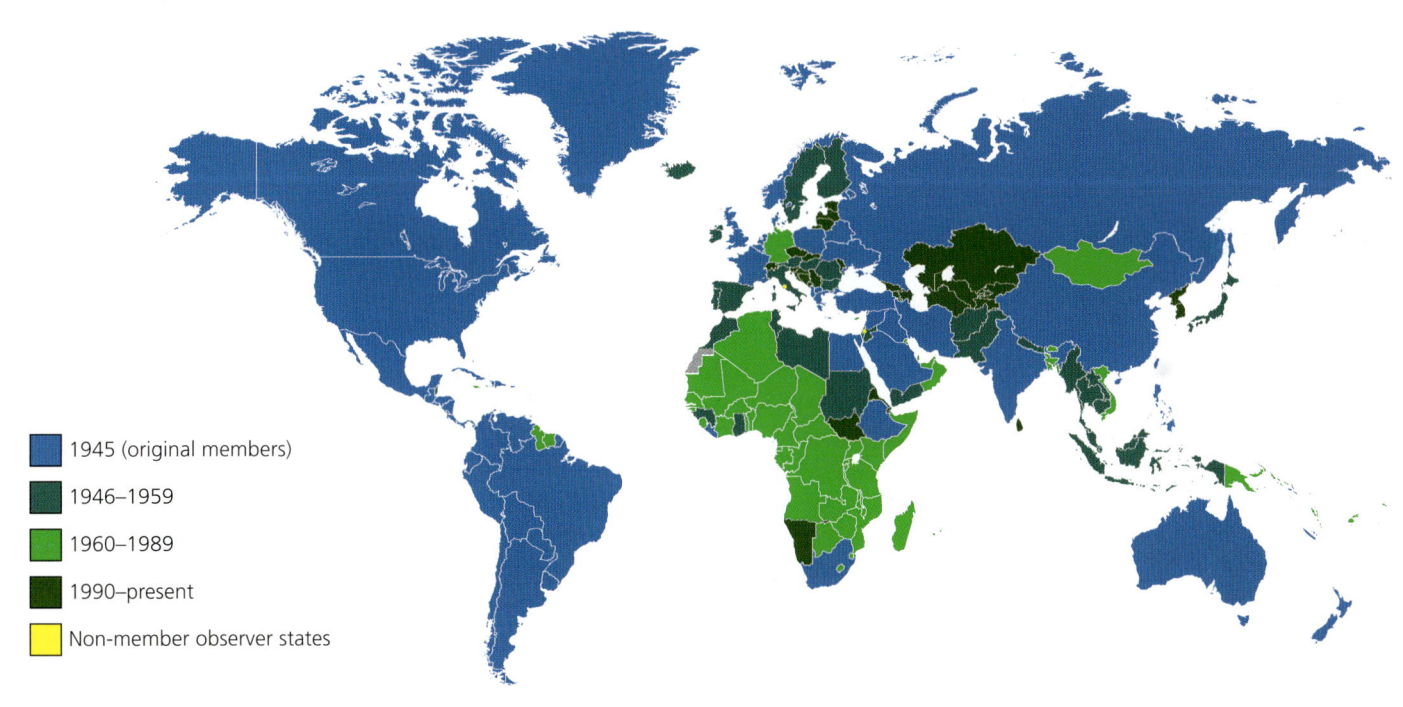

Figure 4.22 Map of the current United Nations' member states by date

Although the General Assembly votes on matters before the UN, decisions made here are not binding. Nonetheless, the presence of developing countries ensures that the UN is often perceived to be more radical than more conservative bodies like the IMF, World Bank and the World Trade Organisation (WTO).

The Security Council of the UN is where the UN's power is most concentrated. The Security Council comprises 15 members, of whom the USA, UK, Russia, China and France are permanent members with the right to veto any amendment. These five permanent Security Council members have at times brought the UN into disrepute through their own nations' actions. All five of these nations can veto decisions made by the council so can effectively reduce the UN to a powerless body. For example, Russia has systematically supported President Assad of Syria and the pro-Russian militia opponents of the Ukraine government. Although developing countries now comprise a quota of the remaining ten non-permanent Security Council members, they have limited influence and power by not being able to veto anything they object to.

Financial and economic IGOs

Financial IGOs include the World Bank, the International Monetary Fund (IMF) and the World Trade Organisation (WTO). These are the three major supra-national organisations which run the world economy. Although they come under the UN system, in practice they operate as autonomous organisations, pursuing a well-rehearsed and prominent neo-liberal agenda. Both the IMF and World Bank were established at **Bretton Woods** when in 1944 delegates from 44 countries met during the Second World War to reshape the world's international financial system. The distribution of power within both the IMF and World Bank is based on financial contributions. This inevitably means they are controlled by the developed countries.

International Monetary Fund (IMF)

The IMF's initial remit was to enforce a set of currency fixed exchange rates that were linked to the dollar. Countries with trade deficits (where the value of their imports exceeded the value of their exports) could receive short-term loans from the IMF to avoid devaluation of their currencies. During the 1970s many countries, including the USA, abandoned fixed exchange rates (allowing their currencies to float on the stock exchange). The IMF continued helping countries cope with major economic crises, including bailing out Britain in 1976 when the nation came close to bankruptcy.

In the 1980s many developing countries encountered a debt crisis. The IMF took on the role of regulating countries in debt and offering them loans in return for structural adjustment programmes (SAPs). The IMF has come in for some vocal criticism about the way it deals with countries in debt. Joseph Stiglitz (2004) believes that with the World Bank and the US Treasury, the IMF embarked on a conspiracy to run worldwide economic reform (the 'Washington Consensus'). He is critical of the IMF's rigid adherence to neo-liberal policies, regardless of their often quite negative consequences for developing nations. Stiglitz argues that SAPs are driven by neo-liberal ideology, but with no apparent concern for the human costs. The IMF's approach to problems seems to be focused on the short term, ignoring the human suffering this can cause and disregarding long-term factors. Postmodernists argue its single approach of neo-liberal solutions ignores the fact that each country is different with unique characteristics and resources (see page 176 re: modernism and development and Ferdinand Tönnies' concept of '**gemeinschaft**'). A one size fits all approach is therefore a very blunt instrument.

The World Bank

The World Bank (officially the International Bank for Reconstruction and Development) was set up to make long-term loans, including the restoration of economies destroyed or disrupted by the Second World War. Such was the success of the US-backed Marshall Plan in assisting European countries' post-War recovery that the World Bank took this as a model to use in helping poor countries develop. The World Bank is owned by its 188 member countries. It raises money on the global financial markets at rates cheaper than individual governments could achieve and passes on this benefit to member countries in the form of cheap loans. Very poor countries receive loans at zero rate of interest from International Development Assistance (IDA). Like the IMF, the World Bank has come under fierce criticism, not least from the close links it maintains with the IMF. It is also obsessed with a neo-liberal economic agenda of structural adjustment programmes, even though these create human suffering and tend to polarise societies (widening the gap between the rich and poor).

World Trade Organisation (WTO)

The World Trade Organisation's origins go back to **Bretton Woods** which proposed the International Trade Organisation to encourage free trade. The USA refused to ratify its charter in 1947 and it was never developed. Tariff reductions were pursued later through the General Agreement on Trade and Tariffs (GATT) treaty which took effect in 1948. GATT survived until 1994 when it was replaced by the World Trade Organization in 1995.

As with the other IGOs, the WTO pursues a neo-liberal agenda, promoting global capitalism. While in theory poorer members have a say and vote, in practice they tend to be excluded. In theory the WTO exists to promote free trade; in reality rich countries and regions like the USA and EU continue with export subsidies and import tariffs. The WTO seems unable to achieve free trade, but it still promotes this as a goal, when critics argue it should be addressing more serious issues like sustainability.

A change in direction?

In 2014 both Christine Lagarde and Jim Yong Kim, heads of the IMF and World Bank respectively, appeared to distance their organisations from neo-liberal policies (see In the News, page 214). However, in terms of actual policy in 2015 the World Bank was still advocating cutting corporate taxes, labour protection and minimum wages; the IMF was still advocating austerity. It would appear there are deep-seated ideological identifications in each organisation.

KEY SOCIOLOGIST

Torfason and Ingram (2010) examined the influence of intergovernmental organisations (IGOs) on the global diffusion of democracy. They claim that IGOs facilitate the spread of democracy through transmitting information between member states. They also claimed that the influence of democratic countries is stronger than that of undemocratic countries. They describe their findings as an important contribution to sociological accounts of globalisation.

CONTEMPORARY APPLICATION

The work of IGOs could be seen to coincide with the eighth Millennium Development Goal of developing a global partnership for development.

STUDY TIP

Differentiate and evaluate the respective roles of IGOs and how they differ to those of NGOs. There will be projects when the goals of IGOs may coincide with those of NGOs.

> **IN THE NEWS**
>
> ### New thinking by IMF and World Bank on global inequality
>
> The neo-liberal 'Washington consensus' of the past is under threat as both the IMF and World Bank soften their rhetoric and pledge that reducing inequality is morally right as well as being economically necessary. Hints that maybe the Washington consensus of neo-liberalism is possibly being re-evaluated arose when both Christine Lagarde and Jim Yong Kim (heads of the IMF and World Bank respectively) both softened their public rhetoric and distanced themselves from the old neo-liberalist arguments.
>
> Ms Lagarde warned of a 'staggering' rise in global inequality with the ghosts of the nineteenth century returning to haunt the twenty-first. Jim Yong Kim pledged to eradicate poverty in a generation while boosting the incomes of the poorest 40 per cent.
>
> Only a short while ago this sort of language would never have been uttered by either the IMF or the World Bank – the Washington consensus banged home its single neo-liberal message that markets had to be liberalised, industry had to be privatised, trade unions had to be restrained and public spending had to be savagely cut. Inequality was rarely mentioned (other than in terms of reflecting meritocracy and promoting ambition) but this too could be left to the free market to solve. Inequality, it was assumed, would promote faster growth through encouraging entrepreneurialism – wealth ultimately trickles down to the poor anyway.
>
> Has the deepest global slump since the 1930s, followed by a weak recovery, finally killed off the Washington consensus? It is too early to say, not least because the consensus still has many influential supporters.
>
> For the Washington consensus to end, policy changes would be necessary both by the IMF and the World Bank and the individual governments who control them. The recent more progressive economic policy of the USA has not been matched by that of Europe. The IMF and the World Bank need to match what they say to what they actually do - the message is one of eradicating poverty, yet the advice is to continue with austerity measures. Until spending and tax policies are in place to redistribute income from the richest to the poorest 40 per cent, the Washington consensus effectively remains.
>
> Adapted from *The Guardian* (2014)

Questions

1. What was the rhetoric and ideas of the old 'Washington consensus'?
2. In what ways have both the IMF and the World Bank softened their rhetoric?
3. What evidence is there of contradictions between what IMF and World Bank say and do?
4. Why is there uncertainty about the future policies of both these IGOs?

Check your understanding

1. How can Schumpeter's concept of creative destruction be applied to TNCs?
2. Why are TNCs attracted to export-processing zones?
3. What are the three strategies identified by Benjamin Selwyn which TNCs adopt to gain global power?
4. What does Naomi Klein mean by the term 'green wash' applied to TNCs?
5. What is an INGO?
6. Why did Graham Hancock refer to NGOs as 'Lords of Poverty'?
7. What is meant by the term global civil society?
8. Which countries hold most power within the United Nations?
9. What is the dominant economic ideology of the financial IGOs?
10. What are structural adjustment programmes of the IMF and World Bank?

Practice questions

1. Explain the meaning of the term 'Washington consensus'. [3 marks]

Read Item A below and answer the question that follows.

Item A

International Governmental Organisations (IGOs) are organisations composed primarily of sovereign states. They include the IMF and World Bank whose contemporary remit is to assist in poverty alleviation in the developing countries. However, they have been criticised for taking on a life of their own in their pursuit of neo-liberal policies.

Applying material from Item A, analyse two ways in which IGOs exert a neo-liberal agenda through their policies on the developing world. [10 marks]

Read Item B below and answer the question that follows.

Item B

TNCs have a reputation for creating productive efficiency by keeping their costs to a minimum. They are attracted to developing countries, especially their export-processing zones, where they can benefit from cheap labour. Many developing countries have lax employment laws, minimal health and safety regulations and often no form of national minimum wage.

Applying material from Item B and your knowledge, evaluate the view that Transnational Corporations (TNCs) play an important role in generating global inequality. [20 marks]

Section 4: Development in relation to aid and trade, industrialisation, urbanisation, the environment, and war and conflict

This section will explore the following debates:
- What is aid?
- What are the arguments in favour of aid?
- What are the arguments against aid?
- What is urbanisation?
- The environment and development
- How do war and conflict impact upon the developing world?

GETTING YOU STARTED

Smokescreen of Western aid to Africa

Health Poverty Action and other NGOs state that Western aid to Africa is masking the 'sustained looting' of the continent to the tune of almost $60 billion annually.

Loans, investment and aid of $134bn reach sub-Saharan countries each year. However, the research found that the region loses up to $192bn in the form of debt repayment, tax evasion, and profits earned by foreign multinationals, amounting to a deficit of $58bn.

Although Western countries give $30bn annually in development aid, the report says that most of the vast amount of money leaving the continent goes back 'mainly to the same countries providing that aid'. Debt repayment alone accounts for $21bn per year.

The report states that the widely accepted idea that the West is helping African countries 'has facilitated a perverse reality in which the UK and other wealthy governments celebrate their generosity while simultaneously assisting their companies to drain Africa's resources'. It is estimated that TNCs profit from $46bn from Africa each year, while $35bn is transferred into global tax havens.

The report calls for the aid system to be completely reformed. It says aid sent in the form of loans serves only to contribute to debt dependency, and recommends a requirement for the donor to put in place transparent contracts to ensure that the government of the recipient country can scrutinise the terms of loans and grants.

'The common understanding is that the UK "helps" Africa through aid, but in reality this serves as a smokescreen for the billions taken out,' said Martin Drewry, director of Health Poverty Action. 'Let's use more accurate language. It's sustained looting – the opposite of generous giving – and we should recognise that the City of London is at the heart of the global financial system that facilitates this.'

According to Drewry, NGOs must also change: 'We need to move beyond our focus on aid levels and communicate the bigger truth – exposing the real relationship between rich and poor, and holding leaders to account.'

Adapted from Anderson (2014)

Questions

1. What evidence supports the claim of 'sustained looting' from Africa?
2. How much do TNCs 'syphon' out of sub-Saharan Africa each year?
3. How much is estimated to move from Africa to tax havens each year?
4. What do NGOs suggest is the best way to tackle inequality between Africa and the rest of the world?

Figure 4.23 Aid such as food, water and blankets can make a huge difference to stricken communities

4.1 What is aid?

Make sure you understand that aid interests are often difficult to disentangle. With the exception of humanitarian/emergency aid in response to natural disasters, aid is rarely given purely for benevolent reasons. Often the economic, political or strategic interests of the donor country are closely tied up with the motive to give aid.

Introduction

'Aid' refers to the flow of resources from the developed to the developing world. Aid can occur in many forms:

- emergency and **humanitarian aid** (short-term response of food, tents, etc. to disasters)
- financial gifts or grants (that do not need to be paid back)
- 'soft' loans (below the commercial rate of interest)
- the writing off of debt
- the loan of expertise and/or technological assistance.

Official Development Assistance (ODA)

This occurs when aid is transferred by **OECD (Organisation for Economic Cooperation and Development) countries** either directly (**bilateral aid**) or through IGOs such as World Bank, IMF, United Nations or the European Union (**multilateral aid**). In addition, NGOs are also important donors and distributors of aid (see page 207), although this is a fraction of the value of ODA.

Sometimes aid is **tied**, whereby the money has to be spent on goods or services provided by the donor country. Cynics argue the purpose of such aid is frequently to benefit the donor country rather than the recipient country. For example if the tractor industry in an industrialised country was in financial trouble owing to a lack of orders, then tied aid could be given to developing countries, providing it was spent on new tractors from the donor country. Tied aid is also often linked in with support for the arms industry. Countries with poor and malnourished populations may be given aid that can only be spent on arms, rather than invested in agricultural infrastructure.

Non-OECD nations can also provide aid. Venezuelan President Hugo Chavez has pursued an alternative to the neo-liberal aid agenda of the 'Washington consensus', freeing Bolivia from its long-standing IMF structural adjustment programme. Cuba trains thousands of doctors each year from the developing

> **KEY SOCIOLOGIST**
>
> **Teresa Hayter** (1971) is a key opponent of aid. She argues that most aid is targeted at the wrong people, so the poor frequently receive no benefit from it all. In addition, she highlights the neo-liberal ideological bias of the World Bank and IMF (the 'Washington consensus'), even though they both claim to be independent of the politics.

world, free of charge, with the sole condition that they return to their countries and practice medicine on the poor. Since 1960 Cuba has dispatched more than 135,000 medical staff to help with humanitarian aid for crises such as earthquakes. In 2014 the World Health Organisation (WHO) thanked Cuba for the largest offer of a foreign medical team from a single country to help with the outbreak of the Ebola virus in Western Africa. The 62 doctors and 103 nurses sent to Sierra Leone are just one part of a 50,000-strong legion of Cuban doctors and health care workers spread across 66 countries in Latin America, Asia and Africa.

The UK's aid budget has been criticised by some members of the public and some political parties like the UK Independence Party (UKIP). They argue for a complete halt in the £12 billion aid budget (2015), arguing it should be spent on projects in Britain. There is also growing opposition generally to giving aid to countries like India and China, who are both embarking on a 'space race', seen to be of little benefit to their citizens.

Much of the UK's aid budget goes to former colonies and could be interpreted as a moral obligation to help provide the basic needs and perhaps compensate for past injustices. By achieving aid donations equivalent to 0.7 per cent of GDP in 2013, the UK was the first G20 country to do so.

> **CONTEMPORARY APPLICATION**
>
> By 2014 the Coca-Cola Corporation had trained around half-a-million poor women in 44 countries in the previous three years in small-scale entrepreneurial ventures. Examples include starting sari-sari convenience stores in the Philippines, farmers growing mangoes in Kenya, and villagers building tiny recycling operations out of discarded bottles from trash heaps in Mexico. In a direct criticism of government aid which was viewed as a wasteful handing out of money, such projects are more about sustainability.

> **STUDY TIP**
>
> Make sure you can identify the different types of aid available as well as considering the arguments for and against aid in general.

IN THE NEWS

In 2013 the value of development aid rose by 6.1 per cent in real terms to reach $134.8 billion in ODA, the highest level ever recorded. This is in spite of continued pressure on domestic budgets in OECD countries caused by the global banking crisis. In 2011–12 many austerity-hit governments had cut their aid budgets.

The average aid budget for OECD countries stood at 0.3 per cent of GNP. In 2013, just five countries met the longstanding UN recommendation for an ODA/GNP ratio of 0.7 per cent. Included for the first time in this five was the UK: its aid budget had risen by 27.8 per cent over the past year.

In terms of bilateral aid, net ODA in the form of grants rose 7.7 per cent in real terms, though by 3.5 per cent if debt forgiveness grants are taken into account. Non-grant aid (including equity acquisitions) rose by about 33 per cent in real terms from 2012.

Bilateral aid to the Least Economically Developed Countries (LEDCs) rose by 12.3 per cent in real terms to about $30 billion. Such aid to sub-Saharan Africa was $26.2 billion, a decrease of 4 per cent in real terms from 2012. It is expected that this trend – a falling share of aid going to the neediest sub-Saharan African countries – is likely to continue in the future.

Adapted from Provost (2014)

Questions

1. Why were governments under pressure to cut their aid budgets around 2013?
2. In two columns outline the arguments for and against maintaining aid at least at 0.7 per cent of GDP.
3. What might be the effects of a falling share of aid going to the neediest sub-Saharan African countries?

4.2 Arguments in favour of aid

Make sure you have a good knowledge of both sides of the argument for and against aid. Remember to link each argument to theoretical perspectives and consider if there is a middle ground between the polar arguments.

The morally right thing to do?

Compassionate people argue that giving aid is simply the morally right thing to do. Given that the wealth of the developed world has been gained through historical processes impossible to justify, such as slavery and the colonial exploitation of land, labour and resources, the rich northern hemisphere is said to have an obligation to redress this and give something back. In addition, the spread of globalisation and environmentalism is highlighting the economic, cultural and political connections that bind us, and the collective interest we have in looking after the planet. Therefore there is a growing call for aid projects to protect rainforests, combat CO_2 emissions and protect endangered species. Global cultural flows highlight to the developing world the blatant global inequalities, fuelling a call for wealth redistribution. In 2015 Oxfam published a research paper claiming the richest 1 per cent will own more than all the rest of the global population by 2016. This 1 per cent have seen their share of global wealth increase from 44 per cent in 2009 to 48 per cent in 2014 – at this rate it will be more than 50 per cent in 2016. Members of this global elite had an average wealth of $2.7 million per adult (2014) when 1 in 9 people do not have enough to eat and more than a billion people still live on less than $1.25 a day.

Modernisation theory support

Modernisation theory is the strongest advocate of giving aid as a means of promoting development and hence helping countries to modernise. In the days of the Cold War (see page 176) modernisation theory advocated aid as a means of providing a non-communist solution to poverty in the developing world. Aid successfully drove development forward: objective measurements, such as global levels of infant mortality, life expectancy and literacy levels all showed an improvement. Modernisation theorists like Walt Rostow advocated aid as a means of driving inward investment that would help stimulate movement through his five stages, especially from stage 1 to stage 2 then onwards to the crucial 'take-off' stage 3 (see Figure 4.6 on page 177).

To modernisation theory, aid is viewed as a crucial component in stimulating the 'four motors of development': investment, education, mass media and urbanisation. Countries are not able to modernise quickly without these four drivers of development playing a crucial role: providing jobs and houses, improving literacy levels and changing cultural attitudes. Aid is therefore viewed as a crucial means helping to shift countries away from traditional values and poverty towards economic progress and 'modern' values such as entrepreneurialism, individualism, consumerism and meritocracy.

Modernisation theory was influential in driving World Bank policies at this time which was particularly focused on developing industry and expanding agricultural productivity. Many countries were still colonies at the time of the Cold War (or gaining their independence) so their European colonisers felt obliged to support their development with benevolent gifts of capital and expertise. Even with a growing recognition of **kleptocracy**, it was assumed by modernisation theorists that wealth would still 'trickle down' to the less well off.

Aid in conjunction with trade

Jeffrey Sachs (2005) strongly advocates Western aid, arguing that it can and does have a positive impact. He supports giving aid as a gesture of philanthropy, helping to solve key problems in the developing world. For example, he argues the case for aid to eradicate measles, malaria and diarrhoea in the developing world, which he estimates would only cost $15 for every person in the developed world. Sachs sees international co-operation and **Official Development Assistance (ODA)** as crucial to ending extreme poverty. He advocates a combination of aid and TNC investment to bring about development. Aid is one development tool among several, he says – it works best in conjunction with sound economic policies, transparency, good governance, and the effective deployment of new technologies. However, as a campaigner for free trade he advocates a change in the rules of trade which, he argues, often unfairly benefit developed nations.

The case for targeted and micro-projects

In contrast to the macro, top-down, Official Development Assistance approach, William Easterley (2006) argues that aid delivered like this invariably fails to get where it is needed most. Aid should be focused and targeted at home-grown, small-scale initiatives, with real accountability to the poor. He advocates the development of micro-projects, such as providing villages with a well that provides safe drinking water or solar panels to generate electricity. However, although such micro-projects are often very successful and can dramatically improve the quality of life for groups of people, critics of such projects complain that though laudable in themselves, they barely make a difference to global inequality.

> **KEY SOCIOLOGIST**
>
> **William Easterly** has long been a vocal opponent of aid, and recently declared that the aid debate was 'over', claiming victory for his theory that large-scale aid projects are doomed to fail. Easterly has become an advocate for small-scale targeted aid, which involves small-scale projects over which there is accountability and control. Such programmes by pass governments and so the chances of kleptocracy are minimised.

The Case for Aid (central node) connects to:

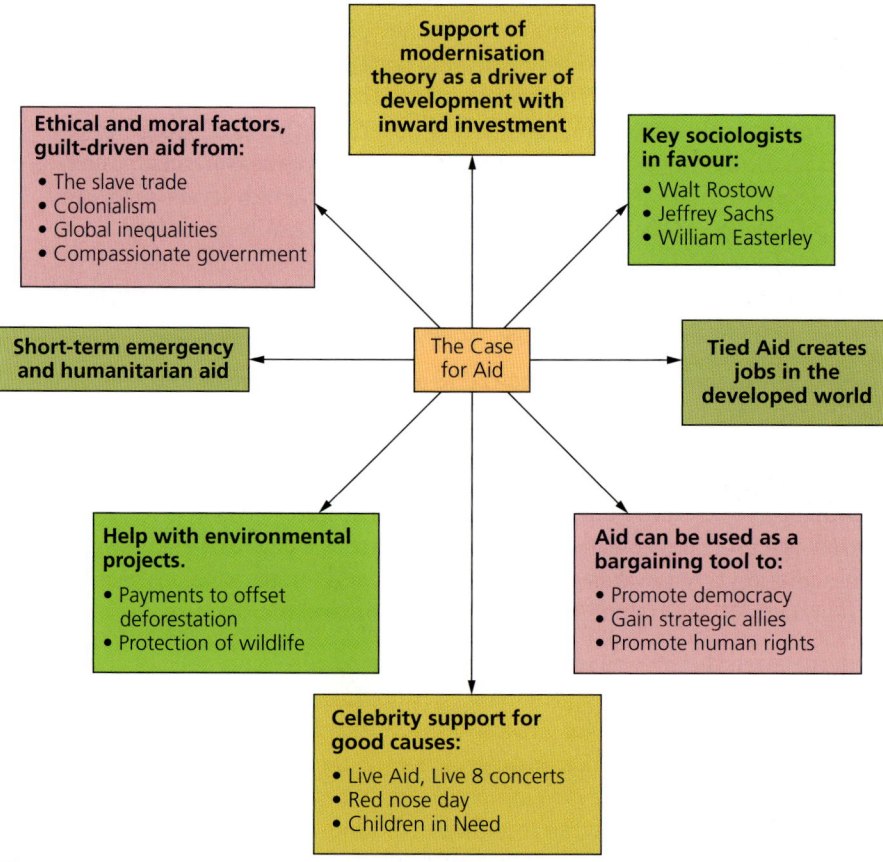

- **Support of modernisation theory as a driver of development with inward investment**
- **Key sociologists in favour:**
  - Walt Rostow
  - Jeffrey Sachs
  - William Easterley
- **Tied Aid creates jobs in the developed world**
- **Aid can be used as a bargaining tool to:**
  - Promote democracy
  - Gain strategic allies
  - Promote human rights
- **Celebrity support for good causes:**
  - Live Aid, Live 8 concerts
  - Red nose day
  - Children in Need
- **Help with environmental projects.**
  - Payments to offset deforestation
  - Protection of wildlife
- **Short-term emergency and humanitarian aid**
- **Ethical and moral factors, guilt-driven aid from:**
  - The slave trade
  - Colonialism
  - Global inequalities
  - Compassionate government

Figure 4.24 The case for aid

CONTEMPORARY APPLICATION

Aid is something of a political issue and there was criticism of the 2010 coalition government's achievement of giving 0.7 per cent of GDP target in international aid for the first time. The 2015–2020 Conservative government has committed itself to continue to meet this 0.7 per cent target. Opponents argue that charity should begin at home and that in this age of 'austerity' the money should be spent on poverty projects in the UK.

STUDY TIP

Remember that although the UK officially does not give 'tied aid, aid is rarely given without some form of strings attached.

IN THE NEWS

Is Britain being too generous with its aid?

Figure 4.25 The UK government is the biggest funder of multilateral aid

With donations totalling £6.3bn in 2013, the UK contributed the most to multilateral aid organisations such as the EU, UN and World Bank. However, a cross-party group of MPs who form the International Development Committee (IDC) feels the overuse of multilaterals has been at the expense of smaller organisations such as NGOs who often operate as specialists in delivering micro-projects. For example, Water Aid told the IDC that the Department for International Development (DfID) spent more of its budget on tackling health emergencies than on the prevention of such emergencies through the setting up of essential sanitation systems.

The IDC said that funding multilaterals was attractive to the DfID as it allowed the use of a system of promissory notes, which count as expenditure on official development assistance (ODA) but do not have to be paid until a request for a transfer is made. The IDC also noted that alongside increased multilateral funding, spending on programmes in sub-Saharan Africa had declined. As a consequence, some key millennium development goals had been missed.

The committee also expressed concern about the fact that DfID provided 13 per cent of the total spent on humanitarian assistance by the Organisation for Economic Cooperation and Development (OECD), stating: 'This is too much and enables other OECD donors to fail to meet their obligations.'

Adapted from Jones (2015)

Questions

1. Why are the MPs in the IDC critical of government aid policy?
2. Why is the government keen on donating aid as multilateral aid?
3. Using this section and your wider knowledge outline the case for giving aid.

4.3 Arguments against aid

Arguments against aid include neo-Marxist (dependency theory) and neo-liberals. It isn't often these two theories align, but their arguments against aid are very different. With the exception of short-term humanitarian and emergency aid, there are many sociologists who are fundamentally opposed to the giving of aid in principle.

Aid as imperialism (neo-Marxist view)

US President Richard Nixon famously admitted: 'Let us remember that the main purpose of aid is not to help other nations but to help ourselves.' Subsequently several US presidents have made no secret of their agreement with Nixon's admission. Neo-Marxists have used Nixon's admission to support their fundamental opposition to aid, which they argue has historically been used as a political weapon wielded by donor countries in their own interests.

The neo-Marxist Andre Gunder Frank argues that aid and debt are the third expression of neo-colonialism (see dependency theory on page 180). Far from assisting countries to develop and industrialise, dependency theory sees aid as serving to maintain underdevelopment. In addition, aid in the form of loans can simply result in a spiralling debt crisis with countries borrowing more and more simply to pay back existing debt. In Africa, many governments have devoted themselves to satisfying the interests of the international donor community without reference to the needs of their own economies and people. Small wonder that so many countries in Africa have failed to prosper.

Teresa Hayter's book *Aid as Imperialism* (1971) describes the conditional nature of aid. The developed world exercises power over underdeveloped countries by giving aid, but with conditions. According to Hayter this is a form of imperialism. In something of an irony, Hayter's neo-Marxist stance echoes the sentiment of right-wing President Nixon: Hayter sees the purpose of aid as primarily to create jobs and export markets for the donor country. She also notes how aid can be used as a lever not just for economic gains but security and strategic interests too: aid might be conditional on a country allowing its territory and air space to be used for military purposes. For example, Australia has threatened to withhold aid from countries that refuse to accommodate its 'offshore processing facilities' where it relocates its illegal immigrants.

The charity War on Want's recent report *Trading Away Our Jobs* (2009) highlights the costs in lost employment and loss of industrial capacity that occurred across Africa as a result of the trade liberalisations imposed by the World Bank and IMF. Far from stimulating growth and development, three in four of the African countries that underwent such economic restructuring experienced a decline in per capita incomes during the 1980s.

Aid and dependency (neo-liberal view)

Although the neo-liberal argument is fundamentally opposed to that of modernisation theory on aid, it does share their view that countries are poor because of 'internal factors'. In a manner reminiscent of the New Right's opposition to welfare, neo-liberal ideology argues that aid serves to compensate for and reinforce internal weaknesses, such as kleptocracy, inefficiencies and lack of entrepreneurial spirit. Neo-liberalists therefore argue that countries become lazy and what emerges is a culture of dependency – they become reliant on ever more low-interest loans from the IMF and World Bank. Neo-liberals advocate that countries should learn to stand on their own two feet. If projects are economically viable, they argue, they should be self-financing through the attraction of private investment. Such an approach would render aid no longer necessary.

One of the strongest advocates of the neo-liberal opposition to aid is Dambisa Moyo (2009). The subtitle to her book *Dead Aid* is 'Why aid is not working and how there is another way for Africa'. She argues that aid to Africa over the past five decades, far from helping, has made the situation decidedly worse. For example, she argues that in 1970 only 10 per cent of Africa's population was living in poverty. Today, despite significant amounts of aid to the continent, the figure is 70 per cent and in the poorest countries as much as 85 per cent are living in poverty. Moyo blames a combination of misdirected aid, kleptocracy on the part of political and government elites, and an over-dependency on loans from the World Bank and the IMF. Robert Calderisi, an ex-World Bank official, supports this view. He sees Africa's poverty and debt as almost entirely self-inflicted. He cites poor economic management of Western aid, especially in sub-Saharan Africa, and a lack of African unity with tribal or border conflicts as key factors.

Peter Bauer (1995) controversially argues that the poorest countries in the world have brought their poverty upon themselves. He even goes so far as to object to humanitarian aid, arguing it is demotivating. He asks why individuals and countries should bother to produce food at all when it is distributed for free whenever a crisis occurs. In terms of conventional aid, he argues 'aid' should really be called 'government to government subsidy', since the money invariably goes to developing world governments, not their people. According to Bauer, the aid industry has developed a momentum of its own because it serves not those who need it, but the vested interests of specific groups, both in the developed world and in developing countries.

Paul Collier (2008) argues that despite billions of dollars in aid, most African countries are poorer today than at the time of their independence. Tribal or border conflicts have undermined the ability of African countries to trade with each other. In addition, he suggests that corruption is endemic in everyday life at every level in Africa. The petty day-to-day corruption that Africans experience hurts the poor the hardest as they have to pay a higher percentage of their income in bribes. Finally he cites lack of good government in the form of dictatorship and kleptocracy as the final factor in accounting for Africa's poor development record. While Collier argues that some aid does make a difference and can even reduce conflict and be used to overcome corruption, he focuses upon why aid has been ineffective in improving the lives of the world's 'bottom billion'.

KEY SOCIOLOGIST

Dambisa Moyo (2009) advocates further integration of African economies into the global market through an expansion in foreign trade. Africa should wean itself off concessional lending from the World Bank and IMF and borrow on international capital markets. Future generations may be crushed by unsustainable levels of debt, but African countries should see their credit ratings improve over time as a result.

CONTEMPORARY APPLICATION

At the height of the Ebola outbreak in 2014 which killed more than 10,300 people in Sierra Leone, a group of MPs criticised the DfID for failing to do more to eradicate female genital mutilation (FGM). UNICEF estimates that some 90 per cent of Sierra Leonean women are subjected to genital mutilation. The DfID is one of Sierra Leone's biggest bilateral donors, but has not used aid as a bargaining tool to get the practice of female circumcision abolished.

STUDY TIP

It is important to be able to argue the case both for and against the giving of aid. It is also important to recognise that there may be different arguments for the various types of aid. Even neo-liberalists, on the whole, support the giving of humanitarian aid.

4.4 Industrialisation and development

To understand industrialisation you need to see it as inherently about the development process. A comparison and contrast can be made about the role and nature of industrialisation according to the different theoretical perspectives.

Introduction

The process of development is effectively that of moving from a rural agricultural society to an urban, industrial society of mass consumption. This was the experience of European countries like Britain, which was the first to go through an Industrial Revolution. It follows that developing countries must go through the same process of industrialisation to become developed. Some of the more advanced developing countries are known as 'emerging economies' and they, by implication, have an established industrial base.

Import substitution industrialisation (ISI)

Dependency theory argues that the countries in the core with their TNCs have a vested interest in keeping the less developed countries in a permanent state of underdevelopment. In response to this, some developing and emerging economies, particularly in Latin America, embarked on a project of setting up their own industries and protecting them from TNC competition through tariff walls. Because the goods produced in these factories would normally have been imported, this policy was known as import substitution industrialisation (ISI).

ISI runs counter to the economic principle of comparative advantage whereby countries concentrate production in what they are most efficient at, then trade with other countries. The countries embarking on ISI sought to increase economic growth by increasing both employment and national output. It was also thought that ISI would bring economic independence, making the countries less reliant upon the world economy. ISIs came to dominate the economies of Argentina, Brazil, Mexico and Chile. Although Duncan Green (2001) argues that ISI has transformed many of the economies of Latin America such as Mexico and Brazil, the general opinion is that embarking on ISI was ultimately doomed to fail. Countries allowed internal competition which meant economies of scale could not be fully exploited. In addition, because of the principle of comparative advantage many companies were simply inefficient. It therefore made more sense to import cheaper manufactured goods, or better still create export-processing zones and invite the TNCs into the developing world.

Export-processing zones (EPZ)

Export-processing zones (EPZs) are customs areas. This means firms can import equipment, without paying import duty, and then manufacture goods for export. Many developing nations in the 1970s and 1980s set up export-processing zones (EPZs) or free-trade zones (FTZs), in which TNCs were encouraged to build factories producing goods for export to the West. TNCs can embrace fully the principles of the new international division of labour by relocating in these purpose-built areas with an abundance of local workers. The attraction of EPZs is that governments liberalise the production process in order to minimise production costs and maximise profits for the TNCs. These include:

- providing cheap labour – about a tenth the rate paid in the developed world
- employing female workers (where there is no equal pay legislation)
- absence of trade unions – these are either weakened or banned altogether

- limited health and safety regulations
- limited or non-existent environmental regulations
- local militias to suppress any worker discontent arising.

The Asian 'Tigers'

From the 1950s a number of newly industrialised countries (NICs) were manufacturing and exporting goods to the rest of the world. Particularly in the Far East, the four most successful countries became known as the Asian 'Tiger Economies'. They were South Korea, Taiwan, Hong Kong and Singapore. These countries were portrayed as economic miracles and have continued to prosper, subsequently achieving the same living standards of European countries like Spain.

The rise of the BRICS economies

BRICS stands for Brazil, Russia, India, China and South Africa, who were all identified in 2001 as large and fast growing economies that will have growing global influence.

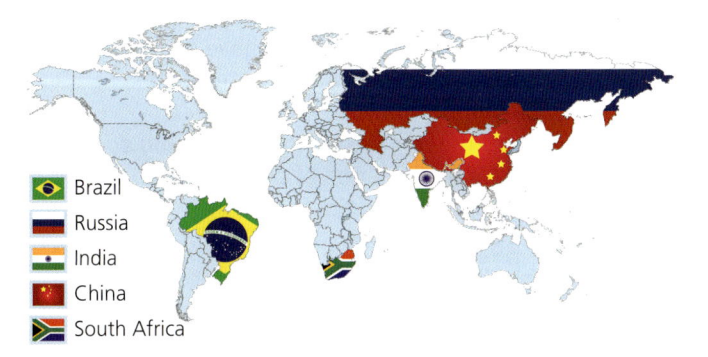

Figure 4.26 The five BRICS countries

Since then China has overtaken the USA as the country with the largest manufacturing output. It has an extremely high rate of investment, currently running at 48 per cent of GNP. Though global demand dipped somewhat following the banking crisis of 2007 China has a phenomenal global export market. The Chinese government wants to move to a slower rate of economic growth and to shift output more towards Chinese consumers.

India has grown less from industrialisation (although it has impressive steel, pharmaceutical and chemical industries) than from developing into a world-class service economy. It has achieved this by using its 250 million strong highly educated middle class.

Brazil has an abundance of iron ore plus agricultural products of soya, coffee and sugar.

Free-market Russia's impressive development since the break-up of the totalitarian communist state of the Soviet Union has been recently undermined by the sanctions imposed following the annexation of Crimea and the military conflict with Ukraine.

The South African economy is different to its sub-Saharan neighbours, in that it is vibrant and successful. Of all the BRICS countries, it is the only one whose growth has not slowed in the decade following 2010.

> **KEY SOCIOLOGIST**
>
> **Charles Babbage** (1835) argued that the division of labour could increase productivity and cut wage costs. He observed that if skilled tasks were only undertaken by skilled and higher-paid workers and less-skilled work given to less-skilled and lower-paid workers, then a hierarchy of wages could be created. Tiger economies and BRICS actively embraced this principle with the new international division of labour and have been described as engaging in 'hyper-Babbagisation'.

> **STUDY TIP**
> Remember the overlaps between industrialisation and development, globalisation and urbanisation.

> **CONTEMPORARY APPLICATION**
> Because of globalisation, the world is becoming hyper-connected through information and communication technology (ICT). With increasing connection to new technology through smartphones and tablets the gulf between the north and south will become narrower. The new international division of labour may be applied to technological industries in the future, just as it is to garment manufacturing today. We are beginning to see this with software and app development occurring in countries like India.

> **IN THE NEWS**
>
> ### As China gets richer, the world gets dirtier
> When the Kyoto Protocol was signed in 2005, it was heralded as ushering in an era of international commitment to tackle climate change and greenhouse gas emissions. However, more than a decade later, the effects of climate change remain a threat.
>
> Since the agreement the economies of China and India have grown, with especially China continuing to generate rising carbon dioxide emissions. Environmentalists warn that failing to reduce these emissions could result in environmental disaster. However, doing so could also put at risk the lifestyles of the millions of people pulled out of poverty by China's rapid industrialisation and growth.
>
> Although India is also experiencing rapid growth, this is likely to pose less of a threat to the environment because its growth, according to Prime Minister Narendra Modi, will not be based on fossil fuels such as coal. Modi has indicated that solar energy will be the foundation of providing electricity to the continent's 400 million people who currently lack access to it.
>
> Adapted from Griffin (2015)

> **Questions**
> 1. What factors are undermining the commitment of the Kyoto Protocol to reduce CO_2 emissions?
> 2. How is the industrial development of India different to China?
> 3. Using the information above and your own knowledge, what are the potential trade-offs of making industrial societies like China 'greener'?

4.5 Urbanisation and development

Urbanisation represents both the process of development and material evidence of development having taken place.

Introduction

Cohen and Kennedy (2013) note that both modernity and industrialisation have been closely linked to growing **urbanisation** for the past 200 years. As of 2009 more than half of the world's population are living in urban environments. Continuing urbanisation is described as an 'unstoppable' process (UNDESA, 2010) with a prediction that by 2050, 70 per cent of the world's population will be urban dwellers. There is also a trend for the growth in megacities – cities of more than 10 million people. As they grow, urban conglomerates sprawl and merge: Cohen and Kennedy cite the merging of Hong Kong, Shenzen City and Guangzhou in China as prime examples of this. The UN estimates that four-fifths of the world's GDP is now generated within urban areas (UNDESA, 2010). The UN also calculates that, in many countries, the bulk of rural income comes from remittances sent back by relatives who work in urban areas. For the first time in human history, there will shortly be a fall in the total rural world population.

Modernisation theory and urbanisation

For modernisation theorists like Walt Rostow the move towards urbanisation is both the path towards and evidence of modernisation. Bert Hoselitz (1960) described urbanisation as the fourth 'motor' of development. Cities are seen to promote economic growth by providing an ample work force available for the factories and businesses.

In addition, cities represent a cultural change from the traditions of rural life and are promoters of the crucial modern values such as individualism, meritocracy and entrepreneurialism viewed as crucial drivers of development to modernisation theory. However, this presents a somewhat romantic view of the city in the developing world. Such a view ignores the fact that although there may be affluent suburbs or apartment blocks (often **gated communities**), the majority of people are living in poverty and often the desperate poverty of **shanty towns**. Indeed the living conditions of the poor in developing cities are often worse than those experienced in rural areas.

Dependency theory and urbanisation

The flow of people from the rural areas to the urban cities is caused by both push and pull factors. Agricultural workers are driven off the land due to a combination of poverty and new developments in agricultural technology; they are also pulled towards the cities by the false hope that their living standards will improve. There is a naïve assumption that there are plenty of well-paid jobs in cities. The reality is that most residents do not have contractual employment at all but scrape a subsistence living from **informal sector employment**. Such jobs consist of unregulated or illegal employment such as in the sweatshops, selling goods on the streets (such as fast food) or services (such as shoe shining or sex working). The poorest and dirtiest work involves recycling and often involves scavenging on rubbish tips. Such is the dire poverty of many urban dwellers that neo-Marxist dependency theory has embraced Karl Marx's concept of the **lumpen-proletariat** – a form of underclass beneath those lucky enough to have contractual employment in the formal labour market. Expressed as neo-colonialism, dependency theory argues that cities in developing countries continue the colonial legacy, serving to facilitate neo-colonial exploitation.

Dependency theory says cities promote underdevelopment of countries – cities monopolise any surpluses generated. The urban poor do not benefit from money that might accrue from investment and aid spent on 'white elephant' projects such as expensive international airports, conference centres and five star hotels. Such projects add to the status of the city, but are irrelevant to the lives of ordinary workers.

However, many developing countries, as they develop, are witnessing a burgeoning professional, technical and managerial class. Such well-paid, secure workers want retail outlets and department stores to buy consumer goods of conspicuous consumption. They also encourage the divisive development of features like gated communities and exclusive restaurants and leisure facilities. Thus the centre of most cities in the developing world looks remarkably like city centres in the developed world: sky scraper office and apartment block, wide streets with expensive shops and shopping malls. Often remarkably close are the slums and shanty towns of the impoverished urban dwellers.

> **CONTEMPORARY APPLICATION**
>
> In their 2013 progress report on the eight MDGs, the World Bank and IMF reported that 'governments should not be afraid of urbanisation', but rather appreciate the positive effects of urbanisation. They state that 'virtually no country has graduated to a high-income status without urbanising and urbanisation rates above 70 per cent are typically found in high-income countries'. The report concluded that incomes are higher in urban areas compared to agricultural wages. In addition, urban areas are more open to upward social mobility.

Global cities

Global cities are also sometimes called 'world cities'. They are characterised, according to Cohen and Kennedy (2013), as attracting both international professional workers, business entrepreneurs and unskilled manual workers to do menial tasks. John Friedman (1986) defined global cities not in terms of their size, but rather by the extent to which they were integrated into the global economy. The most notorious 'primary' examples of core global cities are New York, London, Paris and Tokyo (plus Friedman adds Chicago and Los Angeles). These are all truly globalised cities located in the northern hemisphere and clearly in the developed world. Beneath these six primary core global cities there are semi-peripheral global cities in some emerging countries of the developing world. Not all global cities are capital cities, which is important as it means their status derives from their place in the global international division of labour, rather than as old political, religious or administration centres. As global cities they bring together finance, economic activity and serve as hosts for corporate headquarters. They have dense air links with other global cities and are centres of communication, news bureaux, entertainment and cultural products. Saskia Sassen (2007) describes how these features of global cities become progressively integrated with each other into 'a new geography of centrality' that impacts across all dimensions of global life.

Recent features:
- Emerging middle-classes: (gated communities, disposable Income)
- Flattering projects such as international airports, malls, conference centres, leisure centres

Modernisation theory:
- Urbanisation reflects modernity (Hoselitz, Rostow)
- Cities are progressive places promoting cultural change
- Cities encourage modern values: individualism, entrepreneurialism, achievement
- Humanitarian crises: war, conflict, droughts, etc

Push factors from rural:
- Rural poverty
- Backward traditional values
- Impact of innovative agricultural technology
- Humanitarian crises: war, conflict, droughts, etc

Urbanisation

Dependency theory:
- Urbanisation sustains underdevelopment
- Represents an expression of neo-colonialism
- Most workers poor and exploited: lumpen proletariat
- Urban poor live in slums or shanty towns

Pull factors to urban:
- Attraction of well-paid employment (myth)
- Improved living standards
- Assumed closeness to Western consumer culture
- Access to services such as health care and education
- Urbanisation viewed as closer to Western lifestyle

Global cities:
- Primary core global cities located in developed world
- Financial and economic centres of global trade (TNC headquarters)
- Excellent global transport (air) and communication links

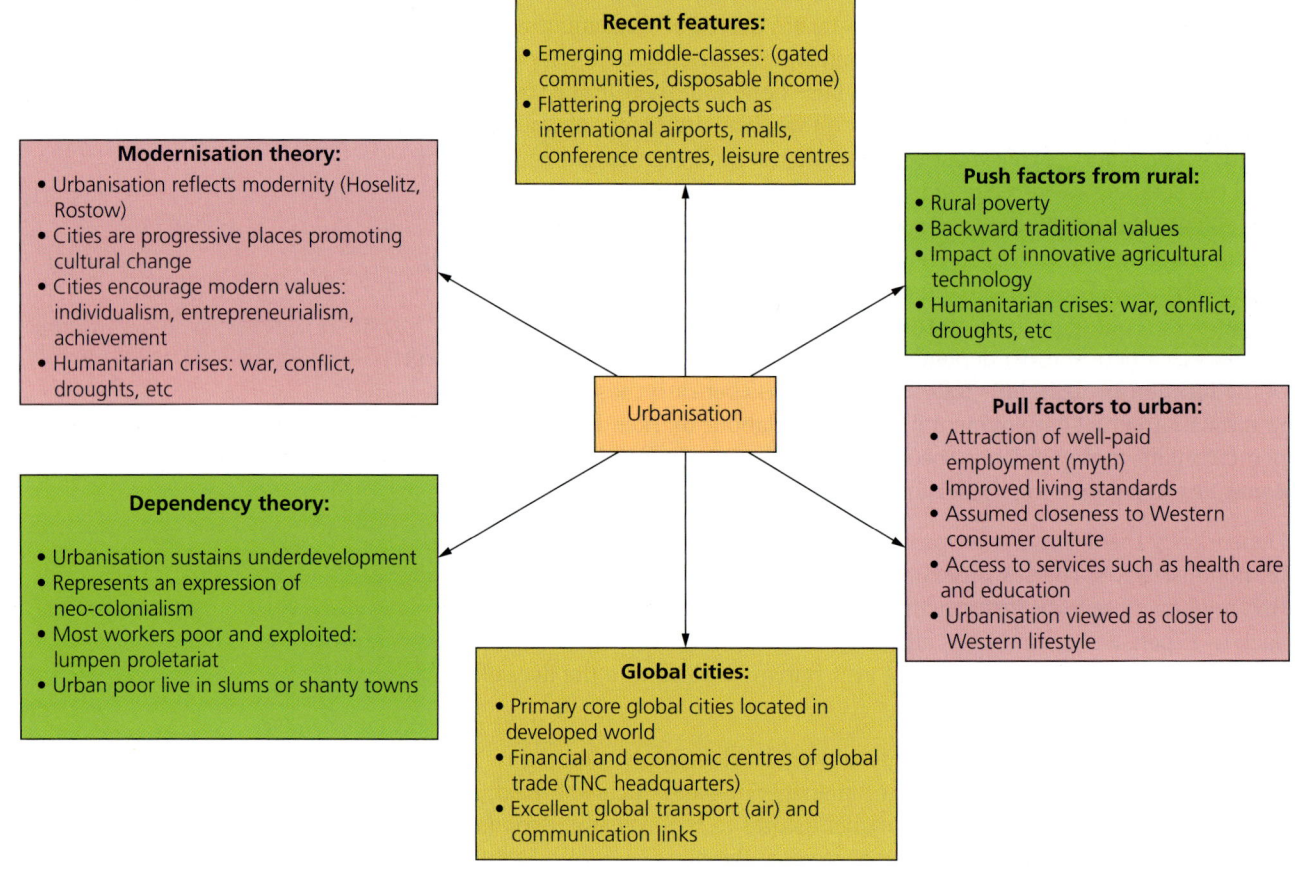

Figure 4.27 Features of urbanisation

KEY SOCIOLOGIST

Benjamin Selwyn (2014) is a Marxist who identifies three strategies adopted by TNCs to gain global power:

1. Lobbying international institutions, such as the World Trade Organisation (WTO) to generate a world market for the protection of intellectual property rights.
2. Selling off core businesses while outsourcing production to the developing world in an attempt to maximise profits.
3. Cutting wage and input costs, and intensifying the exploitation of global labour.

STUDY TIPS

Ensure that urbanisation is discussed in relation to the two key sociological theories of modernisation and dependency. You could also look at women in urban areas from the feminist perspective and explore how postmodern ideas can be applied to urban features.

IN THE NEWS

The destruction of Mecca

Figure 4.28 Abraj Al Bait Towers (Royal Clock Tower hotel)

When Malcolm X visited Mecca in 1964, he wrote that the partly constructed extension to the Sacred Mosque 'will surpass the architectural beauty of India's Taj Mahal' and described the city 'as ancient as time itself'.

However, few visitors today would see evidence of the ancient or of beauty in Islam's holiest city. A huge development of skyscrapers now dominates the landscape. One of the world's tallest buildings, the Makkah Royal Clock Tower hotel presides over the city, rising to 1,972 feet. The concrete and steel of brutalist architecture reign supreme. Expensive hotels and shopping malls catering not to pilgrims but to the 'super-rich' are now seen in the place of the ancient historic and cultural sites.

Mecca's destruction began in earnest when the famous Bilal mosque, which dated from the time of Prophet Muhammad, was demolished in the 1970s. By the end of the 1980s, Mecca was made over into a 'modern city' with multiple traffic lanes and intersections. Today, modern houses stand where the beautifully ornate Ottoman homes once were. Given Mecca's status as a holy place and Islam's history of building mosques of outstanding character, this is a tragedy for the city.

Adapted from Sardarsept (2014)

Questions

1. What point is being made about Mecca in the article?
2. Using your sociological knowledge, explain what factors are driving the building of 'skyscrapers that include offices, luxury shopping malls and hotels' in urban centres.
3. Using your wider sociological knowledge, explain some of the problems that can arise from the modernisation of cities.

4.6 The environment and development

While human behaviour invariably impacts on the natural landscape, levels of economic activity are now so unprecedented that not only is there local degradation of the ecosystem but the very future of the planet is called into question.

Figure 4.29 Pollution is so bad in China it kills up to half a million people each year.

Introduction

The World Business Council for Sustainable Development (WBCSD, 2010) argues that the greatest challenge facing development is that current economic models cannot be sustained since they threaten the ecosystem of the planet.

There is increasing talk of a desperate need for **sustainable development**. Originally defined by the World Commission on Environment and Development (WCED, 1987) (also known as the Brundtland Commission) as 'development that meets the needs of present generations without compromising the ability of future generations to meet their own needs' this definition is now a contested concept. Imran *et al.* (2014) point out that newer definitions of sustainable development have surfaced that emphasise the social, environmental and economic dimensions of sustainability. Whatever the detail, environmental campaigners like Kingsbury *et al.* (2004) argue that the planet's physical capacity cannot support this unprecedented level of growth: certain locations are being despoiled, and elsewhere resources are running out altogether. Some parts of the world are more prone to degradation than others – often the poorer countries, and particularly their rural areas, where degradation of the environment is most serious. And while environmental concerns impact locally, their effects are increasingly being viewed by environmentalists in the West as global.

Measuring CO_2 emissions

In 2014 the annual global CO_2 emissions growth remained stable for the first time in 40 years. The International Energy Agency (IEA) stated that for the first time, greenhouse gas emissions are decoupling from economic growth. It explained the stabilisation of CO_2 emissions at 32 gigatonnes as due to changing patterns of energy use by OECD countries. However, it especially identified the efforts of China moving away from a reliance on coal towards more renewable energy. The UN sought an international climate change agreement in Paris (2014) aimed at limiting the increase of the average global surface temperature to no more than 2 degrees centigrade, compared with pre-industrial levels, to avoid 'dangerous' climate change.

Barrett et al. (2013) argue that talk of cuts in CO_2 in the West is misleading as any such cuts are outweighed by increased CO_2 emissions from the shift of manufacturing to the developing world. For example, although CO_2 emissions in the UK fell by 194 million tonnes in 2012 (compared to 1990) they are outweighed by a rise of 280 million tonnes created abroad during the manufacture of goods imported specifically to Britain. Shifting manufacturing to the developing world, through the international division of labour, has merely transferred CO_2 emissions around the planet: the UK's net traded emissions have doubled in the past 20 years, while emissions within the UK have reduced by 26 per cent.

Environmental issues in the developing world

The very lack of environmental controls has attracted investment from TNCs in developing countries. In 2013 the UN reported that China had replaced the USA as the world's leading manufacturing nation, generating $2.9 trillion in output annually versus $2.43 trillion from the USA. China used its access to cheap coal to achieve this, but at a significant cost to the environment and its population. China's former health minister Chen Zhu admitted in 2014 that between 350,000 and 500,000 Chinese people die prematurely each year because of the country's poor air quality.

China and other dirty developing nations are being forced to embrace renewable energy, sustainable development, environmental change and **green growth**. The latter is now officially embraced by the OECD and refers to a radical approach to development that uses natural resources in a sustainable manner. Fully implemented, a greener economy embraces environmental concerns for jobs, skills, investment, taxation, trade and development. However, it is often expressed as a goal tangential to the pursuit of more environmentally damaging policies and practices. For example, Yang and Cui (2012), for the World Resources Institute, identified that 1,200 coal power stations were still being planned across 59 countries, with about three-quarters to be built in China and India.

In rural areas the production of cash crops is accompanied by the heavy use of environmentally damaging pesticides, polluting rivers and reducing **biodiversity**. The drive by TNCs for cash crops can force local farmers onto marginal land, causing erosion and deforestation for pulp, logging or arable land to grow food. **Deforestation** is a major environmental concern; the World Wildlife Fund (WWF, 2015) estimates 12–15 million hectares of forest are lost each year, the equivalent of 36 football fields per minute. They point out a range of consequences of deforestation:

- As 80 per cent of the world's documented species can be found in tropical rainforests, deforestation puts at risk a majority of the Earth's biodiversity.
- Deforestation causes 15 per cent of global greenhouse gas emissions.
- CO_2 emissions from deforestation account for one-third of total carbon dioxide emissions.
- Disrupted water cycles: trees no longer evaporate groundwater, which can cause the local climate to be much drier.
- Increased soil erosion since deforestation accelerates rates of soil erosion, by increasing runoff and reducing the protection of the soil from tree litter.

- Disrupted livelihoods: millions of people rely directly on forests, through small-scale agriculture, hunting and gathering, and by harvesting forest products such as rubber.

Population growth and food security

The WCED (1987) stated that the 'the world produces more food per head of population today than ever before in human history'. Since the Brundtland Report, global food production has increased faster than the population. There is currently no sign that the Earth has reached its food production limit, or that we are on the brink of a **Malthusian** global food shortage (see Thomas Malthus, page 249). However, despite this abundance of food in 2015, the year when the Millennium Development Goal (MDG7) should have been achieved, around a billion people have an insufficient diet. This undermines their ability to lead a fully productive life. The Brundtland Commission identified that the problem was not insufficient food production or availability, but insufficient income of the poor to purchase food. Global food security also depends on ensuring that all people, even the poorest of the poor, can get food. Poverty and food insecurity tend to be disproportionately rural problems. The biggest concern expressed by the report, however, was whether enough food could be sustainably produced to feed future generations.

Theoretical positions on the environment

As noted above, the prediction of Thomas Malthus (1766–1834) that the population will increase at a faster rate than its ability to feed itself has not transpired. Nonetheless the neo-Malthusian Paul Ehrlich (1968) argues 'the battle to feed all humanity is over'. However, his prediction that 'mankind will breed itself into oblivion' is challenged by anti-Malthusians like Hans Rosling (2014) who predicts the global population will stabilise at 10 billion people. He argues that population growth will stop as child survival in the world rises to 90 per cent and notes that in 2012 the average global family size is just 2.5 children per family. Further, the anti-Malthusians argue that it is not people themselves who destroy the environment through desertification and deforestation but rather the demands from consumerism worldwide.

The neo-liberal response to this is that free-market capitalism will automatically generate solutions to environmental problems. This is referred to as '**technological fix**'. For example, as the rise in car ownership has a long-term impact upon the price of oil (a finite resource) so the market responds with initially more fuel efficient cars and ultimately a new market of electric cars. However, critics argue the market cannot simply redress the loss of rainforests, the melting of the polar ice caps or the growth of greenhouse gases in the environment. Further, critics argue that relying on the free market to solve its problems is naïve, pointing out that it is capitalism, the free market and global consumerism that should be held responsible for the bulk of the environmental destruction. The only real solution, they argue, is through intervention in order to promote sustainable development. Markets alone will only promote environmental change if they have an economic incentive to do so. However, only by adopting a true cost-benefit analysis that takes full account of **externalities** which are ignored in market prices, can truly green growth be achieved.

> **KEY SOCIOLOGIST**
>
> **Wayne Ellwood** argues that by acting in the interests of TNC profitability, the WTO consistently challenges environmental, conservation and food-safety regulations. He notes that when conflicts between environmental and trade policy become too obvious to ignore, the free-traders have pushed the environment debate to the margins within the WTO or isolated it entirely. In addition, any government that violates WTO rules is vulnerable to sanctions – often too severe for even the wealthiest nation to ignore.

> **STUDY TIP**
>
> Environmental issues are closely connected to demographic change. In addition, there is a clear trade-off between high economic growth and environmental damage.

CONTEMPORARY APPLICATION

The World Bank has warned that climate change is particularly affecting developing countries. It points to an increased risk of droughts, floods, sea-level rises and fiercer storms likely to undermine progress especially in the developing world and hit food supply. The World Bank sees climate change as a risk, especially undermining economic development in poor countries, resulting in millions of people around the world being pushed back into poverty.

IN THE NEWS

Developing countries must face up to their responsibility for emissions

A former World Bank chief economist, Lord Nicholas Stern, insists that developing countries including China and India must be accountable for the effects of their expanding industries on climate change. As publisher of the Stern review of the economics of climate change, he argues that climate change could not be avoided even if the developed world reduced their production of greenhouse gases to zero. Emissions caused by the industrialisation of countries such as China, India and South Korea are extremely high. The bulk of the world's greenhouse gases come from the emerging economies. On a more hopeful note, Stern argued that if they adopt new technology, developing countries could continue to grow.

Figure 4.30 A coal plant in India

Adapted from Harvey (2012)

Questions

1. What is the argument being put forward by Lord Stern in the above article?
2. Using your wider sociological knowledge, explain why emerging developing countries like China, India and South Korea are such major polluters.
3. Using the article and your wider knowledge, suggest what needs to be done to address climate change.

4.7 How do war and conflict impact upon the developing world?

Recognise the global context that underpins this new political economy of war. Incidents rarely take place in isolation and are globally connected through ideology, funding and not least global inequality.

Introduction

By the 1990s the issue of conflict had become a central concern within the study of global development. Such conflict could take the form of interstate wars, **civil wars**, **guerrilla warfare**, **ethnic cleansing**, **genocide** and increasingly global terrorism. The funding of modern conflict can also be viewed as global, often sustained by external governments, **diaspora** fund-raising or the redirection of funds intended for humanitarian purposes. Aid agencies are increasingly involved in humanitarian assistance, conflict resolution and the social reconstruction of war-torn societies.

Causes of conflict in the developing world

Explaining this global conflict is complex. Thomas Malthus (1766–1834) predicted that a shortage of food would potentially result in war as people fought over scarce resources. Certainly disputes over access to water are predicted to become an increasingly important factor in driving conflict in the future.

Dependency theory tends to locate the source of conflict in external factors and highlights the fear of underdevelopment as a source of conflict. This can either be about relative poverty from a lack of development, or a reaction to the inevitable hardships from SAPs. Paul Collier (2008) suggests that the Rwandan civil war in the 1990s was linked to the way the Belgians as a colonial power had differentially treated the Tutsi and Hutu tribes. Such tribal resentment had brewed into hostility ever since independence. Modernisation theorists often see the source of conflict as stemming from internal factors. Certainly aspects of global terrorism can be traced, at least partly, back to an adherence to traditional **fundamentalist** values. There is an almost neo-medieval situation with the goal of modernity lost as fragmented factions confront an increasingly weakened central authority pursuing their own traditional religious agendas.

'New wars'

Mark Duffield (2001) argues that the focus of new security concerns is not the threat of traditional interstate 'old wars', but the fear of underdevelopment as a source of conflict, criminalised activity and international instability. He talks about how during the first half of the 1990s conflict took on a different characteristic leading to what he describes as the 'new wars' of the post-Cold War era. The breakdown of order is seen as symptomatic of long-term social processes: economic crisis, the social exclusion of wide strata of populations and internal conflict. Duffield portrays a far-reaching but depressing and pessimistic picture of how the violence and the misery that follow are accepted as normal. He argues that new forms of humanitarian aid intervention, from private aid suppliers, far from solving the problem, accommodate and co-exist with this instability and inequality. Duffield provides the analysis of a realist, offering both insights into the plight of ordinary people caught up in this conflict as well as addressing the policy implications.

The term 'new wars' has been particularly embraced by Mary Kaldor (2006) who defines them specifically as conflict involving both state and non-state networks. She differentiates new wars from old wars where conventional military weapons and battlefield tactics were used between two or more states in open confrontation. New wars are not about attacking other countries, but are internal to countries and invariably stem from competition for resources, political control, or a desire to control through the manifestation of fear and terror. They are, she argues, a political rather than a military challenge. They are about the breakdown of legitimacy. Such new wars are no longer financed through the state but through bodies with a vested interest from the continuation of violence.

Duffield draws attention to the role that **shadow economies** can play in funding rebel movements. Allegations are rife that TNCs are often involved with the illicit activities associated with such shadow economies in return for being able to control the trade in illegal goods like **blood diamonds**, drugs, oil and ivory. Arms manufacturers seem willing to sell to almost anyone with money to pay for arms and governments will supply any rebel group that they favour.

Kaldor argues that any attempt to make sense of this new conflict must be analysed within the context of globalisation. For example, she notes how rebel leaders or **warlords** and their followers often seem well integrated into globalised culture by frequently identifying themselves with global iconic brands, such as Mercedes Benz, Rolex watches and other forms of designer apparel. She argues that the influence of global media cannot be overestimated. She argues that addressing the source and resolving these new wars requires new policy responses. Certainly previous attempts have singularly failed by making the persistent mistake of treating them like old conventional warfare.

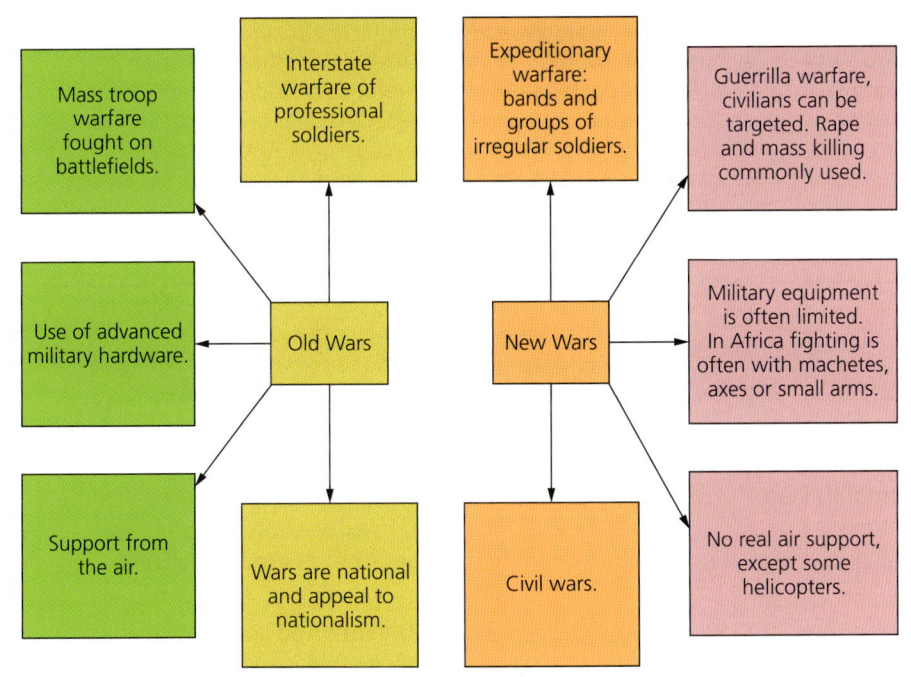

Figure 4.31 Comparison between old and new wars

What conflict costs the developing world

The cost of violent conflict to developing countries is enormous, impacting economically, culturally and disproportionately upon the poor. Gurr and Marshall (2003) argue that conflicts have had a devastating effect upon Africa's development. For example, sub-Saharan Africa has had the lowest GDP for decades, with even some conflict-ridden countries poorer today than they were 30 years ago. Besides the breakdown in social cohesion, the costs of conflicts in terms of the loss of human life and property, together with the destruction of social infrastructure, are enormous. Conflict inevitably leads to the redirection of scarce resources to purchase military equipment, undermining the living standards of ordinary people and at the expense of socio-economic development. Brian Ikejiaku (2012) argues that there appears to be a link between poverty,

> **KEY SOCIOLOGIST**
>
> **Paul Collier** (2008) famous for his focus on the 'bottom billion' has described the effects of violent conflict as 'development in reverse'. He argues that a civil war reduces economic growth on average by 2.3 per cent per annum. Therefore a war that lasts for five years will undermine economic growth by 11.5 per cent.

> **STUDY TIP**
>
> When discussing conflict and war it is important to consider how this overlaps with violence against women, such as rape as a weapon of war. In addition, the refugee problems that can result from conflict link in with both humanitarian aid as well as being a push factor helping to drive populations to urban areas and other countries. The bulk of immigrants who used boats to cross the Mediterranean (2014–2015) to gain access to Europe were refugees from conflict zones in the Middle East and Africa.

conflict and development. Furthermore, poverty is rooted in political corruption – the major cause of Africa's conflict – and this has led to low levels of development.

Impact of conflict on women and children

Another impact of conflict is the traumatic effect it has on children. According to UNICEF (2015) there are an estimated 300,000 children, boys and girls under the age of 18, involved in more than 30 conflicts worldwide. Children are used as combatants, messengers, porters, cooks and for forced sexual services. Another consequence of violent conflict is the increasing amount of sexual violence directed at women. Cohen and Kennedy (2013) note that the rules governing warfare seem to have changed in that in the past combatants tried to minimise harm to non-combatants, especially women and children. Rape, and other forms of violence against women, has become a weapon of war designed to humiliate the enemy. Liz Kelly (2000) notes that women's bodies have become increasingly symbolic of 'territory to be conquered' especially in sub-Saharan Africa. As guerrillas and rival militia advance, often burning villages as they go, surviving refugees increase the risk of disease and epidemics. Etienne *et al.* (2013) writing for the World Health Organisation (WHO) recognise that rape and other forms of sexual coercion can also be directed against men and boys during periods of conflict and war.

> **CONTEMPORARY APPLICATION**
>
> Violent conflict in the developing world is sometimes described as 'low intensity conflict', a term invented by the US Army. It implies that such conflicts do not involve the intense levels of violence found in conventional wars. However, for those caught up in the horrors of 'new wars', the impact can be just as devastating with life-long repercussions. Another disturbing feature of 'new wars' is the systematic raping of women and the involvement of children as child soldiers.

IN THE NEWS

Aid agencies seek innovative strategies as conflicts increase worldwide

With more people across the world currently displaced by crises since the Second World War, aid agencies are looking to innovative humanitarian solutions to assist the affected communities.

The sheer scale of the problem, with requests for aid reaching £10bn annually, and the complex and rapidly changing nature of the issues has meant that the current systems are no longer effective. Programmes set up to help people in rural settings with emergency needs, for example as in the African crises that arose in the twentieth century, are not suited to the very different problems resulting from the present conflicts in Iraq and Syria and Gaza. People displaced by these more recent crises are often highly educated, and over half of the world's refugees now live in urban areas.

Because of this, UN Secretary General Ban Ki-moon has called for 'a more inclusive global humanitarian system' to meet the changing world. In 2016 Istanbul will host the first World Humanitarian Summit. A major theme is 'Transformation through innovation'.

New technologies are increasingly used to help in humanitarian crises, from new imaging systems used to assess damage following earthquakes to mobile technology used in education and to help to reunite family members separated by natural disasters and conflict.

Collaboration between the affected communities and a range of agencies providing aid is of key importance. For the new programmes to work effectively the end users must contribute to their design. A key aim is to enable displaced people to adapt to new situations by using their existing knowledge and skills, rather than being passive consumers of aid.

'People who flee crisis have to adapt, and they often do so in creative and entrepreneurial ways,' says Alexander Betts of Oxford University's Humanitarian Innovation Project. 'Humanitarian innovation begins by understanding the local context and supporting the problem-solving capacities of affected communities themselves.'

Adapted from Madigan (2014)

Questions

1. What examples of innovation are discussed in the above article?
2. Why is there now a greater need for innovation compared to the past?
3. Using your wider knowledge suggest other ways in which innovation could support victims of violent conflict.

Check your understanding

1. What does Hayter mean by the phrase 'aid as imperialism'?
2. Explain the terms: unilateral aid, multilateral aid, humanitarian aid and tied aid.
3. What is the main purpose of aid according to President Nixon?
4. What is import substitution industrialisation?
5. Why are the BRICS economies significant in the global economy?
6. What is meant by sustainable development?
7. What is meant by 'green growth'?
8. Critically evaluate the neo-liberal concept of 'technological fix'.
9. What is meant by 'old' and 'new wars'?
10. Summarise some of the costs of conflict to the developing world.

Practice questions

1. Outline and explain **three** types of aid. [9 marks]

Read Item A below and answer the question that follows.

Item A

Developing countries have long insisted that countries that industrialised sooner, such as the USA and Europe, should make the greatest carbon cuts. They argue that such countries have been responsible for greater emissions over a longer period.

Applying material from Item A, analyse two ways in which the environment is linked to the process of development. [10 marks]

Read Item B below and answer the question that follows.

Item B

Despite sending more than half their aid to countries marked by conflict, donor states have not been successful in promoting peace and building institutions, and this failure risks torpedoing efforts to lift the world's most vulnerable people out of poverty.

Applying material from Item B and your knowledge, evaluate the view that poverty and conflict are connected in the developing world. [20 marks]

Section 5: Employment, education, health, demographic change and gender as aspects of development

This section will explore the following debates:
- The changing nature of employment as a result of development
- The role of education in development
- Health care systems and the nature of health and illness in developing countries
- The significance of demographic change
- The significance of gender in relation to development

GETTING YOU STARTED

Why global violence against women and girls must become new UK priority

Figure 4.32 A woman and a child in Sierra Leone.

The UK lacks a coherent policy on giving aid to countries with a history of violence against women. However, only 14 per cent of the Department for International Aid Development (DfID)'s action plans for countries include strategic plans to tackle violence against woman and girls as a priority.

Adapted from Cansfield (2014)

The World Health Organisation (WHO, 2013) describes violence against women and girls as a global pandemic. They estimate that over a third of women experience violence in their lifetime, typically from their current or former partner. A recent UNICEF study found that one in ten girls face sexual abuse.

The DfID's country plans focus on improving women's access to justice systems. Though this is important in achieving redress for victims, it will by itself have little. Research has found that cultural norms about gender and patriarchal attitudes to power lie behind both partner violence and non-partner rape.

Until attitudes reinforcing the domination of manhood are addressed and tackled, violence against and control over women will continue. Netty Musanhu, director of the Musasa Project in Zimbabwe, sums up the situation saying, 'Men have been socialised that it's OK to beat up women. Women have been socialised to accept it and to normalise it.'

Embarrassment, guilt and shame often prevent women reporting violence. Access to justice isn't enough: prevention will require a transformation of societal views of gender roles and women's rights.

Questions

1. According to critics what is missing from the UK's aid plans to countries?
2. What are the causes of violence towards women according to the article?
3. Suggest ways in which violence against women could be stopped in the developing world.

5.1 The changing nature of employment as a result of development

To understand employment in the developing world, consider economic globalisation and factors like the role of TNCs and the new international division of labour.

Figure 4.33 Female workers share food with their children in Dhaka, Bangladesh

Introduction

The absence of welfare states across most developing countries means that a failure of the poorest households to find some form of remunerative work quickly results in starvation. Many people in the developing world do not have formal jobs as such, but scratch a living selling goods or services in the informal economy; what would be described in the West as casual or irregular work. As countries develop, more secure contractual employment opportunities increase. Initially this is linked to TNCs, although they may outsource production rather than directly employ workers themselves (see page 194).

In general TNCs recruit by applying pre-existing gender practices and inequalities in order to secure workers at the cheapest price. As countries develop further and pass through Rostow's stages of development, so there is an increase in the proportion of public service jobs, such as civil servants, public transport workers, teachers, doctors, nurses, police officers and social workers. The bulk of such workers also reflect a growing middle-class employment sector. Such workers have relatively high disposable income and begin to drive a consumer society creating retailing and service sector jobs. Such workers will seek to show their privileged position through conspicuous consumption.

Formal and informal sectors

Employment in the developing world is divided into a two-sector economy: formal and informal sectors. The formal sector tends to employ a minority of the workforce, increasing as countries progress through Rostow's stages of development. This formal sector is comprised of what limited public sector workers there are plus the major private employers, including TNCs. Such workers usually have low pay and often lack the employment rights workers in the developed world take for granted, such as security of employment, contracts that ensure regular pay, paid holidays and sick pay.

However, the International Labour Organisation (ILO, 2013) says most workers make their living in the informal sector. They estimate that more than half of the developing world's workers are trapped in vulnerable jobs with 397 million workers living in extreme poverty (on less than $1.25 a day), and another 472 million 'moderately poor' living on $1.25 to $2 a day. The majority of workers in the informal sector eek out a subsistence living by selling goods on the street, recycling rubbish, working as sex workers or begging.

The absence of any form of welfare in many developing countries means that people with disabilities, the elderly and widowed women really struggle to make a living. Migrants to the city invariably work in the informal sector and reside in the slums and shanty towns, forming a 'lumpen-proletariat' (see page 227).

Women and employment

Cohen and Kennedy (2013) argue that women in developing countries are subject to other employment abuses that impact directly on them. They state that sexual harassment, violent behaviour (often linked to resisting male demands for sexual favours), working long hours with no concession to family responsibilities, unpaid overtime and unhealthy workplace conditions can all impact more on women than men.

Many young women are sent by their families from rural to urban areas in search of employment. They often reside in dormitories where living conditions are overcrowded, cramped and dangerous. Such young women lack the protection of husbands or male relatives. Trade unions are often banned or, where they do exist, tend to be male-dominated and reluctant to intervene in the support of exploited female workers. Women who complain about employment conditions are often sacked.

Homeworking

The garment industry has a particularly well-developed homeworking sector, often involved in 'finishing' clothes – sewing on labels, sequins or decorations. As in the developed world, where particularly vulnerable workers such as illegal immigrants seem to do homeworking, earnings are very low in the developing world. Homeworkers in the developing world have no employment rights and are heavily penalised if they fail to meet production deadlines. Outsourcing to the homeworker is attractive to companies as, besides encouraging producer flexibility, it can significantly lower costs. Some TNCs and their retailers can make very high profits with huge mark-ups on products partly or entirely home produced. This can be a risky business strategy: upmarket products cannot afford to be tainted by embarrassing allegations of sweatshop conditions, let alone homeworking environments.

Regulating and improving the lot of homeworkers is necessarily difficult, given their dispersion. Some NGOs and fair trade organisations are campaigning on their behalf. The International Labour Organisation (ILO), an arm of the United Nations, ambitiously sets targets for the establishment of worldwide standards of employment.

Working directly for TNCs

Modernisation theorists have traditionally seen TNC employment as liberating – providing jobs and income as well as ultimately driving economic growth as particularly beneficial to women's position. They say it helps give them equality, status, independence as well as opening the door to consumerism. This view assumes income levels are actually large enough to make a difference. Supporters of modernisation and globalisation, like Johan Norberg (2011), see development as a long-term process and even argue that sweatshops are a necessary evil along the road to economic success. Modernisation theorists point out that the most gender-equal societies are the most developed societies.

> **KEY SOCIOLOGIST**
> **Walt Rostow** (1971) sees TNCs as a major contributor to inward investment which he described as a 'motor of development'. TNC manufacturing increasingly becomes a feature of stage 2 in his evolutionary ladder of development. Such investment is necessary to act as the fuel for the crucial third stage of 'take-off'.

Marxist feminists criticise modernisation theory for assuming that development and modernisation are benign processes, pointing out that capitalism and its TNCs involve the oppression and exploitation of all workers, especially women. The Marxist-feminist position has sometimes been expressed as 'exploitation thesis', focusing on new forms of exploitation experienced by women as a result of the global spread of capitalism. They draw attention to the garment sweatshops in South East Asia (especially Bangladesh) which primarily employ young female workers. Diana Leonard (1992) argues that TNCs employ women workers simply to pay low wages. One justification for this low pay is that the highly skilled work women do – such as sewing – is often passed off as unskilled. Female workers in TNCs frequently receive minimal training, low pay and low job security.

Elson and Pearson (1981) note how TNCs base the production in their world market factories on standardised, repetitive processes that are often highly labour-intensive. This stems either from the cheap cost of labour in developing countries or from assembly-type operations which have proved difficult or costly to mechanise further. Rates of pay are about a tenth of the developed world and working hours about double the working week in the West. Elson and Pearson discount the stereotype that women are employed because of their 'nimble fingers' arguing female labour must be more productive and cheaper to employ than comparable male labour. Given the profit and balance sheet approach of TNCs in global capitalism the unit costs of production must be lower with female labour for them to be the favoured worker.

> **STUDY TIP**
>
> When considering employment in the developing world, it is worth stressing that the formal and informal sectors often overlap. The formal sector is often supplied by cheap labour from the informal sector.

CONTEMPORARY APPLICATION

In March 2015 MPs in the Commons' International Development Committee (IDC) stated that population increases, especially in Africa, are making it harder for people to earn a livelihood, let alone find full-time employment. They predicted that in the next decade 600 million young people will compete for a projected 200 million jobs. They describe the problem as a 'ticking time bomb', arguing it should be treated as seriously as humanitarian disasters and global efforts to eradicate disease.

> **Questions**
>
> 1. How does the ILO define middle class?
> 2. Describe the trend of middle-class workers in the developing world.
> 3. Evaluate the impact the middle class have on developing countries.

IN THE NEWS

Developing world's middle class is growing

The emerging middle class in the developing world has more than doubled in size in 10 years. As the total proportion of poor and near poor workers falls (to 58.4 per cent), the remaining 41.6 per cent are defined as middle or upper-middle class – up from 23 per cent 10 years ago. The International Labour Organisation (ILO) defines middle class in the developing world as those earning at least $4 a day. They now make up more than 40 per cent of the developing world's workforce. The ILO forecast this will grow by another 309 million by 2017, with the share of middle-class workers rising to 51.9 per cent. All the dollars figures are calculated at purchasing power parity (PPP) – a conversion rate that eliminates differences in the cost of goods and services between countries by allowing for inflation and what a country's currency will buy.

A growing middle class is predicted to boost consumption and investment, and be an important driver of economic growth in the developing world. The ILO states the middle class also encourage greater spending on health and education. This in turn creates higher productivity and faster development for wider society. An expanding middle class has also been credited with helping to create more political stability through an increased demand for accountability and good governance.

Adapted from Mead (2013)

5.2 The role of education in development

Children in poverty, especially girls, are often excluded from education. Evidence shows that educating girls is one of the best ways of eradicating poverty, reducing family size and encouraging development.

Introduction

Figure 4.34 Some schools in the developing world are modelled on Western values

Education is considered a crucial component for development and was the basis for the second Millennium Development Goal (MDG) (see page 198). Generally, a country's degree of development is reflected in the nature and size of its education system. Very poor countries may lack universal provision of primary schools. The presence of widespread secondary education, further education colleges and higher education demonstrate increasingly significant steps towards development. As countries develop, rates of literacy, numeracy and technological competence increase, and educational attainment continues to rise.

In their annual report on education UNESCO (2014) suggests that 175 million young people lack even basic literacy skills. Their *Education for All* global monitoring report (2014) highlights the state of much of education in the developing world – 'Access [to education] is not the only crisis – poor quality is holding back learning even for those who make it to school'.

Girls and education

Currently, of the 793 million illiterate people in the world, two-thirds are female. Educating girls is considered as one of the most powerful and effective ways of overcoming global poverty. There are numerous barriers to girls' education:

- economic – where education costs money many families in developing countries preference is spending on boys' education. Further, in poor countries girls are often 'traded' for marriage dowries sometimes as young as 12 years old (see page 252)
- cultural – the bias rooted in a tradition that values the education of boys more than girls.

Evidence suggests that by attending secondary school, girls become healthier, have smaller families, earn higher wages and are less at risk of HIV infection. It could also be argued that education enables women to command greater respect and participation in decisions – both within and outside the family.

Long-term, educating girls reduces poverty: it not only creates female workers, but evidence shows that educated women are more likely educate their own children, ending the cycle of illiteracy in one generation. Not surprisingly, Kristof and WuDunn (2009) state that fertility rates tend to fall sharply with greater empowerment of women through education.

Amartya Sen: the benefits of education

Amartya Sen (2003) demonstrates that very poor families often rely on the earning capacity of their children rather than prioritising education. He suggests making education compulsory and promoting the economic benefits of schooling.

This economic connection is particularly critical in a world where workers are increasingly competing with each other in the global labour market. Beyond employment, when people are illiterate their understanding of and power to invoke their legal rights is limited. Sen argues that the very poorest people are disadvantaged by their inability to read and see what they are entitled to. Of course, this phenomenon is not limited to the developing world – it applies the world over. A lack of education can also stifle the political opportunities of the poor, by reducing their ability to express effectively their demands and participate politically. Finally, Sen argues how a lack of education can exacerbate health problems, for instance, where knowledge is lacking on the way infections are spread and how diseases can be prevented.

Applying theory to education

Bert Hoselitz (1960) regards education as one of the four 'motors' of development (see page 227). It is estimated that countries that devote at least four per cent of their GDP towards education are the most successful. The modernists' favoured model of education is one based on the Western system, promoting values such as individualism, meritocracy and entrepreneurialism.

Dependency theory adopts a rather more negative view of Western-style education, seeing it as ideological and serving as a form of **cultural imperialism**. They criticise the form of education introduced by colonial powers. Those schools mimicked European schools, producing an academic elite equipped to help run the countries as colonies. As these countries gained independence, so they changed the education systems to make them more geared to the country's new needs rather than the colonial past.

Education for All global monitoring report (2010)

UNESCO's 2010 report responded to the global banking crisis. It expressed the fear that the global economic downturn was having a negative impact on the education systems in many of the world's poorest countries. The report warned that this crisis could create a lost generation of children whose life chances will have been irreparably damaged by a failure to protect their right to education. The report focuses upon the countries whose children are most at risk of being left behind. It advocates that the global community works with such countries to formulate concrete solutions for making sure that no children are excluded from schooling.

> **KEY SOCIOLOGIST**
> **Daniel Lerner** (1958) envisaged how the traditional-to-modern social change could be catalysed by mass media. He had high hopes that radio and television could be put to use in the world's most disadvantaged countries to help bring about modernisation. He argued that, 'no modern society functions efficiently without a developed system of mass media'. As such the mass media could bring to mankind the infinite vicarious universe of education, essential skills, social unity, and a desire to 'modernise'.

> **STUDY TIP**
> When considering the impact of education in the developing world, consider that much of education provision in the developing world is of a very poor quality (see In the News below).

> **CONTEMPORARY APPLICATION**
>
> The philanthropist and founder of Microsoft, Bill Gates, predicts that new technology will revolutionise the way children in developing countries learn over the next 15 years. This is supported by a report prepared by the mobile phone industry that explores mobile technology's potential to improve access to education for young people in developing countries. As the price of this technology falls, so it opens up its potential to more children in the developing world.

IN THE NEWS

The low quality of education in much of the developing world is no secret

Figure 4.35 Indian children attend a school run under a bridge in New Delhi, India

The Indian NGO Pratham's recent report highlights the poor quality of education locally. It states that more than half of grade five students have a reading level of only grade two. Unfortunately this statistic is a familiar picture across the developing world: much of the education is of a very low quality.

In India there has been a significant move towards universal primary education with more than 90 per cent of children attending – an increase of 36 million children since 2000. There are more than 90 million more children in secondary school now than in 2000. This increase can be explained partly by India's rising population and, until the banking crisis of 2008, growing incomes within India. The government policy of paying a stipend to poor families on the condition that children go to and stay in school has also contributed. However, critics argue that expanding the education system to accommodate more children has been achieved by sacrificing quality.

India's schools seem to be characterised by overcrowded classrooms, under-qualified teachers, not enough teaching materials and high absentee rates among both pupils and teachers. The result is a poor learning environment and low-quality outcomes.

Programmes such as those in Bangladesh and Mexico have had some success in improving school enrolments, especially among girls. However, more needs to be done to provide a good quality education once they are in the classroom.

Adapted from White (2013)

Questions

1. Why has the number of children in education in India increased since 2000?
2. What factors are causing the quality of education to decline?
3. Using your wider knowledge, what did Hoselitz mean by education being a motor of development?
4. How might a Marxist interpret what is going on here in education: expansion but pupils effectively learning little?

5.3 Health care systems and the nature of health and illness in developing countries

Recognise that health differences vary not only between countries but within them too. The poorest parts of developed countries can have health levels equivalent to developing countries. Rich people living in the developing world are likely to enjoy health chances experienced in the developed world.

Introduction

The greatest barrier to good health remains poverty. There is a huge global health divide. Rich countries have an average life expectancy of around 80 years; poor countries' average life expectancy in 2015 was still only 57. Paul Collier's 'bottom billion' (see page 187) remain particularly vulnerable to diseases like malaria and tuberculosis and have a lower life expectancy simply because they live in poor and marginalised conditions. For example, tuberculosis, a disease of poverty, kills over 1 million people every year. Every year more than 2 million children die from diarrhoeal diseases simply because there is not clean water. Ferdinand De Maio (2014.36) notes this level of inequality is 'avoidable, unnecessary and unfair'.

In 2008 the Global Commission on the Social Determinants of Health asserted that equality in health and social justice should be the most important consideration for all countries.

Health and the MDGs

There is a clear correlation between health chances and a country's GNP. Health featured prominently in the Millennium Development Goals:

(4): reduce child mortality
(5): improve maternal health and
(6): combat HIV/AIDS, malaria and other diseases.

Health is also implicitly related to

(1): eradicate extreme poverty and hunger.

The MDGs mainly targeted communicable diseases, such as HIV/AIDS, malaria and tuberculosis. There was no reference to **non-communicable diseases** (NCDs) such as heart disease, cancer, chronic respiratory disease or diabetes. As noted below, these have become major killers in the developing world.

Non-communicable disease in the developing world

While the developing world has traditionally been associated with communicable diseases such as the Ebola outbreak in 2014, cholera, typhoid and tuberculosis, there has also been a significant rise of non-communicable diseases (NCDs) such as cardiovascular diseases (CVD), diabetes and cancer in developing countries. This is known as the **epidemiological transition**, whereby as countries become more affluent a shift occurs from infectious diseases to non-communicable diseases. It is estimated that around 80 per cent of deaths from these NCDs occur in low and middle-income countries, making them an urgent development issue.

There is a perception that cancer and heart disease apply mainly to affluent societies, whereas developing countries are associated with infectious diseases. However, with the urbanisation of many low-income countries this is increasingly not the case. The World Health Organisation (WHO) estimates that 30 per cent of people dying from NCDs in developing world countries are under 60 years old, therefore in their most productive period of life. The financial burden of NCDs can be devastating. For example, in China, expenses from strokes pushed 37 per cent of patients and their families below the poverty line.

Communicable disease

Communicable or infectious diseases affect 1.5 billion people in the developing world and cause an estimated 500,000 deaths a year according to the WHO (2015). In 2012 an initiative began to eradicate or control the 17 **Neglected Tropical Diseases** (NTDs) that impact particularly in the developing world. Most of these diseases occur in rural and poor urban areas disproportionately affecting the poorest groups. NTDs are defined as 'poverty-promoting' through their stigmatising features and their impact on child health and education, pregnancy and worker productivity. Sometimes the cost of treatment is minimal, yet these diseases run rampant, causing anaemia and malnutrition. For example, the cost of treating a child for soil-transmitted worms is only $0.50 for an entire year and can make a huge difference in improving life opportunities.

Mental illness in the developing world

The World Health Organisation states on its website that we are 'facing a global human rights emergency in mental health'. This is supported by the UN which estimates that mental and neurological disorders are the leading cause of ill health and disability globally. Mental health is an invisible problem that has a significant impact in the developing world, but receives little attention from either governments or NGOs. It is suggested that the lack of interest from NGOs is because the allocation of funds is strongly correlated with a project's marketability to the general public.

Despite its prevalence in the developed world, especially in the form of depression, mental health does not appear to generate sufficient empathy to generate donations to NGOs. Unlike an emaciated child, or one forced to drink polluted water, there are no emotive images that can be used to raise funds. As with the developed world there is a stigma around mental health in the developing world. Those suffering can experience widespread discrimination and limited or no treatment. In many parts of the developing world, including sections of Africa, communities can still regard mental health as a misfortune in the family or some sort of divine punishment. Treatment is often delivered by healers rather than trained doctors. Such traditional healers still often interpret mental illness in terms of being possessed or cursed. Patients treated in hospitals can often experience human rights violations. For example, they can be physically restrained, isolated and denied their basic rights.

Brain drain of medical professionals from the developing world

Across the developing world there is little economic incentive for medical professionals to work in poor or rural areas. With their transferrable skills, doctors and nurses from the developing world have valuable qualifications and skills also in demand in the developed world. The WHO (2013) predicts that the current global shortage of 7.2 million health workers will increase to 12.9 million by 2035, with the poorest countries bearing the brunt of those shortages.

Five African countries (Sierra Leone, Tanzania, Mozambique, Angola and Liberia) have expatriation rates of more than 50 per cent – more than half the doctors born in those countries are now working in developed countries. In the UK, the NHS consistently trains insufficient doctors and other medical professionals and relies on migrant doctors and nurses, often from the developing world. This can cause distortions and shortages of medical staff in the poorer areas of the world.

Mensah *et al.* (2005) estimate that the money saved by the UK through the recruitment of Ghanaian health workers may have exceeded the value of aid it gave to Ghana for health. Natalie Sharples (2015) calculates that poverty-stricken and Ebola-hit Sierra Leone has subsidised the NHS by £22.5 million. This is calculated by the fact that 27 doctors and 103 nurses trained in Sierra Leone are currently working in the UK, saving the NHS £269,527 it costs to train each junior doctor and £70,000 to train a nurse.

Health and theory

Modernisation theory would expect developing world health patterns to reflect those followed by the developed world in the past. Just as the developed world passed through the epidemiological tradition, so will developing countries as improvements in nutrition and hygiene reduce death rates from infectious diseases. Modernists assume that progress through the 'stages of development' will promote improved life expectancy and reduce childhood mortality, eventually leading to illnesses of affluence: heart disease and cancers.

Theodore Macdonald (2009) rejects the modernisation theoretical approach and its modern guise of neo-liberal theory. He argues neo-liberalism is incompatible with global health equity. He argues the very structures set up to improve health and reduce inequality have become the main protagonists in widening them. He argues there is an ever increasing need to address this, given the food shortage, environmental damage and conflict on a massive scale and advocates intervention in order to overcome market failure. He broadly supports dependency theory's challenge to the assumption that markets are valid allocators of essentials like health. Markets, after all, peddle unhealthy products, particularly if they are profitable – tobacco products and foods high in refined ingredients, saturated fats, sugar and salt. Pharmaceutical TNCs market their products at prices people and even governments sometimes cannot afford. Finally, SAPs can result in clinics being closed, especially in rural areas.

> **KEY SOCIOLOGIST**
> **Wilkinson and Pickett** (2010) show that health shows no correlation with average income. In other words a country's health does not improve the richer it becomes. Instead, they argue, there is a strong correlation with income inequality. The wider the income gaps between the rich and poor within a country, the greater the social class health gap.

> **CONTEMPORARY APPLICATION**
> Smartphones are being used to check for eye disease in clinics in the developing world. The phone automatically focuses on what it is looking for, such as a cataract or glaucoma, and captures the image, allowing the health care worker to send it on to more qualified experts by email or SMS. This even circumvents the need for a trained ophthalmic, since anybody can conduct the eye exam.

> **IN THE NEWS**
>
> ### Waistlines are expanding at a rapid rate in developing countries
>
> While the first image most people might have of the developing world is one of hunger and malnutrition, the Overseas Development Institute (2014) has found that the number of overweight and obese people in the developing world has more than tripled – from around 250 million in 1980 to almost a billion today. There are almost twice as many overweight and obese people in the developing world than in developed countries.
>
> The explanation for this growth in obesity is a combination of higher incomes, a fall in the real cost of many foods, and more sedentary habits. In addition, with more working women there is less time to prepare meals with an increasing reliance on and consumption of processed foods and take-away junk food. Across the developing world American fast food outlets like McDonald's, KFC and Pizza Hut are expanding all the time. In addition, local shops are increasingly selling products like crisps, white bread and large bottles of fizzy drinks. However, where local traditions remain strong, as in South Korea, eateries for ordinary people still sell fish stews and traditional food. Consequently, Koreans have half the rate of overweight people compared to many Latin American countries where junk food has become embedded into their culture. As a consequence Latin America (along with the Middle East and North Africa) has obesity rates on a par with Europe.
>
> Adapted from Wiggins (2014)

Questions

1. Outline the reasons why obesity is rising in the developing world.
2. Why are obesity levels lower in South Korea?
3. What are the health implications of growing obesity?
4. Can anything be done to redress this trend?

5.4 Trends, causes and significance for development of demographic change

When considering demographic change you need to explore the arguments for and against the view that population will continue to grow.

Introduction

The population in the developed world is stable, or in some countries even falling: population growth is predominantly occurring in the developing world. There has long been concern at the speed of population growth, but this has been particularly strong since 1925 when the world's population passed 2 billion. In 2013 the world's population passed 7 billion level. Although some demographers predict it will rise exponentially, others like Hans Rosling (2012) argue it will level off at 10 billion. The key fear is that the planet will have insufficient resources, especially food, to support the population. So far, food technology has always kept up with population growth: production of food from animals has increased commensurately and production of fruit and vegetables per person has doubled in the past 50 years. Nonetheless, we still live in a world that is unable to ensure everybody gets fed with 842 million going to bed hungry each day.

The WHO (2012) estimates that stunting in childhood (from malnutrition) affects approximately 162 million children under the age of 5 globally. This is not due to a shortage of food, but an inability of poor households to afford it. Poor diet also impacts on adults, for example, in 2011 the WHO estimated that anaemia affected half a billion women of reproductive age worldwide. Anaemia impairs health and well-being in women and increases the risk of adverse maternal and neonatal outcomes.

The Malthusian argument

Thomas Malthus (1766–1834) predicted that population growth would exceed society's ability to feed itself, resulting in inevitable famine and malnutrition. Malthus also saw this shortage of food as potentially resulting in people fighting wars over scarce resources. In order to prevent this he advocated a limit on population growth through delaying marriage until later in life and abstaining from sex. While the dystopian vision of Malthus has generally failed to materialise, there has recently been a revival of his ideas through neo-Malthusians like Paul Ehrlich (1968). His fundamental argument is that the birth rate must be brought in line with the death rate or 'mankind will breed itself into oblivion'.

The anti-Malthusian argument

Anti-Malthusians such as Ester Boserup (1965) argue that it is population that determines agricultural methods. As population grows then public ingenuity would drive improvements in agricultural technology. Boserup was a great believer in necessity being the mother of invention. Thanks to such advancements in agricultural technology, food supply has kept pace with population growth. In terms of overall food supply it is fair to say that recent history has produced the rapid growth of over-nutrition in the developing world.

Anti-Malthusians question global population statistics which they say are unreliable and inaccurate. Cohen and Kennedy (2013) accuse the neo-Malthusians of overstating their argument from using a distorted statistical analysis. They point out that predictions of population explosions are usually based on present trends, which fail to account for changes in people's behaviour in the future. The United Nations Population Division (UNPD) claims to be the most reliable source of population statistics in the world. It notes that population growth is falling and will continue to slow down over the next few decades. It predicts the global population will peak at around 8 billion then begin to fall. Initially the fall will be slow but will then get faster. Population growth was 2 per cent in 1980; the World Bank (2015) expects it to fall to just 1 per cent by 2020 and 0.5 per cent by 2050. All over the world, birth rates have been dropping quickly, and for nearly 50 years now.

Another criticism is the demographic transition. This is the natural process associated with industrialisation and urbanisation that involves a shift from high birth and death rates to low birth and death rates. Because the developing world is currently going through this demographic transition, the global population will continue to rise for a few decades, and then begin to fall. The number of children has stopped growing in the world and will remain constant at 2 billion.

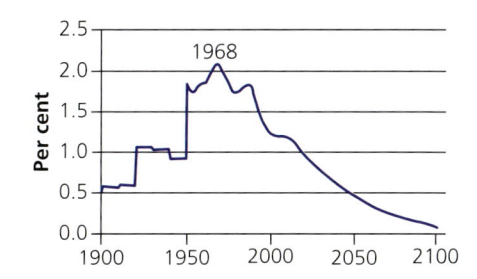

Figure 4.36 World Bank's prediction of how population growth will continue to fall

Therefore the current population growth is due to improved death rates not higher birth rates. As people continue to live longer, global population will continue to rise but then level out.

Population and theory

Modernisation theory links the desire to have large families to traditional values. The solution to rising population is therefore policies like the promotion of contraception, sterilisation, financial incentives to limit family size and some modernisation theorists even advocate the liberalisation of abortion access. As a theory it is highly critical of the influence major religions like Roman Catholicism and Islam can have on population growth. However, Hans Rosling (2012) shows that in the contemporary world religion has little influence on family size. For example, in Christian, Islamic and Eastern religions most countries have low birth rates, but there are also some with very high birth rates. The key factor according to Rosling is poverty. The poorest countries with the highest childhood mortality rate have the fastest population growth.

Dependency theorists like Mahmood Mamdani (2004) point out that modernisation theory ignores that history has shaped current economic inequalities. David Adamson (1986) argues that poverty causes high population growth as families compensate for high childhood mortality. He is adamant that modernisation theory's birth control policies will always fail if poverty is not tackled at the same time. According to Adamson the real problem is not down to overpopulation but the unequal distribution of food and energy. For example, the USA has 6 per cent of the world population but consumes 40 per cent of its resources. In addition, in the absence of welfare and old age pensions, children become an economic asset and necessary to look after people should they live to old age. Cohen and Kennedy (2013) call these offspring 'insurance children'.

> **KEY SOCIOLOGIST**
>
> **Hans Rosling** (2012), an anti-Malthusian, argues that the global population will rise to 10 billion then stabilise. He points out that in 2010, 80 per cent of humans lived in countries where the average number of children was just 2 children per woman. The consequence of this is that the number of children in the world has evened out at 2 billion. The reason the global population is rising is not the birth rate, but increased life expectancy.

> **STUDY TIP**
>
> When writing about population change bring in theoretical analysis as well as statistical evidence in support of the arguments.

> **CONTEMPORARY APPLICATION**
>
> A UN report (*World Urbanization Prospects*, 2014) predicts that the world's urban population, which overtook the number of rural residents in 2010, is likely to rise by about 2.5 billion to more than 6 billion people in less than 40 years. The report highlights how the two continents of Africa and Asia in particular will 'face numerous challenges in meeting the needs of their growing urban populations, including for housing, infrastructure, transportation, energy and employment, as well as for basic services such as education and healthcare'.

5.5 The significance of gender in relation to development

Make sure you can demonstrate the breadth of examples of gender inequity in the developing world. It is also important to see how women can play a key role in driving development.

One of the themes of this chapter has been to show the feminist idea that women are the primary movers of development: working women exert the greatest influence on reducing poverty and the birth rate. At the same time, feminists highlight how women can be the main victims of underdevelopment. In the words of Nikki Van der Gaag (2004) for millions of women in the developing world 'life is still very grim'.

Ruth Pearson (2001) notes that women's issues, previously neglected in development policy, are now at the top of the agenda: gender is now incorporated into the development plans of the UN, World Bank, and many NGO operations. Women's issues formed the basis of two Millennium Development Goals:

(3): promote gender equality and empower women, and
(5): improve maternal health.

Sheryl WuDunn (2010) argues that the central moral challenge of the twenty-first century is gender inequity (compared to slavery in the nineteenth and totalitarianism in the twentieth centuries). The consequences of global policies and actions are now increasingly recognised to have *a gender impact*. For example, Cohen and Kennedy (2013) point out that the impact of SAPs by the World Bank and the IMF hit women the hardest, particularly those living in rural areas and heading households as single parents. SAPs force governments to reduce spending, especially on welfare and food subsidies. This causes the price of food to rise, increased unemployment and reduction in welfare provision, such as rural clinics.

The neo-liberal policies of the World Bank and IMF serve to drive more and more women into the globalised labour market. We have seen how:

- underpaid women form the vast majority of the workforce, particularly in the garment industry (see page 240), and
- TNCs are attracted to employing women as they can pay them less than men (see pages 240–1).

Cohen and Kennedy (2013:159) note:

> It is impossible to disentangle the situation [women] face as workers from the gender inequalities and patriarchal power structures they equally face as women. This is in addition to the low wages, long working hours that often make no concession to family responsibilities.

Women and work

Women's plight working for TNCs has been discussed in some depth already in this chapter (see pages 240–241). Diana Leonard (1992) argues that TNCs aim to exploit women rather than provide them with training, fair pay and job security. She also notes how the development of farming for cash crops in the developing world has led to men rather than women being employed in agriculture.

Women in the developing world undertake almost all of the domestic tasks, such as cooking, cleaning and childcare. In addition, certain tasks are exclusively seen as women's work, such as fetching water or foraging for firewood. This essentially stems from women's lack of power, owing to the combined factors of patriarchy and poverty.

Women are portrayed primarily as mothers, dependent on men. Such ideology is used to justify not sending girls to school, which reinforces men's control over the next generation of women.

Another impact of globalisation has been to create a global market in the services traditionally offered by women. For example, Ehrenreich and Hochschild (2002) describe how millions of women leave developing countries to work as nannies, maids and sex workers in the developed world. They argue that this creates a 'care deficit' in the developing world, as their own families are neglected.

Women lack reproductive rights

Women in the developing world frequently lack reproductive rights – they have no control over their fertility. Men control access to and use of contraception or abortion. Furthermore, the decision about whether to have children, when to have children and how many children they should bear is taken by men. In many parts of the world (in Latin America it is known as '*machismo*') men's status is reflected in the number of children they sire. Girls as young as 12 can be sold off as brides (see page 252) and this can result in children bearing children.

Women in developing countries have little sexual freedom, and lack choices about when they have sex, whom they have it with, or under what conditions and with what outcomes.

Missing women

Nikki Van der Gaag (2004) notes how in many developing countries the birth of a boy is celebrated but the birth of a girl is commiserated. The phenomenon of 'missing women' was first studied by Amartya Sen (1989). Sheryl WuDunn (2010) says in many countries, particularly in Asia, the 'cause of our time' is the fatality that so many people face around the world because of their gender. She points out that demographers have shown that there are 60–100 million missing females in the current population. This is due to **female infanticide** and **foeticide** (foetuses being aborted before they are even born). The Chinese government admits that the country currently has 40 million 'extra' males. According to most predictions, this gap between the number of males and females will only increase with some predicting it will be 55 million by 2020.

Despite being made illegal in 1994, foeticide appears to be widespread in India, although in the poorer areas girls seem to be disappearing just as much from infanticide. In India, while the overall gender ratio is improving, its child gender ratio is on the decline. For example, between 1991 and 2011, the country's female–male gender ratio rose from 927:1,000 to 940:1,000, but its child gender ratio fell from 945:1,000 to 914:1,000. Such is the shortage of marital women that there is a thriving market in bride-buying in the affected states. Most of the brides come from poverty-ridden villages because their families need the money. Despite the prevalence of the dowry system in the north Indian states, men desperate for a wife are more than willing to pay. The outcome, however, is that once purchased the brides have no security and can be exploited and, in many cases, abandoned if they do not produce a son.

Trafficking of women

Slavery, although thought to be a thing of the past, still exists today globally. Sheryl WuDunn (2010) compares the 80,000 slaves exported at the peak of the slave trade in the 1780s from Africa to the New World to the contemporary estimated figure of around 800,000 women trafficked across international borders. Traffickers use force, fraud, or coercion to control other people for the purpose of engaging in commercial sex or forcing them to provide domestic or commercial labour services against their will. Those trafficked can end up working as servants or working on large farms, or in restaurants and hotels.

Significant numbers of trafficked women end up as sex workers in brothels or on the street. In brothels, women are forced to work very long hours, often having unprotected sex; working on the streets and in hotels women have to meet nightly quotas and then turn the money over to their traffickers. Trafficking is very lucrative, estimated to be worth $150 billion a year, since the rewards are high and the risks are low. The Home Office estimated in 2013 that there were up to 13,000 victims of slavery in Britain in 2013, most of them from Albania, Nigeria, Vietnam and Romania.

Maternal mortality

It is estimated by the NGO Women and Children First that between 250,000 and 343,000 women die each year from complications associated with pregnancy and childbirth. Most of the women who die giving birth in the developing world die because they had no access to skilled routine and emergency care. As noted above an impact of SAPs can be the closure of rural clinics, putting pregnant women at risk.

Compared to the developed world, where a woman's lifetime risk of dying during or following pregnancy is one in 4,300, in sub-Saharan Africa that risk is one in 31. Specifically, in Niger one in seven women can expect to die during childbirth. Currently around the world one woman dies each minute and a half from childbirth. Sheryl WuDunn (2010) explains this because women are 'poor, rural and female'.

Gender and theory

Neither modernisation theory nor dependency theory had much to say on gender issues. They were more preoccupied by economic factors and pre-date the influential period of second wave feminism. However, applying the broad brush of modernisation theory, Ester Boserup (1970) advocated the idea that by engaging in the workforce women would not only be emancipated but would help drive forward development. Therefore there is a positive correlation made by modernisation theory, seeing the creation of jobs by TNCs as helping women's position.

Socialist feminists (somewhat influenced by dependency theory) challenged this view as naïve, for viewing the modernisation process as positive and harmless. In addition, Marxist feminists formed exploitation thesis to emphasise how the global spread of capitalism involved the systematic exploitation of women. They argue that when TNCs relocate in export-processing zones (EPZs) it is precisely to exploit the workforce, the majority of whom are young women. Exploitation thesis argues TNCs simply help impose the exploitative system of global capitalism and all this entails on women within developing countries.

> **KEY SOCIOLOGIST**
>
> **Ruth Pearson** originally focused on gender relations in Latin America but has broadened to the Thai-Burmese border and the South Asian diaspora in the UK. She has written extensively on issues such as gender relations, gender and work, reproductive rights, the Indian dowry system, violence against women and women's migration. She is currently researching the position of women in the global economy, home based working and migrant workers' identity.

> **STUDY TIP**
>
> When considering gender inequality it is important to cover issues and examples that can be used to illustrate the marginalisation and exploitation of women. In addition, familiarise yourself with different theoretical analysis, such as whether TNCs contribute to women's emancipation or oppression.

> **CONTEMPORARY APPLICATION**
>
> Purdah is the practice of women covered from head to toe. This can be practised voluntarily, but some women are forced to practise purdah. Thirty years ago Aiden Foster-Carter (1985) described veiling as undermining women's social, economic and political roles, but the debate continues to this day over the rights and wrongs of purdah. The right-wing journalist Julie Burchill once described it as like 'walking around in a prison'. Some feminists, however, have described veiling as liberating since it stops women's bodies being sexualised.

> **IN THE NEWS**
>
> ### Human traffickers may face life sentence under Britain's tough new slavery bill
>
> Under new UK legislation human traffickers can now receive life imprisonment as their punishment. The new law is intended to act as a serious deterrent to modern-day slavery, estimated to be worth around $150 billion per year in the UK and involving at least 13,000 victims of forced labour, sexual exploitation and domestic servitude. The modern slavery bill, passed in March 2015, allows the authorities to seize traffickers' assets and force them to pay compensation to their victims. It also puts the onus on businesses to demonstrate what action they have taken to ensure their supply chains are free of slave labour. With estimates that as many as 36 million people are enslaved globally, pressure has been mounting on the UK government to do something about this growing problem.
>
> Adapted from Nguyen and Guilbert (2015)

Questions

1. What evidence exists to support the idea that slavery is a serious and growing problem?
2. How do you account for the growth in slavery to its current levels?
3. Can you account for why the majority of those being trafficked are female?

Check your understanding

1. Differentiate between the formal and informal sectors of the economy in the developing world.
2. In what ways is women's position in the workforce worse than men's?
3. Why is the education of girls valued less than boys?
4. Why is education so valued by modernisation theorists like Hoselitz?
5. What is meant by the epidemiological transition?
6. What factors are causing obesity to rise in the developing world?
7. Outline the arguments both for and against the Malthusian position on population growth.
8. What is meant by *machismo*?
9. In what ways does modernisation theory see TNCs as helping the emancipation of women?
10. How and why would a Marxist feminist respond that TNCs serve to oppress and exploit women?

Practice questions

1. Outline and explain **two** reasons that can account for the difference in the number of females and males in the global population. [10 marks]

Read Item A below and answer the question that follows.

Item A

Alongside the undoubted difficulties that globalisation imposes on women, it does at least provide a framework on which communication takes place, networks form and institutional links become accessible. These can offer women new opportunities that they may be able to harness to their advantage (Cohen and Kennedy, 2013).

Applying material from Item A, analyse two ways in which globalisation has improved the position of women in the developing world.
[10 marks]

Read Item B below and answer the question that follows.

Item B

Most people think obesity is a problem for countries like the USA and the UK. But the diet and lifestyles that caused the obesity epidemics in affluent nations are being exported all over the world.

Applying material from Item B and your knowledge, evaluate the view that the developing world is acquiring the same health issues as the developed world.
[20 marks]

5 The media

Understanding the specification	
AQA Specification	**How the specification is covered in this chapter**
The new media and their significance for and understanding of the role of the media in contemporary society.	**Section 1: The new media** What is the nature of the 'new media' and how significant is it? To what extent has the new media grown and diversified? Who uses and controls new media?
The relationship between ownership and control of the media.	**Section 2: The relationship between ownership and control of the media** What are sociological views on the ownership and control of the media? What are the patterns of ownership in the media?
The media, globalisation and popular culture.	**Section 3: The media, globalisation and culture** What different types of culture are there and what is the significance of global culture? What is the relationship between the media and global culture? What are sociological views on the social construction of news, including new social media?
The processes of selection and presentation of the content of the news.	**Section 4: What makes the news?** What are sociological views on the social construction of news, including the social media? What is the influence of other groups on the content of the news?
Media representations of age, social class, ethnicity, gender, sexuality and disability.	**Section 5: Media representations of social groups** How are different age groups represented in the media? How are different social classes represented in the media? How are different ethnic groups represented in the media? How are men and women represented in the media? How is sexuality represented in the media? How is disability represented in the media? How have the representations of different groups in the media changed over time?
The relationship between the media, their content and presentation, and audiences	**Section 6: The effects of the media on audiences** What are the different sociological explanations of the effects of the media on audiences? Why might methodological issues arise when researching media effects?

Section 1: The new media

This section will explore the following debates:
- What is the nature of the 'new media' and how significant is it?
- To what extent has the new media grown and diversified?
- Who uses and controls new media?

GETTING YOU STARTED

We're communicating more than sleeping

Digital communications technology has changed the way many people keep in touch. Children aged 12–15 are turning away from voice exchanges to communicating mostly by text. In contrast, adults spend about 20 per cent of the communications time talking on the phone, and 33 per cent on emails. Research by the government-approved Office of Communications (Ofcom) shows that with the success of newer services and portable connected devices, communication choices are evolving further.

Some UK adults now spend more time communicating on social media and other communications technology than they do sleeping. The average time spent on communications by a UK adult is 8 hours and 41 minutes, whereas the average time spent asleep is 20 minutes less than that.

However, mobile communications, superfast broadband, 4G mobile and multi-tasking on different devices has meant that the total use of media and communications averaged even more hours – over 11 daily in 2014 – an increase of more than 2 hours since Ofcom last conducted similar research in 2010.

People aged 16–24 spend the most time on media and communications, using different devices and services simultaneously to clock up an average of 14 hours of media and communications activity into around 9 hours actual time.

Adapted from Ofcom (2014)

Questions

1. Give examples of 'newer services' and 'portable connected devices'.
2. Suggest reasons why the 16–24-year-old age group '… spend the most time on media and communications'.
3. List reasons why the amount of time that people are spending on media and communications has increased steadily over the last 30 years or so.

1.1 What is the nature of the 'new media' and how significant is it?

Make sure you understand what the new media is (its 'nature'), how it differs from traditional types of media and competing views on how beneficial new media might be. It is very important to recognise that not all media is new; for example it would not be appropriate to use newspapers or radio as an example of new media.

The Oxford English Dictionary defines 'media' as 'the main means of mass communication (television, radio and newspapers) regarded collectively'. These forms of media are now sometimes called 'traditional media' to differentiate them from new forms of **digital** communication. Hence '**new media**' means digital technologies which are used for mass communication. This is a wide-ranging term, and could include social networking, blogs, vlogs, digital interactive television, text messaging, websites, online gaming … the list goes on. To put a

> **STUDY TIP**
>
> When writing about new media show an awareness of its rapidly evolving nature. It is more sophisticated to show an appreciation of the complexity of defining 'new media' rather than trying to simplify it into a basic definition. Additionally, you should understand the difference between traditional forms of media and new media.

timeframe on it, the new media includes systems and technologies for delivering information on a mass scale that have emerged in the last 30 years or so. Many forms of 'new' media are actually an evolution of traditional media forms, rather than being brand new. For example, some people now choose to read the news on a website such as www.telegraph.co.uk rather than buying a copy of *The Telegraph* newspaper. It is also important to note that the list of new media devices and technologies is changing frequently, as new technologies emerge, and some fail to succeed in the increasingly crowded media market.

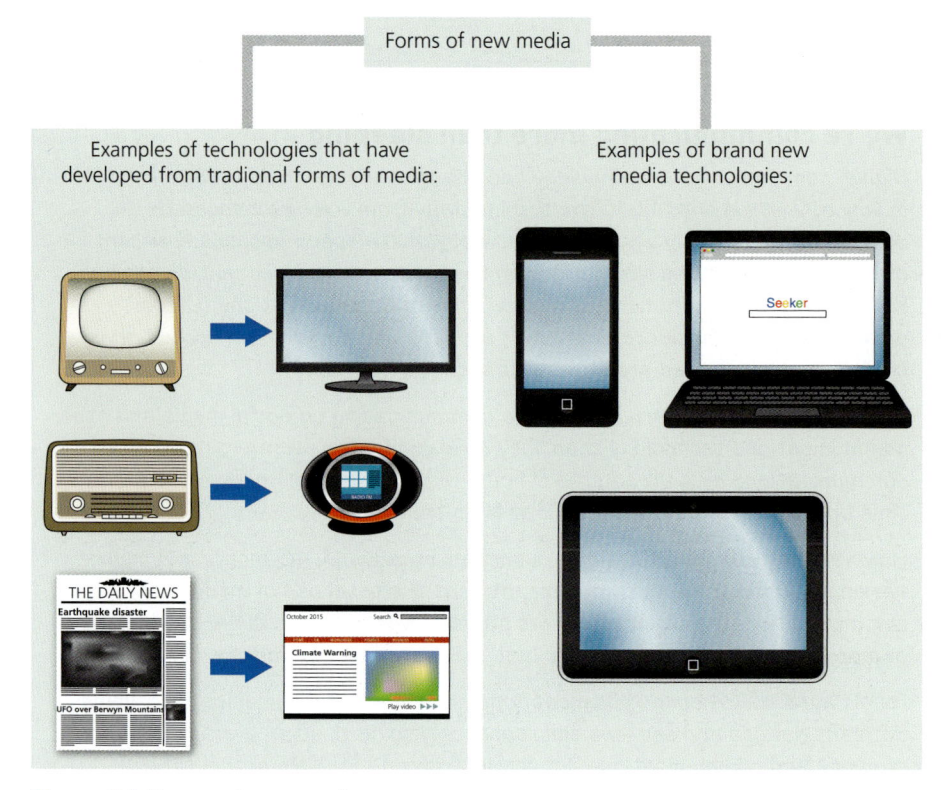

Figure 5.1 Forms of new media

The nature of new media

Most systems and technologies of new media have some common characteristics. One characteristic that differentiates new media from traditional media is the digital nature of new media. According to Curran and Seaton (2010) digitisation has revolutionised the media: whereas information used to be spread in an analogue form, for example, printed words in newspapers, it is now increasingly available in digital formats such as news websites or apps on smartphones. Curran and Seaton note that digitisation allowed new media to develop, by converting 'words, numbers, sounds and images into electronic binary digits'. This led to significant changes for the media, such as the ability to store huge quantities of data in a small amount of space, and reduced costs in terms of production and distribution.

Furthermore, this 'digital environment' (Boyle, 2007) has led to a significant shift in the way that the media operates. For example, via social networks, blogs or websites that are written collaboratively by users (such as www.wikipedia.org), individuals can communicate to large audiences, suggesting that new media is characterised by its **interactivity**. New media offers opportunities for everyday citizens to be actively involved in the information that is being transmitted. For example, the 'red button' on Sky allows viewers to select from a range of football games, and some television programmes feature a live Twitter feed where viewers can submit their opinions. This means that, to some extent, the media is now more individualised, although not all audience members are able to use the interactive features. This might be due to not being able to afford the media services that allow interactivity, or not having the technological confidence to use them.

It is also clear that there are now more media outlets than ever before (for example, the hundreds of television channels on offer on digital systems such as Sky, BT TV or Virgin Media), meaning that another characteristic of the new media is its diversity (see page 261).

As well as there being more delivery systems and technologies than ever, some argue that control and ownership of new media is more diverse and perhaps more democratic than that of traditional media. Boyle (2005) argues that new media has caused a shift in who is in control. The type and timing of television programmes, for example, used to be decided by the owners of the television channels: it was 'supply-led'. Now it is far more **'demand-led'**. This means that users have the ability to choose what they want to watch and when they want to watch it. Examples of this would be BBC iPlayer, Netflix or Sky On Demand, among many. However, other sociologists are critical of this pluralist view (which is explored further in Section 2 of this chapter) and argue that a few multinational corporations continue to control much of the mass media.

Curran and Seaton (2010) argue that different forms of media are no longer separate, but instead new media is characterised by its interconnectivity, for example, a person can send an email through a smart television, or watch television on a computer. Boyle (2005) calls this interconnectivity **'convergence'**.

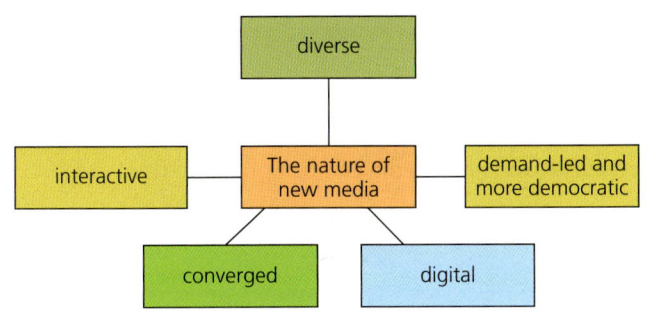

Figure 5.2 The characteristics of the new media

KEY SOCIOLOGIST

Raymond Boyle (2005, 2007) explains in detail the characteristics of new media. With a particular interest in sport media, he takes a chronological approach to examining how new media has changed the nature of communications in the UK.

IN THE NEWS

Pink is beautiful in black

'So What' singer Pink has given a characteristically feisty response to Twitter critics. Her choice of dress and her curvy appearance attracted 'body-shaming' comments on Twitter, with some users expressing the opinion that she was 'fat'.

Quick to respond, Pink replied: 'I can see that some of you are concerned about me from your comments about my weight. You're referring to the pictures of me from last night's cancer benefit that I attended to support my dear friend Dr Maggie DiNome. She was given the Duke Award for her tireless efforts and stellar contributions to the eradication of cancer. But unfortunately, my weight seems much more important to some of you.'

Stating that her black gown 'didn't photograph as well as it did in my kitchen', Pink said she 'felt very pretty. In fact, I feel beautiful'.

Pink has revealed that her husband Carey Hart said he loves her new shape and tweeted his comment: 'It's just more to love, baby'. The couple have a daughter, Willow, born in 2011. Pink reassures her critics that she is perfectly happy with her 'healthy, voluptuous and crazy strong body.'

Figure 5.3 Pretty Pink

Adapted from Hardingham-Gill (2015)

Questions

1. How does this article show that new media is more interactive than traditional media?
2. What other characteristics of the new media can be applied to this news article?
3. Suggest a disadvantage of new media shown by this news article.

The competing views on digital media in contemporary society

Positive views of the new media

For many sociologists, the advent of the new media has brought with it many benefits for individuals and society. Curran and Seaton (2010) use the term 'neophiliacs' to describe those who are positive about new media and recognise the benefits that it may bring. A view often associated with postmodernism, neophiliacs share the belief that new media creates consumer choice and increased participation in the spread of information.

Boyle (2007) discussed how the new media might create consumer choice as the telecommunications industry now aims to produce devices that can be individualised by the user, for example, a seemingly limitless choice of apps on a smartphone. For example, those who grew up in the 1980s had few choices when it came to finding out about current affairs. The news was shown on the four terrestrial television channels once per hour, or daily local and national newspapers could be purchased. Nowadays, media consumers are somewhat spoilt for choice, with multiple 24-hour news channels available on digital television subscription services such as Sky, hundreds of websites dedicated to current affairs, as well as numerous mobile phone news apps which are updated constantly. A wider range of new stories are reported on, as previously the news was limited to how many stories could be slotted into a 10-minute television news slot, or a newspaper with a fixed number of pages. This means that people find out about breaking news stories more quickly, and are able to access news anywhere on portable devices such as mobile phones or tablets, as well as knowing about a more diverse range of new stories from all over the world.

Furthermore, as previously mentioned, new media is characterised by its interactivity and involvement of users. Traditional media was owned almost solely by large corporations, such as Rupert Murdoch's News Corporation which included *The Times*, *The Sun*, the *News of the World*, BSkyB, Twentieth Century Fox and the *Wall Street Journal*. Indeed, it would have been very difficult for an everyday citizen to have their views heard by a large audience. Nowadays, with the development of new media, individuals have opportunities to be involved in the media, perhaps by publishing their own online blog, or by having a large following on Twitter, Instagram or YouTube. Some 'citizen journalists' use this power to spread the word about social issues. Equally the new media has given a platform for experts to easily and widely publish information about their specialism, which could lead to an encyclopaedic source of information. For example, Wikipedia is written by users, not a corporation that owns the website. Anyone can edit a Wikipedia page, they simply need internet access. Jenkins (2008) argues that this 'collective intelligence' could prove to be very beneficial. It is worth noting, however, that Wikipedia contributors are overwhelmingly male – the worldwide Wikipedia Editor Survey 2011 found that 91 per cent of those editing Wikipedia were male. Therefore feminists may question whether women have benefited from new media or whether men use it for their own benefit to spread patriarchal ideology.

Overall, neophiliacs believe that the new media provides consumers with choice and flexibility, as well as the potential to influence which media output succeeds and which fails. It could be argued, therefore, that new media has made the mass media more democratic, both in terms of allowing everyone to have a voice, and in terms of increasing citizens' interest in their society, as they feel they have the means to 'make a difference'. However Curran and Seaton are somewhat dismissive of the claims of neophiliacs, suggesting that neophiliac predictions about the benefits of new media are in some ways naïve.

> **STUDY TIP**
>
> Try to apply these sociological ideas to new media as you use it. For example, as you use social networking, consider what neophiliacs might consider the advantages of it to be.

Critical views of the new media

Curran and Seaton call those who are negative about new media '**cultural pessimists**'. Cultural pessimists share the belief that new media has led to a reduction in quality of popular culture, is poorly regulated, and that a few huge corporations have control of most of the new media, rather than individual consumers.

For example, some cultural pessimists question the quality of information being spread by many of the new media outlets. Keen (2007) refers to the internet as the 'cult of the amateur' and argues that it is leading to the demise of quality information. Similarly, in 2008 *The Scotsman* reported that a study by the Scottish Parent Teacher Council showed that teachers held concerns about their students using the internet as a research tool as some websites hold inaccurate information. Wikipedia was named as an unreliable source as the content on this website is user-generated, so users have a window of opportunity to publish wildly inaccurate information. The article states that the Wikipedia page on Kylie Minogue once claimed that she was Michael Jackson's older sister, and Robbie Williams was accused of eating hamsters in pubs! Additionally, other cultural pessimists argue that even if the information that new media publishes is accurate, it is 'dumbing-down' popular culture. Evidence of this could be the sheer number of websites dedicated to celebrity gossip, which would have made up just a tiny percentage of traditional media stories in previous times. There is little regulation over the internet, and as such, it seems to be somewhat of a breeding ground for poor quality information, and even bullying, harassment and discrimination (Jones, 2013). Keen (2007) suggests that social networking sites are 'becoming infested with anonymous sexual predators and paedophiles'.

Other cultural pessimists are concerned that new media such as digital television has weakened **social cohesion**. This is because, unlike in previous decades when only BBC1, BBC 2, ITV and Channel 4 existed, there are now hundreds of television channels spreading a multitude of beliefs and splitting the public into fragmented groups. However, as Curran and Seaton (2010) point out, the four 'traditional' channels continue to dominate television viewing, with 2013 data showing that BBC1 alone accounted for a 20.8 per cent share of the television audience, and the four traditional channels together attracted 48.6 per cent of the television audience for that year (BARB, 2013).

Indeed, this challenges the neophiliac claim that the new media has reduced the power of large corporations and increased the involvement of individuals in the media. Cornford and Robins (1999) discuss this continuing power of international corporations over the media. Even new media technologies that appear to be user-controlled are owned by corporations who are able to exercise control over them. An example of this is Mark Zuckerberg's *Facebook, Inc*, which owns Facebook, Instagram and WhatsApp. Facebook has recently been criticised for removing photographs which showed women breastfeeding, yet allowing photographs of women in skimpy bikinis. This shows how it is ultimately the decision of large corporations as to what information can be published, something which Marxists would see as evidence of the continuing control of bourgeois corporations over society. Furthermore, as recently highlighted by The Snowden Report, there are concerns about the new media regarding privacy and surveillance.

Different perspectives

Radical feminists would view the media as **malestream**, despite the growth of the new media allowing individual women and feminist pressure groups to have more of a voice. This is because, as argued by Marxists, most of the media seems to still be controlled by just a few large, international corporations, the vast majority of which have male CEOs.

> **KEY SOCIOLOGISTS**
>
> **James Curran and Jean Seaton** (2010) view the internet as the 'single most important development' in the media industry since the 1980s, but also discuss other types of new media, such as the rise of digital television and the hundreds of new channels that it created.

> **KEY SOCIOLOGISTS**
>
> **James Cornford and Kevin Robins** (1999) take somewhat of a cultural pessimist view towards the new media, pointing out how the new media is dominated by just a few huge, powerful corporations, rather than being a way that individuals can have a meaningful influence over the media. They also suggest that new media is not particularly 'new', and is not much more interactive than previous forms of media were.

1.2 How significant is the new media?

For Cornford and Robins (1999), the new media is not as significant or 'new' as it may first appear. Many forms of traditional media, such as the telephone and television, are the basis of new media, and even the idea of audience participation in the media is not particularly revolutionary. For example, readers' letters have been published in newspapers for many decades.

Conversely, Cornford and Robins predicted a 'ubiquitous information appliance', that is, an ever present source of information, which could fulfil every information need, would be invented in the future. By 'ubiquitous', the sociologists mean that the 'information appliance' would be very commonplace, found everywhere. This would make the new media very significant as it would be part of the everyday activities of almost all people. For example, it would be able to show films and television, be used as a telephone, install software, play music, send emails, and browse the web. Eleven years after this prediction, Apple released the first iPad, which seemingly fulfils much of the criteria. Over 225 million iPads have been sold since their release in 2010, along with several million tablets of other brands, but with a global population of 7 billion people, these figures make tablets far from 'ubiquitous'. Furthermore, manufacturers restrict the installation of software of most tablets, and no such device has been invented that all social groups in society have embraced. This again suggests that the new media has failed to be quite as significant as some sociologists predicted.

However, when analysing 2013 data, the Office for National Statistics (ONS) stated that, 'The Internet has changed the way people go about their daily lives. In 2013, more people than ever before used the Internet for reading newspapers or magazines (55 per cent), to access their bank accounts (50 per cent), to seek health information (43 per cent) or to buy groceries (21 per cent). This release highlights that activities previously carried out on the high street, are now increasingly being carried out online.' Postmodernists agree, arguing that we have witnessed a fundamental shift in the way that information and news is collected, analysed and spread over the last 30 years or so. They point to the immediacy of new media, the choices it has given audiences and the way in which it has created connections between distant parts of the globe as evidence of how significant new media has been.

So it could be argued that some forms of new media are significant, but only in certain regions of the world and for particular social groups (namely younger people) in those regions.

1.3 Who uses and controls new media?

When discussing the growth of new media, use statistical evidence to show which types have grown, as well as the reasons behind this growth.

The growth of new media

Since the 1990s, there has been somewhat of an explosion of new media devices and technologies, with the internet in particular growing quickly in popularity. Williams (2001) noted how US households had adopted the internet far more quickly than they had bought into previous new technologies. For example, from the date of invention, it took around 25 years for 30 per cent of US households to have the internet, compared to around 45 years for the same number to have a telephone. Indeed, in the UK, the number of households with the internet grew by over 70 per cent in the 25 years from 1998 to 2013 (see Figure 5.4).

Ownership and usage of internet-ready devices has also grown rapidly. Ofcom's *Communications Market Report* showed how in 2014, 6 in 10 adults owned a smartphone, and 44 per cent of households owned a tablet. Ownership of smart televisions was also on the rise, with 12 per cent of households having one, which was almost double the percentage from the previous year. The graph in Figure 5.5 shows how various types of digital media are being embraced by British citizens.

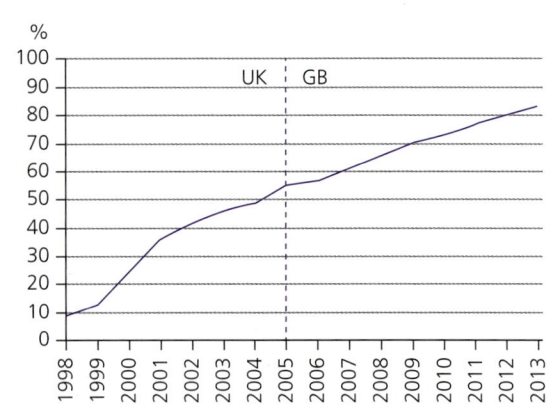

Figure 5.4 Households with internet access, 1998 to 2013

Adapted from ONS (2013)

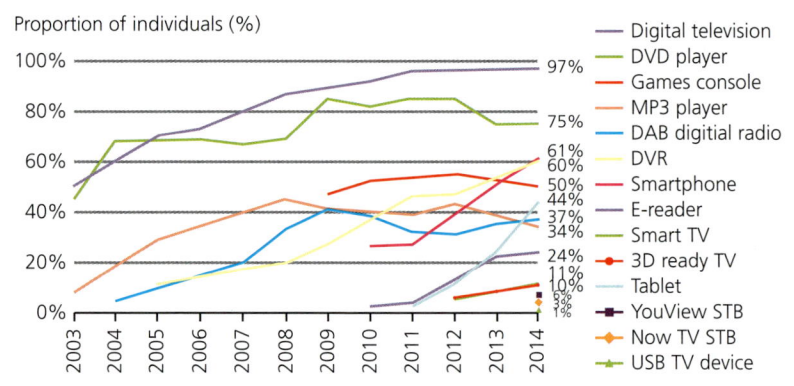

Figure 5.5 Household take-up of digital communication devices: 2003–2014

Adapted from Ofcom (2014)

However, for Boyle (2005), the growth of new media is not as simple as the introduction of new technologies. Instead, he argues that a 'converging media landscape' caused by a digital revolution opened up opportunities to combine previously separate types of media, for example, smart televisions/phones allow users to browse the internet and send emails. Boyle explains how this has also led to economic convergence, with media corporations working together. An example of this would be the links between mobile phone companies and computer companies, for example, Nokia uses Microsoft's platform in its smartphones.

The growth of new media certainly seems to have been encouraged by British governments. Gordon Brown, who was Prime Minister from 2007 to 2010, was quoted in the government's *Digital Britain Final Report* (2009) as saying:

> 'Only a Digital Britain can unlock the imagination and creativity that will secure for us and our children the highly skilled jobs of the future. Only a Digital Britain will secure the wonders of an information revolution that could transform every part of our lives. Only a Digital Britain will enable us to demonstrate the vision and dynamism that we have to shape the future.'

The Digital Britain Final Report explained in detail how the government intended to support and expand the range of new media technologies in the UK, such as the spread of superfast broadband. The report states that its purpose is to outline a 'strategic vision for ensuring that the UK is at the leading edge of the global digital economy'. However, Keen (2007) is less optimistic about using technology to secure future jobs. In fact he notes that the internet may actually be costing jobs, giving the example of advertising: for every free listing on websites such as Gumtree or, in the USA, Craigslist, less money is spent on advertising in newspapers. Furthermore, as films and music are downloaded illegally, profits in production companies fall. The knock-on effect of this 'free' internet could well be the loss of jobs in the future.

> **RESEARCH IN FOCUS**
>
> Ofcom is the British communications regulator, responsible for regulating the 'TV and radio sectors, fixed line telecoms, mobiles, postal services, plus the airwaves over which wireless devices operate' (www.ofcom.org.uk). It is funded partly by taxpayers and partly by fees that the media industry pays.
>
> The Communications Act 2003 made it compulsory for Ofcom to carry out an annual statistical survey on media and communications in the UK and internationally: the *Communications Market Report*. The report is very comprehensive, covering TV, radio, telecoms and the internet, and Ofcom states that the survey enables Ofcom to 'remain at the forefront of technological understanding.' The statistics are collected from industry sources and a survey of approximately 1000 adults, and provide the government and sociologists with a wide array of quantitative and qualitative data on both traditional and new forms of media.

Different perspective

Although statistics show that more households every year are using new media, they also show clear differences in which social groups use and have access to new media. For example, the ONS reported that in 2013, 97 per cent of British households with children had an internet connection. Houses with three or more adults, such as student accommodation, also had a 97 per cent rate of internet access. However, just 40 per cent of households containing one adult aged 65 or over had the internet. Additionally, those aged 16–24 years are almost nine times as likely as those aged 65+ years to use their mobile phone to surf the web:

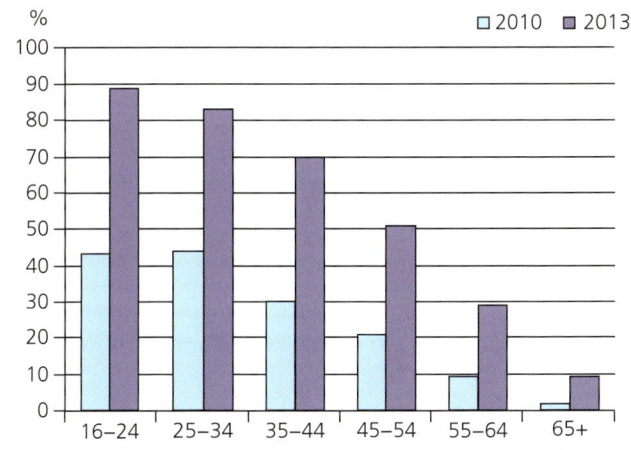

Figure 5.6 Internet use on a mobile phone by age group, 2010 and 2013
Adapted from ONS (2014)

> **CONTEMPORARY APPLICATION**
>
> What is clear is that the new media is a fluid and rapidly evolving industry. Some forms of new media now seem outdated, such as dial-up internet, which was used by almost a third of households in 2006, but in 2013 was used by less than 1 per cent (ONS, 2013). At the same time, it is apparent that new media is continuing to expand, with new technologies and devices regularly coming on to the market. For example, at the time of writing, smart watches are new to the market, and smart glasses are yet to be released. However, we may see a reduction in the speed at which the internet is spreading, as those who have yet to adopt it may face practical barriers such as affordability.

> **Questions**
>
> 1. Why might the British government feel it is important that Ofcom stays 'at the forefront of technological understanding'?
> 2. Suggests ways in which the *Communications Market Survey* might be useful to sociologists who are researching the new media.
> 3. Identify a methodological disadvantage of using secondary data such as the *Communications Market Survey* in sociological research.

Boyle (2007) claims that new media is not causing a generational divide in the way that these statistics seem to suggest, as media in general seems to have always been used differently by different age groups. For example, since the 1950s young people have favoured different types of media to older generations. In fact there was a moral panic when pop music first emerged as parents became concerned about the effects of the music on their teenagers.

The *Communications Market Report* (Ofcom, 2014) agrees that age plays a factor in confidence and usage levels of digital media. In fact, the study found that a range of social variables affected the likelihood of a person accessing the new media:

How social variables affect new media usage

- Young people have higher levels of technological knowledge and confidence than older people, with 14–15 years having the highest levels of confidence
- Males have greater confidence with technology than females
- Those in the highest socio-economic group have greater confidence with technology than those in the lowest socio-economic groups.

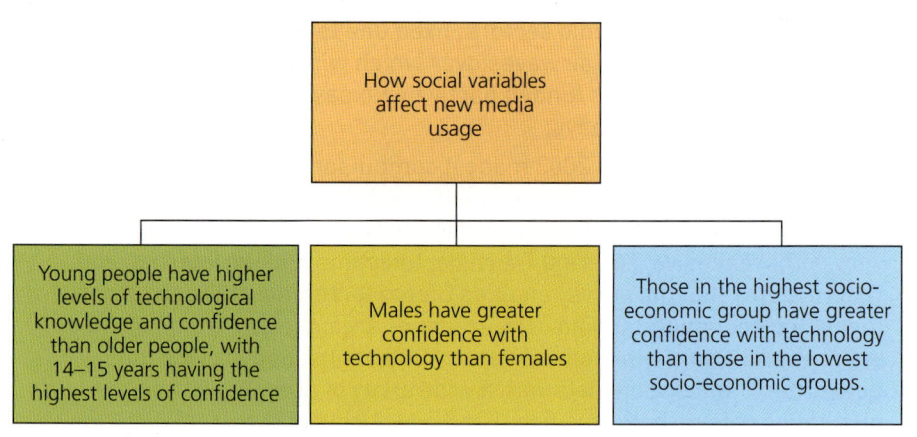

Figure 5.7 Summary of technological confidence levels of different social groups

The government's *Digital Britain Final Report* (2009) expresses similar concerns, stating that the 'online world' '… is moving from conferring advantage on those who are in it to conferring active disadvantage on those who are without.' The report identifies limitations for households that do not have the internet, often due to lack of affordability or technical skills, such as the disadvantage children face when completing homework that their peers have been able to use the internet for, or adults not being able to take advantage of lower bills through price comparison websites. Indeed, of the 4 million households in Great Britain without internet access in 2013, a disproportionately high number were from the lowest socio-economic group. Boyle (2007) agrees that a divide that has increased due to new media is the rich/poor divide: he argues that this creates a digital and cultural divide.

Control of new media

Due to the rise of new media, the mass media is far more diverse, and it is arguably much harder to regulate. This means a significant shift in the ownership and control of media since the 1980s, when the mass media was made up of a relatively narrow range of delivery systems (television, radio, newspapers, magazines and billboard advertising) which were mainly owned by large corporations. The government was able to introduce regulatory bodies such as the Press Complaints Commission and Ofcom to impose some control over the information published by these traditional media corporations.

However, the British government has also introduced a range of measures to try to impose some control over the internet. For example, since 2011 internet service providers (ISP) such as BT, TalkTalk and Virgin Media have been required by the government to force customers to 'opt-in' if they want to view 'sexually content explicit' in a bid to restrict access to pornography. Furthermore, the government is able to prevent consumers from visiting certain websites by asking ISPs to block access to them.

> **STUDY TIP**
> When thinking about how the use of the new media differs between social groups, consider a range of variables, such as gender, ethnicity and social class. You will need to understand both who uses new media more, and why that is the case.

> **STUDY TIP**
> Think about control of the media as a theoretical debate, weighing up different perspectives such as feminist, Marxist and pluralist. These theories are discussed in more detail in Section 2 (see page 268).

As well as the government imposing control over the ISPs, the British criminal justice system has recently set precedents which restrict the information that individuals can publish online. In 2012, the most senior prosecutor in the UK, Keir Starmer QC, announced that he would be publishing new rules on social media for police and courts to use. This came in the wake of Olympic diver Tom Daley being the victim of homophobic abuse by 'trolls' on Twitter. Unfortunately, as Jones (2013) suggests, the internet offers anonymity to trolls, making it very difficult for police to investigate such crimes.

Curran and Seaton (2010) acknowledge that the internet is controlled by the state in some ways, but argue that it is far harder to censor and regulate than offline media because of its global nature. It is true that even though ISPs may block access to some websites, access can still be gained via the use of proxy websites. And the case of www.wikileaks.org editor Julian Assange shows how individuals can overcome government controls on the media: after leaking information on Wikileaks about state secrets, he avoided arrest by seeking political asylum in Ecuador.

Different perspectives

The Marxist perspective could be applied to this topic, as some sociologists are very critical of the extent that the state use new media to collect information about individuals, and use that information to impose control over the masses. For example, in 2013 Edward Snowden leaked information that showed how the American CIA and European governments had set up a global surveillance system, using the internet to spy on citizens. Following on from this, in 2015 a court agreed with pressure group Privacy International that Britain's GCHQ (Government Communication Headquarters) had acted illegally.

However, some liberal feminists would be supportive of new media, in that it seems to have brought more opportunities for women to influence the control of media. For example, Sheryl Sandberg is the chief operating officer of Facebook, and has used her position to encourage women to 'lean in' to their careers. As new media allows people to work more flexibly and remotely, it could be argued that it has helped women who wish to have high-powered careers while also spending time at home with their children.

Check your understanding

1. Suggest ways in which the new media has changed the mass media.
2. Give an example of a new media technology that has evolved from traditional forms of media, rather than being brand new.
3. What is meant by the new media being 'demand-led', and how is this different to 'supply-led'?
4. In what ways is new media characterised by its interconnectivity?
5. Give three advantages of the new media according to neophiliacs.
6. Give three disadvantages of the new media according to cultural pessimists.
7. Why might Keen refer to the internet as the 'cult of the amateur'?
8. Give examples of how the usage of new media is not consistent across social groups.
9. How does the control of new media differ to that of traditional media?
10. Identify one way in which the British government has tried to impose control over new media.

Practice questions

1. Outline and explain two ways in which the new media differs from traditional media. [10 marks]
2. Outline and explain two ways in which the new media might benefit individuals. [10 marks]

GETTING YOU STARTED

Media reform coalition: The elephant in the room

There are growing concerns about the way small numbers of companies own large proportions of the media. This report finds that:

Only three companies (News UK, DMGT and Trinity Mirror) control nearly 70 per cent of national newspaper circulation.

Just five companies control some 70 per cent of regional daily newspaper circulation.

A single news provider, Sky, provides news bulletins for virtually all of national and regional commercial radio.

While the BBC accounts for a majority of television news consumption, a single company, ITV, accounts for a majority of non-BBC TV news consumption.

The report concludes that there needs to be an open debate on media ownership that takes seriously proposals for a range of measures to increase the number of owners of media companies.

Adapted from Media Reform Coalition (2015)

Questions

1. What do the statistics above reveal about the ownership of the media in the UK?
2. What are the effects of this?
3. What recommendations does the report make?

Section 2: The relationship between ownership and control of the media

This section will explore the following debates:
- What are sociological views on the ownership and control of the media?
- What are the patterns of ownership in the media?

2.1 What are sociological views on the ownership and control of the media?

In terms of control of the media, it is important that you discuss and compare the different approaches including Marxism, Neo-Marxism, pluralism and postmodernist views.

The media has a huge influence over the lives of many people. The average viewer in the UK watched three hours and 55 minutes of TV a day in 2014, according to commercial TV marketing body Thinkbox. It is no surprise then that the media acts as a major agency of informal primary and secondary socialisation. This section explores different sociological views on how the media shapes people's identity, influences their behaviour and spreads particular forms of ideological belief.

The Marxist view on the media

Sometimes known as the manipulative or instrumentalist approach, Marxists argue that the very few members of the ruling class are the ones who own the majority of media, and use it to serve their own interests. In this sense, the media is a tool of the ruling class used to maintain their power and control. This means that the ruling class not only use the media to increase and maintain their wealth, but they also use it to manipulate and control the ideas of the working class. Through the ideological control of the working class, the ruling class ensure that their position remains unchallenged. In fact, Marxists argue that the media is a very powerful part of socialisation which ensures that the working class accept capitalist ideology. In turn, the media form part of **false class-consciousness** in which the working class are not aware of their true position of exploitation.

Marxists argue that the ruling classes control the media by deciding on the content, including what is considered to be news and entertainment. The media can and do influence and change the way news is reported which sends powerful and subtle messages to people which shapes their view of the world, for example, broadcasting reports which deflect news attention away from the problems created by capitalism towards other causes of social problems, usually blaming the working class, justifies ruling class control. Marxists argue that the media often reflects the idea that capitalism works and is fair.

Marxists also argue that the media are held in the hands of increasingly small numbers of companies who use the media to reinforce the dominant ideology (see more on these views with the work of Bagdikian, below). Miliband (1973) argues that the owners of the media share particular interests and ideas, known as **cultural capital**. For example, they may have attended similar universities and have a social network based on supporting their own interests. Traditional Marxists argue that new forms of media are in fact simply a continuation of older forms of media in their aims and intentions.

The owners of the media decide on the boundaries of the media, defining what subjects and issues can and cannot be approached. Marxists argue that the owners of the media assume that their audience is unquestioning and passive and as a result, feeds simple, undemanding information to the public. This prevents serious issues being tackled, such as the cause of serious economic inequalities in society. Those working with the media are encouraged to support the views of the media company owners or else face discipline or ridicule. Therefore journalists and editors are likely to report in a way which reflects the views of the company owners rather than providing objective, unbiased views. Those radical groups who try to challenge society through the media are punished severely.

As well as presenting news in a biased way which hides the inequalities in society, Marxists argue that entertainment in the media is organised and presented in such a way which prevents or dissuades people from having serious consideration of any important issues which might reflect problems in society.

One good example of this is the coverage of the conflict in Iraq. The media portrayed the country as potentially developing weapons of mass destruction, which was used as a political justification to bring down the political leaders of the country and invade. The media played a key role in manipulating people into believing the claims of the government, thus supporting their ideas and aims.

This view has been widely recognised as useful and accurate. The media is political and the owners of the media do use their companies to further their political and economic interests. For example, it is widely known that Rupert Murdoch, the well-known **media mogul**, has long influenced much of his media output to support a conservative perspective. However, there are problems with the Marxist view: sometimes the media are responsible for highlighting inequalities within society and do so with some positive effects for the poor and oppressed. Furthermore the media can be seen to reflect a range of ideas, not just those of the ruling class. Another criticism of the Marxist view is that the public are not passive; in fact citizen journalism is an example of how members of the public, non-journalists, are now able to participate in the creation of the news or media and express their own views and thoughts, sometimes challenging the inequalities in society hidden or masked by the media.

The neo-Marxist view of the media

Neo-Marxists agree with traditional Marxists in that the media generally reflects the views of the ruling class; however, they see the relationship as being slightly more complex. Neo-Marxists tend to focus more on the role of the media in enforcing the dominant set of ideas onto the working class. Neo-Marxists argue that the owners of the media exert a subtle influence rather than a direct one. Media owners are rarely taking a hands-on approach in directing output but the fact that they own the company influences the journalists and production teams who generally reflect their views. The neo-Marxist Gramsci calls this **hegemony**, whereby the ideas of the ruling class are perceived to be dominant and therefore widely accepted. In fact, at times, the media even challenge the conventional ruling-class ideology to appear to be providing a balanced view of the world. However, the range of ideas expressed and reinforced reflect ruling-class ideology on the whole.

The neo-Marxist view is generally seen to be more applicable to contemporary society where the media is wide-ranging and more and more complex. These views are more sophisticated in their justification of the capitalist system and are therefore effective in preventing any challenge to the system. However, the actions of media moguls such as Rupert Murdoch (see above) send a strong message to journalists and those working in the media to conform to their views or face being undermined. Therefore neo-Marxists argue that the relationship between the owners and controllers of the media share a mutually beneficial relationship. This relationship involves the negotiation and agreement on certain core values which are then disseminated to the public through the media. For example, the importance of political process which should not be challenged or ideas about the right to privacy of politicians or other public figures. Once these core values have been decided upon, the media managers are allowed a degree of relative autonomy; this means that they can report on what they like providing they stay within the agreed core values.

Neo-Marxists see the class system as more dynamic and changeable, recognising the shifting patterns of class behaviour and alignment. They claim that the media also reflects complex differences of ideas and conflict among the ruling class. For example, the media exposes how some of the ruling class are pro-Europe while others are not. Other neo-Marxists, such as Poulantzas (1975), claim that some academics and intellectuals occupy neither working-class nor ruling-class positions and use the media to explore academic discussions which may or may not support prevailing ideas.

The pluralist approach

The pluralist approach argues that there are a number of different and competing views expressed by different owners of the media. Pluralists argue that competition between different media companies is healthy and creates a balanced range of media which reflects what the consumers of the media want to see and hear. The agenda of the news, for example, is set by the demands and wishes of the wider public, not those who own the media businesses. There are two different groups within the media according to pluralists: there are groups who have an interest in gaining financially or those wishing to gain a shift in social attitudes. The other groups are those seeking to promote the interests of a narrower range of people, for example, trade unions seeking political or social power. These different groups may use the media to promote their interests and pluralists are optimistic that the media can play the role of representing both of these groups.

According to pluralists such as Whale (1997), rather than society being dominated by the ruling class, there are a number of competing groups in society with different views and priorities. They claim that there are a number of measures of the views of the public, such as surveys, which are fed directly back into the type of programmes that are available. Furthermore, pluralists argue that the media is free from political control and therefore able to present a range of views, with freedom and without risk of being challenged. They argue that news values (what is seen as important) is decided by the consumers of the media.

There are clear strengths of pluralists' views: There are many views reflected in the media particularly with the proliferation of multiple channels reflecting an ever wider range of tastes and interests. This approach assumes that the public have the power to decide what they choose to watch and if they do not agree with something they can find an alternative or ignore it.

However, this approach is criticised by Marxists who claim that people are brainwashed into thinking that they have had some control over what is on the media – that it is to some degree democratic. Plus, many people do not relate to what is in the media but have little power in influencing its contents.

The postmodernist view of the media

Postmodernists such as Baudrillard (1994) argue that the media today reflects much of the characteristics of postmodern society. He claims that we live in a media-saturated society where the line between the media and reality is becoming increasingly blurred. We are continually bombarded with images, ideas and information to the extent that the truth becomes very difficult to pick out. Baudrillard therefore argues that the media plays a key role in shaping and distorting people's view of the world. Baudrillard suggests that because of the media saturation, the world we see through the media becomes more real than reality. Baudrillard calls this media-saturated view of the world **hyper-reality**.

Although these ideas are interesting, postmodernists tend to assume that people absorb the media in an unquestioning way without critical appraisal of the contents or a rejection of the ideas expressed there. This is not true for many people who actively choose to avoid engaging with the media.

Different perspectives

Feminists would argue that women are objectified through the media. Given the fact that the majority of the owners of media-based businesses are men, the dominant ideology perpetuated throughout the media reflects a patriarchal view of the world, and women are further oppressed through this institution.

> **KEY SOCIOLOGISTS**
>
> **The Frankfurt School** of neo-Marxist sociologists argue that the media seeks cultural dominance to determine and drive cultural practices and beliefs. These become so engrained by the masses that they become subconscious. The Frankfurt School in general was profoundly pessimistic about the mass media. They argue that the media removes any chance of individualism and reduces any chance of working-class revolution from occurring.

> **STUDY TIP**
>
> Consider the strengths and weaknesses of each approach to the ownership and control of the media. Make sure that you consider how much the media has changed and continues to change.

IN THE NEWS

Ideas, culture and the media under capitalism

The scandal involving News International's phone hacking and corrupt deals with world governments was not the exposure of a 'rogue operator'. Instead it simply exposed, in dramatic style, the underlying basis of the media under capitalism. Run by multinational corporations, their purpose is to promote the interests of their owners who are billionaires. In the 21st century, the links between media and government have confirmed decades of increasing co-operation, overlapping into a revolving-door complex which sees spin-doctors shuttle between governments, media outlets and PR agencies.

The answer to print media's long life lies in the role of ideas in class society. The dominant ideas in any society are the ideas of the ruling class. The reasons are twofold: firstly, membership of the ruling class and privileged layers allows access to education and the leisure to become immersed in all expressions of culture. The second is that it is the capitalists who control the media, either through outright ownership, or through their control of the means of mass production and dissemination (TV stations, satellites, printing presses, art galleries).

But before being exposed to the public consciousness these ideas must be packaged and sanitised by the distribution networks, who are not concerned with such abstract notions as truth or artistic integrity, but the financial impact on the company's profits and image. The arena of distribution and marketing is where the capitalists' power really comes into play in terms of commercial control over artistic content.

Adapted from Tait (2015)

Questions

1. How does this article support the Marxist view of the control of the media?
2. How might pluralists challenge this article?

2.2 What are the patterns of ownership in the media?

Consider both the nature of those who own media companies as well as the extent to which companies are influenced and controlled by political groups, affecting the content of the media.

There are broadly two different types of media ownership: the privately owned and the publicly owned. It is important that you understand the differences between these forms of ownership as it has important implications for not only the content of the news but also whose interests are being served as a result.

Publicly funded media: the BBC

In the UK around 38 per cent of the media is owned by the BBC, the British Broadcasting Corporation which is appointed by the Queen as part of the media trust. What is significant about the BBC is that it is funded by the public. This means that it is very different to privately owned media companies. This means that:

1. There are no commercials used in the BBC.
2. The BBC is intended for public benefit not the pursuit of profit. Therefore it seeks to educate and inform as well as entertain.
3. It is funded by a licence fee.
4. Being funded by the public, it is accountable to the public and therefore is required to be transparent about how it is run, for example, how much it pays those who work for it.

Therefore it is unsurprising that the ethos of the BBC is very different to private companies who are not expected to be as accountable and transparent, and who have less moral imperative to ensure the neutrality of what they present.

Millions of People

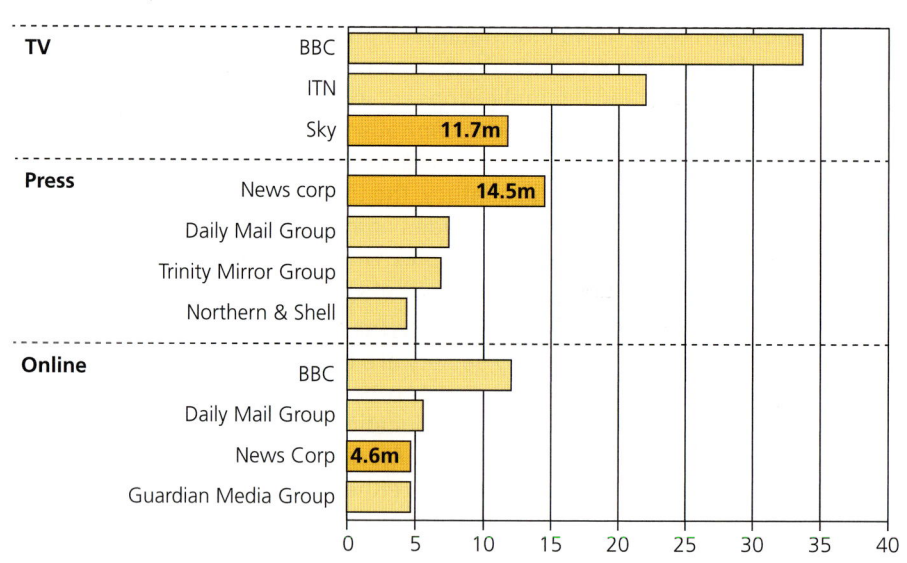

Category	Outlet	Value
TV	BBC	~34
TV	ITN	~22
TV	Sky	11.7m
Press	News corp	14.5m
Press	Daily Mail Group	~7
Press	Trinity Mirror Group	~7
Press	Northern & Shell	~4
Online	BBC	~12
Online	Daily Mail Group	~6
Online	News Corp	4.6m
Online	Guardian Media Group	~5

Figure 5.8 News Corp's media reach in the UK
Source: Ofcom

The BBC is regarded by some as being more sympathetic towards left-wing views, given that it is a publicly funded organisation which seeks to ensure that everyone who pays a licence fee has access to the same quality of media. Being publicly funded the BBC is officially forbidden from taking any political position and is meant to be, instead, politically neutral. However, recent events have meant that the Conservative government, elected in 2015, has been seen to be critical of any political leanings taken by the BBC. For example, the Prime Minister appointed John Whittingdale, a critic of the BBC, as Culture Secretary (see the article on this below).

Privately owned media companies

Unlike publicly owned companies, private companies have the ultimate goal of pursuing profit and they may wield significant power. These companies are by no means politically neutral. There has been a marked change over the past decades in patterns of private companies' ownership of media companies. In his famous book, *The Media Monopoly* (1997), the Marxist Bagdikian argues that there has been a marked decrease in the number of owners of media companies. This means that the owners of these companies have considerable power.

A monopoly is defined as the exclusive ownership of a service or a commodity. Bagdikian applies the concept of monopoly to the media industry. He explores the ratio between profit and the number of companies, which is known as the concentration ratio. According to Bagdikian, the number of companies generally within the media has dropped sharply over the past decades, meaning that the concentration ratio has increased significantly. For example, Bagdikian (2004) reports that in the USA in 1985 there were 50 major media companies, but by 2003 there were only five. Giant companies own almost every mass medium including newspapers, magazines, books, radios, broadcast television, cable systems and programming, movies, recordings. By buying every different medium, these powerful giants communicate messages based on the owner's interest, thus narrowing down the available sources of information. For instance, ABC, CBS and NBC networks control the majority of the national television in the USA. According to Bagdikian, these companies invest millions in different types of media for primarily two reasons: money and influence. The power of these companies is so great that they can strongly influence people's political and social views.

In the UK the picture is similar. The media mogul Rupert Murdoch has become very powerful: he now owns over a fifth of all media in the UK. His media has worked hard to be seen to be taking interest in local issues, however the company is very American. Murdoch has been known to have conservative political views which are reflected in his media.

Ofcom, the communications regulator which was set up in 2003 in the UK, makes decisions to prevent companies such as Murdoch's monopolising media completely. For example, Rupert Murdoch was prevented from placing a bid for Channel 5 television, because of his already dominant position in the media.

There are also European regulations to prevent individual companies becoming too dominant. These controls challenge Marxist views on media domination by a few companies. Furthermore, some of the programmes that are broadcast by dominant companies such as Sky do challenge the system. For example, *The Simpsons*, which reveals dysfunction within so-called 'normal' family life.

The Glasgow University Media Group

The GMG are a group of academics who have carried out extensive research into television-based news coverage. They claim that the news reflects the views and priorities of the owners of media companies, whose ideas are imposed on journalists. These journalists' ideas go on to shape the perspective of their viewers considerably. The GMG argue therefore that television news is far from objective, claiming it is laden with values.

In fact, the GMG suggest that the media goes further and tries to manipulate viewers into a particular emotional response, for example, anger to political issues which work against the interests of the dominant group, thus reinforcing the ideas of the dominant. In their Marxian analysis, the GMG argue that the media encourages viewers to reproduce the views of the powerful which are seen as central to journalists.

Curran (2014) claims that a standard criticism of the press is that it is dominated by rich shareholders, who create a situation where those working in the media are unrepresentative of the public. This distorts the press in mediating public debate, and tends to encourage the promotion of politically conservative or centre-right perspectives. But there is another problem that Curran claims is barely registered. The press has functioned as an extension of government rather than as an independent institution serving the public.

The views of Bagdikian, Curran and the GMG (and Miliband see below) reflect a Marxist approach to the ownership of the media. However, pluralists would argue that a small number of companies owning the media does not necessarily mean that a single set of ideas are transmitted. They claim that the regulatory government bodies, for example Ofcom, ensure that a monopolisation of the media does not take place.

The Marxist Ralph Miliband claims that the media is inherently political and owned by the ruling class who seek to uphold other powerful members of the ruling-class groups such as politicians. In his book, *The State in Capitalist Society* (1969) he writes extensively about the conservative ideological motivations of a capitalist press. He describes how the media attacks anything that does not reflect the views of the government. Miliband was convinced that the mainstream media was a crucial tool used by elites against the working class to fragment, distract and disempower citizens. Miliband also describes the growing influence of advertising and public relations and discusses their role in encouraging people to identify with capitalist society.

Marxist	Pluralist	Postmodernist
Marxists are highly critical of the current patterns in media ownership: ■ Leads to the creation of cultural imperialism/homogenisation, where capitalist ideology is seen as superior and dominant. ■ The concentration of ownership in the hands of small numbers of companies. ■ Unregulated and unchecked media ownership. ■ The illusion of choice in the media – the reality is that these choices (for example in newspapers) are owned by the same companies.	Pluralists argue that media ownership should reflect what the consumers want. Therefore they argue that the ownership of media should provide something for everyone. ■ Companies which own large proportions of the media offer choice in issues, topics and news which allows for a wide range of views including those which challenge mainstream ideas. ■ The changes in current media ownership simply reflect what the public want. ■ There are ever greater ways in which the individual can shape and control the content of the media through bodies such as Ofcom and through citizen journalism.	Postmodernists argue that the increase in choice of different forms of media reflects postmodern society and with it the fragmentation of identities. ■ They claim that new forms of media allow people to express and explore their views therefore giving them 'voice'. For example, citizen journalism. ■ This leads ultimately to the public being able to create and shape news as well as contest what journalists and media owners claim. Thus ensuring that the powerful media owners are not the only ones who have a say in events.

Table 5.1 Summary of different views on changes in media ownership and control

Different perspectives

Postmodernists argue that the ownership of the media is not fixed but is changeable and fluid, therefore they do not see the concentration ratio as a problem, rather, more of a reflection of postmodern society. They point out that new forms of media in fact offer individuals a voice and an opportunity to maintain balance in the views expressed by the media.

IN THE NEWS

Is the BBC safe in the hands of our new Culture Secretary, John Whittingdale?

John Whittingdale's appointment as Secretary of State for culture is likely to be a cause of concern to the BBC and supporters of its place in the cultural landscape of the UK. His appointment precedes the major changes coming up in the way the corporation is run: in 2106 the ten-year charter is due to expire and the licence fee will be frozen. This means that Whittingdale will have a major say about BBC resourcing.

Whittingdale has described the licence fee as 'unsustainable in the long term' and he chaired the Culture, Media and Sport select committee, whose report on the BBC was published in 2015. It is clear that he wants a scaled-back BBC, doing 'less in some areas'.

In addition the culture secretary is reported to have links with Rupert Murdoch's News Corporation, a long-term opponent of the BBC as it stands in the way of the dominance of Murdoch's own companies.

Adapted from Barnett (2015)

RESEARCH IN FOCUS

Murdoch media to control over a fifth of UK news consumption

The proposed merger of the media mogul Rupert Murdoch's media companies would mean that he controls over a fifth of UK news consumption. The question should not be focused on if you like Rupert Murdoch or not but simply whether the companies he owns, News Corp/Sky are too large. Those who have dealt with Ofcom, the communications regulator grappling with the merger of Murdoch's major companies, say that the researchers are trying to understand the issue by producing some data that determines media power and dominance in the UK.

The BBC famously tolerates vast differences of opinion within the organisation, as seen in the public expressions of disagreement between presenters and executives, and controversy surrounding broadcasting standards. While the BBC controls around 40 per cent of the Britain's on air news consumption, its plurality is an issue when some newspapers take decisions about which political party to support right at the top of the organisation.

It is clear that News Corp is a hugely powerful organisation and run along very different lines to the BBC. The question is what Ofcom, and more importantly the government will choose to do about it.

Adapted from Sabbagh (2010)

Questions

1. Why might Whittingdale's appointment as the new Culture Secretary mean that the BBC is no longer 'safe'?
2. What is the difference between the BBC and privately owned companies?

CONTEMPORARY APPLICATION

Ofcom (the Office of Communication) was established as a media regulating body. It is responsible for regulating the TV and radio sectors, fixed line telecoms, mobiles, postal services, plus the airwaves over which wireless devices operate. One of its responsibilities is to ensure that no one media group dominates the media market, and to ensure that the interests of media consumers are maintained. Ofcom also deals with complaints from the public about potentially damaging programmes and makes sure that people involved with the media or affected by it are not unfairly treated.

STUDY TIP

Make sure that you can link the ownership of media to Marxist, pluralist and postmodern theories.

Questions

1. Suggest some reasons why it might be considered a problem for one person to dominate the ownership of the media.
2. How do Rupert Murdoch's media companies differ from the BBC?

Check your understanding

1. Identify three features of the Marxist view of the media.
2. What is the difference between Marxist and neo-Marxist views of the media?

Practice question

1. Outline and explain two views on the control of the media. [10 marks]

Item A

A summary of the media owned by News Corp, Rupert Murdoch's company, in 2010:

MEDIA TYPE	COMPANIES				REVENUE
Book publishing	HarperCollins HarperCollins India				$1.3 billion
Broadcast TV in US	Fox Broadcasting Company MyNetwork TV FOXSports.com 27 Fox TV stations				$4.2 billion
Cable network	Fox News Channel Fox Business Network 8 Fox Cable Network channels 19 Fox International channels National Geographic International				$7 billion
Satellite TV	Sky Italia, BSkyB (39%) Tata Sky (20%) Foxtel (25%)				$3.8 billion
Filmed entertainment	10 film companies including: 20th Century Fox Fox 2000 Pictures Fox Searchlight Pictures				$7.6 billion
Newspapers (including News International)	**Europe** The Times The Sunday Times The Sun News of the World Revenue: $1.61bn eFinancialNews The Times Literary Supplement The Wall Street Journal Europe	**US** The Wall Street Journal New York Post Barron's Community Newspaper Group Dow Jones Local Media Group 7 news information services	**Asia** The Wall Street Journal Asia	**Australia** Approx 150 titles including: The Australian The Daily Telegraph Herald Sun The Advertiser	$6.1 billion
Other	News Corp Digital Media Group (MySpace, IGN Entertainment)				$2.7 billion
				TOTAL	$32.7 billion

Data from News Corporation (2010)

There are growing concerns about the small number of powerful figures who own large proportions of the media. In the UK, for example, the media mogul Rupert Murdoch now owns a fifth of the media, giving rise to concerns that this means that his ideas and agenda are becoming dominant. Others, however, argue that this is not a problem as the media simply reflects what the society wants.

Applying material from Item A, analyse two patterns of ownership of the media. [10 marks]

Section 3: The media, globalisation and culture

This section will explore the following debates:

- What different types of culture are there and what is the significance of global culture?
- What is the relationship between the media and global culture?
- What are sociological views on the social construction of news, including new social media?

Questions

1. Which of the images below are most popular?
2. Why do you think this is?
3. What effect has the internet had on the spread of particular cultural ideas around the globe?

GETTING YOU STARTED

Figure 5.9 [Clockwise from top left] Taylor Swift, Kim Kardashian and Kanye West, people living in a tribe and an orchestra

3.1 What different types of culture are there and what is the significance of global culture?

It is important that you move beyond your basic sociological understanding of culture here to consider the different types of culture that exist today. Be aware of the changes in various types of culture that have occurred and make sure that you consider these in the context of the media.

As you will already know, sociologists define culture as the specific norms and values and way of life of a particular group. There are other types of culture which are explored and understood by sociologists today, including high culture, popular or mass culture and global culture. See page below for more detail on these different types of culture.

High culture

High culture refers generally to what is considered to be middle-class culture. It includes classical music, intellectually demanding books, the theatre and art. Much of what is considered to be high culture often involves abstract thought or relies on other knowledge to understand its meaning. Take a piece of art – its meaning may not be obvious without some social context or at least an explanation of the political and aesthetic implications. High culture is mainly associated with the provision of culture for a general small elite group whose views are expressed, explored and challenged through the media. Marxists see high culture as an important part of cultural capital which are the specific norms, values and attitudes which lead to material rewards in life. Therefore understanding high culture is a way in which the ruling class differentiate themselves from the working class.

Mass culture, popular culture

Once fully industrialised, many societies in the West developed what was known as popular or mass culture, which, as the name suggests, refers to large-scale patterns of cultural practices in the media. According to Storey (2010) there are several characteristics of popular culture in terms of the media which include:

- highly commercialised media, designed to be sold to a wide audience
- simple, accessible, easy entertainment, with a broad appeal, requiring very little abstract thought
- a fast turnover of mass produced products, often considered to be kitsch (inexpensive looking).

Examples include tabloid newspapers, pop music, TV programmes such as soap operas, reality or celebrity-based TV programmes, books and magazines written in an easy and accessible form.

Macdonald (1957) is critical of mass culture arguing that it lacks meaning and, in order to appeal to as many people as possible, appeals to the lowest common denominator. It seeks not to challenge or provoke a strong response – it is generated for commercial purposes and threatens to overshadow and engulf other forms of culture. By strengthening the mass culture, alternative cultural practices and ideas become overlooked or underrepresented. For example, alternative music, food and languages are often ignored by many forms of media. In fact, Macdonald argues that such mass culture can lead to a dangerous state of totalitarianism whereby the media can support the control of a particular group in power in a way that is both dangerous and unquestioned.

Strinati (2004) argues that mass culture has much to offer. He says mass culture is not simply received passively by the unquestioning population in an undiscerning way: critiques of mass culture come from sociologists and others who see the world from their perspective which involves seeing high culture as superior and who therefore judge any alternative to be less important. Strinati points out that within mass culture there are different styles, tastes and options – it is not simply a blanket phenomenon. Strinati also points out that mass culture is not fixed, but fluid and constantly changing and evolving.

Global culture

Global culture is significantly different to the types of culture discussed above; it refers to the process in which various cultures around the world have become increasingly similar as a result of globalisation. It is worth thinking for a moment about the characteristics of globalisation. Globalisation refers to the decrease in distance and time; in other words people are closer and geographical distance is becoming less significant.

It has been suggested that the gulf between high culture and mass/popular culture is less significant than it once was. Some suggest that the distinction between the two was based primarily on class differences which are no longer as significant today. Whereas in the past a person might have had to have the ability to travel and to pay a lot of money to gain access to certain forms of culture, today the internet and new forms of social media have made a wide range of cultural ideas accessible to everyone who has access.

What is the relationship between the media and global culture?

There is much debate in sociology about the significance of globalisation in relation to the media. Lechner and Boli (2012) suggest that there are two main views. Firstly, there is the view that globalisation is simply a number of processes through which more people become increasingly connected in different ways across ever greater distances or alternatively, the more specific view that globalisation is a process through which capitalism expands to a wider range of places around the world to pursue cultural dominance and profit. This section explores these different views with a specific focus on role of the media.

It is important to remember that rapid technological advances have played a significant role in accelerating the globalisation process, and this is significant in terms of both traditional forms of media as well as the new social media. Flew (2002) supports this idea and argues that emerging forms of new media technology have played a central role in the development of a global culture. Technology-based media can be instantly transmitted to a global audience and therefore becomes more efficient in reaching a global audience. Flew argues that one major effect of increasing technological capacity is that the media transmitted often becomes homogenised, meaning that it becomes increasingly similar all over the world. This also means that cultural differences between groups become less pronounced and that similar ideas and products are shared universally. For example, programme formats are used universally, such as the programme *Big Brother* (which was shown in 54 countries) and *Who Wants To Be a Millionaire?* (which has been shown in 106 countries).

Fenton (1999) offers a Marxist view of the global media, arguing that it is an extension of capitalist ideology, offering the ruling class an ever more effective and sophisticated way of maintaining ideological control over the working class in a global context. Fenton argues that the global media simply means Western media, which is based on ruling-class ideology, is being spread to other parts of the world; in a process he calls cultural imperialism. This process is damaging, according to Fenton, since it means that Western culture threatens to dominate over other alternative forms of local culture and worse still, becomes seen as superior to alternatives. This means that capitalism becomes more globalised and less likely to be challenged. Consider examples of global media products such as *Big Brother* and American blockbuster films, which are watched simultaneously all over the world, all selling a particularly Westernised capitalist ideology.

Ritzer (2004) develops Weberian ideas of the world becoming increasingly rationalised to develop the term globalisation, which refers to the tendency of countries, business and other organisations to impose their cultural practices on other parts of the world, a process he sees negatively, as a form of imperialism. Ritzer argues that such imperialism aims to increase profit through cultural homogenisation. He makes it very clear that consumer goods and the media play a key role in spreading a rationalised Western view of the world. Ritzer sees grobalisation as undermining local practices, effectively reducing the value of local culture and ideas.

Different perspectives

Pluralists are optimistic about the impact of globalisation on mass culture, arguing that it provides many people with the opportunity to gain access to the media and to be able to pick and choose which kinds of culture they wish to engage in, positively. Pluralists argue that the choices available allow individuals to engage with a wider range of cultural diversity that may not have been possible before the media became so globalised.

> **STUDY TIP**
> Some arguments suggest that the global media has become increasingly homogenised, resulting in Western culture becoming dominant globally, while others suggest that a global media leads to greater cultural diversity. There is much debate about the significance of global media.

> **RESEARCH IN FOCUS**
> The Global Media Monitoring Project (2010) maps the representation of women and men in news media worldwide. GMMP research has been carried out in five-year cycles since 1995 and relies on the voluntary efforts of hundreds of individuals and organisations, including grassroots communication groups, media professionals and university researchers. The 1995, 2000 and 2005 studies revealed that women are grossly underrepresented in news coverage in contrast to men. The outcome of underrepresentation is news that presents a male-centred view of the world. Only 24 per cent of the people heard or read about in print, radio and television news are female. In contrast, 76 per cent - more than 3 out of 4 – of the people in the news are male. This suggests that patriarchy is evident within global media and that globalisation may be responsible for the spread of the specifically western form of patriarchy.
>
> Who makes the news? The Global Monitoring Project (2010)

Questions

1. What do the findings of this project suggest about global patterns of the news in terms of gender?
2. How might a feminist interpret the concept 'cultural imperialism'?

Check your understanding

1. What is the difference between high culture and popular culture?
2. What are the two views on the relationship between globalisation and the media put forward by Lechner and Boli (2012)?
3. How have advances in technology led to greater globalisation of the media?
4. What is the pluralist view on globalisation and the media?

Practice question

1. Outline and explain two ways in which globalisation may affect the media. [10 marks]

Section 4: What makes the news?

This section will explore the following debate:
- What are sociological views on the social construction of news, including new social media?
- What is the influence of other groups on the content of the news?

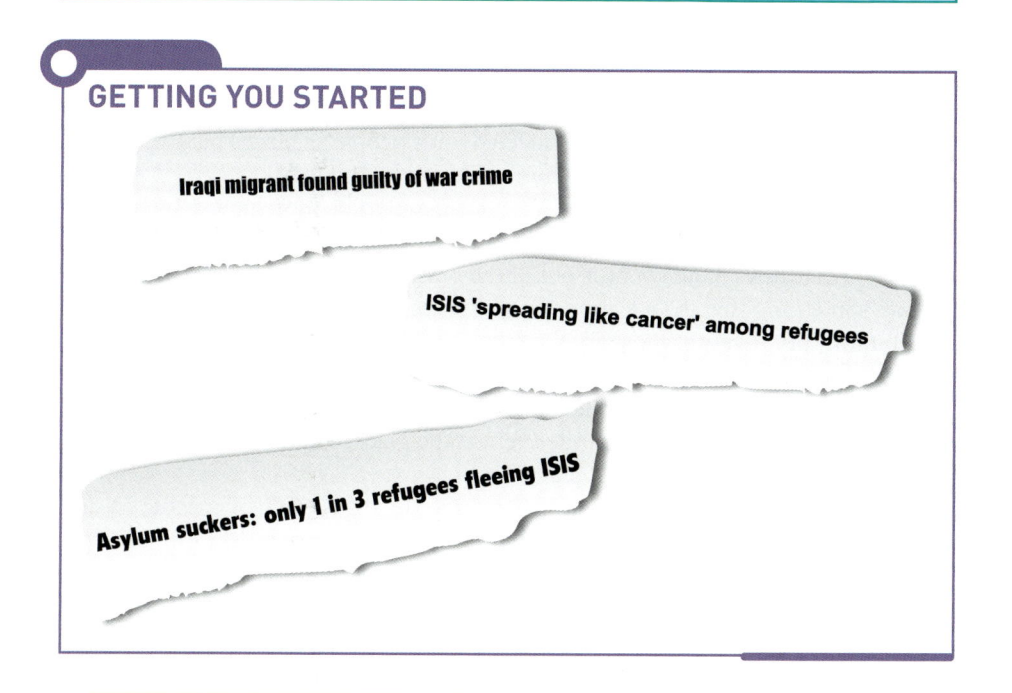

GETTING YOU STARTED

Iraqi migrant found guilty of war crime

ISIS 'spreading like cancer' among refugees

Asylum suckers: only 1 in 3 refugees fleeing ISIS

Questions

Look at the headlines above.
For each, think of three reasons why these events have been chosen to be reported.

1. What does this suggest about what is considered to be 'newsworthy?'
2. What kinds of events do you think might be less likely to be reported in the news?
3. What are the implications of certain events being more likely to make it into the news than others?

4.1 What are sociological views on the social construction of news, including new social media?

The news that we see in newspapers, on the internet and on the television does not reflect the range of events that actually occur; this section examines the process through which certain groups and individuals select particular events which are, for a range of reasons considered to be newsworthy. Therefore the news is socially constructed, it is created by people with a particular value placed on an event, rather than people seeking to carefully reflect a valid reflection of real events. Sociologists examine the extent to which this selection process is designed to further the interests of particular groups. There are a number of reasons why the news is constructed the way it is.

The organisation of the media

Galtung and Ruge (1965) argue that the way that the media is organised lends itself to journalists regarding particular events to be more newsworthy than others. This is reflected in the following criteria (also see the diagram below). They argued that the more of these criteria an issue includes, the more likely it is to appear in the news. However, Galtung and Ruge are criticised for being unable to explain where these priorities and values originate from.

- **Frequency**: Events that occur suddenly and happen to be convenient with the news organisation's timing schedule are more likely to be reported than events that are drawn out more slowly or in a more subtle way or at less convenient times of day or night. Long-term issues are less likely to receive much coverage.
- **Familiarity**: Where events are connected with people or places near to where people live and or work, they are more likely to be reported.
- **Negativity**: Interestingly, bad news is considered to be more newsworthy than good news as it generates greater interest.
- **Unexpectedness**: If an event is out of the ordinary it will have a greater effect than something that is an everyday occurrence, it generates greater interest.
- **Unambiguity**: Events whose implications are clear make for better news than those that are less clear or open to more than one interpretation, or where any understanding of the implications depends on first understanding the complex background in which the events take place. This creates greater ease of access for the audience.
- **Personalisation**: Events that can be portrayed as the actions of specific individuals will be more attractive than one in which there is less human interest. This allows people to identify more closely with the issues.
- **Meaningfulness**: This relates to the sense of identification the audience has with the topic. The closer the issue is to the audience's own culture the more likely it is to be reported – for example, stories concerned with people who speak the same language, look the same, and share the same concerns as the audience receive more coverage than those concerned with people who speak different languages, look different and have different concerns and interests.
- **Reference to elite nations**: Stories concerned with powerful global groups receive more attention than those concerned with less influential nations. For example, killings in developing countries get more media coverage than killings in poorer developing countries.
- **Reference to elite persons**: Stories concerned with the rich, powerful, famous and infamous get more coverage, particularly if the story involved them acting in a way which is transgressive or negative.
- **Conflict**: Where groups or individuals clash resulting in a dramatic effect. Stories with conflict are often considered to be newsworthy.
- **Consonance**: Stories that fit with the media's expectations receive more coverage than those that challenge them. The media are less likely to report events which are harder to report or do not conform to the companies' idea of what news is. This factor seems to conflict with unexpectedness above. However, consonance actually refers to the extent to which the media is willing to report an event.
- **Continuity**: A story that is already in the news gathers a kind of following interest. This is partly because the media organisations are already in place to report the story, and partly because previous reportage may have made the story more accessible to the public (making it less ambiguous). People may like to follow a particular event or issue.
- **Composition**: The media is competitive and therefore there is a competitive element to news reporting. Each media company is competing for the most

popular story. It is the job of the editor to decide how their news coverage is organised to reflect a range of subjects. Some editors may seek to provide a balance of different types of coverage, so that if there is an excess of foreign news, for instance, the least important foreign story may have to make way for an item concerned with the local national news. In this way the space given to a story depends not only on its own news values but also on those of competing stories.

There are also other factors to consider in newsworthiness, such as commercial or professional competition between media companies may lead journalists to endorse the news value given to a story by a rival. Furthermore, a story that is only marginally newsworthy in its own right may be more likely to be covered if it is related to a major running story. Those working in the media need to back up all of their stories with data in order for their news to remain relevant, reliable and to appear unbiased.

What makes something newsworthy?

- Frequency – if the event happened at a regular interval and there is time to place it in the news it is more likely to be included
- Proximity – if the event relates to British/UK culture, consumers are more likely to relate
- The elite and powerful – if the event relates to the wealthy, high status or powerful it is more likely to be included
- The nature of the event – if the event suits the style of the news format of the outlet it is more likely to be included
- Continuous story – if the event is ongoing it may encourage people to watch/read
- Meaning – if the event is considered to be especially meaningful to viewers it is more likely to be covered
- Sensationalism – bad/dramatic events sell more news
- Personal – if it exposes someone's private life, especially someone famous fighting for their privacy – it is more likely to be covered
- Surprise – if the event is unexpected it is more likely to be included due to the 'shock factor'
- Simplicity – if the story is 'accessible' it is more likely to be included
- Is it important enough? If it's a one-off event, probably not, but if an event occurs repeatedly, it is more likely to be included

Figure 5.10 What makes things newsworthy?

The practical organisation of the media

There are several practical issues which shape the media. The media operate on a tight logistical system whereby news has to be reported in time for deadlines before the printing and distribution to occur. This means that traditional forms of media such as newspapers are often quickly out of date. This has become more of an issue with the emergence of 24-hour news programmes and the interest which provide almost instantaneous news coverage. Critics suggest that this means the quality and accuracy of the coverage of news is questionable. Although the internet communications are becoming easier even from very remote regions, the ability to place and control production workers, technical staff and equipment can determine whether a story is covered (Schlesinger, 1987).

Furthermore, the presentation of the news is significant, for example, the news is presented in order of importance and divided up into particular categories which involve the journalists interpreting the information they are presenting. Many forms of news now rely on press or news agencies which supply them with the news which they then present to the public. This can mean that these agencies are very powerful in shaping the news, becoming **gatekeepers** to the issues that occur.

Each media company decides the language and style of their reporting and this can produce powerful effects and reactions in those consuming the media. This becomes particularly important around issues such as immigration where negative language can incite prejudice and discrimination or in other cases, sexism and ageism might be reinforced or challenged.

The owners of the media and the pursuit of profit

Others argue that it is the owners of the media companies who influence the content of their output. This may not occur in a direct way; the owners may not direct journalists regularly to report specifically, however the views and priorities of the owners are likely to be known to journalists and producers who seek to please their bosses. This could involve subtle choices about which stories to prioritise or leave out.

There may be different processes for **agenda setting** within different media companies, with some owners having less input than others. But what remains clear is that different media have different ideological agendas and these reflect their own particular norms and values which are imposed on their audiences. Similarly there may be reasons why the media present events in a particular way in order to improve public relations, for example between different countries where there may be tension.

Similarly the media is run by companies who seek to make a profit. Apart from publicly funded media organisations like the BBC, the media seek to attract as many viewers or readers as is possible and this of course affects what is considered to be newsworthy. One major source of profit is through advertising and so a great deal of attention is paid to seeking the largest audience. The media is well known for being a competitive business and so in order for a newspaper or news programme to survive it needs to prove that it can make enough profit. This may mean that the news becomes distorted in order to attract the audience it needs.

Globalisation, technology and the media

This competition between media companies has been intensified over recent years by the fact that there is now greater access to multiple forms of media offering 24-hour-a-day media. The advances in technology and the expansion of the media now means that there are 24-hour news channels, websites with news being updated as it breaks. This increased choice has only served to make news coverage even more competitive, with each company looking to report the news faster and in ever more interesting ways.

The drive for continuous and rapidly reported news has led some to suggest that the quality of news is actually decreasing. This might suggest that some events may receive too much coverage and other events not enough or that there is a lack of accuracy and detail in the rush to get the news available quickly.

The exaggeration or distortion of events

As we saw earlier, there are a number of criteria which make an event become considered to be more newsworthy. The more newsworthy that a topic is the more likely people are to read or watch the news. This, combined with the drive for profit, can lead to the exaggeration or distortion of events leading to the development of a moral panic. The term moral panic was made well known through the work of Cohen (1972), who showed how media over reactions to particular groups or actions that are seen to be a threat to society and people's safety create pressure on the authorities to act to prevent further such behaviour. Therefore a moral panic is a surge of public concern about an issue which is not proportionate to the actual problem. This of course can lead the police and society to be more vigilant, leading to an increase in the crime rate, making the perception of the problem worse. Recent moral panics have included knife crime, the riots, immigrants, asylum seekers, mentally ill people, dogs being used as weapons and youth crime. These groups become 'folk devils' who are perceived to be a threat to society.

One recent example of this was highlighted through a recent study by the GMG. The study shows how the media are currently reporting disability negatively in the context of government spending cuts, which reveals a major shift in how disabled people are portrayed and the negative impact this is having on public attitudes and on disabled people themselves (Emma Briant, Greg Philo and Nick Watson, October 2011). The media coverage suggests that disabled people are 'state scroungers' living comfortably from state benefits without making any effort to work. This, the authors of the study claim, is grossly over exaggerating the position that many disabled people find themselves in. The study claims that the media encourages the public to think of all disabled people in the same (negative) light, as scapegoats or 'folk devils'. The negativity of the press towards certain groups therefore has a powerful effect on people's behaviour.

Marxists such as Hall (1978) see moral panics as meeting the needs of capitalism to turn attention away from the real causes of problems in society, connected to capitalism, towards blaming the working class. For example, blaming young people's antisocial behaviour for the riots turns attention away from the increasing inequalities in society.

The impact of new social media on news media

With the huge increase in the use of new social media, conventional patterns of news consumption have been challenged significantly, revealing different demands and patterns, for example, between the old and the young, who tend

Figure 5.11 Hyperbole is a feature of some newspapers' headlines

Questions

1. How might each of the headlines above give a distorted picture of reality?
2. What does the language in each headline suggest about the issues raised?
3. What are the likely consequences of such news reporting?

87% of GB adults – 44.8 million people – consume newsbrands

72% of GB adults read a print newspaper

59% consume newsbrands online

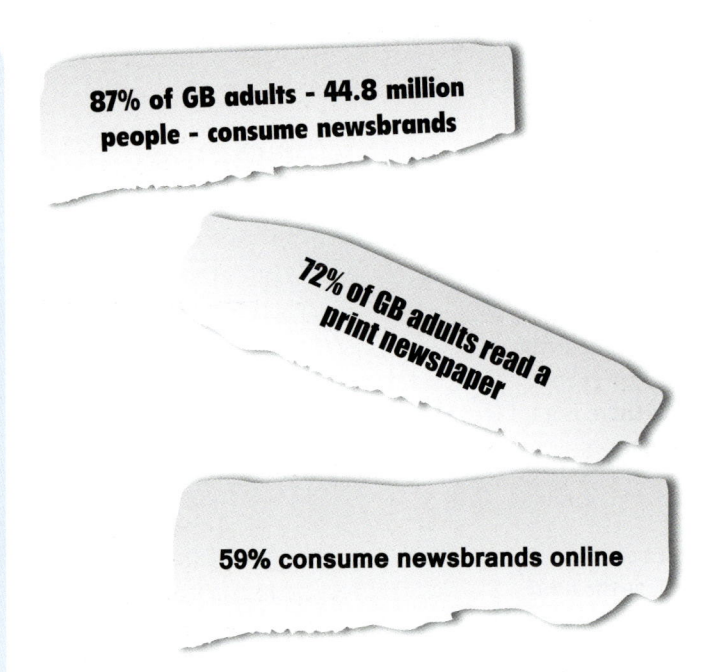

Figure 5.12 News readership figures

KEY SOCIOLOGIST

Greg Philo (2001) of the GMG claims that the news presents news of conflict around the world in a very biased way. As a result, he says people watching the news can have very fixed and overly simplistic ideas about the conflict, often very different to the actual events occurring in the conflict. This view persuaded people to agree with certain political decisions that have been made in relation to responding to these conflicts (see above).

KEY SOCIOLOGIST

Davies (2008) offers a neo-pluralist approach, claiming that journalists are under such pressure that the quality of their work suffers as they do not have the time to check their work properly, leading to inaccuracies and errors. Davies calls this 'churnalism' whereby journalists tend to use facts and statistics from a whole range of sources including the government, without first making sure that they are valid and reliable.

to use new forms of social media in different ways. The new social media provides a range of different platforms from which the news can be accessed which are ever more mobile. There are three key areas in which new social media has had impact:

- newsgathering – it helps journalists gather more, and sometimes better, news material; we can find a wider ranges of voices, ideas and eyewitnesses quickly
- audience engagement – how journalists listen to and talk to their audiences, and allowing them to speak to different audiences
- providing a new platform for media content – it provides a way for journalists to be able to get greater exposure, in short form or as a tool to take people to our journalism on the website, TV or radio. It allows journalists to engage with different and younger audiences.

This different way of gathering and presenting news has already had considerable impact on the reporting of events such as telling some of the major stories of recent times: the Japanese tsunami; the Arab Spring revolution; the Burma uprisings; the Norway shootings and the riots in England.

Recent figures by the National Readership Survey suggest that *The Sun* newspaper lost one million readers over one year, taking its current readership to about six million. The Sun's decision to make its readers pay for the online version has also caused its net readership to fall, bucking the wider trend. Another study, published this month by the Reuters Institute for the Study of Journalism indicated, that just 7 per cent of those polled in the UK said they had paid for news in the past year. However, it added that mainstream news brands still had huge appeal online for the audience, with the Daily Mail, BBC, Sky News, *The Guardian*, Telegraph and the local newspaper category all appearing in their top ten list of most used internet-based sources.

The new social media therefore not only present news differently, possibly reflecting a different agenda and different norms, they are also received by a different audience for example, and they are possibly younger.

KEY SOCIOLOGIST

Nicholas Jones (1986) argues that a revolution has been taking place in the media in terms of the ways events are reported. In his book about the miners' strikes, *Strikes and the Media*, Jones highlights the ways in which the media are used by various groups involved to manipulate the events that occur. Jones argues that the power of the media means that at times journalists themselves are to blame for making already tense situations much worse.

Different perspectives

Marxists would argue that the social construction of news actively deflects interest away from the ruling class and towards the working class. They regard the process of selection of the news as part of the wider ideological conditioning of the working class into accepting the inequalities in society.

IN THE NEWS

Digital news catches up with papers in UK, Ofcom says

Ofcom, the UK's regulatory body for the media, suggests that for first time more people in the UK are keeping up with the news digitally rather than through print. Its annual News Consumption study estimates that internet consumption of news at 41 per cent and those reading newspapers at 40 per cent.

Topping the survey's findings was TV, with 75 per cent of us preferring this method of keeping up with developments. However, the study suggests that the internet was the fastest-growing medium for news, rising from 32 to 41 per cent in just the past year. The only other rise was in radio – but by a much smaller one per cent rise, from 35 to 36 per cent.

Ofcom believes that younger people are largely responsible for the recent increase in digital consumption of news, with two-thirds of people aged 16–24 using social media to keep up to date. This may be due to the fact that more young people than older ones spend time on mobile devices for a wide range of communications purposes. The study indicates that 40 per cent of young people use a mobile phone for news and 15 per cent use a tablet.

Adapted from the BBC (2014)

> **STUDY TIP**
> When considering the construction of the news consider a range of practical, ideological and technological factors that affect the way the news is selected and portrayed.

> **Questions**
> 1. What does the above article suggest about changes in the way news is being consumed by audiences, old and young?
> 2. Name one advantage of news social media being used for news coverage and one disadvantage, in terms of the quality of news coverage.

4.2 What is the influence of other groups on the content of the news?

Consider the role of the government and other groups in shaping the content of the news.

The previous section explored how the media themselves socially construct the content of the news. However, other groups influence the content of the news media in various ways.

The audience

According to pluralists, the consumers are able to not only select the news that they want to see, they also have a wide array of choice in how the news is presented according to the different cultural context they identify with. For example, through the vast array of news channels reflecting different world views such as the BBC, Al Jazeera, Fox, CNN, the audience can find a channel which they can relate to.

Increasingly the audience are able to comment upon the news and the way that it is portrayed. New forms of social media such as Twitter give the public direct access to those in power as well as the journalists themselves and this would suggest that this means they have to be more accountable to be able to respond directly to comments and complaints. This may well create greater clarity and openness as there can be a public dialogue between the public and media, which is known as interactive journalism.

The new social media

The new social media has irrevocably changed how people consume the news. With the distinction between professional journalists and people in the public becoming increasingly blurred, the media react in various ways, with some encouraging the public's participation in news and information gathering while others seek to protect the integrity of professional journalism. What is becoming clear is that being skilled in the use of media, otherwise known as media literacy, is becoming crucial in contemporary society.

The new social media has rapidly changed the way in which news is reported. For example, in relation to social protest in the Middle East. Recent events there have confirmed that social media plays a unique role in giving voice to people who previously had no ability to shape the news.

Before the revolution in the Arab world, the use of social media was described as limited and confined to the social elite. However, the chain of events that occurred across the Arab world in 2011 brought social media to the forefront, with many claiming that Facebook, weblogs, Twitter and YouTube had an important role to play in the revolutions that have taken place. It is hard to understand the extent to which social media have affected events, either through actual protest on the streets or through influencing mainstream forms of media. In the West, headlines were more interested in the impact of social media as the driving force behind many of the uprisings.

In Egypt, for example, through the spread of information online, internet activists were able to establish networks of resistance within Egyptian political society. Despite the relative weakness of the ties between members of these networks, social media emerged as an effective tool to enable collective action. Through being permanently connected to each other, activists were able to access an infinite number of networks of trust and multiply the impact of social protest through the creation of an insurgent community. Internet activism made political action faster and more universal in Egypt. Social media sites became a place where many could express their anxieties and vocalise their feelings.

The question which still needs to be answered is that if journalists have a particular agenda when reporting news, then is it possible that members of the public also have a particular agenda in responding to and shaping the news through new social media platforms?

Advertisers

Advertising is connected to the production of news in an increasingly important way. The giant leap is connected data which is the ability to connect household-level media exposure data, for instance TV viewing, directly to consumer behaviour such as in-store purchases securely, anonymously and at scale. It connects what people see and hear over time, directly to what they do. By understanding how consumers think, media agencies themselves are able to promote certain news stories and to predict what might interest their specific audience on an individual level.

The government

The government has a complex relationship with the media. Each political party has its own manifesto in relation to the media including things like decisions about how much control an individual media company should have. There are two key ways in which the government attempts to control the quality and best practice of the media. Ofcom is the communications regulator in the UK, including regulating the TV and radio sectors, operating under the government legislation, funded by the government. They ensure that there is healthy competition in media providing news and ensure that no one media group monopolises the market. However, they do not regulate the content of television and radio adverts.

There is also IPSO, the Independent Press Standards Organisation, which handles complaints about breaches of the Editors' Code of Practice, for example, dealing with harassment by journalists. Journalists themselves are encourage to alert IPSO if they feel that they are being unfairly pressured into acting in a way they do not see as ethical. IPSO has a board made up of various handpicked legal and media figures. IPSO requires journalists to sign up to its charter.

The efforts of the government to control and regulate the media came after some key events leading to the government led Leveson Inquiry and the subsequent Leveson Report and recommendations.

The Leveson Inquiry

The Leveson Inquiry was a public inquiry into the culture, practices and ethics of the British press following the news of a phone-hacking scandal by News International, chaired by Lord Justice Leveson, in 2011. A series of public hearings were held throughout 2011 and 2012. Following this, the Inquiry published the Leveson Report in November 2012, which reviewed the general culture and ethics of the British media, and went on to make recommendations for a new, independent, body to replace the existing Press Complaints Commission, (IPSO) which will be recognised by the state through new laws.

The inquiry focused on:

- The relationship between the press and the public and looks at phone hacking and other potentially illegal behaviour.
- The relationships between the press and police and the extent to which that has operated in the public interest.
- The relationship between press and politicians.
- Recommendations for a more effective policy and regulation that supports the integrity and freedom of the press while encouraging the highest ethical standards.

The report concluded that a new self-regulation body was recommended, which should be independent of serving editors, government and business. It also concluded that there was no widespread corruption of police by the press. However, it claimed that politicians and the press have had a relationship which was too close. The report found that the relationship between politicians and press over the last three decades has damaged the perception of public affairs, and stated that press behaviour, at times, had been outrageous.

The report represents a clear and strong warning to media companies to act in a more ethical and reasonable way. However, despite the concerns raised in the report, the Conservative government, elected into office in 2015, have not committed to imposing the recommendations of the Leveson Report and have made no mention of media ownership. The Conservative government instead propose to offer journalists protection under the British Bill of Rights, which it wants to replace the Human Rights Act, according to its 2015 election manifesto.

IN THE NEWS

The News International phone-hacking scandal

The UK phone-hacking scandal dates back to 2005 when tabloid *News of the World* published by Rupert Murdoch's News International printed a story about an injury to Prince William's knee, which raised suspicions about how they had come by the details. Following this, employees of the paper were accused of engaging in phone hacking, police bribery, and exercising improper influence in the pursuit of stories.

Investigations between 2005 and 2007 appeared to show that the paper's phone-hacking activities were limited to the British royal family, celebrities and politicians. However, early in July 2011 there was public outrage when it emerged that the phones of murdered schoolgirl Milly Dowler, relatives of deceased British soldiers, and victims of the 2005 London bombings had been hacked. The outcry led to several high-profile resignations, including that of Rebekah Brooks, the chief executive of News International, and Sir Paul Stephenson, commissioner of London's Metropolitan Police Service.

On 6 July 2011, the Prime Minister David Cameron announced the setting up of a public inquiry looking at phone hacking and police bribery by the News of the World. The Leveson Inquiry would also consider the wider culture and ethics of the British newspaper industry. In addition, David Cameron said the Press Complaints Commission (PCC) the voluntary regulatory body for British printed newspapers and magazines, was inadequate. The PCC closed in September 2014, and was replaced by the Independent Press Standards Organisation (IPSO).

On 10th July, following the arrests of managing editor Andy Coulson and royal correspondent Clive Goodman, and with advertisers terminating contracts, the *News of the World* was forced to close after 168 years of publication. Continued public pressure forced News Corporation to drop its plans to take over the British satellite broadcaster BSkyB.

Rupert Murdoch and his son James were among those summoned to give evidence at the Leveson Inquiry. James Murdoch insisted that he had no reason to investigate illegal eavesdropping by employees when he took over News International in 2007. Rupert Murdoch admitted during his testimony that a cover-up had taken place within the *News of the World* to hide the scope of the phone hacking.

Adapted from Wikipedia, News International phone hacking scandal

Questions

1. What does this article reveal about the way that the media operates?
2. Why do you think that phone hacking took place and whose interests did it serve?

According to Greer and Jewkes (2005) the journalists themselves were influenced politically by their media company owners to shape the news in significant ways. News reporting relating to crime is a very clear example of this. According to Greer and Jewkes, one of the most prevalent messages which is shared across much of the UK's contemporary media, especially in the conservative press, is that people commit crimes because 'they' are not like 'us'. Despite having differences, news about crimes share a number of characteristics, one of the most important of which is that they tap into and reinforce cultural fears of 'otherness'.

The media often portrays identities characterised by drawing clear and simplified differences between groups and by the discursive marking of inclusion and exclusion within oppositional classificatory systems: 'insiders' and 'outsiders', 'us' and 'them', men and women, black and white, 'normal' and 'deviant'. Greer and Jewkes analysed UK national press coverage in tabloid (the *Sun*, the *Mirror*, and the *Daily Mail*) and broadsheet (the *Daily Telegraph*, *The Guardian*, and the *Independent*) newspapers, both conservative and liberal, over a three-month period. They found that news reporting reflects a spectrum of deviance, socially constructed ideas of otherness, which exist on a continuum separated by two polar extremes. These are not fixed, but expand and contract with levels of tolerance and concern.

Different perspectives

Bagdikian (2004) argues that the people who own the media form part of a powerful group of elites, including politicians, business leaders and financial leaders, who have similarly conservative values. These values are often expressed through the media in subtle ways which are hard to trace back to the media owner, but are significant none the less. This leads to news which does not challenge inequality or corruption and helps to cover up poor political decisions.

RESEARCH IN FOCUS

Curran *et al.* (2014) argue that the news is created to ensure that the interests of the centre-right political views of the owners who are keen to gain political alliances with the powerful. For example, Curran, has described the government's recent attempt at tackling 'illegal immigrants' with its 'go home or face arrest' van. Curran asks two questions: Why are the vans crowd-pleasers in the first place? Why is there such hostility? The main reason: the media. Coverage of migration, asylum and refugees is often partial, inaccurate and hysterical – as in the tone of this headline from the *Daily Express*: 'UK message to migrants: you are not wanted' (6 June 2011). Government therefore does not simply respond to such coverage, they also promote it.

Curran concludes that the combination of hostile media coverage and tough government policies is counterproductive. They produce fear, attacks upon individuals, depression, anxiety and suicide. Refugees are driven underground, and there is little room for serious discussion about the huge benefits that migration has actually brought to our country.

Adapted from Tiffen *et al.* (2014)

KEY SOCIOLOGISTS

Philo, Briant and Donald (2013) of the GMG explore how migrants have been stigmatised by media coverage, which reflects much mainstream political rhetoric, exploring what is omitted from media accounts, which voices are left unheard, how simplifications and stereotypes are generated, and the consequences of this prejudiced reporting for immigrant communities who feel themselves to be under constant attack.

Questions

1. How, according to Curran *et al.*, is the media used to further political interests regarding immigrants?
2. What is the result of the current coverage, according to the study?
3. How might this be resolved?

Check your understanding

1. What is the difference between traditional Marxist and neo-Marxist views of the ownership of the media?
2. Explain what is meant by newsworthiness.
3. What practical constraints affect the way that news is reported?
4. What impact is global culture having on the media?
5. What is the pluralist view of the media and how might it be criticised?

Practice question

1. Outline and explain two ways in which the news is influenced by different groups. [10 marks]

Read Item A below then answer the question that follows.

Item A

Events that are considered to be news are carefully selected for a range of reasons. For example, newspapers have specific deadlines to meet affecting the extent to which events can be covered. More recently, new forms of social media have provided a new and more instantaneous way of presenting events.

Applying material from Item A and your knowledge, evaluate the factors affecting what is reported in the news. [20 marks]

Section 5: Media representations of social groups

This section will explore the following debates:
- What are the nature, causes, trends and significance of these representations?
- How have the representations of different groups in the media changed over time?

Questions

1. Thinking of recent television programmes that you have watched, suggest three characteristics that children are commonly shown to have.
2. Other than age-related stereotypes, what other types of stereotypes might the media perpetuate?
3. In your opinion, does traditional media spread stereotypical views of teenagers more than new media? Give examples to justify your answer.

GETTING YOU STARTED

Figure 5.13 How does the TV stereotype of children compare to reality?

5.1 What are the nature, causes, trends and significance of these representations?

Question how different age groups are represented in the media. It might be useful to consider the ways in which three broad age groups are presented by the media: children, teenagers and the elderly.

For many sociologists, the media acts as an agency of secondary socialisation: it has the power to shape our norms, values and beliefs. It is therefore of interest to sociologists to investigate how the media represents different social groups, such as age groups, ethnic groups or social classes. These **media representations** are ideological, meaning that those who own and control the media are able to influence how society sees different social groups.

Age and the media

In terms of age groups, it could be argued that the media spreads rather stereotypical views of children, teenagers and the elderly in particular.

Children

Aries (1965) argued that media has the ability to socially construct the meaning of 'childhood': that is, to mould society's view of what it means to be a child. Aries studied paintings from the Middle Ages, and found that children appeared to be treated as miniature adults in that they were partaking in the same work and leisure activities as adults. However, by the 1700s, a market had developed for children's literature, which started to distinguish children from adults. By the 1900s, the mass media was representing childhood as a time of innocence and vulnerability. Some sociologists take this view a step further, arguing that the media represents children as 'perfect angels', downplaying individual variation between children or problems that children might cause. However, television programmes such Jo Frost's 'Supernanny' can be seen to show children as troublesome and badly behaved, rather than angelic.

Teenagers

Wayne *et al.* (2008) noted that the media presents teenagers negatively, 'symbolically criminalising' them by frequently associating teenagers with violent crime. It was also found that the television news rarely offers teenagers the opportunity to have their voice heard: just 1 per cent of all of the television news stories studied by Wayne *et al.* featured a teen's opinion. This means that society starts to view youth as problematic and to be feared, rather than recognise the problems that teenagers experience such as unemployment and mental health issues. This is supported by Cohen's classic study *'Folk Devils and Moral Panics'* (1972) which showed how youth subcultures of 'mods' and 'rockers' were scapegoated by the media as violent criminals who were responsible for many of society's ills. However, Batchelor (1999) found that teen dramas and youth magazines were sensitive and helpful in addressing dilemmas faced by teenagers, even if these media outlets focused to a large extent on the issues that heterosexual teen girls face rather than treating youth as the diverse group that it is.

Figure 5.14 A typical teenager?

RESEARCH IN FOCUS

Television news and the symbolic criminalisation of young people

This essay combines quantitative and qualitative analysis of six UK television news programmes. It seeks to analyse the representation of young people within broadcast news provision at a time when media representations, political discourse and policymaking generally appear to be invoking young people as something of a folk devil or a locus for moral panics. The quantitative analysis examines the frequency with which young people appear as main actors across a range of different subjects and analyses the role of young people as news sources. It finds a strong correlation between young people and violent crime. A qualitative analysis of four 'special reports' or backgrounders on Channel Five's Five News, explores the representation of young people in more detail, paying attention to contradictions and tensions in the reports, the role of statistics in crime reporting, the role of victims of crime and the tensions between conflicting news frames.

Adapted from Wayne *et al.* (2008)

Questions

1. What is the difference between a quantitative and a qualitative analysis?
2. What is meant by 'political discourse' and how does it link to the media?
3. Identify ways in which the media labels young people as folk devils.

The elderly

Elderly people are underrepresented in the media and when they are shown they are often represented in rather stereotypical ways. Williams and Ylänne (2009) conducted a content analysis on five years' worth of advertisements in 121 magazines. They found that the most common media representation of the elderly was as 'golden-agers': 19.5 per cent of the elderly people featured in the magazine adverts were lively, active and enjoying life. Another common representation of the elderly was as wise 'mentors' or 'perfect grandparents', which made up 18.5 per cent and 8.3 per cent of the elderly people in the adverts respectively. Negative stereotypes were less common, but still significant, for example the 9.8 per cent who were portrayed as 'dozy and incompetent'. Therefore, Williams and Ylänne recognise that media representations of the elderly have become more varied, but are concerned that the elderly are usually featured only for age-specific reasons (such as to market a product aimed at the elderly): rather than being depicted as 'just people' the elderly are categorised as somehow separate to other adults. The worry is that this distinction will feed into further ageism and marginalisation of the elderly in our society.

Different perspective

Postmodernists argue that the media is no longer a metanarrative (wide-scale explanation of society) that shapes beliefs, partly as it has become so fragmented: there are so many types of media, and choices that individuals can make when consuming it, that it no longer has the power to spread a dominant set of ideas. The way social groups are portrayed would depend on what type of media an individual chooses to consume.

Social class and the media

In terms of media representations, sociological research tends to focus on the ways in which four broad social classes are depicted in the media, both in terms of frequency of coverage and in terms of the characteristics that are often attached to each socio-economic group:

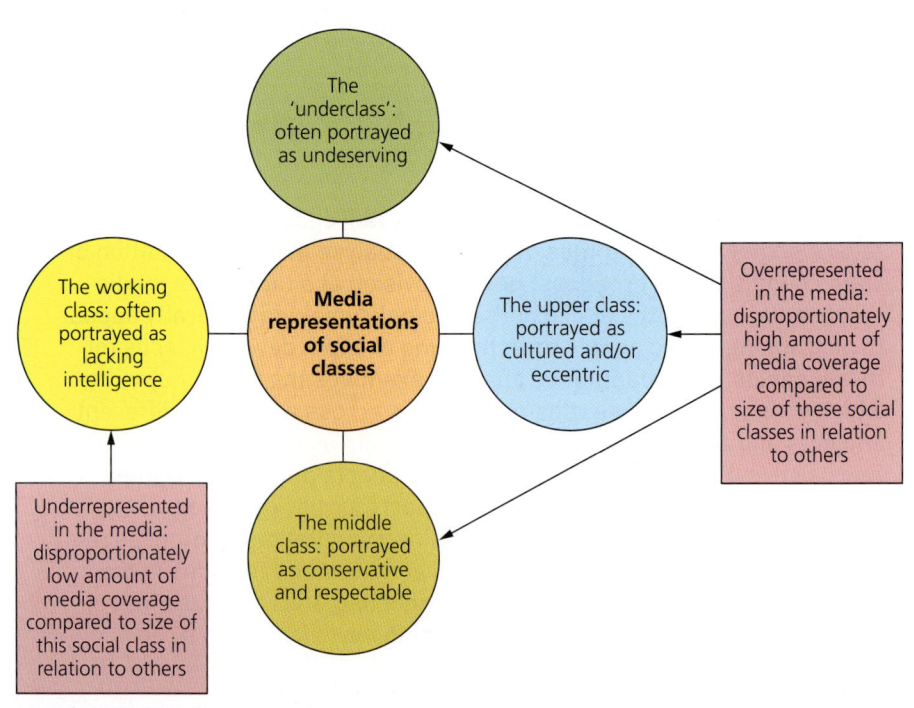

Figure 5.15 Social class representation in the media

The 'underclass'

Figure 5.16 The underclass in the media

Television programmes such as Channel 4's *Shameless* and *Benefits Street* tend to portray the unemployed as feckless, immoral and abusive of state benefits. Rarely do such programmes show any sympathy for people who claim benefits, or investigate the causes of or solutions to, reliance on the welfare state. In the 2015 General Election campaign, David Cameron spoke of the problem of those who 'choose a life on the dole', reinforcing the idea that the underclass are both undeserving of state help and have alternative ways of generating an income. For Marxists, this ideology creates a smokescreen to divert attention away from capitalism as the root of social problems by scapegoating the unemployed.

The working class

Some newspapers are aimed at a working-class readership, such as 'red-top' tabloids like *The Sun*. These newspapers tend to be more simplistic in language than newspapers which are targeted towards wealthier readers, and focus more on sport and celebrity scandal than important current affairs. In addition, although few television programmes focus on working-class people, those that do tend to depict working-class men as thuggish, stupid and deviant. These two factors combine to perpetuate the stereotype of the working class as lacking intelligence and somewhat of a threat to society. For example, similarly to how the media portrays unemployed and impoverished people, Newman (2006) noted that the media tend to focus on the deviance that working-class individuals may commit, such as blue-collar crimes and benefit fraud, rather than the normal, day-to-day activities of this social class.

The middle class

The middle class is usually considered to consist of those with professional jobs who hold university degrees. As most media professionals fit this description, it comes as little surprise that those who make the media tend to use it to produce content that is of interest to them and their peers. As such, the middle class tend to be overrepresented in the media: both in terms of how many middle-class families are featured in television programmes, and how many newspapers

Figure 5.17 Media representations of the middle class

and television programmes focus on middle-class interests. Take for example *The Antiques Roadshow*, advertisements for exotic holidays and the multitude of property programmes such as *Homes Under the Hammer*. This shows how much of the media concentrates on holidays, property investment, antiques, and other material goods that only those with a considerable income could afford. Broadsheet newspapers such as *The Telegraph*, *The Independent* and *The Guardian* also target the middle class. In addition, many soap operas and fictional television programmes feature middle-class families, and usually present them positively, showing the middle class as well-mannered, ambitious, respectable members of society.

The upper class

Altman (2005) was interested in the media fascination with very wealthy people, which might include rich celebrities, billionaires and royalty. He found that in the USA, the proportion of pages of news magazines focusing on celebrities and entertainment had doubled between 1980 and 2003, whereas the coverage of national affairs had dropped by 10 per cent over the same period. It was interesting to note how the news of Princess Charlotte's birth dominated the headlines for a three-day period in May 2015, and as this happened in the same week as the General Election, almost all news stories were about either the royal family or politicians. Taking a neo-Marxist approach, Newman (2006) agrees that the media has somewhat of an obsession with celebrity culture and conspicuous consumption, such as the dominance of television advertisements which focus on high cost items like Caribbean holidays or prestige cars. In addition, both newspapers and the television news broadcast details of daily fluctuations in share prices and the FTSE index, despite the fact that this information is only of interest to the minority who are able to afford to invest in stocks and shares. When celebrities or other wealthy people are featured in the media, it is usually in a positive light, Newman argues. If criticism is made, it might be about trivial issues such as appearance or dress sense, rather than addressing serious concerns about inequality in society. However, some sociologists would argue that the media is obsessed with wealth specifically, not actually social class, and that social class is becoming less significant in contemporary society.

Different perspective

Marxists argue that the positive media portrayal of the wealthy is a deliberate ploy of the capitalist owners of the media. By spreading ideology that wealthy people deserve their wealth, and should be admired for being cultured and successful, the media maintains a false consciousness among the working class. Instead of feeling resentful about the inequality in society, the proletariat are led to believe that society is **meritocratic**, and that the wealthy should be celebrated.

Ethnic groups and the media

Whereas 'race' refers to differences in skin colour, '**ethnicity**' is used to refer to a group that share a cultural heritage, who may or may not have the same skin colour. Therefore, ethnicity distinguishes between groups who hold very different cultural beliefs, norms and values, even though they might share a skin colour. An example of this could be 'black African' versus 'black Caribbean' groups. Until the 1990s, however, sociological research tended to use the term 'race' rather than 'ethnicity'.

> **STUDY TIP**
> Consider not just 'white' people versus ethnic minorities, but examples from a range of different ethnic groups. After all, there are huge variations between different ethnic minorities and how the media portrays them.

The media is sometimes accused of being **ethnocentric**, focusing on white people and their interests, although not all white people necessarily benefit from this as it assumes that white people share the same interests. Furthermore, many newspapers scapegoat ethnic minorities as a 'threat' to white British culture, for example by reducing the strength of Christianity by bringing beliefs from other religions into the UK, or by threatening British values by holding alternative values. Hall (1981) took a **deterministic** approach to explaining how the media portrays people from various ethnic groups. Hall claimed that,

> '…the media construct for us a definition of what race is, what meaning that imagery of race carries, and what 'the problem of race' is understood to be. They help us to classify the world in terms of race.'

For Hall, the media was responsible for creating and maintaining racist stereotypes, and in the process, controlling how people think about race. This enables those in power, who are typically white, to exert their authority and dominance.

For Hall, the media does this by linking skin colour to human 'nature', suggesting that black people and white people are 'naturally' different in terms of their abilities and personalities. This 'fixes difference', meaning that society believes that people from different ethnic groups are fundamentally different, legitimating racist stereotypes. For example, at times, the media show black Caribbean people as laid back and not very hard-working, Chinese people as academic and particularly gifted at mathematics and Muslims as linked to extremist terrorist activity. Consider the last news article you read concerning Northern African or Eastern European immigrants. It is likely they were portrayed as problematic and keen to utilise the welfare systems of European countries such as the UK.

Hall's views are supported by the 2011 REACH Media Monitoring Report carried out by Stephen Cushion *et al.* of Cardiff University. The sociologists carried out a quantitative and qualitative content analysis of 'media coverage of black young men and boys in the British news and current affairs media', along with interviews with those involved with making or reporting the news. The sociologists found that when young black men were featured on the news, 70 per cent of the stories related to crime, particularly knife crime, gang crimes and murders. However, when news stories of boys/young men of all ethnic groups were considered, just 40 per cent were linked to crime.

Different perspective

Functionalists would argue that the media does not construct our views of different groups in society, but merely reflect our views. The media acts as a 'mirror' of society. Therefore, as our views about different ethnic groups change over time, perhaps because of our own personal experiences of people from various ethnicities, media coverage will also change.

Gender and the media

Women

Feminist sociologists consider the media to be **malestream:** made by men, for men, and about men. In terms of how many male journalists, media executives and editors there are in the UK press and television industries this argument seems to hold some weight. Most people might suggest men such as Rupert Murdoch, Max Clifford or Mark Zuckerberg if asked to name someone who is influential in the media, as opposed to one of the few women. Rebekah Brooks has become well known in recent years as the *News of the World* editor who presided over the phone-hacking scandal, but few people would be able to name

> **STUDY TIP**
> Remember that the focus of sociologists has only recently shifted from race to ethnicity. For some sociologists, the concept of ethnicity is just as problematic as the concept of race, as it still infers set differences between groups in society, while ignoring differences within groups.

> **KEY SOCIOLOGIST**
> **Stuart Hall** is a Marxist who suggested that the media played a significant role in painting young, black men as folk devils in the 1980s. Hall argued that the bourgeoisie used the media and police to create moral panic by spreading the ideology that young, black men were causing many of the problems in society. Hall claimed this was a smokescreen to cover up how capitalism had caused the economic decline.

a female media executive who is seen in a positive way. Tuchman agrees, arguing that if the media isn't ignoring women, it is condemning or trivialising them. According to radical feminists, this 'symbolic annihilation' of women perpetuates patriarchy in society, fuelling the belief that women are inferior and simply less important that men.

For Wolf (1990), the media is at least partly responsible for spreading the **beauty myth**. The media publishes photographs of size zero models and of celebrities for whom fitness, nutrition and appearance has become a full-time occupation, most of which are airbrushed to remove any minor imperfection. Women's magazines and newspaper supplements focus on diet and beauty regimes. Pornography suggests that surgically enhanced, waxed women are more beautiful than women in their natural form. In short, women are led to believe that to be beautiful is to be slim yet large-breasted, young, wrinkle-free, tall, with perfect white teeth, and have thick, shiny hair. 'Normal' women see this standard of beauty as necessary to be attractive to men, and to be satisfied and successful. Wolf believes that this beauty myth controls women's behaviour and reinforces patriarchy. One example of this is how there are many more images of near-naked women in the media than semi-dressed men:

> 'To live in a culture in which women are routinely naked where men aren't is to learn inequality in little ways all day long. So even if we agree that sexual imagery is in fact a language, it is clearly one that is already heavily edited to protect men's sexual – and hence social – confidence while undermining that of women.' (Wolf, 1990:139)

Questions

1. In what ways might 'page 3' be seen to have been spreading the 'beauty myth'?
2. Suggest other specific television programmes or types of media that spread the 'beauty myth'.
3. How might Wolf explain Jodie Marsh's reaction to the end of page 3?

IN THE NEWS

The end of page 3: a victory for feminism?

Figure 5.18 Women take a stand against page 3

Although Britain's best-selling tabloid has not confirmed the move, *The Times* reports that it is 'quietly dropping one of the most controversial traditions of British journalism'.

The news was welcomed by shadow cabinet minister Harriet Harman, who has long campaigned against the use of topless pictures in the newspaper. She tweeted: 'Glad that @TheSunNewspaper p3 gone. Women expect to be equal in C21. Not posing half naked.'

On Twitter, Labour MP Stella Creasy said: 'Hey Britain- lets show some love 2 Lucy Ann Holmes of @NoMorePage3 4 helping give the nudge to nipples in our news.'

But former page 3 model Jodie Marsh led the backlash against the move, saying on Twitter that 'telling girls they shouldn't do page 3 is not being a feminist'. In a series of tweets, she said: 'So-called "feminists" really annoy me. Telling girls they shouldn't do page 3 is not being a feminist; women should do whatever they want.' Commenting on her career as a page 3 model, she said: 'I loved doing page 3, it was good money, I felt powerful, I was definitely in control and all the people (mostly women) I worked with were fab. I never felt exploited – in fact the opposite. I thought "Blimey, people are willing to pay to see my boobs." I am very much a feminist. I believe women can do it all and have it all. Women who slag off other women are just jealous and insecure.'

Adapted from Channel 4 (2015)

Men

Men may be overrepresented in the media, but it doesn't necessarily mean they all benefit from the media or that the media doesn't control men too. For Connell, the media promotes **hegemonic masculinity** in society. Men's magazines such as *GQ*, *FHM* and *Men's Fitness* focus on viewing women as a sexual object through a heterosexual man's eyes (**male gaze**), and encouraging men to have interests that will confirm their masculinity: macho competitive sports such as football and rugby, a desire to drive fast cars, a fitness regime that will result in a muscular physique. Men who do not live up to this masculine ideal may feel inferior and abnormal.

Sexuality and the media

Some sociologists are concerned that the media presents unrepresentative and even harmful stereotypes regarding sexuality. For example, as explained the 'gender' section, Connell argues that the media is partly responsible for maintaining the hegemonic masculinity that is evident in our society, by spreading the belief that macho, heterosexual identities are superior to other identities such as feminine or homosexual. However, Batchelor and Kitzinger (1999) might argue that the media's portrayal of teenage sexuality in particular is far more complex than this. For example, Batchelor and Kitzinger found that there were key differences in the way that different types of media represent sexuality. This is shown on the diagram below:

Figure 5.19 One version of how men are seen in the media

Media messages about teenage sexuality

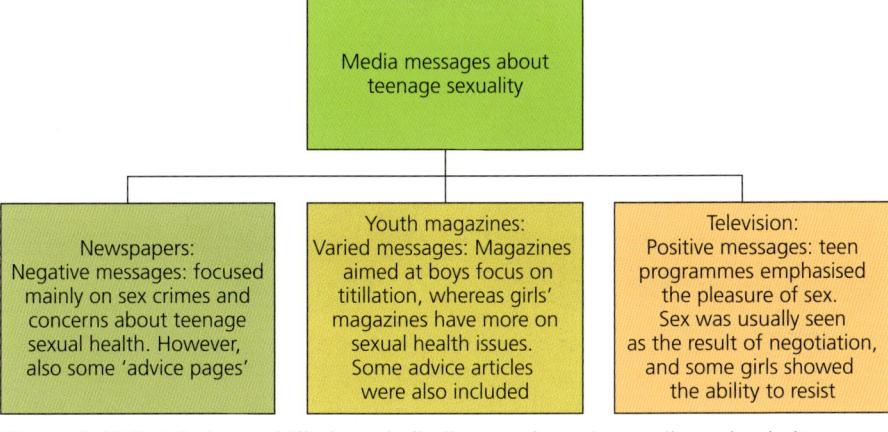

- **Newspapers:** Negative messages: focused mainly on sex crimes and concerns about teenage sexual health. However, also some 'advice pages'
- **Youth magazines:** Varied messages: Magazines aimed at boys focus on titillation, whereas girls' magazines have more on sexual health issues. Some advice articles were also included
- **Television:** Positive messages: teen programmes emphasised the pleasure of sex. Sex was usually seen as the result of negotiation, and some girls showed the ability to resist

Figure 5.20 Batchelor and Kitzinger's findings on how the media varies in its portrayal of teenage sexuality

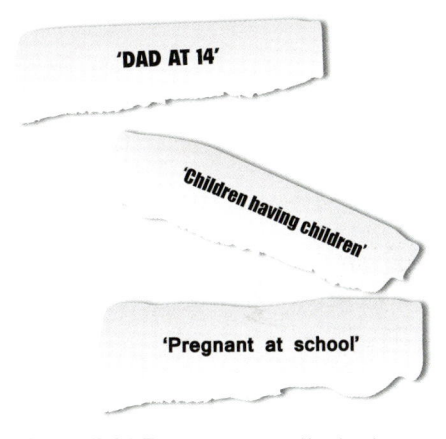

'DAD AT 14'

'Children having children'

'Pregnant at school'

Figure 5.21 Teenage sexuality in the media

KEY SOCIOLOGISTS

Susan Batchelor and Jenny Kitzinger (1999) conducted a content analysis of the media messages in Scotland about teenage sexuality. This included analysing a week's worth of national and regional newspapers, youth magazines and 88 ½ hours of television programmes (at peak viewing times for youth audiences).

KEY SOCIOLOGIST

Raewyn Connell (aka R.W. Connell) is an Australian sociologist who was born Bob Connell. She argues that there are 'masculinities' rather than simply one masculinity, and writes about issues affecting men and boys, such as violence, boys' education and gender equality. She holds concerns that a hegemonic masculinity exists in society, suggesting a gender hierarchy and a lack of gender equality.

Batchelor and Kitzinger suggest that the main media message for adults/parents came from newspapers and emphasised the dangers of teenage sexuality, whereas 'youth media' was far more likely to spread the message to teenagers that sex was pleasurable, but that relationships often brought heartache. There was less on the potential negative physical consequences such as teenage pregnancy or sex crimes.

While Batchelor and Kitzinger's research disputes the idea that all media is one-dimensional in its representations of teenage sexuality (with the sociologists being impressed with girls' magazines and how educational they were for young women), the study did show some support for Connell's view that hegemonic masculinity is evident in the media. For example, most media representations could be seen to be perpetuating a gender divide and stereotypes about sexuality in the following ways:

Common ways in which the media is stereotypical in regards to teen sexuality:

- Homosexuality is shown as a threat to heterosexuality or as a joke.
- Gay teenagers are rarely featured, and if they are, the focus is on anxieties and problems associated with their sexuality.
- The assumption is made that teenagers aged 16+ are sexually active or will soon be so.
- Magazines aimed at girls and boys promoted different agendas, reinforcing a gender divide.
- Lesbianism was presented from a male perspective, as a form of titillation. A 'tolerance' towards lesbians is common.
- Most of the characters were white, thin, conventionally attractive and with no visible disability.
- Young men are usually represented as being focused on sex, as opposed to young women who are interested in relationships.

Figure 5.22 Stereotypes of teen sexuality in the media

In summary, Batchelor and Kitzinger suggest that the media representations of teenage sexuality perpetuate gender and sexual stereotypes and fail to address the diversity of sexual relationships, especially for young men.

Disability and the media

According to 2014 government statistics, there are over 11 million people with a limiting long-term illness, impairment or disability in Britain. Disabled people are less likely to be employed, achieve qualifications, and more likely to experience discrimination and be victims of crime than non-disabled people. Barnes (1992) claimed that disabled people are becoming increasingly aware that the media was a significant contributor to this **institutional discrimination**. For Barnes, the media perpetuates the link between '… impairment and all that is socially unacceptable'.

On behalf of the British Council of Organisations of Disabled People, Barnes carried out an investigation into the extent to which the media spread **disablist imagery**. (For further information on this, see Book 1 page 146 on 'Disability and Identity'.) This research included carrying out a detailed content analysis of previous research of media representations of disabled people, and writing to disability organisations, media organisations and advertisers to request information on media portrayals of disabled people. Barnes was able to identify 11 specific harmful stereotypes of disability that are commonly used in the media. They include (see Figure 5.23):

Consider the last time you saw a disabled character in a television programme. Were they presented in any of the ways listed? Perhaps not, as Barnes also acknowledges that there has been a recent shift to try to show disabled people as 'normal', downplaying their disability and showing them as participating fully in their community. However, Barnes argues that attempts to portray the disabled as 'normal' could be harmful, in that this will not raise awareness of how disabling society is to people with impairments: it is often a lack of understanding of disability, or a lack of provision that prevents those with impairments from participating fully in society, rather than a lack of ability or willingness on the part of the person with the impairment. Furthermore, when disabled people are presented as 'normal', they are unrepresentative of the disabled population as a whole. For example, much of the time disabled characters in the media are white, male, aged 25–40, with physical disabilities. This does little to educate the audience about the wide-ranging and often hidden nature of disability.

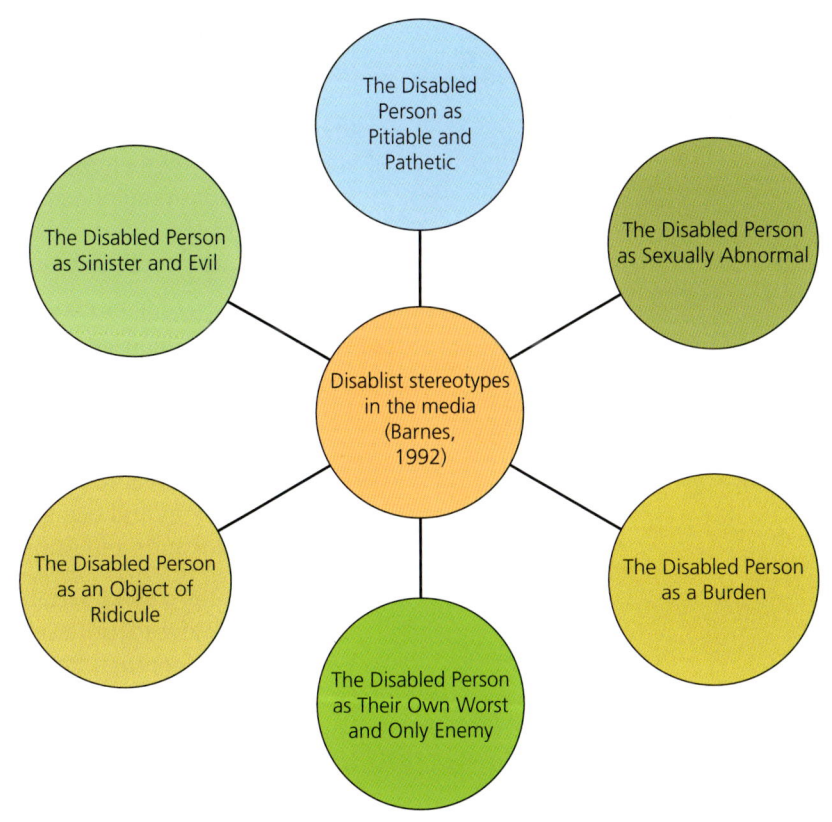

Figure 5.23 Disablist stereotypes in the media

Barnes also notes that the media may be contributing to the **'simultaneous oppression'** of ' …disabled members of the lesbian and gay communities, disabled black people, disabled women and disabled members of other marginalised groupings.' This is because the media can also be held responsible for the spread of racist, xenophobic, homophobic, and sexist ideas. However, Barnes acknowledges that the media alone is not responsible for the spread of negative stereotypes, and that the law, education system and other social institutions are also to blame. However, as the media is so widespread, with 98 per cent of British homes owning a television, it is likely that media is a highly powerful force in shaping how we view people with disabilities.

In conclusion, Barnes argues that 'the vast majority of information about disability in the mass media is extremely negative. Disabling stereotypes which medicalise, patronise, criminalise and dehumanise disabled people abound in books, films, on television, and in the press. They form the bed-rock on which the attitudes towards, assumptions about and expectations of disabled people are based.'

5.2 How have the representations of different groups in the media changed over time?

Postmodernists argue that many of the media representations discussed above were evident in the modern era, but the media and its messages have since become fragmented and more diverse. Whether this is true or not, there is certainly evidence to suggest that media representations change over time.

For example, McRobbie carried out a content analysis of girls' magazines in order to assess the messages that the magazines were passing on to their readers. In the 1960s, *Jackie* focused on romance and boys. By the 1980s *Just Seventeen* seemed to be aimed at a different audience: to girls who were somewhat independent and wanted to control their own bodies, for example, by being educated about sex. The feminist movement had apparently made an impact: girls were now learning about experimentation and self-confidence, and far less magazine space was devoted to articles about love and boyfriends.

In addition, Connell (1995) argued that ideas about masculinity change over time, and are influenced by a multitude of factors, including how women view men. For example, some of the most popular male celebrities over the last decade or so do not completely fit the traditional model of masculinity. David Beckham is 'macho' in some ways (such as his love of football and fast cars), but he also displays some stereotypically effeminate characteristics, such as being in touch with his emotions and being very interested in his appearance and in fashion (wearing headbands and sarongs at times!).

Indeed, a quick consideration of media personalities identifies a wide range of masculine gender identities: from the '**metrosexual**' presenters such as David Walliams and Jonathan Ross, to the camp and homosexual personalities of Graham Norton and Alan Carr. Can the same be said for women though? Young, glamorous and slim would describe most female presenters, and there have been suggestions that the media industry is particularly ageist towards women. Former Sky presenter Anna Ford claimed she felt she had to leave due to her age otherwise she would be 'shovelled off into News 24 to the sort of graveyard shift'. There was also outrage when newsreader Moira Stuart lost her job in 2007, again allegedly due to her age.

Figures 5.24 Different types of masculinity in the media

Furthermore, the media seems to be more politically correct in its representations of minority groups than in the past. Is this evidence of a more democratic media, in which individuals can influence media content by complaining to regulators such as OFCOM and PCC, or even by creating the media themselves, through new media? Recent legal reforms include the introduction of the Equality Act, 2010 which strengthened the law in regards to all forms of discrimination, both in the workplace and wider society. However, it should also be noted that within the press and television sectors, many minority groups are underrepresented in terms of employment within these organisations, and this is likely to cause such forms of media to provide little and/or inaccurate coverage of minority groups, such as people with disabilities.

Check your understanding

1. According to Aries, how does the media represent children?
2. Suggest ways in which the media 'symbolically criminalises' (Wayne et al., 2008) teenagers?
3. Why do Marxists believe that the media scapegoats the working class and underclass?
4. Give examples of ways in which the media perpetuates racist stereotypes.
5. What does Wolf mean when she argues that the media spreads the 'beauty myth'?

Practice question

1. Outline and explain two ways in which the media representations of social groups may be stereotypical.   [10 marks]

Section 6: The effects of the media on audiences

This section will explore the following debates:
- What are the different sociological explanations of the effects of the media on audiences?
- Why might methodological issues arise when researching media effects?

6.1 What are the different sociological explanations of the effects of the media on audiences?

Question the effects of the media on their audience, being sure to show an understanding of the variety of theoretical approaches there are regarding this debate, and the implications of each, as outlined below.

The hypodermic syringe model

The view that the media acts in much the same way as a hypodermic syringe was an early theory developed when radio and newspapers were first starting to become commonplace. This model uses an analogy: that the media is capable of injecting ideas into people's minds, in the same way that a syringe can directly

Figure 5.25 A summary of the hypodermic syringe model

> Media content is designed by journalists and other media professionals, and transmitted to audiences. → The audience passively accepts and internalises the media messages. → The audience's behaviour and attitudes will change to reflect the media messages.

inject drugs. In other words, the audience is passive and the media is a powerful and direct influence on society:

Politicians, campaigners and even the media themselves are often proponents of this theory. For example, the case of the James Bulger murder is often used as 'evidence' to suggest that the media is capable of influencing people's behaviour. James Bulger was 2 years old when he was abducted from a shopping centre, abused and murdered. His killers were Robert Thompson and Jon Venables, both of whom were 10 years old. The media claim that the murderers had watched *Child's Play 3* (a horror film which the British Board of Film Classification had rated as 'suitable only for adults') and their actions towards James Bulger could be considered to be 'copycat' behaviour due to the similarities to the torture methods shown in the film.

However, the hypodermic syringe model has been heavily criticised for being overly simplistic. For example, some sociologists argue that different social groups within media audiences might be affected in different ways by the same media messages. Indeed, of the millions of people who watch horror films each year, the vast majority do not go on to mimic the scenes in the films.

Different perspective

Neo-Marxists argue that the hypodermic syringe model fails to question who has power to control the media. For example Marcuse of the Frankfurt School argue that the mass media is used as a drug by the bourgeoisie to keep the proletariat passive and obedient. Whereas Marx himself claimed that religion was the 'opiate of the masses', religion seems to have lost at least some of its influence in contemporary society, while the mass media has become ubiquitous. Therefore, neo-Marxists agree that the media acts in much the same way as a hypodermic syringe in order to control the masses, but take the theory a step further by questioning who holds power over media content.

Figure 5.26 Can horror films fuel violent impulses?

The two-step flow model

It could be argued that the two-step flow model offers a more sophisticated explanation of media effects than the hypodermic syringe, in that the two-step flow recognises that individuals are not necessarily affected by the media directly, but by the social response to the media. This model was proposed by Katz and Lazarfield in 1955, and suggests that audience members develop an opinion on the media, and some of these are '**opinion leaders**' who express their views to others. Therefore, unlike the hypodermic syringe model, this explanation recognises that audience members are not isolated, powerless individuals, but social beings who have the capacity to form their own opinion on media content. For example, a group of friends may discuss a television series, and these discussions affect their understanding of that series. This means the media may influence people directly, in that opinion leaders may be interested enough by

Figure 5.27 A summary of the two-step flow model

> Media content is designed by journalists and other media professionals, and transmitted to audiences. → Audiences are exposed to the media messages and consider and discuss them. → The views of 'opinion leaders' (people whose views are respected) about the media content affects people's attitudes and behaviour.

the media content to want to discuss it, but the main effects come in a 'Chinese whispers' way when the opinion leaders spread their views to others. Unlike the hypodermic syringe model, this acknowledges that the media audience isn't totally passive, but are affected by their social interactions.

The selective filter model

Klapper (1960) suggests that the audience have some choice over whether they are affected by the media. This is a critique of the hypodermic syringe model, as audience members will not be directly affected by all media content. Instead Klapper argues that media content is only able to influence the audience if it is able to pass through three filters (Figure 5.28).

The uses and gratifications model

The uses and gratifications model is a functionalist model which suggests that the media has a function: meeting people's individual needs. This view suggests that the audience is active, and each person chooses the media they experience to meet their individual needs, for example, the elderly may be more likely to use the media for current affairs, whereas teenagers see it as having more of an entertainment function (Figure 5.29).

Different perspective

Some feminists would argue that the uses and gratifications model is idealistic in assuming that all media content provides positive functions for society and individuals. Radical feminists would suggest that the model ignores how the media is used by powerful groups to spread and maintain patriarchy: male dominance. Rather than individuals being able to actively select the media content to suit their own needs, radical feminists suggest that so much media content is written by men, that patriarchy is embedded in the media and infiltrates our beliefs and culture.

The reception analysis model

Whereas the uses and gratification model suggests that individual audience members use the media in different ways, the reception analysis model proposes that social groups interpret media content in different ways. Morley (1980) suggests that the subcultural groups that an individual belongs to, based on their personal characteristics such as gender, social class, age, ethnicity, etc ... will

Stage 1: selective exposure
The audience must choose to watch, read or otherwise expose themselves to the media message. For example, a Party Political Broadcast by the Labour Party before a General Election can only have an influence on a person's vote if they opt to view it. It should be noted that this may not be entirely a free choice: an audience member's socio-economic background will influence what they choose to watch, and not everyone has access to all media. For example, not all homes have Sky or cable television, so may have little choice over which news programme to watch.

Stage 2: selective perception
Once the audience is exposed to the media message, Klapper suggests they still have the option to reject the message. For example, if watching a documentary on the advantages of immigration, those with far right-wing beliefs are likely to disagree with the content of the programme and not let it influence their existing belief that immigration is inherently problematic.

Stage 3: selective retention
Supposing the audience have chosen to expose themselves to a media message and accept it, the extent to which that message will affect them is still dependent on whether the audience finds it memorable. Some studies indicate the audiences are far more likely to remember media content that is aligned with their existing beliefs. Therefore Klapper suggests that our beliefs are primarily shaped by the social groups we are most attached to. The media is a secondary influence, and can reinforce the beliefs we hold.

Figure 5.28 The stages of the selective filter model

KEY SOCIOLOGISTS

Denis McQuail and Jay Blumler have worked both together and separately to investigate media effects. Taking a functionalist stance, they agree that the media is beneficial to individuals, in that it can fulfil their individual needs. The uses and gratifications model is often attributed to these two sociologists, along with Katz and Lull.

McQuail, Blumler et al. (1972) argue that there are four basic ways in which individuals use the media:

- **Social solidarity:** the media is a key part of our culture, and being able to experience/discuss it with others helps us to feel a sense of commonality with those around us.
- **Entertainment:** e.g. we might turn to a comedy programme to make us laugh, or pick up a magazine because we're bored.
- **Surveillance of the world around us:** e.g. the news helps us to keep an eye on current affairs.
- **Identity:** the media helps us to develop and maintain our sense of self, e.g. being inspired by the dress sense of a celebrity.

Figure 5.29 Potential uses of the media

affect how they interpret media messages. Therefore the reception analysis model suggests that media content is **polysemic**, and that there are at least three ways in which audience members might decode a media message:

Morley's typology of audience interpretations of media content

- **Dominant or hegemonic reading:** The audience member agrees with the 'code' of the programme (its meaning system of values, attitudes, beliefs and assumptions).
- **Negotiated reading:** The audience member broadly accepts the preferred reading, but modifies it to reflect their own interests or socio-economic background.
- **Oppositional reading:** The audience member rejects the preferred reading and the programme's code, instead interpreting it in an alternative way.

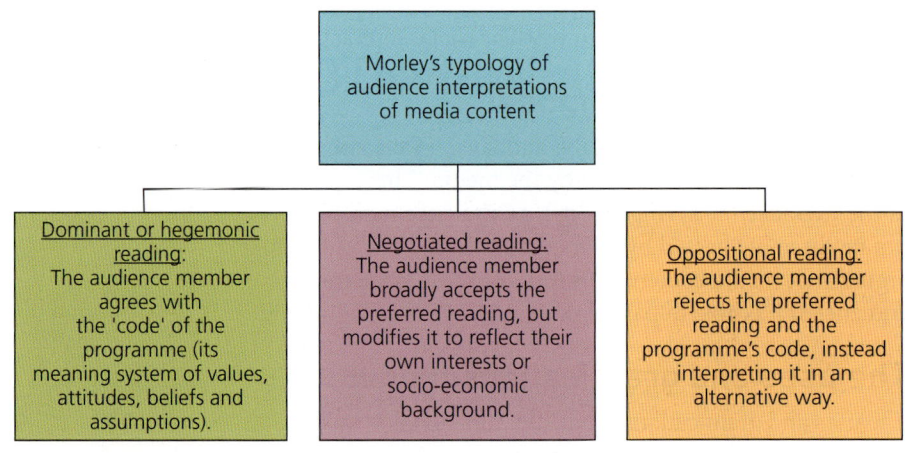

Figure 5.30 Ways in which audience might decode media messages

For example, consider an advert for a luxury steak restaurant. Arguably most people would share the code that the marketing team devised when creating the advert, for example, making people think the restaurant looks appealing and the food sounds delicious. This is the dominant reading. However, how might someone who cannot afford to visit such a restaurant interpret the advert? They might read the advert and negotiate the code, by sharing the view that the food sounds delicious, but think the restaurant is not appealing as it is too expensive. What about vegetarians? An oppositional reading is likely to apply for this subcultural group, who see the both the food and ethics of the restaurant as disgusting and unappealing.

Morley concludes that the way in which media affects audiences is complex, not least because most people belong a multitude of subcultural groups, and their responses may not always be consistent. For example, a young Londoner born to Pakistani parents may feel conflicted when watching a news report on how England defeated Pakistan in a cricket test match.

Questions

1. Morley opted for group interviews because 'much individually based interview research is flawed by a focus on individuals as social atoms divorced from their social context'. What does he mean by this and why might group interviews overcome this problem?
2. The experimental groups in Morley's study watched *Nationwide* in an artificial environment (not in their own homes), with a group of people they did not know well. How might this have affected the results?

RESEARCH IN FOCUS

David Morley: The 'Nationwide' audience (1980)

While working at the Centre for Contemporary Cultural Studies (CCCS) at the University of Birmingham between 1975 and 1979, Morley undertook a detailed analysis of *Nationwide*: a 1970s news programme.

He was interested in discovering '... the extent to which individual interpretation of programmes could be shown to vary systematically in relation to ... socio-cultural background'.

The methodology involved showing two episodes of *Nationwide* to 29 groups then conducting unstructured, group interviews with each. The groups were each made up of people with relatively similar characteristics, for example, 'group 21' consisted of bank managers who were mainly male, aged 29–52, all white and middle class.

Morley found that different groups decoded media messages in different ways, and that media audiences were not passive, but that they used their existing knowledge and prior experiences to come to a decision about whether they agreed with the media messages or not.

Adapted from Morley (1980)

The cultural effects model

The cultural effects model accepts that audience is not a homogeneous group who are all affected in the same way by the media. Instead, a person's social background will affect their interpretation of media messages. For example, some parents may be angered by the violence in traditional cartoons such as Tom and Jerry, whereas children will see it as humorous.

However, the cultural effects model is a Marxist explanation of media effects, and proposes that the media is a very powerful tool in transmitting capitalist ideology in order to maintain a false consciousness in society. As discussed in Section 2 of this chapter, Marxists argue that the bourgeois owners of the mass media use it as a tool of oppression, by spreading capitalist ideology through the television, radio, etc., to encourage the proletariat to believe that social inequality is natural and normal, and that social mobility is possible. This prevents the proletariat from realising that they are being exploited by the capitalist employers, who are paying low wages while reaping the rewards of the profit made.

The cultural effects model disputes that the media has an immediate effect on audiences, as the hypodermic syringe model supposes. Instead Marxists claim that the media has more of a 'drip, drip' effect. In other words, media content gradually spreads capitalist ideological values by transmitting them over a long period of time, so the **cumulative effect** of years of media messages means that most people come to accept the preferred reading of media messages. For example, young children are rarely materialistic, often finding most enjoyment from very simple (and inexpensive) activities such as playing with a cardboard box or chasing each other around. Marxists would argue that the cumulative effect of advertising in the media slowly socialises children to believe that they 'need' material goods such as toys and video games in order to be happy. This benefits the capitalists, who rely on such 'consumption of commodities' to continue to make profit and maintain their wealth.

Philo of the Glasgow Media Group (GMG) studied a range of social groups and found that their interpretation of an intended media message varied depending on their previous knowledge and experiences of that subject matter. In Philo's research, the groups were shown press photographs of the 1980s coal miners' strike, and most participants recognised that the intended message was to blame the proletariat miners, not the bourgeois state or mine owners who may have been responsible. However, those with little experience or knowledge of the strike were most likely to accept the intended media message, whereas those who had previously supported the miners began to question their sympathy for the miners. The remaining few participants vehemently rejected the intended message. This shows how the media is not the sole source of our beliefs, but has the capacity to affect them, especially if we are exposed to consistent messages over the course of many years.

> **KEY SOCIOLOGIST**
>
> **Greg Philo**, part of the Glasgow Media Group (formerly the Glasgow University Media Group), has been very influential in the study of media effects. Taking a Marxist stance, Philo has conducted research into media presentations of the 1980s miners' strike, the Falklands War and the 'troubles' in Northern Ireland.

6.2 Why might methodological issues arise when researching media effects?

A good way to evaluate the sociological explanations of the media's effect on its audience is by questioning how sound the research behind each model is. As shown in this next section, there may be significant methodological issues to be aware of when researching media effects on audiences.

Gauntlett questions whether it is possible to identify any simple mass media effect as many of the sociological explanations outlined above are based on little or flawed research. For a start, much of the research carried out on media effects has been conducted in artificial environments, as shown in Philo's research into the 1980s miners' strike and Morley's research on the 1970s news programme *Nationwide*. In both cases, the participants were shown the media content in groups with people they did not know well, outside of their homes. This is not the way that most people experience the media most of the time, so begs the question of how **valid** the results of the study were. For example, the responses may have suffered from the **'social desirability effect'**, where participants give answers that they think the researchers want to hear.

The social desirability effect may also have been evident in Morrison's study of the Gulf War in 1991. Morrison wanted to establish what media audiences thought the role of the television should be when covering the Gulf War, and how they reacted to television coverage of the Gulf War. This study involved an hour-long structured interview with 1,000 people, and the interviews were conducted in the interviewees' homes. Some of the questions asked the respondents to rate a statement in terms of how strongly they agreed with it, other questions had multiple choice answers.

Different perspective

While methods such as structured interviews are useful for producing quantitative data that is easily comparable (for example to establish differences in responses of social groups), interpretivists would be likely to disapprove of the method as it does not allow respondents to elaborate on their answers.

Gauntlett also criticises many studies of media effects for being rather selective in the media messages they analyse. For example, many sociologists have been interested in the effects of violence in the media on audience members, and there are a multitude of studies into the effects of fictional violence on audience, for example, from horror films and video games, but very little on how violence in factual media such as the news affects audiences. It would be inaccurate to assume that all types of violence in the media, for example, affect all people in the same way, so perhaps some of the models over-simplify media effects.

Research into media effects may also present ethical dilemmas, particularly if vulnerable groups such as children and/or sensitive topics such as violence are to be studied. In 1963, a psychologist named Albert Bandura conducted a laboratory experiment in order to see whether children exposed to violence in the media would imitate the behaviour. The children watched a video that involved a 'Bobo' doll being beaten by an adult, and were then individually taken to a room with a Bobo doll and a box which contained things such as toy hammers. Many of the children began to hit, punch and kick the doll, copying the behaviour they had viewed in the video, and some took the aggression a step further by using the toy hammer to beat the doll too. This study has been heavily criticised for being unethical, and the British Sociological Association's code of conduct states that children should be protected and not exposed to such potentially harmful messages in sociological research. However, it is difficult to imagine a research method which would better show whether violence in the media promotes violence in audience members (and particularly children). Furthermore, not only experiments present ethical dilemmas: a sociologist would need to approach other methods such as interviews and questionnaires with caution, as questioning children (and adults, although perhaps to less of an extent) about how they were affected by violence in the media could lead to distress.

Other sociologists have attempted to overcome the issues highlighted above by using content analysis on secondary data, a research method that does not involve any participants so avoids many of the ethical concerns of other

Figure 5.31 A Bobo doll

methods. Aston University recorded the main news and current affairs programmes over a six-week period in 1991 that coincided with the Gulf War. They then analysed the 300 miles of recordings to look for common themes in the reporting. However, this does not necessarily lead to more accurate data than the experimental methods used by Philo, Morley and Bandura. One main criticism would be that content analysis concentrates on the media message, but not on the meanings that audiences give to media messages, assuming that the audience is passive and not capable of adapting the media content. Therefore, if this method was used to study violence in the media, it would be difficult to draw conclusions of how the content affected the audience without making significant assumptions about the way audiences respond to media messages.

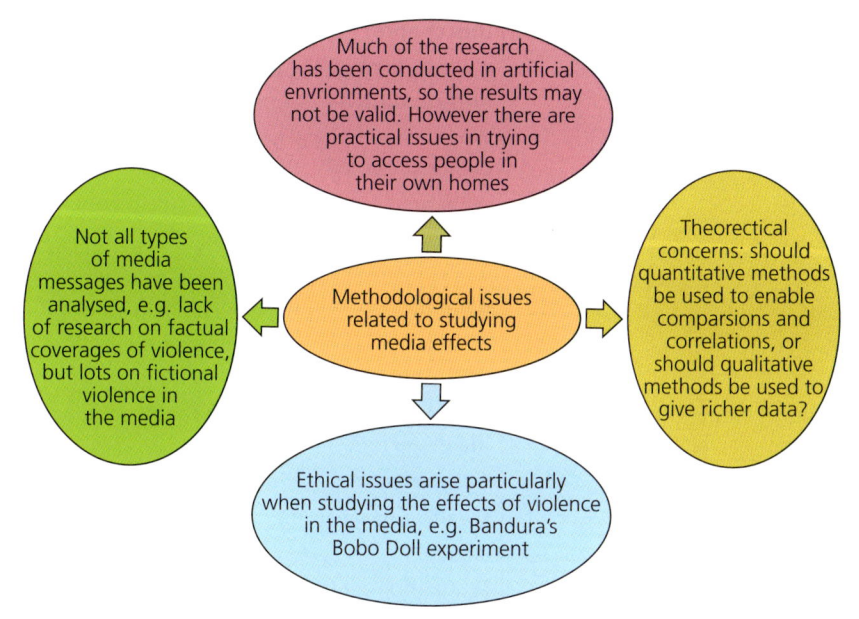

Figure 5.32 Methodological issues and the media

Methodological issues related to studying media effects:
- Much of the research has been conducted in artificial envrionments, so the results may not be valid. However there are practical issues in trying to access people in their own homes
- Not all types of media messages have been analysed, e.g. lack of research on factual coverages of violence, but lots on fictional violence in the media
- Theoretical concerns: should quantitative methods be used to enable comparsions and correlations, or should qualitative methods be used to give richer data?
- Ethical issues arise particularly when studying the effects of violence in the media, e.g. Bandura's Bobo Doll experiment

Check your understanding

1. Suggest ways in which the new media has changed the mass media.
2. What is the difference between traditional Marxist and neo-Marxist views of the ownership of the media?
3. Explain what is meant by newsworthiness.
4. What practical constraints affect the way that news is reported?
5. What impact is global culture having on the media?
6. What is the pluralist view of the media and how might it be criticised?
7. How are men and women represented by the mass media?
8. Using examples, explain how media representations of people from lower social classes differ from those middle or upper classes.
9. Suggest ways in which the two-step flow model is an improvement on the hypodermic syringe model.
10. Identify and explain one similarity and one difference between the cultural effects model and the hypodermic syringe model.

Practice question

1. Outline and explain two models of the way in which audiences are affected by the media. [10 marks]

6 Stratification and differentiation

Understanding the specification	
AQA Specification	**How the specification is covered in this chapter**
Stratification and differentiation by social class, gender, ethnicity and age	**Section 1: Theories of stratification and differentiation** What are functionalist theories of stratification? What are Marxist theories of stratification? What are Weberian theories of stratification? What are feminist theories of stratification? What are postmodernist theories of stratification?
Dimensions of inequality: class, status and power; differences in life-chances by social class, gender, ethnicity, age and disability	**Section 2: How do different factors impact life chances?** Social class? Wealth and income? Gender? Ethnicity? Age? Disability?
The problems of defining and measuring social class; occupation, gender and social class	**Section 3: Definitions and measurements** How should sociologists measure social class? How are occupation, education and social status used in measuring social class? What are the problems of defining and measuring social class?
Changes in structures of inequality, including globalisation and the transnational capitalist class, and the implications of these changes	**Section 4: Structural changes** Have structures of inequality changed? Has the class structure of the UK changed? What is the impact of the global economy on stratification?
The nature, extent and significance of patterns of social mobility	**Section 5: Patterns of social mobility** What are the nature, extent and significance of patterns of social mobility? What are types of social mobility? What are the patterns, changes and impacts of social mobility in the UK? How do we measure and study social mobility?

Section 1: Theories of stratification and differentiation

This section will explore the following debates:

- What are functionalist theories of stratification?
- What are Marxist theories of stratification?
- What are Weberian theories of stratification?
- What are feminist theories of stratification?
- What are postmodernist theories of stratification?

GETTING YOU STARTED

What is a meritocracy?

Figure 6.1 Young's 1958 book, *The Rise of the Meritocracy*

Adapted from Allen (2011)

The concept of meritocracy was developed by Michael Young in his dystopian book, *The Rise of the Meritocracy* (1958), written as a satire of governance of the people by those regarded to possess merit. The point behind the book was precisely to inspire the reader to reflect on the folly of meritocratic life. However, while Young's book succeeded in this respect when it was published in the late 1950s, the word meritocracy has been somewhat reinvented. Much to the anger of Young himself, meritocracy was transformed by neo-liberals and political leaders such as Tony Blair from a negative term into a positive ideal.

The key argument of Young in *The Rise of the Meritocracy* is that a meritocracy only succeeds in perpetuating inequalities, rather than offering a platform of equality of opportunity. Nearly 60 years after its publication many see Young's predictions as remarkably accurate. For example, Britain has an earnings gap between the rich and poor that is wider than most comparative countries. In addition, there are deep-seated and systematic inequalities in income and outcome along lines of gender, ethnicity, social class and geographic location.

But what about the ideal of meritocracy in the twenty-first century? Zygmunt Bauman (2010) neatly sums contemporary society up as one where we no longer 'keep up with the Joneses', but the infuriatingly nebulous idea of 'keeping up with celebrities'. Today individuals have hopelessly naïve ideas about becoming rich, inevitably by becoming a celebrity rather than hard work through the education system. When we live in a symbolic order that stokes up unrealistic aspirations, mundane everyday techniques for maintaining perspective are vital. In the current meritocracy it is necessary to develop practices of self-care that can act to restrain hopes within safe channels.

Questions

1. What was Young's intention in writing his book?
2. How has the word meritocracy been subsequently reinterpreted by neo-liberals?
3. In what ways have Young's predictions proven correct?
4. How is contemporary society summed up by Bauman's quote?
5. Using the item and your wider sociological knowledge, what might the outcome be of such a society with unrealistic aspirations?

1.1 What are functionalist theories of stratification?

Functionalist theories of stratification have positive ideas of inequality and meritocracy in creating a social order that is both fair and efficient in allocating people to their appropriate roles. These ideas will then need to be evaluated.

We saw in Book 1 how the nineteenth-century classical sociologist Emile Durkheim (1857–1917) and the US structural functionalist Talcott Parsons (1951) both saw the function of education as an important agency of socialisation for transmitting common values to the next generation. For Durkheim, schools were like a 'society in miniature' which reinforces norms and values to children in order to bring about value consensus. Parsons, writing in the era of post-Second World War optimism associated with full employment, argued that education prepares children for an achievement-orientated society. In schools, children learn about the importance of hard work, getting on, individualism, and competition. This gives them the values necessary to fit into the achievement-orientated workforce, essential to the smooth running of modern industrial societies. Functionalists like Talcott Parsons view society as a fair and efficient system that benefits the hard working through operating as a **meritocracy**.

Functionalists like Parsons explain the role of meritocracy as twofold: **role allocation** and establishing **social order**. What he saw in his own American society was a coherent and structured social system, held together by a value-consensus whereby the people subscribed to a shared set of norms and values. Functionalists also highlight the specialised **division of labour** which allocates roles on the basis of interdependent skills. Everyone plays their part, from the social elite who organise it all, to the workers in the factories, call centres, retail outlets and services such as health care, education and social care. While society is not equal, functionalists are very positive about the role and functions of society, regarding the rewards from this division of labour as fair. The most talented are assumed to rise to the top of society and therefore deserve to be rewarded with high income and status.

The functionalists Davis and Moore (1945) claim that the primary role of education is to promote a meritocracy by allocating people to this division of labour, via qualifications, to the occupational roles that best reflect their abilities. This process is known as role allocation. By rewarding people differently ensures that the most talented occupy the most challenging roles. Since not everyone has the talent, ability or qualifications to do these functionally important roles of leading business, politics and society generally, those that can should be highly rewarded. Therefore inequality of reward is positively embraced, indeed portrayed as a good thing since it then acts to motivate the rest of society. Society thus functions like an elevator; it lifts those who are capable upwards while bringing the mediocre downwards.

According to Christopher Hayes (2012), for meritocracies to truly measure up to their ideals, they have to comply with two fundamental principles:

1. *Principle of Difference*: whereby the people themselves acknowledge there exists this vast differentiation in merit, talent and aptitude. Having done this, they then have to accept the natural hierarchy that derives from this and allow the system to match the most capable individuals to the most challenging tasks.
2. *Principle of Mobility*: where a competitive selection process enables people to rise and fall along with their accomplishments and failures.

Research evidence shows that most people support the above principles and believe that Britain should be a land of opportunity, where hard work and fairness are rewarded. For example, 2013 research by YouGov found that 78 per cent of the public in Great Britain thinks that 'it should be the government's job to ensure that rich and poor children have the same chances'. However, critical sociologists like Marxists and feminists are very sceptical of the existence of the principle of equality of opportunity. As a consequence they talk of blocked **social mobility** and a risk of 'group think' whereby the elite that runs the country lack an understanding of those with different backgrounds. For society to be more meritocratic, professions like the judiciary, politics, and the media should be more representative of the public as a whole.

Criticisms of meritocracy

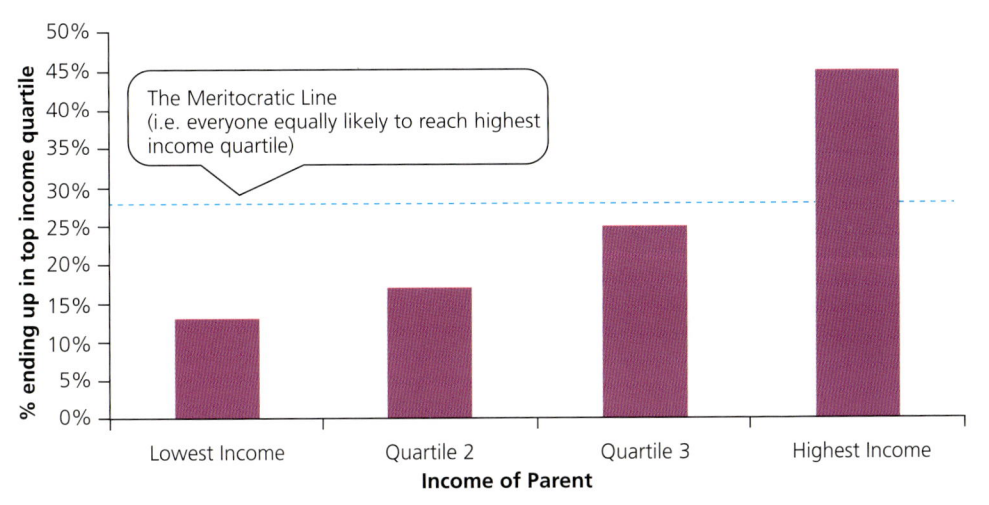

Figure 6.2 The meritocracy myth: children born into high income backgrounds are far more likely to have high income as adults. From Milburn (2014)

- Although only 7 per cent of the population attend private schools, they account for 71 per cent of senior judges, 62 per cent of senior armed forces officers, 55 per cent of senior civil servants, 53 per cent of senior diplomats and 50 per cent of members of the House of Lords.
- Although Oxford and Cambridge educate less than 1 per cent of the population they account for 75 per cent of senior judges, 59 per cent of the Cabinet, 57 per cent of senior civil servants, 50 per cent of diplomats, 47 per cent of newspaper columnists, 38 per cent of members of the House of Lords.
- The implication of this is that there is a huge wastage of potential working class (and to a lesser extent middle class) talent, who are excluded by this private and 'Oxbridge' educated elite.
- Feminists focus on the 'glass ceiling' of sexist prejudice and discrimination that still can act as a barrier to reaching the top jobs. The implication here is of a huge wastage of female talent.
- Researchers of ethnic opportunities still talk of 'snowy peaks' whereby the top jobs are still predominantly occupied by white people. The implication here is a huge wastage of BME talent.

KEY SOCIOLOGIST

Melvin Tumin (1953) found that gender and the income of an individual's family were more important in role allocation than ability. In addition, he was particularly critical of the assumption that the relative importance of a particular job can be derived from its income and status given to those performing it. Instead he turned it around arguing certain jobs appeared inherently important, simply because people received great rewards to perform them.

STUDY TIP

When evaluating meritocracy it is important to retain a sense of balance. While the evidence suggests Britain is 'deeply elitist', this does not mean that it is entirely closed to upward social mobility. As Figure 6.2 portrays, at least 13 per cent of those born into the lowest income quartile (the poorest quarter of society) will rise to the top quartile as adults. However, 75 per cent of society lies below the dotted 'meritocratic line' which represents true equality of opportunity.

Questions

1. Briefly summarise from the item above the findings of Professor Clark.
2. Using the item and your wider sociological knowledge, outline why name may be a particularly important and relevant indicator of social position.
3. Using the item and your wider sociological knowledge, evaluate whether Professor Clark is right about his predictions with regard to children of immigrants.

- Research conducted by the Social Mobility and Child Poverty Commission (2013) found that 65 per cent of people believe 'who you know' is more important than 'what you know'.
- The same report found that 75 per cent of people think family background has a significant influence on life chances in Britain today.
- The very functionalist principle of support for inequality is challenged by the work of Wilkinson and Pickett (2009) who demonstrate that everyone in society (including the rich) are worse off when there is inequality in society. They argue that everything, from life expectancy to mental illness, violence to illiteracy, is affected by how equal society is.

CONTEMPORARY APPLICATION

In 2014 the Commission on Social Mobility and Child Poverty published their report on who is in charge of our country (*Elitist Britain*). It undertook an analysis of the background of 4,000 leaders in politics, business, the media and other aspects of public life in the UK. Its research found a dramatic overrepresentation of those educated at independent schools and Oxbridge across the most influential institutions of Britain. It concluded that Britain is deeply elitist.

IN THE NEWS

Social mobility no easier today than in medieval society

According to Gregory Clark, Professor of Economics at the University of California, who recently presented his results to the Economic History Society at Cambridge, the rate of social mobility in England is substantially slower than most academics believe and possibly worse than in the Middle Ages.

Professor Clark uses the evidence of surnames in England. Starting in the Middle Ages, he looked at three wealthy family names: the Bazalgettes, Du Canes and Willoughby de Brokes. When compared to poorer family names (like Smith derived from being humble blacksmiths in 1300) he found that descendants of those with 'rich' surnames remain substantially wealthier in 2011 and live on average three years longer.

Professor Clark concludes that despite significant state spending on education and health, this has generated no gains in the rate of social mobility. The modern meritocracy is no better at achieving social mobility than the medieval oligarchy. For particularly disadvantaged sectors, like children of recent immigrants, by experiencing possible additional prejudice and discrimination, they have even less opportunities for upward social mobility.

Adapted from Reisz (2011)

1.2 What are Marxist theories of stratification?

Recognise how Marx's dichotomous view of class (as either bourgeoisie or proletariat) could be considered narrow and out of date in discussing the complexities of modern society.

Traditional Marxism

Karl Marx (1818–1883) and Friedrich Engels (1820–1895) did not define social class in terms of income, birth or occupation, but by a person's relationship to the **means of production** (the resources that generate output, such as slaves, land, factories, etc.). Those who owned the means of production become the dominant class. Therefore, all societies with the exception of pre-literate (primitive hunter/gatherer primitive communism) and communism are divided along class lines:

Historical epoch	Dominant class (ruling)	Subordinate class (ruled)
Pre-literate, pre-history	classless – primitive communism	
Ancient society (e.g. Greek/Roman)	master (citizen)	slave
Feudal society (agricultural)	lords	serfs (peasants)
Capitalism (industrial)	bourgeoisie	proletariat
Future communist society	classless – communism	

Table 6.1 Marx's model of historical materialism

Marx's class formation is described as '**relational**', meaning it derives from a person's relationship to the means of production. His concept of class is a **dichotomous** one (there are only ever two classes and people belong to one or the other). The dominant class in every society owns the means of production, whereas the subordinate class owns nothing except its labour power. The two classes are interdependent and, because one exploits the other, **class conflict** inevitably exists. Marx argued that it is this antagonism which provides the driving force for social change.

Marx developed **historical materialism** by borrowing Hegel's idea of the dialectic, which argues that out of conflict of opposing arguments (the *thesis* and *antithesis*) eventually comes new knowledge (*synthesis*). Combining this with the philosophical idea of materialism (that people's behaviour is shaped by the material world around them rather than prevailing ideas) Marx argued that out of class conflict society will inevitably move from one epoch to another. Hence his view that the historical movement from pre-literate to ancient to feudalism to capitalism has been driven by class conflict since the interests of the dominant class can *never* coincide with the subordinate class who have a vested interest in changing society. Marx argued that therefore the shift from capitalism to communism in the future is an inevitable certainty; since capitalism can never be in the interests of the oppressed and exploited proletariat.

For example, under capitalism (which came about when society moved from an agricultural society to an industrial one following the **Industrial Revolution**) exploitation comes about because it is the **proletariat** who produce *all* the wealth. However, the capitalist class or **bourgeoisie** do not pay the workers wages worth the full value of this wealth. Instead they keep the difference as profit (what Marx called '**surplus value**'). Marx described this class

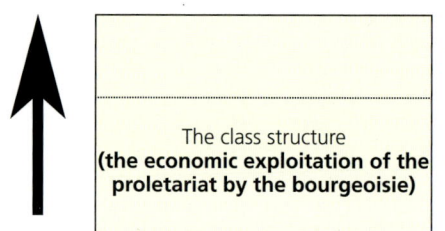

Figure 6.3 Infrastructure and superstructure of Marx's view of capitalist society

relationship which forms the economic base of society as the **infrastructure**. Above the infrastructure lies what Marx called the **superstructure**. This refers to the ideological and cultural ideas that are used to deceive the proletariat into accepting that society is fair. It therefore includes intangible things like political, educational, media and religious ideas that are used to dupe the proletariat through **false consciousness** as to why change (to the fair and equal future society of communism) would be a mistake.

Marx developed the concept of **alienation** to convey how under capitalism people suffer a loss and no longer even know their own self. Alienation has two central and dominant ideas: firstly that alienation is the product of the class structure; and secondly, that as society develops it stands over and against them. The ultimate form of alienation according to Marx is capitalist society where market forces pervade every area of social life and determine how people live and what they do. We lose control over our lives especially in the workplace. Because the proletariat do not own the means of production they have no control over the production process. Their labour is sold for a wage and consequently this becomes a means rather than an end – the focus is to earn income rather than take pride or control in what they do. As workers engage in the cut-throat competition for jobs, promotion and opportunities, self-preservation (keeping your job to provide a roof over your family's head and food on the table) becomes the foundation of **false class consciousness**, undermining any sense of collective class unity or consciousness.

Neo-Marxist models of class

Marx's dichotomous model of class was a fairly accurate description of the nineteenth-century capitalism, but many view it as over-simplistic when applied to the complexities of contemporary society. The American neo-Marxist Erik Wright (1983) begins from the classical Marxist position of seeing society as comprised of two polar classes: the bourgeoisie (upper class) and proletariat (working class). However, Wright recognises certain contradictory class locations that do not fit neatly into either of Marx's dichotomous view of class.

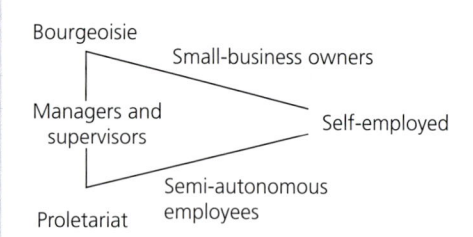

Wright undertook an extensive revision to his model, but again emphasising the need for Marxist class theory to confront the 'problem' of the 'middle classes' - the **contradictory class locations**:

Figure 6.4 Erik Wright's Contradictory Class Locations

Wright (1983)

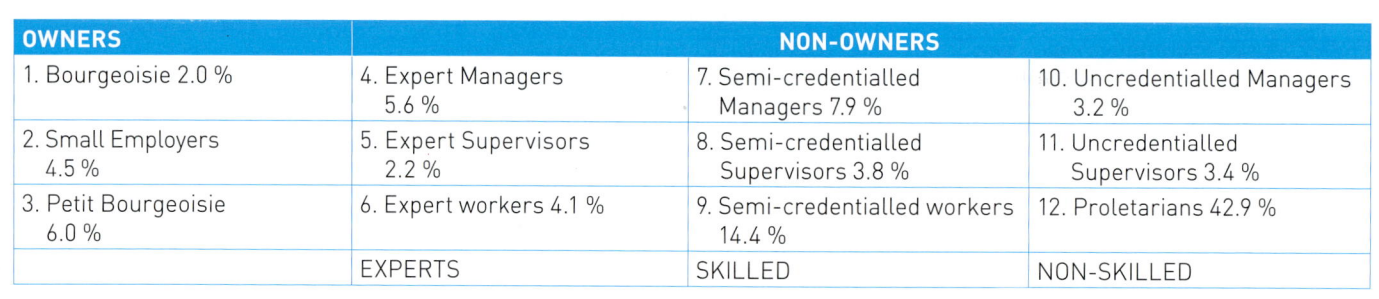

OWNERS		NON-OWNERS		
1. Bourgeoisie 2.0 %	4. Expert Managers 5.6 %	7. Semi-credentialled Managers 7.9 %	10. Uncredentialled Managers 3.2 %
2. Small Employers 4.5 %	5. Expert Supervisors 2.2 %	8. Semi-credentialled Supervisors 3.8 %	11. Uncredentialled Supervisors 3.4 %
3. Petit Bourgeoisie 6.0 %	6. Expert workers 4.1 %	9. Semi-credentialled workers 14.4 %	12. Proletarians 42.9 %
	EXPERTS	SKILLED	NON-SKILLED

Table 6.2 Class Structure and Distribution of Wright's Revised Model

The whole point of his revision was to return exploitation to the centre stage. There are also interesting theoretical aspects of Wright's new scheme with him now favouring a trajectory view of class, rather than a positional one.

Louis Althusser (1918–1990) argued in his book *For Marx* (1965), that the capitalist ruling class maintains its power through state agencies such as education. Althusser referred to any social institution whose purpose was to use ideology to control the working class as an '**ideological state apparatus**' (ISA). The role of ISAs is to reproduce and legitimate (meaning, to justify) the values and culture of the ruling class in such a way that these values are seen by each generation as being natural and inevitable. If ISAs proved insufficient in keeping the proletariat in check, then Althusser notes that governments can use their '**repressive state agencies**' (RSA), riot police and if necessary the armed forces on the streets.

1.3 What are Weberian theories of stratification?

Recognise Weber's contribution of differentiation and his role of taking Marx's ideas forward so that market position and status are recognised as adding layers within social classes.

Max Weber (1864–1920) saw ownership of property as the starting point of defining social class: 'property and lack of property are … the basic categories of all class situations'. In this way his analysis of social class shared the 'relational' characteristics of Marxist theory. However, unlike Marx, Weber believed that there are divisions *within* as well as between social classes. He therefore argues for a more complicated class division based on: 'class, status and party'. Status differences exist within each class, for example linked to rank or skills, and his term 'party' refers to differences in power. Social class, according to Weber, represents a category of people who share a similar market position. Such a market position through determining income, status and power, also shaped a person's **life chances**: things such as good health, employment prospects, housing and living standards.

Weber's approach to understanding social class position is centred on what market situation occupations have. Social class is therefore shaped by factors like levels of pay, status and comparable conditions of employment that employees share. He identified four 'constellations' of social class situations:

- the dominant property-owning and commercial class (similar to Marx's bourgeoisie)
- the property-less white-collar intelligentsia (recognition of the middle class)
- the petty bourgeoisie (owners of small businesses)
- the manual working class (which Weber subdivided according to skill).

For Weber, members of each social class will seek to both protect their market position as well as improving it in terms of the rewards and resources they enjoy. He can thus explain why some manual workers through trade union power have improved their pay and conditions relative to other manual workers. In addition, unlike functionalism and Marxism, Weber can explain the market situation of other groups of workers characterised by factors like gender, ethnicity and age.

Neo-Weberian model of class

John Goldthorpe (1980) developed a schema of class, originally for the Oxford Mobility Study, based on a Weberian framework. It is based on the production of a distinctive set of life chances, lifestyles, socio-political orientation and patterns of association. As a class map it locates in categories occupations that have similar 'market' and 'work' situations.

> **CONTEMPORARY APPLICATION**
>
> With the global rise of neo-liberal ideology, Marx's ideas are currently not very fashionable. There has been an assumption that free-market capitalism results in higher living standards. However, with the gap widening between the very rich and the very poor the gulf witnessed by Marx between the bourgeoisie and proletariat in his lifetime is returning. Between these extremes of wealth and poverty currently lies a heterogeneous and fragmented majority that currently shows no appetite for a communist revolution.

> **STUDY TIP**
>
> Marxist ideas can be difficult to grasp, but they offer a good critique of other theories. By using one theory to evaluate another, you can deepen your understanding of both.

> **KEY SOCIOLOGIST**
>
> **David Lockwood** (1958) applied a Weberian analysis to his classic study of clerks, *The Blackcoated Worker*. This study was centred around the '**proletarianisation**' debate which argued that increasing numbers of white-collar workers saw their work situation as having a lot in common with the working class (or proletariat). Lockwood adopted a Weberian approach in this classic study to show how an occupation's class position derives from a combination of the material (pay) and symbolic (status) rewards.

I	Higher-grade professionals, administrators, and officials; managers in large industrial establishments; large proprietors	Service class
II	Lower-grade professionals, administrators, and officials, higher-grade technicians; managers in small industrial establishments; supervisors of non-manual employees	
IIIa	Routine non-manual employees, higher grade (administration and commerce)	Intermediate class
IIIb	Routine non-manual employees, lower grade (sales and services)	
IVa	Small proprietors, artisans, etc., with employees	
IVb	Small proprietors, artisans, etc., without employees	
IVc	Farmers and smallholders; other self-employed workers in primary production	
V	Lower-grade technicians; supervisors of manual workers	
VI	Skilled manual workers	Working class
VIIa	Semi-skilled and unskilled manual workers (not in agriculture, etc.)	
VIIb	Agricultural and other workers in primary production	

Table 6.3 Goldthorpe's social class schema

> **STUDY TIP**
>
> You should aim to be able to compare and contrast Marxist with Weberian views of stratification, the similarities and differences between them.

> **CONTEMPORARY APPLICATION**
>
> While the Marxist classification remains valid to this day, many felt that this dichotomous view of one class or the other failed to reflect the complexities of contemporary capitalism. The neo-Weberian schema of Goldthorpe does precisely this by differentiating workers (the proletariat) according to their class and market position in the labour force.

1.4 What are feminist theories of stratification?

Recognise not only the role of patriarchy in the oppression of women but the different ways in which the several branches of feminism interpret this source of oppression.

Unpacking patriarchy

The central argument of feminism is that it developed out of the systematic biases and inadequacies of '**malestream**' theories that predominated in sociology before the 1970s. Feminist sociologists argued that it was necessary to develop feminist theories that explain the world from the position of women. As discussed below, there are a range of feminisms, but the one thing they all share is a view that we live in a society dominated by **patriarchy**. This is the assumed superiority of men and therefore how society has been constructed to operate in the interests of men. Feminists argue that society, and even sociology's interpretation of it, has been constructed in a way that reflects the interests of men while serving to conceal women's oppression. Feminist theory is a generalised system of ideas that is a woman-centred perspective in three ways:

1. Its starting point is the position and experiences of women.
2. It views the world from this position of women.
3. It is political; seeking to change the world for the benefit of women.

Kate Millet became a leading light in feminism's '**second wave**', when she published *Sexual Politics* (1970). She documented the inequalities associated with gender and highlighted how patriarchy penetrated society's structures, including literature, philosophy, psychology and politics. Millet saw the family as the key source of women's oppression and portrayed women (as society's key socialisers) ironically complicit in reproducing society's patriarchy. In addition, other agencies of socialisation help reinforce patriarchy. For example, she argued the education system prepared girls for lower paid work in the labour force (a feature that still prevails today with the **gender pay gap**).

Sylvia Walby's (1990) explanation of why gender inequalities exist and how they are sustained centres on the way patriarchy is embedded throughout society. For Walby, patriarchy is a system of six social structures and practices, in which men dominate, oppress and exploit women. Together they capture the depth, pervasiveness and interconnectedness of women's subordination.

Patriarchal mode of production	Relations between women and men in families and households, involving housework, childcare, mothering, etc.
Patriarchal relations in paid work	Horizontal and vertical segregation, unequal pay, sexual harassment, etc.
Patriarchal state	Exclusion of women from access to state resources and power; the state's systematic bias towards patriarchal interests in its policies and actions.
Male violence	Patterned and systematic violent behaviour by men which women routinely experience (wife-beating, sexual harassment).
Patriarchal relations in sexuality	Heterosexuality, with its double standard (one set of rules for women and another for men, which results in men being privileged).
Patriarchal culture	Institutions and practices (the media, religion, education) that create particular representations of women and thereby set out correct forms of conduct for women, shaping their identities and so on.

Table 6.4 Walby's Six Structures of Patriarchy

Figure 6.5 Kate Millet

Walby (1997) would later update her work in order to recognise the impact of an additional third system of oppression of racism. She saw racism as intersecting with capitalism and patriarchy in what she terms her 'Triple Systems Theory'. Walby has been unfairly criticised for focusing primarily on women and their inequalities while ignoring men and masculinities.

Shulamith Firestone (1970) approached gender divisions through the Marxist idea of dialectical materialism. However, where Marx and Engels focused on economic class relations, she argues they failed to recognise the 'sexual substratum' that underpins society. She also challenged Engels' view that male domination came about with private property and the need for monogamous relationships in order for descendants to be identified for inheritance. Instead she argues the biology of childbirth necessitates the inevitable dependence of women and children on men, for protection if not subsistence. As a consequence she makes the bold statement that women will never be liberated until freed from the burden of childbirth.

Ann Oakley wrote *Sex, Gender and Society* (1972) in which she debunked most of the myths that argued gender behaviour was biologically driven. Instead, she showed that gender roles, attitudes and expectations derived from prevailing cultural ideas that were often influenced by traditions and historical precedent.

Figure 6.6 Heidi Safia Mirza

For example, why is it that just because women biologically bear children should they be the ones who rear children? Oakley argues: 'we are now able to disregard (if we wish) almost all the so-called consequences of the reproductive division between the sexes'. She identifies two revolutionary developments, firstly reliable contraception (particularly the pill) that has given women control over their own fertility, and secondly, formula milk powder which now makes it possible to distribute both the work and the joy of childrearing between people regardless of their biological sex. However, the reality is that in the twenty-first century, over 40 years on from Oakley's writing, it is women who still invariably undertake the bulk of childrearing. Oakley sums this up admirably: 'arguments long believed in have an alarming tendency to remain suspended in thin air by the slender string of passionate, often irrational, conviction'. In other words men could share the work (and joys) of childrearing (and some do) but most use the myth of biology and women's 'natural' qualities of nurturing in order to avoid roles and tasks they would prefer not to do. Oakley has continued with this theme through looking sociologically at housework (1974), childbirth (1979, 1980, 1981) and the body (2007).

Heidi Safia Mirza (1992), as a black feminist, played an important role in taking feminism forward into its 'third wave'. She successfully introduced the idea of differentiation, recognising that the female experience was not just shaped by gender, but equally by factors like 'race', faith and culture. Mirza's early work looked at the experiences and attainment of young Black and Asian women in schools. She subsequently went on to research other educational inequalities, including the processes of racialisation in higher education. Mirza can be credited for bringing to feminism postcolonial and black feminist theoretical frameworks. Her work explores and unpacks the inequalities and human rights issues that black and minority ethnic group women experience. Her recent writing continues this theme, exploring key issues associated with multiculturalism and diversity, including issues associated with Islamophobia and gendered violence.

Liberal feminism

A leading liberal feminist is Ann Oakley. While recognising the presence and barriers of patriarchy to establishing a gender-equal society, they are the most optimistic about achieving this goal. They see inequalities stemming largely from male ignorance. Therefore gender inequality can be eradicated through the processes of socialisation, sex-role conditioning and, if necessary, anti-discrimination legislation. Therefore the task of the liberal feminist is to recognise, highlight and challenge all aspects of discrimination and disadvantage experienced by women in their campaign for equal rights. They are essentially reformist, identifying laws and practices that give preferential rights to men and campaigning for these injustices to be removed. Other feminists can be critical of liberal feminism, seeing it as somewhat naïve and lacking in radicalism. As such they can take a more structured view of women's oppression, locating it in the institutionalised ways men have constructed to promote and keep their self-interest.

Marxist/socialist feminism

As their name implies these are both feminists and Marxists. As a consequence they see women as doubly oppressed by both patriarchy and capitalism. They argue that capitalism has created the position of women's dependency on men to fulfil two needs. Firstly, it provides cheap female workers who can be exploited even more than men. Secondly, because housework is unpaid, it ensures that the reproduction of labour (the daily household chore of feeding, cleansing and refreshing workers as well as the long-term rearing of children to become future workers) is undertaken within the family and therefore done cheaply. Consequently, it is far more profitable for capitalism to have women as unpaid domestic labourers than to have to pay male labourers the higher wages they would need to purchase these domestic services in the market place. It is now common for mothers to be workers as well. Veronica Beechey (1977) argues that working mothers are typically in low-paid often part-time work, resulting in them still being financially dependent on their male partners. Beechey refers to women as '**semi-proletarianised**' workers; economically more disadvantaged than even the male working class and constituting a '**reserve army of labour**' (easily hired but the first to be shed in recessions). Marxist feminists therefore see women oppressed not only by the capitalist system but also by the men they live with who expect domestic services. The solution to this oppression is simple: abolish capitalism, the fair and equal society of communism they argue will ensure that gender relations will also become equal.

Radical feminism

This is the most extreme form of feminism which evolved from the Women's Liberation Movement of the 1960s. They hold little sympathy for the Marxist-feminist view that it is capitalism that promotes women's subordination, arguing women were exploited historically long before the origins of capitalism. Instead the source of women's oppression is men and particularly the institution of the family. Some radical feminists see all women in the same sex-class position because of their social control and abuse by men. Patriarchy, they argue, is universal across all societies. Wherever men are, women will be oppressed, regardless of their social class, culture or ethnicity. Radical feminism is based on two important ideas: sexual politics and women's consciousness. Kate Millet sees sexual politics as referring to the unequal power relations that exist between men and women. Men, because of their size and strength, will always be a physical threat to women, including the threat of rape which Susan Brownmiller (1976) argues keeps all women in a state of fear. By raising women's consciousness through sharing experiences, women can develop a sense of shared oppression and sisterhood. Women's liberation can only be achieved by actively challenging the system of patriarchy. Some extreme radical feminists called **separatists** argue that women can only be free when men are isolated entirely from their lives.

Black feminism

As noted above, black feminism came about from a criticism that feminism was preoccupied with the gendered oppression of white women and failed to appreciate that black women are oppressed not only by sexism but racism as well. Black feminists, like Heidi Mirza, became critical of how feminism generally failed to address the interrelations between ethnic group, sex and social class. They argue that in order to eliminate women's subordination, the system of racism must be challenged, alongside patriarchy and capitalism. Black feminists have made an important contribution to examining the specific experiences of black women within families, the education system, sport, the media and paid employment.

Eco-feminism

Vandana Shiva (1999) was one of the first and most prominent eco-feminists. She argues that the attempt to dominate and control nature is a product of a specifically male way of reasoning that developed in Western industrial society. She argues that the rational and scientific thinking associated with industrial

> **KEY SOCIOLOGIST**
>
> **Juliet Mitchell** (1971) used the psychoanalytical ideas of Sigmund Freud to explain why women accept the institutions and ideologies that oppress them. Using Freud's concept of the unconscious she argues that ideas about females and femininity have become so taken for granted that they are unconsciously taken as correct. While the use of psychoanalytic theory still divides the feminist community, growing numbers are using it to explore the psychology of womanhood and femininity.

> **STUDY TIP**
>
> Despite the fact that Marxists largely ignore gender relations and postmodernists regard gender as a concept that is no longer relevant, feminists would claim they have a lot to contribute to our understanding of the meanings and experiences of women.

society was reductionist and based on the suppression of women's ways of knowing the natural world. This scientific and rational worldview is described as androcentric, which means it is dominated by the concerns of men and which marginalises and obscures the interests of women. Eco-feminism therefore works closely with the environment and reflects a desire to protect nature from patriarchal destruction.

> **CONTEMPORARY APPLICATION**
>
> The concept of **post-feminism** suggests that feminism is no longer necessary or relevant anymore. The first argument for this is that 'equal opportunities' have now largely been achieved. For example, girls' performance in education is opening up the workplace, while postmodernist choice offers women escape from men in relationships, marriage, or having children. The second argument is that far from liberating women, feminism has failed them in that they are increasingly burdened with more, not less, work. Thirdly, in something of a backlash against feminism, the New Right identifies feminism as responsible for most of society's problems: such as permissiveness, lone-parent families and rising crime. Feminists would respond that feminism (like women generally) is simply being used as a scapegoat for society's (malestream) problems.

1.5 What are postmodernist theories of stratification?

Evaluate the arguments and evidence in support of the postmodernist idea that class has lost its significance since society has moved from one based on production to an individualistic one centred on consumption.

The essence of postmodernist thinking is that we now live in a significantly different society to the previous modern one based on production and industrialisation. So great is the difference, we can now talk of a distinctly new type of society: *post*modernity. Such a society is characterised by being individualistic and now based on consumption and choice. Whereas previously, the nature of an individual's work would define their status or place in society, now there is much more interest in what people purchase and how they spend their leisure time. It is through their consumption choices that people construct their identity. Sometimes the phrase 'pick 'n' mix' is used to describe the way we shape our identity through the choice we exercise over what we buy. Consequently, postmodernists argue, social factors like social class, gender and ethnicity have ceased to be interesting (or even existent).

Traditionally class has been the key concept for understanding society. However, critics like Pakulski and Waters (1996) argue that it has become a purely historical phenomenon. Used today, they argue, it is reduced to a crude and blunt instrument, incapable of handling the nuances of postmodern society: 'if the proof of the class pudding is in explanatory eating, perhaps the chef needs to be fired' (1996:151). Concentrating on social class is unhelpful since societies are changing from class societies towards ones where stratification is primarily cultural. Societies are increasingly organised around differences of lifestyles, aesthetics and patterns of consumption. In addition, these differences of statuses are reflected in fragmented and complex identities that are fluid, constantly negotiated and changing. The class perspective has become a political straitjacket which diverts attention from more central and morally problematic inequalities.

Consumerism as differentiation: the 'seduced' and the 'repressed'

Zygmunt Bauman (1988) explored the idea of a consumer society and claimed that divisions in society were now formed by creative self-expression through consumption rather than by social class or employment. Such consumer lifestyles are increasingly becoming the means to a sense of belonging, acceptance and membership within society. He called those that are able to consume in an active and effective way the 'seduced' and in this group he included both the wealthy and those with less well-paid jobs but access to credit. Those that are not able to consume effectively he called the 'repressed'; in this group he included not only those on low wages and long-term welfare, but also others who may not be able to consume effectively for other reasons such as the disabled, the elderly and some ethnic minority groups. Status or value is therefore conferred by the way that you spend your money. Moreover, an individual is able to create an identity or image by buying into a particular lifestyle, whereas those that cannot partake may be undervalued or excluded. Thorstein Veblen (1899) referred to the concept of buying into an image as 'conspicuous consumption' when goods are bought solely for their show off rather than intrinsic value.

Style over substance: subjective aspects of differentiation

Dominic Strinati (1999) argues that in postmodernist society surface images and style become important defining features of identity. Iconic symbols and images are increasingly consumed for their own sake rather than for their utility. He argues that usefulness and value gets forgotten since images and signs are consumed precisely because they are images and signs which provide meaning. 'In this process, it is the style not the substance of consumption which matters' (Strinati, 1999:28). Advertising and marketing play an important role here, generating fashions and the latest 'must-have' products that demonstrate style. In addition, television programmes increasingly shape viewers' lifestyles and consumption through coverage of looking good, cooking, shopping, gadgets and fashion. An illustration of this would be the motoring programme *Top Gear* that is preoccupied with top of the range iconic brands of cars and the self-indulgence of its presenters who have become celebrities.

David Grusky (1996) also argues that social class is no longer an effective tool in understanding stratification. As individual identity and choice have become more influential behind lifestyle decisions, so class becomes increasingly redundant. He notes the important role globalisation has played in helping to shape a postmodern consumer society whereby people can access and blend different cultures and ideas through picking and mixing. He contrasts the Weberian concept of life chance with the postmodern idea of 'life choice'. Life choices imply that individuals can exercise a degree of control over their lives, but the outcomes are less certain and carry a degree of risk. So, for example, the pressure to consume makes most two-parent households become dual-earner households. However, working long hours simply to 'keep up' can impact negatively on the relationship between working adults, their children and partners. However, families from all classes will react in similar ways to these challenges; thus bringing about cross-class convergence.

Criticism of postmodernism

Hetherington and Harvard (2014) point out that postmodern society, while apparently enabling people to construct their identities through lifestyle and fashion choices, is just as marked by social divisions and inequalities. While

> **KEY SOCIOLOGIST**
>
> **Jean Baudrillard** (1985) sees the social world in which we live as made up of signs and discourses that refer to each other in a bewildering excess of information and image. Through developments in the media and culture we consume not necessarily objects but these signs and symbols. These signs proliferate over time to the point that we confuse reality with fiction. The images are everything, the reality nothing: a condition Baudrillard terms 'simulacrum'. He gives theme parks (and Disneyland in particular) as an illustration of simulacrum.

> **CONTEMPORARY APPLICATION**
>
> It was thought that shopping malls, sometimes described as postmodern cathedrals for the worshipping of shopping, would cause the decline and end of the department store, a concept that goes back to the nineteenth century. Yet in London both Harrods and Selfridges have never had so many visitors. Selfridges even has a 'click and drive thru' facility.

> **STUDY TIP**
>
> A useful approach to postmodernism is to question to what extent is this a new theory (from a perspective that rejects theory in the first place) or, as critics argue, simply a reorganisation of old and existing structures dressed up as new and different.

> **Questions**
>
> 1. In what ways does this article support or challenge postmodernist views on class?
> 2. In what ways does the school you attend still act as a marker for the rest of your life?

the old class divisions based on production and work might have softened, new social divisions emerge in a market-driven consumer-driven society. Under the banner of freedom of choice, such choices are still largely dependent on income; which for most people is determined by the job they do.

Instead they found that the British class system was becoming more polarised. For example, class divisions were found to be strong and widening, especially between the prosperous elite and the lower classes they termed the 'precariat'. They also found a growing divide between middle and working classes in terms of the amount of cultural and social capital each class possessed and used.

Finally, Marxists like David Harvey (1990) argue that since capitalism is still at the heart of Western society, we can hardly be in a fundamentally new type of postmodern society. Harvey concedes that capitalism operates now under a new flexibility in production with just-in-time delivery, flexible working patterns and zero-hours contracts. However, the cultural changes and growth in individualism and choice are simply capitalism engineering new markets to the pursuit of profit. The diversity, individualism and nostalgia that preoccupy postmodernists, is little more than capitalism manipulating the cultural and social preferences of the moment.

> **IN THE NEWS**
>
> ### Time to stop this obsession with social class
>
> On BBC2's bafflingly pointless documentary series about *Tatler* magazine, one of the staff was worried about which piece of cutlery to use for eating a pear. The answer was quickly resolved by a copy of Debrett's, which each Tatlerite is given upon being hired. If you think it is only the upper classes that have the time to fret about mind-boggling invisible codes involving appropriate behaviour, then consider the media's indignation when ex-MP David Mellor ranted at a London taxi driver. But their indignation was somewhat undermined by their insistence on recording what school and university Mellor attended half a century ago.
>
> Is there another country on this earth that insists on noting what school a 65-year-old man attended in any news story about him? All countries are interested in status – in the USA this is usually expressed by a fascination with money and, increasingly, fame. But only in Britain is there this snobbery over where someone went to school. Class in Britain is defined by seemingly random – but actually deeply significant – things like schools and John Lewis.
>
> When the Labour MP Emily Thornberry took the now infamous photograph during the 2015 General Election campaign of a house in Rochester with a Union Jack and a white van outside the nation spotted the invisible code embedded in that photo and reeled in horror. However, as an outsider I am still at a loss to explain how a text-less photo of a house led to an MP being sacked.
>
> Perhaps Britain's class obsession is a way of consoling itself that old rules still exist, even if the empire doesn't. Heck, you guys can barely hang on to Scotland – no wonder you try to distract yourselves by talking obsessively about schools and cutlery. Oh, and if you are still wondering, the answer to the question of how you eat a pear is with a spoon.
>
> Adapted from Freeman (2014)

Check your understanding

1. What is meant by the term meritocracy?
2. Why do functionalists consider inequality as functional to society?
3. What is meant by Marxists by the term means of production?
4. Briefly explain Marx's model of historical materialism.
5. What does Erik Wright mean by the term 'contradictory class locations'?
6. What are life chances?
7. What did Max Weber mean by market situation?
8. What is meant by third wave feminism?
9. What did Thorstein Veblen mean by the term 'conspicuous consumption'?
10. What does Zygmunt Bauman mean by the 'seduced' and 'repressed' in a consumer society?

Practice questions

1. Outline and explain **two** arguments used to challenge the idea that we live in a meritocracy. [10 marks]

Read Item A below and answer the question that follows.

Item A

The economic base (or infrastructure) is made up of the forces of production. It is argued that development of economic production automatically results in changes in the superstructure; the cultural and political ideas that prevail in society.

Applying material from Item A, identify two key institutions within the superstructure and the ways in which each can promote false consciousness in society. [10 marks]

Read Item B below and answer the question that follows.

Item B

Weber's own view on social class argues that the market is the major determinant of life chances. These can broadly be defined as the chances that individuals have of gaining access to scarce and valued outcomes. Weber argued that the market distributes life chances according to the resources that individuals bring to it. Besides the distinction between property owners and non-owners, people's class position can also be based on skills and other assets. The important point, however, is that all these assets only have value in the context of a market: hence, class situation is identified with market situation.

Applying material from Item B and your knowledge, evaluate the view that a Weberian view of class is more applicable to contemporary society. [20 marks]

Section 2: How do different factors impact life chances?

This section will explore the following debates:
- What is the relationship between life chances and social class?
- What is the relationship between life chances and gender?
- What is the relationship between life chances and ethnicity?
- What is the relationship between life chances and age?
- What is the relationship between life chances and disability?

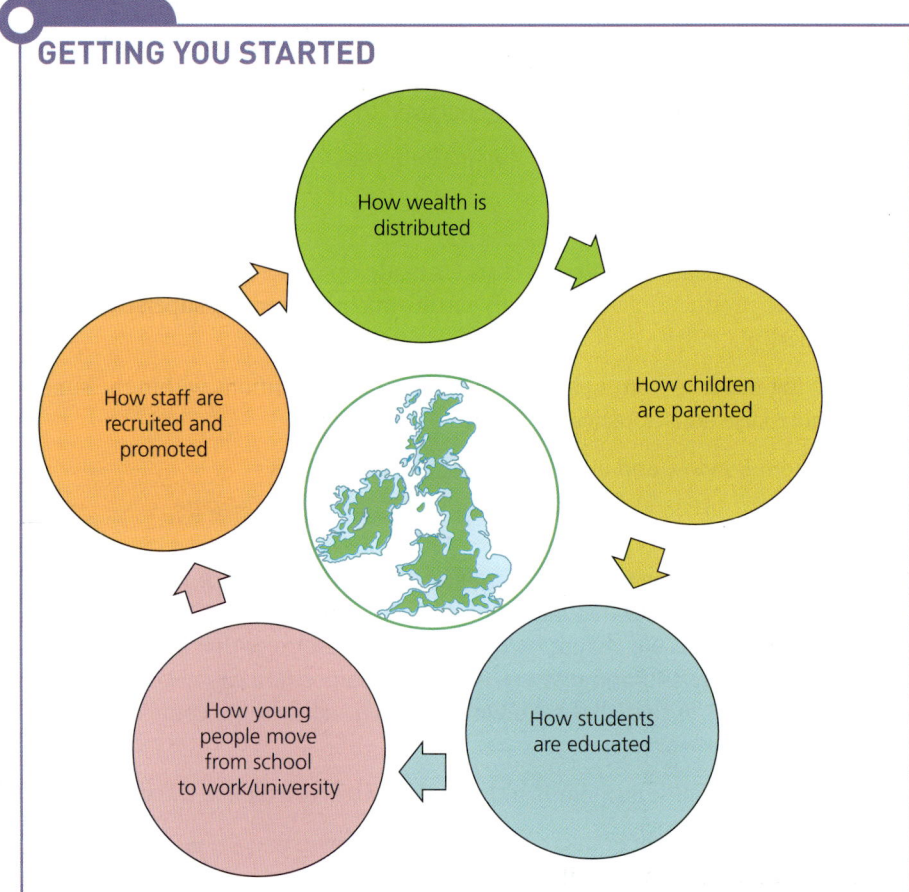

GETTING YOU STARTED

- How wealth is distributed
- How children are parented
- How students are educated
- How young people move from school to work/university
- How staff are recruited and promoted

Figure 6.7 Britain's elite is the product of a complex combination of social factors
Adapted from Milburn (2014)

Questions

Using the diagram above answer the following:
1. How equally is wealth distributed in the UK?
2. How does school and university education shape future life chances?
3. In what ways can home background influence a child's progress?
4. What overall message does this diagram give about opportunities in contemporary UK?

2.1 What is the relationship between life chances and social class?

To explain changes to differences in life chances by social class then you need to examine and discuss explanations of, and changes to, differences in life chances by social class with regard to differences in health, education and work chances.

Social class inequalities, the central concern of Marxists, appear to many sociologists to have little if any relevance to the twenty-first century when so much more is made of racial and gender differences and the focus by postmodernists of highly individualistic lifestyle patterns. This section demonstrates the weakness of such ideas by showing that within Britain a deeply unequal class system survives. At the top is a very rich upper class accounting for the top 1 per cent who own formidable amounts of capital. Beneath them the next 2–3 per cent occupy the elite positions at the top of the professions, senior management in business and the peaks of government and its agencies. Next are those who occupy the next best 30 per cent places in salaried occupations. At the bottom, beneath the proletariat of non-manual and manual workers of differing statuses and incomes, is an underclass of the very poor struggling to live on low wages or long-term benefits. Let us look at each of these classes in more detail.

Upper class

According to Giddens and Sutton (2012) the upper class is shrinking to the point of becoming invisible, however, they concede how they still maintain power and influence. The wealth and exclusivity of this group cannot be exaggerated, although some 'old families' especially of the landed gentry may lack the wealth of past generations. Nonetheless, they are still accepted within this exclusive group for their lineal descent in preference to the 'vulgar rich' of new money. Consequently, an interesting inter-breeding and inter-marriage can occur between new money and families with heritage as they trade wealth for acceptance and respectability. It is sometimes said that this top 1 per cent 'know of' each other and books like *Debrett's*, *Who's Who* and an annual calendar of exclusive sporting and leisure activities enables them to mix socially. Such events also allow the *nouveau riche* (such as celebrities and new money) to participate and, if accepted, join this narrow and closed group of excess and privilege. Through family connections (**nepotism**) and money they have access to an elite education at the top public schools, followed by 'Oxbridge' leading to top jobs (if they choose to work). They embrace and constitute what is known as the **establishment**.

Figure 6.8 The upper class

Middle class

The middle class expanded significantly through the post-Second World War development of a post-industrial society and the growth of service sector employment (see Goldthorpe's schema on page 318). As you learnt in Book 1, the middle classes are seen as sharing certain cultural values in common, such as **deferred gratification** and the importance of **cultural capital** in gaining education success as a means to upward social mobility. However, because of the fragmented and diverse make-up of the middle class, some argue that it is more appropriate to talk about the middle classes. For example, Savage *et al.*'s (2013) classification for the BBC makes the distinction between the 'established middle class' and 'technical middle class'. In

Figure 6.9 The middle class

addition, most (but not all) of the self-employed would classify themselves as middle class. The American Marxist Harry Braverman (1974) notes how many white-collar workers, such as those employed in the lower professions and routine clerical jobs like call centre workers, may be subject to **deskilling** and the process of proletarianisation (discussed in the previous section through the work of David Lockwood (1958)).

Working class

Max Weber's work on market situation highlights the fragmented nature of the working class; made up of skilled, semi-skilled and unskilled manual workers. In the USA skilled manual workers are called 'middle class' and there has been much talk of a blurring between the working and middle class in Britain. For example, the classic *Affluent Worker* study (Goldthorpe *et al.*, 1969) identified the emergence of an instrumental and privatised working class that appeared to show signs of sharing middle-class values. However, the research eventually found strong working class identity with no evidence of **embourgeoisement** whereby manual workers are assumed to take on the attitudes, values and behaviours of the middle class.

Underclass

The very notion of an underclass is controversial. Although the concept itself is Weberian in nature (low status, poor market situation), the most famous proponent of this disadvantaged group beneath the working class comes from the New Right sociologist Charles Murray (1990). Murray adopts a very negative view of such people, seeing them as sharing deviant subcultural values centred on welfare dependency. However, some Marxists, like Jock Young (2007), have also embraced the concept of an underclass. He does not share Murray's disparaging view, but sees them as a particularly poor and disadvantaged group living at the bottom of the class structure. Because their poverty is experienced amid the great wealth of consumer society, he argues the humiliation they feel from in your face capitalism is a 'meta-humiliation' (Bauman and Tester, 2001).

Figure 6.10 The working class

Figure 6.11 The underclass

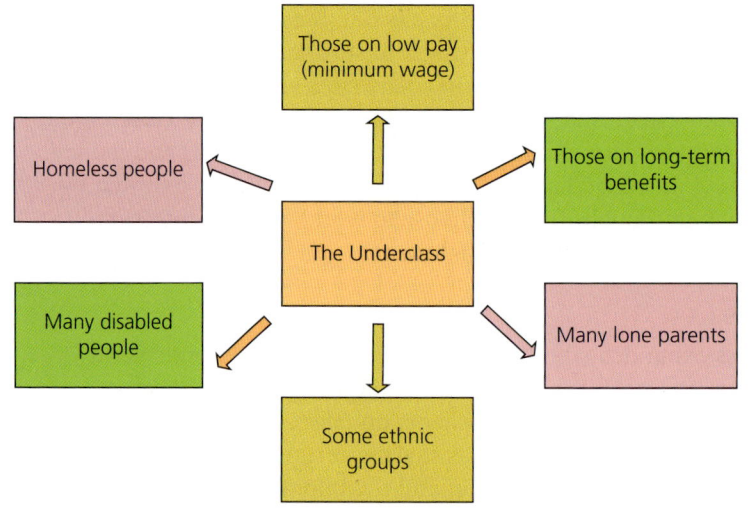

Figure 6.12 The underclass

The Underclass:
- Those on low pay (minimum wage)
- Those on long-term benefits
- Many lone parents
- Some ethnic groups
- Many disabled people
- Homeless people

Social class and life expectancy

Evidence suggests that social class plays a major role in life chances, including life expectancy. The gap in life expectancy between rich and poor is persistent and is larger now than in the early 1970s. Figures from ONS (2014a) show that remarkably 1 in 5 manual workers (almost 20 per cent) die before reaching the current retirement age of 65. This compares to just 7 per cent for professional and managerial workers. After retirement, working-class men and women enjoy fewer years before they die (14 years compared to 18 years for professions like lawyers, teachers and doctors). The Office for National Statistics (ONS) now differentiates between life expectancy (LE) and healthy life expectancy (HLE). This is an important distinction as it highlights that not only do the lower classes not live as long, but may spend a greater proportion of their twilight years in poorer health. The higher social classes therefore live longer and have a higher quality of life after retirement. It is important for the well-being of society that the number of years lived in 'good' health rises faster or at the same rate. If not, then these additional years of life are being spent in poor health and greater dependency, putting additional strain on health and social care resources.

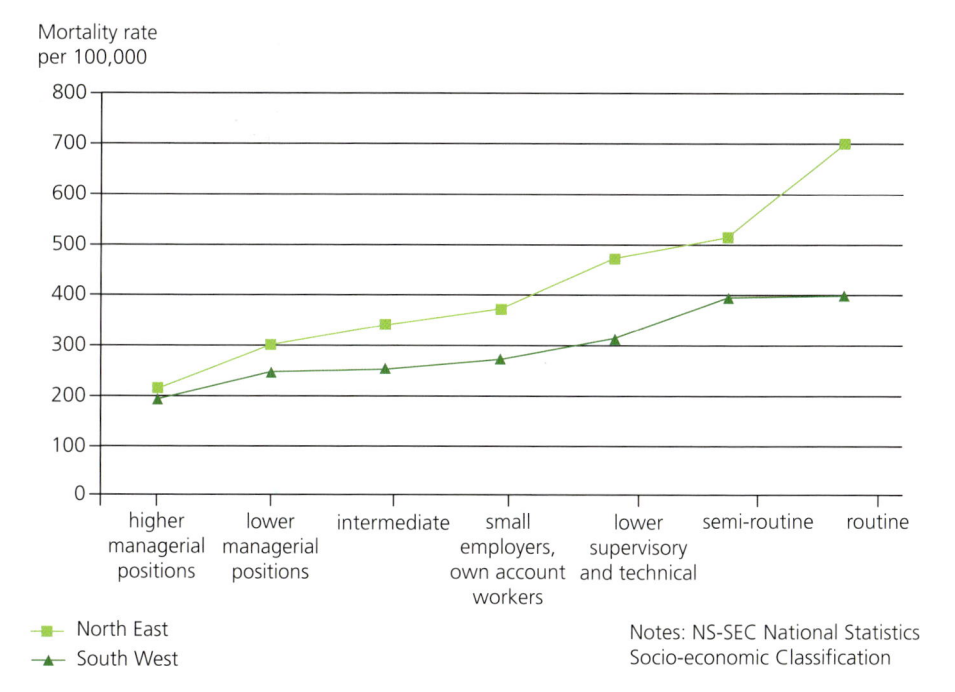

Figure 6.13 The inverse relationship between social class and mortality rate is higher in the North East than the South West. From Marmot et al. (2010)

In research for the Centre for Labour and Social Studies, Danny Dorling (2013) showed that life expectancy is related to the fact that in recent decades, living standards have risen fastest for the richest and only marginally for the poorest (see Oxfam's comparison below). Dorling adds: 'the longer people live in poverty the shorter lives they can expect to live. What we can now be sure of is that as income and wealth inequalities rise, so too do health inequalities'. Wilkinson and Pickett (2009) also regard inequality as harmful because it places people in a hierarchy which increases competition for status, causing stress and leading to poor health. The 2011 Census confirmed that most people experiencing 'not good' health in England and Wales are the least wealthy. Those who had never worked or were long-term unemployed had the highest rates of 'not good' health.

Social class and education

Book 1 showed a clear correlation between social class and education attainment. Children from the higher social classes have much greater levels of achievement. This is due to the rich being able to purchase private education and what is known as 'selection by mortgage' within the state sector, with better schools being generally located in expensive areas to purchase housing. This process becomes self-serving, with middle-class pupils attending the better schools and because of parental expectations and the cultural capital of their homes, boosting the attainment levels of these schools further. Children from the lower social classes, who tend to be served by less well-performing schools, are twice as likely compared to children of higher professional parents to be not in employment, education or training (NEETS).

Distribution of wealth

Wealth is a measure of the value of all of the assets of worth owned by a person and reflects the most unequal distribution and takes the form of money, property, land, stocks and shares and financial bonds. Wealth is therefore a source of **unearned income**. However, defining and measuring wealth is not clear-cut. For example, some people question whether houses and pensions should not be included because of their use-value. So sociologists often refer to **marketable wealth** when talking of wealth. These are assets a person could reasonably dispose of, without interfering too much with everyday life. Housing and pensions are therefore excluded from marketable wealth.

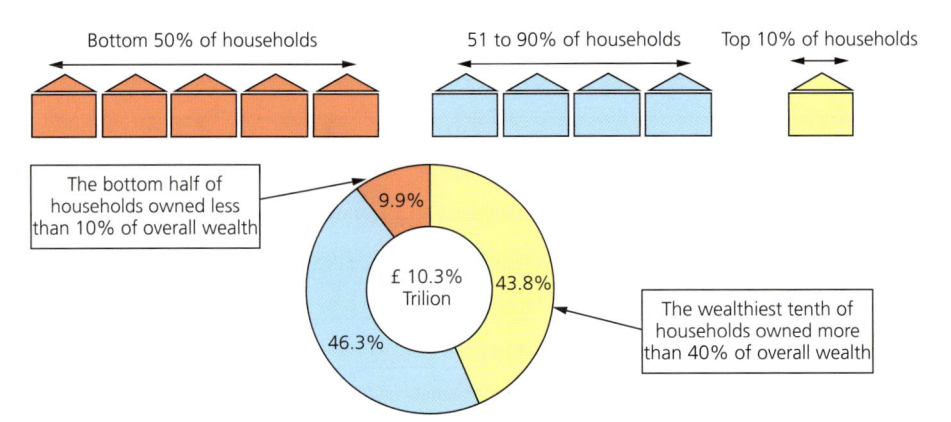

Figure 6.14 Distribution of Total Household Wealth. Adapted from Office of National Statistics (2013)

Bottom 50% of households — The bottom half of households owned less than 10% of overall wealth — 9.9%

51 to 90% of households — 46.3%

Top 10% of households — 43.8% — The wealthiest tenth of households owned more than 40% of overall wealth

£10.3 Trilion

The richest people in the United Kingdom are enjoying record amounts of wealth with the combined wealth of the wealthiest 1000 amounting to £547 billion. To get into the *Sunday Times* Rich List (2015) individuals needed at least £100 million. In 2015 there was a record number of 117 billionaires (in 2005 there were just 60). Many included in the Rich List have come to live in Britain from overseas, often to avoid paying tax by claiming **non-domicile** ('non-dom') status.

The Office of National Statistic (ONS, 2013a) produce a Wealth and Assets Survey (WAS) in order to demonstrate how households manage their wealth in the UK. It divides wealth into four categories:

- property wealth (including second homes, property to rent)
- physical wealth (including household contents, cars, paintings, antiques)
- financial wealth (including savings accounts, ISAs, shares)
- private pensions (the accrued value of private and company pensions).

Personal wealth is very unequally distributed in the UK. For example, the richest family (Gerald Cavendish Grosvenor and family) own more wealth than the poorest 10 per cent of the population (6.3 million people). According to Oxfam

(2014a) the five richest families in the UK are now wealthier than the bottom 20 per cent of the entire population. That means just five households have more money than 12.6 million people put together – almost the same as the number of people living below the poverty line. It is worth remembering that many people within the working and middle classes can have negative wealth. This stems from the common occurrence of large debts associated with loan arrears, outstanding balances on credit cards or student loan debts.

Global wealth inequality

Britain's growth in multibillionaires reflects a wealth explosion occurring globally. Oxfam (2015) reported that in 2014, the richest 1 per cent of people in the world owned 48 per cent of global wealth, leaving just 52 per cent to be shared between the other 99 per cent of adults on the planet. Oxfam argues that if the trend of wealth accumulation of the rich continues then the top 1 per cent will have more wealth than the remaining 99 per cent of people by 2016. The collective wealth of this richest 1 per cent is $110 trillion; 65 times the total wealth of the poorest half of the world's population.

Distribution of income

Whereas wealth is an asset, income is a flow concept, and refers to the incoming flow of resources over time. It comprises four constituent parts:

- earned income from employment (including self-employed)
- income from state support (including benefits, tax credits and state pensions)
- income from private pensions (including occupational and personal pensions)
- income (such as interest from savings or rent from property).

The distribution of income in the UK is drastically unequal. Oxfam (2014) describe income inequality as a serious problem facing the UK. Oxfam go on to point out that between 1993 and 2011 the incomes of the top 0.1 per cent grew by 101 per cent, almost 4 times faster than the incomes of the bottom 90 per cent of the population which grew by 27 per cent. What this means in real terms is that the richest 0.1 per cent saw their income grow in real terms by more than £461 a week, the equivalent of over £24,000 a year (enough to buy a small yacht or a sports car). By contrast the bottom 90 per cent experienced a real terms increase of only £147 a year (insufficient to insure a family car and equating to just £2.82 a week: as Oxfam put it, the price of a large cappuccino).

Explanations for the widening income gap

Since the 1980s there have been successive cuts in **progressive taxation** (whereby tax as a percentage of income increases as income rises) such as income tax. Even the coalition government's policy of raising the threshold at which workers start paying tax from £7,000 (in 2010) to £10,500 (2015) has benefited the higher off more than poorer earners. Firstly, if low-paid workers earn too little to pay income tax, raising the threshold offers no benefit to them at all. Secondly, the poor suffer most from taxes like VAT (currently 20 per cent on most goods and services) and council tax (even allowing for council tax benefits) rather than income tax. Claiming that raising the threshold of income tax takes 'poor families out of paying tax' is misleading as they still pay national insurance, VAT, excise duties such as on petrol, tobacco and alcohol, and council tax. Thirdly, the cost of raising the tax-free thresholds in income tax has been financed by benefit reforms and cuts. Therefore those with incomes in the bottom half have lost more on average from benefit and tax credit changes than they have gained from the higher tax threshold.

Since the 1980s there have been successive increases in **regressive taxation**, such as VAT and excise duties (where tax as a percentage of income decreases as

> **KEY SOCIOLOGISTS**
> **Westergaard and Resler** (1976) undertook a Marxist appraisal of the class structure of Britain. Their evidence supported the fundamental claim of Marx that because of the exploitative nature of the capitalist system, social class is still the main form of inequality in Britain. They found clear evidence of a powerful ruling class based on a concentrated ownership of private capital. Twenty years later John Westergaard (1995) concluded that privately owned wealth had become even more concentrated.

> **CONTEMPORARY APPLICATION**
>
> Statistics from the Department for Education (DfE) show the link between social class and educational attainment. In 2009/10, for example, 76 per cent of children from higher professional backgrounds achieved five or more GCSE grades A*–C, compared with only 32 per cent from routine worker backgrounds. Although the performance of all children has improved, the gap between the top and the bottom is wider and these social class inequalities in educational attainment are more marked than ever. One of the best measurements of social class is eligibility for free school meals (FSM). Only 30.9 per cent of pupils eligible for FSM achieved five or more A*–C grades at GCSE or equivalent including English and mathematics GCSEs, compared to 58.5 per cent of pupils not known to be eligible for FSM.

> **STUDY TIP**
>
> It is worth remembering that social class divisions are the most important and significant. Although there are divisions associated with gender and ethnicity, class will also influence these.

> **Questions**
>
> 1. How much wealth does the richest 10 per cent own compared to the poorest 10 per cent?
> 2. How does the article explain the connection between deprivation and poor health?
> 3. What are the sociological implications made in the last paragraph?

income rises). Everyone pays indirect taxes added to the price of commodities and services, including children, and those on welfare including the unemployed and pensioners. When VAT was raised to 20 per cent in 2010 the coalition government claimed it was a 'progressive tax'. This is clearly untrue because indirect taxes like VAT are regressive because everyone pays the same tax on whatever they buy; it has a disproportionate effect on those on low incomes.

Social class and education

Book 1 showed that social class remains the strongest predictor of educational attainment. According to Perry and Francis (2010) the UK has one of the most significant social class gaps for educational attainment in the developed world. This stems partly from, as noted above, the impact of the private education system whereby those who can afford it purchase privileged education as well as post-school benefits such as 'old school tie networks'. But within the state sector, factors like **deferred gratification**, cultural capital (Pierre Bourdieu) and **selection by mortgage**, collectively ensure that the middle class as a group significantly outperform the working class as a group. Marxists, such as Paul Willis (1977) go as far as to argue the education system is stacked against the working class and indeed designed to fail significant numbers. If everyone achieved the benchmark of 5 A*–C GCSEs (including maths and English) who would do all the low-paid dead end jobs so important to society? In addition, young people categorised as NEET (not in education, employment or training) are disproportionately working class.

> **IN THE NEWS**
>
> ### A 25-year gap between the life expectancy of rich and poor Londoners
>
> The UK now has a staggering and unusually high level of economic inequality: the richest 10 per cent now have 850 times the wealth of the poorest 10 per cent. As economic inequality has risen, so too has health inequality.
>
> Income inequality, relative poverty, unemployment, underemployment, insecure and volatile incomes and the low-pay economy many are now stuck in, all have a negative impact on people's health. Quite understandably, the relentless grind of life at the bottom of the heap takes its toll on a person's physical and mental well-being. The lazy stigmatising of poor people as junk-food munching wastrels hardly helps either.
>
> The solution to health inequalities is not to try and change people's health-related behaviours – a crass, ineffective approach that often fails to address why they have them in the first place. The key is to deal with the underlying issues of economic inequality.
>
> Life expectancy inequalities should be seen as a sort of canary in the coalmine. Not only do they reflect all the other inequalities that afflict the UK – in income, education, social class, social mobility, life chances; but they also point towards future problems.
>
> A country that allows its poorest citizens to die 25 years earlier than its richest is one that is likely to suffer from a worrying breakdown in the social fabric that binds society. This is far more than a health issue; it is an issue of how we see ourselves as a country, and how we treat the most vulnerable in society.
>
> Adapted from Pickett and Wilkinson (2014)

2.2 What is the relationship between life chances and gender?

When writing on gender life chances then you need to credit feminist theory for highlighting examples, evidence and explanations for gender inequalities wherever they exist in society. The expressive role of women, gender socialisation and the reserve army of labour are particular issues. In addition, it is worth emphasising intersectionality; that is, each woman and man's experiences will also be shaped by social class, ethnicity and age.

Gender socialisation and the 'expressive role'

Feminists argue that gender socialisation still plays a major role in shaping life chances, even in the twenty-first century. Ideas like those of Talcott Parsons (1951) that the difference between men and women's roles is innate and biological, were prevalent in the 1950s but receive little support today. However, within common sense thinking there is still support for the expressive role of women as primary homemakers and caregivers, and the instrumental role of men as primary providers and breadwinners (see Book 1, page 177). Parsons argued the naturalness of these roles had to be reproduced through proper socialisation. Nonetheless, society reinforces them by the way women are assumed to be the natural and primary child-rearers, and the way paid employment is gendered. Since then, anthropological studies have brought to light societies where gender roles are expressed entirely differently to Parson's description. For example, Margaret Mead (1935) studied the Mundugumor society in New Guinea where women are as assertive as men and completely lack any maternal desire to bear or rear children. Such examples show that gender roles are learnt and challenge Parsons' idea that they are innate.

Feminists have long pointed out how much of women's paid work seems to be a simple extension of their domestic work: cooking, cleaning, childcare, or clerical work which traditionally involved supporting men. While women's employment has broadened and expanded over time Arlie Hochschild (1983) argues women are more likely to do emotion work for pay. That is, many roles dominated by women are based on or require a large amount of 'emotional labour'. For example, a flight attendant is obliged not only to smile but to try to work up some warmth behind it. According to Hochschild, emotions are reduced to commodities, bought and sold on the market. Once we sell our smiles, we no longer own them, and they are used by capitalists to produce profit. Jobs that call for emotion labour effectively require the worker to produce a positive emotional state in another person. Women seem preferable in this role. Hochschild's ideas are also replicated in George Ritzer's concept of McDonaldisation (see page 194) and Ken Robert's 'new working class' (see page 374).

Feminists argue that gender behaviour is still learned and socialised from an early age. There is clear evidence that children are aware of sex roles by the age of two. A child's early experiences are almost all contained within the family, the primary agency of socialisation and reinforced over time by the secondary agencies like education, peer group and the media. Consequently, social conditioning about appropriate gender roles is both handed out and received in conscious and unconscious ways. The feminist Ann Oakley (1972) identifies four processes of socialisation that take place in the home:

- Manipulation describes how girls receive far more fussing and grooming with regard to their dress and appearance.
- Canalisation refers to the way toys, books and games are often blatantly sex-differentiated.
- Verbal appellation is the gendered language boys and girls (even babies) are spoken about, such as boys tend to be discussed in terms of strength while girls tend to be discussed in terms of appearance and prettiness.
- Activity exposure refers to identifying with and practising specific gender roles, such as washing cars, making cakes.

Postmodernists would argue that such practices are quite stereotypical and emphasise the shift towards individualisation where specific qualities of choice, character and achievement transcend gender. In addition, within their childrearing practices, many parents are actively challenging the more prevailing and ingrained attitudes and values with regard to traditional gender roles (see In the News below). However, it is naïve and simplistic to solely talk about gender socialisation without acknowledging the role of factors such as social class, ethnicity.

IN THE NEWS

Fathers able to share parental leave from April 2015

According to Jo Swinson MP, the coalition government equalities minister, men are too often mocked in the workplace for wanting to go part-time or leaving early to pick up their children. She criticised the 'cultural double-standards' and said it was not right for men to be disparaged for wanting to work less to spend more time caring for their children. Many men now want to leave at a particular time or take an afternoon off to watch the school play but do not feel they can because of workplace and employer attitudes.

Swinson states: 'It is a symptom of how we have cultural double standards in many workplaces, where for women to take flexible working or leaving early on a particular day to pick up the kids from nursery is deemed to be acceptable but for some reason we treat a man who is making the same choice differently.'

The government has now proposed that parents can share 12 months of leave after the birth of a child. Such a proposal is aimed at both helping women return to the workplace and reflects how increasingly men want to have more involvement in caring for new babies. Swinson says more must be done to encourage men to take up their rights and questioned a culture in which men who take their family responsibilities seriously are 'ribbed'.

'Once you had a more diverse mix around the table, when people were acknowledging external responsibilities at the same time as doing an excellent job, men felt like they could also play their role as a father alongside their working role and the two didn't have to be in such conflict.'

Adapted from Mason (2013)

Questions

1. According to Swinson what problem do many men experience in the workplace?
2. Why do you think we have 'cultural double standards' according to Swinson with regard to men and women leaving early?
3. Outline reasons why men might not want to take parental leave.
4. Why do you think employers opposed changes discussed in the article?
5. Evaluate the impact on women of men becoming more home and child-centred.

Gender and life expectancy

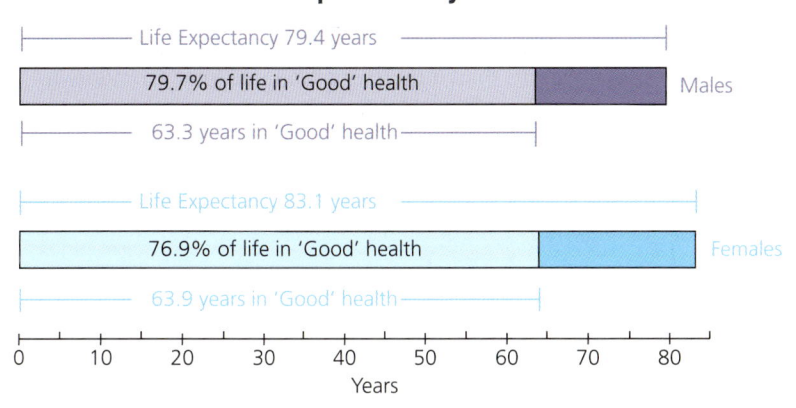

Figure 6.15 Life expectancy (LE), healthy life expectancy (HLE) and proportion of life in 'Good' health for males and females at birth in England, 2011 to 2013. Adapted from Office of National Statistics (2015)

Although females can expect to live a longer life, males generally expect to spend a larger proportion of their lives in 'good' general health compared with females. Life expectancy at birth for both females and males in the UK has reached its highest level on record. Women's life expectancy has increased to 83.3 years (2014) compared to 79.2 years for men. This gender gap in life expectancy is beginning to narrow. Around half the difference in the longevity between the sexes can be explained by smoking and male cessation rates explains why life expectancy has been improving more for men than for women. Other factors include increased alcohol consumption by women and a growth in obesity levels. Although obesity levels are similar between men and women, they can have a greater impact on women because it increases the risks of both hypertension and diabetes. Underpinning these figures is also a person's social class background. Middle-class men and women tend to live longer than working-class men and women.

Gender and education

As noted in Book 1, females outperform males at all levels of education from primary school to university. For example, taking the government's benchmark of achieving five A*–C at GCSE, the female rate in 2014 was 73.1 per cent compared to just 64.3 per cent for males; a gap of 8.8 percentage points. In addition, before the school leaving age was effectively raised to 18, females had a higher staying on rate post-16 and are more likely to go on to higher education (university) than males. The Higher Education Statistic Agency (2013) states that there were a total of 935,920 females on all courses compared to 785,475 males. However, official figures from parliament show that females made up 57.0 per cent of 16–24-year olds classified as NEET, in 2014. 549,000 women aged 16–24 were NEET compared to 414,000 men. Most women who are NEET are inactive, but most men who are NEET are looking for and available to start work. Around 60 per cent of women who are NEET and inactive reported that they are not looking for or available for work because they are looking after family or home.

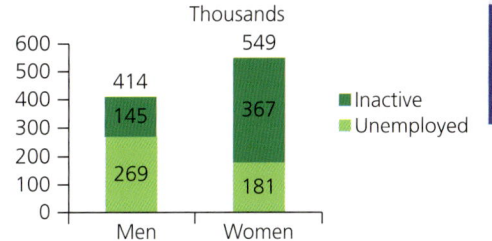

Figure 6.16 Inactive and unemployed NEET by gender, 2014. Adapted from Mirza-Davies (2015)

Gender and work

As the TUC (2012) note 'women's employment has been the great success story of the last 40 years'. According to ONS (2013b) although there are more men in employment (15.9 million compared with 14.0 million women), 67 per cent of women aged 16 to 64 were in work, an increase from 53 per cent in 1971. For men the percentage fell to 76 per cent in 2013 from 92 per cent in 1971 (see also Sara Arber's 'The price of being female', page 363). It notes that because women's income accounted for more than a quarter of income growth in low to middle income households since the 1960s they have been the 'driving force' behind improvements in household living standards. In addition, in 2014 the gender pay gap narrowed, to 9.4 per cent; the lowest since records began in 1997 (ONS, 2014b).

Women as a 'reserve army' of labour

Looking at the workforce more closely, however, tempers this celebration of women's participation: According to the TUC (2012), 28 per cent of women are in low-paid work, compared to 17.2 per cent of men. This is attributed to the high numbers of women who have part-time jobs.

Women's position in the labour market has been described as a '**reserve army of labour**'. A major function of this 'reserve army' is to reduce the wages across the board. Veronica Beechey (1986) identifies a number of ways in which involving women in the workforce helps lower wages. Beechley says women are:

- less likely to be unionised
- easier to 'hire and fire' as part-time workers with fewer employment rights
- able to 'disappear' back into the family as mothers and housewives
- flexible workers prepared to work part-time
- prepared to work for less because they are, in any case, considered 'secondary breadwinners'.

However, **substitution theory** offers a critique of the 'reserve army of labour' concept, pointing out that capitalism benefits from keeping women in employment in recessions as they are cheaper to employ than men. In recent recessions in Britain, for example, women's employment rates have not declined more than that of men.

Vertical and horizontal segregation

Women's position in the labour market is also affected not only by structural factors like **vertical segregation** (where the top jobs in an industry are dominated by men, often protected by a '**glass ceiling**') and **horizontal segregation** (the traditional employment areas that attracted either mainly men or women) but constraints reinforced by stereotypical assumptions of their role within the home. Although Talcott Parsons' (1960) assumptions of an 'expressive role' (to men's 'instrumental role') is now outdated, assumptions about women as the primary child-rearer remain. Consequently women are less likely than men to occupy higher-paid managerial and professional jobs. In 2015 women held only a third of managerial jobs. Women also seem to be located in a narrow range of jobs referred to as the five 'Cs': caring, catering, cashiering, cleaning and clerical work. For example: 19 per cent of women are employed in administrative or secretarial work compared with just 5 per cent of men; 15 per cent of women are employed in the personal services compared to 2 per cent of men, and 10 per cent of women work in sales compared to 5 per cent of men.

Occupation	% Female
Caring, Leisure and Other Services	82%
Administrative and Secretarial	77%
Sales and Customer Service	63%
Professional	50%
Elementary	46%
Associate Professional and Technical	43%
Managers and Senior Officials	33%
Process, Plants and Machine Operatives	11%
Skilled Trades	10%

These occupation groups are dominated by women–…

…–these have a fairly equal gender split–…

…–and these are dominated by men.

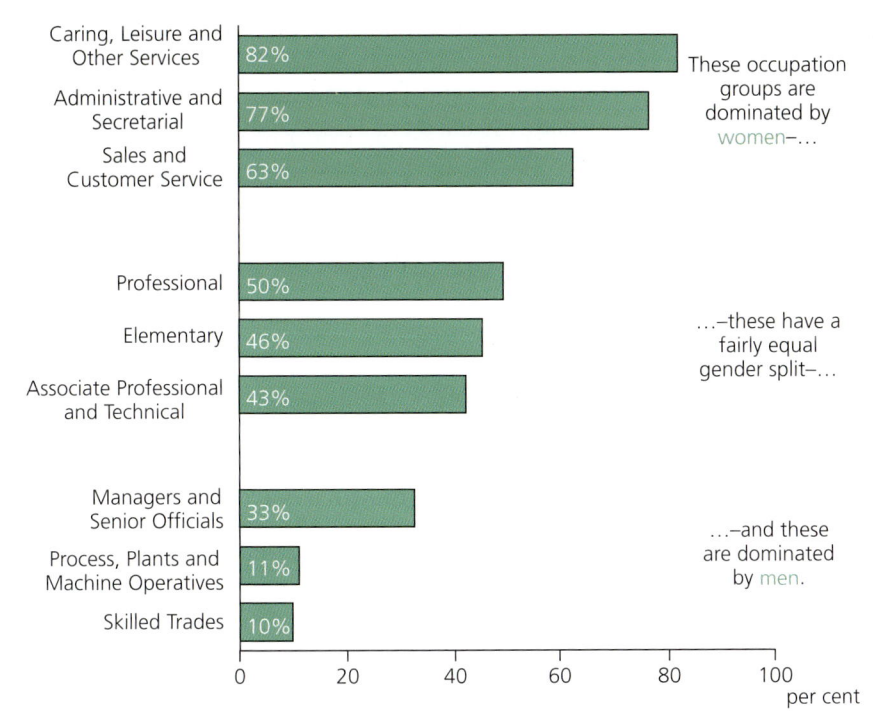

Figure 6.17 The percentage of the workforce that is female according to employment areas (2013). Adapted from Office of National Statistics (2013b)

Barron and Norris (1976) explain women's inferior position in the workplace in terms of their 'dual labour market theory' made up of 'primary' and 'secondary' markets. This is a similar idea to that of Michael J. Piore (1995) studied in Book 1. Many female workers are confined to the secondary labour market characterised by low wages, low status, low skills and insecure employment relationships with little or no prospect of promotion. Barron and Norris liken women's position in the secondary labour market to the Marxist concept of a reserve army of workers serving the profitability of capital by having access to a pool of easily expendable labour. They also refer to the mechanisms by which women remain in the secondary labour market. These include not being promoted and failing to plan institutionally to ensure women are not disadvantaged through child-bearing.

Catherine Hakim (1995) controversially argued through 'preference theory' that women choose to work part-time because of a commitment they feel towards their home and family. She argued that they were 'uncommitted' workers who have chosen flexible hours to fit in with domestic priorities. This implies that many women choose work in the secondary labour market since it can offer flexibility to work around their children's schooling. Hakim argues that it is women's choices (rather than structural constraints) that shape patterns and types of women's work. In addition, the heterogeneity of women's employment statuses derives from the preferences they show towards having a career or choosing to look after children:

> '… there are at least three types of career rather than just one: the *truncated career* that probably ends with (delayed) marriage or babies, the *adaptive career* that demands a large element of work-life balance over the lifecycle as a whole, and what I have called the '*hegemonic*' or '*greedy*' *career* that can easily become all-consuming, especially at senior levels' (Hakim, 2006, **emphasis added**).

> **KEY SOCIOLOGIST**
>
> **Jon Swain** (2014) found that both girls and boys feared being labelled by other pupils as a 'boff'. In addition, girls and boys maintained a precarious balance between achievement and sociability. The majority were not prepared to take the risk of being seen as conforming too closely to the official school regime by working too hard, and often chose the option of playing safe and 'hiding' in the middle. This goes some way to explaining why many girls and boys do not work particularly hard in the classroom.

> **STUDY TIP**
>
> While feminists are right to highlight gender inequalities, it is worth bearing in mind that social class is still the greatest divider in contemporary society.

Sue Sharpe (1981) found that assumptions about women being the primary carer develop in the early months of motherhood, when fathers tend to participate less. This creates an imbalance in the practical and psychological responsibility for the children. Therefore, men are assumed to be less involved in or fulfilled by parenthood than women. It is also assumed that caring for children provides mothers with the greatest satisfaction in their life. For some mothers, this may be the case, but for others it is never so. There is pressure on women to stay at home with their children, whether they want to or not, and this has generated guilt and anxiety in those that return to work.

Changing nature of work for men

Susan Faludi (1999) argues that because of commodification of modern society and rampant consumerism, men are now experiencing a profound crisis of self-doubt as their self-worth and usefulness becomes ever smaller. She sees the workplace as increasingly threatening to men through rising unemployment, shrinking pay, longer hours and perpetual fear of redundancy. All these factors serve to undermine the secure 'breadwinner' role they once enjoyed as males. However, men are also threatened from marriage and relationships, which are no longer as stable as they once were. In addition, men's role in the community – church, politics and local associations – has also been diluted.

The strength of female emancipation, independence and power is perhaps most forcibly expressed through debates that 'men are in crisis', 'men are now the oppressed and weaker sex', and 'men no longer know what women want or how to satisfy them'. The Equality and Human Rights Commission receives more complaints about unequal opportunities from men than women. Web sites like Families Need Fathers highlight how fathers feel the courts treat them unfairly over custody decisions following separation and divorce.

2.3 What is the relationship between life chances and ethnicity?

When writing on ethnicity and life chances prejudice, discrimination and institutional racism are particular issues. Remember intersectionality, experiences within ethnic groups, will also be shaped by social class, gender and age.

The term ethnicity is always preferred by sociologists to 'race'. The use of quote marks around it reminds us of its problematic nature. The concept of 'race' is viewed as a **social construction** because of its limited biological basis. It only becomes an important social category because of the differential treatment people can receive through prejudice and discriminatory behaviour and institutional racism. Robert Miles (1989) argues that the concept of '**racialisation**' (the process of defining people in terms of biological characteristics) should be used instead. Ethnicity derives from the Greek word 'ethnos', and refers to groups who share certain common attributes. It is often associated with strong subjective identification, as well as objective characteristics linked to shared culture, language, religion or geographical ancestry. Issues surrounding 'race' and ethnicity only become problematic when differentiation occurs based on perceived biological differences. Ideas of white supremacy have existed since the days of colonialism and were reinforced by nineteenth-century social Darwinists like Herbert Spencer (1864) who argued the Caucasian race was more evolved than other races. Such ideas have since been discredited, but are still used by racists to justify supremacist positions and behaviours.

Theoretical analysis of ethnicity

Marxists, such as Robert Miles (1993) argue that racial inequality is rooted in the social inequality of the economic class structure. Capitalists are viewed as constructing and exploiting racial divisions in order to set members of the working class (**proletariat**) against each other rather than the system. **Racialism** is therefore viewed by Marxists as a means by which the ruling class maintains control. By creating hostility and conflict, weaker ethnic groups can be blamed for the problems of capitalism such as unemployment, shortage of housing, falling educational standards, etc. Marxists argue that hostility and the scapegoating of minority ethnic groups is evidence of **false consciousness**. However, some neo-Marxists challenge the **reductionist** approach of traditional Marxism. For example, the Centre for Contemporary Cultural Studies (1982) argue that 'race' operates separately from other social relations, but at the same time affects class. The book *The Empire Strikes Back* (1982) advocated that class and 'race' needed to be reconceptualised as relatively autonomous, and could only be understood when analysed together.

Weberians see 'race', like Marxists, as largely an ideological construction that is used to justify discriminatory treatment. If ethnic minorities suffer disadvantage in employment or housing it is because they lack a strong market position. In a classic study, Rex and Tomlinson (1976) studied the Handsworth area of Birmingham and adopted a Weberian approach to BME position in the labour market. They found evidence of exploitation and occupational segregation that rendered minority ethnic groups predominantly within the 'secondary labour market' characterised by low wages, low status, poor working conditions, limited promotion opportunity and more insecurity. Assessing their work, housing and educational disadvantages they were described as constituting an '**underclass**'. BME groups were 'systematically at a disadvantage compared with working-class whites and that, instead of identifying with working-class culture, community and politics, they formed their own organisations and became in effect a separate underprivileged class'.

Prejudice

Prejudice is an antipathy towards another person or group, usually based on unfounded stereotypes or generalisations. Given its unfounded basis, prejudice is inherently unjust and irrational. Ted Cantle (2008) argues that racial prejudice often reflects ancient stereotypes about other nations linked to a 'pecking order' of nations. Prejudices are not fixed but can be fluid and reflective of agendas and subject to cultural adjustment. Ethnic identities are dynamic and constantly changing, and so are prejudices. For example, in the UK, the Irish were subject to considerable prejudice and discrimination in the past from landlords and employers, but currently 'Irishness' enjoys a fashionable status. A contemporary example of prejudice is the degree of Islamophobia which the Muslim community has to endure. Linked to Islamic terrorism it is further provoked by both political events and the demonisation of Muslims within the mass media. Muslims are portrayed as both unbelonging and subject to the process of **othering** as an 'out-group'. The teaching union NASUWT (2014) reported an increase in Islamophobic incidents with the rise of anti-Muslim sentiment causing 'uncertainty and fear' in schools.

Discrimination

Discrimination refers to differential treatment of a people who have been formally or informally classified as a group. M.N. Marger (2000) identifies three categories of discrimination:

- mass societal aggression against certain groups
- denial of access to societal opportunities (such as denying access to schools, jobs, organisations and recreational facilities such as golf clubs)
- use of derogative language judged to be offensive.

In the context of 'other-groups' discussed above, some racial and ethnic groups are subject to discrimination more than others. An obvious example of discrimination is the practice by police forces of stopping and searching black males more than other groups. The Equality and Human Rights Commission (EHRC, 2012) found from a national survey that the police were guilty of racial profiling and up to 28 times more likely to stop and search black than white people.

Discrimination can also be observed applying to ethnic and racial groups in terms of employment. With regard to worklessness and ethnicity, most ethnic minority groups have historically experienced discrimination in the labour market and much higher levels of unemployment. For example, in 2013 unemployment levels in the UK stood at 8 per cent but for ethnic minority groups it was 14 per cent. Specifically, for black ethnic minorities it was 17 per cent and for Pakistani/Bangladeshi ethnic groups it was 19 per cent. Worklessness impacts particularly on young people from ethnic minority groups, with 16–24-year olds having an unemployment rate of 37 per cent, up from 33 per cent in 2012. For the UK as a whole, unemployment in this age group is 21 per cent. Other instances of racial discrimination can occur in the rented housing market and within education.

Institutional racism

Institutional racism describes racism within any of the institutions and organisations that make up society, for instance employers, schools, government agencies and bodies like the police. When racism is institutionalised it means it is embedded within the policies and practices of organisations. This can be either blatant, open prejudice and discrimination, such as blocking promotion of certain groups, or the unchecked, operation of discriminatory policies embedded in everyday routines and formal rules; such as not catering for the diets of certain groups or regularly holding meetings at times of worship for particular groups.

Following the murder of schoolboy Stephen Lawrence, the Macpherson Report (1999) famously declared the Metropolitan Police as institutionally racist. In 2013 the younger brother of Stephen Lawrence accused the Metropolitan Police of still practising institutional racism. He reported how he had been stopped 25 times by the police since passing his driving test aged 17. For a discussion of institutional racism in education see Book 1, page 74.

Ethnicity and life expectancy

As we saw in Book 1 statistics show consistently higher premature death rates for non-white men and women than for white men and women. In particular, people descended from Pakistan and Bangladesh, living in England and Wales, have the highest mortality rates from circulatory disease. This raised risk is due in part to a raised prevalence of diabetes. However, the key factor in mortality rates is the lower social class of most BME groups. Most ethnic groups are concentrated within the working class, so it follows that the factors discussed about class and health are the key determinants of mortality here too.

In terms of poor health BME groups in the UK experience poorer health in general compared to the overall population, although some BME groups fare much worse than others. Pakistani and Bangladeshi groups stand out as having the worst health. The graph below shows for England and Wales combined, age-standardised rates of over 13 per cent for men and over 15 per cent for women, compared to around 8 per cent for all ethnic groups reporting 'not good health'. Chinese men and women report the best health of any ethnic group. In terms of poor health and BMEs, patterns vary from one health condition to the next.

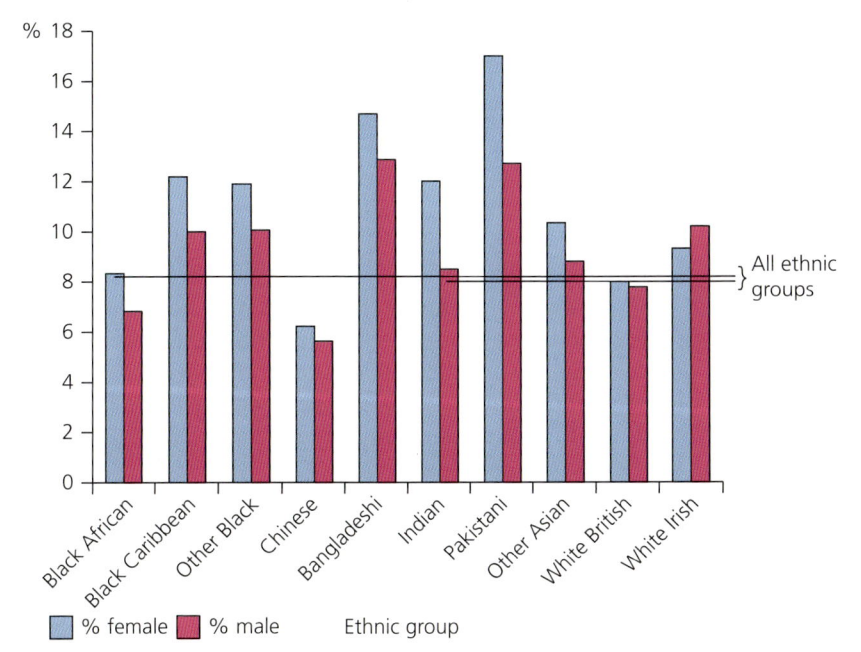

Figure 6.18 Age standardised percentages of people reporting 'not good' health by ethnicity. Adapted from EHRC (2010)

A Weberian sociological approach could offer a useful means of making sense of the general poorer health of BME groups, with its emphasis on class and status differences. The findings of people like Richard Wilkinson and the Whitehall II Study emphasise the importance of status in shaping health chances. Those could be usefully transferred to BME groups. Frequently located in the lower social classes and often subject to discrimination, it is no wonder they often have poorer health chances. In terms of social policy The Acheson Report (1998) was the first health report to specifically make recommendations for reducing ethnic health inequalities.

Ethnicity and education

Tarique Modood et al. (1997) found a close correlation between BME performance in schools and their social class location. Those with the poorest achievement levels tend to be located within the working class. On the other hand, those BME groups predominantly located in the middle class enjoy relative success. Department for Education and Skills statistics highlight the differences in attainment between children from different ethnic backgrounds. Chinese and Indian ethnic groups have the highest Level 2 (GCSE or equivalent) and Level 3 (Advanced level or equivalent) attainment by age 19. Black, Traveller of Irish Heritage and Gypsy/Roma groups have the lowest attainment by age 19. For example the percentage achieving 5 A*– C GCSEs are Chinese (89.9 per cent), Indian (84.4 per cent), White (79.1 per cent), Caribbean (59.5 per cent), Gypsy/Roma (38.6 per cent). However, it is worth noting that within these ethnic groups, besides social class, there will also be differentiation associated with gender. For an example of racial discrimination in education see Gillbourn and Youdell's discussion of the A–C economy in Book 1, page 75).

KEY SOCIOLOGIST

Tariq Modood (2003) provides a postmodern approach to the study of ethnicity. He stresses the benefits of a multicultural society and how globalisation contributes towards the fluid nature of identity. He applauds the contribution of migration while at the same time challenging simplistic assumptions that BME groups are homogeneous. However, despite this disparity of experiences, Modood is very aware of the material and social disadvantages experienced by many ethnic minorities.

CONTEMPORARY APPLICATION

Historically, most BME groups were disadvantaged in terms of education attainment compared with the White British group. However, over the last 20 years educational attainment has been increasing among BME groups. For example, the number of Indian and Pakistani university graduates increased by 27 and 18 percentage points respectively, between 1991 and 2011. The acquisition of education has been associated with the improvement of employment outcomes among BME groups, alongside better income prospects.

STUDY TIP

Remember that there are differences within as well as between BME groups and that it is dangerous and simplistic to assume otherwise.

RESEARCH IN FOCUS

Segregated Britain

Research by Ludi Simpson and Stephen Jivraj (2015) finds that so-called 'segregated' Britain is both more diverse – and home to far wider inequalities – than originally thought. It reviews the previous three censuses and suggests that ethnic inequalities in health, employment and housing remain prevalent in British communities and that discrimination continues to impede certain ethnic minority groups from realising their ambitions of good jobs and decent housing.

They also found that inequalities can be found in more affluent areas of the UK and were not just confined to deprived areas. Despite improvements in health, employment and housing of ethnic minority groups in the last 20 years, clear disadvantage persists when compared with the average experience of the White British group and this is particularly marked in some of the less deprived areas. Ethnic minorities who have managed to overcome barriers to secure housing in better-off neighbourhoods may well feel worse off than those that remain in the most deprived neighbourhoods.

The research also challenges the idea that Britain is becoming more segregated, concluding that most areas are diverse. They argue that diversity is breeding diversity in Britain, with the ethnic group category 'Other' projected to soon become the biggest minority in many local authorities. However, the research found that restructures of the housing and labour markets have failed to improve living standards for ethnic minority populations who, instead, have been disproportionately disadvantaged.

Their research concludes that policy now needs to go beyond the type of legislation that outlaws discriminatory practices to ensure that third and fourth generations of ethnic minorities do not continue to face social inequalities.

Adapted from Care Appointments (2015)

Questions

1. What has happened to ethnic inequalities in health housing and employment over the past three censuses?
2. What policies could be implemented to ensure that 'third and fourth generations of ethnic minorities do not continue to face social inequalities'?
3. How would a Marxist explanation of ethnic inequalities differ to that of a Weberian approach?

2.4 What is the relationship between life chances and age?

Consider the impact of factors like an ageing population, discrimination of the elderly and youth as well as differences in health, education and work chances. When writing about childhood keep your discussion contemporary and avoid getting side-tracked into discussing historical data about children scaring crows or being used to climb up chimneys.

Currently one-in-six of the UK population is aged 65 and over, but by 2050 this will have risen to one in four people. One implication of this for the allocation of resources and demands on taxpayers is that the pensioner population is set to rise. In 2008 there were 3.2 people of working age for every person of pensionable age. This ratio is projected to fall to 2.8 by 2033.

The social construction of childhood

The French sociologist Phillipe Aries (1962) (see also Book 1 page 210) highlights how childhood is a social construction. His research shows that in pre-industrial society the concept of childhood did not really exist. Offspring over the age of five were essentially treated and dressed just like adults and were integrated into the adult world of work, leisure and sexuality. He argues that the concept of childhood evolved in nineteenth-century Britain, when philanthropists began to campaign for their exclusion from employment from particular forms of labour, including in factories and mines and as chimney sweeps. The introduction of mass education served to differentiate them from adults and reinforce childhood as a period before employment. In contemporary Britain, children have become objects of consumption in contrast to their role in production in the past. In addition, childhood has become constructed in modern terms as a period of vulnerability, whereby they are in need of protection from vices and dangers. Aries' research is important since it shows that modern understanding of children as having specialised needs and as 'separate' from adults is a relatively recent way of thinking about them. However, even today the age at which childhood ends and adulthood begins is both fluid and ambiguous. Many rights start at 18, but 'childhood' can end at 14 according to some bus companies or 12 with regard to theme parks.

We saw in Book 1 (see Chapter 5, Families and Households) how sociologists like Neil Postman (1985) argue that 'childhood' is disappearing as it becomes ever shorter as television in particular blurs the distinction between adulthood and childhood. Both television and the internet give children complete access to all information, eroding childhood as a period of innocence. Postman is concerned how modern media gives children unlimited access to an adult world. The impact of this is to undermine children's ability to trust, believe in and rely on the adult world. As a consequence adult authority is lost. Postman thus argues that this leads to children becoming more like adults in relation to their dress and criminality and sexuality, while in contrast adults seem to be regressing into childhood, wanting to look forever young and 'hip'.

Age and health

Because ageing is a biological process it follows that mortality rates by cause of death will increase with age. For young people aged 15 to 29, injury and poisoning account for the highest mortality rates (40 per 100,000 population for men and 10 per 100,000 for women). In adults aged 30 to 44, the leading cause of death for men was injury and poisoning (43 per 100,000 population) whereas for women it was cancers (30 per 100,000 population). For those aged 45 to 64, for both men and women cancers were the leading cause of death (240 per 100,000 for men and 213 per 100,000 for women). Younger men aged 15 to 29 and 30 to 44 had higher injury mortality rates than older men aged 45 to 64.

There are accusations that the elderly can suffer age discrimination in hospitals, either by being denied treatment available to younger people or by negative attitudes of staff towards them. The Care Quality Commission (2011) stated that elderly patients in half of NHS hospitals were being neglected because of a lack of 'kindness and compassion'. The Patients' Association claims that the number of elderly subject to neglect when treated in NHS hospitals is more than 200,000 per year. In addition, 'bed blocking' is causing over 100,000 elderly patients to remain in hospital beds because there is no one to support them at home, or there are no places available in residential homes.

> **STUDY TIP**
>
> Notions of childhood have evolved considerably in the past 100 years. When writing about childhood, it is important to recognise these changes and keep points grounded in their historical context.

> **KEY SOCIOLOGIST**
>
> **Talcott Parsons** saw age (along with factors like sex, race, and family status) as an example of ascription, an inborn quality of an individual. He did not see age as a significant differentiator in modern industrial society with the exception of education which predominantly serves young people. Thus he played down age grading and formal age categorisation, although this does occur with regard to things like voting and retirement ages.

> **CONTEMPORARY APPLICATION**
>
> The Equality Act (2010) permits employers to discriminate because of a person's age in a wide range of situations, if the employer can show that what it has done is justified. For example, it is not age discrimination to pay a young worker the lower minimum wage if that is the rate for which they qualify; this also applies for apprentices who do not qualify for the national minimum wage.

> **STUDY TIP**
>
> Discrimination occurs most at the beginning and end of the life cycle. It is therefore something experienced by the young and elderly rather than the middle aged. However, remember how within these two categories discrimination will also be influenced by factors such as social class (wealth and income), gender and ethnicity.

Age and education

Age has a close correlation with education, since most societies in the developed world have a schooling start age and leaving age for compulsory education. However, recently, the UK government has introduced schemes to promote 'life-long learning', although adult education has experienced something of a decline in recent years. Talcott Parsons (1960) saw one of the roles of schools as an agency of secondary socialisation; taking over this role from the family. He also viewed schools as offering a bridge between the 'particularistic' ascribed values of the family and the 'universalistic' values of achievement characteristic of the workplace and wider society. Education therefore serves to accommodate the transition from the home (where children are treated as individuals) to cope with wider society where no one is granted special considerations and status is achieved rather than ascribed. Children's ten or so years in compulsory education are an important period of maturing, not only biologically, as they evolve into young adults, but socially too as they learn the importance of achievement and how to compete in a society viewed by Parsons as meritocratic.

Age and work

Research from the English Longitudinal Study of Ageing (ELSA, 2014) reveals high levels of age discrimination faced by older people, a situation that worsens as they age. They found that 33 per cent of elderly people experience age discrimination, with less wealthy older men being at highest risk. Retired older people were 25 per cent more likely to report age discrimination than those who were still employed. The research also highlighted that older men faced higher levels of perceived age discrimination in many aspects of their lives in comparison with women.

While children worked in factories, mines and as chimney sweeps in the early period of industrialisation, child labour is carefully controlled in contemporary society; not least because they are legally obliged to go to school. The youngest age a child can work part-time is 13. However, exceptions are made for children involved in areas like television, the theatre and modelling where they are required to have a performance licence. Children are only allowed to work full-time once they have passed the minimum school leaving age and can only work a maximum of 40 hours a week. Once they reach 18, adult employment rights and rules then apply. In 2013, the school leaving age was effectively raised with young people required to do some part-time education or training until the age of 17.

Recent government policy, begun with the coalition government (2010–15), has been to emphasise work over welfare for young people. School leavers have been required to take a job or sign up for training as part of plans to prepare young people for the world of work. Up to 3 million apprenticeships have been planned. Those young people who don't have any work experience will be forced to take part in training or work placements as part of a new, tougher Day One Work Requirement. If they fail to comply they will have their benefits removed. Jobseeker's Allowance will be axed for 18–21-year-olds and replaced with a Youth Allowance that will be time-limited to six months.

> **IN THE NEWS**
>
> ### Age discrimination at work
>
> Research from the Department of Work and Pensions (DWP) shows perceptions towards those aged over 70 are more positive than towards those in their 20s, unless they are in senior roles. The report, based on analysis from the Office for National Statistics' opinions survey, looked at factors associated with age discrimination and prejudice, and compared attitudes towards people in their 20s and those aged over 70.
>
> Perceptions towards those aged over 70 were that they were friendlier, had higher moral standards and were more competent than their younger counterparts. However, when respondents were asked how acceptable they would find a suitably qualified 30-year-old or 70-year-old boss, the results showed a bias towards younger workers. Three times as many (15 per cent and 5 per cent respectively) thought that having a 70-year-old boss would be 'unacceptable' compared with having a 30-year-old boss.
>
> Just over a third of respondents said they had seen some age-related prejudice in the past year. Experiences of age discrimination were more common for younger groups, with under-25s at least twice as likely to have experienced it as other age groups. In general terms, people in their 40s were viewed as having the highest status, while on average people aged over 70 were given a higher status than those in their 20s.
>
> Employers are urged to renew their commitment to building age-diverse workplaces. With the removal of mandatory retirement age a long time ago, it is argued they can reap the benefits of employing a multi-age workforce.
>
> Adapted from Snowdon (2012)

Questions

1. Which age group did the DWP find were viewed most positively?
2. What favourable perceptions were held about people aged over 70?
3. Why do you think 15 per cent of people found a 70-year-old boss 'unacceptable'?
4. Outline some of the benefits of employing a multi-age workforce.

2.5 What is the relationship between life chances and disability?

Consider the impact of factors like social exclusion, poverty and differences in health, education and work chances.

Disablism is the term used by sociologists to refer to the discrimination experienced by people with disabilities. The social model highlights how society can impose barriers against those with impairments, preventing them fully participating in society. The **social model of disability** has now become the ideological litmus test of disability politics in Britain, used by the disabled people's movement to distinguish between organisations, policies, laws and ideas which are progressive and those which are inadequate.

Michael Oliver (1986) notes how the disabled in the past were encouraged to view their situation as loathsome and undesirable. Erving Goffman (1963) famously showed how stigma is used as a marker for 'moral inferiority'.

However, Tom Shakespeare (2002) argues the success of the social model became its main weakness. By becoming a powerful tool, central to the disability movement, it acquired the status of a 'sacred cow'. As such the social model became an ideology which could not easily be challenged. He argues that most supporters of the social model will concede behind closed doors the significance of impairments when they talk about things like 'aches', 'pains' and 'urinary tract infections'. However, they deny any relevance of the body when campaigning in support of the social model. Shakespeare rejects this attempt to dismiss the importance of impairments, arguing if an impairment causes constant pain then how can society be implicated? Similarly, if someone has a significant intellectual limitation, how can society be altered to make this irrelevant to employment opportunities? He argues the need to create a mature society that supports everyone on the basis of the needs they have.

Disability and health

In the past disability was often equated with illness and disease and therefore disabled people were relieved of all normal expectations and responsibilities. This freedom from social obligations and responsibilities was subsequently taken up with disability equated with social deviance. In terms of contemporary social policy, Roddy Slorach (2012) argues that the 2010–15 coalition government's policy of subjecting 2 million people to medical tests in assessment for Work Capability Assessments (WCAs) shows that the idea of disability equalling a work-shy malingerer still carries weight in the twenty-first century.

Disability and education

The origins of special schools for children with impairments implied a philanthropic gesture in response to 'special needs'. However, Michael Oliver (1990) argues it was really a means of removing uneducable and disruptive pupils from mainstream education. Others see it as an outcome of power struggles between doctors, educational psychologists and special education teachers. The prevailing view from some disabled communities is that segregated education is a more efficient and effective form of education; even if expensive and under resourced. It is argued by supporters of segregated education that mainstream schools offer poor quality of service and there is limited meaningful inclusion. In contrast, special schools offer individualised support, an accessible environment and empathetic peer culture.

Critics of segregated education argue that removing disabled children from peers, the local community (and even family in residential schools) has wide-ranging negative effects. It restricts children with disabilities the opportunity to mix and make friends with non-disabled children. The principle of integration within inclusive education was enshrined by the Salamanca Statement and Framework for Action on Special Needs Education (1994) which was endorsed by 92 countries. However, the implementation of this statement requires 'whole school' policies that facilitate meaningful opportunities for children regardless of impairments. It involves inclusive teaching and learning methods as well as good resources and support. It is also argued that when pupils are segregated those with impairments experience a narrower curriculum due to lower expectations. In addition, since levels of attainment by children with disabilities are much lower than their non-disabled peers, in a climate of targets, competition and league tables, they are viewed as an unwanted liability.

Disability and work

Figure 6.19 Remploy workers in Sheffield protest against the closure of their factory

Historically, workers with disabilities have been supported by some aspects of positive discrimination. For example, employment quotas, designated employment and 'sheltered employment' such as Remploy factories. However, government and local authority cuts have dealt a harsh blow to disabled employment prospects. Given that occupation is an important classifier of people in terms of class, status and power, people with disabilities have a level of unemployment far higher than that of able bodied people at around 50 per cent. When they do work, they are overrepresented in low-paid, less-skilled routine work. Disabled people are particularly underrepresented in the professions and management which offer higher earnings and security of employment (vertical segregation). People with disabilities are also subject to horizontal segregation; overrepresented in specific occupations. Their work position has been likened by Mark Hyde (1998) to the Marxist concept of a '*reserve army of labour*', used when needed but often the first workers to be discarded when no longer required.

KEY SOCIOLOGIST

Vic Finkelstein (1980) developed an account of disability based on the Marxist historical materialist account. He argues before industrialisation people with impairments still expected to participate in economic life, working in agriculture. However, with the arrival of the factory system, people with impairments were less productive so struggled to find employment. Therefore the roots of disability are to be found in the rise of capitalism. Those excluded from production became marginalised from wider society and in this way capitalism created disability as a form of social oppression: the 'other'.

CONTEMPORARY APPLICATION

When the government closed all 92 Remploy factories in Britain in 2013, more than 1500 workers with disabilities lost their jobs. Remploy was set up in the 1940s to give disabled soldiers and miners a job for life. For over 70 years they provided employment for thousands of people with disabilities making products such as school furniture and wheelchairs. Two years after the closures, nearly half (733) of those made redundant had not found new employment.

STUDY TIP

When writing about the marginalised position of most people with disabilities in society, equate how their position of social exclusion and poverty is a key factor in shaping their life chances in health, education and work chances.

IN THE NEWS

Toy industry shuts out children with disabilities

There are 770,000 children in the UK with disabilities and more than 150 million worldwide. Yet these children are excluded by the global toy industry, currently worth £2.9 billion. There are no wheelchair-using Barbies, although several years ago there was an American Sign Language Barbie. Playmobil's answer to disability is a boy with a broken leg and an elderly man being pushed in a wheelchair by a young blonde woman. What does this say to children? That only old people need wheels? That childhood disability amounts to a few weeks with your leg in plaster and then goes away?

Using the hashtag #toylikeme, UK journalist, Rebecca Atkinson started to make over children's toys, giving them impairments and posting the results online. The whole thing went viral as parents shared her image of Disney's Tinkerbell with a cochlear implant.

Some small UK toy producers have been quick to answer the campaign call. Arklu, the makers of Lottie dolls, already produce 25 per cent of their dolls with glasses and have agreed to look at ways to make future ranges more disability representative. Makies, the world's only producers of 3D-printed toys, have started producing a series of disability accessories for their existing range of bespoke dolls.

Figure 6.20 This image of a doll with a hearing aid went viral when posted by ToyLikeMe

Adapted from Atkinson (2015)

Questions

1. How many disabled children are there in the UK and worldwide?
2. Why do you think large toy manufacturers are reluctant to produce toys representing disability?
3. In what ways will this absence reinforce ideas of exclusion for children with disabilities?

Check your understanding

1. What is meant by the middle class quality of deferred gratification?
2. What is meant by the term embourgeoisement?
3. Why is the underclass considered to be a Weberian concept?
4. What is meant by vertical and horizontal segregation in the labour market?
5. What claim does Hakim make with her 'preference theory'?
6. What does the term racialisation mean?
7. How has the Marxist concept of 'reserve army of labour' been applied separately to women, BMEs and the disabled?
8. What does Zygmunt Bauman mean by the 'seduced' and 'repressed' in a consumer society?
9. How does Neil Postman see childhood as disappearing?
10. How does the social model of disability argue that society 'disables' people?

Practice questions

1. Outline and explain **two** ways in which women are unequal to men in the labour market. [10 marks]

Read Item A below and answer the question that follows.

Item A

People with disabilities are particularly underrepresented in the professions and management which offer higher earnings and security of employment (vertical segregation). At the same time they are overrepresented in low-paid, less-skilled routine work.

Applying material from Item A, analyse two reasons why people with disabilities are disadvantaged in the labour market. [10 marks]

Read Item B below and answer the question that follows.

Item B

A truly open labour market is one where from an equal base everyone has the same chances of recruitment and advancement. It assumes that workers are employed and progressed on the basis of merit rather than privilege, favour or background.

Applying material from Item B and your knowledge, evaluate the view that an open and non-discriminatory labour market exists in the United Kingdom. [20 marks]

Section 3: Definitions and measurements

This section will explore the following debates:

- How do sociologists measure social class?
- How can occupation, education and social status be used in measuring social class?
- What are the problems of defining and measuring social class?

GETTING YOU STARTED

How the working class are portrayed on television

Figure 6.21 Vicky Pollard is one example of a negative stereotype of a working-class person on TV

Source: Adapted from Foster (2014)

The popular perception of class has shifted from objective classifications based on occupation to being defined by culture. Someone who listens to Radio 4 and owns a cafetière is 'middle class', while someone who reads tabloids and watches soaps is working class.

Worryingly, the term 'working class' has often become equated with the derogatory term 'chav'. Because of this change in the way we see class, the proud traditional of the working class as blue-collar workers has virtually disappeared from our screens.

The schedules have become dominated by 'cops, docs and frocks', with the 'docs' – or documentaries – often being voyeuristic prole-baiting sneerathons. Gypsies, for example, are presented as 'a strange breed to be prodded through the bars of their cages'. Extreme examples of benefit claimants, such as families with a dozen kids, are paraded as the tips of uncouth, freeloading icebergs. It's now the norm for television to depict the working class as ugly stereotypes like Vicky Pollard and those chewed up and spat out by The Jeremy Kyle Show.

Television mirrors and contributes to the current belittling of the working class. We need a return to programming which reflects working-class struggles honestly, and not through the distorting prism of bourgeois ideology. Definitions of class based on 'wealth and power are better than those based on lifestyle'. After all, 'an aristocrat who watches The X Factor is still an aristocrat'.

Questions

1. What problems can arise from defining class in terms of culture?
2. According to Foster how have the working class come to be defined by the media?
3. Do you agree that media portrayal of the working class has become reduced to 'voyeuristic prole-baiting' and 'sneerathons'?
4. What Marxist point is being made by Foster when he describes working-class portrayal as 'bourgeois ideology'?
5. What important point is being made in the last sentence of the item?

3.1 How do sociologists measure social class?

There have been many attempts, both official and sociological, to measure social class in the UK. This section will examine several schemas or models that have been developed by sociologists, including the most recent developed in conjunction with organisations like the ONS, OECD and even the BBC.

Socio-economic classification (SEC) is a descriptive generic term for all the different schemas of stratification discussed below. Although in themselves SECs are non-theoretical, some are shaped by Marxist or Weberian principles. What they all have in common is that they claim to measure and show the principle of stratification. This refers to social inequalities that may be attributed to the way a society is organised.

The most common way of measuring social class is schemas based on occupation in one way or another. However, focusing on employment necessarily excludes those who do not work. For example, SECs typically exclude children, students, those who look after a home, unpaid family workers, the retired, the sick and disabled, the unemployed, and the never employed. They also do not take into account the temporary or fragile nature of some people's employment contracts or status. Consequently, workers in part-time, flexible contracts or on zero-hours contracts may have their social position over or understated. Such jobs may be worked around children at school or a post-retirement source of extra money or may be someone's sole source of income. SECs are inevitably something of a blunt instrument, but can be important to governments in helping to shape future policies.

By focusing on employment, SECs tend to ignore the privileged super-rich elite, referred to as capitalists or the ruling class. Any attempt to theorise class or understand power relations is incomplete without them, but they are missing from conventional class schema. One sociologist who does include them is Erik Olin Wright.

Wright's elaborated class typology

		Owner	Relation to means of production Employees			Degree of control	
Number of employees	Many	Capitalists	Expert managers	Skilled managers	Non-skilled managers	Managers	Relation to authority
	Few	Small employers	Expert supervisors	Skilled supervisors	Non-skilled supervisors	Supervisors	
	None	Petty bourgeoisie	Experts	Skilled workers	Non-skilled workers	Non-management	
			Experts	Skilled	Non-skilled		
			Relation to skills				

Table 6.5 Wright's elaborated class typology (2005)

Evaluation of Wright's schema

Erik Wright's (1997, 2005) approach is avowedly Marxist. We saw his contribution to class with his concept of contradictory class locations (page 316). He subsequently developed a schema based on the idea of exploitation. In order to demonstrate the Marxist principle that exploitation forms the basis of class relations, Wright's second model is based on different forms of assets used in the exploitation process. Employers are shown to own assets in the form of the means of production; managers have access to organisation or managerial assets under their bureaucratic control and professionals have their own assets of skills and expertise.

His model represented in the table below demonstrates the three dimensions which need to be measured. Wright is attempting in this sophisticated model to measure the assets discussed above – property, authority and expertise. To gain his data, Wright had to go beyond questions on occupation and employment status, and gain evidence on factors like degree of workplace supervision, decision-making, specific tasks and educational attainment.

Erikson and Goldthorpe (1992) argue that when collecting data many respondents might be unwilling or unable to give precise details of their ownership of wealth. Runciman has also been criticised for not making it clear how much marketability, power or control a person needs for them to be placed in a particular class. Subsequent schemas, by other people (see below) put the self-employed and small proprietors in separate classes. Runciman rejected this on the grounds that they do not necessarily have similar amounts of economic power to warrant being put in a class by themselves.

Although Wright's purpose with this elaborated schema was to return exploitation to the centre stage, he also broke away from traditional Marxist analysis by favouring a trajectory view of class, rather than a positional one. He argues that class analysis must examine people's pathways through the class structure and take full account of the fact that class positions and their occupants are not identical. What he meant by this is it cannot be assumed that people who occupy the same class position will experience the world the same way. There is a sense in which a female clerical worker aged 60, and with no prospects of promotion as she approaches retirement, is in a very different class position from (say) a young female clerical worker in her early twenties hoping to progress into a managerial career. In this respect Wright is adopting more of a Weberian approach, seeing class interests as **gradational** rather than relational (defined solely by relationship to the means of production). At the same time, as a neo-Marxist he is modifying traditional Marxist class theory to confront the 'problem' of the 'middle classes'.

In response to the criticism Wright received for producing an over-complicated schema, he developed a simpler model:

Relation to authority		Relation to means of production				Relation to authority
		Owner	Employees			
	Hires labour	Capitalists	Expert managers	Non-skilled managers	Has authority	
	Does not hire labour	Petty bourgeoisie	Experts	Non-skilled workers	Non-management	
			Experts	Non-skilled		
			Relation to scarce skills			

Table 6.6 Wright's simplified model of class

Runciman's social classes

W.G. Runciman (1990) developed the Runciman Scale, a combination of both Marxist and Weberian social class analysis. Not only does it measure class in terms of economic power, ownership and control, but it also includes a person's status based on their market position. The scale is based on three categories of economic power:

- ownership of the means of production
- control over others in the workplace
- marketability in the form of the possession of skills valued by society.

In contrast to most other schemas of class, Runciman included as his seventh category the underclass: a group essentially outside the relevance of ownership, control and marketability.

Runciman claimed the upper class was comprised of capitalists (owners of the means of production), but also included very highly paid managers and those with exceptional marketability such as senior partners in accountancy firms. However, he excluded extremely rich celebrities as he argued their role is irrelevant to production, distribution and exchange.

He divided the middle classes into three groups and also includes here small business owners and the self-employed who would not be classified as capitalists. The upper middle class is comprised of higher professionals, senior civil servants and senior managers. In contrast the lower middle class are comprised of routine white-collar workers in 'deskilled' occupations. Runciman argues that the gap in economic power between these two groups is sufficient to justify the existence of a middle middle class. This group includes lower professions and middle managers. Runciman excludes shop assistants, checkout operators and routine clerical workers from the middle class on the grounds that they have insufficient economic power in terms of the marketability of their skills. Instead he places them in the working class.

Runciman divides the working class in two on the criteria of marketability of skill, rendering this aspect of his schema quite Weberian. He put semi-skilled manual workers into the lower 'unskilled' working class as he felt unskilled workers with minimal skills were increasingly defined as semi-skilled. Classification within the working class was based on marketability, control and ownership. Consequently, if a worker had control over the operation of machinery or was in a strong position to market their skills, then they would be placed in the 'skilled' upper working class.

Finally, Runciman distinguishes an underclass at the bottom of the stratification system as a group who have no control ownership or marketability. They are those in receipt of long-term welfare as they are unable to participate in the labour market.

Evaluation of Runciman

The strength of the Runciman Scale is that it uses several factors (ownership, control and marketability) to analyse class. It satisfies the Marxist criteria by including an upper or capitalist class. However, it also embraces Weberian ideas by highlighting the importance of marketability.

Rosemary Crompton (1993) praises the Runciman Scale, arguing it successfully reflects some of the key social changes that have occurred in Britain since the Second World War. These include the blurring of the boundary between manual and non-manual work associated with the routinisation and feminisation of lower level white-collar service sector jobs. She also supports Runciman's recognition of the very poorest and most deprived at the bottom of society characterised by state dependency.

Upper class
Upper middle class
Middle middle class
Lower middle class
Skilled working class
Unskilled working class
Underclass

Table 6.7 Runciman's Seven Class Schema

> **KEY SOCIOLOGIST**
>
> **Charles Murray**, a New Right sociologist, visited Britain in 1989 in search of the 'underclass' courtesy of *The Sunday Times*. In 1993 he returned to warn that the crisis of the 'underclass' was 'deepening'. Murray particularly identified with Runciman's idea that members of the underclass were not simply in receipt of welfare benefits, but were excluded from the labour market on a more or less permanent basis.

> **CONTEMPORARY APPLICATION**
>
> The Great British Class Survey (GBCS, see page 359) based on Savage et al. (2013) dispenses with the traditional upper, middle and working-class categorisation represented in the table above and replaces it with:
>
> - elite
> - established middle class
> - technical middle class
> - new affluent workers
> - traditional working class
> - emergent service workers
> - precarious proletariat.

IN THE NEWS

Why defining social status is so difficult

Figure 6.22 The *Class sketch*, featuring comedians John Cleese, Ronnie Barker and Ronnie Corbett, was a classic TV moment in the 1960s

The concept of social class has become increasingly difficult to define and measure. Two centuries ago those who did not work were the gentry, but in contemporary society those that never worked, along with the long-term unemployed, could be described by some as an 'underclass'. In the past riding a bike and having only one pair of shoes would have located someone firmly in the working class, but now could reflect the ethical and environmental values of a highly skilled professional.

Because the components that now make up class – social, economic and cultural life – are based on subjective judgements as well as objective facts, measuring social class has become extremely difficult. Nonetheless there are some crucial factors reinforcing traditional patterns. A report from the OECD (2012) found that British schools do a remarkably efficient job in reproducing society's inequalities: the rich stay rich, the poor stay poor while those born into the middle class grow up to be middle class themselves.

Any attempt to draw global comparisons of social class is fraught with problems. Almost every study measuring social class is of limited use when making comparisons between countries. Comparing material wealth does not have much value where religion plays a crucial role in determining social status. Even comparing economic indicators between developed countries can be problematic. For example, asking about home ownership might not prove so helpful in a country such as France which has a long culture of renting.

Adapted from Chalabi and Sedghi (2013)

Questions

1. Why is it argued that old classifications of upper, middle and working class are out of date?
2. What evidence is there that traditional inequalities still remain in contemporary society?
3. Why is it difficult to draw global comparisons of social class?
4. What would a traditional Marxist say in response to this article?

3.2 How can occupation, education and social status be used in measuring social class?

Figure 6.23 Occupation has long been used to classify social class

Objective definitions of class

The simplest and most common means of measuring social class has traditionally been achieved using schemas that classify people according to occupational scales. These tend to measure the distributive aspects of inequality and often because they are hierarchical imply status as well as income differentials. These tend to reflect Weberian ideas of social class and are sometimes referred to as gradational. An alternative and second approach are the more Marxist schemas intended to measure how class is relational to economic factors as well as reflecting distributive issues.

Registrar General's Social Class

The **Registrar General's Social Class (RGSC)** was renamed in 1990 as the Social Class based on Occupation. It was originally devised to analyse differences in infant mortality across society and based on the subjective judgement of Dr Stevenson, the Registrar General in 1911. The occupation groups were based on the assumption that society is a graded hierarchy of occupations ranked according to skill. However, no account is taken of differences between individuals in the same occupation group, such as differences in educational qualifications.

I	Professional etc. occupations
II	Managerial and Technical occupations
III	Skilled occupations
	(N) Non-manual
	(M) Manual
IV	Partly skilled occupations
V	Unskilled occupations

Table 6.8 The Registrar General's classification

Although widely used, the RGSC was criticised for the following reasons:

- Being created to describe an industrial society it increasingly failed to reflect a more post-industrial society.
- Far from being objective it is value-laden: based on the assumption of a hierarchy of occupational status, it implies that non-manual work is superior to manual work.
- It is therefore more accurately a *status classification* rather than a class one.
- It does not include those who do not work (for example, very rich, students, unemployed, retired).
- Feminists criticised it for rendering women invisible since it classified households on the occupation of their male partners.
- It was criticised because it had no coherent theoretical basis.

Because of these criticisms associated with the RGSC some sociologists produced their own alternative class and occupational scales which they claimed to be superior in both conception and use.

The Hope-Goldthorpe schema

The most widely used sociological class schema was designed for the Oxford Mobility Study (see page 318). By being based on occupation and employment status it was operationally similar to the RGSC, although it is claimed that the Hope-Goldthorpe schema has a more satisfactory theoretical and conceptual basis. The Hope-Goldthorpe schema is regarded as neo-Weberian since it brings together individuals who share similar work and market situations.

I	Higher professional, administrators and managers	Service class
II	Lower-grade professionals, administrators, higher-grade technicians, supervisors of non-manual employees	
III	Routine non-manual employees	Intermediate class
IV	Small proprietors	
V	Lower grade technicians and supervisors	
VI	Skilled manual workers	Working class
VII	Semi- and unskilled manual workers	

Table 6.9 Hope-Goldthorpe scheme with Erikson's and Goldthorpe's employment relations

The key differences between Goldthorpe's schema and the RGSC are that there are separate categories for two new groups: small proprietors and lower grade technicians and supervisors. Erikson and Goldthorpe (1992) modified the original schema, preferring the concept of employment relations in order to emphasise the idea of a class structure of 'empty places' that individuals fill. Recognising that employers do not treat all employees alike is crucial to Erikson and Goldthorpe's analysis of the employment relations of employees:

'*Service relationship*' refers to how senior employees render a 'service' to the employer in return for high rewards in terms of salary and status. Such employees also receive long-term benefits such as employment security and career opportunities.

'*Intermediate relationship*' refers to employees who combine aspects from both the service relationship and the labour contract. Such employees are typically clerical occupations, technicians, sales and service occupations.

'*Labour contract*' (working class) includes employees who are closely supervised and give discrete amounts of labour in return for a relatively low wage compared to the service class. Payment is calculated on the amount of work done or by the actual amount of time worked.

Because this schema is not based on occupation as such but qualitative differences in employment relationships, Erikson and Goldthorpe (2002:33) note that 'the classes are not consistently ordered according to some inherent hierarchical principle'. However, it follows that Classes I and II have advantages such as income, security of employment and promotional prospects over Classes III, VI and VII.

The National Statistics Socio-economic Classification (NS-SEC)

The Registrar General's classification which has been in use since 1911 was replaced for the 2001 Census by the NS-SEC to reflect the occupational changes associated with the move of Britain from manufacturing to a more service sector economy. It was produced by a group of sociologists led by Gordon Marshall working with the support of the UK Economic and Social Research Council (ESRC). They decided to adapt the Hope-Goldthorpe schema in order to create the NS-SEC because the former was widely used and judged to be conceptually clear. The following diagram shows the eight categories and some examples of occupations for each of the new layers.

1 Higher managerial, administrative and professional occupations

 1.1 Large employers and higher managerial and administrative occupations: company directors, corporate managers, police inspectors, bank managers, senior civil servants, military officers

 1.2 Higher professional occupations: doctors, barristers, solicitors, clergy, librarians, social workers, teachers

2 Lower managerial, administrative and professional occupations: nurses, midwives, actors, musicians, prison officers, police, soldiers (NCO and below)

3 Intermediate occupations: clerks, secretaries, driving instructors, computer operators, telephone fitters

4 Small employers and own account workers: publicans, playgroup leaders, farmers, taxi drivers, window cleaners, painters and decorators

5 Lower supervisory and technical occupations: printers, plumbers, butchers, bus inspectors, TV engineers, train drivers

6 Semi-routine occupations: shop assistants, traffic wardens, cooks, bus drivers, hairdressers, postal workers

7 Routine occupations: waiters, road sweepers, cleaners, couriers, building labourers, refuse collectors

8 Never worked and long-term unemployed

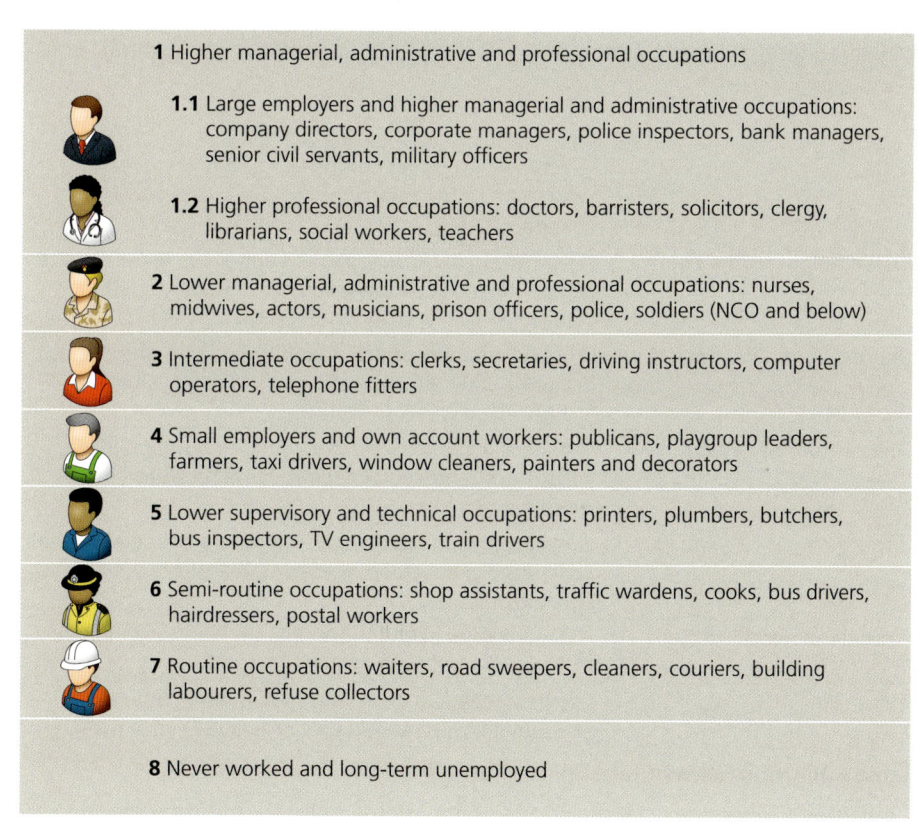

Figure 6.24 National Statistics Socio-economic Classification

Adapted from *The Guardian* (1999)

The NS-SEC makes no reference to either 'skill' or the 'manual/non-manual divide'. This was a deliberate decision by its authors since to use category names which refer to skill would have been inconsistent with an employment relations approach. Changes in both the nature and structure of industries and occupations render the manual/non-manual divide as out of date as well as misleading. For example, category 6 includes many non-manual service occupations. Gordon Marshall (1999) described the new classification as trying to 'unpack the "black box" of social class'. He feels it is a more accurate measurement for putting occupations into classes than the Goldthorpe schema. This is based on factors like promotion prospects, nature of pay scales, job security, and autonomy at work. It also has an additional category for long-term unemployed/never worked (what some people might call the 'underclass'). The NS-SEC can be condensed into three analytic classes:

1. Professional and managerial (classes 1 and 2)
2. Intermediate (classes 3 and 4)
3. Routine and manual (classes 5, 6 and 7).

Great British Class Survey (GBCS)

Savage *et al.*, (2013) developed a class survey based on Pierre Bourdieu's (1984) work when he extended the idea of capital from its usual economic meaning through terms like **social capital** and **cultural capital**. As a classification it is therefore capable of considering people's economic position as well as their engagement in cultural and social life in order to advance or maintain their social position. Respondents were asked about income and savings, house values ('economic capital'), their cultural interests and activities ('cultural capital'), and the number and status of people they know ('social capital'). This data was used to produce a classification comprised of seven classes based on consumption as well as economic factors (combining economic, social and cultural capital). The seven classes are:

Elite	Exclusive grouping comprised of the very wealthy with high levels of economic, social and cultural capital.
Established middle class	High levels of three types of capital but less than the elite. Viewed as a sociable and culturally engaged class.
Technical middle class	High levels of economic capital, but as a group less socially and culturally engaged. Members have relatively few social contacts.
New affluent workers	Medium levels of economic capital, but high levels of cultural and social capital. Members tend to be young and active.
Emergent service workers	Low economic capital but high levels of social capital and 'emerging' cultural capital. Members young and urban.
Traditional working class	Low levels of economic, social and cultural capital. Members tend to be older.
Precariat	Lowest levels of economic, social and cultural capital. Members lead precarious everyday lives.

Table 6.10 Great British Class Survey

Compared to the other classifications, the mapping of levels and type of consumption is far more important. It has been criticised for giving insufficient weight to economic factors. In addition, it has been suggested that the established middle class, which accounts for 25 per cent of the population, could be subdivided further. Others have questioned to what extent the established and technical middle classes differ. The classification offers little insight into how the classes relate to each other or analysis of the power relations that operate between these classes. Geoff Payne (2013) notes that while there are important conceptual and structural differences between the NS-SEC and the GBCS, their findings are remarkably similar:

NS-SEC	per cent	GBCS	per cent
Large employers and higher managerial		Elite	6.0
Higher professional	12.0	Established middle class	25.0
Lower managerial and professional	24.4	Technical middle class	6.0
Intermediate occupations	14.9	New affluent workers	15.0
Small employers	11.0		
Lower supervisory and technical	8.1		
Semi-routine occupations	16.5	Traditional working class	14.0
Routine occupations	13.0	Emergent service workers	19.0
		Precariat	15.0

Table 6.11 Payne's models of contemporary social class

Data from Payne (2013)

According to Savage *et al.* (2013) the inclusion of cultural capital in the GBCS appears to be the most significant difference between the two classifications.

Subjective definitions of class

Subjective definitions of social class refer to the class a person thinks they belong to. Back in the 1970s, W.G. Runciman (1972) undertook a social survey of 14,000 adults in order to evaluate people's subjective class location. A key finding was that people formulated their position in society by making comparisons to reference groups (such as other groups of workers) and evaluated their sense of satisfaction or deprivation. Other findings by Runciman were:

1. People had widely varying ideas about what kinds of people belonged to the different social classes.
2. People only made 'short-range' comparisons between themselves and others. In other words they compared themselves with groups within their everyday range of experience, rather than the very rich.
3. As a consequence, such short-range comparisons failed to generate feelings of the 'unfairness' of society generally.
4. Many manual workers defined themselves as 'middle class', and some non-manual workers saw themselves as 'working class'.

In a more recent survey for the British Social Attitudes (2013) they researched how important a subjective understanding of social class was in shaping social attitudes. They measured subjective social class using responses to the following questions:

1. Which class would you place yourself in, middle class or working class?
2. Among which group would you place yourself, high income, middle income, or low income?
3. To what extent do you think a person's social class affects his or her opportunities in Britain today? A great deal, quite a lot, not very much, or not at all.

Table 6.12 shows that between 1983 and 2012 there has been very little change in the proportion of people identifying as 'middle' or 'working class'. In 2012, 35 per cent of the public saw itself as 'middle class' and 60 per cent view themselves as 'working class'.

	Subjective social class				
	Working class		Middle class		Did not identify with any class
	Prompted working class	Unprompted working class	Prompted middle class	Unprompted middle class	
1983	27%	33%	14%	20%	6%
1987	31%	30%	18%	16%	5%
1991	30%	29%	18%	16%	6%
1997	30%	31%	17%	20%	2%
1998	32%	25%	17%	20%	6%
2012	32%	29%	13%	22%	5%

Table 6.12 Subjective social class 1983–2012. Data from British Social Attitudes 30 (2013)

Table 6.13 below shows a similarly flat trend regarding the income group that people perceive themselves to be in, although there are signs of a slight increase in propensity to view oneself as middle rather than low income. In 2012, 51 per cent of people thought they had a middle income, 44 per cent think low income and only 4 per cent perceive themselves as having a high income.

	Self-rated income		
	Low income	Middle income	High income
1983	50%	47%	3%
1987	46%	50%	3%
1991	57%	58%	3%
1997	n/a	n/a	n/a
1998	43%	52%	4%
2012	44%	51%	4%

Table 6.13 Self-rated income in the United Kingdom (2012). Data from British Social Attitudes 30 (2013)

Likewise there has been little movement since 1983 in whether the public perceives that someone's class affects their opportunities. Throughout the period, a majority of people (around seven in ten) think that social class does affect opportunities, either a great deal or quite a lot.

As the tables above show, people's views on patterns of inequality are very different to most sociologists! However, given that ordinary people's view of inequality is from the vantage point of their own limited (and short-range) life experience, this is not very surprising. It also supports the Marxist concept of false consciousness whereby the ignorance of the degree of inequality in society results in an uncritical acceptance of the inequalities of capitalism. The notion of subjective definition of social class will be returned to in the next chapter when we consider the meanings and definition of the middle class and the working class with particular reference to the concepts of proletarianisation and embourgeoisement.

CONTEMPORARY APPLICATION

The BBC drew on the work of Savage et al. (2013) and operationalised a simplified Class Calculator by which people could calculate their own class position. Nearly 5 million participants undertook the online Great British Class Survey ('GBCS').

STUDY TIP

Feminists are angry at the way most of the classifications above render women invisible by focusing on household social class based primarily on the male breadwinner's occupation. What is clearly needed is individualistic definitions of class.

KEY SOCIOLOGIST

A comparison of the GBCS and NS-SEC by **Geoff Payne** (2013) found that they produce basically similar pictures of class in contemporary Britain. Summarising the findings he argues that 'rather than class being dead, it was more the case that '"Class is dead" is dead'.

IN THE NEWS

Why a Marxist classification is still relevant

The radical understanding of social classes holds that classes do not exist prior to coming into relationship with one another. For example, to a Marxist the proletariat or working class could not exist without a capitalist class. Historically, serfs could not exist without feudal lords. These classes have very specific mechanisms of reproduction, but only in relation to one another: the working class reproduces itself by selling its labour power, which it can only do if there is someone to buy it.

However, recent social classifications have 'classes' that can exist without any relationship to other classes. For example, a technical middle class does not need a new affluent worker, or precarious worker, for it to exist. As these new 'classes' are statistical constructs, their existence implies no necessary relationship to other classes, nor any specific principle of reproduction. The Marxist dichotomous view of class is sometimes mistaken for oversimplification, but it arises from a desire to make class categories explain more. As such it can explain the real development of societies.

For example, consider today's experience of a Tory-led government filled with millionaires, implementing policies designed to enrich the ruling class, and depress the living standards of the working majority. Only by employing a radical class analysis, 'austerity' can be seen as a political class strategy for redistributing the social product and consolidating the wider political and ideological power of the rich. It explains the doggedness of their clinging to policies that 'don't work', and also calls into question what sort of strategies we could activate in opposing 'austerity'. This is what is at stake in class analysis today.

Adapted from Seymour (2013)

Questions

1. What does it mean that 'classes do not exist prior to coming into relationship with one another'?
2. How are contemporary social classifications different to radical classifications?
3. What is the accusation made in the final paragraph about government policy about 'austerity'?

3.3 What are the problems of defining and measuring social class?

Figure 6.25 In the past class divisions were symbolised by 'Toffs and Toughs'

The concept of social class itself is best viewed as a structural position within the overall class structure, represented in the various schemas covered in the previous section. The Danish-American sociologist Aage Sørensen (1991) makes the interesting point that class positions are 'empty places'; existing independently of individual occupants. Class positions are consequently filled when people fulfil the social relationships within markets, especially within labour markets. Classifying people objectively within structural positions reflects the theories of both Marx and Weber, but also later sociologists such as John Goldthorpe, Gilbert and Kahl and Savage et al.

We have seen that trying to measure social class through the various attempts to operationalise the concept is a challenging task. Most attempts to measure social class involve classifications based on occupation. However, as discussed above, a distinction can be made between descriptive models (such as the RGSC) and gradational class schemes (such as Goldthorpe's schema). The big problem with measuring social class in terms of occupation is where to place those economically inactive; such as the very rich, unemployed, sick and disabled and students.

Anthony Giddens: From advocate to adversary of class

Giddens' relationship to class analysis has undergone a remarkable transformation since his early work in the 1960s and 1970s. His early work involved a thorough re-theorisation of class through an ambitious attempt to blend insights from both Marx and Weber. At this time Giddens argued that economic classes were defined in terms of 'market capacities' – factors like property, skills and bargaining power – resulting in individuals who shared similar market capacities forming social classes.

In recent years he has become something of an adversary of class, supporting Ulrich Beck's notion of 'individualisation' (although Giddens does not use the actual term). Giddens' (1991) ideas are crucially reflected in the concept of reflexivity of the self. He argues we are now living in conditions of late modernity where, as a result of globalisation, social class has been 'evacuated' from social life and supplanted by 'a context of multiple choice'. As a consequence, we are all now living increasingly individualised lives, whereby the self has become a reflexive project in which individuals actively choose, sustain and constantly revise their identity. However, Giddens recognises the burdens of such a superficial society – having to constantly reconstruct an 'inherently fragile' narrative of self-identity. By this Giddens reflects on how individuals struggle to live up to their own 'ideal self'. In addition, he argues, this reflexivity takes place within a society he characterises as something of an ethical vacuum.

> **KEY SOCIOLOGISTS**
> **Giddens and Sutton** (2012) maintain that social class continues to play a significant sociological role in any analysis of inequality, simply because evidence shows it still correlates with a wide range of inequalities: educational attainment, health and life expectancy and future employment prospects.

Southerton: the visibility of class

Dale Southerton (2002) argues that social class can be classified from cultural cues, such as everyday practices, leisure pursuits and cultural values. Using simplistic stereotypes, he argues that class (especially those at the bottom of the class structure) is as visible as those the in the image at the beginning of this section:

> 'It sounds awfully snobbish to say, but if you stand behind somebody in Tesco's ... it's blatantly obvious where they live because of the way, there's a different dress code ... you've got this almost downtrodden image ... And you seem to get this overweight syndrome, mum's always got a cigarette in her hand ... even the kids are different, the behaviour, the noise, the way they play' (Southerton, 2002, page 185).

Southerton is being derogatory and patronising to those from the working class. The inference that class can be identified through bodily and behavioural cues is to construct the working class as 'other', or 'not the middle class' who are culturally constructed as 'normal'. By stripping people of social respectability and self-worth, such accounts become a shorthand way of referencing social class without explicitly naming it.

Arber: the price of being female

Attempts to analyse social class alone become complicated when gender relations are considered. The feminist Sara Arber (2008) is particularly interested in the longitudinal picture of gender inequality and how this can change over time, especially as women enter retirement. As discussed in previous chapters, there is a gender division between women and men associated with vertical and horizontal segregation. However, divisions widen further when women retire. What Arber terms the 'price of being female' is exacerbated when the effects of occupational and private pensions are assessed in terms of post-employment income. Therefore, the costs of the sexual division in the labour market and of women's role in the domestic economy ('the cost of caring') are borne by women, particularly as they grow old. Arber concludes that, besides social class, gender and marital status are just as crucial factors in understanding income inequality among elderly people. Occupational and personal pensions are the chief means of perpetuating these divisions into later life.

Wilkinson: Employment 'genderquake'

Helen Wilkinson (1994) notes there has been something of a 'genderquake' in terms of gender relations in education and the workplace. So while in the past measurement of social class tended to render women invisible by naively assuming they took their social class from their husbands, this is no longer applicable for a number of reasons:

- 25 per cent of women aged under 24 earn more than their male partners (2013). A further 22 per cent of couples have equal pay packets meaning that in 47 per cent of households of this age group males are no longer the primary breadwinner.
- Even where women earn less than their male partners their income is equally relied on, thus elevating their economic importance.
- Where couples are in very different occupations it may make sense to allocate individual social class locations.
- The number of stay-at-home mums has fallen to a record low, plunging to just 2 million (2013); the lowest since current records began in 1993. Over the same period the number of stay-at-home dads has almost doubled to 209,000.
- Therefore the number of households with women as the sole breadwinner is increasing, although they will be spread across social class classifications according to their employment status.

Gilbert-Kahl: model of the class structure

Sociologists Dennis Gilbert and Joseph Kahl (1992) developed a social class model for the United States based on Weberian principles. They devised a classification of six classes:

- capitalist class
- upper middle class
- lower middle class
- working class
- working poor
- underclass.

These layers of social class closely tied to occupation and income. Gilbert and Kahl saw class position as fluid and located individuals on their achieved positions obtained during their life course. As a consequence, their social class system allows for some degree of social mobility between classes over the life course. Notwithstanding this, Gilbert and Kahl conceded that inheritance and family position were particularly important factors in determining social position. They also recognised that social class in the USA is also interrelated with such factors as 'race', ethnicity, sex, gender, and national origin. For example, their sixth category of 'underclass' is disproportionately comprised of groups like ethnic minorities, immigrants, female-headed households and children.

STUDY TIP

Be aware of the postmodernist and late modernist contribution to sociology, arguing that some of the modernist assumptions are either outdated or no longer applicable. So ideas that the significance of class has waned as society becomes increasingly individualistic and characterised by choice and diversity become increasingly useful in evaluating traditional class structures.

CONTEMPORARY APPLICATION

As the focus on social class as the key aspect of inequality has declined, sociologists have increasingly embraced the concept of intersectionality. This is the complex way in which diverse social inequalities including gender, ethnicity, age, sexuality and disability are recognised to impact on people's lives. Social class alone cannot explain the complex inequalities experienced in contemporary society.

IN THE NEWS

Is class dead?

Class is a taboo subject in mainstream politics. Britain is adopting the American political dishonesty of disguising ever-widening income differences by calling nearly everyone 'middle class'. The 2011 riots implied there was a respectable middle class with an underclass beneath, quite unconnected to the rest of society.

The convenient political myth says class is dead. The deference of Downton Abbey is no more, with young people embracing a generic 'universal estuary' 'English' accent and mockney. Classlessness may be modern and hip – but the reality is birth determines destiny more certainly than 50 years ago. The great majority of those in the professions and good jobs were born to them. Class matters more, not less, than it did, and it needs saying loudly. Too often 'effort' is over-claimed and luck ignored by those eagerly justifying their class and income advantage over the very hard-working low-paid.

Of those calling themselves 'middle class' they stretch from the highly privileged – the 7 per cent with children in private schools – all the way to families struggling on the edge to pay a mortgage on an ex-council house. Where once the label 'working class' was a badge of pride those self-defining as working class say despondently that it only means 'poor' and 'low-paid' these days.

Class is a tangled web of education, taste, history and illusion – but follow the money, and income matches class pretty accurately. GDP has doubled since 1978, but only the top 10 per cent have seen incomes grow at or above that rate, twice as fast as the median and four times faster than the bottom 10 per cent.

Adapted from Toynbee (2011)

Questions

1. What arguments are used in modern society to imply class is dead?
2. How are the working class and particularly the underclass portrayed in society?
3. What evidence does Toynbee give for claiming class more not less than it did?
4. What point is being made in the last paragraph?

Check your understanding

1. What was Wright's elaborated class typology based on?
2. What were the three categories of economic power used by Runciman in his model?
3. What category included by Runciman was to influence the subsequent work of Charles Murray?
4. What was the Registrar General's Social Class (RGSC) based on?
5. How was the Hope-Goldthorpe scale different to the Registrar General's classification?
6. What was the eighth category in the National Statistics Socio-economic Classification (NS-SEC)?
7. What did Sørensen mean by saying that class positions are 'empty places'; existing independently of individual occupants?
8. How did Anthony Giddens change his view of social class over time?
9. Why was Southerton criticised for claiming social class could be classified from cultural cues?
10. In what ways is a subjection classification different to an objective classification of class?

Practice questions

1. Outline and explain **two** ways in which social class has been measured by socio-economic classifications (SECs). [10 marks]

Read Item A below and answer the question that follows.

Item A

The nature and pattern of women's labour force participation is a combination of structural factors that impact on women's lives and women's choices. The heterogeneity of women's experiences reflects the heterogeneity of the options and choices available to them.

Applying material from Item A, analyse two reasons why gender cannot be ignored from household measurements of social class. [10 marks]

Read Item B below and answer the question that follows.

Item B

Objective classifications attempt to measure class formation, both in the ways in which a structure forms into recognisable classes which are recognisable, and, as a consequence, how classes produce distinctive set of life chances, lifestyles, socio-political orientation and patterns of association.

Applying material from Item B and your knowledge, evaluate the view that objective classifications of social class are a coherent reflection of the inequalities within society. [20 marks]

Section 4: Structural changes

This section will explore the following debates:
- Have structures of inequality changed?
- Has the class structure of the UK changed?
- What is the impact of the global economy on stratification?

GETTING YOU STARTED

Does Parliament reflect the social make-up of the population?

Figure 6.26 Conservative Ministers in Parliament in the UK

MPs are over four times more likely to have gone to a fee-paying school than their constituents. Seven per cent of the general population attended independent schools, compared with 32 per cent of all MPs elected in 2015 to the House of Commons. Among Conservative MPs, this rises to almost half (48 per cent). Of non-Conservative MPs, 24 per cent went to a fee-paying school. Out of all MPs who were privately educated, almost one in ten went to Eton.

MPs educated at comprehensive schools now make up 49 per cent of the House, a rise from 43 per cent in 2010. Almost two-thirds (64 per cent) of those who were newly elected in 2015 went to comprehensive schools.

Nine out of 10 MPs are graduates and over a quarter went to either Oxford or Cambridge. If parliament is truly to represent the whole nation, the best possible representatives should be able to become MPs, regardless of social background. Today's figures remind us how important it is that we do more to increase levels of social mobility and make sure that bright young people from low and middle-income backgrounds have access to the best schools and the best universities.

Source: Adapted from The Sutton Trust (2015)

Questions

1. What percentage of MPs elected in 2015 were privately educated?
2. Why is the intake of newly elected MPs in 2015 encouraging in terms of social mobility?
3. What message is being made by the Sutton Trust in the last paragraph?
4. What does this news release tell us about the openness of British society?

4.1 Have structures of inequality changed?

Since the 1960s there has been talk of the decline of social class, a blurring between the working and middle class and even the radical idea that class is dead. These debates are discussed below along with questioning the extent to which changes in the structure of inequality centres on class. The key factors of gender and ethnic inequalities are examined as well. In the past 50 years or so, several important legislative acts have been passed to assist the breakdown of inequalities. The Equality Act (2010) has embraced and consolidated all previous inequality legislation. Inequalities inevitably take time to eradicate as they reflect vested interests, power structures and ingrained attitudes. This section explores the extent to which inequalities still prevail and the implications of what change has taken place in the move to eradicate such inequalities.

Embourgeoisement: a blurring of the class boundaries?

The **embourgeoisement** thesis can be seen as an early formulation of the idea of 'classlessness'. Its focus was on the disappearance of the working class as a distinct class. Manual workers, it was argued, no longer formed a self-contained and self-reproducing social class, and they no longer had a distinct cultural and political outlook. Changes in the nature of work (particularly the growth of new, light automated industries), real wage rises for manual workers (up 300 per cent in real terms since 1900), increasing educational opportunity, and a growth in consumerism led some people to believe the working class was adopting middle-class norms and values. In short, society was becoming a vast middle-class society, and when we are all in the same class, then by implication, we are a 'classless' or no-class society.

Goldthorpe *et al.* (1969) undertook their classic *Affluent Worker Study* in an attempt to evaluate the evidence for embourgeoisement in Britain. They deliberately chose Luton as an example of an unrepresentative purposive sample. They felt because of its socio-economic characteristics, Luton was so promising a town to find embourgeoisement that if not found there, they could safely conclude it did not occur anywhere in Britain. In the end they found no evidence of embourgeoisement, but did conclude that their affluent workers were embracing some middle-class characteristics. For example, materialism and expressions of self-interest to work and politics ('**instrumental orientation**') seemed important rather than traditional working-class values of social solidarity about 'them and us'.

Goldthorpe *et al.* identified the emergence of an instrumental and privatised working class that appeared to show signs of sharing middle-class values but with no desire to identify with or *become* middle class. For example, they showed little interest in socialising with their middle-class neighbours or acquiring middle-class friends. Most associated either with kin or with individuals of a similar socio-economic status. This lack of involvement in 'middle-class society' was also exemplified by the type of associations or organisations that the manual workers joined, such as working men's clubs, allotment associations, angling societies — all noticeably lacking in middle-class membership. In short, Goldthorpe *et al.* found the social boundaries between the middle and working class strong. However, this study is over 45 years old and its contribution to contemporary class analysis can be drawn into question.

Are we beginning to dis-identify with class?

Savage *et al.* (2010) argue that people generally recognise that they live in an unequal social world. The pervasiveness of inequalities results in encouraging people to embrace certain social identities. They recognise how as we moved into the twenty-first century social class took on an ambiguous nature:

> 'At one level, the idea of class seems to be widely understood and is clearly recognised as an important feature of social inequality. Yet, at the same time, people are generally reluctant to identify themselves unambiguously as members of social classes and class identities do not necessarily seem highly meaningful to them' (Savage *et al.*, 2010).

Savage *et al.* maintain it is not entirely clear whether this dis-identification with class is restricted to just those with working-class identities. As Beverley Skeggs (1997) muses: 'Who would want to be seen as working class?' Because the middle classes are less stigmatised they feel class identity might still be stronger here. In an earlier work Savage *et al.* found that middle classes tended to reject direct middle-class identification, preferring to focus on their 'mobility stories'. The implication of this is that as society has opened up, being 'middle class' is only a temporary position on their upward journey to higher places. As we shall see in Section 5, such imaginations of openness and mobility are delusionary, but it does not mean that they are not real inside people's heads. One could argue that in postmodern society there is a widespread belief that society has changed to the point that everyone feels that they need to distance themselves from the more overt language of class. However, there is a contradiction to Savage *et al.*'s findings. While talking about dis-identification with class, they point out that when asked to classify themselves, over half the population continue to call themselves 'working class'. So despite de-industrialisation and the shrinking numbers of manual workers, it would seem that there has only been a moderate decline in working-class identification since the 1960s.

Is class dead?

Pakulski and Waters (1995) argue that class no longer captures the important dimensions of conflict, stratification and inequality in society. As such it has been reduced to a historical phenomenon, becoming an overly crude concept, no longer capable of handling the nuances of the new identity politics. Their argument is partly influenced by Max Weber who argued that there are a variety of generative structures of social inequality besides social class. Consequently they argue that a sociological concentration on class actually hinders understanding since it diverts attention from other more central and more morally problematic inequalities that pervade postmodern society. Their analysis revolves around three core arguments:

1. That the classness of social inequalities varies historically.
2. That classness peaked in industrial society and has been declining ever since.
3. That contemporary society remains unequal but in a (mainly) classless way.

They are also influenced by the work of Emile Durkheim who argued in his analysis of the division of labour how many processes come to play in the dissolving of class; not least the process of occupational differentiation.

> 'class formation [is] first weakened by occupational differentiation and market fragmentation, then undermined by the unravelling of corporatist deals, and finally destroyed by the decomposition of class elites, organisations (parties and trade unions) and ideologies' (Pakulski and Waters, 1996).

Pakulski and Waters challenge all the traditional Marxist tropes of class in turn.

- They disagree that economic structures are fundamental to the structure of society and the structuring of actions.
- They deny that classes are distinct groups, implying they are little more than theoretical categories.
- With regard to identity, they deny that class shapes individual identities. They find no evidence of Marx's prediction that class will result in collective action in the promotion of social change.

They distinguish four features of this social change:

- *Culturalism*: stratification is now reduced to consumerism, lifestyle and aesthetics.
- *Fragmentation*: in postmodern society people have a variety of statuses based on membership of multiple groups.
- *Autonomisation*: postmodern society is more individualistic, therefore people become more independent in terms of values and behaviour.
- *Resignification*: people can and do change their preferences, resulting in a more fluid and unpredictable society.

Pakulski and Waters centre their argument on what they term 'status-conventional theory'. As social class becomes less important so status becomes more significant. The stratification of postmodern society is therefore primarily cultural; organised around differences of lifestyle and consumption. The old layering of class society has been replaced by a fragmentation of fluid statuses which can overlap and shift. Society is therefore not fixed but subject to negotiation and change. Class is dead as issues relating to gender, ethnicity, age, beliefs, disability and cultural difference and preference have become more important to individuals. In this respect, the ideas of Pakulski and Waters have something in common with those of Anthony Giddens (1991) and his late modern concepts of reflexivity and fluidity.

Critique of Pakulski and Waters

- They have been accused of using inconsistent definitions of class, defining it in economic terms, sometimes defining it in terms of political discourse. Marxists would argue class is a real economic phenomenon based on the relationship to the means of production and cannot be dismissed. Weberians would point to its real and measured impact on life chances in terms of employment, health and education.
- Marxists like John Westergaard (1996) challenge the idea that consumption patterns have become more important than class, since social class still largely determines consumption patterns and lifestyle.
- Harriet Bradley (1997) criticises their work for being superficial and lacking concrete evidence. She describes it as a 'rehashing of the usual postmodern truisms about change involving consumerism, fragmentation and destabilisation' without empirical backing.

KEY SOCIOLOGIST

Beverley Skeggs (1997) argues the case for class and gender being fused together to produce an accurate representation of power relations in contemporary society. She questions how theoretical frameworks were often generated in a manner that did not understand how women live and produce themselves through social and cultural relations. Using detailed ethnographic research she shows how 'real' women inhabit and occupy the social and cultural positions of class, femininity and sexuality.

STUDY TIP

Familiarise yourself with the postmodern argument that people have dis-identified with class to the point that class is dead, alongside the counter argument that class is still a real phenomenon that shapes life chances.

CONTEMPORARY APPLICATION

The BBC in conjunction with sociologists (Savage et al., 2013) devised the Great British Class Survey (see next section) believing that the traditional categories of working, middle and upper class are outdated, fitting just 39 per cent of the population. From a survey of 161,000 people a new model of seven social classes was devised ranging from the 'elite' at the top to a 'precariat' representing an impoverished and precarious proletariat at the bottom.

IN THE NEWS

The more unequal we get, the less we want to talk about it

Being perceived as upper class in contemporary Britain is the kiss of death, and not just in politics. In the same poll, YouGov asked people the question, 'What class are you?' Forty-six per cent said 'working class', 49 per cent 'middle class' and just 1 per cent 'upper class'. I'm surprised the number was so high, frankly. I've been hobnobbing with society types for over 30 years — including dukes, billionaires and minor royals — and I've only ever heard one person describe themselves as upper class. To complicate matters, the person in question was, in fact, middle class.

What polls like this reveal is that we've become a nation of inverted snobs. To be precise, everyone dis-avows the class hierarchy that prevailed until about 25 years ago, but they do so partly because to admit you set any store by it is, in itself, a low class indicator. So the English class system hasn't really gone away, it's just become more insidious. Officially, it's ceased to exist in the sense that no one cares whether you say 'serviette' or 'napkin'. But unofficially, it's still there, casting its ancient spell.

The metamorphoses of the class system from overt to covert, above ground to underground, must be connected to the massive increase in economic inequality in the past 25 years or so.

Adapted from Young (2014)

Questions

1. What does the author mean when he says the class system hasn't really gone away, it's just become more insidious?
2. Does it matter whether you say 'serviette' or 'napkin' in certain social circles?
3. Explain why the massive increase in economic inequality has turned the class system from overt to covert.
4. Besides language what other cultural signifiers of class exist in society?

4.2 Has the class structure of the UK changed?

Postmodernists claim that class is dead but socio-economic classifications continue to highlight the perseverance of a layered society with differential life chances.

The upper class

Aristocratic landed gentry

The wealth of the upper class traditionally derived from rent from land ownership; hence the phrase the 'landed gentry'. Some, like Gerald Grosvenor, the 6th Duke of Westminster, continue to use land to generate wealth. He is the ninth richest man in the UK from owning 190 acres in Belgravia, an area adjacent to Buckingham Palace and one of London's most expensive neighbourhoods worth around £8.65 billion (2015). The 'aristocratic' character of land ownership has been a central feature for upper class social status and political power in Britain for centuries. John Scott (1991) shows how titles and trappings of the landed aristocracy help to disguise the capitalistic nature of ownership and aid the integration of many of the wealthy into a closed status group. Such boundaries of status and social closure, working through kinship, elite education and commercial networks, serve to sustain the British upper class as a clear social entity with special access to power and social influence.

Over time divisions of interest between land and industry have been fundamental to the political development of the upper classes. Marxists, like Westergaard and Resler (1976), argue that capital ownership is the basis of not only division but exploitation in a capitalist society: the interests of capital will always take precedent and be rewarded more highly than that of labour. This continuing relationship between capital and labour means that class divisions will ever be maintained along these lines.

An outdated concept?

Sociologists, like John Goldthorpe in the managerialist tradition, argue the concept of an upper or ruling class is outdated. Some, like John Scott, prefer 'capitalist class' to upper class as this describes their economic basis. According to such theorists, capitalist patterns of control disappeared with the growth of wider share ownership. Goldthorpe somewhat naively saw the managers of his 'service class' displacing the capitalist class from its position of power. Ralph Dahrendorf (1959) even went so far as to describe the creation of the widespread share ownership as 'the half-way stage to communism'. However, the doubling of the wealth of the upper class in the past decade shows the upper class are anything but outdated.

The middle class

The emergence of modern industrial capitalism in the eighteenth century stimulated the growth of the middle class. A second phase of middle-class development occurred in the nineteenth century, with the growth of the non-manual sector. There were simply not enough children from the older middle class to fill these positions so a 'new' middle class of salaried grew to fill the gap.

The middle class can easily be differentiated from the upper class by their lack of ownership of and control over capital. The dividing line between the middle class and the working class has become considerably more complex. Until relatively recently, the distinction between middle and working class was the nature of their work – non-manual as opposed to manual work. However, the distinction between manual and non-manual work has become blurred as factory and manufacturing jobs have significantly declined. Both changes are associated with a shift towards a post-industrial society.

Fragmented middle classes

Savage (1992) argues that the middle class is fragmenting and that it might be much more appropriate to talk of 'middle classes'. Roberts *et al.* (1977) shared this view and from a survey of 243 male white-collar workers found they there were contrasting subjective perceptions of what constitutes the middle class:

1. About a quarter of the sample (in the middle range income bracket for white-collar workers) saw themselves as part of a middle class that was made up of the bulk of the working population sandwiched between a small powerful and very rich upper class, and a relatively impoverished lower class. They made no distinction between manual and non-manual workers.
2. A fifth of the sample felt threatened as part of a 'compressed middle class' squeezed between two increasingly powerful classes of an organised and unionised working class and a rich and privileged upper class. Small business people typically held this compressed middle-class self-image.

3. Around 15 per cent of the sample, typically from well-educated professional workers, saw the middle class as a finely graded ladder containing the upper middle, middle middle, lower middle classes. Supporters of this self-image tended to be relatively high paid.
4. A similarly sized proportion of the sample described themself as 'working class'. They identified with the process of proletarianisation seeing themselves as having more in common with manual workers than with top management and higher professionals. Such people were typically routine non-manual workers with few promotion prospects and relatively low wages.

However, Anthony Giddens (1973) challenges the plurality of middle classes, arguing there is simply a single middle class based on the possession of 'educational or technical qualifications'. Furthermore, they are distinct to the upper class in that they do not own the means of production. In contrast to Giddens, John Goldthorpe (1982) does not distinguish an upper class, but characterises the middle class as a maturing 'service class' made up of large proprietors, administrators, managers and professionals. His schema does differentiate between those in the higher and lower professions and management.

Contemporary middle class

Savage *et al.* (1992) found the middle class was comprised of three distinct groups: those with property assets, those with organisational assets and those with cultural assets. The importance of the latter was central to their later work (Savage *et al.*, 2013) when they developed the Great British Class Survey (GBCS). They built their classification on the work of Pierre Bourdieu and his concepts of economic, cultural and social capital. Bourdieu had shown that besides economic capital the middle class benefit enormously from cultural and social capital that particularly advantages them in terms of educational achievement and credentials. Savage *et al.* differentiated between the 'established middle class' and the 'technical middle class'. In terms of the former, they have been viewed as similar to the elite, but having smaller incomes, fewer saving and living in cheaper houses. In terms of social and cultural capital they do not appear to differ significantly. The technical middle class have high economic capital, very high social contacts, but relatively few contacts reported with only moderate cultural capital. Taken together, these 'middle classes' comprise 32 per cent of the population; a very substantial proportion of UK society.

Middle-class professionals

We saw from the socio-economic classifications discussed previously that higher and lower professions featured predominantly in most of these schemas. The professions and senior managerial positions have always been the target of middle-class children and the motivation to succeed in the education system. The higher professions in particular attract and reproduce the upper middle class, having the high returns in terms of income and status. The lower professions are less well rewarded and often below the income of skilled manual workers like plumbers, plasterers and train drivers. Professional workers remain of paramount importance to the economy, but it is worth emphasising the divisions that exist between the affluent lifestyle of the higher professions and the comfortable existence of the lower professions. A useful means of examining the differentiation within the professions is to embrace Mike Savage's vision of a fragmented middle class made up of several Subdivisions. This pluralistic view of middle classes can then be positioned along the lines of variations in the nature and type of property, public/private employment and degrees of cultural and social capital.

The working class

Traditionally the working class has been defined in classifications like the Registrar General's classification (RGSC) as manual workers. From the various classifications studied in earlier chapters it should be clear that as a group the working class has no uniform or homogeneous nature. They are invariably divided into skilled, semi-skilled or unskilled workers, or alternatively described as semi-routine or routine. The postmodernist concept of fragmentation highlights such diversity within manual workers. However, at the same time, observers have commented on how manual workers of different statuses can share a lot of experiences and embrace a broad culture that can differentiate them from the middle class.

Distinction between manual and non-manual workers

Although postmodernists argue class is dead and that the distinction between working class and middle class has become somewhat blurred, there are still some key differences in the life chances between manual workers and non-manual workers. The obvious one is pay, although some skilled manual workers can earn higher wages. For example, London Underground drivers earn around £40,000 per annum for a four day week (TfL, 2015) compared to an average £34,600 for teachers per annum (DfE, 2015). However, a comparison of wages alone does not take into account factors like promotional prospects, annual increments, pension schemes, expense accounts, paid sick leave, company cars and perks like private medical assurance which many non-manual workers enjoy. In addition, wages of manual workers tend to peak in their thirties whereas earnings of many non-manual workers rise to peak during their forties or later. Finally, non-manual workers tend to have greater security of employment compared to manual workers who traditionally have had a greater risk of redundancy, lay-offs and short-time.

Traditional working class

In the past sociologists like David Lockwood (1966) referred to the working class as 'proletarian traditionalists'. Various studies of this era portrayed the working class as living in close-knit communities producing a shared sense of social solidarity such as trade union support and collective rather than goals. They were portrayed as working in traditional industries and subject to limited social or geographical mobility. Consequently they lived for the moment and adopted the classic working-class characteristic of fatalism. While this image of the working class might have applied in the 1950s by the 1960s sociologists were questioning whether the working class was aspiring to middle-class attitudes, values and behaviours in a process known as embourgeoisement (discussed previously on page 368).

Insiders and outsiders

David Goldblatt (2000) notes how in post-industrial society there has been a huge growth of low-skilled, low-paid workers in the increasingly large service sector. He observes how they are differentiated from higher-paid, skilled workers into an increasingly divided two-tier system he calls 'insiders' and 'outsiders':

> 'In place of a relatively homogeneous semi-skilled working class there now exists a labour market of insiders and outsiders, high-skilled and low-skilled workers, permanent and temporary workers, full-timers and part-timers' (Goldblatt, 2000:131).

Reflecting the concept of a 'reserve army of labour', Goldblatt argues that this allows companies to rebuild their profitability by shifting the problems of flexibility and variation onto those on the edge of the labour market, who work when demand is high and are thrown out when demand is low.

New working class

In contrast to the proletarian traditionalists, the new working class are viewed as more individualistic and many see the decade of neo-liberalism associated with the 1980s onwards as particularly influential in shaping these new developments. Instead of renting social housing, the new working class aspires to homeownership. Rather than working in traditional industries (many of which no longer exist anyway) they now work in service industries. In the past writers (like Young and Willmott (1963) in their study of Bethnal Green) portrayed a male culture spending their evenings drinking down the pub. The new working class is more home and child-centred and spends more time with their partners (as also reflected in Young and Willmott's study of the privatised family life in 'Greenleigh').

Ken Roberts (2001) has put a slightly different slant on what he calls the 'new working class' as a specific type of contemporary worker. He sees them employed as a low-skilled workforce in businesses generally associated with dining, leisure, sport and tourism. He refers to this group of workers as the 'new working class'. Since employment in this service sector often involves low skills, he argues that employers are looking increasingly for aesthetic attributes rather than educational qualifications:

> 'Because of their visibility to the client, young (attractive) people are required to supply aesthetic labour – looking right to boost the company's image and appearing human and interested in their commitment to customer satisfaction' (Roberts, 2001).

According to Roberts, employers increasingly rely more on appearance and accent than on qualifications and corporate image becomes defined through their employees. An example of this was Abercrombie and Fitch who faced legal action in France for only employing 'good looking' staff. In London a female employee with a prosthetic arm was made to work in the storeroom so that she was not seen by customers. Examples like this show that it is now more important to employers that the social role of their employees reflects the lifestyle being sold by the restaurant, cafe or shop they work in than that they have any technical skills. Roberts argues this new working class is fragmented, insecure, typically working part-time and/or unsocial or variable hours. They work to serve the leisure time of others and are frequently on **zero-hours contracts**.

Working class in the Great British Class Survey (GBCS)

The most up-to-date classification of working class comes from Savage *et al.* (2013). They identified three categories of manual workers. The first is 'new affluent workers' who have moderately good economic capital, with a moderately poor mean score of social contacts, though high range. They are described as moderately highbrow and possessing good emerging cultural capital. The second group was termed 'traditional working class' who are deemed to have moderately poor economic capital, few social contacts, low highbrow and an emerging cultural capital. The third category is 'emergent service workers' who also have moderately poor economic capital, though with reasonable household income, moderate social contacts, high emerging (but low highbrow) cultural capital. They may be likened to Roberts' 'new working class' or Goldblatt's 'outsiders'. Beneath the working class, Savage *et al.* have a final layer: the 'precariat' or some would call them an underclass.

The underclass

The underclass is a differentiated layer beneath the working class, reflecting people whose lifestyle (material and/or cultural) is so distinctly different to the rest of society that they constitute a class in their own right. The term 'underclass' was first used in recent times by the Swedish academic Gunnar Myrdal (1963) to describe a group of people driven to the edges or even outside the economy. However, the concept can be traced back to Karl Marx and the 'lumpen-proletariat' (ragged proletariat) a term he used to describe the very poorest workers. Although the underclass is particularly associated with the New Right, it is a Weberian concept reflecting a group at the bottom of society lacking status and market power. Although the late Marxist Jock Young (2007) was happy to use the term underclass to refer to the very poor at the bottom of society, it is a term generally claimed by New Right sociologists like Charles Murray (1990) and Peter Saunders (1990).

Cultural arguments for an underclass

Murray argues that members of the underclass define themselves as different by their own deviant subcultural behaviour. Murray singles out three forms of behaviour that define underclass status:

- Parenting: illegitimate births to young women, with fathers refusing to take responsibility.
- Criminal: habitual crime and particularly violent crime.
- Labour: the refusal of young working class men to enter employment.

The term 'underclass' for Murray represents a certain type of poor person defined not by their condition, but by their deplorable behaviour in response to that condition: welfare dependency and work-shyness:

> 'If illegitimate births are the leading indicator of an underclass and violent crime a proxy measure of its development, the definitive proof that an underclass has arrived is that large numbers of young, healthy, low-income males choose not to take jobs' (Murray, 1990).

The right-wing Anglo-Australian sociologist Peter Saunders (1990) views the underclass in a similar way to Murray:

> 'A stratum of people who are generally poor, unqualified and irregularly or never employed. This underclass is disproportionately recruited from people ... who are trapped in run-down housing estates or in decaying inner cities, and young single people and single parent families' (Saunders, 1990).

Saunders talks about 'four key features' of the underclass:

- multiple deprivation
- social marginality
- an almost entire dependence on state welfare provisions
- a culture of fatalism.

Both Saunders and Murray imply that the poor themselves are to blame for their poverty because they either choose to act in certain deviant ways or they are conditioned to do so by what they both regard as an overgenerous welfare state. It has been recorded elsewhere in this book how Murray's ideas have been criticised for lack of evidence. Alan Walker (1991) sums this up by accusing Murray of relying on 'assertions, anecdotes and innuendos'.

Structural arguments for an underclass

We saw earlier that W.G. Runciman (1990) identified an underclass in the Runciman Scale. He saw the underclass as largely comprising those members of society more or less permanently dependent on welfare benefits. Others like Anthony Giddens linked the underclass to a wider category of those in the secondary labour market. Rex and Tomlinson (1979) in a classic neo-Weberian study of ethnic minorities in the Sparkbrook area of Birmingham concluded that because of their disadvantages with regard to the labour market, housing and education, they constituted a separate underclass beneath the white working class. Official unemployment statistic suggest that ethnic minority males have an unemployment rate which is almost double that of white males.

Jock Young (2007) has a compassionate view of the very poorest members of society. Unlike Murray and Saunders he is non-judgemental, seeing the underclass as casualties of the capitalist system. However, because their poverty is experienced amid great wealth in a consumer society, their humiliation becomes a 'meta-humiliation' (Bauman and Tester, 2001). Young challenges Murray's view that they hold their own subcultural values. Instead he notes how they wholeheartedly embrace mainstream neo-liberal values of individualism and materialism; as a compensation for the humiliation of poverty. Yet the underclass is portrayed as different and feckless, providing an ideal scapegoat for others to blame. When society fails to deliver the material success promised by a mythical meritocracy, instead Young argues a form of social bulimia results. Out of feelings of insecurity and dissatisfaction the oppressed in society look for scapegoats to demonise, with the underclass acting as a prime target for resentment. Media representations of the very poor on welfare imply they are getting exactly what they want without any effort. However, the reality and pain of being poor rarely gets the sensitive coverage it warrants.

KEY SOCIOLOGIST

Marshall *et al.* (1988) support the idea that the working class is divided in accordance with levels of skill involved in their work. For them, class divisions remain important and they believe that competition between different groups of the working class has created divisions lasting from the nineteenth century to the present day. They argue that the working class has always been stratified according to industry, locality, grade and occupation.

STUDY TIP

Having an awareness of social class divisions is important, while recognising the case that such divisions are becoming less important and the boundaries between them increasingly blurred.

CONTEMPORARY APPLICATION

Those at the bottom of society have always been obligingly accepting of their inferior position and lack of radical politics. Richard Hoggart (1957) wrote about the working class in the 1950s: 'they do not quarrel with their general level … the strong sense of the group among working-class people can express itself as a demand for conformity'. The novelist Andrew O'Hagan (2014) writes: 'My contention is that most people [in England] are subjected to a sustained and ever-increasing bombardment of invitations to assume that whatever is, is right, so long as it is widely accepted and can be classed as entertaining.'

> **IN THE NEWS**
>
> ### Thought class was dead?
>
> In his 1989 introduction to George Orwell's *The Road to Wigan Pier*, the academic Richard Hoggart wrote: 'Class distinctions do not die; they merely learn new ways of expressing themselves.' This is as true now as it was 25 years ago, and 25 years before that. 'Each decade,' he continued, 'we shiftily declare we have buried class; each decade the coffin stays empty.' Compare this with: 'We're all middle class now' (except we're not); or 'Playing by the rules' (which are made by, and changed at the whims of, the most privileged); or 'We're all in this together' (unless you're a scrounger).
>
> We need Hoggart now because we have a deceptively flattened media and cultural landscape in which everyone is meant to take a bit, and like a bit, of everything. Twitter and Instagram give the impression of everyone having an equal voice, from the out-of-work plasterer to the millionaire art dealer. A grounding in Hoggart's work blasts through that. He reminds us that access to culture widens and narrows according to who's got the keys – and that is always the people with education, contacts and confidence.
>
> Adapted from Hanley (2014)

> **Questions**
>
> 1. In what respects does the 'coffin stay empty' with regard to social class?
> 2. Outline briefly how a Weberian would argue social class is still a real phenomenon.
> 3. Outline briefly how a Marxist would argue social class is still a real phenomenon.
> 4. What point is the author making in the final paragraph about social class?

4.3 What is the impact of the global economy on stratification?

Migration and stratification are intimately and irrevocably linked through Max Weber's concept of life chances. Migration and immigration can best be understood as motivated by a desire to improve life chances following relocation. Attitudes to migration and especially immigration can be highly variable, more often perceived as a threat to jobs or prevailing cultural practices. As a consequence, immigrants frequently face prejudice, discrimination, racism, social exclusion, separation from family members (including partners and children) and sometimes the denial of citizenship rights. Stratification mechanisms can also impact on who is allowed to migrate, often determined by what skills workers possess and matching these to the demands of the host country. Other migrants may come fleeing brutality and seeking asylum, while citizens of the European Union have freedom of movement to relocate in any member country. Immigration formed one of the key political issues in the

2015 General Election, resulting in a commitment to hold a referendum on EU membership by 2017.

Sociologists examine the process and consequences of migration on host populations, such as degrees of resistance, incorporation and assimilation. Any study of migration must also recognise the impact of inscriptive factors like gender, ethnicity, age and how these impact on life chances such as educational attainment, health, housing, employment and earnings.

A disorganised working class?

The UK is one of the most unequal societies in the Western world and as noted in earlier chapters the share of wealth of the richest one per cent continues to increase. However, despite the widening of the pay gap Ken Roberts (2001) found little evidence of class consciousness among those at the bottom of society. While he found an identification among manual workers with the term 'working class' there was little evidence of any meaningful level of class consciousness. Instead, Roberts uses the term '**disorganised**' to describe their attitude. Roberts' explanation of this is his belief that the working class has become disempowered through its loss of control of key institutions like the trade unions and the Labour Party.

Roberts provides a range of evidence in support of this argument. He states that the Labour Party is no longer the party of the working class. He argues that the Blair years in particular involved a distancing between the Labour Party and rank and file workers through weakening its links to the unions and pursuing policies aimed at appealing to big business and the middle classes. A second factor is the decline in power, influence and membership of the trade unions. Roberts notes that in unions, membership from the middle class is higher than the working class. A third factor according to Roberts is the ideological severance between the working class and the Cooperative movement which has become just another retailer. Fourthly working-class leisure has become fragmented as traditional areas like working men's (sic) clubs have lost out to television and other forms of commercial leisure. Finally the close-knit working-class communities have declined due to slum clearance, the loss of heavy industry and the influx of new residents.

Elective belonging

Savage *et al.* (2005) in their book *Globalisation and Belonging* link issues of stratification associated with long-term residents and recent migrants to important cultural issues of identity, difference, choice and lifestyle. They make the point that in contemporary society relatively few people are born and bred in the place where they still live. Consequently they examine how far-reaching global changes are articulated locally and how people have a sense of elective belonging based on where they choose to put down roots. Those who are seen as transient, with no ties to the place they now live in, are viewed critically. Therefore the concept of elective belonging argues that places are not characterised by tensions between insiders and outsiders but that instead they are defined as locales for people electing to belong (and not just reside) in specific places. The feel of a place is strongly influenced by the values and lifestyles of those migrating to it.

Savage *et al.* found that the way children were brought up helped create this feeling of elective belonging. Migrants talked about how childrearing made them feel at home. In addition, feeling at home was also shaped by the way migrants connected their location to other places that they prized. In a world of global connections, residents routinely associate the place where they live with other places, sometimes of significant distance. Elective belonging involves people moving to a place and putting down roots. Places are defined not simply as sites where one happens to live but the sites chosen by particular social groups wishing to announce their identities.

One clear finding of the researchers was the differentiated nature of the social networks of residents. For example, work and friendship networks rarely overlapped. Within these differentiated fields, residential space became the key arena for the respondents to define their social position. This was because residential space was crucial in allowing people access to other fields such as education, employment and various cultural fields. They looked at people in areas around Manchester and used Pierre Bourdieu's concept of types of capital to differentiate them. For example, Chorlton appealed to those with both cultural and economic capital. Winslow appeals to those with considerable amounts of economic capital and moderate cultural capital. Finally, Ramsbottom is favoured by the upwardly mobile without large amounts of cultural capital. The conclusion is that locational residence is possibly the most crucial identifier of who you are.

KEY SOCIOLOGIST

Research by **Avery et al.** (2012) found that there are complex intersections between immigration and retirement. At a time of increasing immigration and the government extending the retirement age, this poses a double threat to those seeking employment. However, the researchers concluded that besides the threats there were also opportunities for employers, individuals and society at large.

CONTEMPORARY APPLICATION

The middle class has more than doubled in size over the past decade in the developing world. Defined as those living on more than $4 a day, the middle class makes up more than 40 per cent of the developing world's workforce and is predicted by the International Labour Organization (ILO) to account for more than half by 2017.

STUDY TIP

Global trends and patterns will continue to exercise an increasing influence on the UK economy and its workers. The global trend in outsourcing production to the developing world is known as the **new international division of labour**.

IN THE NEWS

It's immigration, not immigrants, that British people say they don't like

A YouGov poll of *Sun* readers produces the entirely unsurprising finding that only 10 per cent think immigration in the past 10 years has been good for Britain, while 71 per cent think it has been bad for us. Despite this opposition to immigration there are still four significant categories where a majority of the population wish to continue to enter Britain in either the 'same or greater numbers than today'. These groups are the wealthy people looking to invest in Britain, people paying to study in British universities, people with high levels of skills and qualifications and people coming to work in British health services.

Hostility to immigration partly stems from a belief that Britain has been overrun with the 'wrong' immigrants, such as welfare tourists who come here for child benefit and jobseeker's allowance.

Evidence shows that many people vastly overstate the numbers of such people. In addition there is a feeling that Britain has 'gone to the dogs' with too few secure jobs and affordable homes, too much crime, overcrowded schools and an overstretched NHS. There is a feeling that life is worse now than for decades.

YouGov's figures for immigrants from non-white countries will also surprise some people. Those from India and the Caribbean produced clearly positive responses, with those from Pakistan being only narrowly negative. Only Nigeria provokes anything like the hostility we accord to people from Bulgaria and Romania. Compared to the 1950s the passage of time and the accumulation of personal contacts seems to have changed attitudes.

Adapted from Kellner (2015)

Questions

1. What types of immigrant do a majority of people still want to continue coming to Britain?
2. According to the article where does hostility to immigration come from?
3. How have attitudes changed since the 1950s?

Check your understanding

1. What does embourgeoisement mean?
2. What were the findings of Goldthorpe *et al.*'s study of affluent workers in Luton?
3. What do Savage *et al.* mean by the term *dis-identification*?
4. In what ways is the work of Pakulski and Waters influenced by the ideas of Weber?
5. Briefly summarise Ralph Miliband's elite theory.
6. Why do Savage *et al.* argue it makes more sense to talk about the middle classes?
7. What does proletarianisation mean?
8. How is the new working class different to the traditional working class?
9. What do Savage *et al.* mean by elective belonging?
10. How did Roberts see the working class?

Practice questions

1. Outline and explain **two** classifications by which social class has been measured in the UK. [10 marks]

Read Item A below and answer the question that follows.

Item A

The middle class is a broad group of people in the middle of a social hierarchy sandwiched between the upper class and the working class. As a group they are cemented together by shared cultural values but are also characterised by considerable internal differences.

Applying material from Item A, analyse two reasons why the middle class is a fragmented social class. [10 marks]

Read Item B below and answer the question that follows.

Item B

Social class was the very basis of past work on the stratification of society. Yet it is increasingly argued that class has become an increasingly outmoded concept. Others argue that through stratification people are still differentiated hierarchically into distinct social classes.

Applying material from Item B and your knowledge, evaluate the view that social class is an out-of-date concept. [20 marks]

Section 5: Patterns of social mobility

This section will explore the following debates:

- What are the nature, extent and significance of patterns of social mobility?
- What are types of social mobility?
- What are the patterns, changes and impacts of social mobility in the UK?
- How do we measure and study social mobility?

GETTING YOU STARTED

Questions

1. Why is it likely that children of the upper class will share their parents' wealth, status and social position?
2. Make a list of factors which can inhibit children from lower class parents becoming higher professionals.
3. Are workers in call centres faced with jobs like this for the rest of their working lives?
4. Why is it that those at the bottom of society tend to reproduce their inequalities to their children?

5.1 What is the nature, extent and significance of patterns of social mobility

'Low social mobility and lack of educational opportunity is arguably the biggest social challenge of our times: the income gap between the richest and poorest in society continues to widen, while education opportunities remain overwhelmingly dominated by children from the most privileged homes' (Sutton Trust website, 2015).

There has been a vigorous debate among sociologists and politicians about the extent and direction of social mobility in Britain over recent decades. Following the optimism that prevailed in the 1950s and 1960s about the opening up of society, research seems to suggest that the UK remains a fairly closed society:

'Low social mobility and lack of educational opportunity is arguably the biggest social challenge of our times: the income gap between the richest and poorest in society continues to widen, while education opportunities remain overwhelmingly dominated by children from the most privileged homes' (Sutton Trust website, 2015).

However, Dorling *et al.* (2007) found more evidence of a slow and steady increase in social mobility when people were classified by address rather than occupation. They argue that the address you are born in matters more now than it did in the past for your chances of dying young, being poor or wealthy and so on. Dorling (2008) also found that wealth inequalities had a bigger impact than income inequalities compared to the recent past.

Generally those who are privileged will seek to preserve their privileged position; for example, by passing on their privileges to their children and mutually supporting each other by closing ranks. However, this goes against three important principles of social justice, economic efficiency and social stability. Because these can all be viewed as beneficial to society as a whole, any attempt to restrict or inhibit these principles undermines the interests of everyone (except the privileged who to stand to lose). The principle of living in a meritocracy implies equality of opportunity and economic efficiency, whereby the rewards for employment reflect a person's actual productivity rather than their ascribed characteristics such as sex or 'race'. Finally, evidence shows that blocking aspirations and opportunities can become a potent source of social dissent and conflict. Lea and Young (1984) support this with their left realist research into ethnic minorities and crime.

Social mobility refers to movement up and down the social scale from one class to another. It is either '**intergenerationally**' which measures mobility between generations, usually between parents and children, or '**intragenerationally**' which is the movement calculated within a person's lifetime. Since the Second World War politicians have talked up the amount of mobility there has been, implying that Britain has become a more '**open society**'. Although an open society implies the existence of a meritocracy, much of the mobility in the past 60 years or so has been short-range and explained by the increased availability of white-collar and professional jobs as the economy moved towards a post-industrial society.

Social mobility is possible in either direction and can be short or long range. Most upward mobility is between the working and middle class since access to top positions in society tends to be blocked by the inherited advantage of existing elites. The few and often well-publicised examples of uneducated entrepreneurs belies the advantages that an exclusive private education still yields in contemporary society. For example, for the poorest fifth in society, 46 per cent have mothers with no qualifications at all whereas for the richest it is only 3 per cent.

Most studies on social mobility refer to men, their occupations and the comparison between father's occupation and son's occupation (intergenerational mobility). Any attempt to measure mobility broadly becomes problematic because it tends to render women and minority groups 'invisible' (although the Scottish Mobility Study (Payne, *et al.*, 1987) and 'Essex Study' (Marshall *et al.*, 1988) both included women). An additional problem is that while people can move up and down the social scale, society itself is subject to change. For example, clerical workers used to outrank manual workers in terms of income and status, but this may no longer be the case. Finally, the biggest problem with studies of social mobility is that they are by their nature either premature or out of date. This is because social mobility can be a lifetime process. It is only possible to measure the extent of a person's mobility when their career is over. Goldthorpe (1980) overcame this problem by assuming that people have little career progression after the age of 35. He used the term 'occupational maturity' to refer to people over this age.

> **CONTEMPORARY APPLICATION**
>
> Social mobility, or rather lack of social mobility, remains a matter of public concern. One of the most controversial conclusions to be derived from all the mobility research has been the lack of openness in society. It had been assumed that industrialism and especially post-industrial society would lead to greater openness or fluidity in society. The Cabinet Office Business Plan 2011–2015 included as one of its priorities the development of a cross-government social mobility strategy.

> **KEY SOCIOLOGIST**
>
> **John Goldthorpe** is noted for grouping social class into just three categories: the service class (professionals, managers and small business people), the intermediate class (technical, supervisory and self-employed), and the working class (semi and unskilled manual workers). As noted above, Goldthorpe with the *Affluent Worker Study* helped dispel the myth of embourgeoisement.

> **STUDY TIP**
>
> There is an obvious connect between social mobility and the quality and openness of the education system. Think about the life chances of those with free school meals (FSM) compared to those from privileged backgrounds and how the education system reproduces inequality at top and bottom of society.

IN THE NEWS

Privilege is the key to landing internships

Given that securing an internship is an increasingly important stepping stone into the labour market for the best jobs, the exclusivity of internships paints a bleak picture of social mobility in modern Britain. Because internships are usually unpaid this effectively denies them to all but the most privileged young people in society. On average, individuals have to complete seven internships before securing their first paid job. This illustrates just how important internships have become in securing full-time employment and the potentially far-reaching consequences for those unable to work for free.

A survey of 5,000 people carried out for the Debrett's Foundation finds that 72 per cent of privileged young Britons admitted to having used family connections to secure an internship work placement. Other factors in landing an internship included attending private school and who you know. One in ten young people said they had completed 15 placements before getting the job they wanted. One in five were not paid anything and one in ten only received travel and lunch expenses.

Debrett's chief executive Joanne Milner, said: '[Because of] the growth of the way graduates get jobs through internships, it's became much more important. I think people in Britain care about meritocracy but all the evidence is very bad – people who don't have those connections are not getting on the career ladder. We're actually going backwards.'

Adapted from Siddique (2015)

Figure 6.27 Getting a professional job often means doing several unpaid internships

> **Questions**
> 1. In what ways are less privileged people denied access to internships?
> 2. How does the growth and restricted access to internships undermine meritocracy?
> 3. Why do you think privileged young people put up with the internship system?
> 4. Do you agree that in terms of social mobility 'we're actually going backwards'?

5.2 Types of social mobility

Absolute mobility

Absolute mobility measures movement from one social location to another, whether 'upwards' or 'downwards'. For the Oxford Mobility Study (1980) John Goldthorpe specifically distinguishes between absolute flows, measured as 'inflow rates' and 'outflow rates'. Inflow refers to where people currently in a social class have moved from. When inflow rates are small this implies that a social class is self-recruiting. Outflow refers to which social class people actually end up in. When outflow rates are broad and extensive, this implies there is equality of opportunity. Absolute rates tend to be driven by structural changes such as the expansion of salaried professional and managerial positions which provide increasing 'room at the top'.

Father	Sons		
	Service	Intermediate	Working
Service	61.7	24.6	13.8
Intermediate	27.9	37.0	35.2
Working	15.0	26.4	56.6

Table 6.14 Sons' jobs compared to their fathers' jobs. Data from Oxford Mobility Study (1980)

Intergenerational mobility for males (Outflow)

The above table shows that British society is reasonably open. However, although there was some long-range mobility, most mobility was actually short-range. In addition, both the service class (professional and managerial) and the working class (semi and unskilled manual workers) have a significant amount of self-recruitment.

Relative mobility

Relative mobility measures the relative chances of individuals from different social class positions ending up in a specific location in the class structure. Relative mobility is essentially the mobility that occurs over and above the mobility that is due to changes in the occupational structure. Consequently, relative mobility is viewed by sociologists as the more appropriate indicator for assessing the openness of a society and the degree of equality of opportunity. One way of measuring relative mobility involves a highly technical measure called the 'odds ratio' which Kellner and Whilby (1980) refer to as the '4-2-1 rule of relative hope' to describe how sons of service class fathers were four times

---

KEY SOCIOLOGIST

Anthony Heath analysed the 1972 Nuffield social mobility survey (with Halsey and Ridge). His work is closely associated with a systematic analysis of the quantitative data associated with analysing large-scale social surveys of class, gender and ethnic stratification. His most recent research focuses on particularly the 'ethnic penalties' that BME groups experience in education and the labour market.

CONTEMPORARY APPLICATION

Governments like to be seen to be taking social mobility seriously – even though levels remain little changed. One way of doing so might be to increase mobility rates by increasing economic prosperity. Other approaches might involve a degree of social engineering whereby the government could encourage or subsidise working-class entry to elite educational institutions like private schools or 'Oxbridge' or professions such as law or medicine.

more likely to be service class themselves than sons of working-class fathers. Sons of intermediate fathers were twice as likely as sons of working-class fathers, and half as likely as sons of service-class fathers, to end up in the service class.

Relative mobility rates seem to be driven by what is referred to as 'inequalities of condition' between the social classes. These refer to the extent of class inequalities with regard to key factors like access to education or restrictive recruitment practices by employers. Education is regarded as the main channel for access to higher-level positions, while the recent favoured fashion of using unpaid internments by employers excludes those without savings or parents who will subsidise them for months. With regard to relative mobility Goldthorpe felt that this had not changed significantly since Glass's study. Although there was clearly some absolute mobility, these observed changes in the overall rates of class mobility were primarily due to changes in the occupational structure, not a shift to a more open society or more equal opportunities.

> **STUDY TIP**
> Recognising that while measures of absolute mobility tell a story, the significant indicator of the openness and meritocracy of a society is through the extent to which relative mobility occurs.

IN THE NEWS

The role of private education

Figure 6.28 Research shows that going to a top private school still opens doors closed to others

The Prime Minister David Cameron speaking about social mobility said: 'You've got to get out there and find people, win them over, get them to raise aspirations, get them to think they can get all the way to the top.' One way, it is argued, of helping the less privileged to achieve social mobility is by offering scholarships to elite schools and top universities like Oxbridge. However, such an approach can be so destabilising that not only is it difficult to adjust to a very different social context, but that even if they do make the adjustment they are then emotionally reluctant or unable to return to their original community and make a contribution.

Adapted from Kynaston (2014)

The second argument is that even if you have a meritocracy, those who are at the top become self-serving, IQ-driven and intolerant. Rewarding the successful excessively privileges the winners, bringing out their least appealing qualities, and badly undervalues the contribution of the losers.

The third argument is that rather than bang on about greater equality of opportunity, what really matters far more to the welfare of most people is greater equality of outcome – a far tougher policy objective, but one almost entirely written out of the political script. Equality of opportunity, when combined with serious inequality of outcome, was described by David Lipset as 'the worst possible recipe for a harmonious society.'

There is also the whole matter of symbolism: as George Orwell reflected soon after the war, the Labour government's failure to abolish first-class rail travel was all too emblematic of its broader failure to carry through an egalitarian social revolution. In 2014 we look at No 10 and see an Old Etonian in situ; we look at London's City Hall and see the same; we look at Lambeth Palace and see the same again ... They may or may not be worthy occupants, but the triple whammy is in its way grotesquely symbolic, telling us something stark and unacceptable about our society today.

> **Questions**
>
> 1. Why are scholarships criticised as a means of promoting social mobility?
> 2. What is the article's argument against meritocracies?
> 3. Why is equality of outcome more important than equality of opportunity?
> 4. What point is being made about symbolism in the last paragraph?

5.3 Patterns, changes and impacts of social mobility in the UK

The Glass mobility study (1949)

The first major study of mobility was undertaken by David Glass (1954) and colleagues in 1949. This pioneering study provided a picture of mobility trends in the first half of the twentieth century. It found that society was relatively closed to mobility with extremely high rates of reproduction and social closure at the top.

> '... the general picture so far is of a rather stable social structure, and one in which social status has tended to operate within, so to speak, a closed circuit. Social origins have conditioned educational level, and both have conditioned achieved social status. Marriage has also to a considerable extent taken place within the same closed circuit' (Glass, 1954, page 21).

Although Glass and his colleagues found some evidence of downward social mobility before the Second World War, they were more optimistic about post-war society. Writing in the era following the 1944 Education Act they expected mobility to increase in the second half of the century. It was widely hoped at the time that this Act would offer greater equality of opportunity for educational success and that this would consequently be reflected in the labour market.

Goldthorpe and post-Second World War mobility

There were a range of mobility studies looking at Britain following the Second World War. Goldthorpe et al.'s (1980) Oxford Mobility Study (conducted in 1972) is probably the most famous, although there were other studies by Goldthorpe and Payne (1986), Heath (1981), the Scottish Mobility Study by Payne, Ford and Robertson (1976) and Hout (1989). The 1972 Oxford Mobility Study showed that Glass's prediction of a more open society after the War had come true. In particular there was more upward mobility into the 'service class'. Overall there was more upward than downward mobility. Goldthorpe et al.'s concluded that the key factor driving this mobility was the expansion of professional and managerial occupations and the decline of traditional working-class industries and their occupations. Hence absolute mobility rates, especially upward mobility, increased substantially in post-war society. However, Goldthorpe et al. found little evidence of relative mobility. What mobility there was stemmed from more jobs at the top, not an equalisation of mobility chances. Consequently, although chances of upward mobility had increased for everyone, the relative competitive chances of people from different social origins had not greatly changed. In this sense Glass's optimism of increased equality of opportunity and openness in post-war society had not been fulfilled.

Payne *et al.*'s Scottish Mobility Study (SMS)

The Scottish Mobility Study (Payne *et al.*'s 1987) found that Scotland showed similar rates of mobility to the rest of the UK. Consequently this meant a growth of white-collar managerial occupations and a decline in blue-collar manual ones, meaning more people experienced upward social mobility than downward mobility. However, there was less upward social mobility into the higher professions. These appeared to engage in a high degree of self-recruitment with predominantly sons of higher professionals gaining opportunities to work as higher professionals. Nonetheless mobility rates, especially upward mobility, increased substantially in the post-war period although the SMS found this was influenced by age and region. It found that social mobility was not only more likely to occur in south east England (compared to the north and Scotland) but was also more prevalent among young people. In addition, although the SMS found evidence of absolute mobility with many more men than before being upwardly mobile, the relative chances of being upwardly mobile had not changed.

The SMS is also noteworthy since it considered women's mobility. When male respondents were married or living with a woman, information was collected about her. The term used by this study of 'female social mobility' refers only to married women or women living with men, not single women. Its research showed that 75 per cent of men experienced downward mobility on their first entry into the labour market, but tended to recover their position after a period of years. 77 per cent of women experienced downward mobility on entry to the labour market, with many remaining there. 40 per cent of sons of professional/managerial workers eventually achieved professional status, but the figure for daughters was only 12 per cent.

The Sutton Trust and social mobility

The Sutton Trust (2012) undertook research comparing children born in the 1950s with those born in the 1970s. It found that the current state of social mobility in the UK was actually quite low. In addition, it highlights the disproportionately favourable effect of attending the most affluent independent schools. Education opportunities remain overwhelmingly dominated by children from the most privileged homes. For example, five elite schools sent more pupils to Oxford and Cambridge universities than nearly 2,000 state schools, which amounts to two-thirds of the entire state sector. They also note that an elite education is not only important to gain entry into the top universities but also into the higher professions as well.

They conclude that limited social mobility and unequal educational opportunity is the biggest social challenge of our times. Those who came from better-off backgrounds experienced most from opportunities offered from higher education. For example, while the proportion of graduates from the poorest fifth of families has increased from 6 to 9 per cent, the richest fifth of the population have seen graduation rates rise from 20 to 47 per cent. In addition, the income gap between the richest and poorest in society continues to widen. The Sutton Trust highlights that the cost of this inequity to the country is not only economic, but has a significant social impact as well.

The Sutton Trust found that social mobility was lower in Britain than in other advanced countries such as Canada, Australia, Germany, Sweden, Norway, Denmark and Finland, and on a par with the United States.

> **KEY SOCIOLOGISTS**
>
> **Anthony Heath and John Ridge**
> (2011) argue that differential rates of social mobility between different groups in society are revealing indicators of a society's character. An open society rewards according to actual productivity rather than to ascribed characteristics such as privileged background, 'race' or sex.

> **STUDY TIP**
> Knowing a range of social mobility studies will be useful in your studies. Get to know the findings they have in common as well as any specific differences between them.

> **CONTEMPORARY APPLICATION**
> Policies aimed at increasing social mobility can either target the 'demand side', such as focusing on admission practices of the more elite universities such as the Russell Group and Oxbridge. On the other hand, 'supply side' solutions might involve increasing educational qualifications of the adult population. Denmark, for example, has successfully achieved this through their educational encouragement of life-long learning.

> **RESEARCH IN FOCUS**
>
> **Li and Heath: Ethnicity and social mobility**
>
> The study also presents new research on some on Britain's largest longitudinal studies. Professors Anthony Heath and Yaojun Li looked at 40 years of data to define rates of social mobility through identifying the percentage who moved up or down from the occupational class of their father.
>
> They found that 43 per cent of white men and 45.6 per cent of white women moved up to a higher socio-economic class than their father and that in contrast, first-generation black African, Indian and Pakistani and Bangladeshi groups had significantly lower upward mobility rates. Just 34.3 per cent of first generation Pakistani and Bangladeshi men and 27.6 per cent of Pakistani and Bangladeshi women moved up from the socio-economic class of their father.
>
> Variations in mobility by gender were also noted by researchers: black Caribbean men (39.3 per cent) and Chinese women (46.8 per cent) were found to experience lower rates of upward mobility than black Caribbean women (67.3 per cent) or Chinese men (56.9 per cent). The study also showed that for second generation south-Asian groups, men had benefited more from upward occupational mobility than women.
>
> Adapted from Li and Heath (2008)

> **Questions**
> 1. What percentage of the white population had upward social mobility?
> 2. Which ethnic groups had significantly lower rates than the white population?
> 3. In what ways does gender impact upon mobility?

5.4 How do we measure and study social mobility?

Gender and social mobility

As noted above, one of the problems with mobility studies is the exclusion of women. For example, for the Oxford Mobility Study (1980) Goldthorpe argued the case that the appropriate unit of stratification in an industrial society is the family. He then classified the class position of the family as determined by the principal breadwinner, typically the male. This position sparked debate, with Britten and Heath (1983) arguing for a joint approach to measuring the shared family class position, in which both spouses, if employed, contribute to family class. In addition, many feminists, such as Michelle Stanworth (see below) contest this rather sexist assumption and argue that men and women should have an individual class location.

In a later work Goldthorpe and Payne (1986) seemed to confirm Goldthorpe's belief that excluding women from mobility studies made no difference. They examined data from the 1983 British Election Survey in three ways. Firstly by including women but classifying them according to their husband's occupation. Secondly, the highest occupation of either partner was used to determine both members of the couple's class position. Thirdly, women were allocated a class position based on their own occupation. Although the last method resulted in very different levels of absolute mobility for men and women, it had little effect upon levels of relative mobility. This showed that the chances of women compared to other women were the same as the chances of men compared to other men.

Feminist response

As a feminist Michelle Stanworth (1984) is critical of the practice of Goldthorpe of classifying women as the same social class of their partners. Evidence would seem to support Stanworth. Goldthorpe used the notion of 'occupational maturity' in his analysis of men's mobility. However, the concept may have less relevance for women's mobility since they work in inferior jobs (often part-time) to their partners who may be pursuing a career. This occurs because many married women leave the labour market, or work part-time, when their children are young and then return to paid employment, but at much the same level as before, in their mid thirties. Consequently society is less open for women than for men. Therefore if occupational mobility of females is measured by comparing her occupation with that of her father, then a skewed picture is going to result as occupational opportunities available to women are different from those of men:

1. There tends to be a downward bias in occupational mobility for women measured against their fathers since men are not burdened by the impact of child-bearing and rearing.
2. The pattern of mobility is ragged since women are especially concentrated into routine and clerical work.
3. Concentration in this type of work serves to act as a buffer zone preventing them rising or falling too far from this middle of the occupational range.
4. Improvement in female education and greater attendance at higher education is having a knock-on effect leading to improvements in women's position in the labour market.

Saunders' defence of meritocracy

The New Right sociologist Peter Saunders (2013) claims that there are no social barriers to social mobility, arguing that the inequalities that we see in society are mainly the result of differences in effort and intelligence. He goes on to highlight four social mobility myths:

1. That the UK has a serious problem with limited social mobility.
2. The problem is getting worse and the working class in particular have poor opportunities for mobility.
3. That intelligence is irrelevant.
4. Education reform is needed to achieve more social mobility.

In challenging the first myth he argues that using Goldthorpe's three class schema (service, intermediate and working class) over half the population are living in a different social class to the one they were born into. He quotes the General Household Survey (2005) that found that 32 per cent of men born into the working class had reached the service class. Similarly the British Cohort Study (1970) found that 45 per cent of men and 39 per cent of women were upwardly mobile by the age of 33. Saunders also points out that class mobility in the UK is equivalent to other countries.

With regard to the second myth, Saunders concedes that there may be a fall in absolute mobility as the middle class shrinks. However, he argues relative mobility, which is the significant measure, has stayed roughly the same.

Saunders challenges the third myth by arguing we would expect to see more people recruited from higher class parents because the parent-child IQ correlation is 0.5. Children from higher class parents would therefore be expected to end up achieving higher success levels.

Finally Saunders rejects all the educational reforms that have been advocated, arguing that there appears to be no bias against the working class. Ability to work hard is much more important in determining destination than class origin. For example, he argues that universities recruit on prior educational attainment rather than class bias.

Saunders' conclusion is that if there is a social mobility problem, then it is confined to the poor and inadequate parenting experienced at the bottom of society, especially associated with lone-parent mothers. So for Saunders it is underclass parenting that is the problem. However, this is to blame poor social mobility on cultural factors rather than the real structural inequalities (poverty, low achieving schools, poor housing, run down neighbourhoods, etc.) faced by people at the bottom of society. The criticisms addressed to Charles Murray in previous chapters apply to Saunders here too.

Migration and social mobility

Lucinda Platt (2002) examined the relative importance of family origins and ethnic group for shaping children's social class destinations. She notes that in a very class-divided society racial inequality may be less of an issue compared to class inequality. However, when it is difficult to transmit class privilege across generations within a potentially marginalised group, then this indicates additional discrimination experienced by that group.

She highlights how first-generation immigrants were subject to significant levels of discrimination on arrival in Britain, and reasons that it would therefore be expected for subsequent generations to experience subsequent upward social mobility. She examines the processes by which such upward mobility is achieved including the use of networks as well as the attainment of educational qualifications. Educational qualifications have been shown to be both a route to upward mobility as well as a means by which privileged classes maintain that privilege. However, Platt recognised how different ethnic groups achieved varying success in terms of qualifications which she argues indicates how society is less open to some groups and how 'ethnicity' outweighs other factors.

In terms of social mobility Platt found that this varied considerably between ethnic groups. In absolute terms Indians did better than all other ethnic groups. Indians, white non-migrants and white migrants were able to retain privileged positions in society while Caribbeans and Pakistanis found it harder. This indicates that ethnic group matters, and is more salient for Caribbeans and

Pakistanis than for other groups. She also examined the chances of becoming a professional or managerial class and found that a child's educational qualifications were a key factor. This indicates that class advantage can be maintained through privileged parents ensuring greater educational success for their children. Platt concludes that class origins continue to matter, but equally so does ethnicity. Most BMEs had a higher chance than their white non-migrant counterparts of ending up in the professional or managerial classes, when comparing like with like. However, the situation for Pakistanis is the reverse, being less likely than their white counterparts to achieve success: even when origins are taken account of, they are doing worse than a model of parity of class processes would suggest and thus, for this group, ethnicity far outweighs class in influencing outcomes. Bangladeshis and Pakistanis were also more likely to be unemployed.

> **CONTEMPORARY APPLICATION**
> The prevailing policy debate about how to promote social mobility ignores wider structural changes to society linked to processes like globalisation and new international division of labour. Furthermore debates ignore the true extent of social inequality and the factors serving to reproduce them.

> **KEY SOCIOLOGIST**
> **Geoff Payne** has played an important role in building our understanding of social mobility. He was a leading sociologist in the Scottish Mobility Study. His recent work is based on the argument that any substantial increase in upward mobility can only occur if the current structural blockages are removed.

> **STUDY TIP**
> Although social mobility is generally measured in terms of social class, it is important to recognise that within social class positions there can still be inequalities like gender, ethnicity, age, disability or regional location that promote or hinder movement.

IN THE NEWS

Supporting low-income parents early on will improve children's life chances

Sir Michael Marmot in a speech to MPs stated that upon the first two years of life, everything else is built. This shows that the first years of a child's life are crucial in shaping their future life chances. In the speech, Marmot outlined what could be done to improve outcomes by creating the conditions for every child to have a good start in life. The case for intervention is growing, with policies aimed at better supporting parents, who in most cases play the greatest role in creating the environment where children grow up.

We need to dispel two damaging misconceptions about a focus on parenting support. First is the idea that concern with family support constitutes some form of moral panic. Recent social transformations have brought greater individual freedom but also greater isolation. As fewer of us grow up in an extended family environment, we have less experience of looking after children, and fewer parenting skills, once cultivated from long before the teenage years. Second, we must be clear that this is not about blaming poor people for their poverty. Understanding how the behaviour of parents affects their child's outcomes is not to deny constraints such as class and income on life chances. It is, rather, a way to be more precise about how these constraints play out in real people's lives.

Adapted from Field (2015)

Questions

1. How would the New Right sociologist Peter Saunders disagree with Frank Field's arguments here?
2. What reasons does Field give for increased parenting problems in contemporary society?
4. What reasons does Field give for not blaming poverty on the poor?
5. If you were a politician how would you improve social mobility for those especially at the bottom of society?

Check your understanding

1. What is the difference between intergenerational mobility and intragenerational mobility?
2. What is absolute social mobility?
3. What is relative social mobility?
4. Briefly summarise the findings of Glass.
5. What differences did the Oxford Mobility Study find to Glass?
6. How was the Scottish Mobility Study different?
7. What are the findings with regard to mobility by the Sutton Trust?
8. What is Goldthorpe's attitude towards classifying women's social class?
9. What is the response of feminists like Michelle Stanworth?
10. What did Lucinda Platt find with regard to ethnicity and mobility?

Practice questions

1. Outline and explain **two** ways in which social mobility can be measured. [10 marks]

Read Item A below and answer the question that follows.

Item A

Women are clearly doing a lot better than they were and now make up nearly half of the workforce. Women are upwardly mobile in absolute terms, but there remains a more sizable gender gap in terms of relative mobility,

Applying material from Item A, analyse two reasons why women may experience less mobility than men. [10 marks]

Read Item B below and answer the question that follows.

Item B

A society is said to be open when there is movement of individuals between identified social strata in a society. Such movement is referred to as social mobility which can be both upward and downwards.

Applying material from Item B and your knowledge, evaluate the view that the United Kingdom is an open society. [20 marks]

Tackling the A-level exam

This section will explore:
- Overview of the A-level
- The skills you will be expected to demonstrate
- The types of questions you will be expected to answer
- How the A-level is different to AS (including how to tackle longer questions)
- Tackling Paper 1
- Tackling Paper 2
- Tackling Paper 3

Overview of the A-level

The exams that you will take at the end of your course reflect that you have studied sociology in some depth. Therefore the demands of the questions are significantly higher than the AS. This is partly because you are able to draw links between the different areas that you have studied, for example, studying different theories through a number of different topics. This section of the book will explore each of the exam papers with a particular focus on the skills, details and depth required.

> **STUDY HINT**
>
> If you have already taken the AS, you will need to make sure that you are clear about the differences in the questions and the increase of demands. Although the topics you are examined have the same content, and possibly similar sounding questions, in which you will be expected to demonstrate greater depth and detail in your answers. It is a good idea to practise thinking and writing at an A-level standard, and to be very aware of the differences between the two courses.

There are three exams that you will take at the end of the course, and each one is two hours long. These exams are worth 80 marks each, in other words, they are 33.3 per cent of your final result.

- In Paper 1 you will answer all questions on Education with Theory and Methods. There is a long essay worth 30 marks that gives you the opportunity to write in more detail and possibly about a wider range of ideas or research relating to education.
- In Paper 2, Topics in Sociology, there are two sections: A and B. You will pick one topic out of the four offered in each section.
- In Paper 3 you will answer all of the questions on Crime and Deviance with Theory and Methods.

Although the three question papers are all quite different in layout, there are many similarities in the types of questions being asked.

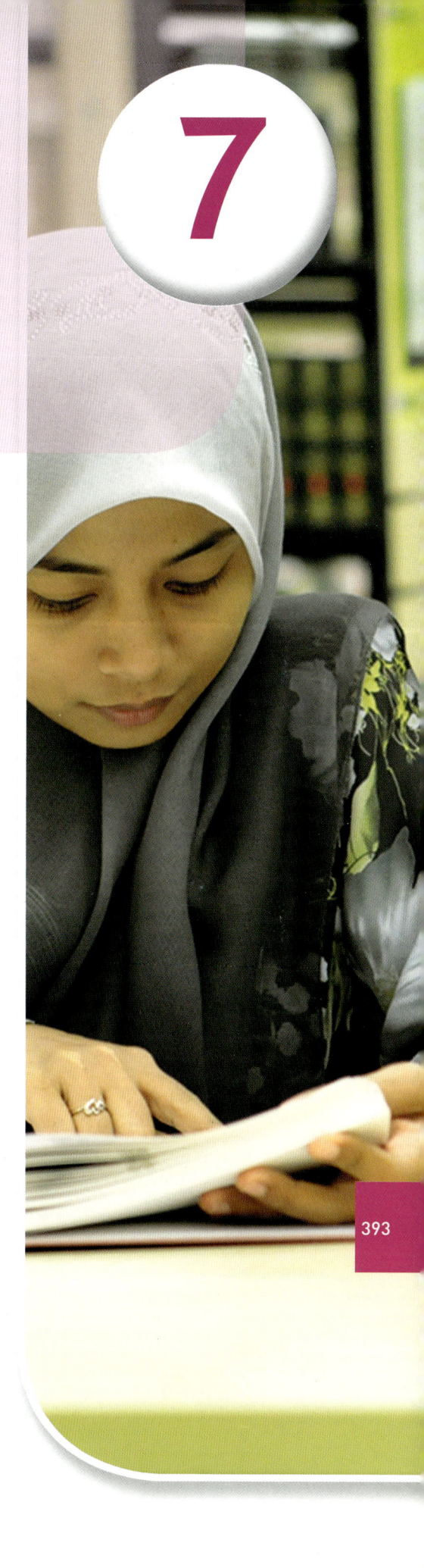

Paper 1 – Education with Theory and Methods, 80 marks (2 hours)

Paper 2 – Topics in Sociology, 80 marks (2 hours)

Paper 3 – Crime and Deviance with Theory and Methods, 80 marks (2 hours)

The skills you will be expected to demonstrate

As explained above, there is a clear need for you to demonstrate greater depth at A-level than at AS.

There are three groups of skills (known as AO1, AO2 and AO3) that you will be expected to demonstrate, and it is worth becoming very aware of these as you work through the course. Each exam question has a different proportion of these skills with varying marks available. It is also important that you become aware of these proportions and write accordingly.

AO1 Demonstrate knowledge and understanding of sociological theories, concepts and evidence

At A-level you will be expected to have greater depth of knowledge than at AS. It can be difficult try to present a good range of knowledge, so manage your time carefully, for example, to make sure that you include evidence from a range of perspectives or both sides of an argument.

You can demonstrate AO1 skills by:

- Writing about the studies and concepts that you have learnt. The way to maximise your marks here is to explain the study accurately, for example, what it found and how it was carried out, and by giving the correctly spelt researchers' names.
  Concepts are a very important way of showing knowledge and understanding and must be used correctly as well as be defined thoroughly and spelt accurately.
- Using knowledge about different theoretical perspectives. Again this should be accurate, and specific. For example, avoid generalising about 'all Marxists' – rather discuss specific Marxists in terms of their unique contribution.
- Using your knowledge of the methodology of sociological piece of research. This may be how a piece of research was carried out, who the sample was made up of, when the research was carried out and where.

> **STUDY HINT**
>
> Make sure that you only pick the knowledge and show understanding of what is specifically relevant to the question. Wasting time writing about less relevant material means less time for detail on more relevant points. Sometimes questions might ask you to draw from a number of different areas of the course and therefore you need to think carefully about which of these parts are most important and try to create a good balance of knowledge and understanding.

Marks can also be given for knowledge and understanding that is linked to the core themes of the course: socialisation, culture and identity as well as stratification and power.

Knowledge and understanding of the development of sociology as a discipline over time is also useful, as is showing you understand the tension between structure and action, or globalisation, for example. This kind of knowledge shows that you understand the subject in a broader sense and can locate your answer within this context.

You can show your knowledge and understanding by mentioning an issue that has recently been in the news or by writing about a relevant policy or law if it is relevant. Make sure that this contemporary issue is clearly relevant to sociology and not based on entertainment, for example.

AO2 Apply sociological theories, concepts, evidence and research methods to a range of issues

Application (AO2) is assessed in two ways. Firstly, where there is stimulus material – that is, an 'item' – you are required to apply your knowledge and understanding to that 'item'. Secondly, where there is no item, AO2 is assessed by linking two content areas of the specification. You would therefore be required to apply your knowledge from one part of the specification to another part of the specification.

Remember that it is really important that you make sure you link every point you make to the question, rather than simply writing down what you know. A good starting point is to ask yourself: what is this question specifically asking me to do?

AO3 Analyse and evaluate sociological theories, concepts, evidence and research methods in order to present arguments, make judgements, draw conclusions

This group is the hardest set of skills to develop. It involves you thinking about weighing up arguments, considering which view is the strongest, looking at a debate in a balanced way and making your work feel discursive, rather than list-like. This might involve you needing to discuss if a theory or evidence is relevant to contemporary society, for example.

Analysis requires you to break down information into its different components and identify the characteristics of these components. It is all about unpacking concepts and theories and separating them into their different parts.

Evaluation requires you to be confident in considering the strengths and weaknesses of ideas and evidence in relation to the question. Simply listing criticisms in a general way is not going to be the best way to demonstrate analysis. You should show that you have understood the specific strengths and weaknesses to the particular angle that the question takes. You need to weigh up the specific question in front of you, show you are considering and comparing various views and coming to a reasoned, thoughtful and clear conclusion. Therefore it is a good idea to get used to evaluating questions that you have not seen before and asking yourself if you are offering evaluations that are specific enough. Analysis and evaluation in themselves, in a general sense, are not as highly awarded as specific, focused analysis and evaluation, which responds directly to the question in front of you.

Examples of analysis and evaluation might include:

- analysis: breaking down ideas, theories, concepts, research or policies *that are relevant to the question*.
- evaluation: offering criticisms of an idea, theory, concept, piece of research or policy *that are relevant to the question*. This might involve criticising the methodology or relevance of the idea/research to contemporary society.
- analysis: considering the strengths of an idea, concept, view, piece of research or policy
- evaluation: deciding which side of an argument carries greatest weight, after carefully considering the merits of both sides
- drawing together a range of views and making an overall statement that takes all of the views into account
- understanding that rather than reaching a yes or no argument, there are a number of competing views on a subject that need to be considered.

> **STUDY HINT**
>
> Look at an essay that you have written and highlight all of the AO3 skills that you can see. Are they general or do they focus on the specific demands of the question? Can you reword any AO3 skills that are general to improve them?

Activity

1. Sort the following sentences into AO1, AO2 or AO3 columns.
   You may find that the sentence has more than one skill. Think carefully about why you've chosen this skill.

Meritocracy refers to an education system that is fair and everyone has an equal chance of success.	On the other hand, feminists argue that the education system reproduces patriarchal ideology.
Cultural deprivation theories can be criticised; some cultures may be different but necessarily inferior.	Globalisation has had a number of effects on education, for example, in terms of policies that have been created.
The gap between boys' achievement and girls' achievement is greatest at GCSE.	Educational policies have not been successful in closing the gap between the middle class and the working class.
The New Right are heavily criticised by feminists.	Differences in achievement among ethnic groups cannot be fully understood without also considering class and gender.
Marketisation policies were introduced by the New Right, but continued into successive governments.	This study suggests that...

2. Have a look at the following issues and topics and design three sentences about each, for each skill. The first one has been done for you.
   a) Functionalist theories of education
   b) Compensatory education policies
   c) The effect of globalisation on education
   d) The male gaze
   e) Gendered subject choices
   f) In school factors
   g) Material deprivation
   h) Feminist views on education

> **Functionalist theories of education**
>
> AO1: Functionalism is a structural, consensus theory that argues that society shapes behavior.
>
> AO2: Parsons argues that the education system is meritocratic, which supports the idea that education functions to raise equality between different social groups.
>
> AO3: Although some functionalist ideas are still relevant in some respects, their views fail to take into account the idea that persistent inequalities still exist in education and society between various groups.

How are marks broken down in A-level Sociology in terms of AO1, AO2 and AO3?

Now that you know what different skills mean, it is important to understand the proportions of each skill that you are expected to demonstrate in each paper. In the A-level course, just under half of the marks available are for AO1, knowledge and understanding, and just over half the marks are for AO2 and AO3, the higher level skills. Therefore it is important that you try to demonstrate all of these skills.

Assessment objectives (AOs)	Component weightings (approx. %)			Overall weighting (approx. %)
	Paper 1	Paper 2	Paper 3	
AO1	15	13	16	44
AO2	11	11	8	31
AO3	8	9	8	25
Overall weighting of components (%)	33.3	33.3	33.3	100

The types of questions you will be expected to answer

Your exam papers use the following command words. It is worth thinking carefully about what each command means. The same questions are used on all three papers which should mean that you get used to them.

Question type	Explanation
Outline	To describe the main characteristics. Write around a sentence or two for each thing that you outline.
Outline and explain	This means to outline (as above) and then develop each outline more fully. Outlining and explaining one factor will probably take one paragraph. In questions worth 10 marks, you should consider material from the wider subject area, not just from the specific part of a topic that is being tested.
Applying material from the item...	This means that you should refer to ideas in the item or go further than the item in developing what is described there. The important skill to demonstrate here is that you are picking out the right information in the item and adding relevant information from your own learning, such as studies, concepts or a contemporary issue.
Analyse	This means to break a topic down into different parts, such as different views or evidence, and examine each in turn in more detail. This may involve including criticisms.
Evaluate	This means to weigh up a particular view or argument or to consider the usefulness of evidence and come to a clear conclusion.
Applying material from Item C and your knowledge evaluate the strengths and limitations of using [method] to investigate [an educational issue].	This question type appears once in the Methods in Context section of paper 1. This question asks you to apply your knowledge of methods to explore the various benefits and problems of using one type of methodology to learn about an educational issue. In other words, is it an appropriate method and why? So you can use your knowledge of both education and methods together here.

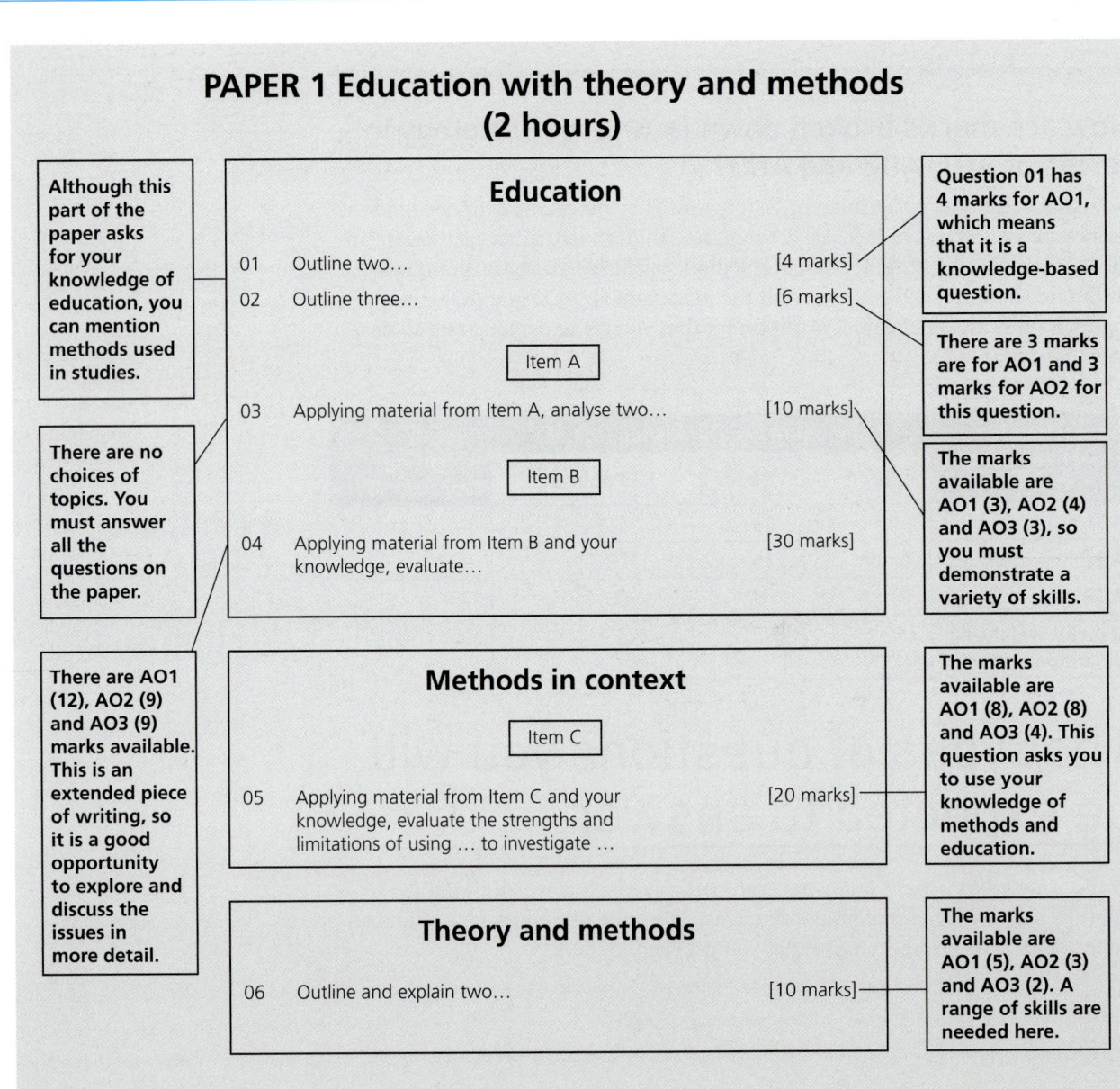

PAPER 1 Education with theory and methods (2 hours)

Education

01 Outline two… [4 marks]
02 Outline three… [6 marks]

Item A

03 Applying material from Item A, analyse two… [10 marks]

Item B

04 Applying material from Item B and your knowledge, evaluate… [30 marks]

Methods in context

Item C

05 Applying material from Item C and your knowledge, evaluate the strengths and limitations of using … to investigate … [20 marks]

Theory and methods

06 Outline and explain two… [10 marks]

Annotations:

- Although this part of the paper asks for your knowledge of education, you can mention methods used in studies.
- There are no choices of topics. You must answer all the questions on the paper.
- There are AO1 (12), AO2 (9) and AO3 (9) marks available. This is an extended piece of writing, so it is a good opportunity to explore and discuss the issues in more detail.
- Question 01 has 4 marks for AO1, which means that it is a knowledge-based question.
- There are 3 marks are for AO1 and 3 marks for AO2 for this question.
- The marks available are AO1 (3), AO2 (4) and AO3 (3), so you must demonstrate a variety of skills.
- The marks available are AO1 (8), AO2 (8) and AO3 (4). This question asks you to use your knowledge of methods and education.
- The marks available are AO1 (5), AO2 (3) and AO3 (2). A range of skills are needed here.

PAPER 2 Topics in sociology
(2 hours)

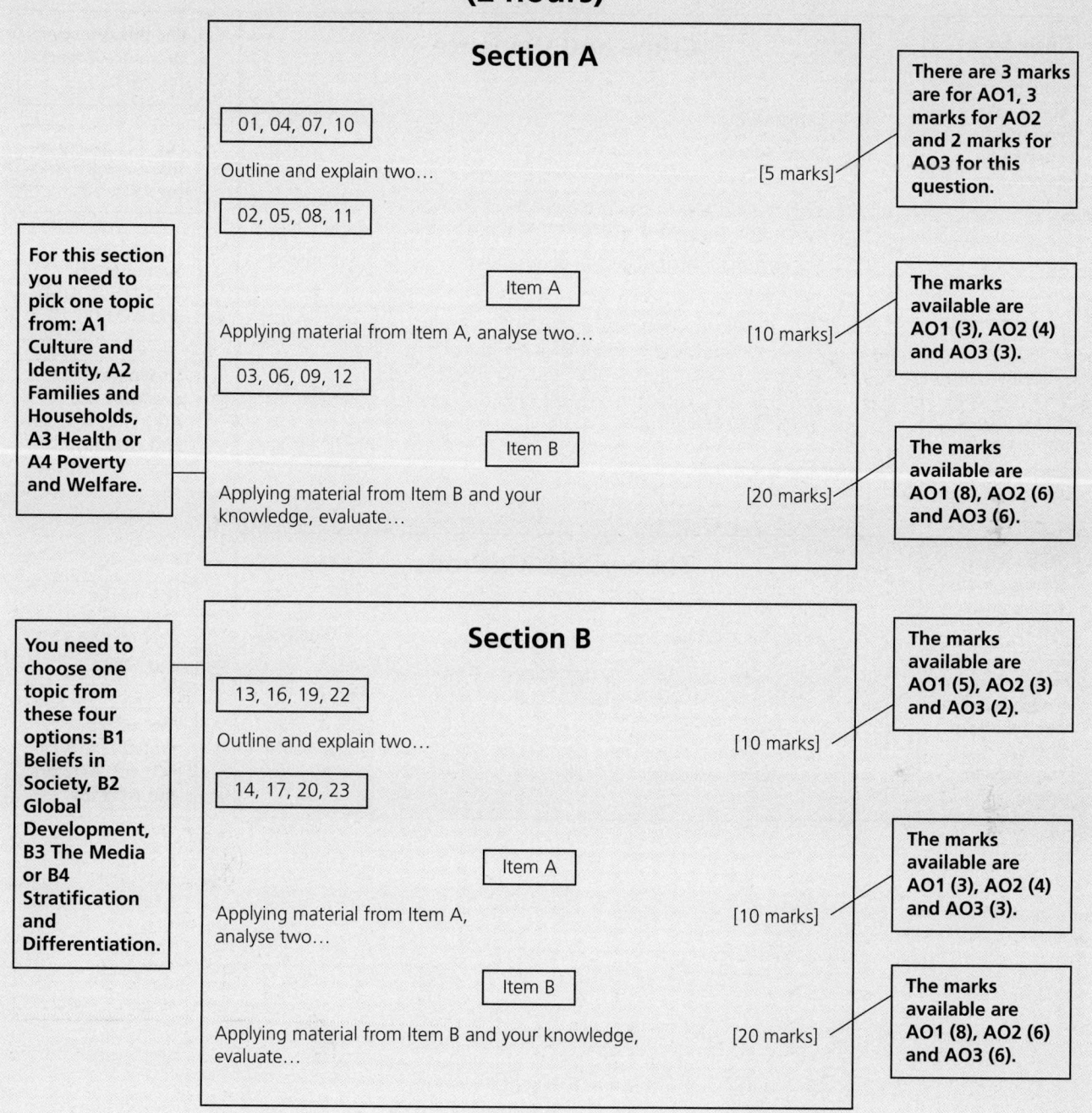

Section A

For this section you need to pick one topic from: A1 Culture and Identity, A2 Families and Households, A3 Health or A4 Poverty and Welfare.

01, 04, 07, 10

Outline and explain two… [5 marks]

There are 3 marks are for AO1, 3 marks for AO2 and 2 marks for AO3 for this question.

02, 05, 08, 11

Item A

Applying material from Item A, analyse two… [10 marks]

The marks available are AO1 (3), AO2 (4) and AO3 (3).

03, 06, 09, 12

Item B

Applying material from Item B and your knowledge, evaluate… [20 marks]

The marks available are AO1 (8), AO2 (6) and AO3 (6).

Section B

You need to choose one topic from these four options: B1 Beliefs in Society, B2 Global Development, B3 The Media or B4 Stratification and Differentiation.

13, 16, 19, 22

Outline and explain two… [10 marks]

The marks available are AO1 (5), AO2 (3) and AO3 (2).

14, 17, 20, 23

Item A

Applying material from Item A, analyse two… [10 marks]

The marks available are AO1 (3), AO2 (4) and AO3 (3).

Item B

Applying material from Item B and your knowledge, evaluate… [20 marks]

The marks available are AO1 (8), AO2 (6) and AO3 (6).

The types of questions you will be expected to answer

PAPER 3 Crime and deviance with theory and method (2 hours)

Crime and Deviance

There are no choices of questions on this paper, so you must answer all questions.

01 Outline two... [4 marks] — For this question there are 4 marks for AO1.

02 Outline three... [6 marks] — For this question there are 6 marks for AO1.

Item A

03 Applying material from Item A, analyse two... [10 marks] — The marks available are AO1 (3), AO2 (4) and AO3 (3).

Item B

04 Applying material from Item B and your knowledge, evaluate... [30 marks] — The marks available are AO1 (12), AO2 (9) and AO3 (9).

This question requires you to go into more depth.

Theory and Methods

This section draws on all topics and issues.

05 Outline and explain two... [10 marks] — The marks available are AO1 (5), AO2 (3) and AO3 (2).

Item C

06 Applying material from Item C and your knowledge, evaluate... [20 marks] — The marks available are AO1 (8), AO2 (6) and AO3 (6).

These questions can be about theory, methods or both.

How the A-level is different to AS (including how to tackle longer questions)

Although some of the questions look the same, the A-level exams reflect the fact that you will have studied sociology in much more detail. In this section we will explore more closely the differences between the AS and the A-level.

The following table highlights key differences.

AS exam	A-level exam
■ 2 components ■ 2 exams ■ More short questions	■ 3 components ■ 3 exams ■ More higher mark questions
Paper 1 Education with methods in context	**Paper 1 Education with theory and methods**
■ 1 and a half hours ■ 60 marks ■ The biggest single question is 20 marks.	■ 2 hours ■ 80 marks ■ This paper has a methods in context question. ■ There is a 30 mark education essay question. ■ There is a 10 mark question on theory and methods.
Paper 2 Research methods and topics in sociology	**Paper 2 Topics in sociology**
■ 1 and a half hours ■ 60 marks ■ Section A: Answer two compulsory questions on research methods ■ Section B: Pick one topic from four and answer all questions on this topic.	■ 2 hours ■ 80 marks ■ There are two sections to this paper, you pick one topic from section A and one topic from section B.
	Paper 3 Crime and deviance with theory and methods
	■ 2 hours ■ 80 marks ■ 50 marks for the Crime and deviance section, which includes a longer 30 mark question ■ 30 marks available for Theory and Methods.
The skills you are expected to demonstrate are more focused on knowledge and understanding. In percentages:	The skills you are expected to demonstrate focus more on application, analysis and evaluation. In percentages:

Assessment objectives	Paper 1	Paper 2	Overall weighting (%)
AO1	22	24	46
AO2	18	13	31
AO3	10	13	23
Overall weighting of components (%)	50	50	100

Assessment objectives	Paper 1	Paper 2	Paper 3	Overall weighting
AO1	15	13	16	44
AO2	11	11	9	31
AO3	8	9	8	25
Overall weighting of components (%)	33.33	33.33	33.33	100

So you can see that apart from pure theory questions and one set of options, the AS and A-level cover similar content. However, there are significant differences in demand at A-level.

Both AS and the A-level require you to:

- Explore many of the same topics.
- Refer to an item to answer questions.
- Go beyond the item and discuss studies, concepts and theories that you have learnt about.
- Use AO1, AO2 and AO3 skills.
- Develop an argument.
- Discuss the strengths and weaknesses of a particular argument.
- Use contemporary examples to back up your argument.
- Come to a clear conclusion in longer essay questions.
- Answer a Methods in Context question with the same wording and skills breakdown at AS and at A-level.

But for the A-level question you might be expected to:

- Demonstrate more detailed AO1 and greater focus on higher level skills (AO2 and AO3).
- Answer questions about Theory and Methods, Crime and Deviance.
- Spend more time on your longer essays, which are worth more marks (about 30 minutes for an AS 20-mark question and about 45 minutes for an A-level 30-mark question).
- Give a more detailed analysis and evaluation.
- Break down concepts further, for example, identify a theory that the concept is associated with or criticise it.
- Draw links between different parts of the course (within the topic of education and possibly beyond).
- Spend time focusing on strengths and weaknesses of ideas, studies and concepts.
- Write about a greater range of sociological ideas.
- Show that you understand how sociological ideas emerged as well as how wider changes in society may have shaped sociological ideas.

Although the questions are going to cover similar issues, you will be expected to present more sophisticated arguments and ideas, especially in the long essay, which is worth 30 marks. Here is an example of a topic and how you might be expected to approach it at AS and also A-level.

AS	Applying material from Item A and your knowledge, evaluate the view that social class differences in achievement are the result of processes within schools. [20 marks]
A-level	Applying material from Item A and your knowledge, evaluate the view that social class differences in achievement are the result of processes within the school. [30 marks]
Item	Social class continues to be a very important factor in explaining differences in education outcome. Some sociologists suggest that there are a number of processes that take place inside the school that lead to class differences, such as the way teachers may treat working class students differently to middle class students.
	However, others claim that other factors lead to class differences in educational outcome, and that these lie outside the school.
How would you use the item? (specific suggestions)	• Point out that social class is important and give a statistic about social class, for example, privately educated school children account for 11 per cent of the population but go on to account for half of the places in elite universities, suggesting that class really does continue to influence educational success • '…the way teachers may treat working class students…' refers to positive and negative labelling by teachers, where middle class students are labelled positively and working class negatively. • Material deprivation can be developed and defined, with evidence used such as poor diet, housing and lack of resources.
Concepts	• internal/external factors • social class • working class • middle class • material and cultural deprivation • social capital • labelling • self-fulfilling prophecy • culture clash • immediate gratification • streaming • ideal pupil • marketisation • hidden cost of education • aspirations • class identity • anti/pro-school subculture
Studies and contemporary issues	• Evans (2009) • Bourdieu (1984) • Reay *et al.* (2005) • Bowles and Gintis (1976) • Ball (1981) • Becker (1971) • Dunn and Gazele (2008) • Ingram (2011)
Conclusions	• Class cannot explain differences in education alone, both gender and ethnicity also impact upon educational achievement. • Both internal and external factors contribute to working class underachievement. • Compensatory education policies are in place, which are designed to reduce class differences and provide a more level playing field.
What ideas might you develop more for the A-level question?	• A more developed critique of labelling theory, for example, as deterministic, exploring a number of possible responses to labelling • More studies developing more complex ideas such as cultural capital • The introduction of theories in more detail, for example, in Marxist views on class differences • An analysis of the studies used, considering their methodology and/or their relevance to contemporary society • A greater range of concepts explored and in more detail, perhaps including criticisms of concepts as well • An evaluation of the various arguments and a clear conclusion arguing for or against the question

Activity

Look at the following statements and develop them to A-level. The first has been done for you. Don't forget that you can add a criticism or evaluate the idea.

AS	A-level
Cultural capital can be described as middle class tastes, values and activities which lead to economic success later in life	Cultural capital is a concept developed by Bourdieu, a Marxist who argued that the middle class possess particular tastes, values and habits that lead to economic success in life. In education this means that children are likely to feel that school is not different to being at home. In fact, they are likely to understand and feel comfortable with the culture of school. Spending time outside school exploring classical music, visiting museums and other educational activities gives these middle class children an advantage at school, as their general knowledge is likely to be broader.
Feminists argue that the education system maintains patriarchy.	
Compensatory education policies are designed to reduce class differences in educational outcome.	
Some ethnic groups are more successful in education than others.	
Educational policies reflect political views of those who create them.	
Labelling theories are problematic as they are deterministic.	
Student subcultures are generally pro-or anti-school.	

Tackling A-level Paper 1

How long should I spend on each section of the exam?

Education

Education: You should spend approximately 1 hour and 15 minutes answering questions 01 to 04.

01 Outline two... [4 marks]
02 Outline three... [6 marks]
03 Applying material from Item A, analyse two... [10 marks]
04 Applying material from Item B and your knowledge, evaluate... [30 marks]

Methods in context

Methods in context: You should spend approximately 30 minutes on question 05.

05 Applying material from Item C and your knowledge of research methods, evaluate the strengths and limitations of using ...to investigate... [20 marks]

Theory and methods

Theory and methods: You should spend approximately 15 minutes answering question 06.

06 Outline and explain two... [10 marks]

Paper 1 questions

In this section you will get some advice on how to approach each question type. Since many of the questions are similar in style, the first paper sets out more detailed tips and guidance. This advice can also be applied to subsequent questions. So, for example, the skills required for short questions remain the same whether they are for paper one, two or three. Be aware, however, of the different marks awarded for different questions, as they indicate the way that marks are given for demonstrating various skills.

Here is some general advice for short questions.

Do:
- Make sure that you answer the question as thoroughly as you can.
- When you are being asked for more than one way, example, factor or criticism make sure that your answers are different and try to avoid answers that are too similar or overlapping.
- Make sure you are accurate when you are defining a concept.
- Avoid wasting time, for example, you do not need to give any additional information if you will not be given any additional marks for it.
- Add an example to support your answer if you are not sure you have answered fully.

Don't:
- Use one-word answers
- Overwrite
- Use the word you have been asked to define in the definition; use alternative words.

01 Outline two... [4 marks]

This is a knowledge-based question about education that asks you to identify ways in which a sociological concept is related to education. All four marks are for AO1.

- Two marks can be given each of two appropriate factors clearly outlined or one mark for appropriate factors partially outlined.

Example question

01 Outline two processes in schools that explain differences in achievement for some ethnic groups. [4 marks]

Answer A

Less value placed on education.

This response does not answer the question as these values are learnt at home rather than being an in-school process.

Answer B

Negative labelling by teachers can affect some ethnic minorities.

This answer clearly identifies a process that impacts on different ethnic groups, however, it does not explain how negative teacher labelling actually leads to lower educational attainment.

Answer C

Labelling by teachers can negatively affect some ethnic groups, such as, Black African and Caribbean boys who are often judged to be negative and unwilling to conform, which leads them to believe that they cannot achieve, resulting in poorer results.

Anti-school subcultures are a part of a process in schools which may be created as a response to racism among some ethnic groups. In these subcultures, students from some ethnic minority groups may act negatively, for example, truanting or breaking the rules, which means that they are less likely to do well at school.

This is a good answer. It clearly identifies two processes that occur within the school and links these clearly to the underachievement of some ethnic minorities.

Practice questions

- Outline two ways in which marketisation may widen inequalities in education.
- Outline two ways in which school prepares pupils for the world of work.
- Outline two ways in which the education system reinforces class differences.
- Outline two ways in which the education system reinforces gender differences.
- Outline two ways in which social policies may make education more meritocratic.

02 Outline three... [6 marks]

This question awards 3 marks for AO1 and 3 marks for AO2 skills, so, as well as showing you know and understand something, you must also apply your knowledge to this specific issue. It is a good idea to get into the habit of setting out your three points separately. You do not have to do this but it really helps to show what you are trying to say in a clear way. This question is marked as two marks for each of three appropriate reasons clearly outlined or one mark for appropriate reasons partially outlined.

- Two marks are awarded for a clearly explained example or one mark for a partially explained example.

Example question

02 Outline three ways in which labelling may affect educational achievement. [2 marks]

Example answers

Answer A

Students from different schools have different experiences.

Some students reject their labels.

Some students accept their labels and then behave in the way that they have been labelled.

The first point is not relevant to the question. The second point is relevant but not developed. The final point is identified clearly and explained, although saying that the process of accepting a label is known as a self-fulfilling prophecy would have been better.

Answer B

Students who are labelled by teachers negatively may join an anti-school subculture.

Labelling can be positive resulting in pupils thinking that they can do well and therefore being more confident and doing well.

The first reason is a partial answer but it does not go on to explain the effect this might have on their educational outcomes. The second point is correct and well developed. Remember not to assume that labelling is always negative.

Answer C

Students who are labelled by teachers as underachievers may not bother working hard, which may lead them to a self-fulfilling prophecy that leads them to do badly in their exams.

Students may reject their label, as Mirza found Black sixth form girls did, and go on to do really well in school despite their negative label.

Students may identify with other peers who have been labelled negatively or positively in pro- or anti-school subcultures, leading them to do worse or better. For example, anti-school subcultures develop disruptive behaviour, which often leads students to underachieve.

This is a good answer because it has three clear explanations; for each it explains the consequences of labelling well.

Here is another example question with candidate answers

02 Outline three ways that gender differences are reinforced in education.
    [6 marks]

- Two marks for each of three appropriate reasons clearly outlined or one mark for appropriate reasons partially outlined
- Other relevant material should be credited.

Student A

Gender refers to the socially constructed ideas about what it means to be a girl or a boy. In education this might mean girls are encouraged to take subjects seen as 'female' by their teachers. Also boys are encouraged to take 'male' subjects. There are lots of things that go on in school, which means that girls do better than boys.

This answer is not set out clearly. The first sentence is not answering the question but does correctly identify that teachers encourage gendered subject choices. But instead of developing this point it simply repeats the same point for boys.

Student B

The ways that girls and boys are treated differently by their teachers affects their results. Also, sometimes textbooks contain pictures of girls and boys that portray them in stereotypical ways, for example, with the girls doing dance and the boys doing science, which reinforces the subjects that girls and boys take.

The student makes a good point in her first sentence, however this point is not developed by saying that by being treated preferably, girls might do better than boys. The second sentence does give a reason (gendered textbooks) and it does explain how this affects the subjects that girls and boys take.

Student C

Girls are labelled positively as more hard-working by teachers than boys, meaning that they are likely to feel more encouraged and do better as a result of the self-fulfilling prophecy.

Girls and boys are made to do different sports at school, such as boys playing football and girls doing dance. This sends messages to girls and boys about boys being more competitive and sporty while girls are more interested in looking nice and doing less competitive activities such as dance.

There are few female head teachers and senior staff in schools, meaning that girls lack powerful role models, which discourages them from going for powerful positions themselves.

There are three clearly stated responses here which are set out carefully. The three ways do not overlap and each point is developed. This is a very strong answer.

Practice questions
- Outline three ways in which material deprivation may affect educational achievement.
- Outline three ways in which the organisation of the school may be seen as ethnocentric.
- Outline three ways in which processes in school create gender differences.

03 Applying material from Item A, analyse two reasons... [10 marks]

This question has 3 marks for AO1, 4 marks for AO2 and 3 marks for AO3. There is a focus on knowing studies, concepts, ideas and policies, but equally it is important to apply this knowledge and weigh up different arguments. You are expected to write in prose, so this is a mini essay that needs to be organised into paragraphs.

Some general advice on how to use the item
This applies to all questions on all three papers with items.

Do...	Avoid...
Use the item at least once.	Copying the item out in your essay, just refer to the ideas in it.
Make sure that you develop ideas mentioned in the item, take them further and add more detail.	Listing points about the item without linking them to the question.
Unpack or explain concepts that you see described or mentioned in the item. Explain how they link to the question specifically.	Agreeing with or disagreeing with the item in an overly simplistic way.

How is this question marked?

There are three mark bands as shown in the table below.

8–10	<ul><li>Answers in this band will show good knowledge and understanding of relevant material, for example, on two reasons.</li><li>There will be two developed applications of material from the item.</li><li>There will be appropriate analysis/evaluation of two reasons.</li></ul>
4–7	<ul><li>Answers in this band will show a basic to reasonable knowledge and understanding of one or two reasons.</li><li>There will be some successful application of material from the item.</li><li>There will be some analysis/evaluation.</li></ul>
1–3	<ul><li>Answers in this band will show limited knowledge of one or two reasons.</li><li>There will be limited application of material from the item.</li><li>Some material may be at a tangent to the question,</li><li>There will be limited or no analysis/evaluation.</li></ul>
0	<ul><li>No relevant points.</li></ul>

> **STUDY HINT**
>
> **Tips for 10 mark questions with items**
>
> These tips are for all 10 mark questions with items that require referral to an item, although you must make sure that you understand that the 10 markers vary in how they are worded, and how the marks are awarded for the different skills.
>
> Do:
> - Make sure that you identify two different points clearly.
> - Evaluate and analyse. For example, make sure that you do criticise the ideas you are discussing.
> - Make sure that you refer to the ideas in the item, or critique them, or alternatively, offer counter views to them.
> - Use concepts clearly and make sure that you unpack them, that is, explain what they mean and make sure that they you explain how they are relevant to the question.
>
> Don't:
> - Spend too long on these questions. It is easy to write too much if you know a lot about the topic. About 15 minutes should be enough.
> - Simply describe a study or an idea. Make it relevant to the specific demands of the question.

Example question

> **Item A**
>
> Despite girls achieving very strong results in education at all levels, wherever there is an opportunity for choice in the subjects to be taken, girls and boys conform to gender stereotypes. Girls overwhelmingly choose subjects that reflect traditionally feminine subjects while boys continue to take subjects that are perceived to be masculine, such as physics and maths. A range of reasons have been put forward, including pupil pressure and teacher labelling, as well as factors outside of school.

03 Applying material from Item A, analyse two reasons why girls and boys tend to choose different subjects. [10 marks]

Example answers

Student A

Gender is an important factor when looking at the different choices people make in subjects. Girls are better at writing and therefore tend to take subjects such as English. This is because they are naturally better at literacy.

The student here correctly identifies that some girls achieve better results in literacy-based subjects. However, the student assumes that the reason is biological, that somehow girls are born differently to girls. There may be a case for arguing that there are some biological factors, but this question is asking students to consider the social reasons for differences in gender and educational outcomes. The student also assumes that all girls are better at literacy than all boys, which is not the case.

Boys like to fight and do sport so they take subjects such as PE. Boys tend to be brought up to be competitive and sporty and this means that they find sitting still and being neat and tidy difficult for long periods of time.

Again, more assumptions about the innate differences between boys and girls. This would better be replaced with a study or a concept that explains the role of differential gendered socialisation in gendered subject choices, such as McRobbie's study of bedroom culture. However, this is one reason, albeit undeveloped with sociological evidence and concepts.

Girls tend to choose subjects that are similar to their career choices, which tend to be about taking a caring role, such as being a nurse or a secretary. This might be because of the pressure put on them by their friends. Girls who choose male subjects often get looked down upon or bullied for being different.

Another reason offered here about conforming to gender roles, however, there is little sociological knowledge here. The student might have mentioned gender domains or subcultures or the male gaze. It also does not explain why boys pick the subjects that they do.

Overall in this answer the knowledge is basic, it refers to sociological ideas but does not offer concepts explicitly or research. It is simplistic, and tends to make generalisations about 'all girls' and 'all boys.'

Student B

The process being described in the item is gendered subject choices. This refers to where students make decisions about the subjects they will take based on assumptions and values informed by home and school influences.

One internal factor is that schools may create or contribute to gender domains, which is imagined territories that are perceived to be male or female. Subjects fall into imagined male or female categories. These are reinforced by teachers who uphold these gender domains in the examples they use in class, or through the advice that they give students, for example, with regards to which subjects they should take.

The item is referred to and developed. The student clearly identifies one reason for gendered subject choices – gender domains – and they demonstrate their understanding of the concept well.

Alternatively, textbooks can reinforce stereotypical ideas about gendered subject choices, as Lobban found in her study of imagery and content in school storybooks. Furthermore, boys and male teachers may regard girls and female students with a male gaze, which means looking at them in a controlling way to ensure that they do not stray from socially expected norms about girls being conformist and well-behaved. If girls do stray from these norms, including in terms of gendered subject choices, they may be teased or worse, bullied.

Another two internal factors are identified here. Lobban's study is used well and the consequences of the male gaze are also well explained.

Outside the school, girls and boys can reinforce stereotypical ideas about gender through, for example, a 'bedroom culture' for girls which McRobbie sees as girls reinforcing ideas about working hard, being worried about doing well and being neat, which ties in with succeeding in literacy-based subjects.

This adds another dimension to the student's answer, through exploring external factors using a relevant study.

In conclusion, gendered subject choices remain significant and are caused by many factors both inside and outside of the school. Things are changing however as women are increasingly successful in a broader range of subjects and beginning to earn more than men in their early twenties. This suggests that gendered subject choices may become less of an issue in the future.

A clear conclusion that recognises that things may be changing. This conclusion also acknowledges that a range of internal and external factors lead to gendered subject choices.

A very strong answer with clear evidence of knowledge and understanding as well as higher level skills.

Practice question

Item A

Bowles and Gintis describe the way in which work mirrors school. They claim that school simply prepares students for the kinds of demands that they will face in work. They argue that the purpose of this is to ensure that the economy runs smoothly to benefit the ruling class. Others see the similarities between school and the workplace more positively, pointing out that, for example, students are rewarded for hard work as they would be in work and that this process provides a bridge between the home and the school.

03 Applying material from Item A, analyse two ways in which education is said to be similar to the world of work. [10 marks]

04 Applying material from Item B and your knowledge, evaluate... [30 marks]

This is a demanding question that requires you to explore an educational issue in significantly more detail. This is an opportunity for you to examine a range of views, concepts and issues in education. The breakdown of marks is as follows: 12 marks for AO1, 9 marks for AO2 and 9 marks for AO3. The item will give you some ideas to develop in your answer, so make sure that you read this carefully before you begin answering the question. You can expect to spend around 45 minutes answering this question, so it should be detailed and thorough.

> **TIPS FOR ANSWERING LONGER ESSAYS**
>
> Do
> - Make sure that you create a debate, with different perspectives included.
> - Ensure that your essay is well organised and structured, with a clear beginning middle and end.
> - Focus on the question throughout – make sure that you do not go off on a tangent.
> - Ensure that you offer criticisms of different perspectives.
> - Use contemporary issues to support or challenge the ideas that you are discussing.
> - Mention the methods used by the sociologists you are discussing if you know it; this is a very good way of developing your analysis.
> - Draw on different areas of the course if appropriate to support your argument.
>
> Don't
> - Forget the importance of concepts being used effectively in a way that shows that you understand the concept.

How is the 30 mark essay marked?

Here are the different mark bands that are used to mark this question.

25–30	<ul><li>Answers in this band will show sound, conceptually detailed knowledge of a range of relevant material. Sophisticated understanding of the question and of the presented material will be shown.</li><li>Appropriate material will be applied accurately and with sensitivity to the issues raised by the question.</li><li>Analysis and evaluation will be explicit and relevant. Evaluation may be developed, for example, through a debate between different perspectives (e.g. New Right, postmodernism, feminism).</li><li>Analysis will show clear explanation. Appropriate conclusions will be drawn.</li></ul>
19–24	<ul><li>Answers in this band will be accurate, broad and/or deep but incomplete.</li><li>Answers will show an understanding of a number of significant aspects of the question; good understanding of the presented material.</li><li>Application of material is largely explicitly relevant to the question, though some material may be inadequately focused.</li><li>Some limited explicit evaluation, for example, of the impact of equality legislation and/or some appropriate analysis, e.g. clear explanations of some of the presented material.</li></ul>
13–18	<ul><li>Answers in this band will show largely accurate knowledge but limited range and depth</li><li>Understands some limited but significant aspects of the question; superficial understanding of the presented material.</li><li>Applying listed material from the general topic area but with limited regard for its relevance to the issues raised by the question, or applying a narrow range of more relevant material.</li><li>Evaluation will take the form of juxtaposition of competing positions or one to two isolated stated points. Analysis will be limited, with answers tending towards the descriptive.</li></ul>
7–12	<ul><li>Answers in this band will show limited undeveloped knowledge.</li><li>Understands only limited aspects of the question; simplistic understanding of the presented material.</li><li>Limited application of suitable material, and/or material often at a tangent to the demands of the question, Very limited or no evaluation.</li><li>Attempts at analysis, if any, are thin and disjointed.</li></ul>
1–6	<ul><li>Answers in this band will show very limited knowledge.</li><li>Very little/no understanding of the question and of the presented material.</li><li>Significant errors and/or omissions in application of material.</li><li>No analysis or evaluation.</li></ul>
0	No relevant points.

Practice question

Item B

Some sociologists argue that the role of education is to provide the right amount of skilled workers for a changing economy. For example, the recent demand for computer literate students has meant that computer skills are taught in compulsory education.

There are sociologists who regard this provision of skilled workers positively, while others disagree and argue that the education system simply reinforces inequalities that occur both inside and outside the education system.

04 Applying material from Item B and your knowledge, evaluate the view that the role of education is to prepare students for work. [30 marks]

Some advice on how to answer this question

For this question you should aim to think about the role or function of education using a number of different theoretical perspectives. These include functionalists (as suggested in the item) and the New Right as well as opposing views from Marxists and feminists. Within each perspective specific concepts and theorists should be referred to, as well as criticisms and evaluations of their views in terms of how relevant they are to today's society.

It would also be a good idea to suggest how education prepares some students more than others in terms of class, gender and ethnic differences in outcome. The postmodern view on the role of education might also be useful here in highlighting how working practices are changing within a global context. Finally, you need to come to a clear conclusion about the view that the role of education is to prepare students for work. Perhaps you disagree and believe that the education system functions simply to reproduce inequalities.

Example questions

Here are some example questions for you to plan (perhaps you can try writing the item that might go with the question).

- Applying material from Item B and your knowledge, evaluate the view that education provides everyone with equal opportunities for success. [30 marks]
- Applying material from Item B and your knowledge, evaluate the view that home factors can explain why working class children underachieve in education. [30 marks]
- Applying material from Item B and your knowledge, evaluate the view that gender is the most significant factor affecting educational outcomes in education. [30 marks]

05 Methods in context [20 marks]

This question is worth 20 marks with 8 marks for AO1, 8 marks for AO2 and 4 marks for AO3. You are expected to demonstrate your knowledge of sociological methods, concepts and examples of research as well as knowledge about a particular educational issue. This knowledge is to be applied to a considering carrying out research in a particular situation, and you should, explain the benefits and limitations of the given research method. This question demands a strong understanding of how the method would actually work in a real context.

Due to this question demanding such different skills, there is a chapter dedicated to this question (see Book 1 pages 90–114).

> **STUDY HINT**
> If you have taken the AS exam, you will be aware of the skills required for this question, but remember that at A-level you will have more detailed knowledge of methods and education and should therefore be able to answer this question in greater detail and with greater confidence.

06 Theory and methods: outline and explain two... [10 marks]

This question requires you to draw on your knowledge of theory and methods. There are 5 marks for AO1, 3 marks for AO2 and 2 marks for AO3. Remember that you will need to use your knowledge of research methods as well as your knowledge of positivist and interpretivist approaches to research. You could be asked about the strengths and limitations of a particular research method, factors affecting the choice of method or questions about a social theory. The table below shows how this question is marked.

8–10	■ Answers in this band will show very good knowledge and understanding. ■ There will be two applications of relevant material. ■ There will be appropriate analysis.
4–7	■ Answers in this band will show a reasonable to good knowledge and understanding. ■ There will be one or two applications of relevant material. ■ There will be some basic analysis.
1–3	■ Answers in this band will show limited knowledge and little or no understanding of the question or the material. ■ There will be limited focus on the question. ■ There will be limited or no analysis.
0	■ No relevant points.

Example question

06 Outline and explain two arguments for the view that a positivist approach is useful in carrying out research. [10 marks]

Some advice on answering this question

- Explain what is meant by positivism.
- Suggest positivist types of research and data
- Use an example of piece of research that uses positivist methodology. Refer to the concepts of reliability, objectivity and value freedom. Criticise the positivist approach using an interpretivist argument, suggest that positivist research lacks validity and verstehen.

Example question

06 Outline and explain two arguments for the view that theories developed in modern society are no longer relevant for understanding society today. [10 marks]

Theories created in the modern era such as Functionalism and Marxism reflect the views of their time. The modern era is seen as stable and both functionalists and Marxists argued that social forces shape the individual, that there was generally value consensus in society, and that people saw the world around them in a similar way. For example, Marx saw society as being based upon class differences, whereas, for most people today, class is not the most important factor shaping a person's identity or life. Similarly, functionalists argued that people experienced a collective conscience, and that they shared a sense of belonging to a wider group, which may not be the case any longer. In sum, modern theories sought to provide a metanarrative or an overarching set of answers to questions in society, which many feel is no longer possible.

> Postmodernists argue that modern theories are no longer relevant as society has changed so much. They claim that society no longer shapes behaviour, rather the individual shapes their life through a series of choices that are available to them. For example, in the family, the postmodernist feminist Stacey argues that this increased choice has led women to be able to make choices about their relationships and family life that are both positive and beneficial for them. As women now work, they are able to support themselves financially and can leave unhappy relationships, which was not possible for many women in the past. This approach shows how traditional modern theories based on metanarratives of feminism or Marxism are no longer useful for understanding society today.
>
> It is clear that traditional, modern theories are no longer useful for understanding a complex postmodern world where people's identity is based around a number of different factors.

This is a well organised answer with two clear arguments and a conclusion. The first point raised is that society has changed and does not share ideas and views as it once did, therefore making modern theories less relevant. The second point raised focuses on the choices possible within postmodern society, which make modern theoretical explanations less relevant. Both points link to the idea that modern theories suggest that society shapes the individual whereas this may well no longer be the case. Concepts are used confidently and there is clear knowledge and understanding. Ideas are applied to the question and the argument comes to a clear conclusion.

Practice questions

- Outline and explain two arguments for the view that consensus theories are useful for understanding society. [10 marks]
- Outline and explain two arguments for the view that theories developed in modern era society are no longer relevant for understanding society today. [10 marks]
- Outline and explain two arguments for the view that qualitative research methods are most useful for understanding society. [10 marks]

Tackling A-level paper 2

STUDY HINT
Make sure that you only answer one set of questions from section A and one set of questions from section B.

In this paper there are two sections: A and B. In each section, you have a choice of topics. You must select one topic from each section and answer all the questions on that topic. Both sections A and B follow the same question pattern, there are two 10 mark questions followed by a 20 mark question.

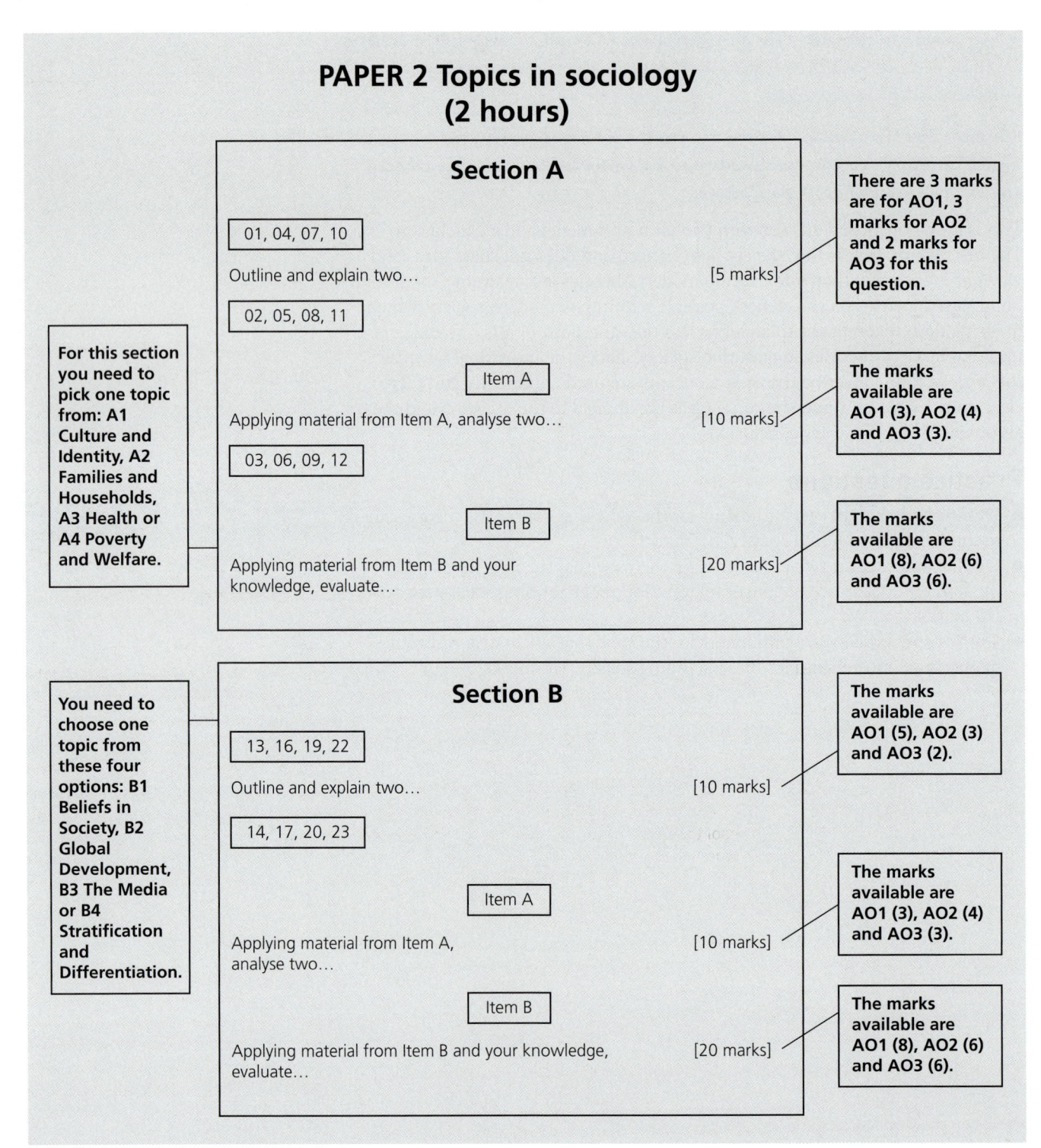

PAPER 2 Topics in sociology (2 hours)

Section A

For this section you need to pick one topic from: A1 Culture and Identity, A2 Families and Households, A3 Health or A4 Poverty and Welfare.

01, 04, 07, 10
Outline and explain two… [5 marks]
— There are 3 marks are for AO1, 3 marks for AO2 and 2 marks for AO3 for this question.

02, 05, 08, 11
Item A
Applying material from Item A, analyse two… [10 marks]
— The marks available are AO1 (3), AO2 (4) and AO3 (3).

03, 06, 09, 12
Item B
Applying material from Item B and your knowledge, evaluate… [20 marks]
— The marks available are AO1 (8), AO2 (6) and AO3 (6).

Section B

You need to choose one topic from these four options: B1 Beliefs in Society, B2 Global Development, B3 The Media or B4 Stratification and Differentiation.

13, 16, 19, 22
Outline and explain two… [10 marks]
— The marks available are AO1 (5), AO2 (3) and AO3 (2).

14, 17, 20, 23
Item A
Applying material from Item A, analyse two… [10 marks]
— The marks available are AO1 (3), AO2 (4) and AO3 (3).

Item B
Applying material from Item B and your knowledge, evaluate… [20 marks]
— The marks available are AO1 (8), AO2 (6) and AO3 (6).

The choices you have for each section are as follows.

Section A	Section B
A1 Culture and Identity	B1 Beliefs in Society
A2 Families and Households	B2 Global Development
A3 Health	B3 The media
A4 Work, Poverty and Welfare	B4 Stratification and Differentiation

	AO1	AO2	AO3	Total
Option 1				
Q01, Q04, Q07, Q10	5	3	2	10
Q02, Q05, Q08, Q11	3	4	3	10
Q03, Q06, Q09. Q12	8	6	6	20
Option 2				
Q13, Q16, Q19, Q22	5	3	2	10
Q14, Q17, Q20, Q23	3	4	3	10
Q15, Q18, Q21, Q24	8	6	6	20
Total	32	26	22	80

> **STUDY HINT**
> Remember that if you took the AS you will have already been examined on one topic from section A. Make sure that you realise that for this paper, at A-level the demand is significantly higher, therefore your work needs more detail and higher level skills need to be demonstrated.

Below are some questions for you to practise.

Section A

Culture and Identity	Families and Households	Health	Work, Poverty and Welfare
Outline and explain two ways in which individuals may be socialised into a social class identity. [10 marks]	Outline and explain two ways in which migration has affected family size. [10 marks]	Outline and explain two ways in which health is socially constructed. [10 marks]	Outline and explain two ways in which poverty can be measured. [10 marks]
Applying material from Item A, analyse two ways in which identity is changing as a result of globalization. [10 marks]	Applying material from Item A, analyse two ways in which the family remains oppressive for women. [10 marks]	Applying material from Item A, analyse two ways in which healthcare is unequally distributed in society. [10 marks]	Applying material from Item A, analyse two ways in which worklessness affects people's lives. [10 marks]
Applying material from Item B and your knowledge, evaluate the view that gender is the main resource for creating an identity. [20 marks]	Applying material from Item B and your knowledge, evaluate the view that social policies support the nuclear family. [20 marks]	Applying material from Item B and your knowledge, evaluate the reasons why mental health is unevenly distributed in society. [20 marks]	Applying material from Item B and your knowledge, evaluate the view that the state should do more to help reduce poverty in society. [20 marks]

Section B

Beliefs in Society	Global Development	The Media	Stratification and Differentiation
Outline and explain two ways in which globalisation affects religion. [10 marks]	Outline and explain two reasons why development projects may fail. [10 marks]	Outline and explain two ways in which the media represents gender. [10 marks]	Outline and explain two forms of stratification in society. [10 marks]
Applying material from Item A, analyse two ways in which religion is a force for change in society. [10 marks]	Applying material from Item A, analyse two ways in which non-governmental organisations affect development. [10 marks]	Applying material from Item A, analyse two ways in which journalists decide what is newsworthy. [10 marks]	Applying material from Item A, analyse two ways in which class based differences are becoming les significant today. [10 marks]
Applying material from Item B and your knowledge, evaluate the view that religion is in decline. [20 marks]	Applying material from Item B and your knowledge, evaluate the view that globalisation has a positive impact upon relationships between different countries. [20 marks]	Applying material from Item B and your knowledge, evaluate the view that news is controlled by the owners of the media companies. [20 marks]	Applying material from Item B and your knowledge, evaluate the view that social mobility is a possibility for all groups in society. [20 marks]

Section A Families and households

Example question

01 Outline and explain two ways in which migration has affected family size. [10 marks]

Migration refers to the movement of people; there are two types, immigration where people move into a place or emigration where people leave a place. Immigration has increased in the UK and this has had a considerable effect on family size. One reason for the increase in immigration was the inclusion of more countries into the European Union, such as Poland, which means that people are able to live in different parts of Europe such as the UK.

One way in which immigration has affected family life is that there is a higher fertility rate among some immigrant groups, on average around 2.3, whereas the average fertility rate for British-born women is 1.9. This has meant that family size in general has increased on average. This has also led to greater demand for school places and greater strain on public services such as the NHS.

Some immigrants however tend to have different family structures such as African Caribbean populations who have a much higher rate of single parent female headed or matriarchal families than average in the UK. However New Right thinkers, such as Murray, would argue that single parent families are inadequate for raising children and that two parents are needed, particularly strong male role models within a conventional nuclear family.

In conclusion, migration has led to greater family diversity and will continue to do so as a result of globalisation.

This answer has two clearly explained ways, as well as clear definitions of migration, immigration and emigration. There is analysis through the perspective mentioned (New Right views) and other effects of immigration are mentioned and developed, such as the impact of increased birth rates. It is clear from this answer that the student has not simply generalised and knows that there are different effects of migration on family size.

02 Applying material from Item A, analyse two ways in which the family remains oppressive for women. [10 marks]

> ## Item A
> Feminists argue that although there have been some improvements for women in society, the experience of family life for women remains negative. They point out the high rates of domestic violence towards women as well as the continued burden on women to perform both paid work and domestic work.

Feminists such as Dobash and Dobash argue that one in four women experience domestic violence at some point in their lives. Feminists argue that the family reflects patriarchal ideology and that this encourages men to assert their power over women in many different ways. However, it is not just women who experience domestic violence, there is a growing number of men who also experience domestic violence as well. Some Marxist feminists such as Ansley argue that women absorb the frustrations their husbands have with capitalism. For example, men are frustrated with their lack of control at work as the ruling class gives men tasks over which they have little control, and they therefore come home and take their frustrations out on their wives. However, not all men do this and some men are happy at work.

As the item suggests, some women feel a tension because they have to carry out domestic tasks as well as paid work, which Oakley calls the dual burden. This is a common way in which women may continue to find family life oppressive as it is exhausting for them to take on this dual burden. However, there are more and more men who feel this way too, as men begin to take more responsibility for the childcare and housework. Gershuny carried out longitudinal research to explore the impact of women's full-time work on men's contribution to housework. He found that there is a time delay between women working full time and men contributing more, which he calls lagged adaptation. Gershuny's work however does suggest that men are gradually helping more and this suggests that the family might not be as oppressive for women in the future.

This is a good answer because it gives two clear ways in which the family remains oppressive, it uses the item and goes beyond it. It analyses both ways, for example, in pointing out that, men may also experience domestic violence and also that, as Gershuny suggests, family life may be improving as men participate more fully in housework as women work full time. There are concepts, perspectives and a sense of change.

The evaluate question

The 20 mark question in Sections A and B places a strong emphasis on higher level skills, with 8 marks for AO1, 6 marks for AO2 and 6 marks for AO3. The question asks you to apply material from the Item as well as your own knowledge to evaluate an idea or view. To evaluate in this sense means to explore different views, looking at their strengths and weaknesses as well as their relevance to the issue. Here are some ideas of how you might approach this skill for this question.

- Take an idea or view expressed in the item and develop it further. That is, go beyond the item by adding more detail, for example, add names, research or concepts that support or challenge the item.
- Comment on the relevance of ideas expressed in the item or within the debate more generally in the context of today's society.
- Consider connections between the question and other areas of the course, be it globalisation, structure, agency, socialisation, culture and identity, for example.
- Focus on the strengths of an idea or argument as well as the weaknesses and consider if there are more strengths or weaknesses overall.
- Come to a clear conclusion that corresponds clearly to the specific question.

Practice question

01 Applying material from Item B and your knowledge, evaluate the view that social policies support the nuclear family (20 marks)

Item B

Social policies are often reveal assumptions and ideas that a government has about what they see as appropriate family life as well as the role of the state. Some governments argue that the state should be involved with shaping family life and helping those out who need it while others argue that the individual should take greater responsibility for their family rather than rely on benefits.

Some advice on how to answer this question

This question is asking you to explore the way different policies have encouraged the nuclear family and/or other family types. It is worth organising your answer in terms of political approach, on the one hand there is the New Right which includes the 1979–97 government as well as the coalition and recent conservative government. Policies created by these governments encourage traditional gender roles, marriage (for example through the married persons tax allowance) and they see the nuclear family as ideal, the cornerstone of society. You should discuss examples of their policies (including recent policies). Alternatively, there is New Labour ideology from 1997 to 2010, which also sees the nuclear family as ideal but also supports women going back to work, more equal gender roles and supports alternatives to the nuclear family. It would be a good idea to include different theoretical perspectives on the role of policies.

Tackling A-level Paper 3

In this paper there are no options, all six questions must be answered. There are two sections of the paper, section 1 includes four questions on crime and deviance (worth a total of 50 marks) and the second section includes two questions on theory and methods (worth a total of 30 marks). This paper reflects A-level demands and therefore you are expected to write in some detail. You may find at times that it is appropriate to draw from other parts of the course to answer the question. This is fine as long as you are careful to relate your ideas to the specific demands of the question. The paper is structured as shown below.

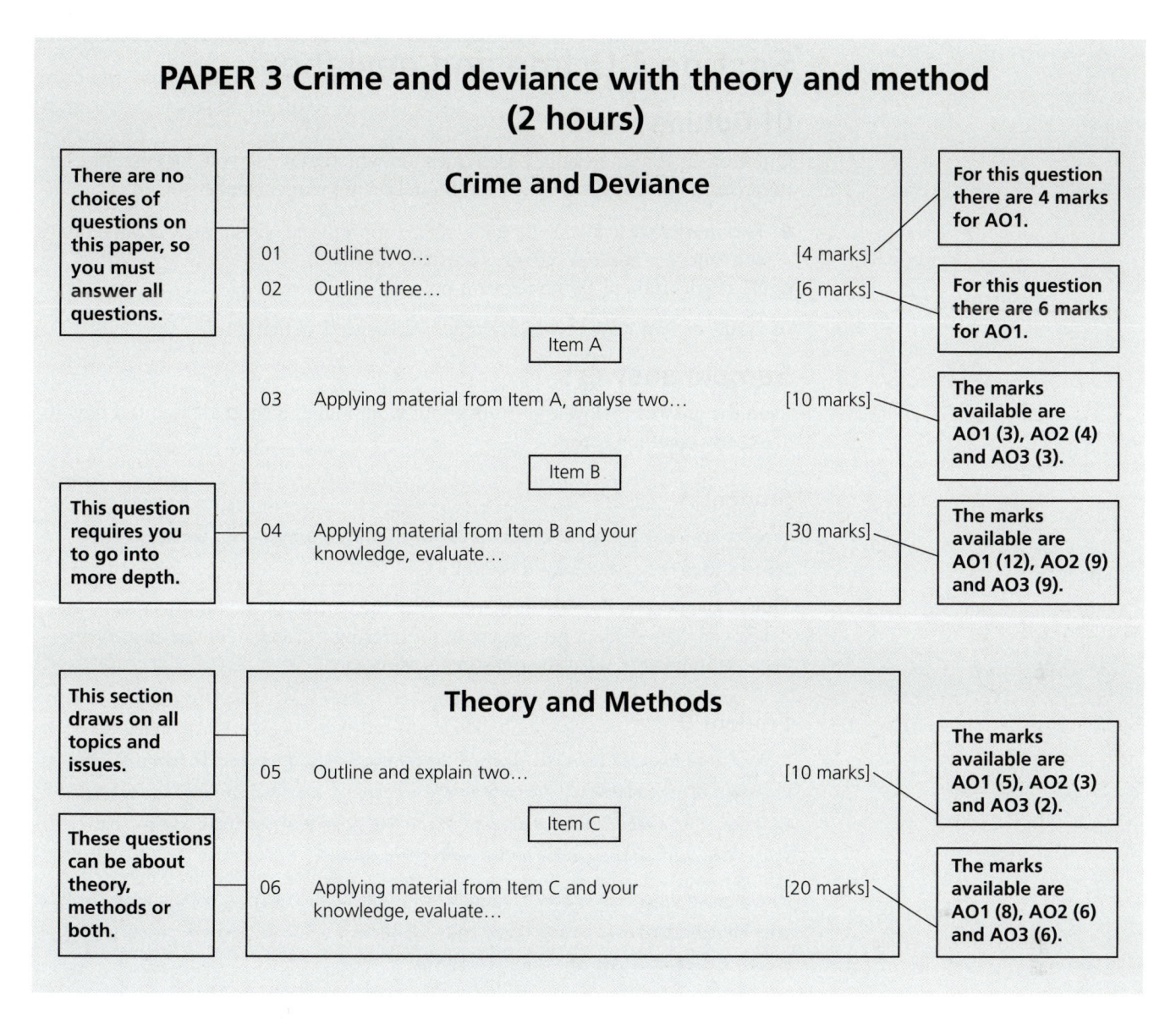

PAPER 3 Crime and deviance with theory and method (2 hours)

There are no choices of questions on this paper, so you must answer all questions.

Crime and Deviance

01 Outline two… [4 marks] — *For this question there are 4 marks for AO1.*

02 Outline three… [6 marks] — *For this question there are 6 marks for AO1.*

Item A

03 Applying material from Item A, analyse two… [10 marks] — *The marks available are AO1 (3), AO2 (4) and AO3 (3).*

Item B

This question requires you to go into more depth.

04 Applying material from Item B and your knowledge, evaluate… [30 marks] — *The marks available are AO1 (12), AO2 (9) and AO3 (9).*

Theory and Methods

This section draws on all topics and issues.

These questions can be about theory, methods or both.

05 Outline and explain two… [10 marks] — *The marks available are AO1 (5), AO2 (3) and AO3 (2).*

Item C

06 Applying material from Item C and your knowledge, evaluate… [20 marks] — *The marks available are AO1 (8), AO2 (6) and AO3 (6).*

The mark breakdown is as follows:

Question number	AO1	AO2	AO3	Total marks
01	4			4
02	6			6
03	3	4	3	10
04	12	9	9	30
05	5	3	2	10
06	8	6	6	20

Section 1 Crime and deviance

01 Outline two...

Question 01 is a knowledge based question which may ask you, for example, for two reasons or ways and which has the following mark scheme:

- Two marks are available for each of two appropriate ways clearly outlined or one mark for appropriate ways partially outlined.
- No marks if there are no relevant points.

01 Outline two ways in which crime is measured. [4 marks]

Sample answers

Read the answers below and think about what makes a good answer and how to avoid any common errors.

Student A

Victim surveys are used to record crime, however, people may lie about the crimes that they have been a victim of.

This answer correctly identifies one way of measuring crime but it is not developed. The student gets no credit for offering a criticism of victim surveys, because that is not what the question is asking for.

Student B

Crime is measured in a number of different ways. The first is through crimes recorded by the police who decide that an event is a crime when it is reported to them. They record it as a crime, which the government then use in their statistics, which they then share with the public.

The second way crime can be measured is through victim surveys where people who have had crimes committed against them self-report crime, often giving a much fuller account of crime statistics.

This answer is accurate and clear. There are two clear ways and these are developed.

Student C

The government recorded crime.

Where people tell a researcher about the crimes they have committed.

This answer does not actually state the measures of crime, which shows how important it is to accurately identify the measure before going on to develop it.

02 Outline three...

This question is also knowledge based and so you might be asked, for example, for three reasons or ways that need to be accurate and clearly different. You need to make sure that these reasons are not too similar or overlapping. Here is an example of this question type with the mark scheme underneath.

- Two marks for each of three appropriate reasons clearly outlined or 1 mark for appropriate reasons partially outlined.
- No marks for no relevant points.

02 Outline three reasons why corporate crime is often undetected. [6 marks]

Sample answers

Student A

Corporate crimes often go undetected because even if people see them happen in business, they may not report them for fear of losing their jobs.

Corporate crimes are often under-reported due to the fact that they are carried out by the powerful who the police are less likely to treat as suspects, therefore, leading to less crimes being revealed.

The police see people working in business as law abiding and they label them positively.

The first part of the answer is relevant and the second reason is appropriate and well developed; however the final reason is too similar to the second.

Student B

Corporate crime is crime carried out in businesses, such as embezzlement, fraud or corruption. This is happening more and more and often by middle class people who carry out the crimes from their laptop, making it hard for the police to see.

Quite often corporate crime happens in private, closed-off business, such as banks, where powerful people use their cultural capital to give the image of being respectable and law abiding.

This answer clearly identifies and explains the reason of being less visible to the police in the first paragraph. The second paragraph correctly identifies two further points but doesn't develop either of these. The student could have set out each reason more clearly.

Student C

Corporate crime is often undetected as it often involves the powerful who are able to use their position to talk their way out of the crime.

Crimes committed by the powerful are often cleverly hidden from view, making it harder for the police to detect that the crime has been committed or how it has happened.

The police may not have the skills, resources or ability to access the inner workings of businesses meaning that many corporate crimes remain undetected.

This is a good answer. It is succinct and each point is separate and well developed.

03 Applying material from Item A, analyse two...

This question is worth 10 marks and requires you to write in prose. It is worth 3 marks for AO1, 4 marks for AO2 and 3 marks for AO3. So although knowledge and understanding are important, so too are showing the higher levels skills that are worth more. As this is an analyse question it means you need to clearly criticise some ideas, concepts or evidence. Now, we will look at an example of this question, with a mark scheme followed by some example student answers. Pay particular attention to the mark bands so you know how to write a top band answer.

03 Applying material from Item A, analyse two reasons why some ethnic groups are over represented in crime statistics. [10 marks]

Item A

Prison populations do not reflect the make-up of different groups in society. In fact, some groups are persistently overrepresented. For example, there are far more men in prison than women. Sociologists suggest a number of reasons for these patterns, for example, structural inequalities in society, which place some groups in a disadvantaged position.

8–10	Answers in this band will show good knowledge and understanding of relevant material on two reasons why some ethnic minorities are overrepresented in crime statistics. There will be two developed applications of material from the item, e.g. status frustration, institutional racism in the police, relative deprivation, rational choice theory or marginalisation. There will be appropriate analysis/evaluation of two reasons, e.g. of how far rational choice may determine decisions to commit crime and how far police discrimination can account for the overrepresentation of some ethnic groups in prisons.
4–7	Answers in this band will show a basic to reasonable knowledge and understanding of one or two reasons why situational crime prevention strategies may not be effective in reducing crime. There will be some successful application of material from the item, e.g. the fact that some ethnic minorities are more likely to be marginalised and therefore more likely to commit crime. There will be some analysis/evaluation.
1–3	Answers in this band will show limited knowledge and understanding of one or two reasons why some ethnic minority groups are overrepresented in prisons. There will be limited or no application of material from the item. Some material may be at a tangent to the question, e.g. there may be some drift into material of other groups in prisons. There will be limited or no analysis/evaluation.
0	No relevant points.

Sample answers

Student A

As Item A suggests, some ethnic groups in society are overrepresented in prisons, including in particular black working class men. There are several suggested reasons for this.

One theory is the left realist argument that ethnic minorities are more likely to be among the relatively deprived in society, which means that they feel that they have less than other people in society and commit crime to feel they have a similar amount of things. Left realists also argue that groups such as black working class men also feel that they are a marginalised group, meaning that they are on the edges of society with relatively few life chances. Functionalist subcultural theorists, alternatively, would call this status frustration, which in a way is similar; some poorer black ethnic minorities commit crime because they cannot see a legitimate way to improve their position in society. These two factors may explain this groups' overrepresentation in prisons. However, others would argue that making such generalisations is wrong, and that there are other more important factors involved, such as the way policing is organised.

There have been several cases of institutionalised racism, which might also explain the overrepresentation of ethnic minorities in prison populations. Institutionalised racism means the conscious or subconscious discrimination of some ethnic groups at an organisational level, for example, the Stephen Lawrence inquest, which revealed systematic racism among the police investigating his murder. This, along with a much higher rate of police stop *and searches of cars with a black male driver, may also reflect discriminatory assumptions or labelling of the police which would therefore lead to higher rates of arrest and prison statistics.*

There are clearly a number of structural factors linked to discrimination in wider society that lead to some ethnic groups' overrepresentation in prisons, but class and gender are also important factors in understanding the types of patterns of who is in prison.

This is a strong, focused answer which uses the item and shows good knowledge and understanding of theories and concepts. The concepts are well explained and relevant. There are two clearly explained reasons, which are applied to the question. There is some analysis, showing that no one explanation of overrepresentation of ethnic minority groups in prison is sufficient. The answer evaluates using the idea that there are other patterns in prison populations which may be relevant. The answer also draws upon a contemporary issue, the Stephen Lawrence case.

04 Applying material from Item B and your knowledge, evaluate…

This question requires you to write in some detail about crime and deviance. There are 12 marks for AO1, 9 marks for AO2 and 9 marks for AO3. You will have around 45 minutes to answer this question. Here are some ideas for how to approach this question:

- This is an evaluate question, therefore there should be a clear discussion and exploration of a number of different views on the issue.
- Use the item and go beyond it by exploring supporting and opposing research, ideas and concepts.
- Consider how relevant the various ideas you are discussing relate to today's society, which is global and possibly, according to some, postmodern.
- Use contemporary examples to support your ideas or arguments, but make sure that they are applied to the question clearly.
- You can draw from different parts of the course, for example, if you feel it is appropriate mention New Right views about the inadequate socialisation of boys in single parent families for crime if you are asked to discuss gender and crime rates.
- You can further develop your concepts, explain them fully, give examples and link them to particular theories or theorists.
- You may find it appropriate to talk about relevant policies or changes in the law which reflect changing ideas about crime and deviance.
- Don't forget that theories of crime all come from a particular context, which may help explain their views, and don't forget to explore the kinds of assumptions that these theories make about society and relate these to the specific demands of the questions.
- Be critical of theories, concepts, policies and ideas.
- Come to a clear conclusion making sure it relates specifically to the question.

04 Applying material from Item B and your knowledge, evaluate the view that Marxist theories are useful for understanding crime in society today
[30 marks]

Item B

Traditional Marxists argue that the cause of crime lies in the way the economy is organised in capitalist society. They argue that capitalism creates a set of ideas which encourage people to want to turn to crime to gain material wealth. Marxists also argue that the police carry out selective enforcement of the law.

However other theorists offer different reasons for crime, such as creating boundaries in society so that people know what is right and wrong, as well as committing crime as a rational choice.

Some advice on how to answer this question

The question asks you to give a detailed discussion of the extent to which Marxist theories of crime are useful in today's (global, postmodern) society. Therefore you should explore Marxist explanations in some detail, including both classical Marxist explanations as well as more contemporary Marxist subcultural theories. Use contemporary evidence that supports and challenges Marxist explanations of crime, such as the overwhelmingly working class prison population or the rising number of middle class people committing new forms of crime. Make sure that you explore the strengths and weaknesses of Marxist explanations of crime then go on to explore how other theoretical perspectives would challenge Marxist ideas. Avoid simply listing information on other theories and hoping that it is relevant, you need to show exactly how it relates to the question. Finally, make sure you explore postmodern theories of crime to explore how modern theories of crime, such as Marxism, may no longer be useful for explaining crime. Come to a clear conclusion.

> **STUDY HINT**
>
> While you may have answered questions at AS on theory and methods, the demand is significantly higher here. You are expected to understand the differences between the demands for A-level, such as considering theory in more detail and understanding and explaining methods using a wider range of concepts.

Section 2 Theory and methods

This section requires you to explore methodological and theoretical issues, by drawing on all areas of the course. The questions may ask you to discuss issues that are both theory and methods related such as asking about the relative importance of positivism and interpretivism. Make sure that you carefully consider including knowledge and understanding from both if it is appropriate.

05 Outline and explain two...

This question is similar to other 10 mark questions that you have answered at A-level. There are 5 marks for AO1, 3 marks for AO2 and 2 marks for AO3. Look carefully at the mark scheme below and think about the students, responses as well.

05 Outline and explain two factors affecting the choice of research method.
[10 marks]

8–10	Answers in this band will show very good knowledge and understanding of two factors affecting choice of research method. There will be two applications of relevant material, e.g. practical and ethical issues. There will be appropriate analysis, e.g. of why ethical issues may be more important than other factors.
4–7	Answers in this band will show a reasonable to good knowledge and understanding of one or two factors affecting the choice of research method. There will be one or two applications of relevant material, e.g. how researcher characteristics affect what is possible in terms of the types of people being researched. There will be some basic analysis.
1–3	Answers in this band will show limited knowledge and little or no understanding of the question or the material. There will be limited focus on the question, e.g. there may be some drift into different research methods. There will be limited or no analysis.
0	No relevant points.

Sample answers

Student A

There are three main factors affecting the choice of research method including practical, ethical and theoretical factors.

Ethical factors, probably the most significant of all factors, relate to the moral issues connected to the research, for example, making sure that the researcher and those being researched are not harmed in the process of the research project. This also relates to deception, so, for example, Humphery failed to tell the people involved in his study of voyeur sex that he was an undercover researcher and this meant that they were deceived; they did not consent to the research. Protecting the identity of those being researched is also an important ethical issue, because if the research write up reveals the identity of those being researched they could be harmed as a result.

Another factor affecting the choice of research method are practical issues that include the social characteristics of the researcher, which may make it harder for them to access particular groups, for example, Sudhir Venkatesh would have found it difficult to conduct his research on gangs had he been a woman. Furthermore, time and money are very real constraints, some subjects are more likely to get funded while others are not, which can lead to people doing certain types of research and not others. Some research, such as Barker's study of the Moonies, took her six years to complete, which is clearly very demanding. Some groups are simply too difficult to gain access to, such as the powerful or criminal groups where a gatekeeper is needed in order to gather a sample to research.

Ethical issues seem to be the most important factor in the choice of a research method as you cannot do research which harms people or is morally wrong in some way. There are also theoretical issues, which can shape the way a sociologist thinks about the world and therefore how they carry out research.

This is a reasonable response. There are clearly two factors affecting the choice of method and these are well organised with a range of examples and studies. There is some analysis and evaluation throughout the response, however, the student could have gone further to provide more detailed criticisms. There are a number of concepts that could also have been mentioned such as positivism and interpretivism, as well as validity, reliability and representativeness, which are quite important in discussing methods.

Practice questions

- Outline and explain two ways in which positivist research may be useful for understanding society.
- Outline and explain two strengths of interpretivist research.
- Outline and explain two problems with using experiments.
- Outline and explain two ways in which postmodern approaches may help sociologists understand society.

06 Applying material from Item C and your knowledge, evaluate...

This question asks you to explore a theoretical or methodological issue in more detail. There are 8 marks for AO1, 6 marks for AO2 and 6 marks for AO3. Given that this is an evaluate question, it is important to make sure that you weigh up different views as well as exploring strengths and weaknesses.

06 Applying material from Item C and your knowledge, evaluate the view that functionalism is useful for understanding society today. [20 marks]

Item C

Consensus theories such as functionalism argue that social forces shape people's behaviour and that on the whole, society benefits individual and the wider group. However, others disagree, for example, conflict theorists argue that society only benefits certain groups in society.

More recently, postmodern theories have challenged the ideas of both consensus and conflict theories and argued that they are no longer relevant for understanding society today.

17–20	Answers in this band will show accurate, conceptually detailed knowledge and sound understanding of a range of relevant material on the usefulness of functionalist theories in our understanding of society. Sophisticated understanding of the question and of the presented material will be shown. Appropriate material will be applied accurately and with sensitivity to the issues raised by the question. Analysis and evaluation will be explicit and relevant. Evaluation may be developed, for example, through a debate between different perspectives, e.g. Marxist, neo-Marxist, feminist, postmodern. Analysis will show clear explanation. Appropriate conclusions will be drawn.
13–16	Answers in this band will show accurate, broad and/or deep but incomplete knowledge. Understands a number of significant aspects of the question; good understanding of the presented material. Application of material is largely explicitly relevant to the question, though some material may be inadequately focused. Some limited explicit evaluation, e.g. from a Marxist perspective, and/or some appropriate analysis, e.g. clear explanations of some of the presented material.
9–12	Answers in this band will show will show largely accurate knowledge but limited range and depth, e.g. a broadly accurate if basic account of functionalist theory. Understands some limited but significant aspects of the question; superficial understanding of the presented material. Applying listed material from the general topic area but with limited regard for its relevance to the issues raised by the question, or applying a narrow range of more relevant material. Evaluation will take the form of juxtaposition of competing positions or to one to two isolated stated points. Analysis will be limited, with answers tending towards the descriptive.
5–8	Answers in this band will show limited undeveloped knowledge, e.g. two to three insubstantial points about Functionalism. Understands only limited aspects of the question; simplistic understanding of the presented material. Limited application of suitable material, and/or material often at a tangent to the demands of the question, e.g. drifting into an answer about social solidarity with limited reference to Functionalism. Very limited or no evaluation. Attempts at analysis, if any, are thin and disjointed.
1–4	Answers in this band will show very limited knowledge, e.g. one to two very insubstantial points about sociological theory in general. Very little or no understanding of the question and of the presented material. Significant errors and/or omissions in application of material. No analysis or evaluation.
0	No relevant points.

Some advice on how to answer this question

Explain how functionalism is a consensus, structural theory and make sure that you explain that functionalism is a modern theory. Explore the different functionalist views, considering the work of Durkheim, Parsons and Merton with relevant concepts that go with each. Criticise each set of views and make sure that you also point out the strengths of this approach using contemporary examples. Draw on other topics where relevant to the question, for example, to show how functionalist ideas may be useful for understanding crime through the role of boundary maintenance. Then use other modern theoretical views, such as Marxism, to evaluate functionalist views, making sure that you do not simply describe other theories but apply them to functionalism. Finally, use postmodern theory to explore the idea that perhaps functionalism is less relevant to understanding society today. Come to a clear conclusion about whether functionalism has more strengths or weaknesses.

Practice questions (perhaps you could try writing the item)

- Applying material from Item C and your knowledge, evaluate the view that sociology is a science. [20 marks]
- Applying material from Item C and your knowledge, evaluate the view that feminism is useful for understanding society today. [20 marks]
- Applying material from Item C and your knowledge, evaluate the view that observation is a useful way of researching society. [20 marks]

Summary

In this section you have learnt about the three A-level exam paper structure and question types. Clearly a key skill at A-level is to make sure that you apply knowledge to the question and avoid creating list-like answers.

As we have seen, there is a significant increase in the level of depth required at A-level compared with AS, so make sure your answers reflect this. Make sure that you practise the sample questions and make sure that you are familiar with how they are marked. It would be a very good idea to have the general advice on writing essays in front of you when you are writing them.

Key terms

Absolute mobility: Movement up or down the social scale, usually measured by comparing children to the position of their parents.

Absolute poverty: When people are so poor they do not have access to the basic necessities of life. Absolute poverty often is represented by a poverty line. Globally this is $1.25 a day.

Acheson Report: Investigation into the nation's health inequalities published in 1998.

Agenda setting: The process through which those working in the media determine what is to be considered important and what to prioritise or overlook in terms of the news. This is very important as it will to some extent determine the views and priorities of the audience.

American Dream: An aspiration for the consumer society of the USA.

Antisocial behaviour: Any behaviour which is disruptive of the peace and causes disorder. It can include litter dropping, noise, vandalism, aggressive dogs among other things.

Asian Tiger economies: Rapidly developing countries such as Taiwan, Singapore, Hong Kong and South Korea.

Beauty myth: Wolf's idea that society socialises women into a quest for an unachievable standard of beauty, suggesting that only by being beautiful can they be happy and fulfilled. The media does this by bombarding women with images of the ideal type of beauty, and this becomes an 'iron maiden': a torture device that traps women and controls their behaviour.

Big stories or **Metanarratives**: What theories like functionalism and Marxism are called by postmodernists. Such theories attempt to explain how society as a structure works.

Bilateral aid: Aid that is given from one government to another.

Bourgeoisie: The dominant social class is the Marxist dichotomous view. The bourgeoisie own and control the means of production (factories and land).

Bretton Woods: Rural town in New Hampshire, USA where 44 countries met in 1944 to shape the international financial system and create the IMF and World Bank.

Broken windows thesis: The belief that if small-scale crimes are detected and punished promptly then there will be less crime. This particularly applies to damage against property which if left, gives the impression that an area is run down, leading to further crime occurring.

Burgernomics: Term associated with Pakko and Pollard as a light-hearted way of demonstrating development. They measured development by the time it took to earn enough money to buy a McDonald's 'Big Mac'. They estimated the cut-off time between developed and developing countries to be 20 minutes.

Calvinism: A group of Protestants who followed the teachings of a preacher called John Calvin. Calvin emphasised hard work and very simple living.

Camera obscura: A camera obscura projects a 360-degree moving image onto a table, but everything is inverted back-to-front. Marx used the analogy of the camera obscura to show how ideology distorted reality by making circumstances 'appear upside down' and 'inverting' our perception. Ideology therefore promotes false consciousness by altering people's perception of the world – their objective social reality.

Canteen culture: The concept developed by Reiner (2000) that among the police there exists a culture in which sexist and discriminatory values are seen as acceptable and which reinforces mistrust of particular groups and consequently shapes racist police practices.

Chivalry thesis: The idea that the legal system treats women more leniently than men, which reflects patriarchal ideas about women being unlikely or unable to commit crimes.

Civil war: Conflict that is normally contained within a country between rival groups, normally involving a rebel faction seeking to overthrow the government or establish self-rule.

Client cults: More organised cults in which the service providers exhibit a degree of organisation in contrast to their clients. The relationship between clients and the leaders of client cults resembles that of patients and therapists.

Cold War: Ideological war between USA and Soviet Union from 1950s to late 1980s. The USA and the Soviet Union (USSR), the two most influential nations at the time, were pursuing different social, economic and political models and vied to get countries around the world to side with them. They each offered financial support and an ideological programme that promised development and sought to entice nations seeking to develop to follow their programmes, bolstering their international profile and potential partners, and legitimising their approaches.

Collective conscience: Term associated with Emile Durkheim that refers to the shared moral values that serve to enforce social integration and order in society.

Colonialism: The taking over of countries usually by military force.

Colonies: Countries that were taken over in the eighteenth and nineteenth centuries by the military and political power of mainly European countries. They were controlled and exploited for the benefit of their colonial power.

Communicable diseases: These are diseases passed from one person to another. They can be transmitted by virus or bacteria through the air, polluted water or by the exchange of body fluids.

Conspicuous consumption: When goods and services are consumed not so much for their intrinsic value but as displays to everyone else of a person's wealth and status.

Core values: The most important and fundamental values of any group of people or society.

Core: Term used by Frank to refer to the rich developed countries.

Corporate crime: Crimes carried out by or on behalf of companies, with the aim of making greater profits for the business.

Corporate responsibility: The ethical obligations of large firms to comply by the law and engage in an approach that is non-exploitative, avoids the use of sweatshops and is environmentally sustainable.

Creative destruction: Term associated with Schumpeter to describe the inherently disruptive nature of capitalism.

Crime: Behaviour which involves the breaking of any formal or written rule or law. What is considered to be a crime varies from time to time and place to place, so, like deviance, crime is socially constructed. For example, taking drugs was not illegal in the past, but drug taking has become criminalised.

Criminal justice system: Many agencies (for example, The Home Office, the police, The Ministry of Justice) working together to ensure that criminals are punished and that the UK remains a safe place for people to live.

Criminal subcultures: A group of people within society whose values run counter to the rest of society in relation to deviant behaviour, which is perceived as an alternative lifestyle and involves a group of criminal or deviant individuals.

Crisis of modernism: Problems associated with modern living such as pollution, mental illness, stress, crime, suicide, etc.

Cultural capital: Term associated with the Marxist Pierre Bourdieu that a particular set of values, interests and knowledge lead to material rewards and success.

Cultural hegemony: The range of ways that a culture communicates, which contains messages and signs that reflect the worldview of the dominant group. Often used to describe the dominant capitalist ideology.

Cultural homogenisation: When cultural practices become more and more similar as a result of an increasingly global media and culture.

Cultural imperialism: The imposition of Western values through institutions like education and the mass media.

Cultural pessimists: Those who hold concerns about the new media.

Cumulative effect: The idea that continued exposure to media messages over a prolonged period of time will mean those messages eventually influence a person's views and behaviour.

Deferred gratification: Practice of making short-term sacrifices for long-term gains, as exemplified by the middle class valuation of education for improved careers later in life.

Deforestation: The removal of forested land for agricultural use or logging.

Demand-led: The way in which audiences are able to choose from a range of media options, and thus influence which become popular and successful, and which fail. This is opposed to the media being 'supply-led', as it was in the past.

Demographic transition: The movement from high birth and death rates to low birth and death rates.

Deskilling: Term particularly associated with the Marxist Harry Braverman to describe the loss of skills among the workforce.

Determinism: The belief that agencies of socialisation such as the media are able to construct reality e.g. views and beliefs, rather than individuals having their own free will.

Deviance: Behaviour that is seen as wrong in a given time and place. What is considered to be deviant changes and is therefore socially constructed. Deviance is complex, for example, certain behaviours in a particular context are considered acceptable but not in other situations.

Deviancy amplification: The process whereby the media exacerbate the crime that they are reporting about, by exaggerating it or reporting it in a distorted way.

Devolution: The shifting of political power from central governments to local or regional areas. In the UK there has been a shift of some power from the Westminster government to Scotland, Wales and Northern Ireland.

Diaspora: Literally means the spreading of seeds; in sociology it refers to the dispersal of people across the globe that retain cultural connections with their ancestral homelands.

Digital: All forms of information that can be reduced to binary code, which can then lead to the proliferation (growth) of small and large-scale phenomena.

Disablist imagery: Messages or ideas that portray people with disabilities in a negative or inaccurate way.

Disorganised: Term associated with Ken Roberts to describe the lack of class consciousness among the working class.

Diversionary institutions: Marxist term for institutions in society that serve to reinforce false consciousness by detracting people's minds from the exploitative and unequal nature of society. Examples would include the family, education, religion and the media.

Diversity: The variety of options and choices available in society.

Divestment: The opposite of investment and involves the selling of stock and shares in corporations engaged in unethical or ecologically unsustainable activities.

Division of labour: How work roles are allocated according to task and authority.

Edgework: A concept developed by Lyng (1990) who suggests that young males are not seeking material reward in committing crime, rather they seek excitement and risk-taking.

Embourgeoisement: The process by which the working class are seen to adopt the attitudes, values and behaviours of the middle class.

Enlightenment: Period between the first and fourth quarters of the eighteenth century when the reason of rational and intellectual thinking increasingly replaced faith in explaining the world.

Epistemological: The nature, source and extent of knowledge.

Establishment: Term for the privileged social elite who exercise considerable power and political influence in society.

Ethnic cleansing: The violent removal of people from an area or country on the basis of their ethnicity.

Ethnocentric: A way of looking at things through your own narrow cultural norms and values. The way in which a social institution, such as the media, revolves around the dominant culture. For example, in Britain, the media may focus on white British culture at the expense of other ethnic groups.

Export-processing zones (EPZ): Fenced-off industrial areas in the developing world where TNCs undertake their manufacturing of goods to be exported to global markets.

Externalities: Term for positive and negative consequences of market decisions which affects other parties without this being reflected in market prices. Negative externalities of driving a car are the pollution produced which others have to breathe and the added congestion to road traffic.

Extractivism: Term that describes the way of running an economy in resource-exporting countries, especially in Latin America.

False class consciousness: a distorted view of reality in which people do not see the true cause of their oppression.

False consciousness: Marxist term that refers to the proletariat's ignorance of their true oppressed class position; a situation that actually causes them to support the economic system of capitalism that is exploiting them.

False needs: Products demanded which might actually be harmful to the individual.

Fatalism: Attitude of living for the moment and enjoying the present time. Stereotypically associated as a working class attitude. The opposite of deferred gratification.

Female infanticide: The practice of killing girls as children.

First wave feminism: Feminist movement associated with the campaign to win the vote for women.

Foeticide: The practice of aborting foetuses before they are born (often done in some cultures to avoid giving birth to a girl).

Folk devils: Groups or individuals who are presented in an exaggerated way as threatening peace and/or safety of society

Foot-loose capital: The view that the productive capacity of TNCs is not tied to any particular location because they no longer need to be close to sources of raw materials, specific labour or markets.

Free-trade zones: Very similar to Export-Processing Zones. Specifically, as their name implies, they allow TNCs to produce without financial or quantitative barriers to imports or exports.

Fundamentalism: An extreme form of (usually) religion that tries to defend a traditional faith against what are understood to be the developments in the contemporary world which threaten it, such as unbelief. Fundamentalism appears to be primary concerned with reclaiming traditional moral and religious values. Adherents usually show a total commitment to traditional values and a literal reading of old texts as a guide for living.

Gatekeeping: With regard to the media, control over the decision-making process regarding what is considered to be news and what is not. It has been suggested by some, such as the GUMG who argue that gate keepers are very unlikely to produce news which damages the interests of their owners or themselves, the ruling class.

Gated communities: Upmarket residential areas that are protected by walls, gates and often security guards; these features reinforce a sense of safety from crime and intruders.

GATT: General Agreement on Trade and Tariffs was a multilateral agreement regulating international trade that preceded the World Trade Organisation.

Gemeinschaft: Term associated with Tönnies to describe the strong tight-knit rural communities that adhered strongly to traditions and values.

Gender Inequality Index: A measurement of disadvantages faced by girls and women associated with participation in the labour market, empowerment and reproductive health.

Gender pay gap: Difference in pay between men and women.

Genocide: The removal of ethnic identity of a particular group in a systematic way. This may involve mass rape, torture, murder or disallowing the use of a particular language or religion.

Geographical mobility: When people can move easily from one area to another. When this occurs it can help development by facilitating the movement of people to where the jobs are.

Global cafeteria: Generic term used by sociologists to describe many choices for people to buy their spirituality.

Global civil society: Broad term for the collection of INGOs, NGOs and global social movements of pressure groups and activists. Their diversity means that it is hard for a coherent message about global issues to come across.

Global commodity chains: Term that describes the subcontracting and outsourcing by TNCs to firms located in the developing world. They are not then *directly* responsible for worker exploitation and the use of 'sweatshops'.

Global criminal organisations: Criminal networks that extend to various places around the globe. Often a step ahead of national governments, these organisations often emerge in the space that was left by the collapse of communist states.

Global culture: Cultural practices, often based on Western culture, that become shared by an ever-growing number of areas around the world.

Globalisation: Term that refers to the increased global interconnectedness of economic, cultural and political structures due to the exchange of views, products and ideas, and other forms of culture.

GNP per capita: The value of national income (GNP) divided by the population to give a figure per head.

Gradational: Basis of Weberian/neo-Weberian class formation, whereby fragmentation and differentiation is recognised within each class. This contrasts with the relational view of class held by Marxists.

Grand theories: The big structural theories of how society works as a system associated with macro-theories like functionalism and Marxism.

Green growth: An alternative approach to economic development that embraces natural resources in a sustainable manner. It is advocated as a global alternative to conventional plans for economic growth.

Grey panthers: Term for those retired with considerable disposable incomes from savings and pensions.

Gross National Product: The total value of goods and services produced in an economy in a year.

Group of 77: An IGO that represents the interests of developing countries. It currently has 134 members.

Guerrilla warfare: When rebel groups adopt a violent oppositional approach to existing governments.

Hegemonic masculinity: The idea that masculinity is the dominant gender identity in society. Men who are strong (emotionally and physically), competitive, ambitious and macho are the most superior of all of gender types in society: women and gay men are inferior.

Hegemony: Concept associated with Antonio Gramsci to explain how dominant groups maintain power through the subtle use of ideas to win the consent of subordinated groups. Ordinary people are led to believe that the prevailing existing order is somehow natural and normal and therefore justified. The idea is that ruling-class ideas become dominant because they are accepted by the rest of society.

High modernity: Term favoured by sociologists like Anthony Giddens over postmodernity in order to stress the continuities society still has with modernity.

Holistic milieu: The range of activities to do with mind, body and spirit associated with new age movements.

Human rights: Basic entitlements of all people to things such as education, health care, freedom of speech.

Humanitarian aid: Similar to emergency aid, it is compassionate money to help with disasters such as tsunamis, famines, earthquakes, droughts, etc., as well as manmade disasters such as hunger brought about by a financial crisis.

Hyper-babbagisation: The process embraced by TNCs and associated with Babbage who argued a division of labour could create cuts in wage costs. By outsourcing production to low-skilled workers in the developing world, TNCs dramatically cut their wage bills.

Hyper-reality: Is a postmodernist term for a media-saturated view of the world that currently exists.

Individuation: The idea of religion as an individual search for meaning. Therefore, the importance of religion has not declined, but its form of expression has changed.

Industrial Revolution: Period of rapid social change from an agricultural to an industrial society. In Britain this happened approximately 1740–1850.

Inflow rates: The rate of people moving into a social class position.

Informal sector employment: Where workers have no contract or guarantee of employment but instead eek out a subsistence living flexible working, trading, recycling or as sex workers.

Infrastructure: Marxist term for the economic base of society essentially made up by the relationship of exploitation between the two social classes.

Institutional discrimination: When the unfair treatment of a certain group, i.e. people with disabilities, is built into the way an organisation operates, e.g. its policies and culture.

Institutional racism: Discrimination against particular ethnic groups or individuals at an organisational level, either intentionally or unintentionally. In terms of crime this may result in greater suspicion of particular groups or a lack of support for certain ethnic groups in their experience of being the victim of crimes.

Interactive journalism: Consists of a dialogue between journalists and the public in which news is defined and negotiated.

Interactivity: The way in which new media allows consumers to be actively involved in the information that is being communicated to them, such as by being able to comment on television programmes by sending a Tweet to a live Twitter feed.

Intergenerational mobility: Mobility between two generations: parents and their children.

Intergovernmental Organisations (IGOs): Organisation composed primarily of sovereign states, also called international organisations. Examples include the United Nations and the World Bank.

Interpenetration: The two-way flows of culture associated with globalisation. Thus the proliferation of fast food outlets from the developing world in the developed world and Brazilian soap operas being popular in Portugal.

Intragenerational mobility: Mobility within a person's lifetime.

Kleptocracy: The corruption and fraud of political elites, who steal from their own people.

Liberation theology: a concept developed by Otto Madura to describe the mixture of Marxist ideology and Christianity that occurred in many Latin American countries in the 1950s and 1960s. This view proposes that the poor take control of their situation and accept responsibility for the end of their poverty.

Lumpen-proletariat: Translates from the German as 'ragged workers'. A term used by Karl Marx to refer to the underclass of the very poorest workers forced into subsistence poverty.

Majority world: Collective term for the developing world because two-thirds of the global population live here.

Malestream: Feminist play on 'mainstream' meaning if a social institution is controlled by men, in the interest of men, women's needs and interests are usually ignored.

Malthusian: Applicable to the ideas of Thomas Malthus who claimed population growth would outstrip food supply leading to widespread starvation.

Marginalisation: The process through which some people find themselves on the edges of society and unable to access rights and services available. This in turn leads to crime becoming seen as more acceptable.

McMafia: A concept developed by Glenny (2009) who draws out similarities between an increasingly globalised food chain and the increasingly globalised criminal underworld. Glenny argues that the deregulation of financial markets and the emergence of capitalism following the collapse of communism left a vacuum that criminals have ingeniously exploited.

Means of production: The key resources necessary for producing society's goods, such as land, factories and machinery.

Mechanical solidarity: Term associated with Durkheim to describe the strong tight-knit rural communities that adhered strongly to traditions and values.

Media convergence: The way in which new media is causing previously separate corporations and forms of media to come together. For example, Samsung mobile phones use Microsoft's Windows operating platform.

Media mogul: An individual who owns a significant part of the media in a given place. This gives them a significant ability to monopolise the agenda and content of the news and prevent honest unbiased reporting and coverage.

Media representation: The way in which the media portrays different social groups, which may be based on stereotypes.

Meritocracy: Term for a society where rewards are based on merit, talent and effort. Those at the top are seen as justly rewarded in terms of income, wealth and status; the most demanding roles are occupied by the most talented people.

Metanarratives: What theories like functionalism and Marxism are called by postmodernists. Such theories attempt to explain how society as a structure works.

Metrosexual: A term used to describe men who are fashionable, urban, heterosexual, liberal and in touch with their emotions. Often used in opposition to traditional masculine traits e.g. aggression and muscular bodies.

Minority world: Collective term for the developed world because around a third of the global population live here.

Modernisation theory: Functionalist-based theory that dominated the development debate in the 1960s. It blames lack of development on internal factors, especially traditional values.

Modernity: Era of industrialisation and urbanisation that followed the period of the Enlightenment. It is consequently characterised by rational thinking of science and technology. Modernity saw change as progress.

Moral entrepreneurs: Coined by Becker (1963) and referring to groups such as the mass media and the police, who have the power and resources to create or enforce rules and impose their definitions of deviance.

Moral panic: Where there is a disproportionate amount of concern attached to a particular issue in society. This is created by the media and politicians who may be trying to divert attention from another social or economic problem.

Multidimensional poverty index: A new and sophisticated measurement of poverty that recognises its multidimensional relationship to factors like living standards, education and health. It replaced the Human Poverty Index.

Multi-faith society: A society that, besides having many different religions, is not dominated by one single religion.

Multilateral aid: Aid that is given by an IGO such as United Nations, European Union, World Bank or IMF.

Naturalisation: Linking a socially constructed idea e.g. about differences between ethnic groups, to nature: the idea that such differences are 'natural' and biological.

Neglected Tropical Diseases: 17 bacterial and parasitic infections classified by the WHO.

Neophiliacs: Those who are optimistic about the benefits that the new media offers.

Nepotism: Being appointed and promoted because of kinship connections.

New international division of labour (NIDL): Trend since the 1970s for TNCs to relocate capital investment in developing countries to benefit from the cheap and docile labour there compared to developed world.

New media: Methods of mass communication which use digital technologies.

New social movements: Pressure and interest groups with an agenda to secure a transformation of society in line with their specific goals. They raise important questions about government policies and increasingly how these impact globally.

News values: The process journalists go through about which events are considered to be important and worthy of reporting in the media.

Non-communicable diseases: Chronic illnesses such as cancer and heart disease. They are non-infectious and cannot pass from one person to another.

Norm setting: The way the media decides upon the norms that it expects people be important then presents media in a way in which encourages people to conform to these norms.

North: Collective term for the developed world which is predominantly located in the northern hemisphere.

Objective: Not influenced by personal feelings or opinions in considering and representing facts.

OECD countries: Organisation for Economic Cooperation and Development was created in 1947 to promote rejuvenation after WW2. Today it promotes the economic and social well-being of people around the world.

Ofcom: The British communications regulator, responsible for regulating the 'TV and radio sectors, fixed line telecoms, mobiles, postal services, plus the airwaves over which wireless devices operate' (www.ofcom.org.uk). It is funded partly by taxpayers and partly by fees that the media industry pays.

Official crime statistics: Drawn from the records kept by the police and official agencies and regularly published for the public to read.

Official Development Assistance (ODA): Aid provided by OECD countries in the form of grants or 'soft' loans. If given directly it is bilateral aid, if donated through IGOs it becomes multilateral aid.

Opinion leaders: Individuals who interpret media messages and pass their interpretations on to others through discussion. These individuals are often viewed as knowledgeable and media-literate, and trusted by others to accurately explain media content.

Organic analogy: The comparison of society to a body. The analogy was originally made by Herbert Spencer and developed by Emile Durkheim.

Outflow rates: The rate of people moving out of a social class position.

Paradigm: A set of values, ideas, beliefs and assumptions providing a model or framework within which scientists operate, and guidelines for the conduct of research, rarely called into question until the evidence against them is overwhelming.

Participatory rural appraisal (PRA): An approach used by NGOs and other agencies whereby the knowledge and opinions of rural people are embraced in the planning and management of development projects.

Passive audience: Those who simply accept and absorb media messages without question.

Patriarchy: Male domination of women or the profit and gain men derive from the oppression and work of women.

Pattern A variables: Term associated with Talcott Parsons for traditional values that hold back development.

Pattern B variables: Term associated with Talcott Parsons for modern values that reflect and promote a developed society.

Periphery: Term used by Frank to refer to the poor and dependent developing countries.

Polarisation: Marxist term for the process whereby the gap between rich and poor widens. Can be applied to countries and people.

Polysemic: The view that a media message can be interpreted in more than one way.

Post-feminism: The view that feminism is no longer appropriate or needed as we now live in a gender-equal society.

Postmodernity: Term used by postmodernists to describe contemporary society. They see society as having distinctly different characteristics to the era of modernity it replaced.

Predestination: The belief that God had chosen whether you were going to heaven or hell before you were born.

Pre-modernity: Period of history before the modern era where society was characterised by myths, legends, superstition and traditions.

Primary deviance: Behaviour which is seen as deviating from the norm which has not yet been labelled as a crime.

Primary green crime: Actions that are not (yet) illegal under international law, but are nonetheless considered to be environmental issues.

Progressive taxation: Where the proportion of income paid in taxation rises as income rises.

Proletarian traditionalists: Term for conventional image of the working class particularly in the past: manual workers who embraced a degree of class social solidarity and worked in traditional industries.

Proletarianisation: Marxist term that describes the process whereby the middle class identify with the class position of manual workers.

Proletariat: The subordinate social class in the Marxist dichotomous classification. The proletariat own nothing except their labour power which they sell for a wage to the owners of the means of production.

Protestant (or Puritan) work ethic: The Protestant belief that work can be spiritual in itself. This is in contrast to the Roman Catholic view that spirituality could only be achieved through religious practice, such as prayer and worship. Protestants developed the idea that hard work was a sign of spirituality and therefore successful workers were godly in character.

Rationalisation: organising something into a logically coherent system

Regressive taxation: Taxation where the proportion paid in taxes declines as income rises.

Relational: Characteristic of Marxist/neo-Marxist class formation, whereby the relationship to the means of production is the key component. This compares to the gradational characteristic of a Weberian class analysis.

Relative deprivation: The perception of an unfair disparity between one's situation and that of others. This has been suggested as a reason behind people committing crimes.

Relative mobility: Refers to the mathematical chances of one class being in a social position compared to another, often calculated using the 'odds ratio'.

Relativism: The belief held by postmodernists that there is no such thing as objective reality or truth. The only truth is the pluralistic character of knowledge.

Religious pluralism: More than one type of religion. According to Steve Bruce, religious pluralism undermines the maintenance of the church type of religious organisation. He believes it is too difficult for the state to lend exclusive support for one religion.

Reserve army of labour: Marxist term that refers to the least secure section of the workforce; employed when the economy is buoyant and dumped when demand for labour is low.

Residualist discourse: Idea linked to neo-liberalist ideology that capitalism provides the solutions to the world's poor. Therefore the problem of development is not capitalism, but exclusion from it.

Role allocation: The idea that education sifts and sorts people into the correct job or role in society.

Ruling-class ideology: In the context of media refers to the way the media reflects the ideas of the powerful in society which are used to dictate what is considered important in society.

Second wave feminism: Feminist movement associated with the Women's Liberation Movement in the 1960s and 1970s.

Secondary deviance: Behaviour which is both regarded as deviant and has been labelled as a crime.

Secondary green crime: Actions that are illegal under national or international law, which may or may not be enforced.

Secularisation: Refers to the suggestion that religion is no longer important in modern societies.

Selection by mortgage: The ability of well-to-do parents to give their children access to the best state schools by moving into their catchment areas.

Self-report study: Research carried out, usually in the form of an interview or questionnaire, that asks people about the crimes which they have committed.

Semi-proletarianisation: Marxist-feminist idea that women are even worse off than men in the proletariat as they are doubly oppressed by capitalism and patriarchy.

Separatism: Extreme form of radical feminism which advocates isolation from men, living in lesbian-based communities, as the only solution to patriarchy.

Service industries: Industries that do not manufacture goods but provide intangible services such as retailing, tourism, finance, health, caring, education, etc.

Shadow economies: Often associated with illegal activities such as drugs, ivory and blood diamonds. Money from shadow economies often ends up funding violent conflicts and civil wars.

Shanty towns: Slums made of self-built houses constructed from whatever materials are available and can be afforded. They rarely have piped water, sewerage or electricity until they have been established a long time and exist outside most large towns and cities in the developing world.

Shifting equilibrium: Term associated with Talcott Parsons whereby he recognises how the forces of social change can evolve societies.

Simulacrum: Term associated with postmodernist Jean Baudrillard meaning the blurring of dreams and reality. An example he gives is of a theme park such as Disneyland, but it can apply to lots of media-related examples as well.

Situational crime prevention (SCP): Refers to strategies which reduce the opportunities for criminals to commit crime, for example, CCTV. The intention being that potential criminals will not commit the crime once they are aware their opportunities are reduced.

Social cleavages: Divisions that exist within society.

Social cohesion: A society that is united by shared beliefs resulting in bonds that link individuals to each other and to society as a whole.

Social control: The formal or informal ways power is exerted over individuals or groups. Formal social control refers to any written rules which are set out, for example laws. Informal social control refers to any unwritten rule that exists.

Social exclusion: Where people, usually from a lower socio-economic position, cannot participate fully in society for example, gaining access to services, gaining a good education and employment. This may place them at greater risk of committing crimes or of being a victim of crime.

Social harm: A term used by postmodernists to describe deviant behaviour which they claim is broader and more flexible than crime and therefore more useful.

Social institutions: The structures that make up society such as the family, education, religion, work and media.

Social mobility: The movement of individuals up or down the social class hierarchy.

Social model of disability: Developed in the 1970s to challenge the individual or medical model of disability that saw disability as a personal tragedy. Instead the social model sees people with impairments 'disabled' by society by not making sufficient adjustments for their needs such as ramps, lifts, electric doors, etc.

Social order: The prevalence of stability and predictability within society, either through reflecting the consensus will of the people or it can be imposed from powerful elements like dictators in a totalitarian society.

Social solidarity: Term associated with Durkheim reflecting a desirable form of social cohesion that exists in a stable society where people are bound together through shared norms and values.

Socio-economic classification (SEC): A descriptive generic term for all the different schemas of stratification discussed.

South: Collective term for the developing world which is predominantly located in the southern hemisphere.

Spiritual marketing: The ability to articulate and convey your authentic beliefs around a service, product or brand transparently, consciously and with the end users benefit in mind.

Spiritual shopper: Suggests the diversity and choice now available to individuals within a postmodern society for those seeking spirituality or spiritual answers. The term implies that people may use consumer culture with regard to religion and shop around from one religious organisation or NAM to another until they find one that offers what they are looking for.

State crimes: Illegal activities carried out by, or on behalf of, the government. These activities break either the rules defined by the government themselves or international laws.

Status frustration: Where individuals feel a tension between the goals of society and their ability to achieve these goals through conventional means. For example, getting a good job to earn financial success when someone has low educational qualifications.

Structural adjustment programmes: Term for the loan agreements stipulated by the World Bank and the IMF whereby money is lent on the grounds that public spending is reduced and countries make an ideological commitment to neo-liberal ideas such as privatising key industries and cutting back on welfare spending.

Subcultures: Smaller groups within society who have alternative norms and values to the majority.

Supernatural: Power above the forces of nature.

Superstructure: Marxist term for the cultural ideas, norms and values that prevail in society. However, these are shaped to reflect the interests of the capitalist class and are therefore reinforced by bourgeois ideology.

Surplus value: Marxist term for profit that derives from the exploitation of the proletariat.

Sustainable Development Goals: New global goals that will replace the Millennium Development Goals.

Sustainable development: When the focus of development is on the ecological factors, the environmental impact and the green economy so that it does not compromise future generations.

Technique of neutralisation: When people attempt to justify their behaviour by removing themselves from taking any responsibility for the act.

Theodicies: The ideas and answers religions provide to the big questions in life about suffering, death and the nature of existence. Theodicy gives meaning to the inexplicable.

Theodicy of disprivilege: The belief of the promise that salvation may be granted as a reward for earthly poverty.

Third wave feminism: Feminism that challenges the idea that women or men are homogeneous groups. The emphasis is on individuality and how gender experience is influenced by factors like income, wealth, ethnicity, religion, locality, etc.

Tied aid: Aid money that is given on the condition that it is spent of goods or services stipulated by the donor country.

Transnational Corporations (TNCs): Companies who operate globally. Their head offices are typically in the West, but production has often shifted over the past few decades to benefit from cheap labour, a long working hours culture, limited health and safety controls and weak trade unions (sometimes banned).

Transnational organised crime: Crime that takes place across many countries and possibly continents. There is general agreement that this new form of criminal behaviour has been made possible because of the receding importance of the nation state.

Underclass: A concept often associated with New Right sociologist Charles Murray, 'underclass' is a derogatory term used to describe unemployed people who are reliant on state benefits. It holds negative connotations such as the view that such people are lazy and a threat to society's morality.

Underdevelopment: Underdevelopment implies an insufficient development of resources, but neo-Marxists argue it is far more sinister and a deliberate outcome of the economic exploitation of the developing world by the developed world who benefit from keeping countries poor. By doing so it is easier to exploit them.

Urbanisation: The spread of towns and cities.

Validity: Whether the data shows a true, accurate reflection of the subject matter.

Value consensus: Agreement within a society about important ideas about how society should be ordered.

Victim survey: Research carried out into specific or general areas about the kinds of crimes people have been a victim of.

Victimology: A branch of sociology concerned with studying the victims of crime and patterns of victimology over time and in different places.

White-collar crime: Crimes of powerful groups, often including individuals who are less likely to be policed and punished in society.

Warlords: Term for rebel leaders in the context of civil or 'new wars'.

Washington consensus: Term for the neo-liberal ideological consensus shared by US-based organisation like the IMF and World Bank.

Zero tolerance: Any policy which states that small-scale crimes should be punished severely to deter people from committing more serious crimes, advocated by right realists.

References

Chapter 1

Althusser, L. (2005) *For Marx*. London: Verso.
Bloor, K. (2000) Feminist analysis of science and the implications for higher education. *Sociological Research Online*, 5 (1).
Blundell, J. and Griffiths, J. (2003) *Sociology AS: The Complete Companion*. Cheltenham: Nelson Thornes.
Castrén. A.-M. and Ketokivi, K. (2015) Studying the complex dynamics of family relationships: a figurational approach. *Sociological Research Online*, 20 (1).
Carter Wall, C. and Whitfield, G. (2012) *The role of aspirations, attitudes and behaviour in closing the educational gap*. York: Joseph Rowntree Foundation.
Davis, H. (2013) Defining 'pimp': working towards a definition in social research. *Sociological Research Online*, 18 (1), 11 (http://www.socresonline.org.uk/18/1/11.html).
Egan, D. (2013) *Poverty and Low Educational Achievement in Wales*. Joseph Rowntree Foundation (http://www.jrf.org.uk/publications/poverty-education-wales).
Fawcett, J. and Downs, F. (1986) *The Relationship of Theory and Research*. Norwalk CT: Appleton Century Crofts.
Goffman, E. (1959) *Presentation of Self in Everyday Life*. New York: Doubleday.
Gouldner, A.W. (1962) Anti-Minotaur: The myth of a value-free sociology. *Social Problems*, 9 (3), 199–213.
Gramsci, A. (1971) *Selections from the Prison Notebooks*. London: Lawrence & Wishart.
Hadfield, P. (2006) *Bar Wars: Contesting the Night in Contemporary British Cities*. Oxford: Oxford University Press.
Hayek, F.A. (1944) *The Road to Serfdom*. London: Routledge & Kegan Paul.
Knight, A., Brannen, J. and O'Connell, R. (2015) Using narrative sources from the mass observation archive to study everyday food and families in hard times: food practices in England during 1950. *Sociological Research Online*, 20 (1) (http://www.socresonline.org.uk/20/1/9.html).
Kuhn, T.S. (1962). *The structure of scientific revolutions* (1st ed.). Chicago: University of Chicago Press.
Locke, R. and Jones, G. (2012) Tackling underage drinking: reflections on one local authority's response. *Education & Health*, 30 (1), 6–10.
Lyotard, J.F. (1984) *The Postmodern Condition: A Report on Knowledge*. Minneapolis: University of Minnesota Press.
Mills, C.W. (1956) *The Power Elite*. Oxford: Oxford University Press.
Popper, K. R. (1959). *The logic of scientific discovery*. London: Hutchinson & Co.
Schuurmans, J. and Monaghan, L.F. (2015) The Casanova-myth: legend and anxiety in the seduction community. *Sociological Research Online*, 20 (1) (http://www.socresonline.org.uk/20/1/1.html).
Sosu, E. and Ellis, S. (2014) *Closing the Attainment Gap in Scottish Education*. Joseph Rowntree Foundation.
Sullivan, A., Ketende, S. and Joshi, H. (2013) Social class and inequalities in early cognitive scores. *Sociology*, 47 (6).
Walsh, M. (2015) *The Devil's Pleasure Palace: The Cult of Critical Theory and the Subversion of the West*. New York: Encounter Books.
White, T. (2006) *Principles of Good Research & Research Proposal Guide*. London Borough of Richmond Upon Thames (www.richmond.gov.uk/research_proposal_guide.pdf).

Chapter 2

Adler, F. (1975) *Sisters in Crime*. New York: McGraw Hill.
Andrews, E. (2012) 'Urban explorer' scales London's 1,000ft Shard. *Mail online*, 9 April (http://www.dailymail.co.uk/news/article-2127056/).
Bauman, Z. and Lyon, D. (2013) *Liquid Surveillance*. Cambridge: Polity.
Beck, U. (1992) *Risk Society: Towards a New Modernity*. London: SAGE Publishing.
Becker, H.S. (1997, 1963) *Outsiders*. New York: Free Press.
Bowcott, O. (2014) Women make up only 25 per cent of judges in England and Wales. *The Guardian*, 9 October (http://www.theguardian.com/law/2014/oct/09/uk-lags-europe-gender-balance-judiciary).
Bowcott, O. and Ball, J. (2014) Social media mass surveillance is permitted by law, says top UK official. *The Guardian*, 17 June.
Bowling, B. and Phillips, C. (2002) *Racism, Crime and Justice*. Harlow: Longman.
Bowling, B. and Phillips, C. (2007) Disproportionate and discriminatory: reviewing the evidence on police stop and search. *The Modern Law Review*, 70 (6), 936–61.
Box, S. (1981) *Deviance, Reality and Society*. London: Holt, Rinehart & Winston.
Braithwaite, J. and Drahos, P. (2000) *Global Business Regulation*. Cambridge: Cambridge University Press.
Carlen, P. (1988) *Women, Crime and Poverty*. Milton Keynes: Open University Press.
Castells, M. (1997) *The Information Age: Economy, Society and Culture: Volume 2 – The Power of Identity*. Malden, MA; Oxford, UK: Blackwell.
Chaiken, J.M., Lawless, M. and Stevenson, K. (1975) *The Impact of Police Activity on Crime: Robberies on the New York City Subway System. Urban Analysis*,3, 173–205.
Chambliss, W.J. (1973) The saints and the roughnecks. *Society: Social Science and Modern*, 11, 224–31.
Christie, N. (2000) *Crime Control as Industry: Towards Gulags, Western Style*. New York: Routledge.
Cicourel, A.V. (1976) *The Social Organisation of Juvenile Justice*. London: Heinemann.
Cloward, R.A. and Ohlin, L.E. (1961) *Delinquency and Opportunity*. Glencoe: Free Press.
Cohen, S. (1971) *Folk Devils and Moral Panics: The Creation of the Mods and Rockers*. London: Routledge.
De Graaf, M. (2013) Gang members to be banned from wearing hoodies. *Daily Mail*, 18 November. http://www.dailymail.co.uk/news/article-2509467/Gang-members-banned-wearing-hoodies-owning-pay-phones-new-crackdown.html.
Durkheim, E. (1947) *The Division of Labour in Society*. New York: Free Press.
Europol (no date) *Europol*. The Hague: Europol (https://www.europol.europa.eu/).
Evans, M. (2014) New domestic violence law will outlaw coercive control. *The Telegraph*, 28 November.
Farrington, D.P. (2001) *What Has Been Learned from Self-Reports about Criminal Careers and the Causes of Offending?* Cambridge: University of Cambridge (http://www.crim.cam.ac.uk/people/academic_research/david_farrington/srdrep.pdf).

Felson, M. and Boba R. (2002) *Crime and Everyday Life*. London: Sage.

Fogg, A. (2014) What is crime? We can't measure it because we haven't defined it. *The Guardian*, 16 January.

Foucault, M. (1991) *Discipline and Punish: The Birth of the Prison*. London: Penguin.

Garland, D. (2001) *The Culture of Control: Crime and Social Order in Contemporary Society*. Chicago: University of Chicago Press.

Gentleman, A. (2014) Change is long overdue for sex abuse victims. *The Guardian*, 2 April.

Glenny, M. (2009) *McMafia: Seriously Organised Crime*. London: Vintage.

Graham-Harrison, E. (2012) Organised crime worth £560bn. *The Guardian*, 16 July (http://www.theguardian.com/world/2012/jul/16/organised-crime-worth-560bn).

Hall, S. et al (1978) *Policing the Crisis: Mugging, the State and Law and Order*. London: Macmillan.

Harrison, E.H. (2012) Organised crime worth £560bn. *The Guardian*, 16 July.

Hayward, K. (2006), The 'chav' phenomenon: Consumption, media and the construction of a new underclass. *Crime Media Culture* 2 (1) 9–28.

Held, D. and McGrew, A. (2002) *Globalization/AntiGlobalization*. Cambridge: Polity.

Helm, T. (2007) David Cameron vows to mend 'broken society'. *The Telegraph*, 25 August.

Hobbs, D. and Dunningham, C. (1998) Glocal organised crime: Context and pretext, in Ruggierio et al (eds) (1998) *New European Criminology*. London; New York: Routledge.

Hutton, W. (2015) Michael Gove has a vision for reforming prisons – and justice. *The Guardian*. 19 July (http://www.theguardian.com/commentisfree/2015/jul/19/michael-gove-justice-prison-system).

INTERPOL (no date) INTERPOL. Lyon: INTERPOL (http://www.interpol.int/).

Jansson, K. (2006) Black and Minority Ethnic groups' experiences and perceptions of crime, racially motivated crime and the police: findings from the 2004/05 British Crime Survey. *Home Office Online Report 25/06*. London: Home Office (http://webarchive.nationalarchives.gov.uk/20110218135832/http:/rds.homeoffice.gov.uk/rds/pdfs06/rdsolr2506.pdf.

Jewkes, Y. (2004) *Media and Crime*. London: SAGE Publishing.

Jones, T, MacLean, B. and Young, J (1986) Islington Crime Survey – Crime, Victimization and Policing in Inner-City London, National Islington Crime surveys (https://www.ncjrs.gov/App/publications/abstract.aspx?ID=102958).

Jones, O. *The Independent* (2015) Riots one year on. *The Independent*, 23 July. HYPERLINK "http://www.independent.co.uk/news/uk/home-news/london-riotsone-year-on-owen-jones-commences-a-series-of-special-reports-7965142.html"http://www.independent.co.uk/news/uk/home-news/london-riotsone- year-on-owen-jones-commences-a-series-of-special-reports-7965142.html.

Jowit, J. (2010) World's top firms cause $2.2tn of environmental damage, report estimates. *The Guardian*, 18 February.

Lea, J. and Young, J. (1984) *What is to be Done about Law and Order?* Harmondsworth: Penguin Books in association with the Socialist Society.

Leach, A (2014) Prison doesn't work 50% of the time, so why do we keep sending people there? *Mirror*, 20 August.

Lemert, E.M. (1972) *Human Deviance, Social Problems and Social Control*. Englewood Cliffs: Prentice-Hall.

Lyng, S. (1990) Edgework: a social-psychological analysis of voluntary risk taking. *American Journal of Sociology*, 95 (4), 887–921.

McLaughlin, E. (2001) Political violence, terrorism and states of fear, in Muncie, J. and McLaughlin, E. (eds) (2001) *The Problem of Crime*. London: SAGE Publications.

Macpherson, W. (1999) Report of the Stephen Lawrence Enquiry (The Macpherson Report). London: Home Office (https://www.gov.uk/government/publications/the-stephen-lawrence-inquiry.

McRobbie, A. and Thornton, S. (1995) Rethinking 'moral panic' for multi-mediated social worlds. *British Journal of Sociology*, 46 (4), 559–74.

Matza, D. (1964) *Delinquency and Drift*. New York: John Wiley and Sons.

Mawby, R.I. and Walklate, S. (1994) *Critical Victimology*. London: SAGE Publcations.

Merton, R.K. (1968) *Social Theory and Social Structure*. New York: Free Press.

Miers, D. (1989) Positivist criminology: a critique. *International Review of Victimology*, 1(1), 3.

Ministry of Justice (2011) *Statistics on Race and the Criminal Justice System 2010, a Ministry of Justice publication under Section 95 of the Criminal Justice Act 1991* (https://www.gov.uk/government/uploads/system/uploads/attachment_data/file/219967/stats-race-cjs-2010.pdf).

Ministry of Justice (2013) *Statistics on Race and the Criminal Justice System 2012, a Ministry of Justice publication under Section 95 of the Criminal Justice Act 1991* (https://www.gov.uk/government/uploads/system/uploads/attachment_data/file/269399/Race-and-cjs-2012.pdf).

Ministry of Justice (2014), *Proven re-offending statistics quarterly bulletin*, April 2011 to March 2012, 30 January. (https://www.gov.uk/government/statistics/proven-reoffending-statistics-april-2011-march-2012.

Murray, C (1989) Underclass. *Sunday Times Magazine*, 26 November

Newburn, T. and Rock, P. (2004), *Living in Fear: Violence and Victimisation in the Lives of Single Homeless People*. Manneheim Centre for Criminology (http://www.crisis.org.uk/data/files/publications/LivingInFear_full.pdf).

Office for National Statistics (2011) *Crime Survey for England and Wales*.

Office for National Statistics (2015) *The British Crime Survey* (http://www.crimesurvey.co.uk.

Potter, G. (2010), What is green criminology? *Sociology Review*, November.

Radford, T (2003) Meet criminals who cost UK £14bn: the middle class. *The Guardian*, 12 September.

Reiner, R. (1984) Crime, law and deviance: The Durkheim legacy, in Fenton, S. (ed.) *Durkheim and Modern Society*. Cambridge: Cambridge University Press.

Rusche, G. and Kirchheimer, O. (1939) *Punishment and Social Structure*. New Brunswick: Transaction Publishers.

Schwendinger, H. and Schwendinger, J. (1975) Guardians of order or defenders of human rights?, in Taylor, I., Walton, P. and Young, J. (eds) *Critical Criminology*. London: Routledge and Kegan Paul.

Shaheen, K. (2015) Isis fighters destroy ancient artefacts at Mosul museum. *The Guardian*, 26 February.

Smart, C. (2002) *Feminism and the Power of Law*. London; New York: Routledge.

Snider, L. (1993) The politics of corporate crime control, in Pearce, F. and Woodiwiss, M (eds) *Global Crime Connections : Dynamics and Control. Basingstoke*: Macmillan.

South, N. and Beirne, P. (eds) (2004) *Green Criminology*. Aldershot: Ashgate.
Sutherland, E.H. (1960) White collar crime, in Wolfgang, M.E et al (eds) *The Sociology of Crime and Delinquency*. New York: John Wiley and Sons.
Taylor, I., Walton, P. and Young, J. (1973) *The New Criminology*. London: Routledge and Kegan Paul.
Taylor, L. (1971) *Deviance and Society*. London: Michael Joseph.
Taylor, L. (1985) *In the Underworld*. London: Unwin Paperbacks.
The Prison Reform Trust (2014) *Prison, The Facts*. Bromley Briefings, Summer 2014.
Tombs, S. and Whyte, D. (eds) (2003) *Unmasking the Crimes of the Powerful: Scrutinising States and Corporations*. New York: Peter Lang.
Travis, A. (2015) Lord Woolf blames 'tough on crime' politicians for poor state of prisons. *The Guardian*, 1 April.
White, R. (2007) Green criminology and the pursuit of social and ecological justice, in Bierne, P. and South, N. (eds) *Issues in Green Criminology*. Cullompton: Willan.
Wikström, P.-O.H. et al. (2012) *Breaking Rules: The Social and Situational Dynamics of Young People's Urban Crime*. Oxford: Oxford University Press.
Wilson. J.Q., and Kelling, G. (1982) Broken Windows. *Atlantic Monthly*, March.
Young, J. (1971) The role of the police as amplifiers of deviance, negotiators of reality and translators of fantasy, in Cohen, S. (ed.) *Images of Deviance*. Harmondsworth: Penguin.

Chapter 3

Aldridge, A. (2000) *Religion in the Contemporary World: A Sociology Introduction*. Cambridge: Polity Press.
Aldridge, A.E. (2004) Defining religion. *Sociology Review*, November.
Arweck, E. (2006) *Researching New Religious Movements: Responses and Redefinitions*. London; New York: Routledge.
Bainbridge, W.S. (1997) *The Sociology of Religious Movements*. New York: Routledge.
Barrett, D.V. (2001) *The New Believers: A Survey of Sects, Cults and Alternative Religions* (2nd edition). London: Cassell Illustrated.
Beckford, J.A. (2003) *Social Theory and Religion*. Cambridge: Cambridge University Press.
Beckford, J. (2010) Cults and normal religions. *Sociology Review*, February.
Bown, D. (2012) *AQA A2 Sociology Unit 3 Workbook: Beliefs in Society*. Deddington: Philip Allan.
British Humanist Association (2014) British Social Attitudes survey finds most people have no religion, just 41.7% are Christian, 17 June.
Bruce, S. (2002) God and shopping. *Sociology Review*, November.
Bruce, S. (2002) *God is Dead: Secularisation in the West*. Oxford: Blackwell.
Browne, K. (2000) Science as social product. *Sociology Review*, 11 (2), 22–5.
Chothia, F. (2014) Will Nigeria's abducted schoolgirls ever be found? *BBC News*, 12 May.
Clarke, L. and Chorley, M. (2014) Lessons in meditation? Schools could teach pupils 'mindfulness' to help them concentrate and deal with stress. *Daily Mail*, 12 March.
Czerniawski, G. 2003) Religion and gender. *Sociology Review*, 13 (2), 6–7.

Davie, G. (1994) *Religion in Britain since 1945: Believing without Belonging*. Oxford: Blackwell.
Garrod, J. (200) Children and religious belief. *Sociology Review*, February.
Giddens, A. (2006) *Sociology* (5th edition). Cambridge: Polity Press.
Gillman, O. and Mullin, G. (2015) Ireland hasn't said Yes, it has said F*** YEAH!': Irish minister joins thousands celebrating as country votes to bring in gay Marriage. *Mail online*, 3 May.
Heelas, P. (1998) *The New Age Movement*. Oxford: Blackwell.
Heelas, P. and Woodhead, L. (2003) The Kendal Project, testing the 'spiritual revolution' thesis, *Sociology Review*, 13 (2), 18–21.
Heelas, P. and Woodhead, L. (2005) *The Spiritual Revolution: Why Religion is Giving Way to Spirituality*. Oxford: Blackwell.
Hunt, S. (2001) *Religion in Western Societies*. Basingstoke: Palgrave.
Hunt, S. (2003) Religion and postmodernity. *Sociology Review*, 13 (1), 12–15.
Holden, A. (2002) Witnessing the future millenarianism and postmodernity. *Sociology Review*, 11(3), 28–32.
Jones, M. (2009) Secularisation. *Sociology Review*, 18 (4), 30–1.
Lyon, D. (1996) Religion in the postmodern: old problems, new perspectives, in Flanagan, K. and Jupp, P. (eds) *Postmodernity, Sociology, and Religion*. Basingstoke: Macmillan.
McGuire, M. (2002) *Religion: The Social Context* (5th Edition). Belmont: Wadsworth.
May, T. (1998) Sociology, science and the social sciences. *Sociology Review*, November.
Maduro, O. (1982) *Religion and Social Conflicts*. Maryknoll, NY: Orbis.
Monnier, C. (ed.) (2010) Religion in global times. *Global Sociology*. https://globalsociology.pbworks.com/w/page/14711246/Religion%20in%20Global%20Times.
Smith, G. (2005) *Children's Perspectives on Believing and Belonging*. London: National Children's Bureau for Joseph Rowntree Foundation.
Walliss, J. (2002) The secularisation debate *Sociology Review*, 12 (1), 12–15.
Woodhead, L. (2008) Britain and secularisation theory. *Sociology Review*, 18 (2), 17–19.
Woodhead, L. and Heelas, P. (eds) (2000) *Religion in Modern Time*. Oxford:Blackwell.
Zuckerman, P. (2008) *Society without God: What the Least Religious Nations can tell us about Contentment*. New York: New York University Press.

Chapter 4

Anderson, M. (2014) Aid to Africa: donations from west mask '$60bn looting' of continent. *The Guardian*, 15 July.
Asian Development Bank (2014) *Key Indicators for Asia and the Pacific 2014*. ADB Publishing.
Babbage, C. (1835) *On the Economy of Machinery and Manufactures*. London: Charles Knight.
Barrett, J. et al (2013) Consumption-based GHG emission accounting: a UK case study. *Climate Policy*, 13, (4), 451–70.
Borger, J. (2011) World Bank urges new focus on global development in fragile states. *The Guardian*, 11 April.
Bauer, P.T. (2000) *From Subsistence to Exchange and Other Essays*. Princeton: Princeton University Press.
Bebbington, A.J., Hickey, S. and Mitlin, D. (2008) Introduction: can NGOs make a difference? The challenge of development alternatives, in Bebbington, A.J., Hickey, S., and Mitlin, D. (eds)

Can NGOs Make a Difference? The Challenge of Development Alternatives. London: Zed Books.
Boserup, E. (1970) *Woman's Role in Economic Development*. London: George Allen & Unwin.
Cansfield, B. (2014) Why global violence against women and girls must become new UK priority. *The Guardian*, 15 September.
Cardoso, F.H., and Faletto, E. (1979) *Dependency and Development in Latin America*. Berkeley: University of California Press.
Castells, M. (1998) *End of Millennium*. Oxford: Blackwell.
Chakrabortty, A. (2014) Why we need a truth on the Clothes Label Act. *The Guardian*, 1 July.
Cohen, G.A. (1981) Freedom, justice and capitalism. *New Left Review*, 1 (126), 3–16.
Cohen, R. and Kennedy, P. (2013) *Global Sociology* (3rd Edition). Basingstoke: Palgrave.
De Maio, F. (2014) *Global Health Inequities: A Sociological Perspective*. Basingstoke: Palgrave Macmillan.
Doane, D. (2014) What's so bad about development?, *The Guardian*, 1 September (http://www.theguardian.com/global-development/poverty-matters/2014/sep/01/development-ngos-third-world-global-south).
Duffield, M. (2001) *Global Governance and the New Wars*. London: Zed Books.
Edwards, M., and Hulme, D. (eds) (1992) *Making a Difference: NGOs and Development in a Changing World*. London: Earthscan.
Elkis, M. (2014) Americans don't have money to burn at casinos. *Economy in Crisis*, 20 September.
Ehrich, P. (1968) *The Population Bomb*. New York: Ballantyne.
Ellwood, W. (2001) *The No-Nonsense Guide to Globalisation*. London: Verso.
Etienne, G. et al (2013) *World Report on Violence and Health*. Geneva: World Health Organisation.
Frank, A.G. (1969) *Capitalism and Underdevelopment in Latin America*. Harmondsworth: Penguin.
Friedman, J. (1986) The world city hypothesis. *Development and Change*, 17 (2), 69–83.
Froebel, F., Heinrichs, J. and Kreye, K. (1980) *The New International Division of Labour*. Cambridge: Cambridge University Press.
George, S. (1976) *How the Other Half Dies*. Harmondsworth: Penguin.
Ghosh, J. (2014) Why Asia is probably poorer than we think. *The Guardian*, 9 September (http://www.theguardian.com/global-development/poverty-matters/2014/sep/09/why-asia-probably-poorer-than-we-think).
Giddens, A. (1999) *Runaway World: How Globalization is Reshaping Our Lives*. London: Profile.
Giddens, A. (2000) *The Third Way and its Critics*. Cambridge: Polity.
Globalisation is Good (2003), Channel 4, 21 September.
Green, D. (1995) *Silent Revolution: The Rise of Market Economies in Latin America*. London: Cassell.
Griffin, A. (2015) As China gets richer, the world gets dirtier – and will have to choose more growth and being green. *The Independent*, 17 February.
The Guardian (2014) Editorial: *The Guardian* view of new thinking on global inequality. *The Guardian*, 13 October.
Gurr, T.R. and Marshall, M.G. (2003) *Peace and Conflict 2003: A Global Survey of Armed Conflict, Global Self-Determination Movements and Democracy*. Centre for International Development and Conflict Management, Department of Government and Politics: University of Maryland.
Hancock, G. (1991) *Lords of Poverty: The Freewheeling Lifestyles, Power, Prestige and Corruption of the Multibillion Dollar Aid Business*. London: Mandarin Books.
Harvey, F. (2012) Lord Stern: developing countries must make deeper emissions cuts. *The Guardian*, 4 December.
Hayek, F.A. (1949) *Individualism and the Economic Order*. London: Routledge & Kegan Paul.
Hayter, T. (1971) *Aid as Imperialism*. Harmondsworth: Penguin.
Held, D. and McGrew, A. (2007) *Globalization/Anti-Globalization: Beyond the Great Divide* (2nd Edition). London: Wiley.
Hoogvelt, A. (2001) *Globalization and the Postcolonial World*. Basingstoke: Palgrave Macmillan.
Hoselitz, B. (1960) *Sociological Aspects of Economic Growth*. Chicago: Chicago Free Press.
Ikejiaku, B. (2012) The relationship between poverty, conflict and development. *Journal of Sustainable Development*, 2, (1).
Illich, I. (1987) *Toward a History of Needs*. Berkeley, CA: Heyday Books.
International Labour Organisation (2013) *Global Employment Trends 2013*. Geneva: International Labour Organisation (http://www.ilo.org/wcmsp5/groups/public/---dgreports/---dcomm/---publ/documents/publication/wcms_202326.pdf.
Izberk-Bilgin, E. (2014) Infidel brands: unveiling alternative meanings of global brands at the nexus of globalization, consumer culture, and Islamism. *Journal of Consumer Research*, (Supplement) 158–82.
Kaldor, M. (2012) *New and Old Wars: Organized Violence in a Global Era*. Cambridge: Polity.
Jones, S. (2015) British MPs urge DfID to think long-term rather than lavish aid money. *The Guardian*, 21 March.
Kelly, I. (2000) Wars against women: Sexual violence, sexual politics and the militarised state, in Jacobs, S., Jacobson, R. and Marchbank, J. (eds) *State of Conflict: Gender, Violence and Resistance*. London: Zed Books.
Kingsbury, D. et al (eds) (2004) *Key Issues in Development*. Basingstoke: Palgrave.
Klein, N. (2000) *No Logo*. London: HarperCollins.
Klein, N. (2014) *This Changes Everything*. London: Penguin.
Kristof, N. and Wudunn, S. (2009) *Half the Sky: Turning Oppression into Opportunity for Women Worldwide*. New York: Knopf.
Lerner, D. (1958) *The Passing of Traditional Society: Modernizing the Middle East*. New York: Free Press.
McLuhan, M. (1962) *The Gutenberg Galaxy: The Making of Typographic Man*. Toronto: University of Toronto Press.
Madigan, S. (2014) As conflicts explode worldwide, the aid industry is turning to the private sector, social media and refugees themselves for innovative solutions. *The Independent*, 18 August.
Mead, N. (2013) Developing world's middle class is growing – but so is its 'near poor'. *The Guardian*, 30 January.
Mensah, K., Mackintosh, M. and Henry, L. (2005) *The 'Skills Drain' of Health Professionals from the Developing World: A Framework for Policy Formulation*. London: Medact.
Miller, M.G. and Newcombe, P. (2013) Billionaires worth $1.9 trillion seek advantage in 2013. *Bloomberg*, 2 January.
Nguyen, K. and Guilbert, K. (2015) Human traffickers may face life sentence under Britain's tough new slavery bill. *The Guardian*, 27 March.

Provost, C. (2014) Foreign aid reaches record high. *The Guardian*, 8 April.
Ortiz, I. and Cummins, M. (2011) *Global Inequality: Beyond The Bottom Billion*. New York: Unicef (http://www.unicef.org/socialpolicy/files/Global_Inequality.pdf).
Przeworski, A. et al (2001) What makes democracies endure?, in Diamond, L. and Plattner, M. (eds) *Divergence in Democracies*. London: Johns Hopkins University Press.
Religion and Babies (2012) Youtube: TED Talks (https://www.youtube.com/watch?v=ezVk1ahRF78.)
Remenyi, J. (2004) What is development?, in Kingsbury, D. et al (eds) (2004) *Issues in Development*. Basingstoke: Palgrave Macmillan.
Rajan, A. (2014) Editor's letter: Suddenly, America is no longer on top. *The Independent*, 6 September.
Ritzer, G. (2007) *The McDonaldization of Society* (2nd edition). Thousand Oaks, CA: SAGE Publications.
Robertson, R. (1992) *Globalization: Social Theory and Global Culture*. London: SAGE Publications.
Rosling, H. (2013) *Don't Panic: The Truth about Overpopulation*. London: BBC (documentary).
Saarinen, J. and Lenao, M. (2014) Integrating tourism to rural development and planning in the developing world. *Development Southern Africa*, 31 (3), 363–72.
Sardarsept, Z. (2014) The destruction of Mecca. *New York Times*, 30 September.
Sassen, S. (2007) *A Sociology of Globalization*. New York: W.W. Horton.
Selwyn, B. (2014) *The Global Development Crisis*. Cambridge: Polity.
Sen, A. (1989) Women's survival as a development problem. *Bulletin of the American Academy of Arts and Sciences*, 43, 14–29.
Sen, A. (1999) *Development as Freedom*. Oxford: Oxford University Press.
Sen, A. (2003) The importance of basic education. *The Guardian*, 28 October.
Sharples, N. (2015) Brain drain: Migrants are the lifeblood of the NHS, it's time the UK paid for them. *The Guardian*, 6 January.
Sklair, L. (2007) *Globalisation, Capitalism and its Alternatives*. Oxford: Oxford University Press.
Stiglitz, J.E. (2004) *Globalization and its Discontents*. London: W.W. Norton.
Swidler, A. and Watkins S.C. (2009) 'Teach a man to fish': the sustainability doctrine and its social consequences. *World Development*, 37 (7), 1182–96.
Torfason, M.T. and Ingram, P. (2010) The global rise of democracy. *American Sociological Review*, 775 (3), 355–77.
Trefis Team (2014) A Uruguayan lawsuit with international Implications for Philip Morris. *Forbes*. 22 September.
UNESCO (2010) *EFA Global Monitoring Report: Reaching the Marginalized*. Paris: UNESCO; Oxford: Oxford University Press.
UNICEF (2015) *Child Labour Factsheet* (http://www.unicef.org/sowc96/2csoldrs.htm. [accessed on 22/03/2015])
UNICEF (2013) *Hidden in Plain Sight: A Statistical Analysis of Violence against Children* (http://www.unicef.org/publications/index_74865.html.)
United Nations (2006) Millennium Project. http://www.unmillenniumproject.org/goals/.
United Nations (2012) *Realizing the Future We Want for All*. New York: United Nations.
United Nations (2014) *World Urbanization Prospects* (2014 Revision). New York: United Nations.

Wallerstein, I. (1979) *The Capitalist World-Economy*, Cambridge: Cambridge University Press.
Warren, B. (1980) *Imperialism: Pioneer of Capitalism*. London: Verso.
Watkins, S.C., Swidler, A. and Hannan, T. (2012) Outsourcing Social Transformation: Development NGOs as Organizations, *Annual Review of Sociology*, 38, 285–315.
Weiss, L. (2005) Global governance, national strategies: how industrialised states make room to move under the WTO. *Review of International Political Economy*, 12 (5), 723–49.
White, H. (2013) Educating the world: how to get pupils in developing countries to learn. *The Guardian*, 26 September.
Wiggins, S. (2014) A weighty problem: how to halt obesity in the developing world. *The Guardian*, 3 January.
Wilkinson, R. and Pickett, K. (2010) *The Spirit Level: Why More Equality is Better for Everyone*. London: Penguin.
World Bank (2009) *Global Monitoring Report 2009 – A Development Emergency*.
World Bank (2015) *The Rapid Slowdown of Population Growth*. (http://blogs.worldbank.org/futuredevelopment/rapid-slowdown-population-growth.)
World Commission Environment and Development (WCED) (1987) *Our Common Future: The World Commission Environment and Development*. New York: Oxford University Press.
World Health Organisation (2000) Sexual violence, in *World Report on Violence and Health*.
World Health Organisation (2012) *Global Nutrition Targets 2025 Stunting Policy Brief* (http://www.who.int/nutrition/publications/globaltargets2025_policybrief_stunting/en/.)
World Health Organisation (2013) *Global health workforce shortage to reach 12.9 million in coming decades*. (http://www.who.int/mediacentre/news/releases/2013/health-workforce-shortage/en/.)
World Health Organisation (2014) *Facts on health inequities and their causes*. (http://www.who.int/features/factfiles/health_inequities/en/ [accessed on 10/11/2014])
World Health Organisation (2015) *Neglected Tropical Diseases*. (http://www.malariaconsortium.org/pages/ntds.htm.)
World Wildlife Fund (2015) *Deforestation* (http://wwf.panda.org/about_our_earth/about_forests/deforestation).
WuDunn, S. (2010) *Global Oppression of Women*. Youtube: TED Talks (https://www.youtube.com/watch?v=nvdUgLEoNEk).
Yang, A. and Cui, Y. (2012) *Global Coal Risk Assessment, Data Analysis and Market Research*. Washington DC: World resources Institute.

Chapter 5

Altman, H. (2005) Celebrity culture: are Americans too focused on celebrities? *CQ Researcher*, 15 (11) (http://www.sagepub.com/upm-data/31937_1.pdf).
Aries, P. (1962) *Centuries of Childhood*. London: Vintage Books.
Bagdikian, B. (2007), *The Media Monopoly*. Boston: Beacon Press.
Bandura, A., Ross, D. and Ross, S.A. (1963) The imitation of film mediated aggressive models. *Journal of Abnormal and Social Psychology*, 66 (1), 3–11.
BARB (no date) All in the family. London: BARB (http://www.barb.co.uk/trendspotting/analysis/share-of-viewing-by-channel?_s=4).
Barnett, S. (2015) Is the BBC safe in the hands of our new Culture Secretary? *New Statesman*, 12 May. http://www.

newstatesman.com/politics/2015/05/bbc-safe-hands-our-new-culture-secretary-john-whittingdale.

Barnes, C. (1992) *Disabling Imagery and the Media*. Halifax: The British Council of Organisations of Disabled People and Ryburn Publishing.

Batchelor, S.A. and Kitzinger, J. (1999) *Teenage Sexuality in the Media*. Health Education Board for Scotland.

Batchelor, S.A., Kitzinger, J. and Burtney, E. (2004) Representing young people's sexuality in the 'youth' media. *Health Education Research*, 19 (6), 669–76.

Baudrillard, J. (1994), *Simulacra and Simulation*. Ann Arbor: University of Michigan Press.

Bauman, Z. (1991) *Intimations of Postmodernity*. London; New York: Routledge.

BBC News (2014) Digital news catches up with papers in UK, Ofcom says. BBC News, 24 June.

BBC News (2011) Inside the Murdoch empire. BBC News, 7 July (http://www.bbc.co.uk/news/uk-14030051).

Bennett, T. (1988) Theories of the media, theories of society, in Gurevitch et al. (eds) (1988) *Culture, Society, and the Media*. London: Routledge.

Boyle, R. (2005) Press the red button now: television and technology. *Sociology Review* 15 (2), 27–9.

Boyle, R. (2007) The 'now' media generation. *Sociology Review*, 17 (1), 17–19.

Channel 4 (2015) The end of page 3: a victory for feminism? 4 News, 20 January.

Cohen, S. (1972) *Folk Devils and Moral Panics*. London: Paladin.

Connell, R.W. (1995) *Masculinities*. Cambridge: Polity Press.

Cornford, J. and Robins, K. (1999) New media, in Stokes, J. and Reading, A. (eds) *The Media in Britain: Current Debates and Development*. Basingstoke: Palgrave Macmillan.

Curran, J. et al (2013a) Auntie knows best? Public broadcasting and public affairs knowledge. *British Journal of Political Science*, 43 (4), 719–39.

Curran, J. et al (2013b) International TV news, foreign affairs interest and public knowledge: a comparative study of foreign news coverage and public opinion in 11 countries. *Journalism Studies*, 14 (3), 387–406.

Curran, J., Gurevitch, M. and Woollacott, J. (1982) The study of the media: Theoretical approaches, in Gurevitch et al (eds.) *Mass Communication and Society*. London: Methuen.

Curran, J. and Seaton, J. (2010) *Power without Responsibility: The Press, Broadcasting and New Media in Britain* (7th edition). London: Routledge.

Cushion, S., Moore, K. and Jewell, J. (2011) *Media Representations of Black Young Men and Boys: Report of the REACH Media Monitoring Project*. London: Department for Communities and Local Government.

Davies, N. (2008) *Flat Earth News*. London: Chatto and Windus.

Davis, M.M. (2010) *Children, Media and Culture*. Maidenhead: Open University Press.

Department for Culture, Media and Sport and Department of Business, Innovation and Skills (2009) *Digital Britain: Final Report*. Norwich: TSO (https://www.gov.uk/government/uploads/system/uploads/attachment_data/file/228844/7650.pdf.)

Department for Work and Pensions and Office for Disability Issues (2014) *Disability Facts and Figures*. London: DWP (https://www.gov.uk/government/publications/disability-facts-and-figures/disability-facts-and-figures).

Fenton, N. (2010) (ed.) *New Media, Old News: Journalism and Democracy in the Digital Age*. London: SAGE Publications.

Fenton, N. (2013) Cosmopolitanism as conformity and contestation: the mainstream press and radical politics. *Journalism Studies*, 14 (2).

Flew, T. (2014) *New Media: An Introduction*. Oxford: Oxford University Press.

Galtung, J. and Ruge, R. (1981) Structuring and selecting news, in Cohen, S. and Young, J. (eds) (1981) *The Manufacture of News: Social Problems, Deviance and the Mass Media*. London: SAGE Publications, 52–63.

Gauntlett, D. (1998) Ten things wrong with the 'effects model', in Dickinson, R. Harindranath, R. and Linné. O. (eds) *Approaches to Audiences – A Reader*. London: Arnold (http://www.theory.org.uk/david/effects.htm).

Global Media Monitoring Project (2010) *Who Makes the News? GMMP Report*. London: World Association for Christian Communication (http://www.genderclearinghouse.org/upload/Assets/Documents/pdf/gmmp_global_report_en.pdf).

Gramsci, A. (1971) *Selections from the Prison Notebooks*. London: Lawrence & Wishart.

Greer, C. and Jewkes, Y. (2005) Extremes of otherness: media images of social exclusion. *Social Justice*, 32 (1).

Hall, S. (1981) *Culture, Media, Language*. London: Routledge.

Hardingham-Gill, T. (2015) 'I feel beautiful': Pink slams critics who brand her fat – says her dress didn't photograph well. *Metro.co.uk*, 13 April.

Jenkins, H. (2008) *Convergence Culture: Where Old and New Media Collide*. New York: New York University Press.

Jewkes, Y. (2014) Punishment in black and white: Penal 'hell-holes', popular media and mass incarceration. *Atlantic Journal of Communication*, special issue on Reframing race and justice in the age of mass incarceration, 22 (1), 42–60.

Jones, M. (2013) New technology and crime: cyber-bullying and the 'antisocial network'. *Sociology Review*, April.

Jones, N. (1986) *Strikes and the Media: Communication and Conflict*. Oxford: Blackwell.

Jones Cere, R., Jewkes, Y. and Ugelvik, T. (2013) Media and crime: A comparative analysis of crime news in the UK, Norway and Italy, in Hough, M. et al (eds) *European Companion of Criminology*. London: Routledge.

Katz, E. and Lazarsfeld, P.F. (1955) *Personal Influence: The Part Played by People in the Flow of Mass Communications*. New York: Free Press.

Keen, A. (2007) *The Cult of the Amateur: How Today's Internet Is Killing Our Culture*. London: Nicholas Brealey.

Khana, A. (2012) Nine out of ten Wikipedians continue to be men: Editor survey. Wikimedia blog, 21 April (https://blog.wikimedia.org/2012/04/27/nine-out-of-ten-wikipedians-continue-to-be-men/).

Klapper, J. (1960) *The Effects of Mass Communication*. New York: Free Press.

Lechner, F.J. and Boli, J. (2005) *World Culture: Origins and Consequences*. Chichester: Wiley-Blackwell.

Lechner, F.J. and Boli, J. (2012) (eds) *The Globalisation Reader* (4th edition). Chichester: Wiley-Blackwell.

Leveson, Lord Justice (2012) *An Inquiry into the Culture, Practices and Ethics of the Press: Report [Leveson]*. London: The Stationery Office.

Macdonald, D. (1957) A theory of mass culture, in Rosenberg, B. and Manning White, D. (eds) *Mass Culture*. New York: Free Press.

McQuail, D., Blumler, J. and Brown, R. (1972) The television audience: A revised perspective, in McQuail, D. (ed.), *Sociology of Mass Communication*. London: Longman.

Marcuse, H. (1972) *One-Dimensional Man*. London: Abacus.
Media Reform Coalition (2015) The elephant in the room. 1 September. http://www.mediareform.org.uk/wp-content/uploads/2014/04/ElephantintheroomFinalfinal.pdf.
Miliband, R. (2009) *The State in Capitalist Society*. Pontypool: Merlin Press.
Morley, D. (1980) *The Nationwide Audience: Structure and Decoding*. London: BFI.
Morley, D. (1992) *Television, Audiences and Cultural Studies*. London: Routledge.
Morrison, D. (1992) *Television and the Gulf War*. London: John Libbey.
Newman, D.M. (2006a) Resource files, Chapter 10: The architecture of stratification: Social class and inequality – micro-macro connection. Study site for D.M. Newman, *Sociology: Exploring the Architecture of Everyday Life* (6th edition). Thousand Oaks, CA: Pine Forge Press, an imprint of SAGE Publications, Inc (http://www.pineforge.com/newman6study, http://www.sagepub.com/newman6study/resources/massmedia.htm).
Newman, D.M. (2006b) *The Architecture of Stratification: Social Class and Inequality*. London: SAGE Publications.
News Corporation (2010) *Annual Report, Year to June 2010*. Guardian/Companies House, PA, AP, Reuters.
Ofcom (2014) Techie teens are shaping how we communicate, in *The Communications Market Report: United Kingdom 2014* (http://stakeholders.ofcom.org.uk/market-data-research/market-data/communications-market-reports/cmr14/uk/).
ONS (2013) Internet access: Households and individuals, 2013, *Statistical Bulletin*, 8 August. Newport: Office for National Statistics (http://www.ons.gov.uk/ons/rel/rdit2/internet-access---households-and-individuals/2013/stb-ia-2013.html#tab-Key-points).
Oxford Dictionaries (no date) Media (http://www.oxforddictionaries.com/definition/english/media).
Philo, G. (2012) The media and the banking crisis. *Sociology Review*, 21 (3).
Ritzer, M. (2004a) *The Globalisation of Nothing*. Thousand Oaks, CA: Pine Forge Press.
Ritzer, M. (2004b) *The McDonaldization of Society*. Thousand Oaks, CA: Pine Forge Press.
Robertson, J., Blain, N. and Cowan, P. (2006) Mum or Eminem? Media influences on today's teenagers. *Sociology Review*, September.
Sabbagh, D. (2010), Murdoch media to control over a fifth of UK news consumption. Organ Grinder. *The Guardian*, 30 December. (http://www.theguardian.com/media/organgrinder/2010/dec/30/murdoch-to-control-22percent).
Scotsman, The (2008) Falling exam passes blamed on Wikipedia 'littered with inaccuracies'. *The Scotsman*, 21 June. (http://www.scotsman.com/news/falling-exam-passes-blamed-on-wikipedia-littered-with-inaccuracies-1-1173782).
Storey, J. (2010) *Cultural Studies and the Study of Popular Culture: Theories and Methods* (3rd edition). Edinburgh: Edinburgh University Press and University of Georgia Press.
Strinati, D. (2004) *An Introduction to Theories of Popular Culture*. London: Routledge.
Tait, K.D. (2015) The socialist youth movement. socialistrevolution.com, April.
The Global Monitoring Project (2010) http://www.genderclearinghouse.org/upload/Assets/Documents/pdf/gmmp_global_report_en.pdf.
Tiffen, R. et al. (2014) Sources in the news: a comparative study. *Journalism Studies*, 15 (4), 374–91.
Tuchman, G. (1978) The symbolic annihilation of women by the mass media, in Tuchman, G., Daniel, A.K. and Bennet, J. (eds) *Hearth and Home*. Oxford: Oxford University Press.
van Dijk, T.A. (1991) *Racism and the Press*. London: Routledge.
van Dijk, T.A. (2000) New(s) racism: A discourse analytical approach, in S. Cottle, *Ethnic Minorities and the Media*. Milton Keynes: Open University Press.
van Dijk, T.A. (2006) Ideology and discourse analysis. *Journal of Political Ideologies*, 11 (2), 115–40.
Wayne, M. et al. (2008) Television news and the symbolic criminalisation of young people. *Journalism Studies*, 9 (1), 75–90.
Whale, J. (1977) *The Politics of the Media*. London: Fontana.
Wikipedia http://en.wikipedia.org/wiki/News_International_phone_hacking_scandal.
Williams, A. and Ylänne, V. (2009) Media representations of older people. *Sociology Review*, November.
Williams, J. (2001) Online communities: The rise and rise of the internet. *Sociology Review*, April.
Wolf, N. (1990) *The Beauty Myth: How Images of Beauty are Used against Women*. London: Vintage.
Woollacott, J. (1982) Messages and meanings, in Gurevitch et al (eds) *Culture, Society and the Media*. London: Methuen.

Chapter 6

Adonis, A. and Pollard, S. (1997) *Class Act: The Myth of Britain's Classless Society*. London: Hamish Hamilton.
Allen, A. (2011) Michael Young's *The Rise of the Meritocracy*: a philosophical critique. *British Journal of Educational Studies*, 59 (4) 367–82.
Aries, P. (1965) *Centuries of Childhood: A Social History of Family Life*. London: Vintage.
Atkinson, R. (2015) The toy industry shuts out children with disabilities. We want to change that. *The Guardian*, 18 May.
Avery, D.R., Volpone, S.D. and Luksyte, A. (2011) Collision course: The impending impact of current immigration and retirement trends, in Wang, M. (ed.) *The Oxford Handbook of Retirement*. Oxford: Oxford University Press.
Banks, J., Nazroo, J. and Steptoe, A. (2014) *The Dynamics of Ageing: Evidence from the English Longitudinal Study of Ageing 2002–12*. London: ELSA.
Baudrillard, J. (1985) The masses: The implosion of the social in the media, trans. M. Maclean. *New Literary History*, 16 (3).
Bauman, Z. (1988) *Freedom*. Milton Keynes: Open University Press.
Bauman, Z. (2010) *Living on Borrowed Time: Conversations with Citlali Rovirosa-Madrazo*. Cambridge: Polity Press.
Bauman, Z. and Tester, K. (2001) *Conversations with Zigmunt Bauman*. London: Wiley.
Beechey, V. (1977) Notes on female wage labour. *Capital and Class*, 3.
Berthoud, R. (2000) Ethnic employment penalties in Britain. *Journal of Ethnic and Migration Studies*, 26 (3), 389–416.
Bourdieu, P. (1984) *Distinction: A Social Critique of the Judgement of Taste*, trans. R. Nice. Cambridge, MA: Harvard University Press.
Bradley, H. (1997) *Fractured Identities: Changing Patterns of Inequality*. Cambridge: Polity Press.
Braverman, H. (1974) *Labor and Monopoly Capitalism*. New York: Monthly Review Press.

Britten, N. and Heath, A. (1983) Women, men and social class, in Gamarnikow, E. et al (eds) *Gender, Class and Work*. London: Heinemann.

Brownmiller, S. (1976) *Against Our Will: Men, Women and Rape*. New York: Fawcett Books.

Cantle, T. (2008) *Community Cohesion: A New Framework for Race and Diversity*. Basingstoke: Palgrave Macmillan.

Care Appointments (2015) Editorial team: 'Segregated' Britain more diverse with far wider inequalities. 14 May.

Castles, S. and Kosack, G. (1973) *Immigrant Workers and Class Structure in Western Europe*. Oxford: Institute of Race Relations.

Chalabi, M. and Sedghi, A. (2013) Classing Britain: why defining social status is so difficult. *The Guardian*, 3 April.

Chartered Management Institute (2014) *Women in Management: The Power of Role Models*. London: Chartered Management Institute.

Crompton, R. (1993) *Class and Stratification: An Introduction to Contemporary Debates*. Cambridge: Polity Press.

Cumming, E. and Henry, W.E. (1961) *Growing Old: The Process of Disengagement*. New York: Basic Books.

Dahrendorf, R. (1959) *Class and Class Conflict in Industrial Society*. Stanford: Stanford University Press.

Davis, K. and Moore, W. (1945) Some principles of stratification, in Bendiz, R. and Lipset, M. (eds) (1967) *Class, Status and Power*. London: Routledge and Kegan Paul.

Delebarre, J. (2015) *NEET: Young People Not in Education, Employment or Training*. London: House of Commons Library. (www.parliament.uk/briefing-papers/sn06705.pdf).

Dorling, D. (2008) Cash and the not so classless society. *Fabian Review*, 120 (2).

Dorling, D. et al (2007) *Poverty, Wealth and Place in Britain, 1968 to 2005*. Bristol: Policy Press.

EHRC (2010) How Fair is Britain, p.261. Data from Census, April 2001, Office of National Statistics.

EHRC (2012) *Briefing Paper 7: Race Disproportionality in Stops and Searches, 2011–12*. London: EHRC (http://www.equalityhumanrights.com/publication/briefing-paper-7-race-disproportionality-stops-and-searches-2011-12).

Erikson, R. and Goldthorpe, J.H. (1992) *The Constant Flux*. Oxford: Clarendon Press.

Erikson, R. and Goldthorpe, J.H. (2002) Intergenerational inequality: a sociological perspective. *Journal of Economic Perspectives*, 16 (3), 31–44.

Fawcett Society (2015) *The Gender Pay Gap* (http://www.fawcettsociety.org.uk/our-work/campaigns/gender-pay-gap/).

Field, F. (2015) Supporting low-income parents early on will improve children's life chances. *The Guardian*, 17 February.

Firestone, S. (1972) *The Dialectic of Sex*. London: Paladin.

Foster, M. (2014) Proper gander: screening the working class. *Socialist Standard*, 1313, January.

Freeman, H. (2014) Come on, Britain – it's the 21st century. Stop this obsession with social class. *The Guardian*, 26 November.

Giddens, A. (1991) *Modernity and Self-Identity*. Cambridge: Polity Press.

Giddens, A. and Sutton, J. (2012) *Sociology*. Cambridge: Polity Press.

Gilbert, D. (1998) *The American Class Structure*. New York: Wadsworth Publishing.

Gilbert, D. and Kahl, J. (1992) *American Class Structure*. Belmont: Wadsworth Publishing.

Gillborn, D. (1990) *'Race', Ethnicity and Education*. London: Unwin Hyman.

Gillborn, D. and Youdell, D. (2000) *Rationing Education*. Buckingham, Philadelphia: Open University Press.

Glass, D.V. (1954) (ed.) *Social Mobility in Britain*. London: Routledge and Kegan Paul.

Goldthorpe, J.H. (1982) On the service class: Its formation and future, in Giddens, A. and Mackenzie, G. (eds) *Social Class and the Division of Labour*. Cambridge: Cambridge University Press.

Goldthorpe, J.H. (2010) Class analysis and the reorientation of class theory: the case of persisting differentials in educational attainment. *British Journal of Sociology*, 61 (s1), 311–35.

Goldthorpe, J.H. et al (1969) *Affluent Worker in the Class Structure*. Cambridge: Cambridge University Press.

Hakim, C. (1995) Five feminist myths about women's employment. *British Journal of Sociology*, 46.

Hakim, C. (2006) Women, careers, and work-life preferences. *British Journal of Guidance and Counselling*, 34 (3).

Halsey, E., Heath, A. and Ridge, J.M. (1980) *Origins and Destinations*. Oxford: Clarendon Press.

Hanley, L. (2014) Thought class was dead? Read Richard Hoggart. *The Guardian*, 13 April.

Harvey, D. (1990) *The Condition of Postmodernity: An Enquiry into the Conditions of Cultural Change*. Oxford: Blackwell.

Hayes, C. (2012) *Twilight of the Elites: America after Meritocracy*. New York: Crown.

Hockey, J. and James, A. (1993) *Growing Up and Growing Old: Ageing and Dependency in the Life Course*. London: SAGE Publications.

Hoggart, R. (1957) *Uses of Literacy*. Harmondsworth: Penguin.

Hyde, M. (1998) Sheltered and supported employment in the 1990s: the experiences of disabled workers in the UK. *Disability and Society*, 13 (2), 199–215.

Hyde, M. (2000) From welfare to work? Social policy for disabled people of working age in the UK in the 1990s. *Disability and Society*, 15, 327–45.

Kellner, P. (2015) It's immigration, not immigrants, that British people say they don't like. *The Guardian*, 2 February.

Kynaston, D. (2014) What should we do with private schools? *The Guardian*, 5 December.

Lea, J. and Young, J. (1984) *What is to be Done about Law and Order?* Harmondsworth: Penguin.

Li, Y. and Heath, A. (2008) Minority ethnic men in the British labour market (1972–2005). *International Journal of Sociology and Social Policy*, 28, 231–44.

LV= Insurance (2013), cited in S. Doughty (2015) One in 4 young women out-earn partners: Quarter of females are now their household's main source of income but many feel under pressure as a result. *Daily Mail*, 30 April. (http://www.dailymail.co.uk/news/article-3061637/One-4-young-women-earn-partners-Quarter-females-household-s-main-source-income-feel-pressure-result.html).

Marger, M.N. (2000) *Race and Ethnic Relations*. Stamford, CT: Wadsworth.

Marmot, M. et al (2010) *Fair Society, Healthy Lives: The Marmot Review*. London: The Marmot Review.

Marshall, G. et al (1988) *Social Class in Modern Britain*. London: Hutchinson.

Mason, R. (2013) Fathers will be able to share parental leave from April 2015. *The Guardian*, 29 November.

Milburn, A. (2014) *Elitist Britain*. London: HMSO (https://www.gov.uk/government/uploads/system/uploads/attachment_data/file/347915/Elitist_Britain_-_Final.pdf).

Miliband, R. (1969) *The State in Capitalist Society: The Analysis of the Western System of Power*. London: Quartet Books.
Mirza, H.S. (1992) *Young, Female and Black*. London: Routledge.
Mirza-Davies, J. (2015) *NEET: Young People Not in Education, Employment or Training*. UK: House of Commons Library.
Modood, T. (2003) Ethnic differentials in educational performance, in Mason, D. (ed.) *Explaining Ethnic Differences*. Cambridge: ESRC and Polity Press.
Murray, C. (1990) *The Emerging British Underclass*. London: Institute of Economic Affairs.
Myrdal, G. (1963) *Challenge to Affluence*. New York: Random House.
Nandi, A. and Platt, L. (2010) *Ethnic Minority Women's Poverty and Economic Well Being*. London: Government Equalities Office.
Oakley, A. (1972) *Sex, Gender and Society*. London: Temple Smith.
Oakley, A. (1974a) *Housewife*. London: Allen Lane.
Oakley, A. (1974b) *The Sociology of Housework*. London: Martin Robertson.
Oakley, A. (1979) *Becoming a Mother* (reprinted 1986 as *From Here to Maternity*). Harmondsworth: Penguin.
Oakley, A. (1980) *Women Confined: Towards a Sociology of Childbirth*. Oxford: Martin Robertson.
Oakley, A. (1981) *Subject Women*. Oxford: Martin Robertson.
Oakley, A. (2007) *Fracture: Adventures of a Broken Body*. Bristol: Policy Press.
Oliver, M. (1990) *The Politics of Disablement*. Basingstoke: Macmillan.
Oliver, M. (1996) *Understanding Disability: From Theory to Practice*. Basingstoke: Macmillan.
ONS (2013a) *Wealth of the Wealthiest (2008–2010)*. Newport: Office for National Statistics.
ONS (2013b) *Full Report: Women in the Labour Market*. Newport: Office for National Statistics.
ONS (2014a) *Life Expectancy at Birth and at Age 65 by Local Areas in England and Wales, 2011–13*. Newport: Office for National Statistics.
ONS (2014b) *Annual Survey of Hours and Earnings, 2014 Provisional Results*. Newport: Office for National Statistics.
ONS (2015) *Healthy Life Expectancy at Birth for Upper Tier Local Authorities: England, 2011 to 2013*. Newport: Office for National Statistics.
Oxfam (2015) *Wealth: Having It All and Wanting More*. Oxford: Oxfam.
Pakulski, J. and Waters, M. (1995) *The Death of Class*. London: Sage.
Parsons, T. (1951) *The Social System*. New York: Free Press.
Parsons, T. (1960) *Structure and Process in Modern Societies*. New York: Free Press.
Payne, G. (2013) Models of contemporary social class: the Great British Class Survey. *Methodological Innovations Online*, 8 (1).
Payne, G., Ford, G. and Robertson, C. (1976) Changes in occupational mobility in Scotland. *Scottish Journal of Sociology*, 1, 57–79.
Perry, E. and Francis, B. (2010) *The Social Class Gap for Educational Achievement: A Review of the Literature*. London: RSA Projects.
Pickett, K. and Wilkinson, R. (2014) A 25 year gap between the life expectancy of rich and poor Londoners is a further indictment of our unequal society. *The Independent*, 15 January.
Platt, L. (2002) *Parallel Lives? Poverty among Ethnic Minority Groups in Britain*. London: Child Poverty Action Group.

Platt, L. (2005) The intergenerational social mobility of minority ethnic groups. *Sociology*, 39 (3).
Postman, N. (1982) *Disappearance of Childhood*. New York: Delacorte Press.
Reisz, M. (2011) Social mobility no easier in England's modern meritocracy than in medieval oligarchy. *Times Higher Education Supplement*, 4 April.
Rex, J. and Tomlinson, S. (1979) *Colonial Immigrants in a British City: A Class Analysis*. London: Routledge, Kegan Paul.
Runciman, W. G. (1997) *A Treatise on Social Theory: Volume 3 – Applied Social Theory*. Cambridge: Cambridge University Press.
Saunders, P. (2013) *Social Mobility Myths*. Presentation to Grammar School Heads Association Annual Conference, London, 19 June (http://www.slideshare.net/saunderspeter/social-mobility-myths-23289638).
Savage, M. et al (1992) *Property, Bureaucracy and Culture. Middle-Class Formation in Contemporary Britain*. London: Routledge.
Savage, M., Bagnall, G. and Longhurst, B.J. (2005) *Globalization and Belonging*. London: SAGE Publications.
Savage, M., Silva, E. and Warde, A. (2010) Dis-identification and class identity in Silva, E. and Warde, A. (eds) *Cultural Analysis and Bourdieu's Legacy: Settling Accounts and Developing Alternatives. Culture, Economy and the Social*. London: Routledge.
Savage, M. et al (2013) *A New Model of Social Class? Findings from the BBC's Great British Class Survey Experiment*. London: Sage.
Scott, J. (1991) *Who Rules Britain?* Cambridge: Polity Press.
Sewell, T. (1997) *Black Masculinities and Schooling: How Black Boys Survive Modern Schooling*. Staffordshire: Trentham Books.
Seymour, R. (2013) What do you mean by 'class'? *The Guardian*, 4 April.
Sharpe, S. (1981) *Double Identity*. Harmondsworth: Penguin.
Siddique, H. (2015) Poll suggests privilege is key to landing internships. *The Guardian*, 30 March.
Simpson, L. and Jivraj, S. (2015) (eds) *Ethnic Identity and Inequalities in Britain*. London: Policy Press.
Skeggs, B. (1997) *Formations of Class and Gender Becoming Respectable*. London: SAGE Publications.
Snowdon, G. (2012) Young and older people 'experience age discrimination at work'. *The Guardian*, 16 January.
Sørensen, A.B. (1991) On the usefulness of class analysis in research on social mobility and socioeconomic inequality. *Acta Sociologica*, 34, 71–8.
Southerton, D. (2002) Boundaries of 'us' and 'them': class, mobility and identification in a new town. *Sociology*, 36 (1), 171–93.
Spencer, H. (1864) *Principles of Biology*. London: Williams and Norgate.
Stanworth, M. (1984) Women and class analysis: a reply to John Goldthorpe. *Sociology*, 18, 2.
Sutton Trust (2012) *The Social Mobility Summit Report*. London: The Sutton Trust (http://www.suttontrust.com/wp-content/uploads/2012/09/st-social-mobility-report.pdf).
Sutton Trust (2015) Press Release: One-third of MPs in new House of Commons was privately educated. 10 May.
Thomas, W.I. and Znaniecki, F. (1927) *The Polish Peasant in Europe and America*. New York: Knopf.
Toynbee, P. (2011) Money busts the convenient myth that social class is dead. *The Guardian*, 29 August.

Tumin, M. (1953) Some principles of stratification: a critical analysis. *American Sociological Review*, 18 (4).
Veblen, T. (1899) *The Theory of the Leisure Class: An Economic Study in the Evolution of Institutions*. New York: Macmillan.
Walby, S. (1990) *Theorizing Patriarchy*. Oxford: Blackwell.
Walby, S. (1997) Gender, class and stratification: Towards a new approach, in Anthias, F. (ed.), *Sociological Debates: Thinking about Social Divisions*. Dartford: Greenwich University Press.
Weber, M. (1892) *Die Verhältnisse der Landarbeiter im ostelbischen Deutschland*. Tübingen: Mohr Siebeck.
Westergaard, J. (1996) Class in Britain since 1979: Facts, theories and ideologies, in Lee, D.J. and Turner, D.J. (eds) *Conflicts about Class*. Harlow: Longman.
Westergaard, J. and Resler, H. (1976) *Class in a Capitalist Society*. Harmondsworth: Penguin.
Wilkinson, H. (1994) *No Turning Back: Generations and the Genderquake*. London: Demos.
Willis, P. (1977) *Learning to Labour*. Aldershot: Gower.
Wright, C. (1992) Early education: Multiracial primary school classrooms, in Gill, D., Mayor, B. and Blair, M. (eds) *Racism and Education*. London: SAGE Publications/Open University Press.
Wright, E.O. (1983) Class, *Crisis and the State*. London: Verso Books.
YouGov (2013) *Public Attitudes Research*. London: Social Mobility and Child Poverty Commission (http://cdn.yougov.com/cumulus_uploads/document/u7f0cyctl1/YGCam-Archive-results-040413-All-Countries.pdf).
Young, T. (2014) Britain's upper class is now too snobbish to speak its name. *The Spectator*, 25 January.
Young, J. (2007) *The Vertigo of Late Modernity*. London: SAGE Publications.

Index

'4-2-1 rule of relative hope' 385

A

A-level exam 394–430
   analysis 396–8, 399, 409–12, 425–6
   application 396, 409–14, 425–7, 429–30
   argument presentation 396–8
   command words 398–9
   conclusion drawing 396–8
   crime and deviance with theory and methods 401, 402, 421–7
   demonstrable skills 395–8
   difference from the AS 402–5
   education with methods in context paper 399, 402, 405, 406–12, 414
   evaluation 396–8, 399, 412–14, 420–1, 426–7, 429–30
   marking schemes 398, 399–401, 406, 410, 413, 417, 422
   methods in context 399, 402, 405, 406–12, 414
   outline 399
   outline and explain two… 415–16, 428–9
   outline three… 407–9
   outline two… 406–7, 423
   overview 394–5
   question types 398–401
   tackling A-level paper 1 405–16
   tackling A-level paper 2 416–21
   tackling A-level paper 3 421–30
   theory and methods 405, 415–16, 427–30
   topics in sociology paper 400, 402
abuse, domestic 51
Acheson Report 342
activity exposure 335
Adamson, David 250
advertising 288
Afghanistan 137
Africa
   and aid 203, 216, 218, 222–3
   and conflict 235–6
   and looting 216
AFTA see American Free Trade Association
afterlife 126
age
   and crime 109
   discrimination 302, 344–6
   and education 345
   and health 344–5
   and life chances 343–6
   media representations 292–4
   and religiosity 150–2, 154, 155
   and work 345–6
agency 33, 35

aggression 308
agricultural technology 249
aid
   to Africa 203, 216, 218, 222–3
   arguments against 218, 222–3
   arguments in favour of 219–21
   bilateral 217, 218
   and conflict 236
   definition 217–18
   and global development 216, 217–18
   humanitarian 217, 218, 223, 236
   micro-projects 220
   multilateral 217, 221
   and sustainability 208, 218
   tied 217
   and trade 220
   and violence against women 238
air pollution 92, 231
alcohol consumption 36
   underage 34
Aldridge, Alan 128
alienation 13, 317
Althusser, Louis 14, 41, 100, 126, 317–18
'American dream' 176, 178, 186, 190, 195
American Free Trade Association (AFTA) 192
Americanisation 137, 190
Amish 142
anaemia 249
anti-Malthusians 249–50
antisocial behaviour 55, 105, 113
Antisocial Behaviour, Crime and Policing Act 2014 113
Arab Spring 288
Arber, Sara 364
Aries, Phillipe 293, 344
AS exam 402–5
Asian Development Bank 175
Asian Tiger economies 178, 181, 197, 225
Assange, Julian 267
atheism, new 161
audiences 286, 287–8, 303–9
   cultural effects model 307
   hypodermic syringe model 303–5
   and the news 286, 287–8
   passivity 304
   reception analysis model 305–6
   selective filter model 305
   two-step flow model 304
   uses and gratification model 305
Australian Aborigines 123
autonomisation 370
Avery, D.R. 380

B

Babbage, Charles 225
Bagdikian, B. 273, 274, 291
Bainbridge 148

Bandura, Albert 308, 309
banking crisis 243
Barnes, C. 300, 301
Barron 338
Batchelor, Susan 299–300
Baudrillard, Jean 23, 271, 325
Bauer, Peter 223
Bauman, Zygmunt 68, 165, 167, 312, 324
BBC see British Broadcasting Corporation
beauty myth 298
Beck, Ulrich 92, 93, 363
Becker, Howard 19, 41
Becker, H.S. 61
Beckham, David 302
Beechey, Veronica 322, 337
belief 114–69, 159, 160
   see also religion
belief systems 122
'belonging without believing' 160
Bentham 101
Berger, Peter 122, 168
Bhutan 174
bias 2, 61–2
Bible 126, 169
'big business' 57
'big stories' 23
biodiversity 231
black civil rights movement 137
black feminism 17, 321, 322
Black and Minority Ethnic Groups (BMEs)
   and feminism 17
   and racial inequality 340, 341–2
   and social mobility 392
black people
   and crime 71, 72, 73, 74, 112
   media representation 296–7
Black Report (1980) 46
Blair, Tony 12, 45, 312
Blumer, Herbert 19
Blumler, Jay 305
BMEs see Black and Minority Ethnic Groups
'bobo' doll study 308
Boko Haram 168
Boli 279
bond ratings 203
Boserup, Ester 249, 253
'bottom billion' 187, 236, 245
bottom-up approach 35
Bourdieu, Pierre 333, 359, 373, 380
bourgeoisie 13, 14, 317
   bourgeois ideology 13, 126
   and exploitation 316
   and the media 304, 307
   see also capitalist class; dominant class; elites; ruling class; upper class

Bowling 112
Bowling, B. 72
Box, Steven 105
Boyle, Raymond 259, 260–1, 264, 266
Bradley, Harriet 370
'brain drain' 246–7
branding 60
brands
   global 190–1, 194, 205, 235
   infidel 205
Brazil 225
Bretton Woods 212, 213
Briant 291
BRICS (Brazil, Russia, India, China and South Africa) 225
British Broadcasting Corporation (BBC) 268, 272–3, 275
British Crime Survey 74, 79, 104, 105, 106
British Election Survey 1983 390
British Social Attitudes Survey 158, 360
British Youth Lifestyles Survey 105
Britten, N. 390
Brixton riots 72
'Broken Britain' 60, 64, 65
'broken window thesis' 65, 99
Brown, Gordon 264
Brownmiller, Susan 322
Bruce, Steve 144, 146, 156, 159
Brundtland Report 232
Bulger, James 304
Burgernomics 194
burglary 109
burka 128
Butler 155

C

Calderisi, Robert 223
Calvinism 134–5
camera obscura analogy 13
Cameron, David 60, 64, 65, 158, 290, 295, 386
Campbell, Colin 146
canalisation 335
cancer 344
Cantle, Ted 340
capitalism 12–14, 17, 192, 316, 325, 372
   and crime 46–7, 57, 59, 92, 100
   and dependency theory 180–1
   and globalisation 181–2, 190–1, 194, 196–7, 241, 279–80
   infrastructure 317
   and the media 271, 279–80, 285, 307
   and neo-liberalism 184, 191
   and the oppression of women 322
   and racial inequality 340
   and religion 133, 135
   superstructure 317
capitalist class 372
   see also bourgeoisie; capitalist class; dominant class; ruling class; upper class
carbon dioxide emissions 92, 226, 230–1

Carlen, Pat 76, 77, 78
Carter-Wall 43
Casanova 160
Casanova-myth 7
cash crops 231
caste system 125–6, 134
Castells, M. 85
Castrén 24
Catholic Church 120, 134, 137
Catholics 132, 138, 156, 159, 160
   see also Roman Catholic Church; Roman Catholicism
causal explanations/relationships 26, 27
CCTV see closed circuit television
Census 2011 156, 330
Chaiken, J.M. 100
Chambers, Roger 207
Chambliss, W.J. 94, 111
charities 206
Chavez, Hugo 217
'chavs' 351
Chernobyl disaster 1986 91–2
Chibok abductions 168
child-bearing 320–1
childhood
   and disability 349
   social construction of 293, 344
childrearing 320–1, 322, 338–9
children
   and conflict 236
   female infanticide/foeticide 252
   'insurance' children 250
   media representation 293
China 203, 225, 226, 231, 233, 252
chivalry thesis 78, 112
Christian Dominionism 131
Christian fundamentalism 166–7
Christianity/Christians
   and the afterlife 126
   churches 139, 140, 143–4
   and conflict 132
   decline 159, 162
   and ethnicity 156
   and globalisation 163
   ideology 118
   intelligent design 118, 119
   Orthodox 132, 143
   patriarchal nature 129
   and young people 151
   see also Catholics; Church of England; Protestants
Christie, N. 106–7
church attendance 126, 150, 159, 162
Church of England 127, 128, 142, 143, 156, 157, 188
churches 139, 140, 143–4
'churnalism' 287
Cicourel, A.V. 61–2
circumcision, female 128, 134, 223
cities, global/world 228
'citizen journalists' 261
civil rights 137

civil society, global 208 9
civil war 234
Clark, Gregory 315
class see social class
class conflict 14, 125, 316
class consciousness 379
classlessness 369
client cults 165
climate change 232
closed circuit television (CCTV) 67
Cloward, R.A. 55, 56
coal 231
coal miner's strike 1980s 307–8
coalition government (2010-2015) 12, 66, 335, 345
Coca-Cola Corporation 218
'coercive and controlling behaviour' 51
Cohen, R. 226, 228, 236, 240, 249, 250, 251
Cohen, S. 54–5, 90, 112, 285, 293
Cold War 176, 179, 219
collective conscience 9, 10, 123, 134
'collective intelligence' 261
Collier, Paul 187, 198, 223, 234, 236, 245
colonialism 22, 164, 180
colonies 180
commodification 192, 339
commodity prices 194
Communications Market Report (Ofcom, 2014) 265, 266
communism 14, 126, 137, 316
comparative advantage 224
Comte, Auguste 26, 32, 39, 42
conditioning, sex-role 17
conflict
   class 14, 125, 316
   and the developing world 236
   and global development 236
   and the news 282, 286
   and religion 124, 132–3, 137–8, 160
conflict theory 12–18, 41, 125, 429–30
   see also Feminism; Marxism
conformity 52
congregational domain 162
Connell, R.W. 299, 300, 302
consciousness 28
   see also class consciousness; false consciousness
consensus theories 9–13, 45, 122, 429–30
   see also functionalism
Conservative government (2015-present) 12
consumer culture 60
consumerism 164–5, 186, 190–1, 324, 339
consumption 22–3
   conspicuous 324
   and identity 323
   mass 176, 178, 186
   and postmodern identity 22
   and urbanisation 227
content analysis 300–2, 308–9
convergence 259

'core' 181, 185, 192, 224
core values 9, 10, 123
Cornford, James 262, 263
corporate responsibility 205
correlations 26, 27
corruption 208
   kleptocracy 178, 207, 219, 222, 223
Courts 110, 111
Creasy, Stella 298
creationism 122
creative destruction 192, 204
Crime and Courts Act 2013 101
crime and deviance 49–113, 179
   control 85, 98–101
   corporate crime 81–5, 93, 424–5
   crime rates 71–81, 89–90
   and the criminal justice system 110–13
   criminal subcultures 55–6
   cultural construction 51
   cybercrime 60, 85
   defining deviance 50
   definition 50
   and ethnicity 71–3, 89, 94, 103, 109, 426
   exam questions 401, 402, 421–7
   functionalist perspective 51–6, 61, 69, 79–81, 100, 111
   and gender 75–9, 109
   and globalisation 84–97
   green crime 91–3
   and labelling theorists 61–2
   and Marxism 46–7, 57–8, 61, 69, 73–4, 79–81, 90–2, 94, 100, 109, 111, 427
   measurement 102–6, 423
   and the media 87–91, 96
   New Right theory of 57
   non-utilitarian crime 58
   organised crime 86–7
   postmodern perspective 66–9
   prevention 67–9, 98–101
   primary deviance 61
   punishment 67, 99–101, 112
   and realism 63–6
   reduction 63
   secondary deviance 61
   situational crime prevention 98–9, 100
   and social class 54–5, 60–4, 78–80, 90, 100, 105, 109, 111
   and social control 50–1
   social distribution 70–83
   and social order 50–2
   and social policy 66, 83, 91, 93, 94–5
   state crimes 94–6
   and structural consensus theories 51–3
   utilitarian crime 58
   victims of crime 63, 106–100
   white-collar crime 57, 81–3, 89
criminal justice system 59, 61–2
   and ethnicity 71, 72
   and new media 267
   racism within 112
   role 110–13
   and women 78, 112

criminalisation 72, 76, 78, 293
Crompton, Rosemary 354
Cuba 203, 217–18
cults 139, 140–1, 148–9
cultural capital 269, 278, 328, 333, 359, 405
cultural cues 363–4
cultural deprivation 73, 99
cultural diversity 147
cultural effects model 307
cultural homogenisation 280
cultural identity 155
cultural imperialism, Western 137, 191, 194, 243, 279
cultural pessimists 261–2
culturalism 370
culture
   global 194, 279–80
   and globalisation 190–1, 193, 194–5, 277–80
   high 278
   mass 15, 278–9
   and the media 277–80
   of modernity 21
   patriarchal 320
   popular 261–2, 278–9
   and religion 155
Curran, J. 258, 259, 260, 261, 262, 267, 291
Cushion, Stephen 297
cybercrime 60, 85

D

Dahrendorf, Ralph 372
Daley, Tom 267
Daly, Mary 129
Darwin, Charles 9, 122
data
   objective 4
   primary 3
   qualitative 6–8, 34
   quantitative 6, 34
   secondary 3–5, 6, 308–9
Davie, Grace 153, 154, 159, 160
Davies, N. 287
Davis, Holly 8
Davis, K. 313
de Beauvoir, Simone 127
death 151
   see also mortality rates
debt 198, 212, 222
debt relief 203
DEC see Disasters Emergency Committee
deductive approach 27–8
deferred gratification 328, 333
deforestation 92, 187, 231–2
'delinquency and drift' 55
demand-led 259
democracy 195, 196, 203, 213
demographic transition 248–50
denominations 139–40, 142–4, 148
Department for International Development (DfID) 221, 223, 238
department stores 325
dependency theory
   and aid 222–3
   and conflict 234
   and education 243
   and global development 180–3, 193, 222–3, 224
   and health 247
   and urbanisation 227, 228
deprivation
   material 99
   relative 63, 73, 81, 146
   social 81, 154, 426
deskilling 329, 354
determinism 14, 297
developing world
   and carbon dioxide emissions 233
   and climate change 232
   and demographics 248
   and disease 245–6
   and employment 239–40
   and mental illness 246
   and the middle classes 241
   and tourism 209
   and urbanisation 227
   and war/conflict 234–6
   women in 251–2
development see global development
deviancy amplification 90
devolution 195
DfID see Department for International Development
dialectic 31, 316
dialectical materialism 320
diamonds, blood 235
diaspora 234, 253
dichotomy, of social class 316, 317, 319
digital communication 257
digitisation 258
disability
   and education 347
   and health 347
   and life chances 346–9
   media representation 300–1
   social model of 346–7
   and work 348
disablism 346–9
disablist imagery 300–1
disaster relief 207
Disasters Emergency Committee (DEC) 207
discrimination
   and age 302, 344–6
   and disability 346–9
   positive 348
   racial 72, 73, 112, 340–1, 426
disease 245
   communicable 245, 246, 247
   Neglected Tropical 246
   non-communicable 245–6, 247
disengagement 151, 160

displacement 99
diversionary institutions 13, 133, 155
diversity 11, 66, 67, 68, 147
divestment 187
domestic abuse 51
dominant class 13, 14, 118, 133, 316, 318
   see also bourgeoisie; capitalist class; elites; ruling class; upper class
dominant ideas 271
dominant ideology 118, 126, 268–9, 271
Donald 291
Dorling, Danny 330, 383
drug trade, illegal 85, 179
Duffield, Mark 234
Dunningham, C. 86
Durkheim, Emile 6, 9, 10, 15, 22, 26, 39, 52, 54, 100, 117, 123, 129, 160, 176, 313, 369

E

Easterley, William 220
'Easternisation' 146
Ebola virus 218, 223, 245, 247
economic growth 172
economy
   invisible 174
   and religion 134–5
   shadow 235
   stratification of global 378–80
edgework 55, 82
education 219, 414
   and age 345
   and the comprehensive school system 46
   and disability 347
   and ethnicity 342, 406–7
   exam questions 399, 402, 405, 406–12, 414
   and functionalism 398
   and gender 336, 408–12
   and gendered subject choice 410–12
   and global development 242–4
   and labelling theory 407–9
   parental involvement 43
   private 314, 315, 367, 383–4, 386, 388
   religious 151
   and social class 331, 333, 356–62
   and social mobility 386, 387, 391–2
   and socialisation 313, 345
Education for All 2010 243
educational attainment 331, 333, 342, 407–8
   gap 47
Egypt 288
EHRC see Equality and Human Rights Commission
Ehrenreich 251
Ehrlich, Paul 232, 249
El Saadawi, Nawal 128
elderly people 150–1, 294, 343–5
elections 195, 196
elective belonging 379–80

elites
   academic 243, 314, 315
   educational 388
   global 196, 197–8, 199, 219
   and the news 282
   and Transnational Corporations 202
   see also bourgeoisie; capitalist class; dominant class; ruling class; upper class
Ellis 47
Ellwood, Wayne 202, 232
Elson 241
embourgeoisement 329, 368, 374
emerging economies 224, 233
emigration 419–20
emotional labour 334
empirical evidence 32
empiricism 26, 29
employment
   formal sector 239–40
   and global development 239–41
   informal sector 227, 239–40
   laws 82
   see also jobs; labour; occupation; work
Engels, Friedrich 316, 320
Enlightenment 21, 120, 121
entrepreneurialism 191, 214, 227
environment issues
   and global development 187, 230–3
   and Transnational Corporations 205
environmental crime prevention 99, 100
environmental degradation 230
environmentalism 187
epidemiological transition 245
epistemological approach 5
EPZs see export-processing zones
Equality Act (2010) 345, 368
Equality and Human Rights Commission (EHRC) 339, 341
equality of opportunity 314, 386
Erikson, R. 353, 357–8
Escobar, Arturo 186
establishment 329
ethnic cleansing 234
ethnicity
   and crime 71–3, 89, 94, 103, 109, 426
   and education 342, 406–7
   and exclusion 314
   and life chances 339–43
   and life expectancy 341–2
   and the media 296–7
   and religion 132, 154–6
   and social class 341, 342
   and social mobility 389
ethnocentricity 17
ethnocentrism 178, 186, 297
eugenics 40
evaluation 42
evangelicals 131, 135
evolution 122
evolutionism 119
exploitation 181, 197

and the bourgeoisie 316
and the dominant class 316
and ethnicity 340
of the proletariat 135, 307, 316–17
and social class 135, 307, 316–17, 352–3
and Transnational Corporations 181, 202, 204–5, 216, 251, 253
and women 320, 321–2
export-processing zones (EPZs) 185, 192, 202, 204, 224–5, 253
expressive role 334–6
externalities 232
extractivism 187

F

Facebook 262, 267
Fairtrade 182
faith 118, 122, 123
   scientific 122
false consciousness 13, 14, 15, 316, 317
   and the media 268, 296, 307
   and racial inequality 340
   and religion 125, 126, 129, 133, 157
false needs 178, 190, 205
falsification 27, 29, 120, 121
Faludi, Susan 339
families 24, 418, 419–21
   nuclear 421
Farr, Charles 91
fatalism 374
fathers 335, 339
Fédération Internationale de Football Association (FIFA) 83
Felson, M. 66, 100
female circumcision 128, 134, 223
female foeticide 252
female infanticide 252
feminism 16–18
   black 17, 321, 322
   and crime 76–8, 107, 112
   criticism 18
   and development 241, 253
   eco-feminism 322–3
   first wave 16
   fourth wave 16
   and gender socialisation 334–5
   liberal 17, 128, 267, 321
   Marxist-feminism 17, 129, 241, 253, 321–2
   and the media 262, 267, 271, 297–8, 302, 305
   post-feminism 323
   postmodern 18
   radical 17, 128, 262, 298, 305, 322
   and religion 127–9, 134, 154
   and science 30
   second wave 16, 253, 320
   and social class analysis 361
   and social control 51
   and social mobility 390
   socialist 253
   and stratification 319–23

third wave 16, 321
and value freedom 41
Fenton, N. 279
FIFA *see* Fédération Internationale de Football Association
finance sector crime 84–5
financial markets, deregulation 202
Findhord Foundation 147
Finkelstein, Vic 348
Firestone, Shulamith 320
Flew, T. 279
foeticide, female 252
folk devils 74, 90, 285, 293, 297
food prices 175, 251
food security 232, 234, 249
Ford, Anna 302
Foucault, Michel 34, 67, 101, 111–12, 129
fragmentation 370
Frank, Andre Gunder 180–1, 222
Frankfurt School 15, 16, 271, 304
free market 11, 12, 232
    global 191, 194, 196, 202
free trade 202, 213
free-trade zones (FTZs) 204, 224
Freud, Sigmund 323
Friedman, John 228
Froebel, Folker 185, 190, 191–2, 204
fully social theory of deviance 59
functional requirements 122
functionalist perspective 9–12, 15, 19, 415, 429–30
    and crime and deviance 51–6, 61, 69, 79–81, 100, 111
    criticism 11
    and education 398
    and the media 297, 305
    and religion 122–4, 134
    and stratification 313–15
    and value freedom 39–40
functionalist subcultural theories 54–6, 79–81, 426
fundamentalism, religious 94, 133, 137, 138, 165–9, 178, 179
funding 41

G

Galtung, J. 282
Gandhi, Mahatma 197
gangs 84
Garland, D. 104, 112
Garrett, Bradley 56
gated communities 227
gatekeepers 284
Gates, Bill 244
GATT *see* General Agreement on Trade and Tariffs
Gauntlett 307–8
gay marriage 136
'gaze of experts' 186
'gemeinschaft' 176, 212
gender
    and crime 75–9, 109

and education 336, 408–12
and global development 250–4
inequality 44, 250–1, 320–1, 337, 364
and life chances 334–9
and life expectancy 336
and media representation 297–9, 302
pay gap 320, 337
and religiosity 152–4
and social class 364, 370
and social mobility 389–90
socialisation 76–7, 334–6
stereotypes 299, 335, 408–11
and work 336–9
gender domains 411
genderquake 364
General Agreement on Trade and Tariffs (GATT) 213
generational division 266
genocide 234
geographic mobility 176
George, Susan 205
Giddens, Anthony 21, 22, 45, 118, 141, 177–8, 184, 193, 363, 370, 373, 377
Gilbert, Dennis 364–5
Gilroy, Paul 73
Gini coefficient 199
girls
    abduction 168
    and education 242–3
Glasgow Media Group (GMG) 4, 273–4, 285, 286, 291, 307
glass ceiling 314, 337
Glass, David 387
Glass Mobility study 387
Glenny, M. 86
global brands 190–1, 194, 205, 235
global cafeteria 147
global cities 228
global civil society 208–9
global crimes 84–97
global culture 194, 279–80
global development 170–255
    and aid 216–23
    contemporary alternative theories 183–7
    defining development 171, 172–9
    and demographic change 248–50
    and dependency theory 180–3
    dependent 181
    drivers of 219
    and education 242–4
    and employment 239–41
    and the environment 187, 230–3
    'four motors' of 219, 243
    and gender 250–4
    and globalisation 189–200
    and health care systems 245–8
    and industrialisation 224–6
    and international governmental organisations 202–3, 210–14
    and Marxism 181–2
    measurement 172–5
    and modernisation theory 176–9

and neo-liberalism 177–8, 183–4, 186, 197
and non-governmental organisations 206–9
'people first' policies 179
and post-development 186
and postmodernism 185–6
resistance to 178
stages of development 177, 239, 247
and transnational corporations 201–6
and urbanisation 226–9
and war and conflict 234–6
world systems theory 184–5, 186
global economy 378–80
global income gap 197–8
Global Media Monitoring Project (GMMP) 280
global pillage 193
global warming 92, 187
globalisation 23, 324, 342
    and capitalism 181–2, 190–1, 194, 196–7, 241, 279–80
    and crime and deviance 84–97
    and culture 190–1, 193, 194–5, 277–80
    definition 190–1
    economic element 190–1, 193–4
    expression 193–6
    and global development 189–200
    and inequity 197–200
    and information and communication technology 226
    and the internationalists 192–3
    and Marxism 191–2, 197
    and the media 277–80, 285
    neo-liberal perspective 191, 197
    pessimist globalists 191–2, 194
    political element 190–1, 193, 195–6
    positive globalists 191
    and religion 163–9
    three-tier social structure 196
    and transformalists 192, 195
    and Transnational Corporations 201
'glocalisation' 191
Glock, Charles 160
GMG *see* Glasgow Media Group
GMMP *see* Global Media Monitoring Project
GNP *see* Gross National Product
GNP per capita 173
God 116, 118, 125, 133, 135, 160
Goldblatt, David 374–5
Goldthorpe, John 181, 318–19, 353, 357–8, 368, 372–3, 384–7, 389–91
Gouldner, Alvin 40, 41
Gove, Michael 100
government 266–7, 289
Gramsci, Antonio 14, 126, 136, 269
grand theories 22
grassroots organisations 207
Great British Class Survey 354, 359–60, 361, 373, 375
Greek Orthodox Church 143

green crime 91–3
Green, Duncan 224
green growth 231, 232
'green wash' 205
greenhouse effect 187
Greer, C. 290–1
Gross National Product (GNP) 172–4, 184, 197–8, 218
　see also GNP per capita
Grosvenor, Gerald, 6th Duke of Westminster 371
Grusky, David 324
guerrilla warfare 234
Gulf War 308, 309

H

Habermas, Jürgen 16, 43
Hadfield, Phil 36
Hakim, Catherine 338
Halevy 157
Hall, Stuart 59–60, 74, 90, 285, 297
Hancock, Graham 182, 207
Happy Planet Index 174
Harman, Harriet 298
Harris, Nigel 191
Harvard 324–5
Harvey, David 325
hate crimes 109
Hayek, Friedrich von 11, 183–4
Hayes, Christopher 313
Hayter, Teresa 218, 222
Hayward, K. 60
HDI see Human Development Index
health 247
　and age 344–5
　and disability 347
　inequalities 46, 330, 333, 341–2, 347
　and poverty 245, 246
　and religion 151
health care systems 245–8
healthy life expectancy (HLE) 330, 336
Heath, Anthony 385, 388, 389, 390
Heelas, Paul 153, 162, 165
Hegel, George Wilhelm Friedrich 31, 316
hegemonic masculinity 299
hegemony 14, 126, 269
Heidensohn 76–7, 112
Held, D. 86, 190, 195
Henry 67, 68
Her Majesty's Crown Prosecution Services Inspectorate 111
Hetherington 324–5
high churches 143
high modernity 22, 23
Hinduism/Hindus 125–6, 132, 134, 138, 155–6
historical materialism 11, 13–14, 316, 348
HLE see healthy life expectancy
Hobbs, D. 86
Hochschild 251
Hochschild, Arlie 334
Hoffman 154

Hoggart, Richard 377, 378
holistic milieu 147, 153, 162
Holm, Jean 127
Home Office 110, 111
homeworking 240
homicide 75
Hoogvelt, Ankie 182, 196, 202–3
Hope-Goldthorpe schema 357–8
Hoselitz, Bert 243
hospital care 344–5
households 418, 419–21
HSBC 60
Human Development Index (HDI) 174
human rights 83, 94–6, 137
　abuses 178
　reproductive 252
human trafficking 85, 86, 87, 252–4
Huntington, Samuel 178
hyper-babbagisation 225
hyper-reality 271
hypodermic syringe model 89, 303–5
hypotheses 26–7, 120–1
hypothetico-deductive method 27–8, 120–1

I

ICC see International Criminal Court
ICJ see International Court of Justice
ICT see information and communication technology
IDA see International Development Assistance
IDC see International Development Committee
ideas, dominant 271
identity
　construction 323, 324
　cultural 155
　Islamic 164
　modern 22
　postmodern 22, 323, 324
　and religion 155
　of resistance 164
　self-identity 165
　social 155
ideological state apparatus (ISA) 14, 100, 126, 318
ideology 14
　bourgeois 13, 126
　dominant 118, 126, 268–9, 271
　and religion 118
　ruling class 74, 136
IEA see International Energy Agency
IGOs see international governmental organisations
ill health 151
Illich, Ivan 205
illiteracy 242–3
ILO see International Labour Organisation
IMF see International Monetary Fund
immigrants, illegal 196, 291

immigration
　and family size 419–20
　and social mobility 391–2
　and stratification 378–80
imperatives (prerequisites) 10, 11
imperialism
　and aid 222
　cultural 137, 191, 194, 243, 279
import substitution industrialisation (ISI) 181, 224
income
　components 332
　distribution 199, 332–3
　gap 197–8, 332–3, 388
　global gap 197–8
　inequality 247, 333
　unearned 331
　see also pay gap; wages
Independent Press Standards Organisation (IPSO) 289
India 172, 225, 226, 231, 233, 244
individualisation 363
individualism 147, 227
individuation 159
Indonesia 197–8
Industrial Revolution 21, 22, 316
industrialisation 191, 192, 224–6
inequality 12, 15
　and capitalism 184
　changing structures of 368–71
　and crime 59, 63, 107–8
　and dependency theory 180
　gender 44, 250–1, 320–1, 337, 364
　global 214, 216
　and globalisation 197–200
　health 46, 330, 333, 341–2, 347
　income 247, 333
　'inequalities of condition' 386
　and meritocracy 312, 313–15
　racial 340–3, 391
　and religion 125–6
　and victims 107
　wealth 330, 331–2, 333
infanticide, female 252
information and communication technology (ICT) 226
infrastructure 13
infrastructure (Marx) 316
INGOs see international non-governmental organizations
Ingram, P. 213
innovation 53
'insiders' and 'outsiders' 374–5
institutional discrimination 300
institutional racism 73, 74, 112, 341, 426
instrumental orientation 369
Integrated Rural Tourism (IRT) 209
intelligent design 118, 119
intensification of flows 190
interactionist perspective 19, 41, 61
interactive journalism 288
interactivity 259

intergenerationally 383
intermediate class 319
International Court of Justice (ICJ) 95
International Criminal Court (ICC), Rome Statute 1998 94–5
International Development Assistance (IDA) 212
International Development Committee (IDC) 221, 241
International Energy Agency (IEA) 230
international governmental organisations (IGOs) 202–3, 207, 210–14
   economic 212–14
   financial 212–14
International Labour Organisation (ILO) 239–40, 241, 380
International Monetary Fund (IMF) 178, 184, 194–5, 198, 222–3
   and gender inequity 251
   and global inequality 214
   role 210, 212–13, 214
   and structural adjustment programmes 251
   and urbanisation 228
international non-governmental organizations (INGOs) 206, 208
International Trade Organization (ITO) 213
internationalists 192–3, 196
Internet 263–7, 344
Internet service providers (ISPs) 266–7
internships 384
interpenetration 194–5
interpretivism 6, 18, 20, 28, 29, 30
   and contemporary society 34
   and crime 105
   and the media 308
   and religion 130
   and sociological method 33
   and value freedom 40, 41
interviews, structured/unstructured 6
intolerance 124
intragenerationally 383
investment 219
iPads 263
IPSO see Independent Press Standards Organisation
IRT see Integrated Rural Tourism
ISA see ideological state apparatus
ISI see import substitution industrialisation
ISIS 167
Islam 128, 129, 159, 164, 205, 250
   see also Muslims
Islamic fundamentalism 94, 133, 137, 138, 167–8
Islamic State 95, 96
Islamophobia 155, 340
Islington Crime Surveys 104
isolation 181
ISPs see Internet service providers
ITO see International Trade Organization
Izberk-Bilgin, Elif 205

J

Jehovah's Witnesses 133, 142, 144, 169
Jewkes, Y. 96, 290–1
Jews 132
   Hasidic 150
jihadists 167
Jivraj, Stephen 343
jobs
   service industry 183
   see also employment; occupation; work
Jones, G. 34
Joseph Rowntree Foundation (JRF) 43, 152
justice, retributive 101

K

Kahl, Joseph 364–5
Kaldor, Mary 234–5
Katz 88
Katz, E. 304
Kautsky, Karl 135
Keen, A. 264–5
Kelling, G. 65, 99, 112
Kellner 385–6
Kendal Project 162–3
Kennedy, P. 226, 228, 236, 240, 249, 250, 251
Ketokivi 24
Keynesian economics 11–12
Khomeini, Ayatollah 164
Kim, Jim Yong 213, 214
King, Reverend Martin Luther 137
Kingsbury, D. 174
Kirchheimer, O. 100
Kitzinger, Jenny 299–300
Klapper, J. 305
Klein, Naomi 203, 205
kleptocracy (corruption) 178, 207, 219, 222, 223
Knight, A. 5
knowledge, social construction 120–1
Koran 127, 128, 137, 167
KORUS see United States-Korea Free Trade Agreement
Kuhn, Thomas 28, 29, 121
Kyoto Protocol 226

L

labelling theory 19, 73
   and crime 61–2, 80–1, 90
   and education 407–9
labour
   division of 190, 194, 201, 203, 204, 313
   dual labour market theory 338
   emotional 334
   and ethnicity 340
   horizontal segregation 337–9
   new international division of 185, 190–2, 194, 201, 203, 204, 224, 380
   primary market 338
   reserve army of 322, 337, 338, 348, 374–5
   secondary market 338, 340
   vertical segregation 337–9
Labour Party 379
   see also New Labour
Lagarde, Christine 213, 214
land ownership 371–2
law
   cosmopolitan 86
   international 86
   and religion 132
Law Offices 111
Lawrence, Stephen 73, 74, 112, 341, 426
Lazarfield, P.F. 304
Lea, John 46, 63, 65, 73, 80, 383
Least Economically Developed Countries (LEDCs) 218
Lechner 279
Lenao, M. 209
Lenin, Vladimir Ilyich 126
Leonard, Diana 251
Lerner, Daniel 243
Leveson Inquiry 289–91
Li, Yaojun 389
liberation theology 126, 136
liberation thesis 77
life chances 318, 327–50
   and age 343–6
   and disability 346–9
   and ethnicity 339–43
   and gender 334–9
   and social class 328–34
life choices 324
life crises 134
life expectancy 153
   and ethnicity 341–2
   and gender 336
   healthy life expectancy 330, 336
   and social class 330, 333
literacy 242–3, 411
   media 288
lobbyists 44
Locke, R. 442
Lockwood, David 319
London riots 2012 54
lone parents 109
Lorenz Curve 199
lumpen-proletariat 227, 376
Lynch 151, 152
Lyng, S. 55
Lyon, D. 68, 161
Lyotard, Jean-Francois 24, 148, 164

M

Macdonald, D. 278
Macdonald, Theodore 247
Macpherson Report 73, 74
macro-theories 13, 15, 32, 35
Maduro, Otto 136
male domination 320
male gaze 299

male violence 238, 320
malestream 16, 41, 262, 297, 319
Malinowski 134
malnutrition 249
Malthus, Thomas 232, 234, 249
Malthusian theory 232, 249
manipulation 335
manual workers 318–19, 328–30, 354, 357–8, 360, 368–9, 373–4
manufacturing, global 190, 191, 225
Marger, M.N. 340–1
marginalisation
   and crime 63, 64, 73, 108, 426
   and religion 127, 129, 136, 146, 154
   and women 127, 129, 323
market capacities 363
marketable wealth 331
Marmot, Sir Michael 392
Marshall, Gordon 358, 359, 377
Marshall Plan 212
Marx, Karl 11, 12–14, 15, 22, 26, 92, 118, 125, 129, 133, 160, 182, 227, 304, 316–17, 318, 320, 333, 370, 376
Marxism 12–18, 19, 415
   and crime 46–7, 57–8, 61, 69, 73–4, 79–81, 90–2, 94, 100, 109, 111, 427
   criticism 15
   and disability 348
   and education 333
   and global development 181–2, 190, 198
   and globalisation 191–2, 197, 198
   and the media 267–71, 274, 285, 287, 296–7, 307
   and racial inequality 340
   and religion 13, 125–6, 133, 135, 136, 157, 304
   social class analysis 352–4, 362, 370, 372
   and social policy 46–7
   and stratification 316–17, 319, 352–4, 362, 370, 372
   and Transnational Corporations 229
   and value freedom 41
   see also Neo-Marxism
Marxist-feminism 17, 129, 241, 253, 321–2
masculinity, hegemonic 299
mass consumerism 176, 178, 186
mass culture 15, 278–9
mass media 15, 61, 68, 219, 243
Mass Observation 5
material deprivation 99
materialism 54, 307
maternal mortality 253
Matza, D. 55
McDonaldisation 194
McGrew, A. 190, 195
McGuire, Meredith 136
McLaughlin, E. 94
McQuail, Denis 305
McRobbie 301–2, 411, 412
McRobbie, A. 90
MCS see Millennium Cohort Study

MDGs see Millennium Development Goals
Mead, George Herbert 19
Mead, Margaret 334
means of production 13, 316, 317
Mecca 229
mechanical solidarity 176
media 256–310
   agenda setting 284
   and the audience 286, 287–8, 303–9
   and competition 283, 285
   and crime and deviance 87–91, 96
   and culture 277–80
   cumulative effect 307
   and globalisation 277–80, 285
   media representation 292–303, 352
   new media 257–67, 287
   news 88, 261, 268, 275, 281–91, 306
   organisation 282–4
   ownership and control 268–76, 284, 291
   polysemic content 306
   and profit 284
   shareholders 274
   smokescreens of the 296
media content analysis 4
media literacy 288
media moguls 269, 270
medical profession 246–7
meditation 147, 148
megacities 226
Members of Parliament (MPs) 367
Mendselsohn 107
mental illness 246
meritocracy 12, 227, 296, 312–15, 383, 386, 390–1
Merton, R.K. 52–4
meta-studies 4
metanarratives 23, 24, 43, 45
   and crime 66
   and global development 185
   and the media 294
   and religion 129, 146, 148, 164
Methodism 142, 144, 156, 157
methods, sociological 2
   A-level exam 396–99, 402, 405–12, 414–16, 427–30
   analysis and evaluation 396–8
   application 396
   choice of 428
   ethical factors 428
   practical factors 428
   theoretical factors 428
   and theory 31–7
Metropolitan Police Force 74–5, 341
metrosexual 302
Michell, Juliet 323
micro-theories 33, 35
microfinance 203
middle class 371
   blurring of the boundaries of 369
   changing structure of 372–3, 380
   contemporary 373

   and crime 78–9, 80, 105
   of the developing world 241
   dis-identification 369
   and education 331, 333
   fragmented 372
   and high culture 278
   life chances 328–9, 331
   measurement 351–65
   media representation 294, 295–6
   professionals 373
   and religiosity 156
   Runciman's analysis of 354
   Weberian theories of 318
Miers, D. 107, 109
migrants, stigmatisation 291
migration
   and family size 419–20
   and social mobility 391–2
   and stratification 378–80
Miles, Robert 339, 340
Miliband, Ralph 268–9, 274
millenarianism 169
Millennium Cohort Study (MCS) 36
Millennium Development Goals (MDGs) 171, 198–9, 228, 232, 242, 245, 251
Miller 60, 154
Millet, Kate 320, 322
Mills, C. Wright 40, 47
Milovanovic 67, 68
mindfulness 148
minimum wage 45–6
Ministry of Justice 110, 111
Mirza, Heidi Safia 321, 322
modern world system (MWS) 185
modernisation theory 415–16
   and conflict 234
   and demographics 250
   and global development 176–9, 193, 195, 219, 227, 240–1
   and health 247
   and mass media 243
   and religion 160, 163–4
   and urbanisation 227, 228
modernism, crisis of 178
modernity 21–2, 23, 25–6
Modi, Narendra 226
Modood, Tarique 155, 342
Monaghan, L.F. 7
monarchy, divine right to rule 134
monopolies 273, 274
Moonies 145
Moore, W. 313
moral entrepreneurs 61
moral panic 59, 74, 90, 285, 293, 297, 392
morality 164, 219
Morley, D. 305–6, 309
Morrison, D. 308
mortality rates 330, 341, 344
motherhood 338–9
Moyo, Dambisa 203, 223
MPs see Members of Parliament
mugging 59, 74, 90

multi-faith societies 159
Mundugumor society 334
Murdoch, Rupert 261, 269, 270, 273, 275, 290, 297
Murray, Charles 64, 79, 112, 329, 354, 376, 391
Muslims 95–6, 155, 167
   and the afterlife 126
   and conflict 132, 138, 160
   and ethnicity 156
   and globalisation 164
   hybrid 155
   Shia 167
   Sunni 167
   women 127
   see also Islam
MWS see modern world system
Myrdal, Gunnar 276

N

NAFTA see North Atlantic Free Trade Agreement
nation states 21, 85, 192
National Health Service (NHS) 247
National Offender Management Service 111
National Statistics Socio-economic Classification (NS-SEC) 358–9
Nationwide (news programme) 306, 308
NATO see North Atlantic Treaty Organization
natural resources, extractivism 187
natural sciences 27–8, 32, 33, 39, 161
needs, false 178, 190, 205
NEET (not in education, employment or training) 331, 333, 336
Neglected Tropical Diseases (NTDs) 246
Nelson, Geoffrey 136, 137
neo-colonialism 181, 222, 227
neo-liberalism 11, 177–8, 183–4, 186
   and aid 222–3
   and gender inequity 251
   and globalisation 191
   and health 247
   and meritocracy 312
   residualist discourse 197
   and Transnational Corporations 202
   see also Washington Consensus
Neo-Marxism 14–16
   and aid 222
   and crime and deviancy 58–60, 73, 90
   and the media 269–70, 271, 296, 304
   models of class 317–18
   and racial inequality 340
   and religion 126–9, 136–7
   and stratification 317–18
   structuralist 14
   see also dependency theory
neo-pluralism 287
neo-Weberian theory 318–19
neophiliacs 260, 261, 262
nepotism 328

new age movements 146–8, 153, 156
new atheism 161
new international division of labour (NIDL) 185, 190–2, 194, 201, 203, 204, 224, 380
New Labour 45, 421
new media 257–67
   control of 266–7
   critical views of 261–2
   forms of 257–8
   growth of 263–5
   nature of 258–9
   news 285–6, 287–8
   positive views of 260–1
   significance 263
   uptake 257
   users 263–6
new religious movements (NRMs) 144–6
   world-accommodating 145–6
   world-affirming 146
   world-rejecting 145
New Right theory 11–12, 329
   and crime and deviancy 57, 60, 64, 79, 112
   criticisms 12
   and families 421
   and feminism 323
   and meritocracy 390–1
   and value freedom 41
new social movements 195
new technology 244, 247
   agricultural 249
   and the media 263–4, 279, 285
new wars 234–5
newly industrialised countries (NICs) 225
news 88, 261, 268, 275, 281–91, 306
   and advertising 288
   and the audience 286, 287–8
   digital 287
   exaggeration/distortion of events 285
   and the government 289
   and the Leveson Inquiry 289–91
   and new social media 285–6
   newsworthiness 282–3, 285
   representation of young people 293
   social construction 281–7
News Corporation 261, 275
News International 271
   phone-hacking scandal 289–90
news values 88, 96, 273, 282–3
News of the World (newspaper) 290
newsgathering 286
newspapers 89
NGOs see non-governmental organizations
NHS see National Health Service
NICs see newly industrialised countries
NIDL see new international division of labour
Niebuhr, H.R. 142, 144
Nixon, Richard 222
non-domicile status 331
non-governmental organizations (NGOs) 179, 216

   contradictory nature 209
   criticisms 207–8
   and education 244
   function 207
   and gender issues 251
   and global civil society 208–9
   international 206, 208
   and mental health 246
   role 202–3, 206–9
non-manual workers 319, 328, 354, 356–9, 372–3, 374
Norris 338
North Atlantic Free Trade Agreement (NAFTA) 183
North Atlantic Treaty Organization (NATO) 195
Northern Ireland 138
nouveau riche 328
novels 4–5
NRMs see new religious movements
NS-SEC see National Statistics Socio-economic Classification
NTDs see Neglected Tropical Diseases
nuclear accidents 91–2
nurturing roles 153

O

Oakley, Ann 320–1, 335
obesity 248
objective data 4
objectivism 39–42
objectivity 37–43, 120
observation, participant 6
occupation
   and social class 356–62
   see also jobs; work
ODA see Official Development Assistance
OECD see Organization for Economic Cooperation and Development
Ofcom 257, 265–6, 273–5, 287, 289
Office for National Statistics (ONS) 109, 330, 331, 336–7, 346
Official Development Assistance (ODA) 207, 217–18, 220, 221
O'Hagan, Andrew 377
Ohlin, L.E. 55, 56
Oliver, Michael 346, 347
ONS see Office for National Statistics
open society 383
operationalise 8
opinion leaders 304
oppression
   capitalist 180, 322
   and dependency theory 180, 181
   of disabled persons 301
   and the media 307
   and religion 125, 126, 129, 133, 136
   simultaneous 301
   of women 129, 322, 323, 420
oral histories 4
organic analogy 9–10, 11, 15
Organization for Economic Cooperation

and Development (OECD) 217, 221, 230, 231
Orthodox Christians 132, 143
Orwell, George 378, 386
other-groups 340, 341, 348
othering 340
out-groups 340
overweight 248
Oxbridge 314, 315, 329, 367, 386
Oxfam 331-2
Oxford Mobility Study 385, 387, 389
ozone layer depletion 187

P

Pakko 194
Pakulski, J. 323, 369-70
paradigms 28, 121
parenting 392
parents 253
    fathers 335, 339
    involvement in education 43
    lone 109
    see also maternal mortality
Parliament 367
Parsons, Talcott 10-11, 123, 176, 313, 334, 337, 345
participant observation 6
participatory rural appraisal (PRA) 207
paternity leave 335
patriarchy 16, 51, 59, 319-21
    and crime 77
    and development 179
    in the family 420
    and the media 280, 305
    and religion 127, 128, 129, 134, 167
pay gap 379
    gender pay gap 320, 337
    see also income; wages
Payne, Geoff 361, 388, 390, 392
Pearson 241
Pearson, Ruth 253
Pentecostalism 155, 159, 164, 168
'people first' policies 179
periphery 181, 185, 192
petty bourgeoisie 318
Philip Morris International 201
Phillips 112
Phillips, C. 72
Philo 291
Philo, Greg 286, 307-8, 309
Pickett, K. 247, 315
pimps 8
Pink 260
Platt, Lucinda 391-2
pluralist approach, and the media 270-1, 274, 280, 287
polarisation 178, 192, 199
police 61, 63
    and corporate crime 424-5
    and crime control and prevention 99
    and crime measurement 102-4, 105, 106, 423

racism 72-5, 103
    role 110, 111
police recorded statistics (official crime statistics) 102-4, 105, 106, 423
politics 204, 221
Pollak 77
Pollard 194
pollution 92, 93, 231
Popper, Karl 27-8, 120
popular culture 261-2, 278-9
    'dumbing down' 262
population growth 232, 248-50
positivism 6, 20, 26-7, 29-30, 415-16
    and contemporary society 34
    and crime and delinquency 105
    and sociological method 32, 33
    and structuralism 35
    and value freedom 41
positivist victimology 107
post-development 186
post-structuralism 34, 101, 111-12
Postman, Neil 344
postmodern feminism 18
postmodernism 21, 22-3, 28-9, 416
    and crime and deviance 66-9, 92, 109
    and development 178
    and ethnicity 342
    and gender socialisation 335
    and global development 185-6
    and the media 263, 271, 274, 275, 294, 301-2
    and religion 129-30, 148-9, 161, 163-5
    and social policy 45
    and stratification 323-5
    and value freedom 39, 41, 43
postmodernity 323
Potter, G. 93
poverty 45-6, 223, 240
    absolute 172, 175
    'bottom billion' 187, 236, 245
    and crime 78-9, 80, 109
    and development 171, 172
    and food security 232
    and globalisation 191, 193, 197, 198
    and health 245, 246
    and life chances 329
    and life expectancy 330
    and new media access 266
    and population growth 250
    and residualist discourse 197
    and social mobility 392
    of the underclass 377
    and victimisation 109
power 19
    imbalance 12, 41
    ruling class 125-6
    of Transnational Corporations 204-6, 229
powerlessness 77, 108
PPP see purchasing power parity
PPT see pro-poor tourism
PRA see participatory rural appraisal

Pratham 244
pre-modernity 21, 23
precariat 325, 359, 375
predestination 135
preference theory 338
prejudice, racial 340
principle of difference 313-14
principle of mobility 313-14
prison system 99-101
    inefficacy 101
    overcrowding 113
    prison populations 425-6
    reform 100, 101, 113
privilege 383, 384, 391
pro-poor tourism (PPT) 209
probation officers 61-2
production, means of 13, 316, 317
profit 316
Project Camelot 40
proletarian traditionalists 374, 375
proletarianisation 319, 373
proletariat 13, 14, 15, 74
    exploitation 135, 307, 316-17
    labour 317
    and the media 304, 307
    and racial inequality 340
    and religion 135, 136
    see also lumpen-proletariat; semi-proletarianised workers
Protestant work ethic 134-5
Protestants 132, 138, 159, 160
Pryce, Ken 155
psychoanalysis 323
punishment 67, 99-101, 112
purchasing power parity (PPP) 241
purdah 253

Q

Quakers 142
qualitative data 6-8, 34
qualitative research 6-8
quality of life 174
quantitative data 6, 34
quantitative research 6, 35
quasi-religions 165
questionnaires, closed question 6

R

race, as social construct 339
racial discrimination 72, 73, 112, 340-1, 426
racial inequality 340-3, 391
racial prejudice 340
racial segregation 343
racialisation 339
racialism 340
racism 17, 40
    and the criminal justice system 112
    institutional 73, 74, 112, 341, 426
    police 72-5, 103
    and Triple Systems Theory 320
racist stereotypes 297

rape 107–8, 112, 236, 322
Rastafarians 155
rationalisation 135, 160, 322–3
rationalism 120
REACH Media Monitoring Report 2011 297
Reagan administration 202
realism
 and crime and deviance 63–6, 79–80, 98–101, 112
 Left 63–4, 79–80, 99, 100
 Right 64–5, 98–9, 100, 112
 and sociological method 33–4
reason 120
rebellion 53
reception analysis model 305–6
reductionist approaches 340
refugees 236, 291
regionalisation 192
Registrar General's Social Class (RGSC) 356–7, 374
Regulation of Investigatory Powers Act (RIPA) 69
Reiner, R. 88
relative autonomy 136
relativism 23, 39
reliability 6
religion 114–69
 and age 150–2, 154, 155
 as belief system 122
 and conflict 132–3
 as conservative force 133–4, 164
 defining 116–19
 and ethnicity 132, 154–6
 functional definition 116, 117
 functionalist theory 122–4, 134
 and gender 152–4
 and globalisation 163–9
 and ideology 118
 and interpretivism 130
 and the law 132
 Marxist theory of 13, 125–6, 133, 135, 136, 157, 304
 and meaning 122, 123
 and the modern world 158–69
 and Neo-Marxism 126–9
 new age religion 146–8, 153, 156
 new religious movements 144–6
 as the 'opium of the masses' 125, 126, 304
 and postmodernism 129–30
 religious organisations 139–49, 159
 and science 118, 120–1, 135
 and social change 134–5, 142
 and social class 156–7
 as social construction 116, 117, 123
 substantive definition 116, 117
religious fundamentalism 133, 165–9
 Christian 166–7
 and conflict 234
 and development 178, 179, 195
 Islamic 94, 133, 137, 138, 167–8
religious organisations 139–49, 159

adventist sects 142
 churches 139, 140, 143–4
 cults 139, 140–1, 148–9
 denominations 139–40, 142–4, 148
 established sects 142
 sects 139–46, 148–9, 150
religious pluralism 147, 154
 limited 160
religious practice 159, 160
Remenyi, Joe 198
Remploy 348
repressive state agencies (RSAs) 100, 318
reproductive rights 252
research methods see methods, sociological
resignification 370
Resler, H. 333
resources
 extractivism 187
 limited 178, 249
retirement 380
retreatism 53, 56
Rex, J. 340, 377
RGSC see Registrar General's Social Class
rich/poor divide 266, 318, 325, 331–3, 379
Ridge, John 388
Rio +20 conference (2012) 199
RIPA see Regulation of Investigatory Powers Act
risk-aversion 154
ritualism 53
Ritzer, George 194
Ritzer, M. 280
Roberts, Ken 44, 372, 375, 379
Robertson, Roland 135
Robins, Kevin 262, 263
role allocation 313
Roman Catholic Church 127, 136, 143
Roman Catholicism 128, 135, 136, 250
Romney, Mitt 166–7
Rosling, Hans 249, 250
Rostow, Walt 177, 219, 227, 239, 240
RSAs see repressive state agencies
Ruge, R. 282
ruling class 57, 318
 and crime 100, 109, 111
 ideology 74, 136
 and the media 268, 269, 271, 274, 287
 and racial inequality 340
 and religion 125–6, 136, 157
 see also bourgeoisie; capitalist class; dominant class; elites; upper class
Runciman, W.G. 353–4, 360, 377
Runciman Scale 353–4
Rusche, G. 100
Russia 225

S

Saarinen, J. 209
Sachs, Jeffrey 220
sacralisation theorists 162
Sandberg, Sheryl 267

Saunders, Peter 376, 390–1
Savage, Mike 361, 369, 372, 373, 375, 379
scapegoats 59, 285, 295
Scarman Report 72
schools
 comprehensive 46
 independent/private 314, 315, 367, 383–4, 386, 388
Schumpeter, Joseph 192, 204
Schuurmans, J. 7
Schwendinger, H. 94
Schwendinger, J. 94
science
 as belief system 122
 characteristics 120
 context 120
 feminist analysis of 30
 natural sciences 27–8, 32, 33, 39, 161
 objectivity 120
 and religion 118, 121, 135, 160, 161
 as social construct 120–1
 sociology as 25–6, 27–31
scientific faith 122
scientific method (doing science) 120–1
scientific theory 120, 146
Scientology 117, 132
Scott, John 371
Scottish Mobility Study 384, 387, 388, 392
SDGs see Sustainable Development Goals
Seaton, J. 258, 259, 260, 261, 262, 267
SEC see socio-economic classification
sects 139–46, 148–9, 150
secular spirituality 151
secularisation 120, 158–63, 165
seduction community 7
segregation, racial 343
selection by mortgage 331, 333
selective filter model 305
self 19
 ideal 363
self-fulfilling prophecy 19, 408, 409
self-improvement 165
self-religions 165
self-report studies 105, 423
Selwyn, Benjamin 229
semi-periphery 185, 192
semi-proletarianised workers 322
Sen, Amartya 174, 243, 252
separatists/separatism 17, 322
Serious Fraud Office 111
service class 319
service sector 23, 374
sex-role theory 76–8, 127–8, 153
sex trade 8, 252–3
sex-role conditioning 17
sexual abuse 110, 141, 238
sexuality 299–300
Shakespeare, Tom 347
shanty towns 197, 227
Sharia law 167
Sharpe, Su 339
shifting equilibrium 176

Shiva, Vandana 322-3
Sikhs 138, 155, 156
Simpson, Ludi 343
simulacrum 23, 325
Skeggs, Beverley 369, 370
Sklair, Leslie 204
slave trade 180, 252-4
Smart, C. 78
smartphones 247, 264
Snider, L. 57, 79
Snowden, Edward 267
social action theory 6, 18-20, 35-6, 40
social capital 359
social change 15, 129
    and development 176
    and Marxism 316-17
    and religion 133, 134-5
    shifting equilibrium 176
social class 13, 14
    blurring of boundaries 368
    changing UK structure 371-8
    class group division 318
    contradictory class locations 317, 352
    and crime and deviance 54-5, 60-4, 78-80, 90, 100, 105, 109, 111
    death of 369-70
    dichotomy 316, 317, 319
    dis-identification with 369
    and education 331, 333, 356-62
    and ethnicity 341, 342
    and exploitation 135, 307, 316-17, 352-3
    and gender 364, 370
    Goldthorpe on 384
    gradational interests 353
    inequalities 328-34, 363, 368-71, 391
    and life chances 328-34
    and life expectancy 330, 333
    Marxist theories of 316-17, 319
    measurement 351-66
    media representation 294-6, 352
    Neo-Marxist theories of 317-18
    neo-Weberian theory 318-19
    objective definitions 356
    postmodern theory of 323-5
    as relational 316
    and religion 156-7
    and social mobility 384-7, 389-90, 391, 392
    subjective definitions of 360-3
    subordinate 13, 14, 316
    and the UK 325
    visibility 363-4
    Weberian theory 317
    see also middle class; precariat; underclass; upper class; working class
Social Class based on Occupation 356-7
social cohesion 262
social construction
    of childhood 293, 344
    of knowledge 120-1
    of the news 281-7

religion as 120, 123
science as 120-1
social control 50-1, 68
    agents of 61-2
    and crime control 85, 98-101
    and the criminal justice system 111-12
    formal 51
    informal 51
    and religion 125, 130, 157
    and the state 94, 112
social Darwinism 339
social democracy 11-12
social deprivation 81, 154, 426
    see also relative deprivation
social desirability effect 308
social exclusion 79
'social facts' 6, 26
social harm 67, 68
    harms of reduction 67
    harms of repression 67
social identity 155
social institutions 10, 64, 317-18
social media 285-6, 287-8
social mobility 176, 314-15, 328, 369, 382-93
    absolute mobility 385, 391
    demand side policies 389
    and education 386, 387, 391-2
    and ethnicity 389
    inflow rates 285
    intergenerational 385
    low 383, 384
    measurement 389-92
    and migration 391-2
    outflow rates 285
    relative 385-6
    and social class 392
    supply side policies 389
    types of 385-7
social networks 380
social norms, diverse 67, 68
social order 18-19, 50-2, 125, 313
social policy 44-8, 66, 83
social processes 59
social solidarity 52, 100, 122-3, 374
social status 356-62
    see also status frustration
socialisation 9, 10, 15
    and crime 73
    and education 313, 345
    and gender 76-7, 334-6
    religious 151
    and TV 268
societal goals 52-3, 55
socio-economic classification (SEC) 352-3
sociology as science 25-6, 27-31
Solidarity 137
    mechanical 176
    social 52, 100, 122-3, 374
Sørenson, Aage 363
Sosu 47
South, N. 92

South Africa 225
Southerton, Dale 363-4
speculators 194
Spencer, Herbert 9, 339
spiritual experimentation 142-3
spiritual marketplace 152, 165
Spiritual Revolution Thesis 162
spiritual shoppers 147, 149
spirituality, secular 151
Stanworth, Michelle 390
Stark 148
Stark, Rodney 160
Starmer, Keir 267
state
    crimes 94-6
    patriarchal 320
    see also nation state
statistics, official 6, 102-4, 105, 106, 423
status classification 357
status frustration 54-5, 60, 73, 79, 81, 146, 153, 426
status quo 14, 74, 79, 126
status-conventional theory 370
stereotypes 61-2
    age-related 292, 294
    of disabled persons 301
    gender 299, 335, 408-11
    racist 297
    teenage sexuality 300
Stern, Lord Nicholas 233
Stiglitz, Joseph 212
stigmatisation 291
Storey, J. 278
Storey, Pat 127
strain, social 52-3, 55
stratification and differentiation 311-93
    definition and measurements 350-66
    feminist theory 319-23
    functionalist theories of 313-15
    and the global economy 378-80
    life chances 327-50
    Marxist theories of 316-17
    Neo-Marxist theories of 317-18
    postmodern theories of 323-5
    social mobility 382-93
    structural changes 367-81
    Weberian theories of 318-19
stretched social relations 190
Strinati, Dominic 278-9, 324
structural adjustment programmes 184, 194, 198, 202, 212, 217, 251
structural conflict theory 12-18
structural consensus theory 9, 15, 20, 35-6, 51-3
structural functionalism 9, 10
structuralist Neo-Marxism 14
Stuart, Moira 302
stunting 249
subjectivism 39
subjectivity 39
subordinate class 13, 14, 316
substitution theory 337

suicide 6, 26
Sullivan, Alice 36
Sun, The (newspaper) 286, 295
supernatural forces 117, 118, 133
superstructure 13
superstructure (Marx) 316
surplus value 316
surveillance 67–9, 101
   liquid 68
   mass media 68, 91
sustainability
   and aid 208, 218
   and development 187, 198, 199, 230, 232
   and tourism 209
Sustainable Development Goals (SDGs) 199
Sutherland, Edwin H. 60, 81, 94
Sutton, J. 363
Sutton Trust 388
Swain, Jon 339
Swidler, A. 208
Swinson, Jo 335

T

Taliban 137
tariffs 213, 224
tax avoidance 57, 60, 80, 216
tax credits 45–6
tax evasion 82
taxation
   progressive 332
   regressive 332–3
Taylor 58
Taylor, L. 85
'techniques of neutralisation' 55
technological fix 232
technology *see* new technology
television 259, 262, 273
   and childhood 344
   representation of social class 295, 352
   representation of young people 293
   smart 264
   and socialisation 268
terrorism 96, 234, 340
textile industry 189, 240
Thatcher, Margaret 12, 46
Thatcher administration 202
'theodicy of disprivilege' 146
theory 1–48
   and the A-level exam 405, 415–16, 427–30
   analysis and evaluation 396–8
   application 396, 399
   conflict theory 12–18
   consensus theories 9–12
   and demographics 250
   and health 247
   and methods 31–7
   and modernity 21–2
   and objectivity 37–43
   and postmodernity 21, 22–3
   primary data 3
   qualitative research 6–8
   quantitative research 6
   secondary data 3–5
   social action theory 6, 18–20
   and social policy 44–8
   sociology as science 25–6, 27–31
   and value freedom 34–43
'third way' 12, 45
Thompson, Robert 304
Thornton, S. 90
tiger economies 178, 181, 197, 225
TNCs *see* Transnational Corporations
tobacco companies 201
Tombs, S. 107–8
Tomlinson, S. 340, 377
top-down approach 35
Torfason, M.T. 213
totalitarianism 131
totemism 123
totems 123
tourism 209
Townsend, Peter 45
toy industry 349
trade 183
   agreements 82
   and aid 220
tradition 164
traditional values 176–7, 179, 250
Transatlantic Trade and Investment Partnership (TTIP) 193
transformalists 192, 195–6
Transnational Corporations (TNCs) 181, 184–5, 190, 192–4, 196, 201–6, 224
   and conflict 235
   effectiveness 202–3
   and employment policies 239, 240–1, 251, 253
   and the environment 205, 231
   and exploitation 181, 202, 204–5, 216, 251, 253
   and export-processing zones 224
   and horizontal flexibility 202
   increasing influence 204–5
   and the media 262
   and politics 204
   power 204–6, 229
   role 202–3
   and taxation 205, 216
   and vertical flexibility 203
   and women 253
Triple Systems Theory 320
Troeltsch, Ernst 143
trolls 267
truth
   religious 118
   scientific 120, 121
TTIP *see* Transatlantic Trade and Investment Partnership
Tuchman, G. 298
Tudor, Andrew 29
Tumin, Melvin 315
Twitter 260, 267, 298
two-step flow model 304

U

UK Independence Party 218
underclass 57
   changing structure of 376–7
   and ethnicity 340
   life chances 329
   media representation 294, 295
   Runciman's analysis of 354
underdevelopment 234
unemployment 341
Unicef 236
Union Carbide disaster 1984 93
United Kingdom 221
United Nations (UN) 87, 93, 174, 175, 178, 198, 200, 208, 216
   and demographics 250
   and employment 240
   and gender issues 251
   and health 246
   role 210–11
   structure 210
   and urbanisation 226
United Nations Convention against Transnational Organized Crime (CTOC) 87
United Nations Educational, Scientific and Cultural Organization (UNESCO) 95, 96, 242, 243
United Nations General Assembly 211
United Nations High Commissioner for Refugees (UNHCR) 236
United Nations Population Division (UNPD) 249
United Nations Security Council 211
United States
   government debt 183
   post-American age 196
   trade 183
United States-Korea Free Trade Agreement (KORUS) 183
upper class 354, 371
   changing structure 371–2
   life chances 328
   measurement 351–65
   and media representation 296
   and religiosity 156
   see also bourgeoisie; capitalist class; dominant class; elites; ruling class
urban explorers 55, 56
urbanisation 219, 226–9, 250
uses and gratification model 305

V

validity 308
Value Added Tax (VAT) 332–3
value consensus 9, 52, 111
   and education 313
   and religion 123, 124, 143
value freedom 37–43
values
   core 9, 10, 123

news 88, 96, 273, 282–3
  traditional 176–7, 179, 250
  Western 191
Van der Gaag, Nikki 250, 252
Vanuatu 174
variables, pattern A/B 176
Veblen, Thorstein 324
veiling 128, 167, 253
Venables, Jon 304
verbal appellation 335
victim surveys 104–5, 423
victim-blaming 45–6
victimisation 72, 73, 75–6, 78, 108–9
victimology 106–10
  critical 107–8
  positivist 107
victims 63, 106–100
  Code of Practice for the Victims of Crime 110
  indirect 108
  primary 108
  social construction of 106–7
violence 308
  against women 238
  male 238, 320
voluntaristic behaviour 19, 33
Von Hentig 107

W

wages
  minimum wage 45–6
  see also income; pay gap
Walby, Sylvia 320
Walker, Alan 376
Wallerstein, Immanuel 184–5, 191–2
Wallis, Bruce 145, 146
Walton 58
war 234–6
'war on terror' 195
warlords 235
Warren, Bill 182
Washington Consensus 184, 191, 210, 214, 217
water pollution 92
Waters, M. 323, 369–70
Watkins, S.C. 208
Watson, Helen 128
Wayne, M. 293
WBCSD see World Business Council for Sustainable Development
wealth 197–8, 219
  distribution 331–3
  inequality 330, 331–2, 333
  marketable wealth 331
Wealth and Assets Survey 331
Weber, Max 6, 18, 19, 26, 28, 33, 35, 40, 94, 122, 133, 134–5, 146, 160, 318, 329, 369, 378
Weberian theory 155
  and ethnicity 342
  and racial inequality 340
  and social class analysis 353–4

and stratification 318
Weiss, Linda 204
welfare 45–6, 64
  absence 239, 240
  dependency 57, 295
  and social control 112
  for young people 345
welfare state, golden age 11–12, 44
Westergaard, John 333, 370
Western values 191
Westernisation 164, 190, 194
Whilby 385–6
White, R. 91
Whitfield 43
Whittingdale, John 273, 275
WHO see World Health Organisation
Whyte, D. 107–8
Wikipedia 261, 262
Wikström, Per-Olaf H. 81
Wilkinson, Helen 364
Wilkinson, R. 247, 315
Williams, John 47
Willis, Paul 333
Wilson, Bryan 142, 158
Wilson, J.Q. 65
Wolf, N. 298
women
  and conflict 236
  and crime 75–9, 109, 112
  and criminal the justice system 78, 112
  dependency 321–2
  and development 250–4
  driving bans 150
  dual burden of 420
  exploitation 320, 321–2
  expressive role 334–6
  marginalisation 127, 129, 323
  media representation 89, 297–8, 302
  missing 252
  oppression 129, 322, 323, 420
  and religion 127–9, 134, 150, 152–5, 167
  and reproductive rights 252
  as reserve army of labour 322, 337, 338
  social mobility 388
  subordination 320, 322
  trafficking 252–3
  violence against 238
  and work 240, 241, 251, 334, 390
  see also girls
Women's Liberation Movement 322
Woolf report 113
work
  and age 345–6
  and disability 348
  and ethnicity 341
  and gender 336–9, 364
  patriarchal relations 320
  service industry 183
  and socio-economic classification 352
  and women 240, 241, 251, 334, 390
  see also employment; jobs; labour; occupation

working class 371
  blurring boundaries of 368
  changing structure of 374–5, 377
  control 318
  and crime 54–5, 60, 63–4, 79, 80, 90, 100, 109, 111
  dis-identification 369
  disorganised 379
  and education 331, 333
  exclusion 314
  life chances 329
  measurement 351–65
  and the media 268–9, 285, 287, 294–6, 351
  neo-Weberian theories of 319
  new 275
  and religion 133, 156, 157
  revolution 126
  Runciman's analysis of 354
  subcultures 60, 63
  traditional 374
  Weberian theories of 318
World Bank 178–9, 184, 194–5, 197–8, 222–3
  and climate change 232
  and gender issues 251
  and global inequality 214
  and modernisation theory 219
  and population 249
  role 210, 212–13, 214
  and urbanisation 228
World Business Council for Sustainable Development (WBCSD) 230
world cities 228
World Health Organisation (WHO) 218, 236, 238, 246, 247, 249
world systems theory 184–5, 186, 192
World Trade Organisation (WTO) 183, 193, 210, 212–13, 232
World Wildlife Fund (WWF) 231–2
Wright, Erik Olin 317, 352–3
WuDunn, Sheryl 251, 252, 253

Y

Yinger, John Milton 117, 142
Young 58
Young, J. 63, 65, 73, 80, 90, 383
Young, Jock 46, 376, 377
Young, Michael 312
young people
  and crime 81, 89, 90, 105
  criminalisation 293
  media representation 293, 299–300
  and religiosity 150–2, 153, 154, 155
youth subcultures 54–6, 90, 293
  anti-school 406

Z

zero tolerance 64, 65, 99
zero-hours contracts 375
Zhu, Chen 231